From These Beginnings...
A Biographical Approach
to American History

From These

A Biographical

Roderick

HARPER & ROW, PUBLISHERS

Beginnings...

Approach to American History

Nash University of California, Santa Barbara

New York, Evanston, San Francisco, London

FROM THESE BEGINNINGS . . .
A BIOGRAPHICAL APPROACH TO AMERICAN HISTORY

Copyright © 1973 by Roderick Nash

Standard Book Number: 06-044725-7

Library of Congress Catalog Card Number: 72-9395

We gratefully acknowledge the use of photographs from the following sources:

Page 1: The Columbus Gallery, Ponce de leon y Laguardia, N.Y. 1893. Page 8: *top*, Map Division, The New York Public Library, Astor, Lenox and Tilden Foundations; *center*, from the Page-Holgate facsimiles of John White paintings, North Carolina, Collection of L. R. Wilson Memorial Library, University of North Carolina, with the permission of The University of North Carolina Press; *bottom*, Reprinted with permission of The Macmillan Company from *Columbus* by Landstrom. Copyright 1966 by Björn Landstrom. Copyright 1967 by Bokforlaget Forum AB. Page 9: *top*, Columbus Memorial Library, Pan American Union; *bottom*, *Narrative and Critical History of America*, Winsor, Houghton, Mifflin, N.Y. 1886. Page 24: New York Public Library Picture Collection. Page 40: The John Carter Brown Library, Brown University. Page 41: *top*, U.S. Department of the Interior; *center*, *The River Towns in Connecticut*, Andrews, Johns Hopkins University, 1863; *bottom*, Massachusetts Historical Society. Page 58: New York Public Library Picture Collection. Page 68: Harry T. Peters Collection, Museum of the City of New York. Page 69: *top*, Henry E. Huntington Library; *bottom*, Library of Congress. Page 87: *top*, Underwood and Underwood; *bottom*, Benjamin Franklin Collection, Yale University Library. Page 100: Frick Art Reference Library, Collection of Charles F. Adams. Page 112: *top*, Library of Congress; *bottom*, John Trumbull, *The Declaration of Independence*, Yale University Art Gallery. Page 113: *top*, New York Historical Society; *bottom*, Thomas Jefferson Memorial Foundation. Page 148: Denver Public Library, Western History Department. Page 156: *top*, Maryland Historical Society; *bottom*, Walters Art Gallery. Page 157: *top*, Henry E. Huntington Library; *bottom*, Denver Public Library, Western History Department. Page 175: *top*, Utah State Historical Society; *bottom*, Union Pacific Railroad. Page 186: The Granger Collection. Page 192: *top*, Library of Congress; *bottom*, The New York Historical Society, Bella C. Landauer Collection. Page 193: *bottom*, Chicago Historical Society. Page 208: Library of Congress. Page 209: *top*, Library of Congress. Page 228: Mark Twain Birthplace Memorial Shrine. Page 238: Harpers Monthly. Page 252: *top*, Harpers New Monthly Magazine; *bottom*, M. H. de Young Memorial Museum, SF. Page 253: *top*, Mackay School of Mines, University of Nevada; *bottom*, Library of Congress. Page 280: Wide World. Page 300: *top*, Lewis Hine, National Child Labor Committee; *bottom*, Library of Congress. Page 301: *top*, Oliver Jensen; *bottom*, *left*, University of Illinois Library, Jane Addams Memorial Collection; *bottom*, *right*, Library of Congress. Page 326: National Forest Service. Page 340: *top*, Bettmann Archive; *bottom*, Oklahoma Historical Society. Page 341: *top*, Culver; *bottom*, Arthur Rothstein. Page 356: *top*, The Newark News, Wisa, Feb. 1910; *bottom*, Tacoma Ledger. Page 376: Greenfield Village and Henry Ford Museum. Page 389: (c) AAA, reproduced by permission. Page 404: Greenfield Village and Henry Ford Museum. Page 405: *top*, UPI; *bottom*, Wide World. Page 422: Wide World. Pages 446–447: Wide World. Page 466: NASA. Page 488: *top*, Wide World; *bottom*, NASA. Page 489: *top*, US Navy; *bottom*, NASA. Page 512: Charles Gatewood. Page 522: *top*, Wide World; *bottom*, Griffiths, Magnum. Page 523: *top*, Laure, Rapho-Guillumette; *bottom*, Wide World. Page 539: Wide World.

All maps by Graphic 70.

For Laura and Jennifer

Contents

Preface

Historians, like beachcombers, are collectors of shells. They commonly gather lifeless outer coverings—reputations and generalizations. The living beings who made and hid under the shells often escape notice. Consequently, the study of history loses much of its significance and fascination. The past dies because we fail to see it as a collection of individuals who loved and hated and achieved and made mistakes and had all the complexity of thought and feeling that we ourselves have.

One way to enliven historical writing is to employ a biographical approach. The logic is straightforward. People are interested in people. History concerns people. The study of history can be made as exciting as life itself if it is conceived in terms of biography. These assumptions underlie the novel structure of this book.

The standard textbook method of dividing the past into periods, eras, or ages has been discarded in the pages that follow. Thirteen often-overlapping lives provide the organizational structure. The larger story of the American experience is woven around these lives. In this way broad concepts are tied to specific examples. The frontier, slavery, and industrialization, for instance, acquire sharp focus when viewed from the perspective of a pioneer, a slave, and an industrialist. Conversely, the narrative of national events deepens understanding of the thirteen individuals. But these personal histories are subordinate to this book's primary purpose, which is to present American history more meaningfully.

One problem in using a biographical approach is finding a happy compromise between "straight" biography and "straight" American history. This is not difficult, of course, when an individual life impinges directly on the course of national events. Thomas Jefferson writing the Declaration of Independence, Henry Ford revolutionizing transportation, and Martin Luther King, Jr. leading the civil rights movement are cases in point. But frequently, even a famous person sinks back into the general citizenry. His life becomes typical rather than unusual. On such occasions I have employed a life-and-times approach consisting of describing the historical context surrounding the individual. The technique is justifiable, I believe, on the grounds that any life is in large part shaped by the stream of events in which it floats. For example, the international relations of the United States in the 1930s and 1940s relate to Neil Armstrong because they shaped the world he inherited as an adult. In the same way, a knowledge of two centuries of black American history is essential in understanding the life and thought of Frederick Douglass.

Another problem came in choosing the thirteen lives through which I would tell the history of the United States. Actually this proved one of the more enjoyable tasks associated with writing the book. For many months I entertained my classes, my colleagues, my publisher, and my family with the question of a suitable cast of characters. The final slate is the result of considerable experimentation, several false starts, much wall-staring, and occasional midnight inspiration. Even so, these thirteen people are not completely satisfactory. There is some comfort, however, in the realization that the choice of individuals is not all-important. A surprising amount of information about the course of national events can be tied to *any* American life. Try it, for example, with your own. As Americans we all affect and are affected by American history.

For research and editorial assistance in the preparation of this book I owe debts of gratitude to Mr. James Joslyn and to my wife, Sandy.

Roderick Nash

Christopher Columbus

*With a rising moon and a strong east wind behind them, the three
ships sailed headlong into history. It was shortly before 2 A.M. on
October 12, 1492, but most hands were on deck. The usual signs of a
landfall—a green branch, a carved stick, many birds—had made
them eager, desperate, for their first sight of land in thirty-three
days. The tall, gray-haired captain braced himself on the sterncastle
of the* Santa Maria. *His face showed the strain of a twenty-year
dream on the brink of realization. Suddenly, a muffled shot from the*

*lead ship, Pinta, broke the rhythmic hiss of the waves. It was the
signal for land ahead, and the Pinta fell off the wind waiting for
the flagship. As she approached, her captain too could see the pale
gleam of limestone cliffs. Christopher Columbus had reached a
new world.*

The son and grandson of humble weavers in the Republic of
Genoa, north and west of Rome, Columbus, one might imagine, had
little reason to anticipate a life of discovery and exploration. But the
Europe into which he was born in 1451 simmered with the forces that
eventually propelled him across the Atlantic. Some were already centuries old. Beginning in 1095, the several crusades to free Jerusalem
from Turkish control had opened European eyes. Nobles and fighting
men who had journeyed to the Holy Land had encountered a whole
new standard of living at this crossroads where East met West. For the
first time, the crusaders saw luxurious silk cloth, which contrasted
sharply with their rough woolen garments such as those Columbus's
family wove. And there were heavy, colorful tapestries that made
ideal wall hangings for dark, drafty European castles and Oriental
spices to preserve as well as flavor food.

The Europeans also saw fabulous quantities of gold and gems.
They heard about still more, especially in the late thirteenth century
when Marco Polo reported his overland journey to China, Japan, and
the Spice Islands. Columbus's copy of Marco Polo's book was under-
lined where the author mentioned "pearls, precious stones, brocades,
ivory, or pepper, nuts, nutmeg, cloves and an abundance of other
spices." He also noted the reference to the palace of the king of Japan
"which is entirely roofed with fine gold, just as our churches are
roofed with lead." This knowledge of Asia whetted the appetite of
Columbus's generation and lifted its eyes to far horizons.

European desire for the treasures of the East could be satisfied by
traders. After goods from Asia arrived at eastern Mediterranean ports
such as Constantinople and Alexandria, merchants from Genoa, along
with those from Venice, Florence, and Pisa, distributed them throughout Europe. Prices, however, were exceedingly high. In addition, Europe soon faced an unfavorable balance of trade: money flowed east

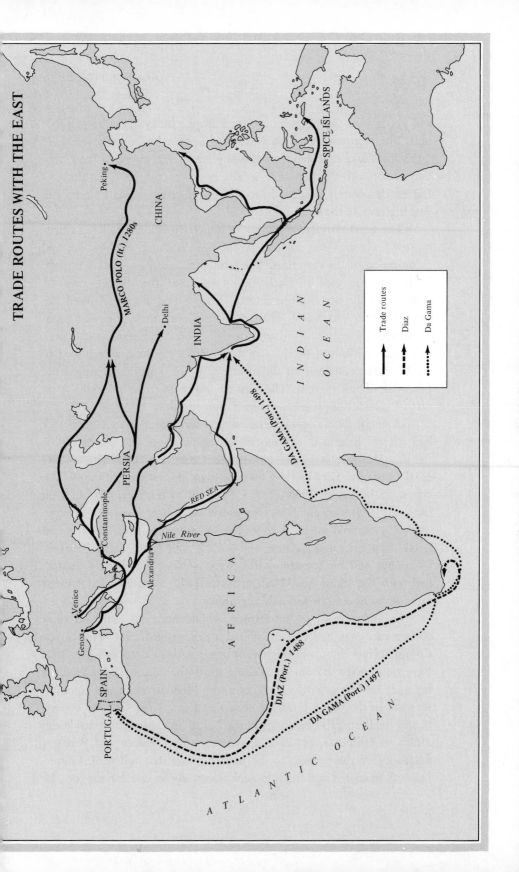

TRADE ROUTES WITH THE EAST

Trade routes
Diaz
Da Gama

PORTUGAL
SPAIN
Genoa
Venice
Constantinople
Alexandria
Nile River
RED SEA
PERSIA
MARCO POLO (It.) 1280s
Peking
CHINA
Delhi
INDIA
SPICE ISLANDS

AFRICA

DIAZ (Port.) 1488
DA GAMA (Port.) 1497
DA GAMA (Port.) 1498

ATLANTIC OCEAN

INDIAN OCEAN

and goods west. Asia had no use for Europe's bulky agricultural products. The economic situation was bad, but to make matters worse, in 1453 the Turks captured Constantinople and thus closed to the Christian Europeans the key link in the route to the East. Columbus's Europe desperately needed cheap and direct access to the Orient. The vast highway of the sea promised both.

The Renaissance also played an important role in readying Christopher Columbus and his society for the discovery, exploration, and colonization of the Americas. The term *renaissance* suggests a rebirth. To be sure, the so-called Dark Ages were not all that dismal except by contrast to the accomplishments of Greece and Rome. Around the twelfth century Arab and Jewish scholars alerted their European counterparts to the cultural brilliance of the classical civilizations. A shiver of excitement spread north from Italy. A society long accustomed to the Christian emphasis on the afterlife, the next world, glimpsed the potential of the present. The idea of improving man's condition on earth—the idea of progress—gained momentum.

A major theme of the Renaissance was pride in man. Christianity had stressed human unworthiness and helplessness, but the heroes of the Rennaissance were Alexander the Great, Aristotle, Caesar, and Mark Anthony. They had not been helpless, but rather had shaped the course of history in their time. Could not fifteenth-century men do likewise? A passion for fame, for glory, for achievement, for mastery gained a foothold in the European mind. It spread from the arts and letters to politics and business, and fed the development of capitalism. Columbus and his contemporaries were restless, increasingly unsatisfied with the status quo. Understandably, this dissatisfaction created an urge for new lands and new beginnings.

Columbus had the restlessness, confidence, and ambition of a Renaissance man and the sea offered a perfect outlet for his energies. Columbus met the sea in the harbor of his native Genoa and may well have transported woolen cloth along the Italian coast. In his twenties he made his first extensive voyages in the Mediterranean as a common seaman. In the year 1476 Columbus sailed in a large Genoese convoy bound for Portugal, England, and the North Sea ports. Just outside the Straits of Gibraltar, however, a war fleet from France and Portugal descended on the convoy. In the furious battle that followed, Columbus was wounded and his ship sunk. Grasping an oar for support, he struggled six miles to the southern coast of Portugal. As he crawled onto the beach of an unknown country, his chances of ever commanding an expedition to the New World seemed remote. But Columbus was an unusual man with a knack for persevering in the face of adversity.

The country Columbus reached in such unpromising circumstances was then the European leader in maritime discovery. Much of the credit for Portugal's eminence goes to Dom Henrique, better known as Prince Henry the Navigator. This talented prince, who died in 1460, personified the spirit of the age of European expansion. From his headquarters on the Atlantic Ocean he sent expeditions into the unknown. Some went north, and developed a brisk trade with England and Iceland. Others pushed west, a thousand miles into the open ocean, to find the Azores. But Prince Henry reserved his keenest enthusiasm for those who sailed south to coast along the dark continent of Africa. At the time of his death, his captains had reached within ten degrees of the equator.

The Portuguese also achieved preeminence in developing the sciences of sailing and navigation. Not only exploration, but the entire colonization movement depended on establishing safe and reliable sea transport. Prince Henry created a fifteenth-century equivalent of Cape Kennedy, gathering around him the best navigational minds in the Western world. The charts, tables, and astronomical observations they compiled made possible long expeditions on the open ocean without the need to stay close to shore. The refinement of the astrolabe, for example, permitted a captain to determine his latitude on the basis of star sightings with considerable accuracy. Equally important were the institutions of early capitalism, the banks and joint-stock companies that enabled Portugal to finance far-flung exploration. A shipwreck, ironically, had left Columbus in the best place to pursue the life of an explorer.

Within six months of dragging himself onto the Portuguese beach, Columbus recovered his health and once again put to sea. This time Iceland was the goal and trading the purpose. During the next few years he mastered Latin and Spanish, married into a prominent Portuguese family, and gained respect both as a gentleman and a seaman. He lived on one of the Madeira Islands west of Gibraltar for a year or more and, in the early 1480s, made at least one voyage around the hump of West Africa to Guinea and the Gold Coast. The African experience added greatly to his skill as a sea captain. It also produced an unexpected dividend. Columbus noticed that south of the Canary Islands the prevailing winds always blew from the east. Further north, off England and Portugal, they came out of the west. Gradually it dawned on him that to sail west into the North Atlantic winds was foolish. A far better course would be to sail south to the trade winds and then west on their wings. To return, one had simply to set a northerly course, catch the west wind, and ride it back to Europe.

Driftwood that storms frequently cast on European shores provided exciting evidence that Columbus was right in his theory that land lay to the west. When he lived on Madeira he could scarcely avoid noticing the huge tropical canes, seed pods, and tree trunks that we now know came from Central and South America. Even carved wood had been found, and on one occasion, two flat-faced human bodies, of an appearance strange to Europeans, washed onto the beach. The significance of all this was not lost on Columbus.

Returning from Africa with knowledge about wind patterns, Columbus gave increasing attention to the possibility of sailing west to reach the Far East. The roots of this idea lay in his understanding that the world was round. Educated Europeans had taken a spherical earth for granted for two thousand years; Columbus simply attempted a feat discussed for centuries. The size of the earth, however, and the distribution of its land masses were still hotly debated among the foremost scholars of Columbus's time. "Knowledge" tended to be a blend of fact, myth, and wishful thinking.

In constructing his conception of world geography, Columbus drew on a variety of ancient and contemporary sources. He owned an early fifteenth-century translation of the work of the Greek mathematician Ptolemy, whose calculations fell short of the earth's actual size. He also owned the standard geography of the Late Middle Ages, Pierre d'Ailly's *Imago Mundi*, which was written in 1410 but not printed until 1480. Columbus pored over his copy, making marginal notations on almost every page. "The earth is round and spherical," he jotted at one point, ". . . between the end of Spain and the beginning of India lies a narrow sea that can be sailed in a few days." Further confirmation of this error came from the renowned Florentine physician and geographer Paul Toscanelli, to whom Columbus wrote for information some time in 1481. Toscanelli stated confidently that the voyage Columbus proposed "is not only possible to make, but sure and certain, and will bring inestimable gain and utmost recognition." He also sent a map that Columbus used to calculate the distance from Portugal to Marco Polo's gold-roofed Japan as 3000 miles. This was only 9200 miles short!

Toscanelli's correspondence with Columbus perpetuated another geographical mistake. According to the Florentine, only open ocean lay to the west between Portugal and Japan. Most fifteenth-century Europeans agreed that at least an island or island group lay between these limits of geographical knowledge. No one, however, had conceived of a continent dividing the sea into the Atlantic and Pacific Oceans. Even if Columbus and his contemporaries knew of the Irish and Viking contacts with North America dating possibly from the sixth century and certainly from the eleventh, they did not realize it was a continent. Yet ignorance, in this case, proved advantageous. Rightly informed, Columbus would more than likely never have ventured west.

Myth also played an important role in his motivation. In company with Europeans since the Greeks, Columbus believed in an earthly paradise. Life was good in paradise, really good. Ripe fruit hung heavy on every bough. The climate was delightful, flowers perfumed the air. Precious stones and quantities of gold could be picked up at will. In some paradise traditions, these sensual joys were subordinated to spiritual ones. Paradise became a place where sin was unknown and men lived in accord with God's commandments. Those lucky enough to enter paradise, it was thought, left behind all worry, fear, and discomfort—even death was unknown.

According to the Christian tradition, man once occupied paradise, but somewhere along the way he had become separated from it. Adam and Eve, for instance, were driven from the Garden of Eden by an angry God. Later generations, however, remembered—or at least they dreamed. Almost every culture in Western history has subscribed to the idea that paradise still existed: somewhere there was an island or a mountain or an enchanted valley. . . . If men could only find it, the good life could be regained. The thought was irresistible, particularly so when parts of the earth were yet unknown. It was tempting

7

Many Europeans of Columbus's time believed that along with the economic, political, and scientific opportunities inherent in discovering new lands went a religious responsibility. Christianity had to be extended to the heathen. In this sketch from a 1500 map of the world, Columbus is shown wading ashore in the New World with an infant Christ on his shoulders. Appropriately, Columbus's first name was Christopher—literally, "Christ bearer."

Only the blind or the extremely biased could have regarded the North American Indians encountered by the first Europeans as wild animals. Many did so, however, in spite of the sophistication of villages such as this one in North Carolina.

The whole age of discovery and exploration depended upon a device as relatively simple as a compass. This reconstruction of a late fifteenth-century model, similar to the one Columbus used, consists of a wooden bowl, an iron needle, and a thin directional "rose" made from wood or paper. The rose could be turned to compensate for magnetic variation.

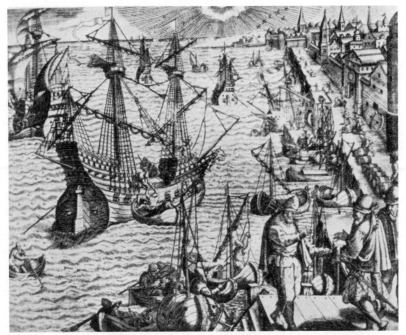

Lisbon, Portugal was one of the most exciting places in fifteenth-century Europe. It was a jumping off place—a Cape Kennedy of its time. This 1590 engraving shows Columbus's fleet returning from his first voyage to the New World. The ships are caravels, about 75 feet long.

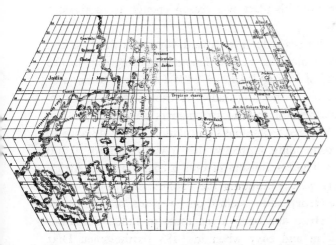

Columbus received this map from the geographer Paul Toscanelli and used it as evidence of the feasibility of sailing west to reach the Far East. The map accurately portrayed this possibility, but it contained two glaring errors. Using the grid-shaped pattern for measurement, "Zipangu" (Japan), the other Spice Islands, and the Asian mainland were located over 9000 miles closer to Europe than in actuality. The second error was the complete omission of North and South America. The large island in the center of the map existed only in European legend.

and easy to believe that paradise lay around the next bend, over the known horizon.

The idea of going *west* to find the lost paradise had existed for centuries before Columbus's venture. The Jews, wandering in the desert after fleeing Egypt, traveled back in that direction to find Canaan—their promised land of milk and honey. The Greeks, Romans, and Phoenicians had similar traditions of an earthly paradise to the west. These mythical places even appeared on maps, set in the middle of the Atlantic under the names of Antilla, Atlantis, the Islands of the Blest, Elysium, and the Isle of Fair Women. In the sixth century an Irish monk named St. Brendan supposedly sailed west in an attempt to reach the paradisiacal Fortunate Isles. According to the legend that grew up around this voyage, Brendan crossed the North Atlantic to Newfoundland, struck south to Bermuda, and then west to Florida. When he arrived, he found a settlement of Irish monks already enjoying the luxuriance of the tropics. True or not—and there is some evidence that Europeans of this time really did reach North America, if not paradise—the prospect of finding it continually fired imaginations. In Columbus's time serious discussions of the location and characteristics of paradise were common in every European port. *Imago Mundi*, for example, declares that "the Earthly Paradise is an Elysian spot . . . far distant from our inhabited world both by land and sea." To be the discoverer of this place was reason enough to motivate a man like Columbus.

To implement his plans for a westward voyage to the East and perhaps to paradise, Columbus needed financial backing. He turned first to King John II of Portugal. Late in 1484 Columbus enthusiastically unfolded his plan to the king's advisory committee. This distinguished group of mathematicians and astronomers was not impressed. In particular, they doubted Columbus's calculation of the distance to Japan and China, contending, correctly, that it was closer to 10,000 than to 3,000 miles. The commission favored a course around Africa. Portuguese mariners were continuing the explorations to the south begun under Prince Henry, and it seemed only a matter of time before they would round Africa and open a sea route to India. Columbus watched in frustration and envy when in 1488 Bartholomeu Díaz sailed triumphantly into Lisbon after performing this feat. Now Portugal had no further use for Christopher Columbus.

At this low point in his career, Columbus became the beneficiary of Europe's changing political structure. Before the fifteenth century an endless series of nobles, barons, earls, and dukes vied for dominance within particular regions. The abundance of leaders scattered wealth and power into small and relatively weak units. From this feudal chaos, however, kings and nations began slowly to emerge. By the late fifteenth century a few families had proved superior in the political struggle for existence. Forcing subservience on what became the lesser nobility, they created a series of hereditary monarchies. Extremely competitive and ambitious, these emerging national rulers aspired to the Roman example of world domination. Discovery and expansion appealed to them as avenues to glory. The nation that could find an easy route to Asia and establish lucrative trading colonies would have an immense advantage over its rivals.

Columbus saw the personal advantages in this political situation. Portugal's good fortune in its African venture in 1488, he thought, might increase the appeal of his scheme elsewhere. So Columbus dispatched his brother to the courts of Henry VII in England and Charles VIII in France. He himself went to Spain, where Ferdinand and Isabella were ending a successful struggle for control of a kingdom.

At first, Columbus made little headway. Ambitious and conceited, he insisted, as a prerequisite for any voyage, on a guarantee of three fully equipped ships, one-tenth of all the treasures he might find, an appointment as governor and viceroy of the lands discovered, and a place in the Spanish nobility with the title Admiral of the Ocean Sea. Detractors raised the old question of distance; Columbus was again accused of unwarranted optimism. But other voices in the Spanish court, impressed with his brash confidence and aware of the need to compete with Portugal, were reluctant to dismiss him. Skepticism vied with desire. Now Columbus probably played his trump—the pattern of the winds. He explained *how* to reach Asia by following the northeast winds in the South Atlantic. Even if the trip proved longer than anticipated, it would be easy to turn north and ride the west winds home.

The king's treasurer, Luis de Santángel, thought it was worth the risk. He pointed out that the surrender of Granada, the last stronghold of African Moors in Spain, on January 2, 1492, had freed the nation's resources for discovery. The voyage just might prove a bonanza.

Moreover, Columbus could be Spain's vehicle for spreading Christianity to heathen peoples. Considerations of gold, God, and glory, Santángel concluded, lent Columbus's proposal irresistible appeal.

The monarchs agreed. Queen Isabella even offered to pledge her jewels. Columbus, already on his way to France, was recalled by royal messenger. Ferdinand and Isabella accepted his terms in a formal agreement of April 17, 1492; and with ample money and connections, his pent-up energy exploded into action. Less than three months after arriving in the port of Palos, Columbus was ready to begin his quest.

Two of the three ships in his expedition, the *Pinta* and *Niña*, were caravels. Light and narrow, these vessels of approximately seventy-five feet had been designed for extended voyages. They were swift and could sail almost directly into the wind. Columbus's flagship, the *Santa Maria*, was longer, bulkier, and slower. The shipowners of Palos apparently were unwilling to risk a third caravel on so dubious a venture. Still, ninety men volunteered for the crew. On August 3, 1492, they left Palos bound for the unknown.

Just as he had proposed, Columbus led his expedition on a southwest slant to the Canary Islands, then due west along the 28th parallel of latitude. The winds proved favorable, as predicted, and the ships made good time. Of course, there were misgivings. Columbus had continually to restrain the crew from altering course to search for islands that seemed just out of sight. As the days stretched into weeks and no land appeared, whispers and then open complaints spread among the men. The sailors did not fear a sudden drop off a flat earth or sea monsters; they were simply a long way from home across an open ocean.

Responding to these challenges, Columbus offered reminders of the riches that lay ahead in Asia. He also deliberately falsified his log to make the distance back to Spain seem shorter. But ultimately it was a question of will. Columbus was committed. Only death or mutiny could have forced him to turn around in mid-passage. His spirit sustained the crew. Then San Salvador loomed into sight on the morning of October 12, and the misgivings temporarily disappeared.

After sighting the island, Columbus wisely furled sail and drifted until daylight. With the reefs and shoals now visible, he cautiously rounded the southern end of San Salvador and coasted up its western side in search of an anchorage. A break in the reef finally appeared;

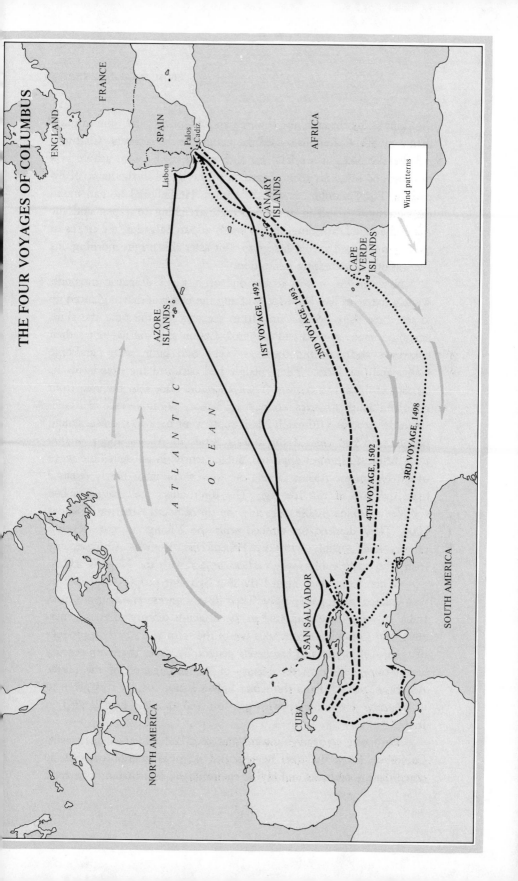

THE FOUR VOYAGES OF COLUMBUS

ENGLAND

FRANCE

SPAIN

Lisbon

Palos
Cadiz

AFRICA

CANARY
ISLANDS

CAPE
VERDE
ISLANDS

Wind patterns

AZORE
ISLANDS

1ST VOYAGE, 1492

2ND VOYAGE, 1493

A T L A N T I C

O C E A N

4TH VOYAGE, 1502

3RD VOYAGE, 1498

NORTH AMERICA

SAN SALVADOR

CUBA

SOUTH AMERICA

the ships sailed through and lowered anchor for the first time in more than a month. Columbus sensed the gravity of the moment. Clad in a red doublet brought specially for such occasions, he went ashore in a rowboat and solemnly took possession of the island in the name of his patrons. For Columbus, it was the climax. He believed he had found the outermost island in an archipelago stretching to Japan and the Asian mainland. Standing on the beach at San Salvador, the riches of the Orient seemed within his grasp. But after this bright morning, his life was one of increasing frustration.

Nevertheless, it was surely one of history's dramatic moments when a native of San Salvador, walking the beach at dawn, glanced up to see three ships approaching from the east. By the time the ships anchored, many natives had gathered. Columbus's journal notes their nakedness and describes them as "very well built, with handsome bodies and fine faces." These people had occupied the islands of the Caribbean for only a century. Their ancestors came into the area from mainland South America, conquering a more primitive race of islanders in the process. Ultimately, their roots went back to the Mongoloid people who had crossed the Bering Strait to Alaska about 40,000 years before Columbus appeared. Subsequently, in an incredible wave of expansion, the Asians fanned out over a continent newly released from the grip of the Ice Age. The forerunners may have reached California around 30,000 B.C. and the tip of South America by about 7000. Their descendants clashed with the Vikings in the eleventh century and possibly with the Phoenicians, Romans, Chinese, and Irish who conceivably made earlier contact with the New World.

When Columbus termed the San Salvador people "Indians," he was, unknowingly, partly right. Their distant ancestors *had* come from India (a term loosely applied in the fifteenth century to Asia generally). But Columbus's conscious use of the term was strictly a product of wishful thinking and erroneous geography. As a twentieth-century Sioux, commenting on the history of the subjugation of the native American, put it, "Even the name Indian is not ours. It was given to us by some dumb honky who got lost and thought he'd landed in India."

European arrogance toward the so-called Indians began with Columbus. From the start he regarded them as inferior even as he noted their good looks and idyllic environment. Nonchalantly he took possession of a land they had occupied for thousands of years. And while gathering specimen flowers, fruit, and birds to take back to Europe, he also collected seven natives. In his mind they were just another type of animal, and his journal contains frank speculations on the ease with which they could be enslaved. "These people," he noted on October 14, "are very unskilled in arms, . . . with fifty men they could all be subjected and made to do all that one wished." The statement proved a grim prophecy.

The first island disappointed Columbus. There were no treasures of the Orient. But he saw what he wished to see, what *must,* he felt, be there. The Indians wore small gold ornaments. By signs, they gave the strangers to believe that much more could be found elsewhere. Columbus assumed that Japan was close at hand. On the afternoon of October 14 he left San Salvador intending to island hop to Asia. The Spaniards cruised among several smaller islands and then, following native directions, pushed on to Cuba. When its high blue mountains appeared to the south, their goal once more seemed on the brink of realization. But again disappointment followed exaggerated expectation. No Grand Khan, wallowing in gold, could be located. Parties sent on inland explorations of Cuba returned with the same depressing story of poor natives and forbidding jungle.

The island of Hispaniola to which the explorers sailed next proved more promising. The Indians had considerable gold and told Columbus of rich mines in the interior. But just when success seemed imminent, the *Santa Maria* ran aground on a reef and was abandoned on Christmas Day in 1492. Columbus made a quick decision. He would plant a colony, called Navidad, and leave forty men on Hispaniola to find the gold and ascertain the location of Asia. On January 16, 1493, the *Pinta* and the *Niña* began the voyage home.

Columbus's arrival in Lisbon on March 4 triggered a surge of excitement. People debated whether he had found the outskirts of Asia or islands midway between Europe and Asia or a whole new continent, but few remained indifferent. Hunger for the Oriental trade combined with Renaissance curiosity and political ambition to create a climate in which Columbus's reports ignited imaginations. Europe was ripe for the news he brought. This had not been true at the time of the earlier discoveries of the New World. When the Vikings, for example, made contact in the eleventh century, Europeans were not straining impatiently at their physical and intellectual bounds. Asia and its riches were unknown. The Crusades had not begun. Neither capitalism nor nationalism had appeared. Open-ocean navigation was a risky, hit-or-miss operation. Consequently, the Viking feat had little impact on history. Christopher Columbus, on the contrary, had the good fortune to sail at a time when Europe was ready. His "discovery" began the continuous European expansion that led directly to the formation of the United States. Not literally, then, but significantly, Columbus discovered America.

After completing his first round trip to the Caribbean, Columbus could have retired with his laurels, but for a man of his temperament, the first voyage could only be prelude. Ferdinand and Isabella were similarly inclined. Their Admiral of the Ocean Sea had come to Barcelona and astounded them with his collection of strange fish, wood, and fruit. Columbus spread gold before the monarchs, assuring them that it was but a token of what existed. The Indians Columbus displayed to the court provided additional incentive. On command, they recited the *Ave Maria* and crossed themselves. In the eyes of fervent Catholics like Ferdinand and Isabella, this was reason enough to continue the western exploration. A whole civilization of heathen seemed to be waiting for conversion to Christianity. And by a Papal Bull of May 4, 1493, which set a Line of Demarcation one hundred leagues west of the Azores, Spain was given exclusive right to exploit and colonize the new lands.

With the stakes so high, Columbus found little difficulty in assembling the men and means to support his return to the Caribbean. On September 25, 1493, seventeen ships and between 1200 and 1500 men left the Spanish port of Cadiz. Once again the ocean crossing caused no problem, but the expedition failed to fulfill expectations. Neither the Asian mainland nor Japan materialized, although the search was much more extensive. The amount of gold was far smaller than Columbus expected. The Indians, moreover, proved as poor subjects for missionary work as the Spaniards proved missionaries. Columbus fought the cannibals of the Leeward Islands, and made them slaves and concubines. The Indians, however, turned the tables at Hispaniola. When Columbus returned to his Navidad colony, he found nothing but bones and charred timbers. Every Spaniard had been killed or carried off into the jungle.

Columbus's fortunes went from bad to worse. He attempted to start another colony, called Isabella, on Hispaniola, but his men suffered from sickness, dissension, and apathy. When they realized that gold could not be picked up on the beaches, they quickly became disenchanted with the New World. Actually, their situation was a symptom of the more general failure of the trading-post colony in the Americas. In wealthy and sophisticated societies like those of India and coastal Africa, Europeans simply set up shop and traded for valuable goods. Amid the comparatively poorer and more primitive peoples of the Caribbean and North America, however, there was little for which to trade. Men would have to *work* for wealth in these places; they would have to invest time, effort, and money before they could expect returns. Columbus unconsciously realized this in one of his official reports. Hispaniola, he declared, "is a wonder, with its hills and mountains, plains and meadows, and a land so rich and fertile for planting and sowing, for raising livestock of all sorts, for building towns and villages." But for over a century neither he nor his followers proved capable of translating this vision into reality. The lure of quick, easy wealth blinded them to the real abundance of the new land.

Troubled by discontent among his men, Columbus had to face the additional problem of full-scale war with the Indians. The missionary ideal broke down completely. Headstrong men, thousands of miles from home, did not respect Ferdinand and Isabella's directive that their new subjects be treated gently. Between 1494 and 1496, about a third of the 300,000 natives of Hispaniola were slaughtered, and the remainder enslaved in the gold mines. Fifty years later, only 500 Indians remained. Shortly thereafter, they were exterminated and replaced as a labor force by enslaved blacks from Africa.

As a colonial governor Columbus proved an almost total failure. Yet for a time he retained the confidence of Ferdinand and Isabella. In 1498 and 1502 the Admiral led new expeditions west, but he no longer pioneered. He had shown the way, and now others followed. His authority continued to dwindle, and at one point he was actually arrested and sent back to Spain in chains. Eventually he lost his position as governor.

Even Columbus's own assurance that he had found the edge of Asia began to waver. On his third voyage in 1498 he made the first recorded sighting of the South American continent. At first he supposed it another island, but there was disconcerting evidence to the contrary. Far from the coast, Columbus was amazed to find the sea fresh and suitable for drinking. He concluded, correctly, that the flow of a river had temporarily overcome the salinity of the ocean. But what a river! Columbus knew that only large land masses could produce rivers of this size. The experience forced him to admit that this land might be a continent, "another world," as his journal expressed it. But the old dream died hard. Perhaps, Columbus desperately reasoned, he had found a magic island not far from Asia that was none other than the earthly paradise.

Apart from such thoughts, there was little to cheer his declining years. Queen Isabella, whose faith in Columbus had been instrumental in making his first voyage possible, died late in 1504, and the Spanish court became increasingly deaf to the Admiral's pleas for restoration of his former incomes and positions. And then his health failed. Embittered and disappointed, yet still proud, Columbus gave up the struggle on May 20, 1506, in Valladolid, Spain. But the cruelest slight came a few years later. Martin Waldseemüller, a renowned German geographer, drew a map and wrote a book in which he mistakenly attributed the discovery of South America to Amerigo Vespucci, a vain and deceitful man who actually followed in Columbus's footsteps. By the time Waldseemüller realized his error, it was too late. Europeans were using "America," not "Columbia," to refer to the entire New World.

Columbus opened the door for further European discovery and exploration of the Americas. The little-known John Cabot, probably a Genoese like Columbus, carried England's flag along the northern route of the Vikings to Newfoundland in 1497. He sailed along the coast and may have reached Maine before returning. A year later Cabot was back, searching for Japan and the Spice Islands, but finding Delaware and the Chesapeake Bay instead. Although he died before completing his second voyage, Cabot laid the basis for England's claim to North America north of Florida. English colonization, however, did not start for almost a century. When it did, in the 1580s, Sir Walter Raleigh learned that the New World could deal lethal doses of the unexpected. His settlement on Roanoke Island off the North Carolina coast met the same fate as Columbus's Navidad. And only relief expeditions and radical reassessment of its purpose saved James-town, Virginia, from similar extinction during its "starving time" from 1607 to 1609. Europeans needed time to learn how to pioneer in a wilderness.

French contact with the New World began with fishing expedi-tions to Newfoundland's Grand Banks as early as 1504, but a formal effort at discovery awaited the appointment by Francis I of Giovanni Verrazano, another Genoese mariner, as national explorer. In 1524 Verrazano became the first to sail the whole coast of North America from Florida to Newfoundland, but he found no northwest passage to Asia. Jacques Cartier tried again in the 1530s, sailing as far as the first rapids on the St. Lawrence River and solidifying the French claim to Canada. As in the Caribbean, the northland spawned rumors of fabu-lous golden kingdoms that vanished like mist as the explorers pene-trated the wilderness. In the end France had to be satisfied with fish and fur.

For the Portuguese, the urge to explore the New World lessened considerably when in 1498 Vasco da Gama actually reached India after rounding Africa. But the Spanish successors to Columbus con-tinued to search for the elusive passage *through* the Americas. The pace of this quest increased after 1513 when Vasco Nuñez de Balboa struggled across the narrow isthmus of Panama and became the first European to see the Pacific Ocean from the west. The unlucky Co-lumbus had spent the entire winter of 1502–1503 sailing up and down the Panamanian coast, unaware that he was only forty miles away from a clear passage to India.

Despite the failure to find India, Spain lost no time in improving on the opportunities Columbus had created in the Caribbean and the adjacent mainlands. Juan Ponce de León, a member of Colum-bus's second expedition, found little except mangrove swamps in Flor-ida in 1513, but Hernán Cortés in Mexico (1519) and Francisco Pizarro in Peru (1531) struck it rich. The gold they stole from the Aztecs and Incas, respectively, made Spain the foremost power in Europe. It also sustained the New World treasure hunt through a succession of wild goose chases. In 1527–1528, for example, Pánfilo de Narváez led four hundred men through present-day Florida and Georgia and along the Gulf Coast to Texas. Disaster piled upon dis-aster until only two men remained. They staggered into Mexico City in

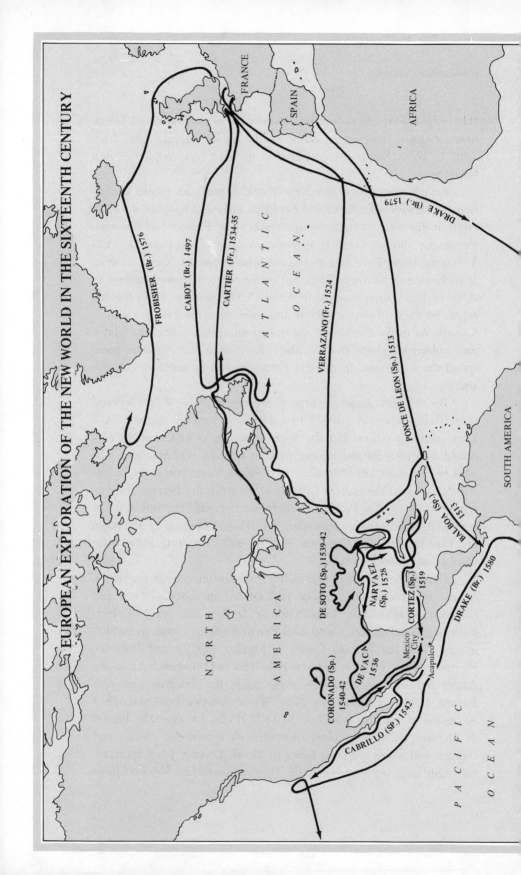

EUROPEAN EXPLORATION OF THE NEW WORLD IN THE SIXTEENTH CENTURY

FRANCE

SPAIN

AFRICA

DRAKE (Br.) 1579

FROBISHER (Br.) 1576

CABOT (Br.) 1497

CARTIER (Fr.) 1534-35

ATLANTIC OCEAN

VERRAZANO (Fr.) 1524

PONCE DE LEON (Sp.) 1513

NORTH

AMERICA

SOUTH AMERICA

BALBOA (Sp.) 1513

DE SOTO (Sp.) 1539-42

NARVAEZ (Sp.) 1528

CORTEZ (Sp.) 1519

DRAKE (Br.) 1580

CORONADO (Sp.) 1540-42

DE VACA 1536

Mexico City

Acapulco

CABRILLO (Sp.) 1542

PACIFIC

OCEAN

1536, after having traveled great distances with Indian tribes. One of these survivors, Cabeza de Vaca, returned with an incredible pack of lies about the Seven Cities of Cibola, where kings bathed in gold dust. The governor of Cuba, Hernando de Soto, could not resist. In 1539 he landed on the Florida coast with six hundred men. In the next four years de Soto marched north to the Appalachian Mountains, then west through the Mississippi Valley and finally as far as Oklahoma. At the same time, Francisco Vásquez de Coronado sought the mythical Seven Cities from the west. He traveled north from Mexico City into Arizona, discovered the Grand Canyon, and pushed east into Kansas only to return empty-handed in 1542. The accompanying sea voyage by Hernando de Alarcón up the Gulf of California and into the Colorado River was similarly unrewarding. Undaunted, the viceroy of New Spain immediately sent Juan Rodríquez Cabrillo sailing up the California coast past San Francisco Bay. Again there was no gold, but much frustration.

The false expectations of Columbus lived on in men like de Soto, Coronado, and Cabrillo. In spite of their courage and persistence, they failed to see the real potential of the New World. They set their sights fixedly on gold. They did not understand that in their disappointment they walked over and sailed along some of the most fertile land in the world—land capable of sustaining a great civilization. The problem, of course, was that, beginning with Columbus, the Spaniards were *conquistadores*, not farmers and settlers. Their purpose was the collection of treasure, not the extension of civilization. Even when souls, not gold, were the objective and priests rather than soldier-adventurers the agents, the Spanish proved inept colonizers. Their idea of a settlement was a virtual prison that forced both labor and religion down the throats of bewildered Indians. A triumphant return to the Old World, not a permanent place in the New, was the primary concern of Spain's men in the Americas. The ultimate cost of such conduct was the loss of North America to the English latecomers who, after a few false starts, learned to accept the land for what it was. Christopher Columbus and his Spanish successors never even tried. Their dreams stood in the way.

SELECTED READINGS

The Person

JANE, LIONEL CECIL (ed.): *Select Documents Illustrating the Four Voyages of Columbus* (2 vols., 1930–1933). A comprehensive collection of letters, dispatches, log books and journals. A shorter collection is *John M. Cohen (ed.): *The Four Voyages of Christopher Columbus* (1969).

LANDSTRÖM, BJÖRN: *Columbus* (1967). A biography embellished with dozens of magnificent, full-color drawings and maps.

MORISON, SAMUEL ELIOT: *Admiral of the Ocean Sea: A Life of Christopher Columbus* (2 vols., 1942). The best biography and one of the most impressive examples of biographical writing we have. Abridged as *Christopher Columbus, Mariner* (1955).

SMITH, BRADLEY: *Columbus in the New World* (1962). A spectacular photographic record of the lands and seas Columbus saw.

The Period

*BAKELESS, JOHN: *The Eyes of Discovery: America as Seen by the First Explorers* (1950). A unique description of the environment the first Europeans encountered in the New World.

BREBNER, JOHN B.: *The Explorers of North America, 1492–1800* (1933). The best general account.

*CRONE, G. R.: *The Discovery of America* (1969). The best short account of the background and aftermath of Columbus's feat.

HOLAND, H. R.: *Explorations in America before Columbus* (1956). A review of the numerous claims of North American contact by Europeans before 1492.

*JONES, HOWARD MUMFORD: *O Strange New World* (1964). The The impact of North America on the European imagination.

*PARRY, J. H.: *The Age of Reconnaissance* (1963). A survey of European culture at the beginning of the age of discovery and exploration.

* Available in paperback.

*PENROSE, BOIES: *Travel and Discovery in the Renaissance, 1420–1620* (1952). A competent survey that puts Columbus's voyages in the perspective of an expanding Europe.

* Available in paperback.

CHAPTER ONE

John Winthrop

*It was a Sunday morning in the spring of 1630, and the faithful
gathered for worship. Being in the middle of the North Atlantic
on the* Arbella *made little difference to Puritans. Religion came
first, always. The preacher was a layman, but governor of the
migrating band, and they quieted as he mounted the forecastle.
Pausing, John Winthrop looked out at the expectant faces and
beyond to the open ocean. These people had cast their lots with the
New World. Unlike the Spanish gold seekers, they came as*

*settlers, hoping to find freedom to live according to their ideals.
These involved nothing less than the continuation of the
Protestant Reformation and the creation of a godly society.
Winthrop fully appreciated the obstacles in their way, and as he
began to speak his tone was grave. He tried to show his followers
how the very freedom that made the North American wilderness
attractive could also prove a liability. It would be easy to forget high
purposes. Discipline and unity were consequently cardinal virtues.
If the colonists weakened, he warned, God's special protection would
be replaced by the full measure of His special wrath. Near the
end of the shipboard sermon, Winthrop created a striking metaphor
that has reverberated through American history. "For we must
consider," he shouted against the sound of waves and wind,
"that we shall be as a city upon a hill, the eyes of all people are
upon us." Here was recognition of the unprecedented opportunity
as well as the awesome responsibility that went with a fresh start
in a new world. While he lived, the force of John Winthrop's
conviction and character played a major role in sustaining the
Puritans in this self-conceived mission. Inevitably, that zeal waned
and with it the tight social control Winthrop prized, but not before
Puritanism made a deep impression on the American character.*

The year of John Winthrop's birth, 1588, proved exceptionally exciting for his native England. Queen Elizabeth had occupied the throne for three decades, and under her guidance the nation had become the most powerful in Europe. English "sea dogs," notably John Hawkins and Francis Drake, brazenly pirated Spanish galleons in Caribbean and South American waters. In 1580 Drake returned with a cargo of Spanish gold after circumnavigating the globe. A proud Elizabeth promptly knighted him. Spain, however, was furious and in 1588 sent a mighty fleet against the upstart English. But the quick British warships, with help from the weather, demolished the Spanish Armada. Now England ruled the seas, and, armed with a different philosophy of colonization, prepared to replace Spain as the dominant power in North America.

At home, England's economy was flourishing under the influence of a burgeoning capitalism. The effects were at once invigorating and dislocating. Prices and profits soared during the sixteenth century. With the woolen industry leading the way, manufacturing became a large-scale enterprise. To supply the mills with raw material, fields once used for crops were fenced (the sixteenth-century term was *enclosed*) for sheep pastures. Some farmers suffered, but for others change created opportunity. John Winthrop's grandfather Adam, for example, quit farming early in the sixteenth century to try his luck in commerce. He did well. Entering the clothworkers' guild, or union, as an apprentice, he subsequently became a journeyman and then a master clothier. He also became rich enough to purchase the manor of Groton in Suffolk, acquire a coat of arms, and join the landed gentry.

John Winthrop grew up in the comfortable, rustic setting of Groton. As his parents' only son and heir, John seemed destined for a life devoted to the gentlemanly art of estate management. At fifteen he journeyed to Cambridge for the traditional two years of polishing in that university's Trinity College. In 1605, at the age of seventeen, Winthrop married Mary Forth, a bride carefully selected by his father for her economic assets and social connections. Ten months later there was a baby, and John Winthrop appeared ready to settle down in Suffolk. At this point, North America seemed totally irrelevant to his life, but he was soon to encounter an influence that ultimately transformed the country gentleman into a wilderness colonizer. The new force was the Protestant Reformation, and it led John Winthrop to the New World, just as the Renaissance spirit of discovery and glory had led Christopher Columbus.

The Reformation began in Germany in 1519 with the work of Martin Luther. Fed as well by the ideas of the French theologian John Calvin, it spread rapidly throughout Northern Europe. Numerous variations in doctrine existed, but in general, Protestants favored reducing the elaborate organization Catholicism placed between the individual believer and God. Their goal was recovery of the simplicity and sincerity of the original Christian faith.

In England, the Reformation quickly acquired political as well as theological importance. Henry VIII, king since 1509, had little sympathy for Protestant ideas, but he coveted power and property. The Catholic Church in England had both in plenty. And Henry harbored personal grounds for resentment: the Pope refused to grant him a divorce. Finally, in the 1530s, Henry made his move. Defying Rome, he appointed himself head of the Church in England, granted himself a divorce, and confiscated all the property of the Catholic Church, which amounted to about a quarter of the entire kingdom. One beneficiary of the confiscation was John Winthrop's grandfather, who bought the old monastic estate of Groton from Henry in 1544.

It remained for Henry's daughter Elizabeth to pursue the Reformation in England. In 1559, at the beginning of her reign, Elizabeth established Anglicanism (the Church of England) as the nation's official religion and proceeded to define what and how Englishmen could worship. The penalty for disobedience was fine and imprisonment. For most Protestants this arrangement proved satisfactory, since the Church of England did eliminate some of the hierarchy and ritual of Roman Catholicism. But the more radical regarded Anglicanism as little better than what it replaced. Many of these dissenters joined hands after 1560 under the banner of Puritanism with the intent of purifying Christianity. In terms of doctrine, this meant accepting the Bible as the sole source of authority and eliminating the hierarchy of church officials in favor of government by local congregations. Since under Anglicanism the king headed the church, Puritans tended to oppose monarchical authority. Here lay the seeds of strife—and also the beginnings of New England.

Puritanism touched the life of John Winthrop in 1606, when he was eighteen and just settling down as squire of Groton. His diary gives the details. On February 2, "a seacret desire after pleasures & itchinge after libertie & unlawfull delightes" on Winthrop's part coincided with his wife's illness. The latter, he assumed, must be a warning to him from the Lord. But his "sinnes" continued, and he himself fell ill. Finally, on April 20 John Winthrop made an agreement (Puritans called it a *covenant*) with God. Winthrop would undertake to purge himself of "pride, covetousnesse, love of this worlde, vanitie of minde, unthankfulnesse [and] slouth . . . both in His service & in my callinge." The Lord's contribution, Winthrop continued, was the provision of "a new heart," strength to resist the temptations of the "Divell," and forgiveness in case Satan temporarily triumphed. "God give me grace to performe my promise," the entry for April 20 concluded, "& I doubt not but he will performe His. God make it fruitfull. Amen."

Winthrop's personal covenant, painstakingly set down as a constant reminder, reflected the core of the Puritan mind. Following Calvin, he assumed that original sin damned all men and destined them to hell's fiery pit. All, that is, but an undeserving few whom God regenerated and granted salvation. These heaven-bound "elect" or "saints," as Winthrop frequently called them, did not in any sense earn their pardon. The best any man could do was to make his covenant, have faith, and seek in the course of his life some sign of the Lord's predetermined decision respecting his fate. Good deeds, a godly life, and success in one's career were such signs—the evidence, not the cause, of salvation. As a saying popular in Winthrop's time went, "a good man does good works, but good works do not make a good man." Living with this paradox was part of being a Puritan.

Once planted in Winthrop, Puritanism took root rapidly. Even as he became absorbed in a career of law and the management of Groton, his concern for religion increased. His central problem was how to live in the real world without loving worldly pleasures too much. This is not to say that Puritans like Winthrop had to be the solemn, gloomy, self-righteous killjoys of the stereotype. The important thing was to love God above all. If a man could enjoy a tankard of ale, a good dinner, a pipe, and his wife without lessening his enjoyment of God, fine. The danger lay in forgetting one's first duty. John Winthrop, who was by his own admission strongly drawn to the lusts of the flesh, teetered between secular and spiritual delights for most of his early life. The pattern was cyclical: after a bout of sensuality, Winthrop's conscience drove him to a period of monastic abstinence. But his resolve always weakened, and the cycle continued. After thirty years of struggle with himself, Winthrop concluded that the key virtue was discipline. Since sinful man could not be continually good, he had to learn to deal with his lower desires and channel their energies upward whenever possible.

While the individual soul dominated the attention of English Puritans, the condition of society also concerned them deeply. Winthrop and his fellows believed it their duty to make the world as godly as possible. The welfare of a nation depended on a social or group covenant between God and its people. Just as in the case of the individual covenant, God was thought to protect and sustain an entire people who endeavored to live according to His laws. Conversely, if society broke those laws, a wrathful God was expected to dispense lethal punishment. Government, then, was crucial as a way of ensuring godliness.

With the stakes so high, Puritans like Winthrop looked with growing uneasiness at the course of English political history in the early seventeenth century. In 1603 James I succeeded Queen Elizabeth, and religious dissenters hoped the change meant greater sympathy for their cause. But in January 1604 at Hampton Court James made his position clear: "I shall make them conform themselves," he declared in reference to the Puritans, "or I will harry them out of this land, or else do worse." Winthrop was only sixteen at the time, but as a member of a Puritan family, news of James's pronouncement must have sent cold chills along his spine. As his involvement with Puritanism grew, he knew he was inviting royal displeasure or, as James had said, "worse." The cells in the Tower of London and the executioner's block provided vivid illustrations of the king's meaning. Yet Winthrop could not think of abandoning his covenant with God. Almost as distasteful was the prospect of watching his country forget the Reformation and perhaps slip back to Roman Catholicism. What could be done?

The alternatives, at least, were not hard to discover, and Winthrop surely weighed them on the long, solitary rides from Groton to his law duties in the Court of Wards in London. One possibility was revolt. In the seventeenth century, however, kings cast awesome shadows. One did not dismiss their authority lightly. Even when Charles I, James's successor, married a Catholic and in 1629 dissolved Parliament, Winthrop could not entertain revolutionary thoughts. A decade later bolder and more desperate English Puritans would overthrow the throne, but by this time Winthrop had found a different solution.

Another alternative Winthrop considered was separating from England and leaving that unhappy country to the bitter fruits of its own ungodliness. Many precedents existed in the Christian past for this kind of response to evil. Hermits and monks had repeatedly fled to lonely retreats to make their separate peace with God. Occasionally an entire group of people, following the example of the Israelites, escaped from persecution. After James's ominous pronouncement at Hampton Court, some radical Puritans from the village of Scrooby in Nottinghamshire organized under the leadership of William Brewster,

William Bradford, and John Robinson. Extremely dissatisfied with the incomplete purification of the Anglican Church, they determined to reject it entirely.

Although these Separatists desired only to be left alone, the Anglicans harassed them unmercifully. In the winter of 1608–1609 they left England for the more permissive climate of Holland. But their troubles continued. The materialistic Dutch culture offered many temptations, and Catholic Spain threatened to conquer the country and crush all forms of Protestantism. The Separatists finally decided that their best hope for freedom was a complete break with Europe. They would seek the wilderness of the New World. Securing a grant of land from the settler-hungry Virginia Company, thirty-five Separatists and sixty-seven other colonists (we have come to call them all Pilgrims) sailed for New England in the fall of 1620 on the *Mayflower.*

The Pilgrims proved the feasibility of separation, but John Winthrop remained unconvinced. He could not escape a sense of responsibility to his fellow-man. No matter how ungodly society had become, the true Christian, as Winthrop defined him, could not turn his back. The goal, after all, was the reformation of Christendom. The purification of a tiny part of it had no meaning. On a more fundamental level, Winthrop perceived that all men were united by original sin. Man could not escape from evil in the world any more than he could flee from evil in himself. Both had to be confronted. Winthrop knew that in this respect the Separatists on the *Mayflower* had failed. They had simply deserted England. In quest of the perfection of their little group, they had forgotten the meaning of the Reformation.

Yet Winthrop could not but envy the Pilgrims their opportunity to build a society according to their understanding of God's wishes. Musing on this apparent dilemma in the 1620s, he gradually formulated a solution. Suppose he left England in order to create a model Christian community that by its very godliness would command the attention and admiration of the rest of the world? Eventually, Winthrop reasoned, other societies would follow the New England example in their own homelands. Surely this would be a contribution to the Reformation. Leaving in order to lead and ultimately to save all mankind—here was an alternative he could support.

Although Winthrop had found good grounds to justify migration, he remained uncommitted at the beginning of 1629. The events of the next ten months, however, forced a decision. During this time the New World became an increasingly familiar subject of conversation around the Winthrop table. A group of Puritan merchants known to the Winthrop family had formed the New England Company and were already involved in colonization. John Winthrop, Jr., even toyed with the idea of joining the company outpost at Salem, Massachusetts. Eventually he declined, but not before his father had reviewed the enterprise favorably. The elder Winthrop also thought a stint in the wilderness would serve to cool the blood of another son, Henry. But in the spring of 1629 Winthrop could think of himself only as squire of Groton and attorney to the court of Charles I.

After two earlier marriages left him a widower, he had finally found in Margaret Tyndal a woman who not only survived, but understood Winthrop's determination to enjoy worldly pleasures without being absorbed by them. As a consequence, he was only mildly interested when on March 4 the New England Company secured a new royal charter confirming its grant and renamed itself the Massachusetts Bay Company. Six days later, however, Charles I dissolved Parliament. Now there was nothing to stand between the Puritans and the hostility of the king. Suddenly New England acquired much greater appeal for John Winthrop.

As the English political climate chilled for men of his persuasion, Winthrop resigned his position as a royal attorney (or perhaps he was fired). Returning to Groton, he contemplated an uncertain future. His friends in the Massachusetts Bay Company, however, knew exactly what Winthrop should do. A man of his substance and experience, they pointed out, was needed in the colonial enterprise. He might well become its leader. And thousands of miles from Charles I and the Anglican Church, such a leader could use his own ideals to shape society. The prospect appealed to Winthrop, as did the argument that his participation was crucial to the success of the entire effort. He was told, probably with some truth, that many Puritans were reserving judgment about America until after John Winthrop decided. For someone with his sense of social responsibility, this situation generated considerable pressure.

But for Winthrop, the central question was how the Massachusetts Bay Company would be governed. He knew what had happened in the case of the Virginia Company's colony on Chesapeake Bay. In 1624, after seventeen years of existence, James I simply voided its charter, disbanded its representative assembly (the House of Burgesses), and placed a royal governor in control. If this could happen to Massachusetts Bay, Winthrop reasoned, then there was no point in proceeding further with plans for a Puritan community. It would be crushed by the Crown. He was right, of course, but in July of 1629 those interested in securing his support made a telling bid. A careful reading of the March 4 charter, they explained, revealed no provision regarding the location of the company's government. Normally, the directors were Englishmen who remained at home under the watchful eye of the king. Yet it appeared that the Massachusetts Bay Company had the option of directing itself from a New World location far removed from royal scrutiny. Winthrop relished this prospect. Here was assurance of the independence he considered essential for the success of a spiritual experiment. In August 1629 Winthrop cast his lot with the New World and began preparations for departure.

It was difficult enough to conclude his personal affairs, but on October 20 the General Court (assembly of members) of the Massachusetts Bay Company elected him governor. "So it is," he wrote to Margaret, "that [it] hath pleased the Lorde to call me to a further trust in this business of the plantation, than either I expected or finde my selfe fitt for."

Despite this initial lack of confidence, Winthrop proved an extremely able governor in the busy months before the Puritan exodus. He understood his first task was recruiting colonists for the holy experiment. Turning to the pen, Winthrop wrote down the reasons for migrating. Widely circulated among Puritans, these "Conclusions," combined with Winthrop's prestige, proved highly persuasive. He began by pointing out that the New World offered few temptations to the younger generation, whereas England was full of "evill examples." Indeed, the corruption of church and society in Europe invited an unfavorable judgment from the Lord. Perhaps the Old World was doomed. New England, Winthrop argued, might be the refuge God provided for those "he means to save out of the generall callamity." Elsewhere in his "Conclusions" he relied on the rivalry between religions in the seventeenth century to drive home the point that if Protestants did not colonize the New World, Catholics would.

Worldly considerations also figured in Winthrop's inducements. He emphasized the depressed English economy and how a man could scarcely earn a living even with hard work. Better to seek new fields where success—that sign of God's pleasure—might crown one's efforts. Moreover, in the New World land was abundant and free. For those who argued that the land belonged to Indians, Winthrop replied according to Scripture. He interpreted Genesis 1:28, the first commandment of God to man, to give Christians the right to conquer and subdue those parts of the world that "lie waste without any improvement." The North American wilderness, in Winthrop's mind, was intended by God to be colonized, civilized, and made fruitful by people like himself. The heathen Indians did not count—except as subjects for conversion. Finally, Winthrop answered the charge that he was deserting Europe with the assertion that the Puritans were actually spearheading the Reformation.

In addition to recruiting colonists, he was responsible for provisioning and partly financing the expedition. Like Noah and the Ark, he had to think of everything necessary to begin civilization anew. Seeds, livestock, tools, books, even limes to ward off scurvy went onto his careful lists and into the holds of the ships. Also needed were representatives of the various crafts and professions, and Winthrop chose his colleagues with this in mind. As a result, the thousand Englishmen who gathered in April of 1630 at Cowes to board the eleven ships of the Massachusetts Bay Company were a society in miniature.

Thus far John Winthrop's energy and idealism had been equal to the task of leaving England. But when the Puritan fleet left Cowes on April 8, his challenge had only begun. In quiet moments, gazing over the ocean, thinking of Groton and of Margaret who remained behind temporarily, misgivings crowded in upon him. He knew the difficulties encountered in previous efforts at colonizing North America. The complete disappearance of Sir Walter Raleigh's 1585 settlement on Roanoke Island was an extreme example, but subsequent English outposts in the New World had fared only slightly better.

The Virginia Company's colony at Jamestown was started in May 1607, when 105 survivors of a voyage that claimed 39 lives landed on the north bank of the James River a few miles upstream from Chesapeake Bay. Their troubles began at once. The site chosen for the colony was a tidal marsh characterized by foul water and

34

malaria-bearing mosquitoes. Tied as they were to ships, the colonists hesitated to move inland to better locations. But attitude as well as environment produced the nightmare of the next several years. Self-styled gentlemen and adventurers in the *conquistador* mold, the first Virginians balked at performing tasks such as farming that were essential for survival. Their supplies dwindled. Disease swept the colony. By January of 1608, only 38 of the original contingent remained. At this point, realistic, hard-boiled John Smith engineered a temporary improvement with his insistence that Jamestown make crops and livestock, rather than gold, its principal concern. But in 1609 Smith was ousted and sent back to England. Now exposed to the full force of their ignorance, the settlers entered upon a "starving time." The winter of 1609–1610 reduced them to a diet of rats, snakes, horsehide, and even human flesh. Of approximately 500 colonists, only 60 survived, and they were en route back to England when they met a relief expedition entering the mouth of the James. Conditions improved slowly, but only because the London Company pumped a stream of new men into Virginia to replace the discouraged and the dead. By the 1620s people no longer starved and tobacco production flourished, but the settlement still clung tenuously to the edge of the wilderness.

As he sailed for America, John Winthrop was keenly aware of the difficulties in Virginia. Indeed, one of the "Objections" in his 1629 argument for migrating had been that "the ill success of other Plantations may tell us what will become of this." But his "Answer" pointed out that most of Virginia's problems "happened through . . . slouth and security." The Puritans, never forgetful of their duty to God and the rest of mankind, would, Winthrop hoped, avoid these perils. Yet only a fool would make light of the immense obstacles associated with New World colonization. A wilderness environment demanded radically different skills and temperaments than rural England. English country squires did not immediately become American frontiersmen. Acknowledging this in his "Conclusions," Winthrop faced the fact that the Puritan endeavor "is attended with many and great difficulties." But his answer to this objection went right to the point: "soe is every good action." This frame of mind gave promise of the physical and mental toughness necessary for survival.

The record of earlier settlement north of Virginia likewise offered little cheer. They knew that in 1607 English merchants had sent colonists to Maine, only to see them straggle back after a few miserable months. The story of the Pilgrims in 1620 was almost as discouraging. The *Mayflower* transported William Bradford's little group to New England at the worst possible time of the year—November. With snow already on the ground and a slate-gray sky promising more, Bradford described the New World as "a hideous and desolate wilderness." Half the Pilgrims died that first winter. Summer brought crops and the assistance of Indians such as Squanto, but the precariousness of their hold on the land gave the celebration of the first Thanksgiving in 1621 a hollow ring. From such experiences, Winthrop learned the full price of religious freedom.

After the frantic months of preparation, the slow Atlantic crossing afforded him an opportunity to meditate on the problems ahead. But Winthrop would not have been on the *Arbella* without a sense of the bright promise of new beginnings. The concept of mission, so central to Puritan thought, captured both these moods. In Winthrop's mind mission resulted from a covenant with God. It meant the responsibility of performing special work for Him and the opportunity of receiving His special protection. Winthrop and the migrating Puritans believed they were a chosen people. God, they thought, had singled them out to lead mankind. And He had given them an almost incredible opportunity. The New World was a vacuum, a clean slate on which man could write a fresh and, perhaps, a better record. None of the mistakes of the past need be made again. For John Winthrop in the seventeenth century, the New World was like another habitable planet for us. But in Winthrop's mind the most logical analogy to the New World was the Garden of Eden. And he was a latter-day Adam. The New World gave him and all mankind another chance.

Winthrop expounded the theme of mission and some of its consequences in a mid-Atlantic sermon, "A Modell of Christian Charity," on board the *Arbella*. He began by enumerating the purposes of the migration: to serve the Lord, to preserve themselves from "the common corruptions of this evil world," and to "work out our salvation." The core of the sermon was the covenant struck between the America-bound Puritans and God. If God brought them safely across the Atlantic, then they had the obligation to keep the faith. For Puritans this was no casual agreement, but a solemn promise that touched every aspect of their lives. "Thus stands the cause between God and us," thundered Winthrop. "We are entered into covenant with Him for this work; we have taken out a commission." Every aspect of Puritan policy was directed to this end. Again and again Winthrop stressed the importance of discipline and unity if the mission was to be accomplished. "We must be knit together in this work as one," he insisted. "We must delight in each other, make others' conditions our own, rejoice together, mourn together, labor and suffer together; always having before our eyes our commission." Of paramount importance, Governor Winthrop continued, was the need for the people to obey their governors and for the governors to obey God. If they did, God would adopt and protect the wilderness colony as He had the ancient Jews. The result would be a model society, "a city upon a hill."

No one knew better than John Winthrop that the extraordinary opportunity of the New England Puritans also meant extraordinary responsibility. Because of this chance to build a godly society, failure would be especially loathsome in the eyes of the Lord. Winthrop felt certain that breaking the covenant and ignoring the mission would bring divine wrath crashing down on their colony. If we "embrace this present world," he warned, "and prosecute our carnal intentions," an angry God will "be revenged of such a perjured people" by stranding them without protection in a wilderness.

As the *Arbella* drew near New England, such considerations became increasingly real. On June 6, 1630, Winthrop's shipmates enjoyed their first sight of land in almost two months. They struck the coast well north of their destination and for the next several days sailed southwest along the coast of Maine. On June 12 the ship anchored off John Endicott's Puritan outpost at Salem, and the passengers feasted on venison and wild strawberries. In time, the other vessels straggled into port, and by the end of the summer the population of New England more than doubled. The previous occupants were only a few Pilgrims under William Bradford at Plymouth, a scattering of survivors from the unsuccessful fishing and trading settlements of Sir Ferdinando Gorges's Council for New England, and gentlemen of wealth and independence like Samuel Maverick and William Blackstone. Winthrop's initial problem as governor was to keep up morale. The long ocean voyage had sapped the Puritans' physical strength and the vigor of their ideals. Face-to-face contact with the New England wilderness further eroded their resolve. Was the migration a huge mistake, the "city upon a hill" a sorry joke? When strong leadership was imperative, Winthrop took command.

His first decision was to find a better location than Salem. Exploration southward into Massachusetts Bay revealed the land around the mouth of the Charles River to be rich, flat, well-watered, and abounding with good harbors. Winthrop approved, and the Puritans quickly spread out around the bay. After a few false starts, the Governor located himself immediately south of the Charles on a narrow-necked peninsula he called Boston. Though death claimed eleven of Winthrop's servants and some two hundred other Puritans the first winter, compared to the "starving times" of earlier settlers, this survival rate was good. Not being first had some great advantages. Older New England hands, some with ten years of pioneering under their belts, helped with advice and gifts of food.

The Puritans were also relatively rich and could buy supplies from England. The arrival of a ship bearing reinforcements of goods and people in February 1631, for instance, contributed a great deal to maintaining the settlement through the first winter. Even so, by spring some of the Puritans were weary of being God's guinea pigs and booked passage back home. Winthrop stood firm. He believed that merely surviving the winter signified God's pleasure with New England. "I would not have altered my course," he wrote to his third and much loved wife, Margaret, "though I had foreseen all these Afflictions: I never fared better in my life, never slept better, never had more content of minde." Only Margaret herself was missing, and on November 4, 1631, she arrived in Boston harbor with the rest of the Winthrop family. The reunion was a joyous time of feasting for the entire colony—the Puritan equivalent of the Pilgrim thanksgiving ten years before.

Margaret Winthrop arrived in Boston as part of a growing stream of Puritans fleeing political adversity in England. Throughout the 1630s Charles I ruled without Parliament, while William Laud, Bishop of London, and after 1633 the powerful Archbishop of Canterbury, harassed Puritans continually. The combined oppression of state and church drove about 20,000 Englishmen to America before 1640. John Winthrop was glad to see them come. The newcomers not only brought sorely needed supplies and skills, they also reinforced the cherished city-upon-a-hill concept. In the 1630s, with immigrants continuously arriving, Massachusetts nearly approached Winthrop's hope for it as a refuge and an example. Yet the growth of Massachusetts Bay created problems for leaders like Winthrop. They found that ideals and realities, theory and practice, did not often correspond in the New World. European plans shattered on the rocks of American circumstances. Winthrop learned this lesson quickly in regard to government.

The charter of the Massachusetts Bay Company gave John Winthrop and a few other "freemen" full authority to legislate for the colony and to choose its governor. In theory, this oligarchic arrangement suited the purposes of the holy experiment quite well. Puritans believed that among the several covenants ordering their lives was one respecting the relationship of people and their governors. It held that God's laws could be enforced among imperfect men only if they agreed to submit to political leaders who could best interpret divine will. Governors, in Puritan thought, were like Old Testament prophets, chosen by ballot. Though they were elected by the people, their authority, drawn from God, was unquestionable.

The first years of Massachusetts Bay revealed the presence of forces working against this political arrangement. The New World situation, in the first place, gave the individual, no matter what his previous status, potential. On the clean slate of the American wilderness he had opportunities unimagined in the older, established European society. Pioneering placed a premium on performance. On the New England frontier a man believed he succeeded or not according to his ambition and ability. Under such circumstances, the successful —and mere survivors were successful at first—gained self-respect. These individuals began to chafe under ideas and institutions that stifled initiative. The wilderness also had a way of blurring the social distinctions so carefully maintained in older civilizations. Equality meant more in the New World than it did in the Old. Men sensed the difference as soon as they landed, and the impact on politics showed almost immediately.

On October 19, 1630, Governor John Winthrop opened the first meeting of the General Court of the Massachusetts Bay Company. Seven other "assistants" attended. Under the terms of the company's charter, these few prepared to conduct the business of the colony. But other men also came. Some drew Winthrop aside and let him know

Any modern camper has his choice of a variety of what-to-take lists and guides designed to facilitate his stay in the wilderness. But the first settlers in the New World wilderness had none until this 1622 broadside was printed in London for the use of the Virginia Company. We can suppose that John Winthrop provided similar information to prospective colonists a decade later.

THE INCONVENIENCIES
THAT HAVE HAPPENED TO SOME PER-
SONS WHICH HAVE TRANSPORTED THEMSELVES

from *England* to *Virginia*, vvithout prouisions necessary to sustaine themselues, hath greatly hindred the *Progresse* of that noble *Plantation*: For preuention of the like disorders heereafter, that no man suffer, either through ignorance or misinformation; it is thought requisite to publish this short declaration: wherein is contained a particular of such necessaries, as either priuate families or single persons shall haue cause to furnish themselues with, for their better support at their first landing in Virginia; whereby also greater numbers may receiue in part, directions how to prouide themselues.

Apparrell.

		li.	s.	d.
Apparrell for one man, and so after the rate for more.	One Monmouth Cap	00	01	10
	Three falling bands	—	01	03
	Three shirts	—	07	06
	One waste-coate	—	02	02
	One suite of Canuase	—	07	06
	One suite of Frize	10	00	
	One suite of Cloth	15	00	
	Three paire of Irish stockins	—	04	00
	Foure paire of shooes	08	08	
	One paire of garters	—	00	10
	One doozen of points	—	00	03
	One paire of Canuase sheets	08	00	
	Seuen ells of Canuase, to make a bed and boulster, to be filled in *Virginia* 8.s.			
	One Rug for a bed 8. s. which with the bed seruing for two men, halfe is	08	00	
	Fiue ells coorse Canuase, to make a bed at Sea for two men, to be filled with straw, iiij.s.			
	One coorse Rug at Sea for two men, will cost vj.s. is for one	05	00	
		04	00	00

Victuall.

		li.	s.	d.
For a whole yeere for one man, and so for more after the rate.	Eight bushels of Meale	02	00	00
	Two bushels of pease at 3.s.	—	06	00
	Two bushels of Oatemeale 4.s. 6.d.	—	09	00
	One gallon of *Aquauitæ*	—	02	06
	One gallon of Oyle	—	03	06
	Two gallons of Vineger 1.s.	—	02	00
		03	03	00

Armes.

		li.	s.	d.
For one man, but if halfe of your men haue armour it is sufficient so that all haue Peeces and swords.	One Armour compleat, light	—	17	00
	One long Peece, fiue foot or fiue and a halfe, neere Musket bore	01	02	—
	One sword	—	05	—
	One belt	—	01	—
	One bandaleere	—	01	06
	Twenty pound of powder	18	00	
	Sixty pound of shot or lead, Pistoll and Goose shot	—	05	00
		03	09	06

Tooles.

		li.	s.	d.
For a family of 6. persons and so after the rate for more.	Fiue broad howes at 2.s. a piece	—	10	—
	Fiue narrow howes at 16.d. a piece	—	06	08
	Two broad Axes at 3.s. 8.d. a piece	—	07	04
	Fiue felling Axes at 18.d. a piece	—	07	06
	Two steele hand sawes at 16.d. a piece	—	02	08
	Two two-hand-sawes at 5. s. a piece	—	10	—
	One whip-saw, set and filed with box, file, and wrest	—	10	—
	Two hammers 12.d. a piece	—	02	00
	Three shouels 18.d. a piece	—	04	06
	Two spades at 18.d. a piece	—	03	—
	Two augers 6.d. a piece	—	01	00
	Six chissels 6.d. a piece	—	03	00
	Two percers stocked 4.d. a piece	—	00	08
	Three gimlets 2.d. a piece	—	00	06
	Two hatchets 21.d. a piece	—	03	06
	Two froues to cleaue pale 18.d.	—	03	00
	Two hand-bills 20. a piece	—	03	04
	One grindlestone 4.s.	—	04	00
	Nailes of all sorts to the value of	02	00	—
	Two Pickaxes	—	03	—
		06	02	08

Houshold Implements.

		li.	s.	d.
For a family of 6. persons, and so for more or lesse after the rate.	One Iron Pot	—	07	—
	One kettle	—	06	—
	One large frying-pan	—	02	06
	One gridiron	—	01	06
	Two skillets	—	05	—
	One spit	—	02	—
	Platters, dishes, spoones of wood	—	04	—
		01	08	00

	li.	s.	d.
For Suger, Spice, and fruit, and at Sea for 6.men	00	12	06
So the full charge of Apparrell, Victuall, Armes, Tooles, and houshold stuffe, and after this rate for each person, will amount vnto about the summe of	12	10	—
The passage of each man is	06	00	—
The fraight of these prouisions for a man, will bee about halfe a Tun, which is	01	10	—
So the whole charge will amount to about	20	00	00

Nets, hookes, lines, and a tent must be added, if the number of people be greater, as also some kine.

And this is the vsuall proportion that the Virginia *Company doe bestow vpon their Tenants which they send.*

Whosoeuer transports himselfe or any other at his owne charge vnto *Virginia*, shall for each person so transported before Midsummer 1625. haue to him and his heires for euer fifty Acres of Land vpon a first, and fifty Acres vpon a second diuision.

The marshy flats of the lower James River just above its entrance into Chesapeake Bay were a poor place to plant a colony. But by 1620, the approximate date this modern painting depicts, the Virginia Company's settlement was beginning to show signs of permanency. Houses are spreading outside the protective confines of James Fort (left foreground, behind the stockade), and some attempt has been made at clearing fields for the tobacco plants John Rolfe introduced in 1612. But the ocean-going vessel at the main dock suggests the continued dependence of the colony on the mother country.

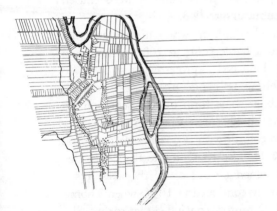

John Winthrop and his Massachusetts Bay contemporaries had an obsession about orderly existence. When a new town was "planted" in the wilderness, an elaborate survey preceded settlement. Each settler was assigned his designated parcel of land. Other parcels were reserved for the church, schools, and the "commons" that everyone shared. This was the plan for Wethersfield, Connecticut.

Colleges ranked high on the list of early American priorities. They were regarded as evidence that civilized standards could and would be maintained in the New World wilderness. Harvard College, founded across the Charles River from Boston in the community of Cambridge in 1636, was the showpiece of seventeenth-century Massachusetts Bay. This view of the college in 1726 reveals buildings that must have been among the most imposing in the colony. They were tangible evidence of the determination of New Englanders to succeed in their colonizing endeavor.

their desire to have a voice in the affairs of the plantation. It was difficult to refuse. These people, after all, were Winthrop's colleagues in colonization. They had dared together. Many had come as a direct result of his encouragement. They were partners in performing God's work on earth. And, Winthrop realized, the Massachusetts Bay Company was not just a joint stock company, but in the New England context, a civil government. Still, he was no democrat. Sovereignty rested with God, not the people. Strong, theocratic leadership, based on a correct reading of God's will, must continue.

The solution, he decided, was to broaden the base of government by creating a new political category, the *freeman*. Any adult male, indentured servants excepted, who was a member of the Puritan church could apply for such status. As a consequence, the second meeting of the General Court in May 1631 included 118 freemen. They had no legislative authority, but they could elect the assistants who did. Election of the assistants also indirectly influenced the choice of governor. Thus, less than a year after its beginnings, Massachusetts government had moved in a republican direction.

The new arrangement pleased Winthrop, who remained governor, but his liberalism soon received a harder test. In 1632 various communities in Massachusetts Bay launched a protest against a tax assessed by Winthrop and his fellow assistants. According to the disgruntled colonists, taxation without some form of representation was contrary to the tradition of English liberties. Winthrop gave ground grudgingly. He finally agreed to consult with two representatives from every town before the next tax. He also consented to the direct election of the governor by the freemen instead of by the assistants.

The drift away from oligarchy continued in 1634, when Thomas Dudley, a political opponent of Winthrop, concluded that the wording of the Massachusetts Bay charter gave all freemen, not just the assistants, the power to make laws. Winthrop balked at this idea. God's will, not the public's, he believed, should determine policy. The people might select their leaders, but once selected, the leaders must answer only to God. The laws of men were not acceptable substitutes, in Winthrop's opinion, for the laws of God.

Respected as he was in Massachusetts, Winthrop could not prevent the continued erosion of his political ideas. Most of those who migrated to New England had come in search of freedom from the power of a king or an archbishop. Their deep-rooted aversion to arbitrary authority did not end with the trans-Atlantic crossing. Indeed, the lack of restraints inherent in a wilderness situation encouraged an even more passionate dedication to liberty. God's authority, of course, went unquestioned, but increasing numbers felt they too could discern His will, and demanded a role in translating it into law. This attitude, in fact, was part of the priesthood-of-all-believers concept of the Protestant Reformation, and one that especially influenced the congregational theory to which the American Puritans subscribed. Even Winthrop's repeated assurances that he and the other assistants best knew God's desires did not placate popular suspicion. There seemed to be too much arbitrary power in an arrangement under which a small group ruled at their own discretion.

In 1634 Winthrop was pressured into permitting each of the ten towns to send two deputies to the General Court. These deputies actually made laws along with the assistants in a semirepresentative assembly. The same year Thomas Dudley, the beneficiary of political criticism of John Winthrop, replaced him in the governor's chair. For the next three years, Winthrop was merely one of the assistants.

During this time the freemen took steps to base the government of Massachusetts Bay on explicit law, rather than the judgment of an oligarchy. Nathaniel Ward of Ipswich prepared the Body of Liberties, which spelled out the rights and obligations of citizenship. In the manner of the English Magna Carta (1215), it reflected the idea that a government of laws offered better protection for popular liberties than a government of men. Winthrop, who regained the governorship in 1637, fought the Body of Liberties doggedly. It was not that he quarreled with its substance, but rather that he believed such rules should result from the slow accumulation of the magistrates' interpretation of the Bible. Time and place, however, were against him. In December 1641 the General Court adopted Ward's code of laws.

Continued sparring between leaders and followers in Winthrop's New England resulted in 1644 in the division of the General Court into two houses—into a bicameral legislature. Winthrop and the other assistants in the upper chamber benefited from this arrangement because they secured a veto over laws made by the deputies in the lower house. The following year, however, the deputies struck back, and again the controversy revolved around Winthrop. The trouble began in the town of Hingham when the people refused to accept the militia officer appointed by Winthrop and the assistants. In his place they nominated another man. Feelings ran hot on both sides. One citizen of Hingham vowed to "die at the sword's point, if he might not have the choice of his own officers." Another simply rejected the idea that the Boston officials had anything to do with the affairs of Hingham. This was the beginning of frontier independence. But for Winthrop, it was a serious breach of the covenant that merited the strongest punishment. The men of Hingham responded by accusing Winthrop of overreaching the powers granted him in the Body of Liberties. Whereupon the lower house of the General Court impeached John Winthrop! A remarkable trial followed. Those who feared concentrated and continuous power hoped to clip Winthrop's wings. Others believed the kind of authority he represented was essential to the Puritan mission. The stormy trial sessions therefore went far beyond the Hingham mutiny. Finally, on July 3, 1645, the General Court was ready with its verdict: not guilty. Winthrop must have anticipated it, because he was ready with what he termed a "little speech." It was one of his greatest moments.

"I entreat you to consider," he began, "that when you choose magistrates, you take them from among yourselves, men subject to like passions as you are." Of course assistants, or "magistrates" as Winthrop called them, could make mistakes. Winthrop even implied that he regretted some of his own recent actions. But, he quickly countered, "when you see infirmities in us, you should reflect upon your own." It was the Puritan mind at its best and worst. Winthrop then advised the people that once they had selected a leader, the terms of the social covenant obliged them to "run the hazard of his skill and ability" as long as he tried to follow God's law.

The second part of Winthrop's speech took up the vexing problem of liberty. In Winthrop's view, there were two kinds. "Natural" liberty belonged to man as it did to "beasts and other creatures," and simply meant to do as one pleased. Good might result, Winthrop conceded, but more frequently evil did because no restraint stood between desire and action. Natural liberty, then, left man's imperfect nature uncontrolled and in time made men "worse than brute beasts." Such considerations were not academic in the wilds of America. The other kind of liberty, which Winthrop called "civil or federal," meant the freedom to do what is "good, just and honest." The definition of "good, just and honest" came from God through the medium of those who could best discern His purposes—magistrates like John Winthrop. In accepting this more restricted form of liberty, man showed his ability to rise above the animals, restrain evil tendencies, and fulfill the terms of the covenant with God. "So shall your liberties be preserved," Winthrop concluded, "in upholding the honor and power of authority amongst you." Thus rebuked, the Hingham radicals subsided.

European feudal and monarchical tradition figured more prominently in Winthrop's 1645 speech than did the currents of individualism and popular sovereignty already percolating through New World society. But of course, all but the children in Massachusetts Bay in 1645 *were* Europeans. Coupled with Winthrop's personal prestige and the unifying concept of mission, this fact served to delay social and political change in New England.

Elsewhere in North America, however, Old World expectations and institutions collapsed more quickly. Indeed, in the light of the experience of other plantations, Winthrop had reason to be encouraged with the Massachusetts record. The original plans of the Virginia Company, for instance, called for a military dictatorship combined with feudal landholding policies. In 1619, however, settlers demanded and received from the London-based directors of the company a representative assembly, the House of Burgesses. The same year, local political authority was removed from Jamestown and given to the several counties. The change indicated a trend. Virginians desired autonomy and continued to resist European directives. By 1624, a frustrated Virginia Company gave up its attempt to control the unruly Americans and turned the colony back to the king. But royal agents proved no more successful. From their wilderness environment, the Virginians derived a passion for independence and a driving ambition. Both tendencies led them to question any authority other than their own.

Further north on Chesapeake Bay, Sir George Calvert, Lord Baltimore, and his son launched Maryland at the same time Winthrop founded the Puritan plantation. Their early histories differed sharply. The Calverts held complete power and intended Maryland to be a feudal estate on the European model, complete with a landed gentry,

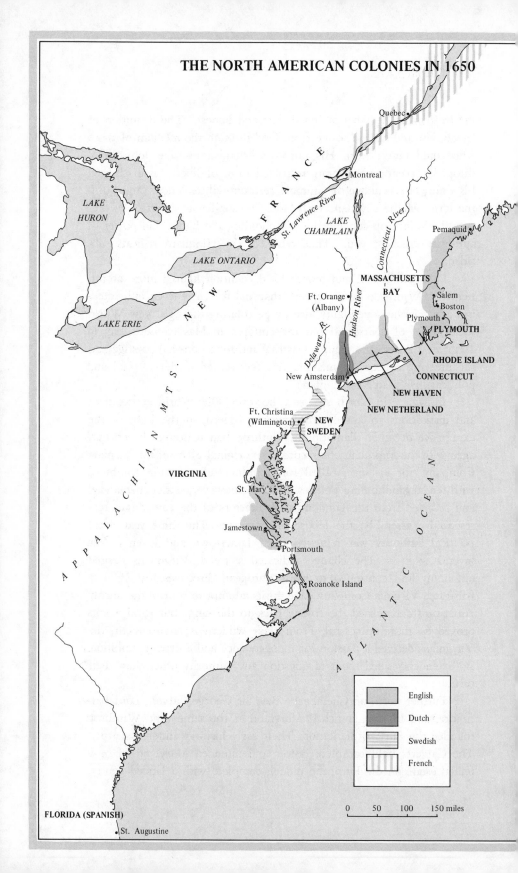

THE NORTH AMERICAN COLONIES IN 1650

LAKE HURON

LAKE ONTARIO

LAKE ERIE

Quebec

F R A N C E

Montreal

St. Lawrence River

LAKE CHAMPLAIN

N E W

Pemaquid

Connecticut River

Ft. Orange
(Albany)

MASSACHUSETTS BAY

Salem
Boston
Plymouth
PLYMOUTH

Hudson River

Delaware R.

New Amsterdam

RHODE ISLAND

CONNECTICUT

NEW HAVEN

NEW NETHERLAND

Ft. Christina
(Wilmington)

NEW SWEDEN

A P P A L A C H I A N   M T S.

VIRGINIA

St. Mary's

C H E S A P E A K E   B A Y

Jamestown

Portsmouth

Roanoke Island

A T L A N T I C   O C E A N

A T L A N T I C

English

Dutch

Swedish

French

FLORIDA (SPANISH)

St. Augustine

0   50   100   150 miles

serfs, and feudal dues. The scheme existed only on paper. The proprietors and their agents were first simply ignored, then defied, and at length made to concede the rights of land ownership and meaningful political representation to most of the settlers.

Neither Maryland nor Virginia became a democracy overnight. Aspirations remained aristocratic, but they were not limited to an aristocracy. Everyone wanted to skim the cream off the top. Men had not crossed 3000 miles of ocean merely to change masters. Political authority that stood in the way of individual ambition was among the first casualties of the American experience. Winthrop would have preferred it otherwise, but he understood the mood of the people. This realism coupled with the spiritual commitment of the Puritans allowed him to retain the essence of oligarchic authority in Massachusetts long after it had faded elsewhere.

We have evidence of this in Winthrop's high-handed treatment of Robert Child. In 1645, while Winthrop was lecturing the General Court on the meaning of liberty, Child, a physician, wrote a "Remonstrance and Humble Petition" that challenged the basis of the entire Puritan political system. It spoke for the rights of those who were not church members and therefore not voting freemen. Either suffrage or church membership ought to be expanded, Child argued. And for good measure he challenged the right of the General Court to legislate without regard to Parliament. He even threatened to return to London and tattle on the colony. Winthrop lost no time in clamping down on the upstart. Arbitrary seizures, fines, and imprisonment were the colony's answers to Child. Before being sent back to England in 1647, he was thoroughly discredited. Time and America, to be sure, were on Child's side, but in the 1640s his challenge to authority brought the conservatism latent in Puritan political theory crashing down on his defenseless head. Winthrop found the result immensely satisfying. The Lord's will was upheld, the unity of the New England way preserved.

Despite the attention paid to politics, the dominant concern of Winthrop's Massachusetts Bay was religion. Churches were the core of New England intellectual and social life and consisted of the "saints" and their ministers. Others might worship in the congregation, hoping for that searing flash of regeneration that would qualify them to sit among the elect. Yet membership in the church was restricted to those who succeeded in convincing themselves and their peers that they had been regenerated or saved. Over time, the restrictions disintegrated. More and more people joined the church under compromise arrangements such as the Half-way Covenant of 1662, whereby children of regenerate parents were automatically included in the elect. In the 1630s and 1640s, however, the lines remained firm. One consequence was an intense intolerance in the Puritan mind. They believed, quite literally, that they and they alone knew God's will. Anyone who disagreed with Puritan theology was not only wrong, but in league with evil. As Nathaniel Ward put it in 1645, "poly-piety is the greatest impiety in the world." A man who tolerated other faiths could not be sincere in his own. Toleration was thought to be particularly unbecoming in a society that regarded itself as God's chosen, a city upon a hill. This left dissenters from Puritan orthodoxy with little choice but to leave. In Massachusetts, religion was far too weighty a matter for variations to be allowed.

As governor, Winthrop carried the responsibility of preserving the plantation's piety, a task that brought some of his most trying moments. The first crisis involved a personal friend, the brilliant and charismatic Roger Williams. Only twenty-seven years old when he came to Massachusetts Bay in 1631, Williams fused the intense idealism of youth with a religious fervor exceptional even among Puritans. His conflict, in fact, resulted from his high standards. Williams began by refusing to associate with those who would not denounce and separate from the Church of England. This included Winthrop and most of the colonists in Massachusetts Bay. Displeased as they were with Anglicanism and Archbishop Laud, they took pains to make clear that in leaving for New England, they were not abandoning the church back home. They preferred to think of themselves as good examples, not deserters. Williams could not live with this compromise, and his zeal led him to other unorthodox stands. He declared that a saint must not even pray in the company of unregenerate people and thus challenged the structure of all New England churches. Scrupulous in every ethical matter, Williams even went so far as to question the legitimacy of taking land from the Indians. Perhaps the whole political edifice of the New World colonies rested on the sands of injustice. Before leaving England, Winthrop had attempted to bury such doubts. Roger Williams had a disconcerting knack for unearthing them.

On several occasions in the early 1630s Winthrop attempted to

48

moderate his idealistic young friend. Experience had taught the governor that a man must live with and try to correct the evil he finds in the world and in himself. Removal to America in search of a clean slate was all right, but ultimately a man had to take a stand. The holier-than-thou attitude of Williams, Winthrop argued, might result in personal salvation, but the proper concern of the godly man should be world reformation. Williams in turn advised Winthrop to "abstract yourselfe with a holy violence from the Dung heape of this Earth." Winthrop balked. His style was to clean dung heaps, not flee them.

Williams first tried Boston, but found that settlement cool to his ideas. Next he moved to Plymouth, where the Pilgrims had at least fully separated from the Church of England. But in time, predictably, Williams found imperfections there too. He moved on to Salem, and here he made his strongest impression. Captivated by the charm and sincerity of the young zealot, the citizens of Salem chose him as their minister. Winthrop's eyebrows must have risen at the news. One dissenter was bad enough, but now Williams threatened to convert an entire congregation. In 1635, Winthrop and the General Court ordered Salem to dismiss Williams. The town exploded. In its eyes, this was not only an intrusion of the state into church affairs, but a violation of the principle of congregational autonomy. Salem prepared to elicit sympathy for its cause in other communities, and the fate of Massachusetts Bay hung in the balance. In fact, Williams explicitly called for those who agreed with him to withdraw from Massachusetts Bay into a purer independent organization. The self-styled leaders of the Reformation were themselves to be reformed. For most Puritans, this was too much. Williams lost support even in Salem.

At this juncture the General Court chose to have it out with Roger Williams. No one, especially not Winthrop, wanted to punish this sweet-tempered visionary. If only he would retract his extreme statements and work for the colony. But Williams was unyielding: Massachusetts, he insisted, should work with *him*. This left the General Court with no choice. In October 1635 Roger Williams was banished and given six weeks to leave the colony.

The Williams decision pained John Winthrop. He knew at first hand the passion that impelled the man. He too had been young and idealistic—sufficiently so to migrate 3000 miles to the New World. He too dreamed of a city upon a hill. In Winthrop's eyes, Williams was not a sinner; his error was an excess of virtue. So while Winthrop the magistrate sternly banished the young upstart, Winthrop the man privately suggested where he might go to find a sanctuary: Narragansett Bay, now Rhode Island. Winthrop, moreover, may have been instrumental in blocking a move on the part of his more conservative colleagues in the General Court to send Williams back to England. Part of Winthrop wanted to see Williams succeed—as long as he left Massachusetts. Besides, in the 1630s there was sufficient wilderness in North America for a variety of Zions. So it happened that in January of 1636 Roger Williams and four followers trudged through the snow toward Narragansett Bay in pursuit of perfection. They bought, rather than took, land from the Indians and founded a town, Providence, that attracted a steady flow of refugees from the northern colonies. Even Winthrop, whom Williams still greatly admired, was invited to join. He refused, of course, but with a certain wistfulness.

Winthrop followed the history of Providence with considerable interest. For a time, Williams spiraled into ever narrower circles of perfectionism and intolerance; at one point he found himself conscience-bound to worship with no one except his wife. But time taught him that absolute purity was, after all, unattainable, and tolerance accompanied this realization. In the end, the toleration of Williams far surpassed that of the Puritans.

Even as Winthrop was breathing a sigh of relief over the departure of Roger Williams, another religious tempest loomed on the horizon. William and Anne Hutchinson arrived in Boston on September 18, 1634. The man was totally undistinguished, but his wife proved one of the most remarkable women in American history. Even Winthrop, who came to loathe her, conceded that she possessed "a ready wit and bold spirit." Anne Hutchinson also had an abundance of charm and, in common with Roger Williams, a natural talent for leadership.

The doctrine she advocated was known to the seventeenth century as *antinomianism*. According to the antinomians, salvation was entirely a product of God's mysterious grace. A man could not earn entrance into Heaven. This was orthodox Puritanism, but antinomians like Anne went further. The behavior of a man on earth, they alleged, bore no relation whatsoever to his ultimate fate at God's hands. Orthodox Puritans vigorously protested this conclusion. In the first place, it seemed to divest the individual of all moral responsibility. If conduct was meaningless even as a sign of salvation, then why worry about being good at all? The prospect horrified John Winthrop, who envisioned wholesale anarchy and immorality. Moreover, antinomianism undermined the whole structure of Puritan civil and church government, which was based on the idea of leadership by God's elect. Anne Hutchinson said in effect that the most flagrant sinner might be the very person that God in his mysterious wisdom would choose to save. And John Winthrop might not. Indeed, Anne implied, most of the ministers and magistrates in Massachusetts were only self-styled saints. At any rate, no one could know for sure.

Obviously, these ideas did not endear Anne to the Puritan leaders. Neither did her claim of the power to receive private revelations directly from God. But this persuasive woman attracted a growing following in the church at Boston. At first she merely interpreted the sermons of its minister and her hero, John Cotton, but gradually her weekly discussions acquired a bolder and more original quality. By the autumn of 1636 the majority of the members of the Boston church accepted her interpretations. Had Anne Hutchinson been a man, she would probably have been chosen minister at Boston, but instead her brother-in-law, John Wheelwright, was proposed for the position. Now Winthrop made his move. It seemed to him that the colony stood on the verge of a fatal split.

Throwing the full weight of his reputation against Wheelwright, Winthrop succeeded in blocking his election. The resulting bitterness divided Massachusetts Bay into hostile factions. In May 1637 Winthrop regained the governorship in a tense election. Patiently, even in the face of personal insult, he set about undermining the antinomians. A colony-wide convention of clergy met in August and supported his stand. Encouraged, Winthrop convinced the General Court that Wheelwright should be banished. But the root problem remained, and in November 1637 Anne Hutchinson was summoned to a showdown before the court. The confrontation was packed with drama. Repeatedly, the nimble-minded woman parried the charges of the magistrates or trapped them in their own logic. But as the relentless questioning continued, Anne lost her poise. In a hysterical flood of words, she defiantly told the court that God spoke to her directly and that He would "ruine you and your posterity, and this whole State." That was enough for Winthrop, and he called the court into private session. Its verdict: banishment. But the court at least postponed the sentence to allow Mrs. Hutchinson to deliver the baby she carried.

Winthrop's victory over Anne Hutchinson was hardly one of the mind. The real reason she could not remain in Massachusetts was the threat she posed to order, unity, and authority—and ultimately to covenant and mission. The threat disappeared when in March 1638 the Hutchinsons and a few disciples left for Rhode Island, which was fast becoming a refuge for Puritan castoffs. Winthrop rejoiced greatly in his triumph. He had brought the colony through its most serious spiritual crisis. But Anne Hutchinson's troubles continued. After a series of controversies in Rhode Island, she moved in 1642 to Dutch-controlled New York, where the following year she fell victim to an Indian massacre. Winthrop reacted to the news with the smugness so characteristic of the Puritan mind. The judgment of Massachusetts, he reasoned, must have been confirmed by the Lord.

A different kind of threat to John Winthrop's conception of a covenant community came from Robert Keayne. A genuinely self-made man, Keayne overcame his beginnings as a poor London butcher's helper to become one of the wealthiest men in New England. His trade was the importing business. The colonists were desperate for manufactured goods such as cloth, pots, glass, guns, and saws. Keayne had these items in stock, and he knew the laws of the marketplace. He charged high prices and made high profits. It was good business, but unfortunately for Keayne, Massachusetts Bay was not a business venture. It was not that Puritans opposed material success; rather, they insisted that all such worldly accomplishments must be subordinated to spiritual ones.

In regard to business, John Calvin and other leaders of the Reformation in Europe had carefully instructed the faithful with a doctrine later labeled the "Protestant ethic." Keayne, Winthrop, and their colleagues believed that worldly success was related to virtue, diligence, and the blessing of the Lord. They also knew that a man might strive to succeed in his calling provided he did so for the glory of God and not his personal gain. The Protestant ethic also required that a businessman observe fair "rules for trading," as Winthrop called them. The first was restraint: one must not press an economic advantage to the utmost, but should rest content with a "just" price and profit.

The Keayne case first came to John Winthrop's attention in 1639, just as the colony was relaxing from the tension of the Hutchinson controversy. Various reports reached the governor that the merchant was reaping too large a profit. Word had it that he went so far as to double his own cost in pricing an item. One Boston widow accused Keayne of seizing her prize pig when she could not meet his exorbitant charges. Winthrop responded by calling Keayne before the General Court and conducting a full inquiry into his business practices. At its conclusion, according to Winthrop, the merchant "did, with tears, acknowledge and bewail his covetous and corrupt heart." He was, nonetheless, severely reprimanded and fined.

In Winthrop's eyes, Robert Keayne was a frightening example of how the New World's economic opportunities could lure even a member of a holy experiment away from godliness. Keayne put personal considerations ahead of those of the commonwealth. He was so severely rebuked, one suspects, because Winthrop wanted to make him an example to those who might be tempted to imitate his enterprising practices. Still, the economic individualism Keayne represented was not easily put down. New England merchants proved increasingly unmanageable, and invariably took a stand against the Puritan oligarchy and the repressive authoritarianism it represented. All but the most devout had taken the side of Anne Hutchinson in 1637 because they thought her doctrine promised less centralized control of economic life. And in the late 1680s, when the structure of New England government underwent reorganization, the merchants even sided with English royal authority in preference to that of the American Puritans. By that time, of course, it was becoming clearer that for better or for worse the Robert Keaynes of the New World would prevail over the John Winthrops.

Different as they were, Winthrop's experiences with Roger Williams, Anne Hutchinson, and Robert Keayne taught a common lesson: individualism, "separatism" in seventeenth-century terms, posed the greatest threat to New England's covenanted purposes. Winthrop had anticipated this on board the *Arbella* when he underscored the need for keeping "knit together" in Massachusetts. But at that time he could not have anticipated the full force of the frontier against his ideal of unity and godliness. In a wilderness, he quickly discovered, there was no order except that which the newcomers established. And the structure was always tenuous. It was so easy for someone to spin off the approved track. Total freedom, unprecedented in the Old World, lay only a few miles away in the forest. Consequently, the American Puritans worked at maintaining standards with an urgency born of desperation.

One result of this mentality was the rigid supervision Winthrop and the General Court gave the process of westward expansion. Town "planting" involved a series of careful steps. First, the area to be settled was selected and the boundaries of fields laid out. Sites for homes and, most important, a church were designated, and some construction begun. Then an entire community moved into the wilderness. In numbers, Puritans thought, lay the strength to resist barbarism. Nonetheless, the pioneers were carefully instructed "to carry and behave yourselves as good and sober men" and reminded that "you are in this voyage concerned not only for a worldly interest but . . . for the translating of Christ's ordinances and worship into that country." Here was an extension of the mission idea that applied originally to the planters of the seaboard towns. Puritan pioneering was a controlled, group effort. The Daniel Boone type of frontiersman, whom later generations of Americans celebrated, was definitely not heroic to John Winthrop and his contemporaries. On the contrary, such men appeared to have forgotten the holy mission, followed their own conception of liberty, and become, in Winthrop's words, "worse than brute beasts."

After 1640 when the Puritan Revolution in England caused Massachusetts to lose its appeal as the cutting edge of world Protestantism, orderly settlement of the frontier became even more important. The transformation of wilderness into civilization became the core of a concept of a new mission. And such a restatement was sorely needed. Winthrop himself felt the pangs of uncertainty. In the 1630s the most important English Puritans, including Oliver Cromwell, had at least contemplated moving to New England. But in the next decade the action shifted to England, and it was Winthrop who contemplated a move. That he remained in the New World was due in part to his ability to redefine the Massachusetts mission in terms of westward expansion. Replaced as a city upon a hill by events in England, Americans could still take satisfaction from expanding the boundaries of Christendom.

Frontiersmen were especially suspect, but the American Puritans also considered it essential to discipline individuals in the older towns. Winthrop's journal history of Massachusetts Bay is full of entries describing the General Court's efforts to stamp out sin. Its tool was a body of regulations on personal conduct known retrospectively as "blue laws." Perhaps the most interesting of them stipulated that every person in the colony had to be a member of a family. It was illegal to live alone. If a person lacked a spouse or relatives with whom he could live, he was obliged to join a family as a serving man or maid. The theory behind the law was that the family would provide an excellent means of social control. There were other laws regulating sexual practices, the use of alcohol, and recreation on the Sabbath. It is, however, a mistake to regard Winthrop and his group as sour-faced enemies of fun. They simply felt that their situation and purpose made it imperative not to relax one's guard. Against the dark background of the wilderness, the flame of civilization seemed tiny and fragile. Unpoliced frivolity could lead to abandonment of standards, and individuals could not be entirely trusted with their own policing. The blue laws provided an incentive to preserve order in a potentially chaotic environment.

The struggle against barbarism also entailed reconstructing the full range of civilizing and humanizing institutions known in Europe. Simple survival, even prosperity, was not enough. A city upon a hill required more. As a 1643 tract explained, "after God had carried us safe to *New England,* and wee had builded houses, provided necessarries for our livelihood, rear'd convenient places for Gods worship, and setled the Civill Government: One of the next things we longed for, and looked after was to advance *Learning* and perpetuate it to Posterity." One of the first results of this determination was the founding of Harvard College in 1636. Retrospectively, it is astonishing that only six years after Winthrop and the bulk of New England's settlers came to the wilderness, they created a college. No better indication exists of the Puritan temperament. Virginia, in contrast, did not found a college (William and Mary) until 1693. Massachusetts' first press was operating in 1639; Virginia's, in 1729. The Puritans also prized elementary and secondary education. A grammar school began in Boston in 1636, and eleven years later a Winthrop-led General Court required every town of one hundred families to establish a school.

With such institutional support, lofty purposes and the discipline essential for their achievement could be maintained.

John Winthrop's beloved Margaret died in 1647, after three decades of married life that in its joyous warmth belies much of the Puritan stereotype. A year after her death the lonely governor married for the fourth time and, at the age of sixty, fathered his sixteenth child. But the driving energy that had carried Winthrop so far was running low. A six-week bout with fever preceded his death on March 26, 1649. It was a timely end. The great age of Puritan mission was gradually fading. Second-generation New Englanders, born in America, could not know the strength of the vision that carried their fathers to the wilderness. Other-worldly ideals gave way before considerations of the present. John Winthrop, Jr., for instance, allowed both science and industry to rival religion as the dominant concern of his life. But the temperament if not the creed of his father proved difficult to dislodge from the American character. Commitment, discipline, and self-righteousness, along with a contradictory sense of guilt and inadequacy, all topped with an obsession for perfection, were a lasting legacy.

SELECTED READINGS

The Person

*DUNN, RICHARD S.: *Puritans and Yankees: The Winthrop Dynasty of New England, 1630–1717* (1962).

*MORGAN, EDMUND S.: *The Puritan Dilemma: The Story of John Winthrop* (1958). The most satisfying (and succinct) biographical study.

*MORISON, SAMUEL ELIOT: *Builders of the Bay Colony* (rev. ed., 1946). Contains chapters on Winthrop, on John Winthrop, Jr., and on other leaders of early Massachusetts.

The Winthrop Papers (5 vols., 1929–1947, published by the Massachusetts Historical Society). The most authoritative edition of

* Available in paperback.

John Winthrop's journal, which records the main events of New England's early history.

The Period

*BAILYN, BERNARD: *The New England Merchants in the Seventeenth Century* (1955). Documents the tension between secular and spiritual success in early New England society.

*BOORSTIN, DANIEL: *The Americans: The Colonial Experience* (1964). An interpretive study of American history in the seventeenth century.

*McGIFFERT, MICHAEL (ed.): *Puritanism and the American Experience* (1969). An excellent recent collection of primary and secondary writings.

*MILLER, PERRY: *Errand into the Wilderness* (1956). The essence of the ideas of this foremost scholar of Puritan thought in the New World. See especially Chapter One, "Errand into the Wilderness," and Chapter Three, "The Marrow of Puritan Divinity."

*NASH, RODERICK: *Wilderness and the American Mind* (1967). Attitudes toward the New World environment at the time of colonization.

*POWELL, SUMNER CHILTON: *Puritan Village: The Formation of a New England Town* (1963). A study of everyday Puritan life.

ROWSE, ALFRED L.: *The Expansion of Elizabethan England* (1955). The background of English expansion to New England.

* Available in paperback.

BENJAMIN FRANKLIN, LL.D. F.R.S.

CHAPTER TWO

Benjamin Franklin

Busying himself in the rear of his brother's printing shop, the sixteen-year-old apprentice kept an ear cocked on the conversation in the front of the store. Some literary gentlemen were excitedly bending over a lengthy letter he had secretly slipped under the door the previous night as a contribution to the New England Courant. *The letter purported to be the work of a Mrs. Silence Dogood, but in the early eighteenth century every satirist used a pseudoynm. Guesses as to the identity of the author ranged over the*

*most talented writers in Boston, and with each name mentioned,
the apprentice's amusement and pride increased. Yet his
understanding of human nature kept him silent. On April 2, 1722,
"Mrs. Dogood's" first letter appeared in the* Courant. *The practical
apprentice was on his way to becoming Benjamin Franklin.*

In origin, station, and ambition, the Franklin family typified much
of American society at the beginning of the eighteenth century. Their
nationality was English; Franklins have been traced back to the 1550s
in the parish records of Northamptonshire. Their religion was Protestant, but stopped short of the purifying zeal of people such as John
Winthrop. The Franklins had accepted Anglicanism and remained in
England while the first waves of settlers began New England's history.
The decision to stay did not involve much strain of conscience, for the
Franklins as a rule were more concerned with being artisans and
farmers than theologians. But near the end of the long reign (1660–
1685) of Charles II, Josiah Franklin, Benjamin's father, experienced
religious conversion and began to attend illegal meetings of dissenters
from the Anglican Church. In 1683 he opted for America, and moved
his family to Boston in pursuit of the goals of religious freedom and
economic opportunity. He found a measure of both, establishing a
soap and candle shop on Boston's Milk Street and, in 1694, gaining
admission to the Old South Church.

Although Benjamin Franklin later wrote in the manner of the
English demographer Thomas Robert Malthus about the danger of a
population explosion, the circumstances of early eighteenth-century
America encouraged large families. There was, after all, a continent to
fill, and work for many hands. Josiah had seven children by his first
wife and ten by his second. Benjamin, born in 1706, was the youngest
son of the second union.

Franklin later recalled that his father intended him to be "the
tithe of his sons to the service of the church," a kind of human
offering. So while the other Franklin boys were apprenticed to various
tradesmen in Boston, Benjamin received instruction in reading at
home. "I do not remember," he declared in later life, "when I could
not read." At a time when literacy was a luxury, this ability was a

great advantage. In his eighth year Franklin attended the Boston Grammar School, an institution founded in the 1630s in informal association with Harvard College and concerned chiefly with the intricacies of Latin. The year at Boston Grammar proved profitable. Franklin notes, characteristically, how he had "risen gradually from the middle of the class . . . to be at the head." But lack of money obliged Josiah to end Benjamin's formal schooling before it had hardly begun. At the age of ten, he entered the family business. A refined hatred of the mindless work with wax and tallow was the immediate result. At twelve, seeking an avenue of rebellion, Benjamin threatened to go to sea. Josiah reacted intelligently. His son's apprenticeship was transferred to the printing business of an older brother, James.

It was a brilliant solution. A self-styled "bookish lad," Benjamin thrived in an environment of words. As part of a campaign of self-education, he read voraciously—often, with the aid of his father's candles, far into the night. Franklin also tried his hand at writing. Obtaining a copy of Joseph Addison's and Richard Steele's satiric London periodical, *The Spectator*, he tried to imitate its pithy style. Taking notes on the essays, he reconstructed them in his own words and then compared his efforts with the originals. After some weeks of practice, Franklin could report that he "sometimes had the pleasure of fancying that in certain particulars of small import I had been lucky enough to improve the method or the language." The deceptively unassuming language hid pride and ambition of colossal proportions. Coupled with enormous energy and considerable talent, these traits led both to his success and, in certain quarters, to his unpopularity. The same might be said, parenthetically, about his nation.

Occupied by his apprenticeship, Franklin had to steal the time for self-improvement. The principal victims were his sleep and his religion. Although raised by strict Puritan principles, he found it tempting to cut corners. On Sundays, while his family worshipped at the Old South Church, Franklin read and wrote in the quiet of the closed printing shop. It was not that he denied or despised religion; simply that new gods and new goals arose to challenge the old ones. In Franklin's words, "I still thought [public worship] a duty, though I could not . . . afford the time to practice it."

As horrifying as this attitude would have been to John Winthrop's generation, Benjamin Franklin spoke for growing numbers of his contemporaries. The ninety years that separated Winthrop's Boston from Franklin's witnessed a gradual erosion of spiritual energies. The initial New England ideal of a closely knit, covenanted community proved difficult to maintain in the face of economic growth. The Puritan old guard, fearful of worldliness, tried to bridge the gap between the sacred and the secular with the Protestant ethic and the idea of a Christian calling. But glorifying God with worldly success did not provide a clear means for choosing *between* God and success. Franklin's experience comes immediately to mind. If one could get ahead by skipping church, why not? Was this kind of diligence in one's work evil?

The tendency to answer in the negative was apparent even in Winthrop's time, when New England merchants reacted with amazement and resentment to charges that they were making too much money. The business community also resented the way the church controlled the politics of Massachusetts Bay. At every opportunity, the merchants sided with those who favored greater toleration rather than with the defenders of rigid Puritan orthodoxy. In the 1630s, this had meant supporting Anne Hutchinson; forty years later, it meant defending Charles II's Lords of Trade and that body's colonial agent, Edward Randolph, against the Puritan Establishment. When the Massachusetts charter, which John Winthrop had defended so vigorously, was finally revoked in 1684, the reaction in the colony was mixed. Though they were unhappy to lose a measure of their independence to England, many merchants welcomed anything that promised relief from the strait jacket of Puritanism. In the long run, economic freedom proved more potent in Massachusetts Bay than either spiritual purity or political autonomy.

As shipowners and shopkeepers, both sides of Benjamin Franklin's family experienced the tension between the sacred and the secular. Benjamin's maternal grandfather, Peter Folger, even wrote caustic verses attacking the magistrates of Massachusetts for their intolerance. The Franklins and Folgers, then, were not unhappy at the prospect of colonial reorganization in the late 1680s. The Dominion of New England, as the revised plan came to be called, placed all colonies north of New Jersey under a royal governor. Representative assemblies were eliminated, but the prospect of escaping the Puritan oligarchy sweetened even this pill enough for merchant tastes. They could not, however, stomach Sir Edmund Andros, the Dominion's tactless governor. Miraculously, he managed to alienate all factions. In 1688 Bostonians responded to news of the revolution in England against James II by imprisoning Edmund Andros. Three years later, Massachusetts Bay received a new charter that amounted to a compromise between the Puritan system of government and the Dominion. For people like the Franklins, the new arrangement was a signal improvement; property rather than godliness became the criterion for suffrage.

With the yoke of Puritanism partially lifted, Franklin's Boston surged ahead in pursuit of the main chance. By 1720 the population numbered more than 10,000 persons, and in terms of shipping the city was one of the busiest ports in the British Empire. Secular concerns seemed to carry all before them, but Puritanism had been too strong for too long to vanish overnight. James Franklin and his apprentice were made aware of this late in the spring of 1722, when the *New England Courant* drew the fire of the conservative Boston clergy and the General Court. The leading spokesman of Puritan orthodoxy, Cotton Mather, cited the appearance of disrespectful articles, some of the most subversive of which appeared under the name of Mrs. Silence Dogood. For example, the disguised Benjamin Franklin had written: "It has been for some time a question with me whether a commonwealth suffers more by hypocritical pretenders to religion or by the openly profane. But some late thoughts of this nature have inclined me to think that the hypocrite is the more dangerous person of the two, especially if he sustains a post in the government."

Of course, the *Courant* took pains to accompany such statements with a defense of freedom of thought and speech. Nevertheless, James Franklin was arrested and imprisoned after his June 11 issue appeared on the streets. For a month he languished in jail while Benjamin carried on the paper. Unrepentant after his release, James continued his jibes at the Establishment. Finally, in January 1723 an order from the General Court prohibited him from printing in the city of Boston. Not so easily defeated, the Franklins quickly arranged for Benjamin to assume ownership of the business. The subterfuge saved the *Courant* but fed the apprentice's already burgeoning ego to such an extent that coexistence with James was no longer possible. After repeated quarrels and some blows, Benjamin determined to find another master. The

63

printers guild, however, closed ranks; when Benjamin applied for work, no Boston printer needed help.

At this low ebb in Franklin's life, the repulsive soap and candle business loomed ominously in the future. But Benjamin was nothing if not self-confident. A plan took shape in his mind. He would sell some of his precious books to raise a little money and, with nothing more than a rumor of a printing job in New York as encouragement, leave his native city for the first time. In the fall of 1723 he slipped quietly out of Boston to take on the world. Three days on a fast sloop brought him to New York. The city and colony had been in British hands since the ouster of the Dutch in 1664, but the pattern of large semifeudal landholding that persisted discouraged settlers. New York supported only a few printers, and Franklin found no openings. Undaunted, he pushed on to Philadelphia.

As a foil to his later achievements, Franklin's *Autobiography* takes pains to detail the lowly circumstances of his arrival in the Pennsylvania capital in October 1723. Dirty, disheveled, and dog-tired, the runaway apprentice, all of seventeen years old, staggered up Market Street. With the last of his money he bought three large rolls. Franklin's appearance as he wandered aimlessly through the streets munching his rolls amused an attractive girl standing at the doorway of her father's house. Later she would become Mrs. Franklin, but for the moment he was too tired to care. As he went along, a crowd appeared in the streets. Franklin followed it to the large Quaker meeting house. The service began with a period of quiet meditation that was too great a temptation for the exhausted apprentice. Sprawling out on an empty bench, he fell sound asleep.

The Philadelphia into which Franklin straggled so inauspiciously was the leading city of a colony that had made a comparatively late entry into North America. Yet Pennsylvania was already among its most vigorous settlements. The keys to success in this case were a favorable location and the genius of William Penn. The son of an admiral in the British Navy and a member of a radical Protestant sect called the Quakers, Penn wanted to found a colony based on the principles of religious freedom and popular sovereignty. In 1681 Charles II granted him a charter to a huge tract of exceptionally fertile land west of the Delaware River. It came to be known as "Penn's woods," or "Pennsylvania." The colony's liberal and tolerant policies, so markedly different from those of early Massachusetts, attracted large numbers of immigrants. Speaking a dozen languages and worshipping in different ways, they spread into the hinterland and used some of the richest soil on the continent to raise wheat, corn, hemp, and flax, as well as livestock. Others were city-oriented people who built a vigorous tradition of trade and craftsmanship in Philadelphia.

Two decades before Franklin arrived, Penn had taken the unusual step of responding to criticism by permitting his colonists to draft their own plan of government. They responded, as expected, with a proposal that elevated the representative assembly at the expense of the power of the governor and proprietor. Nonetheless, Penn approved this plan of government in 1701, and his colony prospered. Penn's administrative wisdom extended even to land policy: He stipulated that for every 5 acres of forest cleared, 1 acre be left with trees. In such concern for conservation, Penn was at least two centuries ahead of his contemporaries.

In 1723, then, Benjamin Franklin entered a permissive, rapidly expanding, highly mobile, and commercially oriented society that perfectly suited his ambitions and abilities. He lost no time in capitalizing on his good fortune. Upon awakening from his nap in the Quaker meeting house, Franklin proceeded to the printing shop of Samuel Keimer and immediately found employment. Quick, hard-working, and affable, Franklin made friends easily and moved ahead at a phenomenal pace. He became the New World's typical rags-to-riches success story, the creator of a legend that has shaped the aspirations of Americans ever since.

Arriving literally in rags at the age of seventeen, Franklin at twenty-four owned his own printing business and newspaper. At twenty-seven his name was known throughout the colonies as the creator of Poor Richard, of almanac fame. Three years later Franklin obtained the clerkship of the Pennsylvania Assembly, a post that proved a stepping stone to elected membership. By the age of forty-two he had accumulated sufficient wealth to reach his goal of the "free and easy life." Turning the printing business over to a manager, Franklin began new careers as scientist, inventor, statesman, and diplomat.

Benjamin Franklin succeeded not only because he lived in a favorable time and place, but also because of his character and guiding principles. As early as 1726, three years after his arrival in Philadelphia, Franklin referred in his journal to the necessity of fixing "a regular design in life . . . that, henceforth, I may live in all respects like a rational creature." In language as well as concept such a statement places Franklin squarely in the Enlightenment. This movement in the history of ideas took recognizable shape in the 1690s with the work of Isaac Newton in the physical sciences and John Locke in the social sciences. Enlightenment thought rested on the assumption that all phenomena operated according to permanent designs or laws. Rational man could discern these regularities and understand the cause and effect relationships that followed from them. According to the Enlightenment credo, everything had an explanation. All problems could be solved. Reason and the scientific method were the keys to knowledge.

Benjamin Franklin made a science of the conduct of his life. He began by fixing an ultimate goal—happiness. For Franklin, the chief components of the happy life were health, wealth, wisdom, and usefulness. He also included the principle of utility in his method for achieving the desired end. If a belief or course of action proved useful in securing happiness, it was good in Franklin's eyes; if not, it was bad. In this system of ethics there were no other criteria. Vice and virtue, Franklin believed, had little meaning if divorced from the particular time, place, circumstance, and desired result. This was the essence of relativism. Franklin made his judgments according to how something worked, and in this emphasis on results, he anticipated the philosophy of pragmatism. More exactly, the growing American tendency that Franklin personified—to judge by performance—was later given formal expression by the pragmatic philosophers. Franklin even extended this attitude toward individuals: "do not inquire concerning a Stranger," Franklin wrote in his *Autobiography, "what is he?* but, *what* can he do?" Imperfectly executed as this dictate was and is, it nonetheless constitutes one of America's most praiseworthy ideals.

Franklin's *Autobiography* records that about 1728 he conceived the "bold and arduous project of arriving at moral perfection." The brash confidence of the Enlightenment permeated the plan. Franklin really wished "to live without committing any fault at any time." To carry out the idea, he systematized his beliefs into thirteen "virtues": temperance, silence, order, resolution, frugality, industry, sincerity, justice, moderation, cleanliness, tranquillity, chastity, and humility. These were essential, he believed, for attaining happiness, and for the purpose of measuring his progress in this direction he devised a weekly chart on which he recorded his performance. He devoted a week to each of the thirteen virtues and repeated the course four times a year. The whole undertaking simply extended the campaign for self-improvement Franklin had launched as a teenager in the Boston printing shop.

At first glance, it appears that no two Americans could be more dissimilar than John Winthrop and Benjamin Franklin. The printer's goals and conduct seem to represent the final collapse of the Puritan life style. To some extent, of course, this is true. Success in this world, not salvation in the next, anchored Franklin's philosophy of life. And in sharp contrast to the Puritans, he believed that a man could improve himself, even approach perfection, by his own efforts. For Franklin, God's saving grace was the relic of an unenlightened age. Predestination made no sense to a self-made man. Franklin also rejected the idea of divinely inspired Scripture as part of his rejection of all systems of fixed moral precepts. "Revelation," he declared, "had . . . no weight with me as such." So much for the Puritans' sacred Bible.

A closer examination of Franklin's philosophy, however, reveals some close parallels to Puritanism. Many of the virtues Franklin adopted on the basis of utility proved to be precisely those prescribed by Revelation and stated in Scripture. Franklin saw that the Puritan virtues had utilitarian value, that they were often the means to ends he desired. The *Autobiography* presents Franklin's reasoning succinctly: "vicious actions are not hurtful because they are forbidden, but forbidden because they are hurtful, the nature of man alone considered [and] . . . it was therefore in everyone's interest to be virtuous who wished to be happy even in this world." Starting from a secular perspective, Franklin arrived at a position much like that reached by Winthrop. Their missions differed, but they pursued them with common means and a common zeal.

Another trait that links Franklin to the Puritans and partially redeems him from a degree of self-esteem that borders on the insufferable is his willingness in the long run to admit failure. After years of effort, Franklin abandoned his campaign for moral perfection. Charac-

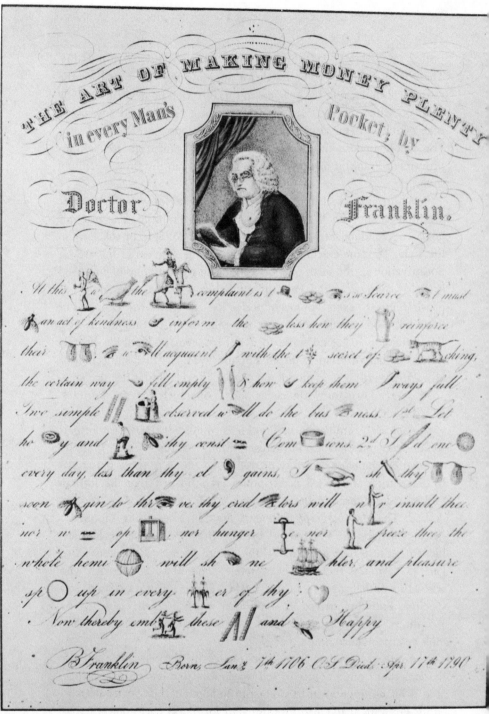

As a printer as well as a self-made man, Franklin must have been pleased with this
handsome lithograph. In elevating money-making to the status of an art, it substituted
a whole new set of values for those of Winthrop's generation. From such publications
stem the popular image of Franklin as a man obsessed with material concerns and,
too, the American reputation for materialism.

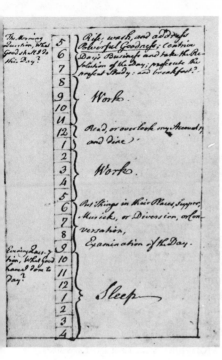

The Morning Question, What Good shall I do this Day?

5	Rise, wash, and address Powerful Goodness; Contrive Day's Business and take the Resolution of the Day; prosecute the present Study; and breakfast?
6	
7	
8	Work.
9	
10	
11	
12	Read, or overlook my Accounts, and dine.
1	
2	Work.
3	
4	
5	Put Things in their Places, Supper, Musick, or Diversion, or Conversation,
6	
7	
8	Examination of the Day.
9	

Evening Question, What Good have I done to Day?

10	
11	
12	Sleep
1	
2	
3	
4	

In the autobiography he wrote as an old man, Franklin included this breakdown of his typical day. The legend of Franklin as a person of superhuman discipline and organization has arisen from such evidence. Note this very secular man's way of referring to God and also the moralism of his morning and evening questions. Although worlds apart in the matter of ends or goals, Franklin and John Winthrop had much in common in regard to means.

From Massachusetts to the Carolinas the American colonists rebelled against the Stamp Act of 1765 as a classic instance of taxation without representation. In this scene sheaves of stamps, or possibly documents bearing them, are being burned on the cobblestones of a town square. The sticks and axes and pitchforks in the background suggest that the mob was bent on more violent expression of its displeasure, probably directed against the person and property of the local stamp agent.

teristically, he made his point with an anecdote: A man with a rusty ax, Franklin began, desired to have the whole head as bright as the cutting edge. He took it to a blacksmith who agreed to polish the steel, provided the owner turned the grindstone. The process went on and on, but specks of rust persisted. At last the owner became exhausted and declared that he would take the ax in an unfinished condition. " 'No,' says the smith, 'turn on, turn on; we shall have it bright by and by; as yet 'tis only speckled.' 'Yes,' says the man, *but I think I like a speckled ax best.'* " So with Franklin, who gave up his idea of perfection and concluded he really liked himself best with a few bad habits. Rationalizing his decision on the familiar grounds of usefulness, Franklin pointed out that "a perfect character might be attended with the inconvenience of being envied and hated; and that a benevolent man should allow a few faults in himself, to keep his friends in countenance." While hardly an admission of original sin, Franklin's statement showed he had nonetheless come to terms with human frailty just as had John Winthrop.

As for his formal religion, Franklin began to question many of the assumptions of traditional Christianity while still a Boston apprentice. He turned initially to deism, whose followers believed that the natural world was God's creation and that its design and function was all the evidence one needed of God's wisdom and power. Indeed, deists rejected all forms of revelation, along with creeds, mysteries, myths, and rituals, as unreasonable and unscientific. The organized church, as the embodiment of arbitrary authority, also suffered eclipse. Deists preferred their truth to be self-evident. They acknowledged a God, but He was a Creator or First Cause—a master mechanic who set the universe in motion and then withdrew to watch it work according to natural laws. Deism, in sum, was a scientific religion for rational men. It suited a young Benjamin Franklin perfectly.

With maturity, however, Franklin's dissatisfaction with deism increased. Observing the conduct of professed deists, he noticed a tendency to make virtue and vice "empty distinctions." The absence of an immediate God dispensing reward and punishment encouraged moral anarchy. "I began to suspect," Franklin commented, "that this doctrine, tho' it might be true, was not very useful." Again considerations of utility shaped Franklin's opinions.

What, then, was a useful religion in Franklin's terms? After considerable reflection, he decided it had to be based on the assumption that a deity or, as Franklin put it, "SOMETHING" existed, that it governed the world, and that "all crime will be punished and virtue rewarded either here or hereafter." The last point ensured socially acceptable behavior. Perhaps some individuals could sustain their morality without a God, but Franklin believed most people needed Him. "If men are so wicked *with religion*," he observed, "what would they be if *without it?*" On another occasion, Franklin wrote to the atheist Thomas Paine that "talking against religion is unchaining the tiger. . . . the beast let loose may worry his liberator." Whether real or not, God was useful. Franklin felt the same way about Jesus. Near the end of his life he remarked that regardless of the truth, he saw no harm in believing Christ to be the Son of God, since it had the "good Consequence . . . of making His Doctrines more respected and better observed." As an afterthought, he added that at the age of eighty-four he was not overly concerned about Jesus and life after death, for "I expect soon an Opportunity of knowing the Truth with less Trouble." The comment struck to the core of Franklin's practical attitude toward religion.

As might be expected, Franklin had little interest in the colony-wide religious upsurge of the 1730s and 1740s known as the Great Awakening. The emotionalism of the revivals offended Franklin's reason, and the emphasis revivalists like Jonathan Edwards placed on human helplessness ran counter to his creed of self-help. Franklin did, however, admire and become lifelong friends with the Reverend George Whitefield. Yet what attracted him was not Whitefield's theology, but his prowess as a public speaker. As for doctrine, Franklin much preferred the position of the liberal opponents of the Awakening, who held that God was forgiving and predestination absurd.

Franklin adroitly shaped his faith to support his style of life. In 1728 he resolved "to be virtuous that I may be happy, that I may please Him, who is delighted to see me happy." The ultimate purpose of religion thus became not the worship of God or even the salvation of man, but man's well-being on earth. Like a warm coat, religion was useful in the here and now. Unwilling to renounce faith, Franklin tailored it to suit his purposes. He stands as a transitional figure between men for whom religion was an obsession and those for whom it was a bore.

During his Philadelphia years, which lasted into the 1750s, Franklin's philosophy was compressed into his most famous publication: *Poor Richard's Almanac*. First published in 1733, the annual quickly developed a colony-wide and even an international reputation. In a real sense, Franklin's almanacs were the first distinctively American literary productions and certainly the best-known American books of their time. "As Poor Richard says" became a preface for maxims throughout the Western world.

To call Richard Saunders "poor" as Franklin did was to camouflage the fact that from the perspective of success he actually dispensed advice on how to get rich. In 1757 Franklin collected the best of *Poor Richard* under the title "The Way to Wealth." This how-to-do-it essay became a bible for the ambitious. It preached the gospel of getting ahead. "The sleeping Fox catches no Poultry," Franklin admonishes, adding "there will be sleeping enough in the Grave." Much of *Poor Richard* is based on the idea that "there are no Gains without Pains." But the almanacs also imply that unless the effort is guided by intelligence, it will come to nothing. Franklin therefore urges his readers to live simply and frugally: "a fat Kitchen makes a lean will." He also provides advice on the management of money, marriage, and friendship to the end that one's pains may indeed produce gains.

On the basis of the almanacs, it is easy to brand Benjamin Franklin hopelessly materialistic. After all, "nothing but money is sweeter than honey," as Poor Richard says. Yet there is more to Franklin than mere acquisitiveness. He is not entirely the "snuff-coloured little trap" that his critics (in this case, D. H. Lawrence in 1923) have alleged. Money for Franklin was important—but as a means, a tool for other tasks. Reflecting the old Protestant ethic, and revealing in the process another tie with Puritanism, Franklin believed that by being successful and socially useful a man pleased his Maker.

In this sense the most immediate influence on Franklin's thought was the Reverend Cotton Mather. A pillar of the Puritan Establishment in the late seventeenth and early eighteenth centuries, Mather in 1710 published a tract entitled *Essays to Do Good*. It elaborated upon the idea that the Christian "may glorify God by doing of *Good* for *others*, and of *Good* for *himself*." Franklin encountered Mather's work as a Boston apprentice and took it to heart. His earliest religious creed declares that "the most acceptable service of God was doing good to man." Years later Franklin again acknowledged his intellectual debt to Mather in a letter to Mather's son in which he said that the *Essays to Do Good* "gave me such a turn of thinking, as to have an influence on my conduct through life; for I have always set a greater value on the character of a *doer of good*, than on any other kind of reputation; and if I have been . . . a useful citizen, the public owes the advantage of it to that book." As he would judge all things by their usefulness, so Franklin would have himself judged. As preparation, he launched a multifaceted campaign of public service. It became his major altruistic outlet and a primary ingredient in his growing reputation.

Franklin began his career as a "doer of good" in 1727 when he organized a "club for mutual improvement" called the Junto among Philadelphia's younger artisans and intellectuals. This harbinger of the Junior Chamber of Commerce had as one of its "standing queries," which Franklin wrote, the problem: "do you think of any thing at present, in which the Junto may be serviceable to *mankind?*" The initial project the Junto undertook was Franklin's plan for a circulating subscription library, the first of its kind in American history.

Thereafter, the club became a seedbed for most of Franklin's community improvement efforts. They included a fire-fighting organization, a night watch, and a street-lighting company. Not the least of his contributions was the spearheading of a movement to pave Philadelphia's dusty streets. In 1749 Franklin took the lead in drafting plans for the Pennsylvania Academy, which was opened two years later. Its course of study reflected some of Franklin's practicality and utilitarianism, although less than he would have preferred. In time, the academy evolved into the University of Pennsylvania. A city hospital and improved medical treatment occupied Franklin's abundant energy in the early 1750s. In every case, he contributed his money and his talent for raising money along with his ideas. "Avarice and happiness never saw each other," said Poor Richard, and Franklin did not forget his own maxim. After all, the three-part goal for which one went "early to bed and early to rise"—health, wealth, and wisdom—was only one-third material. And the almanacs just pointed the way to wealth; once arrived, Franklin expected people to know how to apply their means to worthwhile ends.

The money-making talent that freed Franklin to serve his society also gave him the leisure to pursue scientific investigations. American interest in science, or "natural philosophy" as it was more commonly called, received its initial impetus from the newness of the New World. In an unknown land, mere observation was discovery. Botany and zoology, as a consequence, became the mainstays of early American science. Astronomy also ranked high, since the different perspective of North American observers resulted in data of great comparative interest to their English and Continental counterparts. The Puritans proved eager and talented natural philosophers. John Winthrop, Jr., who corresponded frequently with Sir Isaac Newton himself, became a charter member of his world's leading scientific organization, the Royal Society, in 1663.

Puritans like the younger Winthrop had no difficulty squaring their science with their religion. Nature was God's handiwork; its processes showed the effect of His guidance. Consequently, to study natural phenomena was to observe the wisdom, power, and glory of God. Science for the Puritan mind was an act of worship. But so, in theory, was making money, and just as the Protestant ethic gave way to outright materialism, the reconciliation of naturalism and supernaturalism proved equally temporary. Earthquakes and comets, for example, were either sent as portents by an angry God or solely the products of natural processes. If investigation supported the latter explanation, why involve God at all? In the seventeenth and eighteenth centuries most Americans did not pursue such questions, but rested content with a reconciliation of religion and science.

Benjamin Franklin's career as a scientist began with youthful curiosity. He wanted to know not only how things worked, but how such knowledge could be put to use. Young Franklin, for example, was an excellent swimmer, but unlike the other boys who used the ponds around Boston, he studied the mechanics of propulsion in water. As a result of these observations, Franklin constructed "oval palettes" for his palms and "a kind of sandals" for his feet—the ancestors of swim fins. He also discovered that a flying kite would draw its holder across a body of water "in a very agreeable manner."

In 1724 Franklin made an economically disappointing trip to London. From the standpoint of his interest in science, however, the experience proved immensely stimulating. London in the 1720s rode the crest of the Enlightenment. Newton was the most celebrated figure of an age in which every thinking man knew and respected the scientific method. Franklin's hopes for meeting Newton personally did not materialize, but he did make contact with other members of the Royal Society. When he returned to Philadelphia in 1726, he brought with him the habits of careful observation and logical analysis. He began in fact to apply them, as his journal shows, on the return voyage.

Back in Philadelphia, Franklin used the Junto as a forum for discussing scientific problems ranging from the nature of sound to the causes of earthquakes. Many of his experiments had practical consequences. His investigations of the circulation of air and the transference of heat led to his invention of the Franklin or Pennsylvania stove in the winter of 1739–1740. By 1743 Franklin thought it time that American scientists establish their identity and a means of communication. So he drafted "A Proposal for Promoting Useful Knowledge among the British Plantations in America." Franklin prefaced the document with the accurate observation that "the first drudgery of settling new colonies, which confines the attention of people to mere necessaries, is now pretty well over." It was also apparent that "there are many in every province in circumstances that set them at ease, and afford leisure to cultivate the finer arts and improve the common stock of knowledge."

The American Philosophical Society, which emerged in 1744 from Franklin's "Proposal," was designed to bring these unoccupied, curious, and intelligent minds together through the medium of the mails. Franklin's utilitarianism was evident in the suggested list of subjects for discussion and correspondence. As deserving of particular attention, he mentioned the production of ciders and wines, assaying of ores, draining of meadows, and clearing of land. More abstract questions had their place too, particularly in the thought of such members as the botanist John Bartram and the mathematician Thomas Godfrey, but for the most part the group directed itself to practical questions and applied science—"useful knowledge," in Franklin's terms.

In one notable instance, however, Franklin pursued the truth first; practical applications came later as a byproduct. His fascination with electricity began in 1743, when he witnessed some demonstrations by a touring Scottish lecturer. The man could perform remarkable feats with his primitive generator, but he had no idea how it worked. Franklin determined to find out. He bought the Scot's apparatus and devoted his spare time to investigation. After his retirement from the printing business in 1748, he became a full-time scientist. The next four years were filled with electrical experiments. The field was new, and Franklin quickly moved beyond existing knowledge. Rejecting the prevailing notion of two kinds of electricity, he proposed the idea of a single fluid with two forms, and he coined the words *positive* and *negative* to describe them. To illustrate his points, he performed the first analysis of the principle of the Leyden jar, an electrical generator and condenser.

Communicated to the European scientific community in 1751 by Peter Collinson of the Royal Society, Franklin's discoveries attracted immediate and widespread acclaim. Indeed, the slender volume Collinson had published for Franklin was the most widely hailed American book of the eighteenth century—next to *Poor Richard's Almanac*. Yet on both the intellectual and the popular level, Franklin's reputation as a scientist rested chiefly on his investigation of lightning. As his knowledge of electrical phenomena grew, Franklin began to suspect that lightning was actually electricity. In 1751 he suggested a way of testing the hypothesis by erecting an iron rod on the steeple of a high building. A team of French investigators performed the "Philadelphia experiment" successfully in May 1752. Franklin did not know this, however, when on a sultry evening in June he went into the fields near Philadelphia with his famous kite and key. As a thunderhead approached, Franklin flew the kite, but the first clouds passed overhead with no apparent effect. The second did the job. An electrical charge surged down the string and leaped from the key into Franklin's hand. After rain had wet the string, electricity flowed abundantly into the collecting device. Franklin succeeded on two counts: The hypothesis was confirmed, and the investigator escaped the electrocution that later killed a Swedish scientist engaged in an identical experiment.

Only after several years of work with the theory of electricity did Franklin draw the practical application in the form of the lightning rod. Yet so widely known is this invention that it is commonly believed Franklin was a tinkerer who experimented in order to produce lightning rods—for sale, of course. Nothing could be more unjust. Franklin was a "pure" scientist and a good one; he was also a practical man. When the time came, he made the transition from theory to practice, and as in the case of his almanacs, his lightning rods soon appeared in almost every home. Franklin's own version was equipped with bells that clanged when electrically charged, much to the distress of his wife.

The honors Franklin gleaned from his scientific avocation were legion. Harvard, which he had spurned as a critical apprentice, awarded him an honorary degree, as did Yale and the College of William and Mary. Oxford and St. Andrews topped these with advanced degrees, and Franklin quickly added "Doctor" to his name. The Royal Society conferred a medal and a membership. Yet probably his most cherished honor was his contemporary reputation as "the Newton of electricity." But success did not satiate Benjamin Franklin. In later years, when time permitted, he investigated theoretical problems in astronomy, geology, and botany. He also kept the practical side of his nature alive; he invented a glass harmonica, bifocal eyeglasses, and a "long arm" for grasping books on high shelves.

Franklin's decade of concentration on science, 1743 to 1753, brought many satisfactions, not the least of which was a buoyant feeling of contributing to human progress. Writing to fellow scientist Joseph Priestly, he regretted that he had been born so soon. "It is impossible to imagine," Franklin continued, "the height to which may be carried, in a thousand years, the power of man over matter." Musing on the theme, he forecast the airplane: "we may perhaps learn to deprive large masses of their gravity, and give them absolute levity, for the sake of easy transport." And there were other wonders: "agriculture may diminish its labour and double its produce; all disease may . . . be prevented and cured . . . and our lives lengthened at pleasure even beyond the antediluvian standard."

The optimism of the Enlightenment bubbles over in such statements. But Franklin was too wise in the ways of men to pretend that science held all the answers. "O that moral science were in a fair way of improvement," he continued to Priestly, "that men would cease to be wolves to one another, and that human beings would at length learn what they now improperly call humanity." With the hope, we may believe, of lessening the wolfish tendency in men and in nations, Franklin turned the energies of his later years more and more to public affairs. Undoubtedly he also foresaw in statesmanship new levels of success for Benjamin Franklin.

In 1751 the voters of Philadelphia elected the best-known mem-

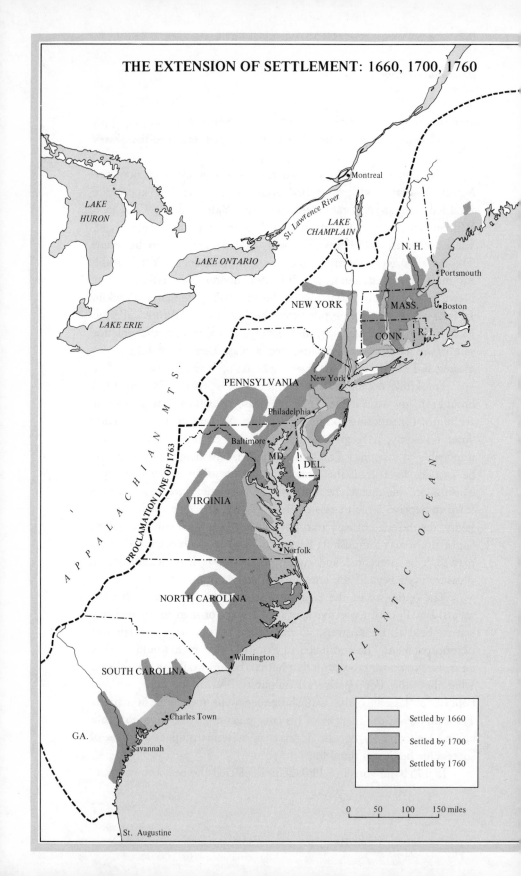

THE EXTENSION OF SETTLEMENT: 1660, 1700, 1760

LAKE HURON

LAKE ONTARIO

LAKE ERIE

Montreal

St. Lawrence River

LAKE CHAMPLAIN

N. H.

NEW YORK

MASS.

Portsmouth

Boston

CONN.

R. I.

PENNSYLVANIA

New York

APPALACHIAN MTS.

PROCLAMATION LINE OF 1763

Philadelphia

Baltimore

MD.

DEL.

VIRGINIA

Norfolk

NORTH CAROLINA

Wilmington

SOUTH CAROLINA

GA.

Charles Town

Savannah

St. Augustine

ATLANTIC OCEAN

Settled by 1660

Settled by 1700

Settled by 1760

0   50   100   150 miles

ber of their community to the Pennsylvania Assembly. For Franklin, it marked a major triumph. At a time when gentlemen-aristocrats dominated politics, he had climbed the ladder from an apprenticeship. More exactly, Franklin became a one-generation aristocrat, proving in the process the exceptional fluidity of the American social structure. His first important assignment in government came in 1754, when the Assembly chose him to be its representative at the Albany Congress. The background of this strange gathering in the wilds of northern New York lay in the tangled world of international relations 3000 miles away. Ever since the 1690s, France and England had been engaged in a series of wars and hostilities. At stake was the so-called European balance of power. Neither nation wanted the other to gain dominance. North America figured only marginally in the conflict as far as Europeans were concerned, but for the American colonists, the struggle became vital because both sides endeavored to enlist the assistance of the Indians. For communities on the outskirts of civilization, this meant the prospect of Indians swooping out of the forest for a massacre. Indians, indeed, held the key to power on the North American frontier during the period of European rivalry.

The immediate roots of the Albany Congress lay in France's determination to enhance her position with respect to England after the unsatisfactory Peace of Aix-la-Chapelle ended the War of the Austrian Succession. North America seemed a promising starting place for France in her renewed quest for power. With the aid of Indian allies, perhaps England could even be forced out of the New World entirely. In the early 1750s, therefore, the French began pushing south from their Canadian stronghold into western New York and along the Appalachian Mountains, building forts and making Indian friends. The prospect of a French-Indian alliance on their unprotected western flank terrorized the English colonists. In a powder-keg atmosphere of rumor and fear, England called the Albany Congress in 1754 to counter the threat. Iroquois chiefs from the Six-Nation Confederacy attended, along with representatives from most of the colonies. The point was to prevent collaboration between the Indians and the French.

For Benjamin Franklin, the Albany Congress provided an opportunity to broach a plan for intercolonial organization. As early as 1751 he had suggested such a union to deal with questions of defense. His appointment two years later to the office of joint deputy post-master-general of North America increased his awareness of the need for and possibility of mutual cooperation. So did his involvement in intercolonial scientific enterprises. As he rode to Albany in June of 1754, then, Franklin's mind dwelled on the problem of unification. By the time he reached his destination, he had an ambitious idea. His Albany Plan of Union called for the establishment of an intercolonial council with authority over defense, western expansion, and Indian relations. Representing the assemblies of the various colonies and headed by the king's representative, the council would maintain an army and navy, build frontier fortifications, execute Indian treaties, and buy western lands. Funds for these purposes would come from a tax levied by the colonists' representatives. Anticipating later developments in English-American relations, Franklin summarily rejected the idea of taxation without representation as inconsistent with the tradition of English liberty.

The gravity of the crisis in 1754 prompted the Albany delegates to adopt Franklin's plan. But when they carried it back to their respective assemblies, the reception was cool. An American national consciousness was in its infancy. The various colonies still eyed each other suspiciously, particularly with respect to western land claims. In reality, of course, the issue of intercolonial union was academic. Even had the assemblies cooperated, England would certainly have vetoed the proposed organization. It held forth the prospect of too much colonial power and, although few admitted it at the time, of independence. Franklin took the rebuff philosophically. The assemblies, he pointed out, "all thought there was too much *prerogative* in it, and in England it was judged to have too much of the *democratic*."

In Pennsylvania the Indian problem of the 1750s sharpened the chronic tension between governor and assembly. William Penn's successors as proprietor lacked his facility for dealing with popular demands. In a squabble over the tax exemption of the proprietor's huge landholdings, the governor refused to pass bills funding frontier defense. With the French and Indians at the colony's western doorstep, this was a serious matter. Unable to resolve the differences in America, the Pennsylvania Assembly instructed Benjamin Franklin to go to England and plead its case directly with Parliament.

When Franklin sailed for England in 1757 to present the Pennsylvania Assembly's grievance against its governor, he became involved in long-standing problems in the English-colonial relationship. The difficulties centered on the gap between the theory and the practice of colonialism. Theoretically, colonies were supposed to be the obedient and grateful servants of their mother country. The idea received economic expression in the theory of mercantilism, according to which colonies were supposed to assist in the maintenance of the favorable balance of trade—a surplus of income over expenses— on which national power was thought to depend. The colonies would supply raw materials to the mother country and consume its manufactured goods. They would neither compete with the industries of the home country nor turn to other nations for supplies and markets. The outposts were to be subservient satellites.

Franklin was well aware of the history of mercantilism in British North America. As early as the 1620s Parliament passed laws limiting Virginia's lucrative tobacco trade to England and stipulating that it be carried only on English ships. Beginning with the passage of the first laws in 1651, a body of legislation known collectively as the Navigation Acts spelled out the economic basis of the colonial relationship. Product after product was "enumerated"—its sale or purchase restricted. To some extent this policy proved advantageous to the American settlements. They enjoyed, after all, a guaranteed market and membership in the Western world's foremost commercial empire. Yet in the minds of the colonists it was security of the feudal variety—purchased at the expense of freedom—and they openly flaunted the economic regulations.

England occasionally, as in the Dominion scheme for New England, attempted to strengthen enforcement, but bribes and smuggling permitted the colonists to do much as they pleased. In practice, 3000 miles from home, mercantilism failed. Virginia, for example, sent its tobacco where it could get the highest price, frequently the Netherlands. And the New England merchants who were engaged in a triangular trade involving rum, slaves, and West Indian molasses customarily obtained the latter from the French West Indies in preference to the British islands. The 1733 Molasses Act, designed to curtail this practice, failed completely. Even with the expense of bribing customs agents added to its cost, French molasses was still cheaper than British. England fumed but, before 1761, took little positive action. For the most part, the colonies went their own way, and when

Franklin arrived in England in 1757 he became the target for British indignation at the uncooperative colonial members of the empire.

A gap between theory and practice also existed in the matter of Franklin's immediate area of concern as Pennsylvania's agent: government. Theoretically a colony existed under a governor who either represented Parliament and the Crown directly (the royal governor) or, in thé case of chartered or proprietary colonies, ruled at Parliament's pleasure. The governor was in control. He might appoint a few local leaders to a council, and most charters provided for an assembly representing the propertied citizens. Still, in theory, these groups had only advisory roles. They were regarded by the British as liberal concessions. Authority resided in England.

Franklin had observed colonial politics long enough to know that this theoretical political structure in reality quickly dissolved into more democratic forms. The colonists, in fact, regarded the assembly as their *right*—as a regularly constituted institution with the job of tempering the governor's will. This it did with a vengeance, using its power to introduce legislation, tax, and appropriate money to counter the governor's veto. As a result of this continual skirmishing with the assembly, the position of governor lost power steadily in the eighteenth century. Occasionally an exceptionally strong figure like Franklin's friend Thomas Hutchinson of Massachusetts would halt the trend temporarily, but the erosion of absolute authority in the colonies was irreversible.

Resistance to monarchical authority was not, of course, restricted to the American colonies. In his efforts to curb the power of the Pennsylvania proprietors, Franklin had the support of a tradition of English constitutionalism dating back to the thirteenth century. It received a major boost in 1688 when the English Whigs, or liberals, deposed King James II on the grounds that he had disregarded man's natural rights of life, liberty, and the possession of property. Immediately following the revolution, John Locke gave natural rights theory classic articulation in his famous *Treatises*. In the eighteenth century English journalists such as John Trenchard and Thomas Gordon publicized a variety of Lockean liberalism.

By 1760, when Franklin's case finally came to a head at Court, a sizable number of Englishmen were jealously guarding their constitutional liberties and closely scrutinizing the conduct of the king. Franklin sensed the mood and took pains to phrase Pennsylvania's case against the Penns in terms of "essential liberty" set against the vestiges of feudalism. After months of hearings and haggling, he succeeded in winning his point: the proprietor's lands would be subject to taxation like those of any man. Franklin's broader objective of eliminating the proprietary authority altogether proved premature. Still, he could declare the British Empire to be founded on "the greatest political structure human wisdom ever yet erected." Time would alter this opinion, but in 1760 Franklin was proud to be a subject of the king.

In 1762 Franklin returned to an America significantly changed from the one he had left five years before. The French and Indian War, which had begun inauspiciously for the English, was nearly over. At the very time Franklin was in Albany at the Congress, a young colonel of the Virginia militia named George Washington surrendered ignominiously to a French force in western Pennsylvania. General Edward Braddock repeated this act in 1755. With the advent of the William Pitt ministry three years later, however, England's fortunes took a turn for the better. In 1758 James Wolfe and Jeffrey Amherst captured the French fortress of Louisbourg, and the following year Wolfe took Quebec. Montreal fell September 8, 1760, and with it the entire French empire in North America.

It was a great victory for an imperial-minded England, but there were unexpected consequences that boded ill for the future of British colonialism. In the first place, the war was expensive, and England was determined to make the Americans, who benefited directly from the victory, pay a substantial part of its costs. As a means of raising money, England decided to dust off and strictly enforce the old Navigation Acts. Especially after a century of indifference, the tough new policy harbored the seeds of conflict.

The second unpleasant result of England's victory became apparent after the Treaty of Paris (1763) eliminated French power from North America. With the enemy gone, the colonists were less dependent on the protection of England. They could afford to treat English authority less seriously. Instead of their savior from Frenchmen and Indians, England seemed more and more an expensive encumbrance. Finally, the French and Indian War created a basis for American unity and American pride. The colonists worked together and played a major role in the victory. Moreover, they saw the British redcoats utterly frustrated by backwoods warfare. If the occasion ever demanded, perhaps even England could be defeated. In 1754 Franklin failed to arouse a sense of American identity. Eight years later, he sensed the beginnings of a more receptive climate of opinion.

The combination of England's need for revenue and the growth of colonial impatience with Parliamentary control led to trouble even before Franklin's 1762 return. Beginning in 1759, England actively attempted to control colonial elections and courts. On top of this, English customs agents, using "writs of assistance" to search homes and warehouses, cracked down on suspected smugglers. A colonial merchant accused of violating the Navigation Acts faced the prospect of being tried in the vice-admiralty court, without a jury, and in far-away Halifax, Nova Scotia. This was tantamount to conviction. Doubtless there were abuses on both sides. Merchants accustomed to being left alone bitterly resented the tightened regulations and redoubled their efforts to avoid them. England's officers retaliated with spies, frame-ups, and tight harbor patrols.

Emotions ran especially high over the Sugar Act of 1764, a revenue measure with which Treasury Minister George Grenville hoped to defray the cost of maintaining a standing army in the colonies. Americans liked neither the means nor the end involved. Another sore point of the early 1760s was the campaign of the Church of England to extend its influence in the colonies. With the exception of the first generation of Puritans, Americans distrusted state religions, and the prospect of enforced Anglicanism united all dissenters in opposition. The issue of westward expansion also contributed to the growth of animosity. England hoped to delay settlement of the trans-Appalachian region until such time as the Indians could be pacified and orderly procedures established. To this end, the Proclamation of 1763 forbade occupation of the West, and American frontiersmen boiled in anger.

Meanwhile, Pennsylvania experienced its own version of discontent in another dispute with its proprietors. Hoping to have the Penns' original charter revoked, the assembly once again dispatched Franklin to London. He arrived in the closing weeks of 1764 and was immediately caught up in the controversy swirling around Grenville's newest proposal, a stamp tax. Planned for institution in the fall of 1765, it required the purchase of a stamp for every kind of legal document, newspapers, pamphlets, even almanacs. At first Franklin accepted the idea calmly, advising a friend that "we might as well have hindered the setting sun." He even recommended an acquaintance as Philadelphia's stamp agent, and bought a supply of stamps for his own printing business. But for once Franklin was out of touch with the American temper. His countrymen regarded the Stamp Act as an outrage. They took it to be a form of "internal" taxation as opposed to the "external" variety regulating trade. The latter had at least some justification under mercantilism, but the stamp tax seemed a blatant revenue measure. Moreover, it appeared to the colonists to violate a basic tenet of English constitutionalism and natural rights theory: the sanctity of property. Since Americans were not represented, it was argued, Parliament had no right to take their property through taxation. Again and again the colonists insisted that if only they could levy their own taxes in their own representative assemblies, they would be willing to go a long way toward meeting England's fiscal demands. Otherwise, it was "no taxation without representation." Americans had found a principle on which to stand.

As the date for instituting the stamp tax approached, some Americans organized boycotts of the offending articles. Others supported an intercolonial Stamp Act Congress which, after pledging "all due submission" to Parliament, resolved that this did not include acceptance of internal taxes or of juryless admiralty courts. The mood at the gathering was one of firm, united resolve. American nationalism had made considerable gains since Franklin's abortive efforts in Albany eleven years earlier. Still other colonists resorted to violence in that tense autumn of 1765. In Boston a mob destroyed the home of the local stamp agent and threatened his life. He resigned the following day. Observing such developments from England, Franklin also got the message. Repenting of his earlier support of the tax, he prepared to lobby for its repeal. An opportunity arose in February 1766. The House of Commons was holding hearings on the controversial tax, and Franklin appeared to testify. Questioned by several members of Parliament, Franklin made plain that his countrymen would not pay the tax unless compelled by armed force. He also used the occasion to review the events of the past decade. Before 1763, Franklin declared, the colonists thought their government "the best in the world." They submitted willingly to Parliamentary authority and were governed easily "at the expense only of a little pen, ink and paper." Not only "respect," but "affection" existed for the mother country. Then came the end of the French and Indian War, the need for revenue, new taxes, and strict enforcement procedures. As a result, Franklin continued, the American attitude was "very much altered." Parliament had betrayed their trust. Franklin concluded his testimony with his conviction that all the colonists desired were their rights as Englishmen, specifically the right of representation in taxing bodies.

At the February hearings many members of Parliament assured Franklin that there was no difference between tax laws and other kinds of legislation. If the colonists accepted the regulation of trade, for instance, they should not resent the Stamp Act. These Englishmen also made it clear to Franklin that although Americans might not have "actual" representation in Parliament, as members of the empire, they were "virtually" represented. The colonists' situation, they insisted, was analogous to that of people in England who had lost their personal representative to Parliament as the result of boundary changes, but could still count on Parliament as a whole to defend their interests.

Franklin could not accept such reasoning. In his eyes and those of his countrymen, Americans were second-class citizens. They did not enjoy, Franklin insisted, "all the privileges and liberties of Englishmen," and they would rebel before conceding the point. First, however, they would refuse to purchase England's manufactured goods, and by means of this economic boycott put the power of the purse behind their cause. Franklin made the point neatly in examination form: "Q. What used to be the pride of Americans? A. To indulge in the fashions and manufactures of Great Britain. Q. What is now their pride? A. To wear their old cloaths over again, till they can make new ones."

In retrospect, Franklin thought his testimony in Parliament on the Stamp Act "contributed much to its repeal." Actually, the replacement of Grenville by the Marquis of Rockingham, a man who opposed the stamp idea from the beginning, combined with widespread realization that the act did not work, sealed its fate. In March 1766 the Stamp Act was repealed to the cheers of grateful Americans. But Franklin knew that the good feeling was premature. Parliament was not about to concede its principle. At the same time it withdrew the

newly-independent American colonies could not have chosen a better
resentative to send to France in 1776 than Benjamin Franklin. French society was
zled by the unassuming wit and wisdom of the man from the "wilds" of America.
elegant receptions such as the one depicted here, Franklin gave his nation's appeal
support in its revolution a mighty assist.

nklin the scientist and inventor applied
s talent to the problem of efficient home
heating. Fireplaces were very inefficient,
cause only one of the sides opened on a
m. Franklin's alternative was this stove,
which stood in the center of a room and
radiated heat from all its surfaces.

stamps, Parliament passed the Declaratory Act, which stated England's power to legislate for the colonies in "all cases whatsoever." "In my Opinion," Franklin wrote, "it will meet with the same Opposition, and be attended with the same Mischiefs that would have attended [the Stamp Act]." Again he misjudged public opinion. The Declaratory Act was pure principle, unlike the Stamp Act, it did not touch American pocketbooks. It engendered much less opposition in the colonies, a circumstance that suggests an intimate relationship between economic self-interest and constitutional principle in motivating American resistance to English government.

The situation changed radically, however, in 1767, when England's continuing search for revenue led its new treasurer, Charles Townshend, to secure the passage of duties on lead, paint, paper, glass, and tea imported by the colonists. Townshend also took steps to enforce the unpopular Quartering Act of 1765, under which American families were required to feed and board English soldiers. Finally, he expanded the customs service and the hated admiralty courts with the object of putting teeth in the new duties.

Again the colonies exploded. American merchants and consumers devised nonimportation agreements designed to choke off trade with England. The plan proved highly effective. England not only failed to collect the anticipated duties, but lost thousands of pounds worth of colonial business. On March 5, 1770, the first blood of the independence movement was drawn when a group of Boston citizens, spurred by the inflammatory rhetoric of Samuel Adams, clashed with British soldiers. Only five Americans died in the so-called Boston Massacre, but the term reflects the depth of colonial bitterness.

For Franklin, who remained in London as agent for several colonies, the clash was deplorable. As a man who made a religion of reason and order, he preferred peace at any price. Yet it was becoming clear to him that "no middle ground can be well maintained. . . . [either] Parliament has a power to make *all laws* for us, or . . . it has a power to make no laws for us." And, he added, "I think the arguments for the latter are more numerous and weighty, than those for the former." This conclusion, of course, supported independence, but in company with most of his countrymen in the early 1770s, Franklin did not as yet regard the prospect seriously. Surely men of good will on both sides would smooth out their differences. After all, the colonists were Englishmen. They wanted to remain loyal subjects of King George III, whom Franklin as late as 1768 termed "the best King . . . any nation was ever blessed with." If only George would protect their rights from an indifferent Parliament and a rapacious bureaucracy, the empire could enter a golden age.

As the 1770s progressed, however, such hopes became unrealistic. True, the Townshend taxes, except for that on tea, were repealed as the decade began. Yet the English government and society Franklin observed from his London vantage point seemed incapable of effective colonial administration. Bloated from a century of profit-making and empire-building, most Englishmen paid little attention to American grievances. Fewer still brought any consideration except profit to the colonial relationship. Again and again Franklin saw the protests and petitions of his countrymen brushed away like so many mosquitoes. Rare indeed were men like Edmund Burke and William Pitt, who with their keen sense of colonial realities could accept some limitation on British authority as the price for retaining any authority at all. As for George III, his empire was simply too large for more than cursory royal attention to American affairs. Franklin probably helped spread the story that the king persistently confused the Himalayas with the Appalachians and the Ganges with the Mississippi.

In the face of such ineptitude, Franklin lost patience and lashed out at what appeared to him to be England's mismanagement of her North American empire. The Tea Act of May 1773 was a particular sore point. The measure permitted the giant East India Company to sell tea directly to Americans at an extremely low price. Even with customs duty, the East India Company tea was cheaper than the untaxed product of non-British nations. As Franklin and his contemporaries saw it, the Tea Act was a deliberate attempt on the part of Parliament to make Americans buy taxed tea and thereby implicitly accept the principle of Parliament's taxing authority. Furious, Franklin wrote some tracts designed, in his words, to provide "a Looking-Glass in which some Ministers may see their ugly Faces, and the Nation its Injustice." The first essay was "Rules by Which a Great Empire May be Reduced to a Small One." The second, "An Edict by the King of Prussia," used a transparent disguise to jab at England's edicts. It concluded with an expression of incredulity that a nation "so wise and liberal in its sentiments, so just and equitable towards its neighbors, should, from mean and injudicious views of petty immediate profit, treat its own children in a manner so arbitrary and tyrannical!"

Words came easily to Benjamin Franklin, but his countrymen frequently turned to deeds to express their opposition to British policy. The taxed tea met with a hostile reception as it arrived in America. In some ports citizen groups forced the ships to return to England without unloading their cargoes. Other communities locked the crates of tea in storehouses and defied anyone to remove them for distribution and sale. In Boston, where Samuel Adams and his Committees of Correspondence kept alive a tradition of radicalism, there were more serious consequences. On December 16, 1773, a band of enraged colonists disguised as Indians boarded the tea ship, hacked open the boxes, and dumped them into Boston harbor.

The "tea party" elicited a mixed reaction. To radical colonial eyes it was a stroke of genius, a way of putting teeth in the American grievances. But for many Americans, and almost all Englishmen, the destruction of the tea was an outright crime. Franklin personally sided with the shocked moderates, branded the tea party "an act of violent injustice" perpetrated on the owners of the tea, and demanded "speedy reparation." In Franklin's opinion, the events of December 16 cost the American cause considerable sympathy throughout Europe. From oppressed disciples of natural rights, they had descended to behaving like anarchists and thieves.

England's response to the tea party, however, made Franklin change his mind. In quick succession early in 1774 Parliament closed the port of Boston, revised the Massachusetts constitution to reduce popular sovereignty, curbed the authority of local juries, and appointed General Thomas Gage, the commander of British troops in North America, as governor of Massachusetts Bay. The colonists labeled these measures the Intolerable Acts, and Franklin agreed that their severity shifted the burden of reconciliation from New World to Old. The Quebec Act added further fuel to the fire. Also passed in 1774, it finally settled the matter of governing the territory won from the French a decade earlier. The act made the governorship a permanent position, abolished representative assemblies of any kind, and encouraged the Roman Catholic Church. Although they were not directly affected, most Americans regarded the Quebec Act as a bad omen, particularly since it applied to all the land west of the Appalachians and north of the Ohio.

Massachusetts' misfortunes generated a wave of sympathy throughout the colonies. The Intolerable Acts created an atmosphere in which the kind of unified action Franklin dreamed about at Albany twenty years before became feasible, and the First Continental Congress assembled at Philadelphia in September of 1774. Many viewpoints were represented, but the delegates shared a sense of fear, anger, and determination to prevent further loss of their rights as Englishmen and as men. Among its first actions was institution of a tight boycott on all trade with England. The delegates also voted to support Boston in resisting the Intolerable Acts. Turning to long-range solutions, Joseph Galloway, an old political ally of Franklin's, tried to secure support for an intercolonial assembly to act in conjunction with Parliament as a kind of lower house. If adopted on both sides of the ocean, Galloway's plan might well have averted the impending revolution. American radicals, however, resented its concessions to Parliamentary authority, and the idea failed by a single vote. Franklin was just as glad. He wrote to Galloway early in 1775: "when I consider the extream corruption prevalent among all orders of men in this old rotten state, and the glorious public virtue so predominant in our rising country, I cannot but apprehend more mischief than benefit from a closer union."

But independence for Franklin did not necessarily entail war. He consistently hoped that an adjustment of America's political status could be negotiated in the conference room by diplomats rather than contested on the battlefield by soldiers. Divorce, not murder, was the sensible alternative in his opinion, and during his final months in England he poured all his skill into this approach. The current, however, ran the other way. Sentiment on both sides was hardening rapidly. Moreover, Franklin operated in 1775 under a cloud of suspicion cast by his recent involvement in the publication of some purloined letters of former Massachusetts governor Thomas Hutchinson. Sensing the futility of his compromise efforts and fearing imprisonment or worse if he remained in London, Franklin sailed for Philadelphia on March 20. While he was in mid-ocean, full-scale war began in Massachusetts between Gage's troops and amateur colonial soldiers massed, thanks in part to Paul Revere's ride, at Lexington, Concord, and along the road to Boston.

Franklin landed in Philadelphia on May 5, 1775, and before he had unpacked he was elected a delegate to the Second Continental Congress. This body found itself in charge of governing a nation at war. Its first order of business was providing for the common defense. Franklin and his colleagues organized the Massachusetts militia into the Continental Army, appointed George Washington commander-in-chief, and issued paper money to finance the fighting.

Before Washington could take charge, however, Gage's force at Boston engaged the colonists in the Battle of Bunker (actually, Breed's) Hill on June 17. The Americans retreated, but not before offering fierce resistance. Following reports of the action closely, Franklin concluded that the British must be "convinc'd by this time, that they have Men to deal with, tho' unexperienced, and not yet well arm'd." The Battle of Bunker Hill also pushed Franklin further toward a commitment to independence. Contemplating the ravages of the British in Charlestown, Massachusetts, following the colonial retreat, he remarked to a countryman in July 1775, "I think I am not half so reconcileable now, as I was a Month ago." To an English correspondent, however, Franklin revealed a rare streak of emotional anger: "you have begun to burn our Towns, and murder our People. —Look upon your Hands! They are stained with the Blood of your Relations!" Yet Franklin and the Second Continental Congress only slowly abandoned the hope of reconciliation. In July the congress addressed a petition to George III acknowledging its loyalty and begging for a restriction of Parliament's power over Americans to matters of trade only. If this were to happen, the petition made clear, Americans would gladly remain English.

Franklin supported the July petition and regarded it as a "Golden Opportunity" for England. Yet he was realistic. He knew the climate of opinion in that nation, and in his judgment, "she has neither Temper nor Wisdom enough to seize" the possibility of reunion. He was right. George III and his ministers were determined to put the unruly and ungrateful colonists in their place and insisted on Parliament's full power to make laws and assess taxes. England replied to the petition by adding 25,000 troops to her North American force.

By 1776 Franklin, with most American colonists, was convinced that independence offered the only long-term solution to their problems with England. But untying the knot promised to be painful. Revolution was a serious matter in the late eighteenth century. The idea of the divine right of kings, of their absolute sovereignty, lingered on in the popular mind as a legacy from the Middle Ages. One did not defy a monarch casually. Moreover, the cultural background of most Americans was English. Mental as well as physical preparation for separation had to be made. Thomas Paine's *Common Sense*, published in January 1776, helped in this respect. Franklin contributed directly to the appearance of the tract, since his letters of introduction had smoothed Paine's move to the colonies from England two years earlier. Franklin also provided Paine with notes and documents for writing a summary of the Anglo-American relationship. Indeed, when *Common Sense* appeared anonymously, many supposed Franklin the author. But the emotional tone of the piece should have dissuaded readers. Paine lambasted kings as the oppressive relics of an unenlightened age. Monarchy, he insisted, was inconsistent with liberty. Americans should pursue the republican way as more in keeping with their respect for the individual.

June of 1776 found Franklin enmeshed in the affairs of the Continental Congress. His tasks included membership on a committee charged with the preparation of a declaration of independence. Thomas Jefferson drafted a document that incorporated many of Franklin's suggestions. The most important involved an opening statement of principles with which the rebels hoped to justify their course of action to the rest of the world and to themselves.

Jefferson wrote: "we hold these truths to be sacred and undeniable, that all men are created equal, that they are endowed by their Creator with certain unalienable Rights, that among these, are Life, Liberty, and the pursuit of Happiness." Franklin argued successfully for substituting "self-evident" for "sacred and undeniable." It was a significant and fortuitous change. Jefferson's wording implied a divine origin for men's rights. Franklin used a term from science and based the rights on reason. All men, he implied, could investigate and prove the proposition. Franklin made natural rights sacred because they were true, while in Jefferson's version they were true because they were sacred. It was a change consistent with both the character of Franklin and the experience of his countrymen.

On July 2, 1776, the Continental Congress adopted Richard Henry Lee's motion for independence. Two days later it approved the Declaration. At the signing ceremony John Hancock supposedly warned, "we must be unanimous. . . . we must all hang together." "Yes," Franklin replied, "we must, indeed, all hang together, or most assuredly we shall all hang separately." With the deed now done, the rebels set about the enormous task of justifying their action with success. Among the most pressing needs was a military and financial alliance with a foreign power. France, the chronic opponent of England in the eighteenth century, offered the best prospects, and late in 1776 Benjamin Franklin once again received his country's call for help. Would he, nearly seventy years old, join a delegation to Paris? "I am but a fag end," Franklin replied with characteristic understatement, but "you may have me for what you please." Franklin's record in France showed that he retained considerable vitality. Arriving in December of 1776, he was immediately swept up in a wave of popular adulation. The French, who knew Franklin from his almanac and his electrical papers, regarded him as a homespun disciple of the Enlightenment, a kind of noble savage, an American Socrates. The envious John Adams, who joined the American delegation when Franklin's popularity had peaked, observed: "his reputation was more universal than that of Leibnitz or Newton, Frederick or Voltaire. . . . his name was familiar . . . to such a degree that there was scarcely a peasant chambermaid or scullion in a kitchen who was not familiar with it, and who did not consider him as a friend to human kind. . . . they seemed to think he was to restore the Golden Age." Hardly one to let such a chance slip by unused, Franklin wore a little fur cap and played the role of backwoods sage to the hilt. He reaped dividends both romantic and diplomatic. The latter climaxed in a treaty of alliance with the French government, signed February 6, 1778, four months after the key American victory in the Battle of Saratoga.

French aid sealed England's fate in the American war. A series of campaigns in the central and southern colonies led Charles Cornwallis's British force to a dead end on the Yorktown Peninsula in Virginia with George Washington in pursuit and a French fleet offshore. Surrender came October 19, 1781.

With the fighting finally over, Franklin turned to the more congenial task of peacemaking. His frame of mind is revealed in a letter to an old English friend: "let us now forgive and forget." Both countries, he believed, could help each other move on to great if separate futures. As one of the official negotiators of the peace, Franklin was instrumental in bringing about the agreement of September 3, 1783. It recognized the United States as a sovereign nation with a northern boundary along the Great Lakes–St. Lawrence waterway and a western one at the Mississippi River. Spain remained on the south and west, and England retained Canada, but the first nation independent of a European power was carved from the New World. Franklin, for one, looked forward to a brilliant future. Three years before his death he participated in the Constitutional Convention of 1787, which restructured the federal government of the United States.[1] According to Thomas Jefferson, Franklin took a moment of the closing session to call the assembly's attention to the painting of a sun on the back of President George Washington's chair. "I have often and often," he declared, ". . . looked at [it] . . . without being able to tell whether it was rising or setting. But now, at last, I know that it is a rising . . . sun."

America changed greatly during Benjamin Franklin's lifetime. He was born in 1706 into a society that still defined its purpose largely in spiritual terms, but the old Puritanism was losing its hold. Yet Americans were loathe to lose the messianic role assumed by the Puritans; a mission lent dignity and significance to their endeavor in the wilderness. As a people on the outskirts of civilization, they both wanted and needed the buoyant feeling of being singled out to lead mankind to a better world. As a result, Americans groped throughout the eighteenth century for a new mission. They found it in the Enlightenment concept of natural rights. Liberty rather than salvation became the new goal. Success rather than salvation motivated Franklin's society. He died in 1790 in a society which had turned from building a holy community to building a free and prosperous one. The good life replaced the godly one.

Nobody reflected this redefinition more clearly nor promoted it more vigorously than Benjamin Franklin. When he wrote at the height of the Revolution that "our Cause is the Cause of all Mankind,

---

[1] For a discussion of the Constitution of 1787 and of the Articles of Confederation government which preceded it, see pages 119–128.

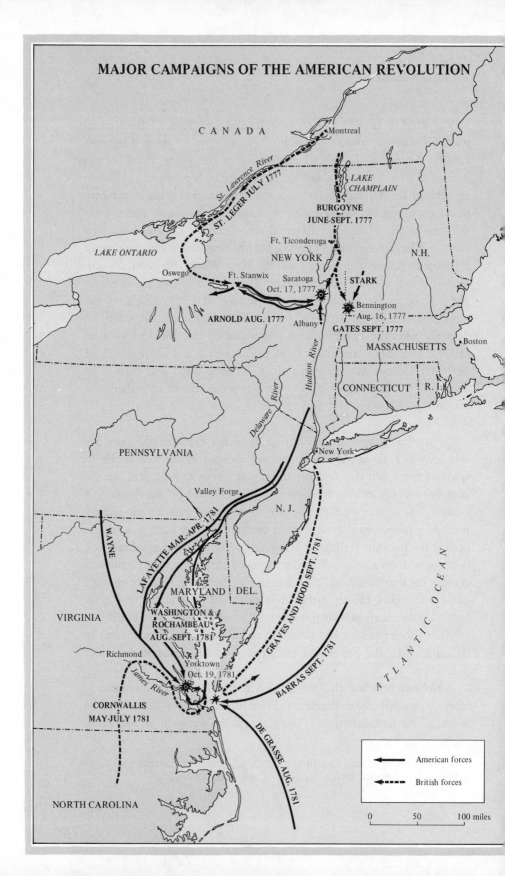

MAJOR CAMPAIGNS OF THE AMERICAN REVOLUTION

CANADA

Montreal

St. Lawrence River

LAKE CHAMPLAIN

ST. LEGER JULY 1777

BURGOYNE JUNE-SEPT. 1777

Ft. Ticonderoga

LAKE ONTARIO

NEW YORK

N.H.

Oswego

Ft. Stanwix

Saratoga Oct. 17, 1777

STARK

ARNOLD AUG. 1777

Albany

Bennington Aug. 16, 1777

GATES SEPT. 1777

MASSACHUSETTS

Boston

Hudson River

CONNECTICUT

R. I.

Delaware River

PENNSYLVANIA

New York

Valley Forge

N. J.

LAFAYETTE MAR.-APR. 1781

WAYNE

MARYLAND

DEL.

GRAVES AND HOOD SEPT. 1781

WASHINGTON & ROCHAMBEAU AUG.-SEPT. 1781

VIRGINIA

Richmond

BARRAS SEPT. 1781

James River

Yorktown Oct. 19, 1781

CORNWALLIS MAY-JULY 1781

DE GRASSE AUG. 1781

ATLANTIC OCEAN

NORTH CAROLINA

⟶ American forces

⟵--- British forces

0   50   100 miles

and we are fighting for their Liberty in defending our own. Tis a glorious task assign'd us by Providence," he echoed John Winthrop. America was still a city upon a hill, but with a new message for the world.

SELECTED READINGS

The Person

*CRAŇE, VERNER W.: *Benjamin Franklin and a Rising People* (1954). A short interpretive biography.

JACOBS, WILBUR (ed.): *Benjamin Franklin: Statesman, Philosopher or Materialist* (1972). A recent collection of analytical essays.

LABAREE, LEONARD W., and WHITFIELD J. BELL, JR. (eds.): *The Papers of Benjamin Franklin* (1959–   ). The most complete and authoritative multivolume collection of Franklin's writing.

*LEMISCH, L. JESSE (ed.): *Benjamin Franklin: The Autobiography and Other Writings* (1961). A useful edition of Franklin's famous self-portrait, along with selections from his scientific, religious, and political thought.

*VAN DOREN, CARL: *Benjamin Franklin* (1938). The most detailed biography.

WRIGHT, ESMOND: *Benjamin Franklin and American Independence* (1966). Franklin's contributions to the revolutionary process.

The Period

*BAILYN, BERNARD: *Ideological Origins of the American Revolution* (1966). Traces the intellectual roots of independence.

*BRIDENBAUGH, CARL, and JESSICA BRIDENBAUGH: *Rebels and Gentlemen: Philadelphia in the Age of Franklin* (1942). Social history that emphasizes the development of the American city.

GIPSON, LAWRENCE H.: *The British Empire before the American Revolution* (15 vols., 1939–1970). The standard source for colonial political history.

GREENE, JACK P. (ed.): *The Reinterpretation of the American Revolution, 1763–1789* (1968). A collection of the most significant recent assessments.

* Available in paperback.

*HINDLE, BROOKE. *The Pursuit of Science in Revolutionary America* (1956). A thorough examination of eighteenth-century American science.

*MILLER, JOHN C.: *Origins of the American Revolution* (1957). A reliable general survey of the road to independence.

*MORGAN, EDMUND S.: *The Birth of the Republic* (1956). A clear and readable interpretation of the American Revolution.

* Available in paperback.

CHAPTER THREE

Thomas Jefferson

The crowd that had gathered for breakfast at Conrad and McMun's boardinghouse rose with one accord as the lanky, broad-shouldered Virginian descended the stairs. Nervously the hostess gestured to a chair left vacant at the head of the table. Thomas Jefferson dismissed the offer, and chose instead a seat along the side with the other diners. After the meal he strolled outside, squinting into the March sunlight at the collection of half-finished buildings, swamp, and forest that for less than a year had served as the capital

*of the United States. Elaborately uniformed grenadiers paraded
in the muddy streets, doing their best to dignify the occasion.
George Washington and John Adams, the two previous Presidents,
coveted such trappings, with their connotation of Old World
aristocracy. Four years earlier Adams rode to his inauguration in a
luxurious coach drawn by six horses. But the election of 1800
defeated the Federalists and brought a different temper to American
life. Jefferson reflected it as he left Conrad and McMun's for the
day's business. Spurning the suggestion of a coach and ignoring
the grenadiers, the President-elect walked to his inauguration.*

On a clear day you can see a long way from Thomas Jefferson's
beloved hilltop home, Monticello. Immediately below, the town of
Charlottesville, Virginia, nestles in the soft-forested folds of the Southwest Mountains. To the west, dominating the horizon, lies the Blue
Ridge, backbone of the southern Appalachians. When Jefferson was a
boy in the 1740s, those hazy mountains marked the edge of settlement. Few even knew what lay beyond: A few decades earlier Virginia's Governor Alexander Spotswood and his expedition had topped
the Blue Ridge in full expectation of seeing the Pacific Ocean. The
creeks and streams south and east of Monticello joined to form the
James River, then flowed onward to the Atlantic. A seedbed of American settlement, the James was also a key artery for subsequent development. Great planters like William Byrd and Robert Carter, whose
holdings included hundreds of thousands of acres of rich bottomland,
located their mansions on its shores. Ocean-going ships served these
plantations, carrying hogsheads of tobacco to eager Old World markets. Tidewater and navigation ended where the James plunged over
the edge of the Piedmont Plateau in a series of waterfalls and rapids.
Richmond, located at this transition point, became the nerve center for
the tidal lowlands and the interior.

With visions of tobacco profits luring them on, planters pushed
up the James so quickly that by the 1730s, when Thomas Jefferson's
father, Peter, sought land, he had to journey some 100 river miles
above Richmond to a tributary called the Rivanna. Peter Jefferson
exemplified the one-generation aristocrat so often encountered early in

the history of a developing nation. Starting as a surveyor, Peter acquired land, cleared it, built houses, bought slaves, and eventually gained political and military office and the status of squire. The country was new, and he grew up with it almost exactly as did another surveyor-soldier-squire in the adjacent Shenandoah Valley named George Washington.

A man of prodigious physical strength, Peter Jefferson could simultaneously push two thousand-pound hogsheads of tobacco from a prone to an upright position. On the frontier, where performance determined reputation, news of such feats spread rapidly. But Peter also used marriage as an avenue of advancement. Jane Randolph, who became his wife in 1739, belonged to the upper crust of eighteenth-century southern society—the First Families of Virginia. The Randolph pedigree extended far back in Great Britain as well as Virginia —"to which," Thomas Jefferson later advised, "let everyone ascribe the faith and merit he chooses." His own preference inclined him toward the self-made man, a natural aristocrat in his father's mold.

Peter and Jane Randolph Jefferson celebrated the birth of their first son, Thomas, on April 13, 1743, at Shadwell, the estate they had carved from the wilderness of the upper James River. The boy grew up with all the advantages of a gentleman at Shadwell and at Tuckahoe, the sprawling Randolph holding downstream. Private tutoring began at the age of five, intensive instruction in Greek and Latin when he was nine. A smattering of French, some contact with the English classics, and the customary heavy dose of religion completed Jefferson's early formal education.

But he had other teachers. His father, whom he revered, was a living example of the rewards of resolution, diligence, and organization in the manner of Benjamin Franklin. And there were the red-earth hills of Albemarle County and the Blue Ridge country of Virginia. Because Jefferson's perspective on this environment was that of the gentleman rather than the frontiersman, he found delight, not challenge, in nature. Living comfortably amid cleared fields in the aftermath of the first wave of settlement, he could love the frontier in a way quite foreign to the man who did the clearing. The freedom and simplicity of the American wilderness permeated Jefferson's life style, while its mysteries sparked a lifelong interest in science and exploration, and its beauty inspired an intense patriotism.

In 1760, at the age of seventeen, Thomas Jefferson left the quiet foothills of the Blue Ridge for two years of instruction at the College of William and Mary in Williamsburg. Founded in 1693, William and Mary was the pride of the South and, next to Harvard, the oldest collegiate institution in North America. Jefferson made the perfect student. Intensely serious and capable of sustained study, he became enthralled with the world of scholarship and refinement. To be sure, there were parties, girls, and drinking, but hangovers only seemed to drive a contrite Jefferson to greater concentration on his courses. His intelligence impressed all his associates, in particular George Wythe, a professor of law.

Wythe also enjoyed good living and high thinking, and he introduced his students to the circle that gathered from time to time at the home of Francis Fauquier, Royal Governor of Virginia. In these occasions, brilliant by eighteenth-century provincial standards, Jefferson took special delight. He contributed to the musical entertainment, partook of the fine food, and participated enthusiastically in the spirited discussions. Jefferson's life and the history of his country were caught for a moment in a quiet eddy. As the music and laughter drifted from the governor's palace into the velvet of a Chesapeake evening, Concord and Lexington seemed inconceivable. And George Wythe could hardly have imagined that in a dozen years he would sign a declaration of independence from England written by his red-haired student from the backwoods academies of Albemarle County.

Jefferson's college idyll ended in 1762, but he continued to study, reading law with George Wythe. Two years later he assumed title under the terms of his father's will to an estate of several thousand acres and several hundred slaves—and became one of the colony's most eligible bachelors. But even this windfall did not bring Jefferson luck in love. After months of agony his passion for sixteen-year-old Rebecca Burwell produced, he ruefully admitted, only "a few broken sentences, uttered in great disorder" as the couple danced at a Williamsburg ball. Reconciled to being single, Jefferson continued his legal studies with even fiercer determination. When he finally took the bar examination in 1767, he probably knew more than his examiners.

The ineptness Jefferson demonstrated in the presence of Miss Burwell undoubtedly led him to admire masters of the spoken word. One of the best in Jefferson's time was another back-country boy named Patrick Henry. Jefferson first encountered this firebrand, seven years his senior, at a Christmas party in the late 1750s. He at first felt Henry to be somewhat coarse and crude, especially when he passed his bar examination after only five weeks of study. But in 1763 Henry impressed Jefferson, Virginia, and the colonies with a brilliant performance in a case known as the Parsons' Cause. The parsons were the Anglican clergymen in Virginia; their cause was to secure a higher salary from hostile local taxpayers. Americans distrusted any hint of an established religion and readily associated the Anglican Church with English government. At the climax of the dispute Patrick Henry addressed a jury sitting to decide the amount of back pay to award a disgruntled parson. In an emotional flood of eloquence, Henry accused King George III of having "degenerated into a tyrant" by overruling a Virginia law respecting the pay of clergy. The jury responded by awarding the beleaguered clergyman the grand total of one penny. Americans chortled gleefully, and Henry became a hero overnight.

He did not rest on his laurels for long. In 1765 the House of Burgesses in Virginia took up the question of Parliament's right to impose a stamp tax on the unrepresented colonists, and Henry assumed leadership of the radicals. On May 30 Jefferson was standing in the doorway of the Burgesses' chamber as a spectator when Henry arose to defend a set of seven resolutions repudiating the Stamp Act. "Caesar had his Brutus," he allegedly thundered, "Charles the First his Cromwell, and George the Third. . . ." Jefferson was aghast, and cries of "Treason!" rang through the assembly, but Henry continued: ". . . and George the Third may profit by their example." Then, turning to his hecklers, Henry shouted, "If this be treason, make the most of it." After more heated exchanges the sharply divided Burgesses passed four of Henry's resolutions and thereby helped define the ideological grounds on which the American Revolution was subsequently fought. Jefferson was moved. Henry, he confessed, "appeared to me to speak as Homer wrote." And soon after hearing Henry's tirade before the Burgesses, Jefferson adopted as his personal motto: "Rebellion to tyrants is obedience to God."

The friction between Patrick Henry and the more conservative Virginia politicians that surfaced during the debate on the Stamp Act Resolutions was part of a pattern in many colonies in the decade before independence. As historian Carl Becker has put it, men were concerned at this time not only with the question of "home rule," but also with "who should rule at home." In other words, there was an internal or domestic aspect to the Revolution paralleling the external conflict with Great Britain. At stake at home was political leadership and the power, privilege, and prestige that accompanied it. Prior to 1760 the keys to such power were held by royal officers, sometimes in collaboration with important colonists. In many colonies a single man or family controlled the political machine. Jefferson's Virginia, for instance, was run by John Robinson, treasurer and speaker of the House of Burgesses. Few went far in Virginia politics without his blessing. Although younger, ambitious men were frustrated, the Robinson-led gentry held tight rein.

About 1763, however, the issue that was to upset the traditional power structure—American independence—appeared. The young insurgents recognized its potential as an avenue for political advancement: If they could associate the colonial establishment with England, patriotism could be used to engineer its downfall. Natural rights might cut a wide swath and level the colonial oligarchy as well as Parliament and George III. Indeed, some old-line American leaders came to regret their championing of John Locke and the entire independence movement. Better to suffer English rule, they concluded, than to risk losing their favored position in a reshuffling of the American deck.

Before the Revolution Patrick Henry led the forces of internal insurgency in Virginia. It is significant that he came from the western upcountry and had the backing of small farmers and traders. The tension between this geographic and economic group and the tidewater aristocracy of great planters had long been a fact of political life in Virginia and other southern colonies. A century before Henry, for instance, Nathaniel Bacon led frontier forces in an abortive revolt against the coastal elite that was no minor squabble. In the aftermath of Bacon's Rebellion, twenty-three men were executed.

The "young hotheads," as Governor Fauquier termed them, did not precipitate such a direct confrontation in the 1760s and 1770s, but Virginians looked worriedly at neighboring North Carolina, where an association of western farmers known as the Regulators fought a pitched battle with tidewater planters. Patrick Henry, however, preferred more subtle means. Associating the oligarchy with British authority, he succeeded in swinging the balance of power in the House of Burgesses to the "hotheads." The Stamp Act debates of 1765 proved that John Robinson's system of government was on the wane. The next year the old elite received a further jolt when an examination of Robinson's accounts revealed considerable corruption. The tidewater gentry never fully recovered. By the mid-1770s, when vital questions about the English relationship had to be decided, the House of Burgesses was in the hands of radical newcomers—Patrick Henry, Richard Henry Lee, Francis L. Lee, George Mason, George Washington, and Thomas Jefferson. Without the loosening effect of the American Revolution on the internal power structure of the colonies, it is possible that none of the these men would have achieved political leadership.

Thomas Jefferson first assumed political office in 1769, when Albemarle County elected him a member of the House of Burgesses. Only twenty-six at the time, he won the approval of both gentry and plain people. Such double backing was common in the eighteenth-century South and proved effective in identifying political talent. The necessity of pleasing both camps discouraged the haughty aristocrat and also the popular rabble rouser. The final products of the system were leaders who, like Jefferson, combined the best of democracy and aristocracy and in so doing defined an American political ideal.

As Jefferson gained experience and confidence as a Burgess, he lent more and more weight to the protest against England. In 1773 he joined Patrick Henry and Richard Henry Lee in calling for a Committee of Correspondence to solidify the colonial cause. Samuel Adams had begun this practice in Massachusetts the previous year, but confined the communications to towns within the colony. The Virginians had an intercolonial organization in mind, and Jefferson personally helped get it under way with his facile pen. In the process he began to acquire a reputation outside Virginia.

The first months of 1774 brought the disquieting news of the Boston Tea Party and Parliament's punitive response. Jefferson was among those who strongly sympathized with the people of Massachusetts, and he represented their plight as an American problem rather than a local one. He also sponsored a measure in the House of Burgesses calling for twenty-four hours of fasting in Virginia on June 1, 1774, the day the Boston Port Act went into effect. An enraged Governor John Dunmore dissolved the Assembly, but its members defied him and regrouped in the Raleigh Tavern next door. There they proposed an intercolonial congress and resolved that "an attack on any one colony should be considered as an attack on the whole." Although few realized its implications, this breakdown of the royal governor's authority was Virginia's revolution.

Later in the summer of 1774, representatives of the various Virginia counties convened in Williamsburg to choose delegates to the Continental Congress. In preparation for the meeting, Jefferson wrote *A Summary View of the Rights of British America*. The tract was intended as a handbook for Virginia's members at the congress, but in pamphlet form it quickly reached a much wider audience on both sides of the Atlantic. In *A Summary View* Jefferson stood squarely on natural rights philosophy as he had learned it from John Locke and other English constitutional theorists. He began by pointing out that the English settlers who emigrated to the New World had not thereby relinquished their liberties as Englishmen and as men. Specifically, they had not agreed to be governed by an assembly—Parliament—in which they were not represented. As for George III, Jefferson made it clear that in his view "kings are the servants not the proprietors of the people." Submission to monarchs was voluntary and could be voluntarily abandoned if the relationship threatened natural rights. Clinching his argument, Jefferson asked: "can his majesty . . . put down all law under his feet? Can he erect a power superior to that which erected himself? He has done it indeed by force, but let him remember that force cannot give right."

These were strong words, but Jefferson stopped short of actually proposing revolution. He referred to the colonies as "British America," and called for the end of Parliament's power to tax and regulate trade rather than for outright independence. Yet even this seemed too much to the majority of the Williamsburg gathering, which adopted resolutions that in Jefferson's opinion were mild as a "sucking dove." In a candid moment, however, Jefferson admitted that the leap he proposed in *A Summary View* was "too long as yet for the mass of our citizens." In 1774 all but a radical fringe of colonists regarded themselves as loyal British subjects and stood by the distinction conceding Parliament the right to impose "external" taxes concerning trade, but not those affecting only the "internal" life of the colonies. A conception of American nationality was, however, growing steadily. Thomas Paine expressed it in *Common Sense.* "In no instance," he wrote, "hath nature made the satellite larger than its primary planet; and as England and America, with respect to each other, reverse the common order of nature, it is evident that they belong in different systems. England to Europe: America to itself."

Jefferson soon had an opportunity to take the leading role in implementing this idea of independence. He arrived in Philadelphia in June 1775 to sit as one of Virginia's delegates to the Second Continental Congress. Although he was the second youngest member of the assembly, necks craned as Jefferson entered the hall. His reputation for logical thought and, in John Adams's words, a "masterly pen," had preceded him. Shortly thereafter Congress entrusted Jefferson with the drafting of several important papers, including the rejection of a proposal of conciliation from England's Prime Minister, Lord Frederick North.

On June 7, 1776, the congress passed Richard Henry Lee's motion that "these United Colonies are and of right ought to be free and independent states." A five-man committee, including Jefferson, John Adams, and Benjamin Franklin, was instructed to draft a formal declaration of the Congress's intent. Franklin, whom Jefferson revered, might well have done the writing, but he was ill at the time. Jefferson then proposed that Adams undertake the task, after which, according to Adams's recollection, the following dialog ensued:

ADAMS: Oh! no.
JEFFERSON: Why will you not? You ought to do it.
ADAMS: I will not.
JEFFERSON: Why?
ADAMS: Reasons enough.
JEFFERSON: What can be your reasons?
ADAMS: Reason first—You are a Virginian, and a Virginian
             ought to appear at the head of this business. Reason sec-
             ond—I am obnoxious, suspected, and unpopular. You
             are very much otherwise. Reason third—You can write
             ten times better than I can.
JEFFERSON: Well, if you are decided I will do as well as I can.

So it was that on June 11 the thirty-three-year-old Thomas Jefferson retired to the tiny parlor of his lodgings at Seventh and Market and began to write his way to immortality.

For over two weeks Jefferson's quill pen scratched out draft after draft of a declaration. Eighteen hundred highly polished words finally emerged. Franklin, now in good health, Adams, and the rest of the committee looked at them and made several suggestions. On June 28 the Congress scrutinized Jefferson's work. He must have cringed inwardly as his painstaking efforts were criticized, revised, and abridged. Yet the version signed on July 4, 1776 was a monument to one man.

Jefferson, to be sure, was modest. He never pretended that the Declaration of Independence was anything but a compilation of the ideas of others, a summary of the spirit of the time and place. Years afterward he wrote of the Declaration: "neither aiming at originality of principle or sentiment, nor yet copied from any particular and previous writing, it was intended to be an expression of the American mind." Jefferson's most obvious intellectual debt was to John Locke and the other Enlightenment philosophers of natural rights. But the Virginian did alter the usual trio of life, liberty, and property to read "life, liberty, and the pursuit of Happiness." George Mason had made the same substitution in his Virginia Bill of Rights of June 12, 1776, and Jefferson clearly used his friend's manifesto as inspiration and guide. Still, the flowing, compelling style of the Declaration of Independence was Jefferson's alone. Although the word was yet to be coined, he had produced a masterpiece of *propaganda*—a justification as well as a declaration.

That Jefferson was well aware of his function as a propagandist is evident in his opening lines. "A decent respect to the opinions of mankind" is stated as the reason for the Declaration. Jefferson knew that "a candid world" as well as reluctant revolutionaries at home would look at the document as an explanation of the legitimacy of the revolution.

Indeed, many colonists were frankly pro-British and loyal to George III. These Tories had no desire for independence and actively discouraged the movement. Their opposition made it imperative that the revolt be made respectable, a matter of duty rather than choice. The action of the colonies had therefore to be defended on the highest grounds of universal principle. British taxation, for example, was disliked because it flattened the colonists' purses, but economic self-interest was an unacceptable reason for a revolution. Good revolutionary technique required the expression of grievances in terms of violations of "the laws of nature and of nature's God." Using Lockean theory, Jefferson sublimated self-interest (taxes, loss of property) to principle (the natural right of the sanctity of property, liberty). Using Enlightenment ideas, he made George III appear to be not merely an inconvenience in certain ways, but a threat to a widely held ideal of human freedom. Indeed, George emerged from Jefferson's scathing pen a tyrannical ogre. Much could have been said for the English side, of course, but in writing the Declaration Jefferson's purpose was persuasion, not scholarship.

With independence declared, Jefferson, like other newly minted Americans, faced the sobering task of justifying the revolution with success. Not only did the proclaimed state of independence have to be confirmed on the battlefield, but the new nation suddenly had a host of awesome responsibilities thrust upon it. These ranged from creating a viable economy to establishing a workable system of government based on republican principles. Thomas Paine had written ecstatically in *Common Sense* about the glorious opportunity an independent America had to "begin the world over again." Doing it, however, was another matter. From our present status as a superpower we can hardly imagine the anxiety existing among Jefferson's contemporaries in the decade after independence. It may help to compare the fledgling nation with a teen-aged couple just starting married life after a bitter family war and a hurried elopement. It was thrilling in prospect and at the dramatic moment of separation, but now, alone in the quiet of a cheap apartment, the full impact strikes home. Food, clothing, order, and security no longer appear automatically from father and mother. Bills must be paid and relations with society established. To make matters worse, all the relatives and neighbors express open doubts about the eventual success of the new union and volunteer numerous predictions of its early demise.

For another perspective on the challenge of separate existence, consider that England, with its long experience in government and its immense resources, had been unable to solve many of the problems inherent in the American situation. Mercantilism had proved unworkable; the economy was in chaos, with thirteen separate and self-seek-

A Declaration by the Representatives of the UNITED STATES OF AMERICA, in General Congress assembled.

When in the course of human events it becomes necessary for one people to dissolve the political bands which have connected them with another, and to assume among the powers of the earth the separate and equal station to which the laws of nature & of nature's god entitle them, a decent respect to the opinions of mankind requires that they should declare the causes which impel them to the separation.

We hold these truths to be self-evident; that all men are created equal, that they are endowed by their creator with equal creation they derive inherent & inalienable rights, that among these are life, liberty, & the pursuit of happiness; that to secure these rights, governments are instituted among men, deriving their just powers from the consent of the governed; that whenever any form of government becomes destructive of these ends, it is the right of the people to alter or to abolish it, & to institute new government, laying it's foundation on such principles & organising it's powers in such form, a to them shall seem most likely to effect their safety & happiness. prudence indeed will dictate that governments long established should not be changed for light & transient causes: and accordingly all experience hath shewn tha

This is a portion of Jefferson's original four-page draft of the Declaration of Independence, which he began composing June 11, 1776 in Philadelphia.

John Trumbull's painting Declaration of Independence *was executed in the 1780s, partly while Trumbull was in Paris as a guest of Thomas Jefferson. A perfectionist, Trumbull painted thirty-six of the figures from life. Facing John Hancock (standing, right) are, from the left, John Adams, Roger Sherman, Robert Livingston, Thomas Jefferson, and Benjamin Franklin.*

As the high point of their efforts in the War of 1812 the British captured Washington, D.C. (August 24, 1814) and burned the public buildings as shown here. President James Madison and other officials fled in disgrace. But three weeks later Americans regained some measure of pride when they successfully defended the city of Baltimore against a British attack. At the conclusion of the battle Francis Scott Key observed the American flag still flying over Baltimore's Fort McHenry and composed the words for the Star Spangled Banner. Set to the tune of an old drinking song, it became the national anthem.

Among the many skills the versatile Jefferson perfected were architecture and horticulture. His own home, Monticello, overlooking Charlottesville in Western Virginia, is a monument to its owner's sense of grace and proportion. The house, which has become a Jefferson museum, is shown as it looks today.

ing entities each going its own way. The same internal discord had doomed any permanent effort at unified government of all the American colonies. England, moreover, had failed to discover ways of raising revenue for defense and administration. And there was the western land issue, which had simply been swept under the rug with the Proclamation of 1763. Inexperienced Americans were now confronted with all these same problems. Moreover, the wealth and leadership ability of 80,000 Tories, or Loyalists, who fled the country during and after the Revolution were no longer available to help build a nation.

Amid the doubt and uncertainty Jefferson's America could count a few assets in facing the formidable task of creating a nation. One was determination to establish the legitimacy of the revolution, to prove the scoffers and the critics wrong, to erase self-doubts. In addition, Jefferson and his contemporaries clung to the old idea that they were God's chosen people, destined to lead mankind in the paths of righteousness. From this perspective, the entire world had a stake in what happened on the edge of the North American wilderness. "The cause of America," as Paine put it, "is in great measure the cause of all mankind." And Philip Freneau, whose newspaper Jefferson later sponsored, solemnly proclaimed American independence an event commensurate in importance to the birth of Christ. True or not, the belief of many Americans in this rejuvenated conception of mission was one of their chief advantages in meeting the responsibilities of nationhood.

Despite all the talk about America, the united colonies, and the Continental Congress, when Thomas Jefferson thought of his country in the late 1770s, he had Virginia in mind. Most of his contemporaries shared this geopolitical orientation. Their loyalty to their respective colonies was, after all, of much longer standing than that to the larger, united body. Indeed, there were serious doubts about whether there would be unification after the fighting ended. Perhaps the various colonies would go their separate ways in the manner of the smaller European nations. Understandably, then, Jefferson's thoughts turned to Virginia immediately after publication of the Declaration of Independence. In his view, the reshaping of Virginia's laws and polity "is the whole object of the present controversy; for should a bad government be instituted for us . . . it had been as well to have accepted . . . the bad one offered to us from beyond the water." Jefferson also knew that the end of British rule meant a rare opportunity to translate political and social ideals into reality. He grew restless in Philadelphia throughout the spring and summer of 1776. Even as he wrote the Declaration of Independence he yearned to be in Williamsburg, and at the first convenient moment after its adoption, he resigned his seat in Congress.

Happily returned to Virginia, Jefferson at once launched a comprehensive effort to bring the new state's laws and institutions into conformity with republican principles and natural rights. His first target was the Virginia aristocracy. Although part of it himself, Jefferson realized that true liberty could not exist in a society dominated by an entrenched oligarchy. It was not the concept of an elite to which Jefferson objected, but rather the fact that the elite was established and perpetuated by artificial means. Instead of earning a silver spoon, its members were born with one in their mouths. What Jefferson hoped to do was "to annul this privilege, and instead of an aristocracy of wealth . . . to make an opening for the aristocracy of virtue and talent." The result should be a "natural aristocrat"—a happy blend of Jefferson's contact with both Enlightenment philosophy and the American frontier.

The foundation of Virginia's pre-Revolutionary aristocracy was land—huge holdings that passed from generation to generatoin according to the rules of entail and primogeniture. In this arrangement, which dated from feudal times, estates passed intact from the owner to his first-born son. They could not be subdivided nor sold outside the family.

In Jefferson's words, primogeniture and entail operated to create "a distinct set of families who, being privileged by law in the perpetuation of their wealth, were thus formed into a Patrician order, distinguished by the splendor and luxury of their establishments." Such a situation not being consistent with the right of every man to life, liberty, and the pursuit of happiness, Jefferson proposed the abolition of both entail and primogeniture. The oligarchy, of course, was suspicious; only his popularity and political tact, eventually pushed the bills through.

Religion also attracted Jefferson's reforming energies. For more than a century the Church of England had enjoyed a favored position in Virginia. Anglicanism was, in fact, the established religion, virtually a branch of the government. Jefferson deplored this situation. A disciple of the Enlightenment doctrine of freedom of thought, he believed that truth needed no enforcement other than its own inherent logic and reasonableness: "it is error alone which needs the support of government. Truth can stand by itself." This was the sense of the words "self-evident" that Jefferson, at Franklin's suggestion, used in the Declaration of Independence.

Jefferson was therefore bitterly opposed to any government effort to enforce or even assist a particular creed not only as a violation of individual liberties, but also as a poor way of making converts. Illustrating his point from the history of science, Jefferson pointed out that "the Newtonian principle of gravitation is now more firmly established on the basis of reason than it would be were the government to step in and to make it an article of necessary faith." Throughout history, Jefferson concluded, force in matters of belief only made "one half the world fools, and the other half hypocrites. . . . Reason and free inquiry are the only effectual agents against error." He held that a man's religion did not fall under the jurisdiction of civil authority. "The legitimate powers of government," he explained, "extend to such acts only as are injurious to others. But it does me no injury for my neighbor to say there are twenty gods, or no God. It neither picks my pocket nor breaks my leg."

To implement his ideas, Jefferson drafted a bill for establishing religious freedom in Virginia. After a ringing preamble, it declared in part that "all men shall be free to profess, and by argument to maintain, their opinions in matters of religion." Here was a guarantee of freedom of conscience for every citizen, be he Hindu, Christian, or atheist. Even more, Jefferson's arguments and his sweeping definition of free thought supported the principle that the opinions of men on *any* subject were not the concern of civil government.

When Jefferson's bill finally became law in 1786, it was a major milestone. The young nation had lived up to the promises of Roger Williams and William Penn. To the delight of Jefferson and his countrymen, the Virginia Statute for Religious Freedom was translated into several languages and circulated widely in Europe. Several publishers reprinted the document as an expression of Enlightenment philosophy. Jefferson believed this particular law put Americans a thousand years ahead of Europeans in respect to human freedom. "It is comfortable," he wrote to James Madison in 1786, "to see the standard of reason at length erected, after so many ages, during which the human mind has been held in vassalage by kings, priests, and nobles." And with an eye to the American obsession with justifying the revolution with success, he added: "it is honorable for us to have produced the first legislature who had the courage to declare that the reason of man may be trusted with the formation of his own opinions."

Jefferson regarded education as another key to the transition from a monarchic to a democratic society. He was convinced that a people could not be both ignorant and free. Indeed, he wrote to Wythe, the most important part of the whole revision of Virginia's code of laws concerned "the diffusion of knowledge among the people." There was much to support his view. Democracy meant popular sovereignty—government by the people. Yet if the people were uninformed and incapable of making judgments about their own lives, unscrupulous opportunists could lead them into tyranny. History, he knew, offered many examples of the enslavement of an uneducated citizenry. And Virginia society, like the rest of the new states, was composed of a few islands of refinement in an ocean of ignorance. Such gross inequality created ripe soil for oppression.

As a remedy Jefferson proposed three years of free education for every white child in the state. The basic skills of reading, writing, and arithmetic would be emphasized, but so would the study of the past, for Jefferson believed that "history, by apprizing [children] of the past, will enable them to judge of the future . . . it will qualify them as judges of the actions and designs of men; it will enable them to know ambition under every guise it may assume; and knowing it, to defeat its views." Though only three years of free elementary schooling were provided, the educational ladder would have more steps. Jefferson felt students on the intermediate level would come from families "in easy circumstances" who could afford to pay tuition and board, but he stipulated that up to seventy of the best poor students in Virginia be given full scholarships. After a year the state-supported scholars would be pared to the twenty "best geniuses." They would study for five more years. Finally, a select group of ten scholarship students would receive a free education at the College of William and Mary.

It was a brilliant and farsighted plan, "adapted," as Jefferson declared, "to the capacity, and the condition of every one and directed to their freedom and happiness." Unfortunately, Virginia adopted only portions and those only gradually. Not until 1825 did an aging Jefferson have the satisfaction of seeing the University of Virginia, an institution he created almost single-handedly, open in Charlottesville as the capstone of the state's educational pyramid.

In 1779 the Virginia legislature called Thomas Jefferson to succeed Patrick Henry as governor. He assumed the office in an atmosphere of fear and gloom. The war with England was not going well. Supplies and money had run short. Even General George Washington's repeated and personal pleas for aid found Governor Jefferson helpless. His own plantations were stripped on behalf of the Revolution, and he had many companions in poverty. Less than half of Virginia's counties paid taxes in 1780. The state militia could be equipped with only one rifle for each five men. On top of this, the British decided to shift the focus of their military efforts to the south. Charleston, South Carolina, fell on May 12, 1780, to a naval strike under Generals Henry Clinton and Charles Cornwallis. On December 30 a fleet of twenty-seven British ships appeared at the mouth of Chesapeake Bay. Virginia could offer no resistance, and the force, under the American deserter Benedict Arnold, sailed up the James toward the capital city of Richmond. Jefferson supervised the removal of the state papers, transferred his family to a safe location upriver, and then returned to watch despondently from across the James as Arnold's men burned the city.

In the dark months of early 1781 it must have seemed to the harassed Jefferson that America's hopes for winning its independence were also going up in smoke. No sooner did he move the seat of government to Charlottesville than Cornwallis was at its door. On June 4 Jefferson slipped away from Monticello only minutes before a British force arrived to capture him. Seven legislators were taken. But even as the remainder fled across the Blue Ridge, the tide was turning in the southern theater of war. Tough American mountaineers under Generals Nathaniel Green and Daniel Morgan had already decisively defeated British regulars at King's Mountain, Cowpens, and Guilford Courthouse in the Carolina back country. The Charlottesville raid, in fact, was the last offensive move Cornwallis made. Less than four months later he stood defeated at Yorktown while the military bands played "The World Turned Upside Down."

With the fighting and his term as governor both at an end, Jefferson retired to Monticello, his family (he had married a young widow in 1772), his library, his horses, his music, and his science. Never again, he vowed, would he leave his hilltop oasis for the hurly-burly of public service. With enthusiasm he turned to writing *Notes on the State of Virginia*, a proud answer to a European's inquiry about the ideals and circumstances of the new society. The book was printed privately in Paris in 1785. He entertained another European, the traveling Chevalier de Chastellux, at Monticello. After four days of companionship the visitor wrote: "let me describe to you a man, not yet forty, tall, and with a mild and pleasing countenance . . . an American, who without ever having quitted his own country, is at once a musician, skilled in drawing, a geometrician, an astronomer, a natural philosopher, legislator, and statesman . . . in voluntary retirement from the world."

A classic portrait, but Jefferson was unable to play this idyllic role for long. The first crack came late in 1782 when his fragile and lovely wife succumbed to a long illness. Not long afterward, another opportunity for public service, this time in the national arena as a congressman, came Jefferson's way. At first he refused, claiming both personal grief and pique over criticism of his governorship as reasons for aloofness. But interesting developments were taking place on the federal level, and just as in the case of Virginia's government, he realized that the success of the whole revolutionary effort hinged on whether satisfactory political forms could be devised. Here was a challenge calculated to stir Jefferson to action. He knew that republics were rare in the history of civilization. Men had always relied more on authority from above (monarchy, oligarchy, theocracy) for government. In fact, the Greek city-states were the only examples of true republics in history, and these had been small units of several thousand citizens in which popular sovereignty had had great meaning. America, however, proposed to govern 3 million people in a republican framework. There were no precedents for such an undertaking, and many felt a republic on this scale would degenerate inevitably into either anarchy or tyranny.

The Continental Congress began to experiment in national

government immediately after proclaiming independence. John Dickinson of Pennsylvania proposed a strong central government in which the states had little power. Some of his colleagues, however, thought such an arrangement too similar to the one they had just overthrown. They countered with the Articles of Confederation, which deliberately created a weak national government. Under the Articles, the government had no courts, no executive leadership, no power to regulate trade and commerce, and no independent source of revenue apart from requisitions from the states. Moreover, on most important issues the approval of *all* the member states was required. This plan for a spineless central government was submitted to the states in November 1777 and, with unanimous approval finally obtained, instituted on March 1, 1781. For Americans like John Dickinson, who thought in terms of the nation rather than the states, it was not a cause for celebration. In their estimation Americans had overreacted, had rushed headlong from one undesirable extremity of the political spectrum to the other.

Thomas Jefferson reentered the national political arena in December 1783, when he rode to Annapolis, Maryland, to take his seat in Congress as a delegate from Virginia. Widely respected throughout the country, he immediately assumed a major role. One of his first assignments was to arrange for the visit of General George Washington. Already a demigod in American eyes, Washington came to Annapolis to relinquish his sword to Congress. The ceremony of December 23 was charged with emotion. Many men wept openly in gratitude. To Jefferson, however, Washington's appearance had a deeper significance. By turning over his sword, the general in effect rejected the idea that he become a military dictator. In the 1780s, with an insecure nation yearning for leadership, this was not far-fetched. In the winter of 1782–1783 a group of army officers, joined by proponents of strong central government, had approached Washington with the idea of seizing power. The general had made his disapproval very clear. Now at Annapolis the one American who had the popularity to undermine republicanism formally and publicly made his commitment to a republic. Like Jefferson, Washington had rebelled in the name of republican principles, and he meant to give them a fair trial. Had he been otherwise inclined, American history could well have been totally different.

While adamantly opposed to monarchical substitutes, Jefferson remained critical of the central government established under the Articles. As a congressman he had ample opportunity to study its weaknesses. Some problems, he believed, were related to the time and circumstance. Congress, for instance, had no money, but only because the war-ravaged state economies were temporarily in disorder. The financial position of the central government would improve with that of the country in general. A more serious difficulty was the contemptuous attitude of many of the states. Some did not even bother to send representatives to Congress. Jefferson, however, was present and determined to make the best of the Articles. His service to the new government was, typically, brilliant. One of his reports made order out of the chaotic coinage system of the time by proposing the adoption of the "dollar," divided into tenths and hundredths, as the basic unit.

Of still greater consequence was Jefferson's influence on western land policy. Congress inherited this thorny problem from Great Britain when several states, led by New York and Virginia, ceded their western land claims to the central government. The cession itself was a triumph for federalism, but it obliged America to become an imperial power with all the attendant responsibilities. The western territories, in other words, bore the same relation to the United States as the thirteen colonies once had to Great Britain. There was the same perplexing question of management, the same danger of rebellion should Congress become as unsatisfactory as Parliament.

The colonial policy that emerged owed a great deal to Thomas Jefferson. On March 22, 1784, he submitted a plan of government for the territories. Its genius was embodied in the provision that the western lands would be organized into states which, when they had a sufficient number of settlers, would be welcomed into the union *on an equal basis* with the original thirteen. No virtual representation, no taxation without representation, no second-class citizenship, but rather an invitation to join the empire. Had England granted as much in the early 1770s, the professed need for the American Revolution would have been eliminated and war, in all probability, averted. Jefferson's plan had the further advantage of encouraging settlement of the West by assuring those who migrated that they would suffer no loss of rights or liberties. It even guaranteed manhood suffrage in the territories—a step toward democracy that none of the original states had yet taken. Himself a slaveowner, he proposed that slavery be prohibited in the western territories after 1800. Finally, Jefferson, a disciple of order, suggested a rectangular survey system for the unsettled land.

The essentials of Jefferson's western plan were incorporated in the Land Ordinance of 1785 and the Northwest Ordinance of 1787. These great laws, the high point of government under the Articles of Confederation, made possible one of the most successful colonizing

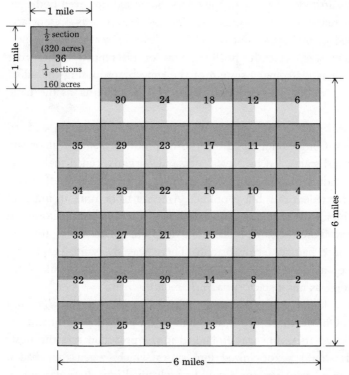

The influence on Thomas Jefferson of the Enlightenment and science generally is evident in his plan for surveying the unoccupied territory of the West. Adopted by Congress as the Land Ordinance of 1785, its geometric regularity shaped the landscape of an expanding nation. The entire six-mile square was called a "township" and consisted of thirty-six "sections," each one mile square. These in turn could be divided according to the detail in Section 36. One disadvantage of Jefferson's system was that its rigid structure did not take the natural features of the environment into account. The lines ran straight regardless of rivers, mountains, or lakes.

efforts in history. The United States expanded from the Appalachians to the Pacific without losing a single acre to an independence movement. Every territory ultimately entered the union in preference to forming a separate nation. As students of Great Britain's imperial misadventures, Jefferson and his colleagues learned their lessons well.

Valuable as Jefferson was at home, Congress needed able representatives abroad, and on July 5, 1784, he sailed for France. After assisting John Adams and Benjamin Franklin for a year negotiating commercial treaties, Jefferson took Franklin's place as American ambassador to France. It was a happy choice. Although lacking Franklin's enormous popularity, Jefferson's reputation as an architect of American independence endeared him to French liberals. As the French Revolution gathered momentum, Jefferson's counsel was increasingly sought. He personally believed that "the American war seems first to have awakened the thinking part of the nation . . . from the sleep of despotism in which they were sunk." Young French officers, Jefferson explained, had returned from service in the New World enthusiastic about the republican regime they saw in operation. When they joined other republicans in launching a revolt against *their* king, Jefferson was understandably delighted. Even as the course of the French Revolution turned toward the guillotine, he never lost faith that its basic energies sprang from the same concepts of human dignity and freedom that had motivated Americans.

Jefferson remained abroad five years. His characteristic response to what he termed "the vaunted scene of Europe" was awe. Patriotic as he tried to be, he could not help but be reminded of his provincialism by the brilliance of European cultural and intellectual life. "Were I . . . to tell you how much I enjoy their architecture, sculpture, painting, music," Jefferson wrote in 1785, "I should want words." He also coveted European books, and returned from Paris with enough to fill 250 feet of shelves at Monticello. And there were the charms of sophisticated European women, notably Maria Cosway, the wife of an English painter, with whom Jefferson traveled through France in the summer of 1786.

But at the same time Jefferson almost desperately resisted European attempts to turn his attention from his own country. Groping for ways to maintain pride in America, he pointed out that his countrymen enjoyed greater civil and economic equality than in the Old

World, where everyone "must be either the hammer or the anvil." Americans were also more moral, Jefferson generalized, and in their natural environment they possessed a resource of matchless beauty. If not culture, then nature would distinguish the young nation on the edge of the wilderness. Still "the vaunted scene" was compelling to the self-styled "savage of the mountains of America." Not for many decades would Americans acquire the cultural confidence to trust their own judgment and taste.

Returning to the United States in 1789, Jefferson enjoyed a brief rest at Monticello before resuming his career in the national government. Much had happened during his absence. Dissatisfaction with the weak central government under the Articles of Confederation grew through the decade. No matter how well it functioned, Congress simply did not possess the power to coordinate state economic policies or protect the nation's commercial interests abroad. Moreover, the mob rule that critics of democracy constantly predicted seemed on the verge of breaking out. In Massachusetts the winter of 1786–1787 brought a pitched battle between impoverished western farmers, organized under Daniel Shays, and the state militia.

Actually, Shays's Rebellion was simply a continuation of the internal contest over who should rule at home that had accompanied the larger struggle with Great Britain. Both the Shaysites and the Boston establishment understood their cause to be sanctified by natural rights and thus in keeping with the principles of the American Revolution. The problem was that this doctrine made no distinction between human rights and property rights. Both were sacred, and if the two came into conflict (as they did, for example, in debtor-creditor relationships), there was no easy solution. Those responsible for the Declaration of Independence and the Articles of Confederation assumed that men of good will could work together in interpreting and institutionalizing natural rights. But Shays's Rebellion, and the prospect of similar mass uprisings elsewhere, suggested that the spirit of 1776 had not erased old social and economic tensions.

The fundamental tension juxtaposed those traditional antagonists, the haves and the have-nots. Shays, representing the latter, preferred a weak central government with its assurance of a maximum of local control by the people. He had the support of men like Jefferson who leaned toward a human rights interpretation of Locke and who

124

trusted democracy. Commenting on Shays's Rebellion while in Paris, Jefferson even went so far as to declare that "the spirit of resistance to government is so valuable on certain occasions, that I wish it to be always kept alive. It will often be exercised when wrong, but better so than not . . . at all. I like a little rebellion now and then. It is like a storm in the Atmosphere."

John Adams, on the other hand, spoke for the forces of law, order, and property rights. Even after independence, he remained highly suspicious of popular sovereignty. For Adams, the Shaysites were "ignorant, restless desperadoes, without conscience or principles, . . . mobish insurgents [who] are for sapping the foundation and destroying the whole fabrick at once." Americans of Adams's persuasion were not opponents of democracy, but they did insist that the voice of the people be diluted—sifted, so to speak, through the medium of a strong central government. Washington spoke for this viewpoint when he observed: "we have errors to correct; we have probably too good an opinion of human nature in forming our Confederation."

If the critics of the Articles of Confederation had a low opinion of human nature, they had a high one of human reason. With it, they believed, man could build a system of government capable of curbing his passion, greed, and selfishness. Armed with this conviction, twenty-nine men (later joined by twenty-six others) gathered in Philadelphia in May 1787 to reconstruct the government of the United States. Fortunately for the outcome of their efforts, they were agreed in certain crucial areas. All were advocates of a strong central government. Most also agreed that the Articles were so deficient in this respect as to be totally useless. It was better to start from scratch than to revise and repair. In this reconstruction, the members of the convention believed, two principles must be incorporated: First, the new constitution must be the supreme law of the land, its power unquestionably greater than that of the various states. Second, the constitution must be a combination of monarchy, aristocracy, and democracy so arranged as to prevent the dominance of any one of these political options.

Nobody in Philadelphia seriously doubted that the people should be the basis of sovereignty in the new government. The question was how to check and balance popular opinion in the interest of the nation's well-being. Here was where reason came into play. Rather than trust men to know and work for the good, the founding fathers assumed with Lord Acton that "power corrupts." They also took pains to remove direct elective power from the people—three stages in the case of the President, four in the case of judges. Like engineers, the Constitution makers of 1787 built a series of automatic cutoffs into their power system. The result, approved September 17, was a masterpiece. In a single summer and without precedents or guides, the Constitutional Convention created a framework of government that has lasted, with only minor amendment, for almost two centuries.

Jefferson, following the Constitutional Convention from Paris, had mixed reactions. He liked the tripartite division of power between the executive, legislative, and judicial branches. He approved of giving the new legislature the power to levy taxes, and he was "captivated" by the compromise that established a bicameral legislature with the states represented on the basis of population in one house and equally in the other. But other aspects of the Philadelphia convention disturbed him deeply. In the first place, he did not agree with most of the delegates that the country teetered on the brink of anarchy in 1787. The Articles of Confederation, in Jefferson's opinion, had not been all that bad. "I would rather be exposed to the inconveniences attending too much liberty," he tartly observed, "than those attending too small a degree of it."

He felt the convention would have done better to have patched up the Articles of Confederation. As for the new system, Jefferson disliked the executive position created in Philadelphia. "Their President," he wrote to John Adams in November, "seems a bad edition of a Polish king." One man might be elected to the office every four years for life. Jefferson's major complaint, however, was the failure to specify the rights and liberties retained by individuals. "A bill of rights," he told James Madison, one of the prime movers at Philadelphia, "is what the people are entitled to against every government on earth . . . and what no just government should refuse, or rest on inferences." Civil liberties, after all, were the reason for the American Revolution for Thomas Jefferson. If a strong central government destroyed them, there was no point to independence.

Jefferson therefore followed the controversy over ratification of the Constitution closely and anxiously. He noted with approval that in

Thomas Jefferson

Virginia patriots like Richard Henry Lee and Patrick Henry spoke emotionally against ratification. Lee referred to the proponents of the Constitution as "a coalition of monarchy men, military men, aristocrats and drones whose noise, impudence and zeal exceeds all belief." This was extreme. Of all the so-called Federalists, probably only Alexander Hamilton considered monarchy a serious possibility. But, as historian Charles A. Beard pointed out in 1913, most of those who designed and favored the Constitution were men of means who stood to benefit economically from the stability and protection of a strong central government. Some even held for speculation Congress's paper money, the value of which was directly proportional to the vigor and power of the United States. This is not to say that economics alone explains the new Constitution, but rather that economic self-interest was evident along with idealistic principle in the summer of 1787. No contemporary of Jefferson would have found this point far-fetched; only those who insist on sanctifying America's beginnings with totally idealistic explanations profess shock at an economic interpretation of the Constitution.

Those who took Jefferson's position ultimately lost the struggle over ratification. Although its margin was narrow (89–79 in the Virginia ratifying convention, 187–168 in Massachusetts), the new government went into operation in 1789 without a bill of rights. But shortly thereafter, James Madison, who had opposed a listing of individual rights as unnecessary, noted the widespread national displeasure at its omission and decided to correct the matter himself. He wrote a declaration of rights and sent a copy to Paris for Jefferson's comments. The reply, full of praise, contained a few suggestions for improvement. Madison took them and in June 1789 introduced the Bill of Rights in Congress. Two years later, after approval by the states, it became the first ten amendments to the Constitution.

Positive action on the Bill of Rights greatly encouraged Jefferson, and the selection of George Washington as the first President in 1789 further reduced his anxieties about the new government. Washington, he felt confident, had no ambition to become a king. Indeed, the more Jefferson thought about how the Constitution of 1787 smoothed out the institutional wrinkles in America's republican experiment, the more enthusiastic he became. The Constitution, he declared, was "unquestionably the wisest ever yet presented to men." How it would work in practice, of course, no one yet knew.

George Washington was determined that Jefferson should take a leading role in establishing the new central government. He invited Jefferson to become secretary of state on his return from France. Given his interest in the success of the American experiment, Jefferson could not resist. After a brief stay at Monticello he made his way north to New York, then the federal capital. There was a dramatic meeting en route at Philadelphia between Jefferson and an aged Benjamin Franklin. The two friends talked largely of mutual acquaintances and politics in France. Franklin was particularly excited about the burgeoning French Revolution. "They served their apprenticeship in America," he observed, "and now they mean to set up for themselves."

Pushing on through a snowstorm, Jefferson arrived in New York in March 1790 to take charge of a State Department consisting of five clerks. The government was already well underway. In Jefferson's opinion, however, it manifested some disturbing tendencies. Most of them stemmed from the activities of Alexander Hamilton, Washington's wartime assistant and now his secretary of the treasury. Jefferson hardly knew the ambitious and talented Hamilton when he joined the administration, but soon the two of them were "daily pitted in the cabinet like two cocks." The conflict was predictable. In direct contrast to Jefferson, Hamilton made no secret of the fact that he despised the mass of common men, distrusted democracy, and preferred an aristocratic or, better yet, a monarchical regime. Saddled with the Constitution, Hamilton determined to make the most of an imperfect situation. This meant maximizing the strength of the central government and encouraging the development of a wealthy elite.

To these ends, Hamilton pushed through Congress a program for funding the debt of the United States at its full face value. He also successfully advocated federal assumption of all state debts incurred in the war for independence and the creation of a government-dominated national bank. Expensive as these measures were, they established the national credit, asserted federal superiority over the states, and brought men of wealth, chiefly northern businessmen, to support the United States. In 1791 Hamilton's Report on Manufactures proposed a protective tariff and a system of bounties, both to encourage domestic manufacturing. Jefferson was able to help block this plan, but he could not prevent Hamilton from obtaining in the same year a 25 percent excise tax on the domestic production of whiskey. This levy struck particularly hard at small farmers, who were accustomed to converting their grain into alcohol. When a group of several hundred farmers in western Pennsylvania came to Hamilton's attention for tax evasion, he personally led a force of 13,000 militiamen to crush the Whisky Rebellion.

Jefferson looked askance at these developments. From his perspective it appeared Hamilton was creating a far stronger central government than necessary—one, in fact, that posed a threat to individual liberties and republican principles. Hamilton's advocacy of manufacturing, cities, and high finance, moreover, ran directly counter to the Virginia planter's precept that "those who labor in the earth are the chosen people of God." Agriculture, Jefferson insisted, had to be the backbone of any happy society. "Let our workshops," he declared, "remain in Europe." America could trade for needed manufactured goods. For Hamilton himself, Jefferson grew to have a well-honed contempt. In as strong language as he ever used, Jefferson labeled the secretary of the treasury "not only a monarchist, but for a monarchy bottomed on corruption." With far more regret Jefferson said almost as much of his old Revolutionary colleague John Adams, whose doubts about democracy had increased substantially. Even Washington's head seemed to have been turned by a vision of grandiose living in the ceremonial manner of Old World courts.

With the tide thus running against republicanism, Jefferson struggled desperately. He had a few allies. Friends of his ideals in the Senate who refused to be pressured by a President eager for certain decisions established a precedent for legislative autonomy. These senators also resisted attempts to make Washington's official title "His Elective Majesty" or "His Most Gracious Highness," in the manner of European kings. The designation "highness," one skeptical legislator dryly remarked, should be reserved for the tallest man in a company. This viewpoint ultimately prevailed, and the accepted form of addressing the President became, to Jefferson's delight, simply "Mr. President."

After 1791 Jefferson also had the support of Philip Freneau and his newspaper, the *National Gazette*. In fact, Jefferson gave Freneau a position in the State Department and helped him start the paper as a challenge to John Fenno's *Gazette of the United States,* which Hamilton patronized. In the hallowed tradition of eighteenth-century journalism, the papers abused each other unmercifully and in vituperative language. Washington, for one, was shocked and disappointed. He had expected, somewhat naively, that political parties would not develop in the United States. Yet by 1792 it was clear that the Federalists, grouped around Hamilton and Adams, and the Jefferson-led Republicans (sometimes called Democratic Republicans) were determining the course of national politics. This realization led a reluctant Washington to agree to a second term as President. He knew he was the only American capable of holding back the partisan deluge.

Questions of foreign policy added fuel to the political fires of the 1790s. Once again, Hamilton and Jefferson squared off. The secretary of the treasury tended to admire and favor England both as a commercial power and as a monarchy. Jefferson, on the other hand, supported France and its revolution on both philosophical and personal grounds. Even after the execution of Louis XVI in 1793 and the massacres by the Jacobins, Jefferson's loyalty held firm. But in Federalist circles around the capital and among the upper classes generally, Jefferson was a marked man. People crossed streets to avoid encountering the "Jacobin," and Hamilton exploited his advantage to the hilt. As a result, when war broke out between France and England, Jefferson was at a severe disadvantage. He attempted to obtain sympathy for France by reminding Washington of the 1778 treaty of alliance that had been so helpful to the American revolutionary cause. Hamilton countered with the argument that the old treaty had been made with the now-dethroned French monarchy and was, consequently, void. When Washington supported this interpretation, Jefferson had little choice but to resign as secretary of state, a step he took at the end of 1793. By this time the brazen behavior of the French emissary, Citizen Edmond Genêt, in commissioning American privateers to prey on English shipping had alienated even Jefferson.

In 1794 a pro-British foreign policy seemed likely, but England did little to cultivate American support. In fact, she harassed the United States both on the high seas, where American ships were seized, and on the northwest frontier, where Indians were encouraged to take the warpath. War with England seemed imminent in 1794, but

John Jay warded off hostilities by negotiating a controversial treaty. It succeeded in removing the British from frontier forts in the Ohio Valley, establishing formal commercial relations, and settling boundary and war debt questions remaining from the Revolution. On the burning issue of maritime rights, however, the Jay Treaty said nothing. It also ignored the fact that Canadian fur traders had unrestricted access to American soil and freely sold arms and ammunition to the Indians.

Leading the Republican opposition, Jefferson branded the Jay Treaty neocolonial. The Senate barely approved the agreement in June 1795. Washington, too, was torn, but finally yielded to Hamilton's arguments and signed the document in the face of widespread national criticism. His decision almost certainly postponed a second war with Great Britain, the major objective of Federalist foreign policy. When the second war finally came, in 1812, the young nation was strong enough to hold its own. Washingtonian diplomacy was further distinguished in the 1790s by the favorable Treaty of San Lorenzo (the Pinckney Treaty) of 1796. According to its terms the United States received important concessions from Spain regarding rights and boundaries in the West. The final movement in the diplomatic minuet of the 1790s involved the United States in an undeclared war with France. An insult to America's foreign ministers by Talleyrand (the XYZ affair) led to a state of open maritime conflict for several years.

John Adams and the Federalists won the Presidential election of 1796, but under the awkward electoral college system Thomas Jefferson, the Republican nominee for President, became Adam's Vice-President. From this vantage point of honored obscurity, Jefferson had ample opportunity to observe federalism play itself out.

Using the threat of war with France as an excuse, the Federalists in the summer of 1798 pushed through the Alien and Sedition Acts. The former were designed to weaken the political influence of immigrants, who generally were Republicans, by giving the President the power to imprison and deport dangerous noncitizens. The Alien Acts also lengthened the residence requirement for citizenship from five to fourteen years. Far more sinister, in Jefferson's eyes, was the Sedition Act, for under its terms the federal government could suppress American citizens. The Sedition Act provided for fines and imprisonment for persons composing, printing, or uttering "any false, scandalous, and malicious writing or writings against the government of the United States, or the President . . . with intent to defame . . . or bring them . . . into contempt or disrepute." The law, in other words, sought to end criticism of the government.

Jefferson was enraged, the more so when Matthew Lyon, a Republican congressman from Vermont, was actually jailed for verbal attacks on his Federalist opponent. In Jefferson's eyes the Alien and Sedition Acts made a mockery of those cherished principles of the American Revolution embodied in the Bill of Rights. Freedom of speech, press, and even thought were denied for purely partisan purposes. In November 1798 Jefferson channeled his wrath into the Kentucky Resolutions. Taking the position that the federal government had assumed undelegated powers in passing the acts, he set forth the doctrine of nullification. The illegal measures, Jefferson wrote, are "altogether void and of no effect," at least as far as Kentucky was concerned. Writing for Virginia, James Madison promulgated a similar doctrine. The other states did not follow suit in 1798, but the controversy raised questions about the nature and purposes of the union that would not be settled conclusively until the Civil War.

The Alien and Sedition Acts prompted some Republicans, chiefly in the South, to give serious consideration to leaving the union. Jefferson, however, believed the Federalists had dug their own grave. The great majority of Americans, he felt, would not accept such curtailment of their hard-won liberties. "A little patience," he advised his more radical colleagues, "and we shall see the reign of the witches . . . pass over and the people . . . restoring the government to its true principles." Events proved him correct, for during the closing years of the 1790s the Federalists committed one political blunder after another. They levied heavy taxes on personal property, then used the revenue to support a large standing army. In 1799 that army marched against a group of protesting Pennsylvanians under John Fries, and cries of tyranny rose on all sides.

Federalism also suffered from divisions in its own camp. After a brief trial, President Adams found he could not stand Alexander Hamilton. Adams also wanted to extricate his administration from the undeclared war with France. The "High Federalists" resisted the idea, but Adams finally repudiated his advisors and concluded a satisfactory peace. The Republicans meanwhile prepared for the election of 1800 by developing an effective party organization. There were local and statewide committees, some of them holdovers from the Democratic Clubs that had appeared earlier in the decade in support of Jefferson, republicanism, and the French Revolution. Several influential Republican newspapers sprang to life and, in defiance of the Sedition Act, attacked the Adams Administration for monarchical ambitions. The Federalists replied in kind and organized their own party. The stage was set for a showdown political battle.

The election of 1800 was unprecedented in several respects. It was the first to take place outside the shadow cast by George Washington, for with him in December 1799 died the last gentlemanly reservations about the propriety of partisan politics. Previously neither Republicans nor Federalists had quite dared bring their animosities into the open. Now it was bare knuckles. In addition, 1800 was the first election in which the contesting parties took their campaigns to the people. It was to be more of a national election and less an agreement among political insiders. With Adams put forward for reelection by the Federalists and Jefferson the natural choice of the Republicans, the start of the new century promised to be exciting.

The Federalists understandably chose to base their campaign on their opponents' shortcomings rather than on their own record. The charges against Jefferson were predictable. For one, he had spent too much time in close association with the radical democracy of France. If Jefferson were elected, charged the Federalists, guillotines would appear in the squares of the major cities, and the privileged classes could expect the worst. Another favorite Federalist smear involved Jefferson's alleged atheism. Actually he was a deist who demanded that his religion, like his other beliefs, be supportable by reason and evidence. In Federalist eyes, however, it was a question of "God—and a religious president; or . . . Jefferson—and no God!!!" One hysterical Adams partisan went further, forecasting that if Jefferson were elected, "murder, robbery, rape, adultery, and incest will all be openly taught and practiced, the air will be rent with the cries of distress, and the soil will be soaked with blood."

Perhaps the most credible Federalist charge concerned Jefferson's philosophical nature and agricultural orientation. The Virginian, it was contended, would be too impractical for the Presidency, and his rural bias would spell hardship for America's struggling commercial and industrial enterprises. Giving no quarter in their struggle for political survival, the Federalists also attacked Jefferson's personal morality. It was alleged that the master of Monticello had defrauded a poor widow of her inheritance and had fathered several children by one of his slaves. The first charge could be dismissed quickly, for Jefferson kept himself in chronic poverty as a result of honoring financial promises made to unlucky acquaintances. As for the illegitimate children, substantial evidence suggests that as a widower in the 1790s Jefferson enjoyed a mutually satisfying intimacy with a black girl named Sally Hemings, who was the half-sister of his deceased wife and who had been with him for part of his stay in France.

The Republican campaign of 1800 was based on the simple promise to return the nation to the path of freedom from which it had strayed under Federalist guidance. Hamilton, Adams, even Washington were accused of undermining the intent of the American Revolution. The strategy proved successful. Not even the forest fires the Federalists lit on election day to preoccupy the country people who were largely Republican could prevent Jefferson and his running mate, Aaron Burr, from sweeping to victory with 73 electoral votes each. The unanticipated tie threw the election into the House of Representatives. The embittered Federalists tried every means to block Jefferson's bid, but after more than 30 inconclusive ballots, he emerged as President.

In later years Jefferson spoke of the outcome of the election as the "revolution of 1800," adding that it was "as real a revolution in the principles of our government as that of 1776 was in form." In one sense, of course, this was incorrect. The election of Thomas Jefferson took place under procedures established by the Constitution. There was no overthrow of the government's principles. No secession or civil war followed the counting of the votes. Neither did the new President revolutionize economic or legal procedures. Jefferson himself interpreted the national mood quite accurately in his inaugural address, when he declared that "every difference of opinion is not a difference of principle. . . . We are all Republicans, we are all Federalists."

Still, a social and intellectual change of such scope that some might call it revolutionary did occur in 1800. The Federalists were an avowed aristocracy. Openly distrusting the masses of common men, they took as their model the privileged upper classes of the Old World.

They insisted that men must keep their place. Those who owned the country ought to govern it, and challenges should be summarily crushed. The Jeffersonians, on the other hand, drew their inspiration from the New World. They had confidence in the reasonableness of mankind and advocated an open, fluid social order. Their elite would be a natural one, the product of talent and diligence. Every man should, they believed, enjoy equality of opportunity and the freedom to exploit his potential to the fullest. Under federalism, in sum, the nation drifted away from democracy. After 1800 the cause of the people was in the ascendancy, at least as an ideal.

President Jefferson surrounded himself with a distinguished group of associates headed by James Madison as secretary of state and Albert Gallatin as secretary of the treasury. Among the first problems facing their administration was one created by a Federalist-dominated national judicial system. John Adams, tired and bitter at the close of his administration, deliberately filled the national courts with Federalist judges. These "midnight" appointments were designed to give the Federalists a measure of influence in Jefferson's administration. Already suspicious of the judiciary because of its distance from popular control (judges had life tenure), the Republicans attacked. At one stroke Congress abolished sixteen circuit courts and their sixteen Federalist judges. The House of Representatives moved on to impeach the highly partisan Supreme Court Justice Samuel Chase, but after a sensational trial, the Senate wisely refused to supply the necessary confirmation.

The real center of judicial power, however, was John Marshall, Chief Justice of the Supreme Court. Marshall was a Virginian and a distant relative of Jefferson, but there was no love lost between the two. A leading Federalist and Adams's secretary of state, Marshall was appointed in the closing weeks of the Adams administration. For the outgoing President's purposes, the choice was brilliant. Marshall, who dominated the Supreme Court for thirty-four years, handed down a series of decisions that institutionalized the Federalist interpretation of the Constitution. His first important ruling, and the foundation of many of the rest, concerned the power to determine the constitutionality of laws passed by Congress. Jefferson believed the authors of the Constitution intended that all three branches of the federal government work together, checking and balancing, to determine the meaning of that document. Marshall took the position that the Constitution was "superior paramount law," unalterable by legislative act or executive order. Hence only the judicial branch could pronounce on the question of constitutionality.

In 1803 Marshall found an opportunity to create a precedent. The case of *Marbury* v. *Madison* involved William Marbury, a Federalist who had received one of Adams's controversial appointments, and the secretary of state, James Madison, who refused to honor his appointment. Marbury went straight to the Supreme Court with the intention of using a section of the Judiciary Act of 1789 to force the executive branch to honor the commitment. Marshall agreed that the law was on Marbury's side, but ruled against him on the grounds that the Judiciary Act gave the Supreme Court an unconstitutional power. The Chief Justice thus decided against both his party and the power of his court, but he established a far more important principle—the right of the judicial branch to decide if an act of Congress was in conformity with the Constitution.

After *Marbury* v. *Madison* Jefferson and his Republican successors to the Presidency could only chafe in frustration as the "crafty chief judge," in Jefferson's words, handed down a series of major decisions. *Martin* v. *Hunter's Lessee* (1816) and *Cohens* v. *Virginia* (1821) resulted in the establishment of the right of the Supreme Court to review, and if necessary to reverse, the decisions of state courts respecting the Constitution. The ruling confirmed the principle of federal supremacy. In *Fletcher* v. *Peck* (1810) and *Dartmouth College* v. *Woodward* (1819), the Marshall Court protected the structure of American business by affirming the obligation of contracts in the face of popular criticism. Hamilton would have been delighted. *McCulloch* v. *Maryland* (1819) set forth the broad or "loose" interpretation of the powers of the federal government under the Constitution. If the purpose was legitimate and constitutional, Marshall ruled, then Congress had the power to take any constitutional action necessary to achieve that purpose. The decision was a direct slap at the Jeffersonians' narrow or "strict" interpretation of constitutional authority.

The Jeffersonians in theory were proponents of weak central government. But relative positions had much to do with this preference. When the Federalists held the national reins, the Jeffersonians opposed a strong central government. Once in control themselves, a powerful nation acquired much greater appeal. In fact, the deposed Federalists soon became the new critics of strong national authority.

The course of events soon substantiated this reversal of roles. In contrast to what many had hoped—or feared—the Republicans did not use their control of Congress and the Presidency to undo major Federalist policies and institutions. The Bank of the United States was left intact, and in 1816 Jefferson's successor, James Madison, created a central bank more than three times the size of Hamilton's prototype. Neither did Jefferson change the Federalist objectives of upholding the national credit, assuming state debts incurred in the Revolutionary War, and encouraging shipping and commerce. In time, the Republicans even instituted and improved upon a Hamiltonian ideal, a protective tariff to encourage manufacturing. The new President did reduce the size of the army as part of his plan for federal economy, yet he took a leading role in establishing the United States Military Academy at West Point, New York. Jefferson also started a sixteen-year plan to abolish the national debt the Federalists had deliberately created for the purpose of securing loyalty to the central government. Secretary of the Treasury Gallatin worked brilliantly at the reduction plan and, for a time, succeeded. But a final accounting showed that Jefferson and Madison were as skillful spenders as the Federalists. After the allotted sixteen years, the indebtedness of the United States had never been higher.

Jefferson's foreign policy also changed with his acquisition of power. Previously sympathetic toward France, he turned hostile when Spain's sale of Louisiana to France became public. Jefferson even contemplated alliance with his old nemesis, Great Britain, to prevent the French takeover on the western border. Napoleon, however, solved the problem. In 1803 France gave up plans for a New World empire and sold all of Louisiana (later carved into thirteen states) to the United States for $15 million. This incredible bargain violated Jefferson's ideals of frugality and constitutionality. And, the Federalists, of all people, accused Jefferson of going beyond the limits of his authority in buying land. In truth, there was nothing in the Constitution sanctioning such action. Jefferson wrestled with the problem for several months, finally rationalized the Louisiana Purchase as an extension of the "empire of liberty," and pushed the required treaty

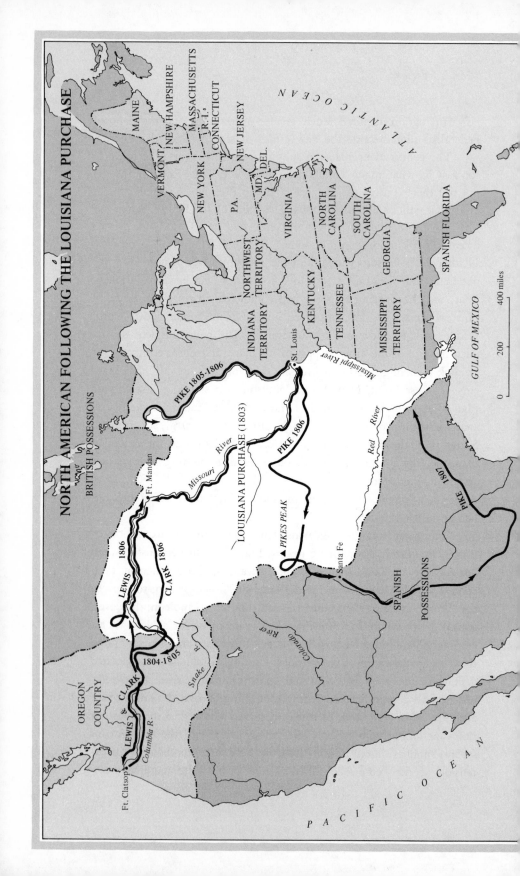

NORTH AMERICAN FOLLOWING THE LOUISIANA PURCHASE

BRITISH POSSESSIONS

ATLANTIC OCEAN

MAINE
VERMONT
NEW HAMPSHIRE
MASSACHUSETTS
R.I.
CONNECTICUT
NEW YORK
NEW JERSEY
PA.
MD.
DEL.
NORTHWEST TERRITORY
VIRGINIA
NORTH CAROLINA
SOUTH CAROLINA
GEORGIA
INDIANA TERRITORY
KENTUCKY
TENNESSEE
MISSISSIPPI TERRITORY
SPANISH FLORIDA

St. Louis

PIKE 1805–1806

Missouri River

Ft. Mandan

LOUISIANA PURCHASE (1803)

PIKE 1806

Mississippi River

Red River

GULF OF MEXICO

0   200   400 miles

PIKES PEAK

Santa Fe

PIKE 1807

SPANISH POSSESSIONS

LEWIS 1806

CLARK 1806

1804–1805

LEWIS & CLARK

OREGON COUNTRY

Ft. Clatsop

Columbia R.

Snake R.

Colorado River

PACIFIC OCEAN

Gratefully retired to Monticello after four decades of continuous public service, Jefferson eagerly turned to his library, his gardens, his inventions, his science, the founding of the University of Virginia, and a correspondence that amounted to over a thousand handwritten letters a year. There was also a steady stream of visitors paying homage to the Sage of Monticello. As a participant in the beginnings of the controversy, Jefferson took a keen interest in the War of 1812.

Its formal outcome, embodied in the Treaty of Ghent, December 24, 1814, was inconclusive and unsatisfying. But Americans proved adept at finding, or perhaps making, glory. Oliver Hazard Perry was elevated to the rank of national hero after his September 1813 victory over the British fleet on Lake Erie. A year later the invasion of Baltimore was repulsed, and Francis Scott Key created a song that later became the national anthem. But from the standpoint of the national ego, nothing compared to the Battle of New Orleans. Jefferson shared the thrill that rippled through the nation when news arrived that on January 8, 1815, Andrew Jackson and an untrained force of frontier riflemen had crushed the cream of the British army. Two thousand Englishmen died in the encounter and only six Americans—one of the most lopsided victories in military history. Newspapers headlined their accounts of the battle "Almost Incredible Victory!!" and "Rising Glory of the American Republic."

Few could doubt it, and in the aftermath of the War of 1812 a feeling of national unity and well-being prevailed. President Madison and Henry Clay advanced an "American System" under which domestic manufacturing and consumption were encouraged by protective tariffs and improvements in internal transportation. The last vestiges of the Federalists as a national political party withered in the sun of the new nationalism. One indication was the collapse of the plan for revising the Constitution that a group of New England Federalists formulated at Hartford, Connecticut, late in 1814. Representatives of the gathering arrived in Washington at the same time as news of New Orleans, and the Federalists attracted only jeers. This is not to say, however, that the United States entered a political "era of good feelings" after 1814. Jefferson, for one, knew better. Factionalism was inherent in politics. Beneath the veneer of national solidarity were ambitious men eager to crack the hold of Virginia (of the first five

through the Senate as quietly as possible. Even he realized that theory had to give way occasionally to practical considerations.

Planning for the exploration and settlement of the West was considerably more enjoyable for Jefferson. In 1804 he fulfilled a dream by sending an expedition under his private secretary, Meriwether Lewis, and William Clark to the headwaters of the Missouri and thence down the Columbia to the Pacific Ocean. Two years and over 7000 miles later Lewis and Clark returned from the wilderness with a wealth of information. Zebulon Pike brought back additional data from his expeditions to the source of the Mississippi and to the Colorado Rockies. The blank map of the American West was gradually being filled in, and Jefferson was delighted both as a citizen and a scientist. He also took pleasure in the thought that the virgin land to the west would soon support a population of hardy yeoman farmers, those mainstays of the republic. To help them the Jefferson administration altered the land laws to make possible the purchase of small farms at attractive prices. Under the Land Act of 1804 a man could obtain title to 160 acres for as little as $80 (one-fourth the purchase price) down.

As the pressures and conflicts of national politics swirled around him, there were times when Jefferson thought wistfully of Monticello —if not of Lewis and Clark's lonely camps. The strange case of Aaron Burr caused him special pain. A suicidally ambitious man, Vice-President Burr became disenchanted with the Republicans midway through Jefferson's first term. Seeking a fresh ladder, he turned to a group of embittered Federalists who were exploring the possibility of persuading New York and the New England states to secede from the union. In the course of this plot Burr's enormous ego ran afoul of Hamilton's, and a feud quickly developed. The climax was a duel July 11, 1804, on the western bank of the Hudson River. Hamilton reputedly fired first and missed, whereupon Burr coolly delivered a fatal shot. He next appeared in the Mississippi Valley, again investigating the chances for leading a revolt from Jefferson's government. The complex deal, involving both Spain and England, collapsed in 1806, and Jefferson ordered Burr arrested on charges of treason. But Chief Justice Marshall, before whom the case was tried, defined treason so narrowly as to ensure Burr's acquittal.

Jefferson was deeply embarrassed, but the bulk of the American people, those who had swept him to a decisive victory in the election of 1804, stood behind their President. Burr was nearly lynched and was eventually obliged to leave the country. Jefferson and his party stood unchallenged. The citizenry had become fond of the President's understated, effective, and unmistakably American style. They liked his abolition of the weekly "levee," a Federalist holdover from the fashionable world of European courts. They chuckled at his insistence on a round table for state dinners so no guest would have precedence over another. And they roared with glee when the new British ambassador, dress sword and all, was received by Jefferson in bedroom slippers!

It was one thing to slight England at a diplomatic reception, something else again on the high seas. In 1805 Lord Nelson reconfirmed British mastery of the oceans with a smashing victory in the Battle of Trafalgar. But Napoleonic France remained the master of continental Europe, and war between the powers continued. One result was that American ships engaged in international trade were subject to seizure by one or the other of the belligerents. It was not a trifling matter for President Jefferson. Between 1804 and 1807 over 1500 American vessels were seized and searched. The British went further, "impressing" American seamen. Under this ancient practice the captain of a warship could in time of emergency compel service from any of his countrymen. Theoretically, then, only Englishmen could be impressed, but on the high seas such niceties were often ignored. Many American citizens found themselves working for the British navy under circumstances that amounted to slavery.

In June 1807 Jefferson received word that the British frigate *Leopard* had dared to fire upon and search America's *Chesapeake* within sight of the Virginia coast. Three Americans died in the encounter, and four men were impressed. The people were furious. Jefferson noted that "never since the battle of Lexington have I seen this country in such a state of exasperation." There was more than enough support to declare war on England, but Jefferson stood by his opposition to America's "entangling" herself in the affairs of Europe. Instead of taking sides in the Anglo-French conflict, he proposed an embargo on all American trade with Europe. Jefferson hoped that the boycott would force respect for the rights of neutral nations.

Instituted December 22, 1807, the embargo proved a failure. The volume of American trade was too small to cause France or England

real economic hardship. Moreover, the United States was not united behind the policy. Shippers and merchants, especially those in New England, regarded the whole idea as a Jeffersonian plot to destroy commerce and punish the Federalists. Many merchants simply resorted to smuggling to move their goods. Still, American exports dropped by 80 percent and bankruptcies rose by an equal amount. Jefferson received a torrent of abuse. "You Infernal Villain," one New Englander wrote, "how much longer are you going to keep this damned Embargo on to starve us poor people."

The election of 1808 reflected this criticism. Jefferson declined renomination, feeling that Washington had set an admirable precedent in limiting his service to two terms. Instead he advanced the candidacy of his secretary of state. Madison won, but New England was solid in its opposition. It appeared to Jefferson that continuation of the embargo would only further divide the country, so he repealed it March 1, 1809, three days before leaving office. Now, an observer rather than a participant, Jefferson watched as the final acts of the diplomatic drama were played out to a sad conclusion. Madison tried several modified trade boycotts without success. Impressment continued. Finally, Napoleon maneuvered Madison into believing that France would cooperate in respecting neutral rights. Madison thereupon sided with France and severed diplomatic relations with England. In good time England also repealed its offensive maritime policies, but too late. Before news of the repeal reached America, Madison asked Congress for a declaration of war. In June 1812, for the second time in less than forty years, America was at war with England.

Both Jefferson and Madison were well aware that the explanation for the War of 1812 was more complicated than violation of maritime rights. Many westerners were anxious to remove the British from Canada. There was the danger of English-inspired Indian attacks from this quarter; moreover, there was the prospect of annexing Canada. Henry Clay and the other "War Hawks" in Congress effectively marshaled this sentiment into an argument for war. Another motive was the vague but potent sense of national honor. Regardless of where they lived or how they made their living, Americans resented being treated as if they were still colonists. Perhaps, they reasoned, a second war of independence was needed to convince the world that the new republic meant to be taken seriously.

Presidents, only John Adams had come from a different state) and the Republicans on the central government.

Sectionalism offered one means of shaking up this political status quo. In his declining years Jefferson observed a sharp intensification of sectional consciousness. The financial panic of 1819 and the subsequent depression set hard-pressed westerners and laborers everywhere against eastern financial interests. Far more serious in Jefferson's estimation was the crisis of 1819 and 1820 occasioned by the application of the territory of Missouri for admission to the union. At issue was the geographical extension of slavery.

As a young man Jefferson, along with most national leaders, entertained the vague hope that slavery would gradually disappear. To this end Jefferson wrote a passage for the Declaration of Independence attacking the international slave trade as a violation of the "sacred rights . . . of a distant people." Although the passage was deleted from the final version of the document, Jefferson continued his campaign. In 1784 he called for the exclusion of slavery from the western territories, and he applauded the action of the Constitutional Convention of 1787, which did provide for cessation of the slave trade after twenty years. But all the while Jefferson struggled with massive uncertainties. If the slave *trade* and the *extension* of slavery were wrong, what about slavery itself? Jefferson the philosopher of liberty and natural rights answered this question one way; Jefferson the southerner and owner of some two hundred slaves answered it another. The latter viewpoint prevailed, but only because Jefferson carefully created and maintained in the face of increasing evidence to the contrary the myth of innate black inferiority. All men were created equal, in other words, but blacks were not fully men. This shabby reasoning was the only way Thomas Jefferson could reconcile his conflicting beliefs.

Contrary to Jefferson's expectations, the passage of time did not bring the weakening of slavery. The advent of large-scale cotton production in the early nineteenth century underlay a dramatic rise in the value of slaves. Moreover, the abolition of the slave trade in 1808 was more than offset by rising birth rates among the black population and smuggling. By 1820 most southern slaveowners regretfully accepted black bondage as an unpleasant necessity, and some had come to see it as a positive good. Considerations of fear as well as economics shaped their point of view. Jefferson and his fellow slaveholders disliked and

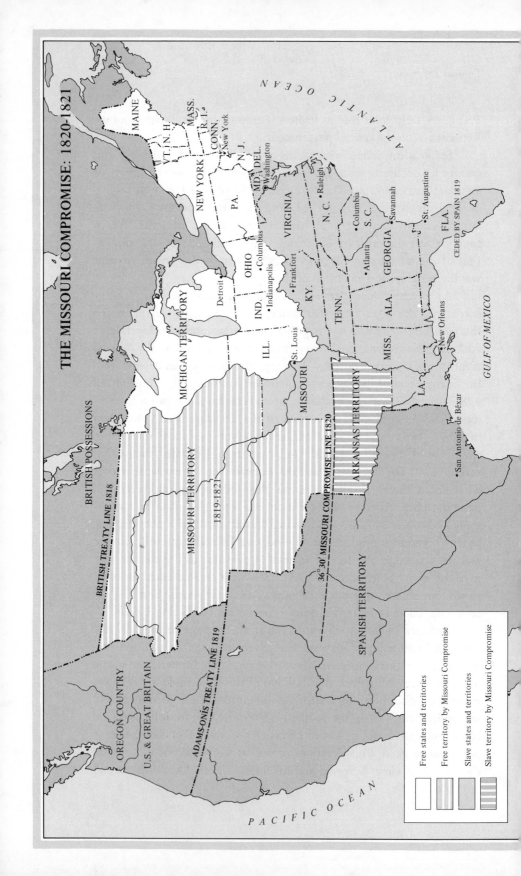

THE MISSOURI COMPROMISE: 1820-1821

ATLANTIC OCEAN

MAINE

VT. N. H.
MASS.
R. I.
CONN.

NEW YORK
•New York

N. J.
PA.
MD. DEL.
•Washington

OHIO
•Columbus
VIRGINIA

•Raleigh
N. C.

•Columbia
S. C.

•Savannah
•St. Augustine

FLA.
CEDED BY SPAIN 1819

MICHIGAN TERRITORY
•Detroit

IND.
•Indianapolis

ILL.

•Frankfort
KY.

•Atlanta
GEORGIA

TENN.

ALA.

MISS.

•St. Louis

MISSOURI

ARKANSAS TERRITORY

LA.
•New Orleans

GULF OF MEXICO

BRITISH POSSESSIONS

BRITISH TREATY LINE 1818

MISSOURI TERRITORY
1819-1821

36°30′ MISSOURI COMPROMISE LINE 1820

SPANISH TERRITORY

•San Antonio de Béxar

OREGON COUNTRY

U.S. & GREAT BRITAIN

ADAMS-ONÍS TREATY LINE 1819

PACIFIC OCEAN

Free states and territories

Free territory by Missouri Compromise

Slave states and territories

Slave territory by Missouri Compromise

feared blacks. Even if they had wished to do it, slavery could not have been abolished without creating in the South a large population of free blacks who would, southern whites believed, run rampant over every civilized value and institution. Colonization of freed blacks in Africa had long been considered a solution to this dilemma, but it had never materialized. White America, it appeared, was stuck with blacks and, because of the supposed need for their social control, with the institution of slavery. "We have the wolf by the ears," Jefferson lamented in 1820, "and we can neither hold him, nor safely let go." Then, in a comment that penetrated to the heart of his personal dilemma, he added: "justice is in one scale, self-preservation in the other."

With a Jefferson one might hope the former would take precedence, but the plain fact is that it did not. During the Missouri controversy he joined the most closed-minded southerners in regarding the whole issue as a Federalist plot and resisting any limitation of slavery. Henry Clay eventually bailed the nation out with a compromise proposal that accepted slavery in Missouri, balanced that state's admission to the union with the inclusion of Maine, and set the latitude 36°30′ as henceforth the northern limit of slave labor in territory acquired in the Louisiana Purchase. Jefferson doubted the compromise would work. He knew that an arbitrary line was no way to settle a difference of moral principle. The Missouri debates, "like a fire bell in the night," filled Jefferson with terror. "In the gloomiest moments of the Revolutionary War," he wrote in 1820, "I never had any apprehensions equal to what I feel from this source." Upon the shoals of the slavery issue, he predicted, the union would founder.

In October 1823 Jefferson, now eighty years old, was flattered to receive a communication from President Monroe soliciting his advice on a delicate question of foreign policy. England, it appeared, was concerned that Spain, with assistance from France, Austria, and Russia, might try to recover her rebellious colonies in South America. The British foreign minister approached the United States with the idea of issuing a joint declaration opposing any further changes in the political geography of the New World. Jefferson thought the proposal had much merit, and advised Monroe to abandon for once the policy of nonentanglement. An alliance with powerful England would be of considerable assistance in keeping the New World independent.

The President tended to Jefferson's position, but Secretary of

State John Quincy Adams opposed it on the grounds that the United States should not preclude her *own* territorial expansion by agreeing to preserve the current arrangement. Florida, he argued, had been acquired from Spain in 1821, and there was reason to believe that Cuba, Texas, and perhaps all South America would one day join the union. Moreover, Adams did not favor riding England's coattails in this matter. Why not, he asked, make a separate statement that the Western Hemisphere was not open to further colonization by any European power? In the end Adams prevailed. The Monroe Doctrine of December 2, 1823, rejected England's proposition, affirmed the principle of New World autonomy, and kept the door open for American expansion.

Late in June 1826 Thomas Jefferson marked the approach of the fiftieth anniversary of American independence by writing a brief statement for the celebration of July 4th. The American Revolution, he reflected, had been a "signal" for oppressed people everywhere to burst their chains and "assume the blessings and security of self-government." Reason and the free exchange of opinion had been substituted for ignorance, superstition, and fear. Because of July 4th, Jefferson continued, "all eyes are opened, or opening, to the rights of man."

John Adams knew that few men had played a more important role in this process than his old friend and sometime opponent, Thomas Jefferson. On July 4, 1826, Adams lay dying at his home in Quincy, Massachusetts, and his mind wandered back to the stirring days of the Revolution. His last words were, "Thomas Jefferson still survives." But just a few hours earlier, also, curiously, on the fiftieth anniversary of the day he had done so much to distinguish, Jefferson too had died.

SELECTED READINGS

The Person

*BOORSTIN, DANIEL J.: *The Lost World of Thomas Jefferson* (1948). Places Jefferson in the context of the American Enlightenment.

* Available in paperback.

BOYD, JULIAN (ed.): *The Papers of Thomas Jefferson* (1950–).
The authoritative collection, expected to reach fifty volumes.

*KOCH, ADRIENNE: *The Philosophy of Thomas Jefferson* (1943).
An analysis of the many facets of Jefferson's thought.

KOCH, ADRIENNE, and WILLIAM PEDEN: *The Life and Selected
Writings of Thomas Jefferson* (1944). The best one-volume
treatment.

MALONE, DUMAS: *Jefferson and His Time* (1948–). A definitive multivolume biography.

PETERSON, MERRILL D.: *Jefferson and the New Nation* (1970). The
most recent biography.

The Period

*ADAMS, HENRY: *History of the United States during the Administra-
tions of Thomas Jefferson and James Madison* (9 vols., 1889–
1891). One of the classics of American historical writing. Adams
treats social and intellectual as well as political and economic
history in an elegant literary style.

*CUNNINGHAM, NOBLE: *The Jeffersonian Republicans* (2 vols.,
1957–1963). The rise to power of a political party.

*DANGERFIELD, GEORGE: *The Era of Good Feelings* (1952).
National political developments in Jefferson's declining years.

*HORSMAN, REGINALD: *The Causes of the War of 1812* (1962).
One interpretation of a much-discussed war.

*JENSEN, MERRILL: *The New Nation* (1950). The achievements
of Americans in constructing their first federal organization.

*MOORE, GLOVER: *The Missouri Controversy, 1819–1821* (1953).
An exploration of the beginnings of sectionalism.

NETTELS, CURTIS P.: *The Emergence of a National Economy* (1962).
A reliable survey of the nation's early economic history.

*NYE, RUSSEL B.: *The Cultural Life of the New Nation* (1960).
Intellectual and social history.

*WOOD, GORDON: *Creation of the American Republic 1776–1787*
(1969). Political theory and political institutions.

* Available in paperback.

CHAPTER FOUR

Jim Bridger

Booming southwest through the narrowing Cache Valley,
the Bear River gathered speed. Jim Bridger also quickened
his step. Tall and spare, with long hair protruding beneath a beaver
hat, he rounded one last bend and overlooked a great plain
extending as far as he could see. In the center, also fading into the
horizon, lay an enormous body of water. Bridger's pulse leaped at
the discovery. Breaking into a jog, he wove through the sagebrush
to the water's edge. Kneeling, he drank, then spat in disgust. Salt!

But in a second Bridger's disappointment turned to awe.
Hurriedly returning to his trapping companions, who were camped
that fall of 1824 in the upper Cache Valley, Bridger reported that
he had found an arm of the Pacific Ocean! Only later did
further exploration reveal what Bridger's "ocean" really was: Utah's
Great Salt Lake.

In 1804, the year of Bridger's birth, the American frontier
began at St. Louis, and Lewis and Clark were making plans to
explore the great unknown to the west. When Bridger died
seventy-seven years later, his nation had spanned the continent, and
the frontier was rapidly becoming history. Bridger figured
prominently in this process of discovery, exploration, settlement, and
development. He neither read nor wrote, but in his time and
circumstance it mattered little. Like Christopher Columbus and Neil
Armstrong, Jim Bridger had the good fortune of living in an age
of expanding horizons.

On March 17, 1804, in a small room over a roadside inn near Richmond, Virginia, Chloe Tyler Bridger, a distant relative of the tenth President of the United States, John Tyler, gave birth to her first son, James. The family owned the inn, but business was poor. Travelers using the James River as a highway into the interior generally carried their own food and saved money by sleeping in their wagons. The Bridgers existed largely on the trade of "locals" who purchased occasional shots of whiskey and mugs of beer. Young Jim and two other children helped with the chores (school was out of the question), but the family slipped steadily further into poverty. Jim's father tried to make ends meet by working a small farm near Fredericksburg, but a century and a half of continuous tobacco production had exhausted the soil. Surveying, which the elder Bridger also tried, proved little better in an old community where boundaries were long established. The cheap, fertile land that underlay the Jeffersons' wealth had vanished east of the Appalachians. Finally, the hard times that accompanied the economic boycotts preceding the War of 1812 added further burdens.

In this dark picture there was one bright spot—the West. People like the Bridgers talked about it as a dreamland of opportunity. As the New World once attracted Europe's dissatisfied, so the land beyond the Appalachians beckoned failures in the seaboard states. The urge to move was a compound of pushing and pulling forces. Adversity in the East pushed pioneers westward, while visions of success across the mountains drew them like a magnet. In 1812 the Bridger family succumbed to the dual force, packed its belongings into a red Conestoga wagon, and sought a new start in the West.

As they left Virginia, families such as the Bridgers took advantage of several policies of the United States. Two of these were the systems of land sale and territorial government established in the 1780s and now functioning with great success. Low minimum acreage requirements, cheap prices, and liberal credit allowances permitted men of modest means to get a start on the public domain. Granted that extreme poverty, such as that of some immigrants and factory laborers, precluded pioneer farming, it was possible for people like the Bridgers, who could sell eastern property, to raise the requisite capital. As for government, stories such as that of the growth of Ohio to independent statehood impressed everyone. A wilderness in 1790, the territory claimed 60,000 settlers in 1803, enough for statehood under the terms of the Northwest Ordinance. By 1810 the population of Ohio stood at 231,000.

A major factor in this growth was the improvement of overland transportation to the Ohio Valley. Graded, paved all-weather roads facilitated the movement of people and produce. Many of these were privately built "turnpikes" that charged tolls, but the condition of the trail-like alternatives made the private roads cheap at almost any price. In 1806 Congress authorized government financing for a road from western Maryland across the Appalachians to Wheeling on the Ohio River. Although delayed by the War of 1812, the National Road soon became the primary artery of east-west travel.

The gradual establishment of the authority of the United States in trans-Appalachia was another precondition to migrations such as that of the Bridgers. French western intrigue ended in the mid-1790s when George Washington and Thomas Jefferson blocked the efforts of Citizen Edmund Genêt to recruit a private army in support of the French Revolution. Spanish claims were weakened in 1796 with the approval of the Treaty of San Lorenzo (the Pinckney Treaty). The new states of Kentucky (1792) and Tennessee (1796) were now safe from Spanish intrigue and the possibility of secession. Also by this treaty the United States obtained a promise of free navigation on the Mississippi River and the right to deposit goods for transshipment at New Orleans, a port essential to the western economy. Spain's sale of Louisiana to France in 1800 and the resale of it to the United States three years later substantially ended the claims of both foreign powers to trans-Appalachia. Spain did retain possession of East Florida and claimed a strip of land along the Gulf of Mexico (West Florida) until the invasion by General Andrew Jackson in 1818 and the negotiation of the Adams-Onís Treaty the following year. As for England, she was slow to evacuate her frontier posts following the American Revolution and, with a foothold in Canada, retained an active interest in the Ohio Valley until the conclusion of the War of 1812.

For the Bridgers and other frontier families, however, the gravest threat came not from a European power, but from a native one—the American Indians. What was euphemistically called Indian "removal" had, of course, gone on since 1607, but after the American Revolution opened the possibility of rapid westward expansion, the problem intensified. In 1792 General "Mad" Anthony Wayne, a Revolutionary hero, received orders to remove the Indian obstacle to settlement in the West. His responsibility was great, particularly because the crushing defeats of Josiah Harmer and Arthur St. Clair in the early 1790s had sent frightened settlers scurrying to the relative safety of Cincinnati. England was delighted and urged the creation of an English-controlled Indian buffer state in the Ohio Valley. Determined to establish his country's claim to the Northwest, Wayne methodically built and trained an army. In June 1794 he advanced against the confederated tribes and at Fallen Timbers in present-day southern Michigan administered a decisive defeat. Moreover, the Indians realized that despite their encouragement and promises, the British were not about to offer active assistance in fighting the Americans. Wayne capitalized on his victory the following spring. In the Treaty of Greenville, representatives of all the important Ohio Valley tribes yielded more than two-thirds of their homeland to the United States.

In the next fifteen years a series of so-called treaties forced Indians from Georgia to Wisconsin to cede land they had occupied for thousands of years. But resentment at the frequently fraudulent tactics of United States negotiators such as Indiana's territorial governor William Henry Harrison increased steadily. About 1805 a Shawnee chief named Tecumseh and his brother, the Prophet, emerged to lead the Indian resistance. Calling for unification of the various tribes, maintaining contact with the British, and urging a fight to the death against the invading white man, Tecumseh whipped the frontier into a frenzy. In 1811 Harrison defeated some of Tecumseh's followers at the Battle of Tippecanoe, but the chief retaliated with a series of guerrilla strikes all along the Ohio frontier. The Bridgers were on their way west at this very time, and their night camps were filled with terror.

After 1812 the Indian war merged with the Anglo-American conflict, and the balance gradually swung in favor of the United States. In 1813 Harrison defeated a combined British and Indian force at the Battle of the Thames near Detroit. One of the casualties in the encounter was Tecumseh. The loss from the Indian standpoint was major. A brilliant organizer, orator, and statesman, Tecumseh possessed talents that overcame some of the frontier hatred of "yeller devils." Even William Henry Harrison, looking back on the life of his former adversary, characterized Tecumseh as "one of those uncommon geniuses, which spring up occasionally to produce revolutions and overturn the established order of things. If it were not for the vicinity of the United States, he would perhaps be the founder of an Empire that would rival in glory that of Mexico or Peru." But the Indian civilization was in the path of American expansion, and Tecumseh became a victim of white ambition. There was no Tecumseh on the southern frontier, where Harrison had a counterpart in Andrew Jackson, who defeated the Creeks in 1814 in the Battle of Horseshoe Bend. Pockets of Indian resistance persisted east of the Mississippi for several more decades, but frontiersmen like the Bridgers took comfort in the belief that time was on their side.

The Bridgers' route west in 1812 took them across the Appalachians, along the route of the National Road, and to the Ohio River. There they sold the red Conestoga and procured passage on a flatboat. The moving carpet of water carried them swiftly to the confluence of the Ohio and Mississippi. Progress upstream was more difficult, but at last the family arrived at St. Louis. Located near the strategic junction of the Missouri and Mississippi rivers, St. Louis already claimed several thousand inhabitants and a settled hinterland extending up and down the Mississippi for 40 miles. The Bridgers bought a small farm at the northern edge of the settlement. Although subject to seasonal flooding, the soil was rich, and the future of this new enterprise seemed bright. James Bridger, Sr., found steady employment as a surveyor, and young Jim toiled at the farm chores. Just breaking the tough prairie sod was a monumental task. For women, frontier farming was particularly demanding, and Chloe Bridger died in 1816, when Jim was twelve. An aunt arrived from Virginia to help raise the children, but by Christmas 1817 Jim's father and younger brother were buried near his mother.

Although Jim Bridger matured quickly on the farm, he was now placed in the position of fending entirely for himself. At first he obtained a canoe and ran a muskrat and mink line in the Mississippi bottomlands. However, by 1817 thirty to fifty wagons filled with immigrants were crossing the Mississippi at St. Louis daily, and Jim saw profit to be made in their service. Ferrying people and their belongings across the river became his principal occupation in the summer months. In winter Jim labored in a blacksmith shop, building heavy muscles and a knowledge of both horses and men. There was considerable talk around the shop and in St. Louis generally about the Far West. Lewis and Clark, of course, were legendary names in the city, and there were later explorers and trappers, dressed in the buckskins of the mountainman, who spoke of a wilderness of snow-capped peaks and roaring rivers. As he repaired their traps and rifles at his forge, Jim Bridger, like Ben Franklin in the printing shop, developed the ambitions that shaped his life.

Fur was the principal product of St. Louis in Bridger's time. After the return of Lewis and Clark, numerous expeditions pushed northwest on the trail of the beaver. Every spring they left the city, poling and pulling keelboats laden with trade goods and traps. One of the first to organize the business was Manuel Lisa, a man whose Spanish heritage did not preclude a Yankee eye for the dollar. In 1807, just a year after the return of Lewis and Clark, Lisa followed the Missouri and the Yellowstone to the mouth of the Bighorn River in present-day Montana. There Lisa built a fort, which he modestly named Fort Manuel. He then sent John Colter, a veteran of the Lewis and Clark expedition, up the Bighorn and into the Yellowstone country. Traveling alone in midwinter with only a 30-pound pack, Colter covered 500 miles and returned with stories of geysers and boiling springs that men found hard to believe. But the unbelievable was always part of the New World's fascination, and when Colter's report reached St. Louis, it only increased the determination of the adventurous to go west.

Jim Bridger's opportunity came in 1822, when an advertisement appeared in the *Missouri Republican*. William H. Ashley, the lieutenant-governor of the new state, was seeking "one hundred young men to ascend the Missouri River to its source, there to be employed for one, two or three years." Excitedly, Bridger sought out Ashley's associate in the trapping venture, Major Andrew Henry, and signed on. The departure date was only a month away, in April. From Pittsburgh, Ashley had acquired two 65-foot keelboats with a loading capacity of 25 tons, equivalent to an entire wagon train. Bridger was assigned to help maneuver the heavy boats upstream against the power of the Missouri. As one man kept the boat in the water with the use of a sweep-rudder, the others trudged along on shore pulling long ropes attached to its bow. It was an exhausting business requiring the men to stumble over rocks and fallen logs, wade side streams, and climb steep embankments. Occasionally an upriver wind and a crude sail would offer some relief, but otherwise it was blisters and sweat.

On May 1, 1822, the Ashley-Henry party reached Fort Atkinson near Council Bluffs and the Platte River. The garrison at the fort had warnings of Indian hostility, and some of the men in the party chose to return to St. Louis. Jim Bridger, however, was just warming up. With the remainder of the Ashley-Henry group he continued up the Missouri and into the Dakotas, where the Mandan Indians made their home. Among these friendly tribes Bridger began to gain the knowledge of native tongues and customs that played a major role in his later success as a scout and guide. Pushing on to the mouth of the Yellowstone, the Ashley-Henry men constructed shelters and ran trap lines. Before winter there was a rich harvest of pelts to send back to St. Louis. There were also Indian problems. Outraged at the white man's invasion of their traditional hunting grounds, the Arikaras and Blackfeet struck back. In one surprise attack the Indians killed fourteen Ashley trappers. Bridger managed to survive, and joined a force of trappers, Sioux Indians, and federal soldiers under Colonel Henry Leavenworth in the destruction of the Arikara village. Nevertheless, Ashley decided

Even more than at other times America seemed to be on the move
in the early nineteenth century, and the direction of travel was invariably
west. This is the Fairview Inn on the National (or Cumberland) Road
near Baltimore. The high-wheeled Conestoga (or "covered") wagons
(right) are similar to the one the Bridger family used to travel over this
route from Virginia to the Ohio River in 1812.

In 1837 a young Scottish-born painter, Albert J. Miller, accompanied
the Scottish nobleman William Drummond Stewart to the fur traders'
annual rendezvous. Among the participants that year was Jim
Bridger (left foreground), dressed, in Miller's sketch, in the suit of
armor Stewart presented him.

J. Goldsborough Bruff was one of the thousands who responded to the news of the discovery of gold in California. A genuine "forty-niner" (he went west in 1849), Bruff's sketch shows how the travelers "circled up" for the night as a precaution against Indian attack. There is a sense of vastness in the sketch, a feeling for the bigness of the sky and the insignificance of the pioneers.

The construction of this fort on a tributary of the Green River in 1843 marked Jim Bridger's transformation from trapper to trader. Located just west of the continental divide, Fort Bridger became a popular way station for travelers on the Oregon and California trails.

to move his operations from the northern to the central Rocky Mountains, where Indian opposition was less intense. In the winter of 1823–1824 he dispatched Bridger, Thomas Fitzpatrick, Jedediah Smith, and several others to probe the country west of Wyoming's Wind River Mountains.

Hiking along the eastern face of the towering Wind River range and up the Sweetwater River, Bridger and his companions discovered South Pass, a low and level route across the Continental Divide and the key to the opening of the West. Its significance was not lost on the trappers. Here, they realized, was a route by which loaded wagons could reach the Columbia River watershed and the Pacific Northwest. Later, South Pass became the gateway to the Oregon Trail and an important factor in Bridger's career as a provisioner and guide. But in 1823 it led only to the headwaters of the Green River and to beaver country of a richness beyond Bridger's wildest dreams. So enthusiastic was his report that Ashley determined to send scores of trappers into the area the following season. Reluctant to build Indian-provoking forts, he hit upon an ingenious plan for exploiting the fur resources. Under the rendezvous system trappers like Bridger were dispatched in small groups to work widely scattered waterways. In the early summer they gathered at a prearranged spot in the mountains for several weeks of trading, gambling, boasting, drinking, and sex. The wagons that had brought trade goods from St. Louis were ready to return loaded with beaver pelts. The first rendezvous, held in July 1825 at Henry's Fork on the Green River, attracted over a hundred trappers and Indians. Bridger was there and became a center of attention with his tale of Great Salt Lake. In subsequent years the annual rendezvous grew larger and more profitable. After the 1826 season Ashley retired, a wealthy man, to St. Louis and a political career. Jedediah Smith, David Jackson, and William Sublette assumed direction of his Rocky Mountain Fur Company.

The decade after 1825 marked the high point of the fur trade and the mountain man. Jim Bridger rose with the tide. He was fearless, tough, and wise in the ways of a wilderness that usually permitted a man only one mistake. He had a knack for geography, an innate sense of direction, and after a decade in the West probably had in his mind the best single map of that region. When asked specifically about a certain area, Bridger would squat on his haunches and sketch in the dirt a remarkably accurate description of the country in question. He put the same talent to work on his own travels. For example, in 1825, when Bridger became the second man after Colter to explore the Yellowstone country, he confirmed his belief that the Missouri, Green, and Snake rivers rose within a few miles of each other on this continental rooftop. At the next rendezvous this information became common property.

Conversely, Bridger learned from his colleagues. In 1826, Jedediah Smith left the rendezvous in Cache Valley, Utah, with fifteen men, a Bible, and plenty of rifles to explore the Southwest. Skirting west of the Wasatch Range and the high plateaus of central Utah, Smith reached the Virgin River and then the Colorado. The next leg of the journey carried him across the Mojave Desert, through Cajon Pass, and into the Los Angeles basin. The Mexicans were surprised, to say the least, at the appearance of the first Americans to make the overland crossing to California, and they requested Smith to leave *pronto* by the same route he had entered their territory. Blithely disregarding the orders, Smith led his men up California's Central Valley and then, in an incredible feat, over the main crest of the Sierra Nevada and across Nevada's arid Great Basin, where they nearly died of thirst, to the 1827 rendezvous at Bear Lake in southern Idaho. A few days swapping adventures with Bridger and others, and the remarkable wanderer set out again. This time Smith traveled from southern California to the Columbia River, sold his furs to the Hudson's Bay Company, and threaded his way through the mountains and canyons of Idaho to the rendezvous at Pierre's Hole.

Hostile Indians were part of the life of the trapper. Bridger fought them doggedly for years. Once he and the black trapper, Jim Beckwourth, led two hundred of their fellows in pursuit of a band of Bannock and Snake Indians accused of stealing pelts to an island in the Green River, where they collected an alleged 488 scalps. But sometimes the tables were turned. At the 1835 rendezvous Dr. Marcus Whitman, the Oregon missionary pioneer, extracted a 3-inch Blackfoot arrowhead that had been embedded in Bridger's back for three years. Others were not as lucky. After he had "retired" to the supposed safety of the Santa Fe trade, Jedediah Smith was slain by Comanches at a water hole on the Great Plains. And every rendezvous produced stories of trappers whose hair had been "lifted." Indeed,

Jim Bridger was an exception among the trappers in that he died of old age. Yet in the final analysis the mountain man had much in common with the Indian. Jim Beckwourth actually joined the Crow tribe. Bridger lived happily with three Indian wives and was devoted to his several "half-breed" children.

It is easy and has long been the custom to style mountain men like Jim Bridger carefree primitivists, and the fur trade a romantic adventure. The western trapper seemingly had cut the ties with civilization and, by virtue of his leap into the wilderness of the Far West, stood apart from the mainstream of American life. Actually, the mountain men and the residents of the eastern states had a great deal in common. The trapper was a highly skilled professional, motivated by the same considerations of monetary gain that moved his eastern countrymen in the era of Andrew Jackson. And the fur trade was a sophisticated industry, in the forefront of the evolution of American economic life toward patterns at once larger and more integrated. Fur was among the first American businesses to function on a nationwide scale. The values and institutions known as Jacksonianism, in short, extended across the wide Missouri to both shape and reflect the aspirations of Jim Bridger and his colleagues.[1]

In 1828 and again in 1832 Andrew Jackson—Tennesseean, Indian fighter, hero of the Battle of New Orleans—was elected President of the United States. Especially in comparison to the previous occupant of that office, the staid New Englander John Quincy Adams, Jackson appeared to be the man of the people, a champion of democracy. What Jackson really championed was equality of opportunity. He and his followers believed in loosening the hold of an entrenched, privileged, and usually wealthy elite on American political and economic life. When he attacked the most glaring special interest of the time—the Bank of the United States—in 1832, Jackson himself declared that he opposed those "artificial distinctions" whereby the "rich and powerful" came to dominate and suppress the ambitions of the "humble members of society." Jacksonians did not mean to imply by this that they opposed all privilege or that they rejected the concept of failure. Rather, they felt that privilege and prosperity should be the result of ability and ability alone. Failure should result from inability. Distinctions between men, in other words, were to be natural.

[1] For the meaning of Jacksonianism for Mark Twain see pages 231–233.

The Jacksonian philosophy was an extension of the Jeffersonian concept of a natural aristocracy, and it was therefore essential that everyone (and Jackson defined this term more liberally than Jefferson) have a chance at success. Its pursuit, furthermore, was to be regulated by rules that ensured the triumph of the talented. Jacksonianism did not pit the poor against the rich; it was the attempt of the poor to *become* rich. The liberation, not the destruction, of capitalism and its rewards were the objectives of the Jacksonian democrat. Typically, he was an ambitious entrepreneur. Hardly a revolutionary or anarchist, he wanted to tear down privilege and interfere with private property only when he believed they blocked his own pursuit of these goals. Jacksonianism, in sum, defined human rights as the free opportunity to get rich. It was the perfect philosophy for an acquisitive society such as Jim Bridger's.

To examine the evolution of the fur trade and the lives of the mountain men is to see excellent examples of Jacksonianism in practice. The West in the early nineteenth century meant equal opportunity. Special interests, family, and background counted for little. Performance—what a man could *do*—mattered. The wilderness played no favorites, and only the talented succeeded and survived. It was the ideal Jacksonian situation. Consider Bridger. The advertisement that induced him to go into the mountains was headed "To Enterprising Young Men!!!" and the young men who responded were economically on the make. Contrary to romantic legend, they did not go west to escape from civilization, but rather to extend it and rise within it. Beaver pelts were not an excuse for a wilderness outing to Bridger but, in his jargon, "hairy bank notes," cold cash. Risks were great, but so were returns. A few boat- or wagonloads of pelts in St. Louis meant affluence.

In this environment the capitalistic entrepreneur, so crucial a part of the age of Jackson, flourished. Manuel Lisa is an example. He was the first trader to recognize that only large, well-organized, and well-heeled companies would succeed in exploiting the fur potential of the Rockies. Another economic visionary was John Jacob Astor, who in 1808 organized the American Fur Company. Astor planned to construct a chain of forts from the Great Lakes to the Pacific Northwest and compete with the Hudson's Bay Company. He sent a land and a sea expedition to the Columbia River and founded Astoria at its mouth. But the War of 1812 ruined Astor's plans, and Indian hostility frustrated Lisa. Still, these entrepreneurs were portents of the new economic order that began to flower during Jackson's presidency.

A sure sign of the presence of Jacksonian aspirations among the mountain men was the fact that few of them passed up the opportunity of entrepreneurial leadership. The pull of power and position almost always overcame the call of the wild. Jim Bridger was no exception. Beginning as a hired hand with Ashley and Henry, he moved up quickly to the leadership of one of their brigades. In this capacity he directed the operations of a group of trappers and earned the nickname "Old Gabe" from Jedediah Smith, who knew that the angel Gabriel was the communicator of God's will to his subordinates. In modern terminology, Bridger was a good "organization man."

In 1830 Bridger *became* the organization. Smith and his associates transferred their interests in the Rocky Mountain Fur Company to Bridger and several others. Now in command of six hundred trappers, Bridger combed over the last untouched beaver country. But he soon learned an axiom of capitalism: where there were profits, there would be competition. It came first in the form of smaller companies whose agents began to appear at the annual rendezvous and bid for the trappers' harvests. After 1832 the American Fur Company offered stiffer competition. With the large and diversified Astor assets behind it, American Fur was in a position to outbid and outlast Bridger and Rocky Mountain Fur. Its advantage increased when its steamboat, *Yellowstone,* reached the confluence of that river and the Missouri in June 1832. Not the smallest dividend of the unprecedented voyage was the awe that the "Fire Boat That Walked on the Waters" produced among the Indians, who now confined their trade to American Fur agents.

After several more years of fierce competition, Bridger saw that he was losing ground. In 1834 he sold out to and became an employee of his larger rival. But the climax of the economic war over fur came with the entrance of the venerable Hudson's Bay Company into the Rocky Mountain arena. Beaver were disappearing in the Pacific Northwest, and the Bay's men moved farther and farther up the Snake River. A race began. Frantically, American trappers pursued the remaining beaver, to the detriment and near destruction of the resource on which they depended. By the late 1830s the end was in sight for those who could bring themselves to look. The 1840 rendezvous was the last. The trappers became disgruntled, and with easy profits gone, few elected to live the free wilderness life that legend has them loving for its own sake. Instead, these Jacksonians pursued opportunities in ranching, farming, shopkeeping, politics, banking, and even opera house management. They developed the West.

While Jacksonianism was influencing the frontier, the frontier style was shaping national politics. Jackson was the first President from a nonseaboard state and the first to step out of the gentlemanly tradition of the Virginia dynasty (Washington, Jefferson, Madison, Monroe) and the Harvard line (John Adams, John Quincy Adams). Hardly embarrassed at this fact, Jackson based his 1828 campaign on his experience as a man of action, a warrior-hero, and a supreme individualist who blended nature and civilization into a new, allegedly superior, and distinctively American character. The fact that in the winter of 1814–1815 he defeated both the powerful Creek tribe (at the Battle of Horeshoe Bend) and the best of England's army (at the Battle of New Orleans) lent substance to this claim. In the person of Jackson, the frontiersman acquired the status of a superman.

Next to Old Hickory, as Jackson was called, the hero of the 1830s was unquestionably Davy Crockett, king of the wild frontier. Crockett deliberately turned down an honorary degree from Harvard and cultivated a demagogic, bombastic, and often fraudulent political style in his congressional campaign. But at a time when the spread of universal white male suffrage was transforming the guiding values of politics from gentlemanly idealism to win-at-any-price, Crockett succeeded in spectacular fashion. Jackson's momentum carried his Vice-President, Martin Van Buren, to the Presidency in 1836. By this time opponents of Jackson and the Democrats had organized the Whig party around Henry Clay, Daniel Webster, and John C. Calhoun, none of whom gained the highest prize in American politics. That was reserved, in 1840, for the old Indian-fighter and hero of the Battle of Tippecanoe: William Henry Harrison. Discarding gentlemanly politics, the Whigs elected Harrison with a grass-roots, frontier-style approach. Their campaign of 1840 featured log cabins (Harrison was born in one) and the frontier wine—hard cider. Harrison's running mate, John Tyler, was reputedly a distant relative of Jim Bridger's mother. Four years later the Jacksonian faction regained the

White House with James K. Polk of Tennessee, an enthusiastic exponent of the expanding American frontier.

Jim Bridger was among the last of the mountain men to accept as fact the demise of trapping. For several years after dissolving the Rocky Mountain Fur Company, he struggled against decreasing beaver and increasing competition. Seeking financial backing for his trapping ventures, Bridger floated down the Missouri to St. Louis in 1839. For seventeen years he had been in the wilderness. Now he could scarcely recognize his former home. Its population had grown to 384,000. The river bottoms where a teen-aged Bridger set traps and paddled his canoe now teemed with steamboats at the wharves. The explorer wandered, lost, through the wilderness of city streets, but he succeeded in finding financial backing for another trapping venture on the upper Green River. The past and the future intersected one day on the Green, when Bridger and his trappers met an old colleague, Tom Fitzpatrick, leading a group of emigrants to Oregon. The year was 1840, and this was the first true emigrant train—a long string of dusty, white-topped wagons filled with men, women, and children. The sight must have reminded Bridger of his own family's westward trek a quarter-century ago and 2000 miles to the east. Fitzpatrick told Bridger the settlers were desperate for equipment and provisions and pointed out that the future lay in providing these wants rather than in fur.

At first Bridger scoffed at Fitzpatrick's suggestion. But in 1842 he again met his old partner on the trail near Fort Laramie with an even larger emigrant train. Soon afterward he encountered another mountain man, Kit Carson, guiding a group of United States Engineers under Lieutenant John C. Frémont. These soldier-explorers were scientifically mapping the West and laying the official basis for its settlement. Frémont was called the Pathfinder, but men like Carson and Bridger knew the territory. Jim began to see a new field for his abilities. But the summer of 1843 again found Bridger plying the trapper's trade. This year, however, he built a fort on Blacks Fork on the Green River, to the west of South Pass and on the best route to Great Salt Lake, Oregon, and California. When he returned to the fort in the early fall, Bridger learned that over a thousand emigrants had passed by, as well as another contingent of army engineers. In December 1843 Bridger made his decision. He would turn Fort Bridger into a

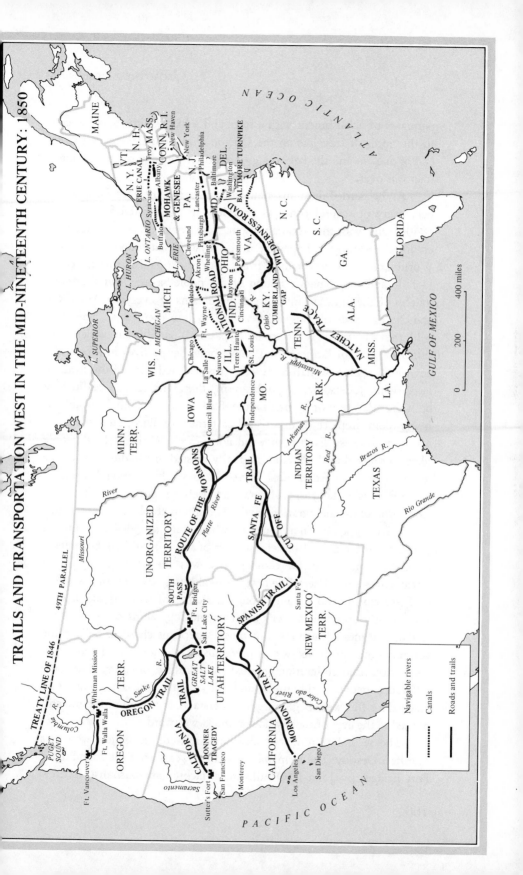

TRAILS AND TRANSPORTATION WEST IN THE MID-NINETEENTH CENTURY: 1850

ATLANTIC OCEAN

PACIFIC OCEAN

GULF OF MEXICO

MAINE

N.Y. VT. N.H.

MASS.

CONN. R.I.

Troy

Albany

New Haven

New York

ERIE CANAL

Syracuse

L. ONTARIO

Buffalo

MOHAWK & GENESEE

PA.

Philadelphia

Lancaster

N.J.

DEL.

Baltimore

MD.

Washington

BALTIMORE TURNPIKE

L. ERIE

Cleveland

Pittsburgh

Akron

Wheeling

NATIONAL ROAD

OHIO

Dayton

IND.

Cincinnati

Portsmouth

VA.

Ohio R.

WILDERNESS ROAD

KY.

CUMBERLAND GAP

N.C.

S.C.

GA.

ALA.

NATCHEZ TRACE

TENN.

MISS.

LA.

FLORIDA

L. SUPERIOR

L. HURON

L. MICHIGAN

MICH.

WIS.

Chicago

Toledo

Ft. Wayne

ILL.

La Salle

Nauvoo

Terre Haute

St. Louis

MO.

IOWA

Council Bluffs

MINN. TERR.

Missouri River

Mississippi R.

Arkansas R.

Red R.

ARK.

INDIAN TERRITORY

TEXAS

Brazos R.

Rio Grande

UNORGANIZED TERRITORY

ROUTE OF THE MORMONS

Platte River

SOUTH PASS

Ft. Bridger

SANTA FE TRAIL

CUT OFF

Santa Fe

SPANISH TRAIL

NEW MEXICO TERR.

Salt Lake City

UTAH TERRITORY

GREAT SALT LAKE

Colorado River

MORMON TRAIL

CALIFORNIA TRAIL

DONNER TRAGEDY

Sacramento

Sutter's Fort

San Francisco

Monterey

CALIFORNIA

Los Angeles

San Diego

OREGON TRAIL

Snake R.

Columbia R.

Ft. Walla Walla

Whitman Mission

OREGON TERR.

Ft. Vancouver

PUGET SOUND

49TH PARALLEL

TREATY LINE OF 1846

River

0   200   400 miles

Navigable rivers

Canals

Roads and trails

permanent establishment with a store and a blacksmith shop and cater to the needs of travelers on the Oregon Trail. For Bridger it was the end of one era and the beginning of another. The day of the mountain man was over.

As he settled into his new vocation, Jim Bridger became the beneficiary of several concepts prevalent in the United States of the 1840s. One was the agrarian myth. The roots of this complex of emotions, values, and hopes lay in the mystique surrounding the New World and drew sustenance from both the Spanish mirage of El Dorado and the romantic notion of the noble savage. But the major sources of the agrarian myth were the dreams of everyday Americans and the promises of those who wished to lure them west. The myth held the American West to be a pastoral paradise in which self-sufficient yeoman farmers lived wholesome, happy lives in a beautiful environment close to nature. It was a rose-colored view of the frontier, laced with Jeffersonian republicanism, that ignored the realities of both the West and of human nature. Still, around the kitchen table or living-room fireplace of dissatisfied easterners or Europeans, the myth was hard to resist. Even if they did not move west themselves, people liked to think that the idyllic life really existed in the direction of the setting sun. For Americans, it was a basis for national pride.

Obviously, land speculators and western developers benefited from promoting the agrarian myth. The innumerable emigrant guidebooks that appeared in the nineteenth century sounded a chorus of praise for life on the frontier. In most of the descriptions Eden itself paled by comparison. Of course, there was the counterimage of a Great American Desert filled with bloodthirsty savages and wracked by fierce storms and searing droughts. Bountiful harvests did not always spring up at the sower's bidding, and log cabins could be intellectual and moral vacuums. But most Americans chose to believe the contrary, and the belief was a prerequisite to undertaking the major dislocations that emigration entailed. Jim Bridger, of course, knew the difference between the myth and the reality. The emigrants who reached his fort were beginning to understand, but some of the fire still burned in the eyes of those who continued westward.

The second complex of ideas that moved the nation west was Manifest Destiny. The term was coined two years after the founding of Fort Bridger by John L. O'Sullivan, a Jacksonian journalist. It drew heavily on the old idea of American mission and the belief that the nation had a right, indeed a duty and God-appointed destiny, to expand across the continent to the Pacific Ocean. Proponents of Manifest Destiny argued that because America had a mission to lead mankind to a better life, the expansion of American civilization was unquestionably good. Freedom and democracy as well as heavenly purposes would be served. There was, to be sure, the problem caused by previous occupants of the land. But expansionists using the Manifest Destiny doctrine blithely dismissed the claims of the Indians, the Mexicans, and the English with the argument that although American civilization might not be immediately appreciated, it would eventually benefit those to whom it was given. Skeptics contended that Manifest Destiny was merely a rationale for American land hunger, intellectual oil to assuage guilty consciences and smooth the way west, but most of Bridgers' contemporaries did not question the legitimacy of such a convenient idea.

The expansion of the United States, which opened a new career for Jim Bridger, inevitably pressed at the territory of Mexico, its neighbor to the south and west. That nation won its independence from Spain in 1821 and at first welcomed American settlers to the northeastern part of the state of Coahuila, which was called Texas. Moses Austin and his son Stephen took advantage of the opportunity and in the early 1820s led the first Americans into Mexico. By 1825 about two thousand Americans, a quarter of whom were slaves, lived south of the border. Cotton production flourished, but the settlers, predictably, chafed under Mexican rule, and compared their situation to that of the American colonists before 1776. After 1830 the Mexican government, aware of a problem, tried to discourage American immigration, but it was too late. The combination of an authoritarian Mexican ruler, Santa Anna, and the inclination to autonomy characteristic of frontiersmen proved too much for the tenuous relationship.

On March 2, 1836, the American-Mexicans declared their independence. In the ensuing war, Santa Anna killed every one of the 200 Texans defending the Alamo mission, including frontier heroes Davy Crockett and Jim Bowie, but at a cost of 1544 Mexican lives. Crying "Remember the Alamo!" aroused Americans organized under Sam Houston, and on April 21, 1836, crushed Santa Anna at the Battle of San Jacinto. Mexico still did not officially recognize Texan independence, but on the frontier possession and strength counted heavily. The Americans had both, and in the fall of 1836 they created the Republic of Texas with Houston as president. A movement for joining the United States began at once, but antislavery interests opposed the addition of another slave state and the consequent disruption of the delicate sectional balance. As a result, Texas existed under its own Lone Star flag until 1845, when a joint resolution of Congress approved annexation.

"Make way, I say, for the young American Buffalo," an eastern politician shouted during the heyday of Manifest Destiny, "he has not yet got land enough." Ironic as the remark sounds in the light of the near extermination of the buffalo by Bridger and his kind, it is true that the annexation of Texas seemed only to whet the nation's appetite for expansion. One logical outlet for these energies was the Southwest. Santa Fe, located on the upper Rio Grande at the eastern edge of the Rocky Mountains, was a focus of interest. Spain had not permitted economic intercourse with the United States, but with the advent of Mexican control, restrictions were relaxed and the Santa Fe trade begun. Every spring a long wagon train assembled at Independence, Missouri, for the journey over the plains. Many of Jim Bridger's fellow trappers found employment on the Santa Fe Trail. Indian attacks, such as the one that claimed the life of Jedediah Smith, were a chronic problem, but the traders learned to draw their wagons into a tight circle when protection was required. Santa Fe, and the community of Taos to the north, were also known to the mountain men as sources of provisions, equipment, and recreation hundreds of miles closer to the trapping grounds than St. Louis.

The other object of American interest in Mexican territory was California. Ecstatic reports of this lotus land beyond the mountains had filtered back east as a result of early commercial contacts involving sea otters, whales, and cattle. A few gentleman-adventurers added embellishments, most notably Richard Henry Dana in *Two Years before the Mast,* which described an 1835–1836 journey. "In the hands of an enterprising people," Dana exulted, "what a country this might be!" The Mexicans, in his estimation, were charming but ill-equipped to spearhead progress. After the pathbreaking overland journeys of Jedediah Smith (1826), James Ohio Pattie (1828), and Joseph Reddeford Walker (1833), the number of Americans living in California gradually increased. Remembering Texas, the Mexican government exhibited a marked coolness toward them, but the immigration persisted. In 1841 John Bidwell led the first emigrant party over the Sierra and into the promised land. Luck, rather than geographic knowledge or wilderness skill, explained Bidwell's successful migration, but after 1843 California emigrants had the benefit of Jim Bridger's fort and advice to help them over the last thousand-mile leg of the journey.

Advice of a different quality came from one Lansford W. Hastings. Hastings made the California trek in 1843, after which he wrote *The Emigrant's Guide to Oregon and California* and set himself up as the resident expert at Fort Bridger, dispensing advice at $10 per person. The gist of it consisted of a recommendation to abandon the accepted California Trail, which ran north from Fort Bridger to the Hudson's Bay Company's Fort Hall and then followed the Humboldt and Truckee rivers to the Sierra Nevada. Hastings instead advocated a cut off through the rugged Wasatch Mountains, south of Great Salt Lake, and across the most arid part of the Great Basin. This was the route that had almost killed Jedediah Smith on his return from California in 1827, and Bridger knew it to be virtually suicidal for slow-moving emigrant parties. Still, the promise of cutting hundreds of miles off the California trip appealed to trail-weary travelers.

Among those who took Hastings's suggestion were a group from Illinois under the leadership of George and Jacob Donner. Leaving Fort Bridger very late in the summer of 1846, the Donner party wasted precious time struggling through the Wasatch range, only to spend six waterless days on the desert west of the Great Salt Lake. The ordeal broke the emigrants' spirit and discipline. They quarreled incessantly and refused to share precious supplies. By now fall was well advanced and the Sierra still blocked the way to California. Tragedy was in the making. A heavy snow trapped the Donner party in the mountains, and the death toll mounted. Of the eighty-nine who started from Fort Bridger, forty-five survived, and some of these only by cannibalism. Blame for the Donner tragedy was subsequently laid at Bridger's door, but he maintained it was Hastings who had urged the ill-fated detour. Certainly Jim had too much respect for geography to deliberately tempt the fates in the manner of the Donners.

By the time the remnants of the Donner party straggled down from their nightmare in the Sierra, the California question was entwined with the larger issue of the war with Mexico. James K. Polk's election to the Presidency in 1844 was pivotal, since the only question in his mind was *how* to get New Mexico and California. First he tried negotiation; John Slidell was sent to Mexico City in 1845 with a cash offer and other concessions. But the Mexicans, already incensed at the annexation of Texas, were not about to cooperate. Enraged at what he considered a snub, Polk began to make ready for war. A skirmish between American and Mexican troops on disputed land facilitated his job. On May 13, 1846, the United States declared war on Mexico. Even at this height of Manifest Destiny many Americans were ashamed of the bullying tactics and the undisguised land greed of the Polk Administration. Only the Vietnam conflict has approached the Mexican War in domestic unpopularity. The Massachusetts legislature, for instance, solemnly proclaimed it "hateful in its objects . . . wanton, unjust, and unconstitutional," and New England refused to provide dollars and troops for what it regarded as a fight to extend slavery. Henry David Thoreau, the mild-mannered Transcendentalist, went to jail rather than pay taxes in support of the Mexican War. But the South and the West were generally for the war, and their support enabled Polk's Army of the West under Stephen W. Kearny to capture Santa Fe and march on California.

Before reaching it, however, Kearny encountered Kit Carson and a band of mountain men heading east. They reported that the weak Mexican government in California had already fallen to the United States Navy and to resident Americans who had organized the Bear Flag Revolt with the assistance of the explorer John C. Frémont and these same mountain men. Delighted, Kearny pushed on to claim California for the United States and the governorship for himself. Official confirmation of the conquest, however, awaited the fall of Mexico City to General Winfield Scott on September 14, 1847, and the signing of the Treaty of Guadalupe Hidalgo on February 2, 1848. According to the agreement, the United States, for $15 million, received California, the sprawling New Mexico territory, and the Rio Grande as the southwest border to Texas. All of Mexico might have been annexed had not Polk's repudiated agent, Nicholas Trist, defied recall and negotiated a treaty without proper authorization.

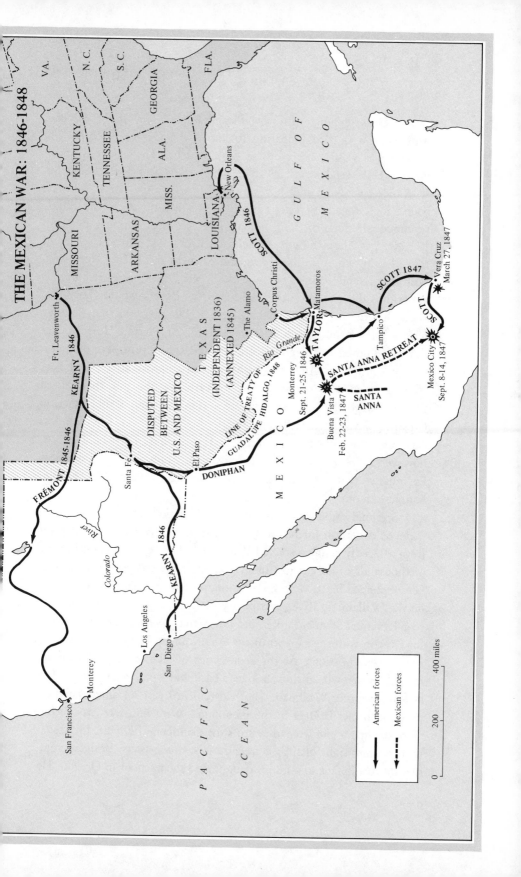

THE MEXICAN WAR: 1846-1848

VA.

N.C.

S.C.

GEORGIA

FLA.

KENTUCKY

TENNESSEE

ALA.

MISS.

MISSOURI

ARKANSAS

LOUISIANA

New Orleans

Ft. Leavenworth

KEARNY 1846

GULF OF MEXICO

SCOTT 1846

Corpus Christi

T E X A S
(INDEPENDENT 1836)
(ANNEXED 1845)

The Alamo

Matamoros

TAYLOR

Rio Grande

LINE OF TREATY OF

GUADALUPE HIDALGO, 1848

Monterey
Sept. 21-25, 1846

Tampico

SCOTT 1847

Vera Cruz
March 27, 1847

SANTA ANNA RETREAT

SCOTT

Mexico City
Sept. 8-14, 1847

SANTA
ANNA

Buena Vista
Feb. 22-23, 1847

DISPUTED
BETWEEN
U.S. AND MEXICO

FRÉMONT 1845-1846

Santa Fé

El Paso

DONIPHAN

M E X I C O

Colorado

River

KEARNY 1846

Los Angeles

San Diego

Monterey

San Francisco

P A C I F I C

O C E A N

American forces

Mexican forces

0   200   400 miles

While stepping with seven-league boots into the Southwest, Americans were also preparing to annex the Oregon country. Jim Bridger was well aware of these developments. He had been at the Pierre's Hole rendezvous in 1832 when the Cambridge, Massachusetts, merchant Nathaniel J. Wyeth rode in with a few dozen followers bound for Oregon. Wyeth's expedition was a response to the frantic promotional efforts of Congressman John Floyd of Virginia and Hall J. Kelley, a Massachusetts schoolteacher obsessed with the idea of transplanting an entire New England town to the Pacific Northwest. Both Floyd and Kelley, along with Wyeth, were convinced that if Americans did not settle this region, Great Britain would. They also knew that the flag followed the fireplace. But the wilderness journey took a toll of the Wyeth party's idealism. At Pierre's Hole Bridger listened, amused, as the group bickered and finally split over the question of continuing. At last Wyeth and ten companions reached Fort Vancouver on the Columbia, only to learn that the ship that carried their heavy goods had been lost attempting to round South America. Crushed, Wyeth returned overland to Boston, but in 1834 he was back, and this time the ship arrived. His trading and fishing efforts, however, were frustrated by the powerful Hudson's Bay Company. Eventually that organization's wily manager, John McLoughlin, bought him out.

Spiritual rather than economic considerations motivated the next wave of American interest in Oregon. In the early 1830s bogus pleas from allegedly religion-starved Flathead Indians elicited contributions of thousands of dollars to Christianize the heathen. Jason and Daniel Lee responded in 1834 with a mission, school, and temperance society on the Willamette River, a tributary of the Columbia. The following year Reverend Samuel Parker and Dr. Marcus Whitman took the trail for Oregon with the support of the American Board of Commissioners for Foreign Missions. At the rendezvous of that year, Whitman removed the arrowhead from Bridger's back and won his friendship. The following spring Whitman, who had returned east for additional support, again met Bridger in the mountains. With him was Mrs. Whitman, the first white woman to cross the Continental Divide. Impressed with his first sight of such a creature in a dozen years, Bridger promised the Whitmans to send his daughter to their school in Oregon. He was as good as his word, too, but Mary Ann Bridger died in 1848 in the aftermath of the massacre of the Whitmans by Cayuse Indians.

Before this unhappy ending Whitman had done his best to promote the settlement of the Pacific Northwest. In 1843 he personally guided a long emigrant train over the Oregon Trail. Its one thousand members paused gratefully at Fort Bridger, which was 1070 miles from the jumping-off place, Independence, Missouri, and almost exactly as far from their destination, Fort Vancouver and the Willamette. In the next two years about four thousand more emigrants came over the trail and, in terms of residents, gave the United States an approximate parity with Great Britain. The growth also increased the urgency of solving "the Oregon question." The key was what parallel of latitude would be established as the boundary between the United States and Canada. President Polk and other expansionists wanted to secure all the Oregon country up to the southern boundary of Russian-held Alaska, or latitude 54°40′. England favored the opposite extreme; the northern boundary of California, which was latitude 42°. The settlement of 1846, designating 49°, was a reasonable compromise, since it extended the eastern Canadian-American boundary to the Pacific.

From the standpoint of the Oregon pioneers, the boundary settlement did not rank in importance with the details of local government. Contrary to their reputation in song and story and on television, frontiersmen were not a lawless lot. On the contrary, for every outlaw with smoking six-shooter, there were a dozen families and businessmen determined to put local affairs on an orderly basis. The extreme individualism of Jim Bridger's generation of mountain men typified only the first wave of pioneers—men who lived a nomadic, wilderness existence and, because they were few, could literally be a law unto themselves. But when settlers arrived they quickly erected a legal framework and enforced it, when necessary, with informal but effective vigilante justice—posses and hangmen's nooses. In Oregon the need to dispose of the estate of a man who died without leaving a will occasioned the first steps toward political organization. In true social compact tradition, the neighbors of the deceased convened to decide the issue. Someone vaguely recalled the New York law dealing with unbequeathed property, so that statute became the Oregon guideline. In 1843 a First Organic Law was pieced together from the fragmentary legal knowledge of the community. Two years later a more complete set of laws regularized such matters as marriage, landholding, and criminal procedures. Taxation was voluntary, but with the understanding that those who did not pay had no vote and no recourse to the law for any purpose. Under such conditions, few refused. The machinery of government was therefore well established by 1848, when Oregon finally became a territory of the United States.

Another example of the orderly extension of civilization occurred in the Great Basin west of Fort Bridger. This time religion provided cohesion and order. The Church of Jesus Christ of Latter-Day Saints had begun in the "burned-over" district of western New York, a region frequently marked by the "fire" of reformers and religious zealots who bore the intellectual legacy of New England Calvinism. The sect had its origins in 1830 in the mind of Joseph Smith, who claimed mystical intimacy with the word of God. Transcribing the Book of Mormon from golden plates he alone had seen, Smith attracted 15,000 followers and moved them successively to Ohio, Missouri, and Illinois. But Smith's advocacy of polygamy and his acceptance of dictatorial authority to the extent of defying federal law subjected the Mormons, as outsiders termed them, to fierce criticism and, ultimately, violence.

In 1844 a mob murdered Smith and sent the Mormons, in the manner of the Puritans, searching for a sanctuary where they could live according to their beliefs. The trans-Mississippi West was an obvious candidate, and in Brigham Young the Mormons had a leader with the brilliance and tenacity to effect the migration. Like John Winthrop over two centuries before, Young was prepared to stake everything on the American wilderness. Midsummer 1847 found him and a well-organized pioneer band at Fort Bridger conversing with the proprietor about the prospects of settling thousands of people in the Salt Lake Valley. Bridger scoffed at the idea. The country was too arid, its discoverer explained, and to dramatize his point he allegedly offered Young $1,000 for the first ear of corn it produced. Bridger suggested the Mormons try Oregon's rich Willamette Valley, but the saints were not easily swayed. Their primary requirement was isolation, and Salt Lake had that in abundance.

The Mormons counted on Jim Bridger's personal guidance through the mountains, but the plans did not materialize. Trusting instead to their God, the emigrants missed the easier routes and strug-

Salt Lake City, Utah, shown here in 1853, was something of a miracle. Less than a decade before, only lizards and jackrabbits had occupied the arid sagebrush benchland between Great Salt Lake and the Wasatch Mountains. The growth of the town was a tribute to the perseverance of the Mormons—one of the most effective groups of pioneers in American history.

[Th]e meeting of the rails of the Union Pacific and Central Pacific railroads at [Pro]montory, Utah, north of Great Salt Lake, on May 10, 1869 was an unmistakable [sign] that the American frontier was vanishing. Americans at the time celebrated the [eve]nt with as much enthusiasm as later generations displayed in the aftermath of [Nei]l Armstrong's walk on the moon.

gled through the tortuous Emigrant Canyon to their haven. Once installed in Salt Lake Valley, however, they made few mistakes. Hard work, a genius for irrigation, and the assistance of a timely invasion of insect-devouring sea gulls solved the agricultural problem, and the relieved settlers joked about Bridger's $1,000 ear of corn. In 1848 the main body of migrating Mormons filed past Fort Bridger in a caravan that one observer described as being "six hundred miles and forty days long." Brigham Young proved a skillful administrator, able to subordinate individual desires to the welfare of the community. The result was rapid and efficient Mormon colonization of the Great Basin from Idaho to southern California. When the United States acquired this territory at the end of the Mexican War, the worried Mormons proposed the creation of a gigantic State of Deseret including all of present-day Utah, all of Arizona, most of Nevada, and parts of Idaho, Wyoming, Colorado, and California, with an ocean port at San Diego. Congress disapproved, but in 1850 President Millard Fillmore did make Brigham Young governor of the more modest Territory of Utah.

As Brigham Young became more powerful in the Great Basin, his initial dislike of Jim Bridger grew into active hostility. The men had little in common. In the eyes of the easy-going, hard-living mountain man, Young seemed stiff, self-assured and incredibly "green" in the ways of the West. The saint, on his part, regarded Bridger as an unregenerate libertine little better than the animals he hunted and trapped. In time Young openly accused Bridger of arousing the Ute Indians against his people. Young was jealous of Bridger's position of authority in territory he was coming to regard as a Mormon empire. There was also an economic factor in the antipathy. Instead of trading at Fort Bridger, the migrating Mormons relied on relief caravans sent east by their brothers at Salt Lake. Mormon traders also endeavored to intercept non-Mormon emigrant parties before they reached Bridger's post. In 1849 the economic war was sharpened as some 40,000 Americans streamed west in quest of the gold that had been discovered the previous year on the property of John A. Sutter near Sacramento, California. As a rule, the Forty-Niners were abysmally prepared for the transcontinental journey and sorely in need of food, equipment, and draft animals when they reached the Green River–Salt Lake frontier. Moreover, the travelers frequently had furniture, machinery, and manufactured goods which they had to unload and would sell at any price before crossing the desert and mountains to California. For the Mormons, the result was affluence; for California, with 100,000 residents by 1850, it was statehood.

As a territorial governor Brigham Young felt it within his power in 1853 to order Jim Bridger arrested on the grounds of instigating Indian attacks. In August a posse of Young's "destroying angels" arrived at Fort Bridger, but found that Jim had headed for the hills. Frustrated, they burned most of the fort to the ground. Jim subsequently returned and sadly kicked through the ashes as he contemplated the perils of property ownership. In the old days such an insult would have been met with immediate retaliation. But the Mormons were too strong. Just as the Indians found themselves crowded into the unwanted corners of their lands, so Jim Bridger was made to yield to a variety of progress he did not fully understand.

In 1857 Bridger had a measure of revenge when he received an appointment as a guide and Indian interpreter in the United States Army. His mission was to lead 2500 troops under Colonel Albert Sidney Johnston against the Mormons, who enjoyed an uncontested theocracy. The soldiers stood firm against a series of Mormon guerrilla attacks and then made winter camp near the ruins of Jim Bridger's old fort. While waiting for spring to open the passes and—it seemed inevitable—a full-scale war, news came of the massacre of 120 emigrants by Mormons in southern Utah. But instead of precipitating bloodshed, the Mountain Meadow Massacre convinced a cool-headed Buchanan Administration, preoccupied, it must be said, by the impending sectional conflict, that civil war in the West had to be avoided. Mediation hurriedly took place in the winter of 1857–1858. Much to Bridger's amazement and disgust, Brigham Young was pardoned and in practice allowed to rule Utah. What Bridger did not understand was that the principle of federal authority had been unequivocally asserted and reluctantly accepted.

After the "Mormon War" Jim Bridger turned to guiding as his principal vocation. A full 6 feet in height, lean and rawboned, with greying hair and a detailed knowledge of the Rocky Mountains, Bridger was a wilderness veteran who commanded respect in any company. A large proportion of his clients were in the transport business. Western developers and proponents of Manifest Destiny had always recognized the need for reliable overland transportation. The frontier, almost by definition, receded as the transportation network advanced. First to appear were the road builders and the organizers of stage-coach lines and express companies. Bridger helped them find key routes, and in the process left his name on western maps. The Bridger Trail ran north from the North Platte River and the Oregon Trail to the Yellowstone River and Bozeman, Montana. Bridger's Ferry took the Oregon Trail across the North Platte. As an all-weather alternative to that famous pathway, Bridger blazed a route from western Nebraska to northern Utah over Bridger's Pass. In 1861, along with Captain E. L. Berthoud and the Central Overland, California, and Pike's Peak Express Company, he laid out the Bridger-Berthoud Road west from Denver. And the South Pass–Green River–Salt Lake corridor that Bridger discovered in the early 1820s became the major east-west transcontinental route.

By 1860, thanks to generous federal subsidies, people and light produce were moving along these roads on a more or less regular basis. The glamour company was the Butterfield Overland Mail, whose horse-drawn coaches in 1858 raced from Missouri to California in twenty-four days. "I congratulate you on the result," a proud President Buchanan wired Butterfield, "it is a glorious triumph for civilization and the Union." But even this achievement paled in comparison to that of the Pony Express, whose team of daredevil horsemen carried the mail across the same distance in just ten days in 1860. A year later the time was cut to seconds when wires were joined on the first transcontinental telegraph.

The efficient transport of items heavier than paper and people awaited the railroads. The two decades before the Civil War saw track mileage in the United States leap from 3,000 to 30,000. These years also witnessed the birth of a plan for a transcontinental railroad, but it foundered on the rocks of sectional competition and uncertain financing. When the Civil War eliminated the first problem and federal subsidies the second, the plans revived. In the mid-1860s the Central Pacific began its push east from California. Generous grants of the public domain, which made the railroads the largest landowners in the West, and federal loans on a per-mile basis encouraged construction. In 1867 the Central Pacific's tracks extended across the Sierra. Meanwhile, the Union Pacific was advancing west from Omaha, Nebraska.

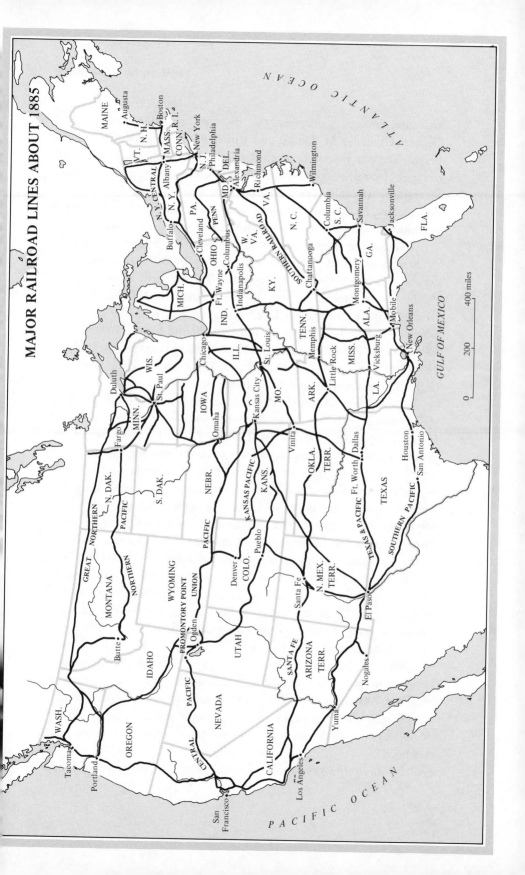

MAJOR RAILROAD LINES ABOUT 1885

Its route, through South Pass, was the one Jim Bridger had showed General Grenville M. Dodge and Union Pacific officials a few years before. The competition between the Central and Union crews resulted in rapid, if careless, construction which over favorable terrain reached the rate of 10 miles per day. The lines met on May 10, 1869, at Promontory, Utah. Only forty-five years before Jim Bridger had stood at almost the same place, the first white man to see Great Salt Lake.

Even as the golden spike was driven at Promontory, other railroads were being lengthened westward to provide the transportation network on which settlement depended. To the north of the Central Pacific–Union Pacific axis, the Northern Pacific and James J. Hill's Great Northern opened the Dakotas and Montana. In the south the Santa Fe Railroad followed the route of the old Santa Fe Trail, and the Southern Pacific claimed the Texas-California traffic. A Bridger-discovered route from Denver to Salt Lake City became the main line of the Denver and Rio Grande Railroad.

The advent of rapid, dependable, and relatively inexpensive transportation of heavy, bulky items helped make possible a series of economic bonanzas in the West. Like the fur trade, which began the process, each bonanza brought a wave of civilization surging westward across the Great Plains or eastward from California and Oregon. When the exploitable resource was depleted the wave receded, but not without leaving a residue of permanent settlement. Second only to the trappers were the miners. After the great California gold rush of 1849, there were similar mineral booms in Nevada, Colorado, Arizona, Idaho, Montana, and Wyoming. Denver developed from gold strikes that attracted frontiersmen like bees to honey, and so did Helena, Montana, and Boise, Idaho. The richest concentration of gold and silver was struck on the eastern slope of the Sierra—the fabulous Comstock Lode. Thanks to the miners who flooded in, Nevada became a state in 1864. Thanks to Mark Twain, the state, and especially Virginia City, became an American legend. Life in all the mining camps was rough and tumble, with the usual frontier assortment of gamblers, whores, and outlaws, but the need for a framework of law and order to protect the gains of the fortunate quickly spawned simple democracy, vigilante justice, and—in time—territorial status and statehood.

By 1875 the easy pickings were over. The early arrivals had

skimmed the cream off the West's mineral riches, just as they had its furs. The next bonanza involved production, rather than mere gathering, and was concentrated on cattle. Southern Texas was the seedbed of the business. For two decades after the Civil War cowboys drove huge herds north along the Chisholm and other trails to the railhead towns of Abilene and Dodge City, Kansas. But the increase of settlers with their barbed wire fences spelled the end of the open range and the cattle bonanza.

Wheat, corn, and hay figured in the next economic era. Making farming possible were technological improvements such as the windmill pump, the Oliver deep plow, and large-capacity planters and threshers. The development of both irrigation and dry-farming techniques also proved vital. But farmers were necessary too, and the Homestead Act of 1862, with its promise of virtually free land to anyone who would reside on and improve it, helped draw them from the eastern states and Europe. For unsurveyed land the Preemption Act of 1841 recognized land titles on a first-come basis. Of course these acts, and others like the notorious Desert Land Act (1877) and the Timber and Stone Act (1878), did not prevent choice western lands from falling into the hands of speculators and quick-profit exploiters. The West, with its apparently unlimited and certainly unclaimed abundance, seemed to encourage such behavior. Bridger and the mountain men showed the way with their trap-out-and-get-out methods of operation.

Along with the entrepreneurs of western transportation who made resource exploitation possible, the other major client for Jim Bridger's guiding skills was the United States Army, which was engaged in its chronic campaign of Indian "removal." The sad process began under President Andrew Jackson with the systematic destruction of the Creek and Cherokee nations in Georgia, Alabama, and Tennessee. The Indians protested the seizure of their lands and actually won a favorable judgment in John Marshall's Supreme Court, but frontier bias prevailed in practice. Even after they accepted a peaceful agricultural existence, the southeastern Indians blocked expansion of the cotton kingdom. A series of forced treaties cleared the way for pushing the protesting Indians—"for their own good"—west of the Mississippi. One of the ugliest chapters in American history was the herding of the Cherokee along the Trail of Tears from their Ten-

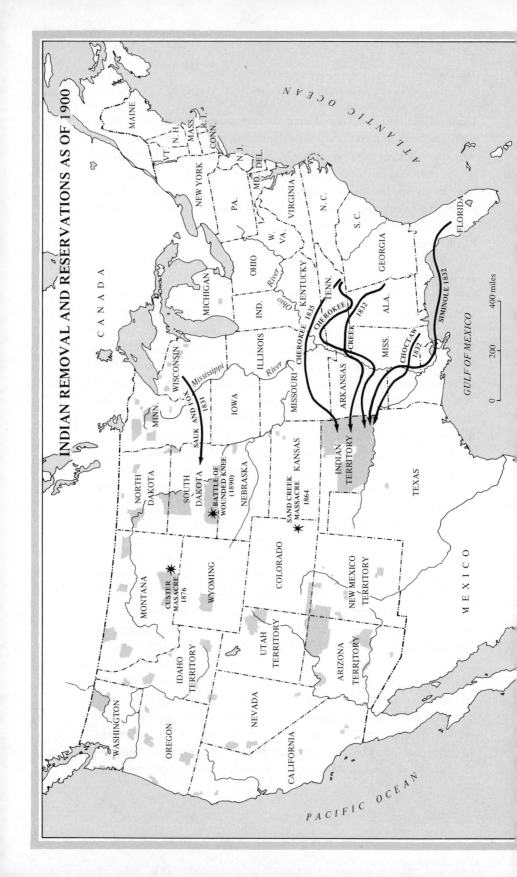

INDIAN REMOVAL AND RESERVATIONS AS OF 1900

nessee homeland to Oklahoma in 1835. Mop-up operations against Florida's Seminoles and their talented leader Osceola continued until 1842. On the northern plains Chief Black Hawk and his Sac and Fox tribesmen made an attempt to revive the spirit of resistance exemplified by Tecumseh twenty-five years earlier, but they too were forced from their homeland.

Of course, the removal of the Indians west of the Mississippi was not a solution. The "permanent Indian frontier" remained only until the white man was ready to cross it. Jim Bridger and the mountain men proved that. But while Bridger and his peers fought the trans-Mississippi tribes on roughly equal numerical terms, time brought increasing advantage to the white man. By the 1860s the pressure of miners and railroad builders on the western Indians was such as to precipitate a series of bloody clashes. The first occurred in Colorado in November 1864, when Colonel J. M. Chivington butchered a Cheyenne village. The army followed this Sand Creek Massacre with a campaign against the Sioux in northern Wyoming and southern Montana—the Powder River country. Jim Bridger knew this region like the back of his hand; he also had a knack for understanding the Indian way of warfare. Pressed into service by the Army, he led several successful marches against Chief Red Cloud's Sioux. When Bridger's advice was disregarded, as it was in 1866 by Captain William J. Fetterman, eighty-one soldiers were surprised and killed. General warfare continued on the western plains throughout the next decade. The climax came in June 1876 when Chiefs Sitting Bull and Crazy Horse killed Colonel George A. Custer and all his 265 men in the Battle of the Little Big Horn.

The victory only delayed the inevitable. Four months later General Alfred H. Terry forced the surrender of the bulk of the Sioux nation. The white man's proposal for small reservations could now be instituted without resistance. The Dawes Act (1887) delivered the final blow at the Indian life style by attempting to destroy tribal identity and assimilate the Indians into American civilization as citizens and small farmers. But for the Great Plains Indian it mattered little. The buffalo that had sustained his civilization had been virtually exterminated in less than fifteen years of hide, meat, and trophy hunting.

For Jim Bridger, too, it was the end of the game. His way of life, like that of the Indians, depended on a quantity of wilderness that was incompatible with an expanding American civilization. After guiding in the Indian wars, Bridger returned to his Missouri farm. The last decade of his life was spent quietly at home with his innumerable stories and a cluster of children fascinated with tales of a life they could never lead. Friends who knew of Bridger's contact with the region may have told him that in 1872 the federal government set aside 3000 square miles in northwestern Wyoming as Yellowstone National Park. This need for protection of a region that only John Colter, Jim Bridger, and a handful of others had seen before the 1870s was a sure sign that the frontier was vanishing.

In 1875 Bridger went totally blind. Weather permitting, he spent his remaining six years on the porch of his farmhouse, leaning forward in a chair, chin resting on a cane. His visitors reported that he always faced west.

SELECTED READINGS

The Person

ALTER, J. CECIL: *Jim Bridger* (rev. ed., 1962). A reissue, with illustrative material and maps, of the first biography.

CAESAR, GENE: *King of the Mountain Men: The Life of Jim Bridger* (1961). The most recent biography.

ISMERT, CORNELIUS M.: "Jim Bridger," in LeRoy R. Hofen (ed.): *The Mountain Men and the Fur Trade of the Far West* (8 vols., 1965–1971). Vol. VI, pp. 85–104. A good short biography.

*VESTAL, STANLEY: *Jim Bridger, Mountain Man* (1946). A rather romanticized account.

The Period

BILLINGTON, RAY A.: *Westward Expansion* (rev. ed., 1967). The best general treatment of America's frontiers.

CHITTENDEN, HIRAM M.: *The American Fur Trade of the Far West* (2 vols., 1935). An old but thorough account.

*DE VOTO, BERNARD: *Across the Wide Missouri* (1947). The

* Available in paperback.

early history of the Far West. De Voto's *The Year of Decision, 1846* (1943) examines a pivotal point in the nation's history.

*GATES, PAUL W.: *The Farmer's Age* (1960). Agricultural history before the Civil War.

*MERK, FREDERICK: *Manifest Destiny and Mission in American History* (1963). Examines two concepts of great import for the West.

*SMITH, HENRY NASH: *Virgin Land: The American West as Symbol and Myth* (1950). Explores the idea, as distinct from the reality, of the West as held by Americans in the eighteenth and nineteenth centuries.

*TAYLOR, GEORGE R.: *The Transportation Revolution, 1815–1860* (1951). An examination of the most important factor in the opening of the West.

* Available in paperback.

Engraved by J. C. Buttre

CHAPTER FIVE

Frederick Douglass

The tall teen-aged slave had one foot on the stable loft ladder when he felt a hand close about his ankle. A quick pull brought him crashing to the floor. From a prone position Frederick Douglass looked up at the grinning face of Edward Covey, professional slavebreaker. The white man began to slip a noose over Douglass's legs in preparation for yet another session of the torture that had made the first six months of 1834 a nightmare of pain. Only two days before Douglass had lain half-dead in the woods near Covey's.

187

It was the low point of his life. "I would have exchanged my manhood," he later recalled, "for the brutehood of an ox." Now, lying on the stable floor, Douglass was seized by a blinding anger. Springing away from the noose, he grappled with the surprised Covey. For the better part of an hour the men struggled desperately. Finally Covey staggered away. Douglass, by his own admission, was a changed man. The act of resistance "recalled to life my crushed self-respect and my self-confidence, and inspired me with a renewed determination to be a free man." *Four years later he escaped to freedom. Four decades later he stood as the foremost spokesman of black America.*

"Genealogical trees," Frederick Douglass wryly observed, "did not flourish among slaves." Few knew their ancestry or even their age. Douglass was no exception. He believed he was born in 1817. His mother was black and a slave. He saw her only a few times. He supposed his father was white, and he was told that Indian blood ran in his veins.

For his first seven years Frederick Douglass lived a relatively comfortable life with his grandmother on a plantation in Maryland's Talbot County, east of Chesapeake Bay. Fishing and watching squirrels and playing on the dirt floor of his grandmother's cabin, he did not understand what it meant to be a slave. Gradually, however, his child's mind learned there was someone called "Old Master." This vague figure, he found out, owned not only the land and the cabin, but his grandmother, his playmates, and his own self. It seemed inconceivable. The older slaves tried hard to shield Douglass from the full implications of his condition. Still, it was impossible to miss the involuntary shudder that invariably accompanied any discussion of Old Master. "Thus early," Douglass remembered, "did clouds and shadows begin to fall upon my path."

At about the age of seven Douglass began a more intensive course of instruction in the meaning of slavery. On what he clearly remembered as a beautiful summer morning, he was taken from his grandmother's cabin to Old Master's plantation. The master in this case was Captain Aaron Anthony, who owned several farms and some thirty slaves. But Anthony, in turn, reported to an even bigger master, Colonel Edward Lloyd. A power in eastern Maryland, Lloyd held twenty-five farms and over a thousand slaves. And as it happened, Lloyd made his personal residence on Anthony's plantation, and Douglass received a memorable impression of the Old South at its zenith.

The grandeur of the place astonished the boy. Like most large Southern plantations of the 1820s, Lloyd's gardens and pastures, mills and craft shops constituted a nearly self-sufficient economic unit. Old Master lived in "the great house," which was built of white-painted wood. Three spacious wings branched out from a broad front porch with its row of white columns. Leading from the porch to the gate a quarter-mile distant was a graveled driveway and a lush lawn planted with trees and flowers. In imitation of English nobles, Lloyd released rabbits, deer, and other game to roam the estate. To the rear of the great house another lawn ran down to the Wye River, Lloyd's chief artery of communication and trade. From his landing the tobacco that sustained the plantation was shipped to market. A pleasure sloop, the *Sally Lloyd,* swung at its mooring, a rowboat trailing behind.

Taking all this in, Douglass could not suppress a thrill at the "elaborate exhibition of wealth, power, and beauty." For him and his fellows, however, home meant one of the miserable slave huts scattered, half-hidden, about the plantation. And Douglass quickly learned that beneath the genteel surface lay a tangled skein of brutality, passion, and blood. Shortly after his arrival at Lloyd's, a young black woman who worked on another farm had been savagely beaten by an overseer. The girl knew she belonged to Lloyd, and with blood streaming down her face and back, dragged herself 12 miles to seek his protection. Douglass was there when she arrived. Lloyd refused to acknowledge her presence, and turned the problem over to the chief overseer, Anthony. Up to this time Douglass had entertained a favorable image of Anthony, who sometimes led him by the hand and patted his head in a paternal fashion. Now he saw the other side of the man. Cursing the bleeding girl, Anthony declared that " 'she deserved every bit of [the beating], and if she did not go home instantly he would himself take the remaining skin from her neck and back.' "

Douglass realized that the girl had no alternative but to return the 12 miles to still more floggings. Absolute repression, he saw, was the keystone of the slave system.

In the next few years Douglass's perspective on slavery expanded considerably. He saw mothers tied to trees and whipped to unconsciousness in front of their crying children. He learned that when his beloved grandmother became too old to work, she was left in a hut in the middle of a forest to die of starvation. He watched an enraged overseer shoot and kill a slave who dared to run from a threatened flogging. Maryland justice did not regard this deed as a crime. Douglass never knew a slave murderer to receive the slightest punishment. Rape of black women (sometimes for the purpose of breeding) was common and also outside the law. But Douglass noted that the offspring of such unions caused Old Master some embarrassment. Although the children were black, they were usually exempt from the punishment dealt other slaves. Problems invariably followed. Lloyd was finally obliged to slip one of his troublesome black sons enough money to buy his freedom.

Douglass noticed that Lloyd's house servants always received preferential treatment on the plantation. In contrast to the field hands, these favored slaves rendered personal service in the great house. Many deliberately copied Old Master in dress, speech, and mannerisms and hardly deigned to associate with their brothers in the fields. But the house servants' social superiority was entirely self-assumed. The master race was blind to anything but color.

The potential for atrocities, Douglass believed, made the slaveholder as well as the slave a victim of the system. There was no chance on either side for character development. "Reason," he wrote, "is imprisoned here, and passions run wild." The slave experience, he concluded, made livestock of human beings. Indeed, the slaves had a worse fate. Old Master's "horses and dogs," Douglass maintained, "fared better than his men."

The slave system in which Frederick Douglass found himself mired in the 1820s had its American origins in 1619, when the captain of a Dutch ship sold twenty bewildered Africans to the tobacco planters of Jamestown, Virginia. The slave trade was already well established. Portuguese and Spanish traders carried human cargoes from West Africa's Gold Coast to Europe as early as the fifteenth century.

Native black kings along the African coast made the trade possible by selling their own slaves or procuring them from the interior. Without exonerating whites for their role in slavery, we cannot ignore evidence that the profit motive which fed the trade existed irrespective of color.

The settlement of the New World opened new opportunities for slavery. Initial hopes centered on easy wealth from a paradisiacal land. Slaves had no role in this economy. But the dreams faded quickly under the impact of the New World reality: men would have to *work* for a living. However, the gentlemen-adventurers who composed the first waves of settlers in the Caribbean and in England's southern colonies were not inclined to perform the hard field labor that the production of sugar, tobacco, and later cotton demanded. Moreover, it was difficult to convince immigrants from their own countries to be employees. In America everyone wanted to be an employer. Slaves filled the resulting labor vacuum.

An estimated 15 million blacks came to the Americas in the three centuries of slave trade. The typical commercial pattern began with the shipment of liquor and manufactured goods from England or her American colonies to Africa. The next leg, the middle passage, took slaves to the markets in the Americas. Hundreds of thousands of blacks died in the foul holds of crowded ships on the journey, but the profits in the business sustained it even if only half the cargo survived. Completing the economic triangle, sugar, tobacco, and cotton were then shipped in the slavers to commercial centers of Europe and the northern colonies. Frederick Douglass's ancestors reached America as a result of these exchanges.

The social status of the first black Americans was not immediately clear. There is some evidence that the African immigrants were regarded by their seventeenth-century contemporaries as indentured servants rather than slaves. In other words, the blacks, like white servants, owed a certain amount of labor to the person who paid their way to America, but they were not his property. They possessed the rights and immunities of human beings. In time, they could expect to earn their freedom. Their children, in any case, were free.

On the other hand, there is also evidence that all seventeenth-century servants were not equal. The black ones had fewer rights from the beginning. In a very short time, their inferior status jelled into hereditary lifetime service. They became property. The reason for this

RAFFLE

Mr. Joseph Jennings respectfully informs his friends and the public that, at the request of many acquaintants, he has been induced to purchase from Mr. Osborne, of Missouri, the celebrated

DARK BAY HORSE, "STAR,"

Aged five years, square trotter and warranted sound; with a new light Trotting Buggy and Harness; also, the dark, stout

MULATTO GIRL, "SARAH,"

Aged about twenty years, general house servant, valued at *nine hundred dollars*, and guaranteed, and

Will be Raffled for

At 4 o'clock P. M., February first, at the selection hotel of the subscribers. The above is as represented, and those persons who may wish to engage in the usual practice of raffling, will, I assure them, be perfectly satisfied with their destiny in this affair.

The whole is valued at its just worth, fifteen hundred dollars; fifteen hundred

CHANCES AT ONE DOLLAR EACH.

The Raffle will be conducted by gentlemen selected by the interested subscribers present. Five nights will be allowed to complete the Raffle. BOTH OF THE ABOVE DESCRIBED CAN BE SEEN AT MY STORE, No. 78 Common St., second door from Camp, at from 9 o'clock A. M. to 2 P. M.

Highest throw to take the first choice; the lowest throw the remaining prize, and the fortunate winners will pay twenty dollars each for the refreshments furnished on the occasion.

N. B. No chances recognized unless paid for previous to the commencement.

JOSEPH JENNINGS.

Twenty Dollars Reward.

RAN away from the fubfcribers, living at New Rochelle, on Sunday evening, the 9th inftant; two indented GERMAN SERVANTS: John Jacob Wittmer, belonging to Mr. Lifpenard, about five feet five inches high, well fet, has a remarkable large head, fhort neck and broad face; halts as he walks, his right leg being much fhorter than the left; had on, or took with him when he went off, a bhie broad cloth coat, with brafs buttons, fhort white waiftcoat, with red embroidered flowers; corduroy breeches; light coloured worfted ftockings; new fhoes, and new round hat, with a band and buckle. Mr. Williams's fervant is a tall flim fellow, five feet eleven inches high; fomewhat freckled; long hair, tyed behind; had on a mixed blue and white coat; black breeches; and took with him a pair of clouded overalls, red, blue and white, which he may probably wear. Whoever apprehends the above fervants, and will bring them to their mafters, at this place, fhall receive the above reward, or ten dollars for either of them, with an allowance for all reafonable charges.

LEONARD LISPENARD, jun.
DANiEL WILLIAMS.

New Rochelle, October 13, 1785.   33-6

Essentially, slavery was a form of livestock business, with institutions comparable to those associated with the management of cattle or horses. There were auctions (opposite, top), in which the merchandise was freely examined and sold to the top bidder. An advertisement for such an event (opposite, bottom) underscores the close association in the white South's mind of horses and slaves. Both kinds of livestock occasionally ran away, but the human fugitives proved much harder to catch. Despite newspaper notices and rewards (above), many escaped slaves were never recovered. One reason was the existence of the "underground railroad" (below). This was actually a loose organization of Northerners who assisted fugitives in their flight to freedom.

LIBERTY LINE.
NEW ARRANGEMENT---NIGHT AND DAY.

The improved and splendid Locomotives, Clarkson and Lundy, with their trains fitted up in the best style of accommodation for passengers, will run their regular trips during the present season, between the borders of the Patriarchal Dominion and Libertyville, Upper Canada. Gentlemen and Ladies, who may wish to improve their health or circumstances, by a northern tour, are respectfully invited to give us their patronage.

SEATS FREE, *irrespective of color.*

Necessary Clothing furnished gratuitously to such as have *"fallen among thieves."*

"Hide the outcasts—let the oppressed go free."—*Bible*

☞For seats apply at any of the trap doors, or to the conductor of the train.

J. CROSS, *Proprietor.*

N. B. For the special benefit of Pro-Slavery Police Officers, an extra heavy wagon for Texas, will be furnished, whenever it may be necessary, in which they will be forwarded as dead freight, to the "Valley of Rascals," always at the risk of the owners.

☞Extra Overcoats provided for such of them as are afflicted with protracted *chilly-phobia.*

rapid hardening seems to be a deeply rooted bias in the Anglo-American mind against black men. Part of it stemmed from their color itself. In the eyes of whites, a black man was at once shocking, inexplicable, and frightening—associated because of his color with the powers of darkness. Given this bias, slavery seemed a way for white society to live with the disturbing strangers in its midst. Also significant in stamping slavery on the African was his social visibility. A white servant at least looked like everyone else. Taken from his place of servitude, he blended into society. He could thus reap the benefits of the fluid social and economic structure of a growing country. But the black was a marked man. His color constantly testified to his menial origins. It was easy to pin on him the label "slave." In any event, by 1700 it was clearly understood throughout the American colonies that slavery concerned blacks only. The slave, as Frederick Douglass learned at a very tender age, had lost his manhood.

But the young Douglass also learned that there were varieties of slavery, some more pleasant than others. While still a boy he was sent from the Lloyd plantation to Baltimore and the home of Hugh Auld. Specifically, Douglass was a gift to the Aulds' young son, Tommy. In this capacity he lived a better life than he had thought possible. He had clean clothes, regular food, a bed, and a mistress who at first treated him more as a stepson than a slave. Mrs. Auld even began to teach Douglass to read. She made the mistake, however, of informing her husband of the boy's rapid progress. Auld became enraged and forbade the lessons. "Learning," he declared in Douglass's presence, "will spoil the best nigger in the world." If the boy learned to read the Bible, Auld continued, "it will forever unfit him to be a slave." Education, Auld concluded, could only make slaves "disconsolate and unhappy."

Frederick Douglass, however, chose this path. He sensed that the reason slaveholders opposed educating blacks was a fear it would promote a desire for freedom. Douglass agreed and redoubled his efforts to read and write. His teachers were the street society of Baltimore and a battered copy of Noah Webster's famous spelling book that he somehow acquired and carefully hid. Instruction in writing came from copying the letters on the sides of shipping crates on Baltimore's docks. When he was thirteen, Douglass earned his first money blackening boots and used it, in the manner of Benjamin Franklin, to buy a book: *The Columbian Orator.* The volume contained stirring speeches advocating natural rights, and some of the orations even concerned the abolition of slavery. Exposure to them heightened Douglass's desire for freedom. No matter how kind his treatment, he knew he was someone's property, and the thought incensed him. Precisely as Auld predicted, education and slavery were poor partners.

About the time he learned to read and write Douglass left the Auld household to work in the shipyards of Baltimore. He thereby joined the ranks of a select group—the city slaves. These blacks constituted a substantial percentage of the slave labor force. They worked in the cities and towns of the South, but under conditions different from those of the plantation slaves. Normally the city slave had his own quarters and the liberty to come and go in the town as he pleased. His labor was frequently "hired out" to businessmen in the community, the wages accruing to the master. But occasionally a slave would be permitted to work part of the time for himself and in this way accumulate the funds to buy his freedom. Such self-freed blacks were not common in the South, but their presence constitutes evidence against the interpretation of American slavery as a completely closed, spirit-breaking system.

For a time in Baltimore Douglass entertained hopes of being permitted to earn the money to buy himself from his master. His growing skill as a caulker of ships lent substance to this dream. But in 1833 Douglass's luck took a turn for the worse. His master died, and the resulting adjustments sent him back to a farm. Having tasted the liberal variety of slavery in Baltimore, resubmission to the harsher rural pattern was doubly hard. Douglass tried to maintain his dignity. He organized a Sunday school class for black children on the plantation, but saw it disbanded by an angry mob of pious leaders of the local church. Moreover, Douglass's new master warned him in no uncertain terms that such behavior would bring him to the same fate as Nat Turner.

Nat Turner was not just a name in the South in 1833, but the foremost symbol of the greatest horror a southern white could imagine: slave revolt. Try as he might, the southerner could not deny the possibility of black insurrection. Slaves, after all, were not like other livestock. They could think, plan, organize, kill, rape, and plunder. And the slave system was not the benign, paternalistic welfare institu-

tion its apologists maintained. Behind the façade of moonlight, mag-
nolias, and happy darkies singing for a beloved Old Master was force
and fear. To understand the white viewpoint, it is necessary only to
note that in many parts of the South blacks outnumbered whites.
Indeed, in the tidewater region where Douglass lived and in the Mississippi Valley, the ratio rose to as much as 9 to 1. If the blacks in
these areas had rebelled, they could have easily crushed the white
establishment. Whites knew this far better than blacks, and they
exerted every effort to keep the South a white man's country. American slavery was as much a means of social control as it was a method
of economic exploitation. Any sign of slave resistance, especially organized group resistance, met with hysterical repression.

The pattern became clear as early as 1739, when one Cato led a
group of South Carolina slaves on a rampage of killing and destruction. Reacting immediately, the white community crushed the revolt
and slaughtered every black even remotely associated with the disturbance. In the 1790s a full-scale racial war swept over the island of
Hispaniola in the Caribbean. The leader of the blacks, Toussaint
L'Ouverture, eventually established political control. Frightened
American slaveowners took pains to keep news of the conflict out of
southern newspapers and even out of southern conversation for fear of
inspiring local blacks. But the American tradition of slave rebellion
was extended by Gabriel's Revolt in 1801, the Denmark Vesey Conspiracy in 1822, and particularly by the Nat Turner Insurrection of
1831. It was the last that touched the life of Frederick Douglass.

Turner was a slave in Virginia. He knew how to read, studied the
Bible, and found in it a justification for slaves turning against tyrannical masters. Turner was also a preacher with a considerable following in the black community of his region. In August 1831 he struck. A
force of slaves descended on a series of plantations, knives in hand. In
a short while fifty-seven whites, mostly women and children, lay dead.
Turner hoped his example would provoke a general slave revolt, but
the whites retaliated with a crushing show of force. For a time, any
black in the vicinity of the insurrection was shot on sight. Throughout
the South terrified slaveowners searched for the slightest indication of
insubordination and met it with whips, guns, and rigid codes defining
acceptable behavior. Nat Turner brought the fear latent in the slave
system into the open.

The Turner revolt coincided with and contributed to a gradual hardening of southern attitudes toward slavery. To be sure, the "positive good" argument was well established in 1820 at the time of the Missouri Compromise. But up to the 1830s many Southern whites were at least willing to weigh the advantages and liabilities of the system and to contemplate its eventual elimination. Indeed, before 1830 the American abolitionist movement centered in the South. Of 130 early antislavery societies in the country, 100 were Southern. But after Nat Turner, Southern criticism of slavery gradually stilled. Like Thomas Jefferson, many Southern whites reached the conclusion that slavery might not be desirable, but it was necessary. Others went still further, defending slavery as a positive good.

Economics, particularly the cotton boom, figured in this shift of attitude. So did the multifaceted proslavery argument that drew on sources as diverse as Scripture and physiology. Slaves, it was argued, had the minds of children and needed the protective guidance of masters. The upshot was the collapse of the colonization movement and with it the hope of sending freed slaves back to Africa. This, in turn, killed Southern abolitionism, the whole point of which had been to get blacks out of the South. Also influential in the closing of the Southern mind regarding slavery was the marked increase of Northern criticism of the institution. Self-criticism, they discovered, was one thing; outside denunciation of their life style something quite different and quite intolerable. Furiously, Southerners pointed out that William Lloyd Garrison began publication of his rabidly antislavery newspaper *The Liberator* a few months before the Nat Turner Insurrection. The effect of such external criticism was to silence the internal kind. By the time Frederick Douglass was a teenager, slavery was untouchable, a topic on which objective discussion was impossible in the South. The need for keeping a feared race permanently subordinated transcended all other considerations.

With the specter of Nat Turner seared into the Southern mind, the emergence of Frederick Douglass as a literate, outspoken black with a taste for religion and a talent for leadership aroused instant suspicion. The consequence was a term at Edward Covey's slave-breaking establishment. But in this instance it was Covey who broke, and Douglass left his farm determined to be free. His first attempt to run away, however, proved a dismal and almost disastrous failure. In

1836 Douglass and five fellow slaves laid plans to escape to the North by boat up the Chesapeake Bay. But one of the blacks disclosed the plans to his master. Douglass landed in jail with every expectation of being sold "down the river" to the cotton plantations of the Deep South. But, almost miraculously, he received a reprieve from the Aulds, who recognized that slavery would be considerably safer *without* men of Douglass's spirit and intelligence. Auld arranged for Douglass to return to Baltimore and accumulate money as a hired-out laborer. He would be set free, Auld promised, at the age of twenty-five.

In Baltimore again Douglass's life became entangled in the relationships of Southern whites. The central fact here was that although slaveholders comprised a very small percentage (about 10 percent) of all white southerners, these same slaveholders were an elite which dominated the power structure of the section. They maintained their favored position only by resisting the challenge of the nonslaveholders. Sometimes the clash was direct, as in Virginia where in early 1832 the legislature debated a resolution abolishing slavery in that state. The tidewater planters lined up solidly against the proposal, but the non-slaveholding upcountry farmers were just as solidly for it. The latter believed, with good reason, that their opportunities would be increased by the elimination of the slave oligarchy.

The Virginia vote was surprisingly close, 73 to 58, and slave-owners throughout the South took steps to protect their status. One involved convincing the nonslaveholders that the perpetuation of slavery served their interests too. The technique was to argue, according to Douglass, that "slavery was the only power that could prevent the laboring white man from falling to the level of the slave's poverty and degradation." In other words, without slavery there would be several million blacks competing with whites for jobs and for status in the South. With slavery, even the lowliest Southern white had a social cushion securely beneath him. The planters also made it clear that if a black insurrection came, it would engulf all whites, not just slaveholders. The Southern way of life was at stake, alleged the slaveholders, and they represented themselves as its champions and defenders. These arguments proved effective. By 1836 in Baltimore the hatred of nonslaveholding whites for blacks both slave and free had been honed to a fine edge. When Douglass began work in the city's shipyards, he was met by a team of white workers who beat him unmercifully as fifty of their fellows cheered.

The experience in the shipyards discouraged Douglass about the chances of earning freedom in the South, and once again his thoughts turned to escape. In addition, he had met a free black woman, Anna Murray, whom he wished to marry as a free man. On September 3, 1838, Douglass made his move. From a free black sailor of his acquaintance he borrowed a suit of clothes and a set of "protection" or "free" papers. Thus equipped, he boarded a train for Philadelphia and New York. In the course of the trip he encountered several white men who knew him, but he remained unrecognized. His closest call came just south of the Mason-Dixon line separating Maryland from Pennsylvania and slavery from freedom. In making a routine check, a conductor asked Douglass for his free papers. Comparison of the description of the rightful owner with Douglass's appearance would have revealed the subterfuge immediately, but the conductor only glanced, nodded, and moved on up the car. Frederick Douglass was a free man.

The North to which Frederick Douglass immigrated in 1838 was already fully aware of, and uneasy about, the South he left. The tension generated by the Missouri crisis eighteen years before still lingered. Indeed, the intervening years sharpened sectional consciousness. The election of 1824 found no less than five candidates, each with strong sectional ties, in the running. John C. Calhoun and William H. Crawford represented the South in their distrust of strong central government, high protective tariffs, and manufacturing. Henry Clay and Andrew Jackson drew the largest part of their support from the West and the more commercial Middle Atlantic states. The Northeast backed John Quincy Adams, who ultimately won the election after a widely criticized bargain that made Clay secretary of state.

During Adams's administration, the tariff continued to be a focus of sectional dispute. An analysis of congressional votes shows the South solidly against high tariffs, the Middle Atlantic states just as solidly for them, and New England mixed but shifting toward a protariff stand as its stake in manufacturing increased. The climax came in 1828, when Congress enacted the highest tariff yet in American history. Southerners immediately branded it the Tariff of Abominations. Led by Vice-President Calhoun of South Carolina, they argued that the levy on foreign goods was, in effect, a tax on southern planters for the benefit of northern manufacturers. A high tariff had the effect of raising the price of foreign goods southerners consumed. Many also believed that by reducing the income of European textile manufacturers, the tariff prevented their buying more southern cotton. Moreover, the South saw Congress's power over the tariff as a bad omen for the future of other southern interests, particularly slavery. The extent of the South's displeasure became clear in Calhoun's 1828 essay, "The South Carolina Exposition and Protest." In it he argued that a state which judged the federal government to have exceeded the powers granted under the Constitution of 1787 might nullify a federal act. This was the ultimate in states rights, a political posture that became increasingly important to the South as its consciousness of its minority status in the nation increased.

The first chance to test the doctrine of nullification came in 1832, when Congress passed a new tariff bill unacceptable to the South. Led by Calhoun and Senator Robert Y. Hayne, famous for his debates with Daniel Webster over the nature of the federal union, the South Carolina legislature nullified the law, and Calhoun resigned as Vice-President. In a rage, President Andrew Jackson threatened to hang Calhoun, dispatched a fleet of warships to Charleston, and declared it his intention to lead an overland force against the rebels. For a few anxious months at the beginning of 1833, the fate of the union hung in the balance. But South Carolina's position was weakened by the fact that no other southern state came to its support, and on March 15 the legislature accepted a compromise engineered by Henry Clay. Fortunately, the tariff was an issue susceptible to compromise; one could easily find the middle ground between a duty of 50 percent and one of 30 percent. But there were other issues coming to the fore for which such compromises were impossible. As Frederick Douglass knew so well, a man was either slave or free.

The exhilaration Frederick Douglass initially experienced on reaching New York quickly gave way to frustration and despair. In terms of the position of the black, he found the city in many ways an extension of the South. Slavecatchers, eager to return runaways to their masters, were everywhere. No one could be trusted. For a few dollars some blacks would even betray their brothers. Moreover, the country was in the throes of financial depression following the Panic of 1837, and jobs were scarce. For blacks it was worse. Just as in Baltimore, white laborers made sure that black ones were the last to be hired and the first to be fired. Douglass walked the streets for a few days until his money ran out. Then, in desperation, he turned to David Ruggles, a local black leader. Ruggles sheltered Douglass and arranged for his marriage to Anna Murray, who had arrived from Maryland. He also advised the newlyweds to leave New York for a safer location farther north.

Following Ruggles's suggestion, the Douglasses pushed on to New Bedford, Massachusetts. In this maritime center, the capital of the American whaling industry, Douglass hoped to find a chance to exercise his trade as a skilled caulker of ships. But on applying for a job, he learned that all the white workers in the yards would quit if a black one were hired. Douglass had to eke out a living sawing wood, shoveling coal, and sweeping chimneys. Anna served as a domestic when she was not caring for her two babies. Besides the economic struggle, there were other disturbing facts of northern life. Most of the churches refused to accept blacks as members of the congregation. Public transportation was also segregated. Douglass learned that even if he purchased a first-class train ticket he was obliged to sit in the uncomfortable segregated car, reserved for blacks only. He concluded that northern society, lacking slavery, had been adept at finding alternate means to express its prejudice.

Still, there were reasons to take heart. A passion for reforming man and his institutions flourished in the North at the time Douglass arrived. "In the history of the world," Ralph Waldo Emerson wrote in 1841, "the doctrine of Reform had never such scope as at the present hour." What Emerson had in mind was a series of interrelated ideas centered on the possibility of human betterment. The reformer of the 1830s and 1840s believed that every man was basically good. Strip away handicaps such as ignorance or lack of opportunity, and the innate goodness would shine through. No one was hopeless, no one beyond help. Each individual contained what Emerson and his fellow Transcendentalists termed a "spark of divinity." It followed that the poor, the drunk, the insane, and the black were all susceptible to improvement—perhaps, the most enthusiastic reformers believed, even to perfection. Reform philosophy exuded a confidence stemming at once from the Enlightenment, Romanticism, and the American sense of mission. As a celebration of individual potential, it was entirely consistent with American circumstances and ideals.

The abolition of slavery had a place of special importance in the galaxy of American reform crusades. In the abolitionist mind both the slaveholder and the slave were ripe for improvement. Slavery, they believed, was a sin. Moreover, it was a blot on the American record of championing individual rights and freedoms, an embarrassing anomaly in a nation dedicated to liberty. By denying a person control over his own destiny, slavery went against the grain of the entire New World experience.

Abolitionism as an organized reform movement began among the Quakers in the eighteenth century. At the time of the American Revolution they did not hesitate to point out the contradictions between slavery and the ideals motivating American independence. There was some response: most Northern states declared slavery illegal before 1800. Some went further, and agitated for national emancipation. Pennsylvania's antislavery society had Benjamin Franklin as its president in 1787. In the South, however, abolitionism was considerably less successful. Even blacks did not support it because of the plan for colonizing freed slaves in Africa that was invariably part of southern abolition. Douglass, for instance, declared: "we are *American* citizens, born with natural, inherent and just rights; and . . . the . . . intolerable scheme of the American Colonization Society shall never entice or drive *us* away from our native soil." The more radical white reformers, believing that colonization was a poor substitute for full freedom for all men in the United States, shared this opinion.

The debate over colonization came to a head in Baltimore at the very time Frederick Douglass was enslaved there. He did not know it, but Benjamin Lundy, a New Jersey Quaker, edited an antislavery newspaper entitled *The Genius of Universal Emancipation* in that city. Lundy believed in gradual, compensated emancipation of slaves and their subsequent colonization in Africa. His co-editor, however, disagreed violently. Indeed, violent disagreement was characteristic of William Lloyd Garrison. In sharp contrast to Lundy, he defended immediate, total, and uncompensated emancipation; rejected colonization; and denounced the United States Constitution, which he regarded as proslavery, as "a covenant with death and an agreement with hell." Aggressive to the point of belligerence, convinced he was morally right, and driven by an obsession with becoming famous, Garrison broke with Lundy and went North to enter the abolition business on his own.

In 1831 Garrison launched a weekly antislavery newspaper, *The Liberator*, in Boston. Totally committed, he gave no quarter and asked none. "I *will*," he thundered in the first issue, "be as harsh as truth, and as uncompromising as justice. On this subject, I do not wish to think, or speak, or write with moderation. . . . I am in earnest—I will not equivocate—I will not excuse—I will not retreat a single inch— AND I WILL BE HEARD." Shortly after starting the newspaper, Garrison organized the New England Antislavery Society. Its agents fanned out and organized enthusiastically. They drew encouragement from the news that in 1833 the British abolition movement had borne fruit with the emancipation of slaves in the British West Indies. By the time Douglass came to New England in 1838, about two thousand local societies with a membership of nearly 200,000 existed in the North.

Garrison and Wendell Phillips dominated the movement in New England, Gerritt Smith and the wealthy Tappan family in New York, and Theodore Dwight Weld in the Ohio Valley. Yet abolitionism was not universally popular in the North. Quite probably a majority of northerners saw Garrison and his colleagues as irresponsible fanatics —revolutionaries who would tear the fabric of American political, social, and economic life in their intemperate zeal to end slavery. In 1835 Garrison was mobbed and beaten by his critics. He escaped lightly, however, compared with Elijah Lovejoy, who was killed in an encounter in Illinois two years later.

Frederick Douglass's first contact with abolitionism occurred early in 1839, a few months after his escape, when a copy of *The Liberator* fell into his hands. He had not known about Garrison before, but the position of the newspaper moved him so deeply that despite his poverty he became a regular subscriber. "The paper became my meat and drink," Douglass later wrote. "Its sympathy for my brethren in bonds—its scathing denunciations of slaveholders . . . sent a thrill of joy through my soul." Douglass also joined the local abolition society in New Bedford and, in his words, "took right hold of the cause." By March 1839 he was addressing meetings of New Bedford blacks on the disadvantages of colonization. He also used these occasions to commend Garrison as a man "deserving of our support and confidence."

The first meeting between Douglass and Garrison occurred on August 9, 1841, when the abolitionist leader came to speak in New Bedford. "No face or form," Douglass acknowledged, "ever impressed me with such sentiments." Two days later both men were again together at an antislavery convention on the island of Nantucket. Friends persuaded Douglass to address the gathering, and at last he came forward, hesitant, embarrassed, and so nervous he could hardly stand. As Garrison remembered, Douglass's first words were apologetic. "Slavery," he said, "was a poor school for the human intellect." Then, drawing himself up to his full height of over 6 feet, he began to narrate his experiences as a slave. The audience was transfixed by the simple presentation. At its conclusion, Garrison himself arose to declare that "Patrick Henry . . . never made a speech more eloquent in the cause of liberty, than the one we . . . just listened to from the lips of a hunted fugitive." Capitalizing on the drama of the situation, Garrison next asked the assembly: "Have we been listening to a thing, a piece of property, or to a man?" A thousand voices responded "A man! A man!" Would the audience allow Douglass to be taken back into slavery? "No!" came the roaring response.

In the evening session of the convention Douglass spoke again. By this time Garrison and the other officers of the Massachusetts Antislavery Society were convinced that the young black with the deep voice might be one of the most potent weapons in their arsenal of persuasion. They offered Douglass a job as a lecturer on the antislavery circuit at a salary of $450 a year. But the astonished Douglass accepted only a three-month appointment, convinced that he would be of limited value. As it turned out, he greatly underrated himself. The opportunity opened at Nantucket launched Frederick Douglass on a lifelong career as a liberator of his people.

The life of an antislavery lecturer, particularly a black one, was hardly dull. Many of the audiences Douglass faced were openly hostile and came armed with eggs and rotten vegetables. In 1843 Douglass and his colleagues were occasionally run off the stage and even beaten. It was during this sustained tour that people began to doubt Douglass's assertion that he was really an escaped slave. Sensing this reaction, his fellow abolitionists tried to persuade him to use more of the speech and mannerisms of the plantation. Douglass, they bluntly declared, was supposed to be an exhibit to accompany the presentations of the white speakers. But Douglass refused to hide his talents. In answer, he wrote his autobiographical *Narrative of the Life of Frederick Douglass: An American Slave.* Wendell Phillips advised him to burn the manuscript, since it could well lead to his capture and return to slavery. Douglass, however, published his book in 1845 and watched with pleasure as sales quickly mounted to 30,000 copies. He did heed Phillips's advice to the extent of seeking temporary sanctuary in England, where for two years he enjoyed a huge success as a lecturer on a variety of reform subjects. Douglass returned to his family and country in 1847 with enough money to purchase his freedom. This was duly accomplished with the transmission of $710.96 to the Auld family in Baltimore. For the first time in almost a decade, Douglass emerged from the shadow of reenslavement.

Ambitious and determined after his sojourn abroad, Douglass decided to set his own course within the abolition movement. Late in 1847 he moved to Rochester, New York, and began publication of his own newspaper, *The North Star.* Many white abolitionists objected, but Douglass defended his venture as providing evidence of the black man's capability. Only by such independent participation in American life could blacks foster a sense of pride and self-reliance. His goal, he made clear, was not just freeing slaves, but permitting a life of dignity for all black people throughout the nation. The newspaper, and plans for the education of free blacks whom Douglass sponsored, contributed to this end. *The North Star* also aided Douglass in formulating and expressing his own reform philosophy.

For a decade, he was a Garrisonian. By the late 1840s, however, he had developed doubts about Garrison's rejection of political action as an abolitionist weapon. Garrison burned the Constitution, but in Douglass's opinion that document could be construed as a guarantee of freedom to all Americans regardless of color. The problem was to allow everyone to share the liberties it defined. For this reason Douglass felt political action was needed along with moral persuasion. Garrison stood on the principle of "no union with slaveholders." Douglass felt that southern institutions could be changed through the political process by pressure from the majority of Americans. It was essential, therefore, to extend the vote to all adults.

When Douglass called for extension of the vote, he had women in mind as well as blacks. In his eyes these two social groups occupied a similar relationship to the white, male establishment. They also constituted the majority of the population. Douglass believed that there was strength in unity, and he pressed for civil rights on both fronts. In fact, *The North Star* carried on its masthead the slogan "Right is of no sex—Truth is of no color." In 1848 Douglass proved the sincerity of his belief: he was the only man to take an active part in the Seneca Falls Convention that launched the women's rights movement in the United States.

While Frederick Douglass labored in Rochester on the broad front of reform, the course of national politics once again brought sectional competition into prominence. The catalyst of the renewed tension was westward expansion. Both North and South knew that western resources, commerce, and votes were vital to achieving national dominance. At first, the South had enjoyed a major geographical advantage. The Appalachian Mountains, slanting northeast-southwest across the eastern United States, posed a major barrier to communication and trade between the North and the West. Southerners, on the other hand, were connected to the West by the Mississippi River. Places as widely separated as western Pennsylvania and northern Wisconsin could ship their products down the Mississippi to the port of New Orleans. But in the early nineteenth century the Mississippi was a one-way street. Rivermen took their wooden flatboats down with the current, sold them for lumber, and walked back north along trails such as the Natchez Trace. In 1811, however, the first steamboat on the Mississippi enabled goods to move upstream. Commerce between West and South was possible, and political alliance seemed sure to follow.

The South's early success in the competition for the western trade and vote stirred the North to action. In 1825 New York completed the Erie Canal between Albany on the Hudson River and Buffalo on Lake Erie. This easy route west facilitated communication with the whole Great Lakes watershed. Moreover, the Erie Canal led to an excellent market and manufacturing center—New York City. New Orleans lacked these characteristics. In addition, the South and the West, both producers of raw materials, were not economically compatible. This became increasingly apparent after the opening of the Erie Canal. In

1838, the year Douglass came north, receipts at Buffalo exceeded those at New Orleans for the first time. It was a poor omen for the South. By this time, too, Pennsylvania's Main Line of canals and roads from Philadelphia to Pittsburgh was open for business. But the outcome of the North-South struggle for the West awaited the trans-Appalachian railroads in the 1850s. The systems developed by the New York Central, Pennsylvania, and Baltimore and Ohio Railroads made it impractical to use the Mississippi except for passenger traffic and local trade. A revolution in technology and transportation left the South economically and politically isolated.

Nervous about this situation, Southerners reacted angrily in 1846 when David Wilmot of Pennsylvania rose in the House of Representatives to propose that slavery be prohibited in any part of the territory to be acquired from the Mexican War. President James Polk attempted to soothe the South by suggesting that the land in question was unsuited to slavery for reasons of climate and soil. Cotton, tobacco, and slavery, he argued, had reached the natural limits of their expansion. Southerners were not so sure. In the first place, slave-owners saw no reason why slaves could not be used for tasks other than picking cotton. Black bondsmen like Frederick Douglass had long worked effectively in cities, and their potential as miners, lumber-jacks, and ranchers in the West was apparent. It was conceivable, John C. Calhoun argued, that slavery could become the normal institution for managing all labor in the United States. Furthermore, there was the question of property rights. Calhoun again led the way, a year after Wilmot's suggestion, in arguing that Congress had no authority to limit slavery and thus deprive a citizen of his right to move where he pleased and take his property, slaves included, along. In effect, Calhoun was saying that the Missouri Compromise of 1820 (which prohibited slaves north of 36°30′) was unconstitutional.

The issue of slavery expansion became pressing in 1849, when California applied for admission to the union as a free (nonslave) state. The South objected strenuously, and threatened secession. For a few anxious months at the beginning of 1850, the Union teetered on the brink of dissolution. But Henry Clay, Daniel Webster, and Stephen A. Douglas engineered a compromise in the Unted States Senate. As signed by President Millard Fillmore in September 1850, the series of acts admitted California as a free state, organized the remaining terri-

Frederick Douglass helped raise black soldiers like these for the Union cause in the Civil War. Although the victims of blatant discrimination on the part of their white colleagues, the black regiments distinguished themselves on numerous occasions. By 1865 blacks comprised almost a fifth of all Union troops.

During the Civil War era photography became a major source of historical documentation. This excellent print shows President Abraham Lincoln at the headquarters of the Army of the Potomac, October 4, 1862. Notice how the lanky Lincoln, even without his top hat, towers over his companions.

The enormous physical, social, and intellectual task called "reconstruction" is dramatized in this photograph of Charleston, South Carolina after its surrender on February 18, 1865. The end of the Civil War was less than two months away, but the problem of rebuilding American society was just beginning.

Here former slaves are registering to vote in Macon, Georgia under the supervision of the Union Army. The date is September 1867. Two years later Congress proposed the Fifteenth Amendment (ratified 1870) with the intent of guaranteeing black suffrage. But left to Southern whites, rather than the army, black voting rights quickly became a travesty.

tory acquired from Mexico without restrictions on slavery, abolished the slave trade (but not slavery) in the District of Columbia, and strengthened the procedure for returning fugitive slaves to their masters.

For Frederick Douglass, the most important part of the Compromise of 1850 was the Fugitive Slave Law. Deliberately favorable to the slaveowner, the measure was intended as a sweetener for an otherwise pro-North compromise. It was aimed at stopping the operation of the underground railroad. This shadowy volunteer organization assisted blacks fleeing slavery by passing them from hand to friendly hand until they were safe. In 1838 Frederick Douglass received help of this kind in New York City from David Ruggles. Not really a railroad, the enterprise supposedly received its name from the complaint of a frustrated slaveowner whose failure to trace his fugitives prompted him to remark that once in the free states, slaves vanished as if they had boarded a subterranean train. But the hunters often captured their quarry, and there were countless narrow escapes. A "conductor" on the underground railroad might awaken in the middle of the night to find a frightened fugitive in his yard and the owner's forces in hot pursuit. He then had to hide the slave in an attic or secret stairwell. The following night the slave might be buried under a wagonload of hay and carried to the next "station."

In southern minds such assistance to fugitive slaves was outright stealing—a violation of the natural law respecting the sanctity of property. The Fugitive Slave Law of 1850 reflected this viewpoint. Recapturing escaped slaves became a national rather than a state process. This policy bypassed the personal liberty laws with which many northern states blocked the operation of earlier fugitive slave legislation. The new measure created commissioners who could issue warrants for the arrest of fugitives, and who also served as judges in cases involving runaways. But there was no jury, and the testimony of blacks was not admitted as evidence. Finally, the Fugitive Slave Law provided that any white who aided a fugitive (even by looking the other way as he passed by) was subject to fine and imprisonment, and forced to reimburse the slaveowner for the full value of his lost property.

Attitudes toward the Fugitive Slave Law differed sharply. Southerners and Northern moderates regarded its successful operation as vital to the effectiveness of the Compromise of 1850 and consequently to the existence of peace and union. Extremists spoke openly of secession if the law was not obeyed. "Before God and man," a Raleigh, North Carolina, editorial warned, ". . . if you fail in this simple act of justice, THE BONDS WILL BE DISSOLVED." In antislavery circles, on the other hand, opposition to the law was equally intense. "This filthy enactment," declared the normally mild-mannered Ralph Waldo Emerson, "was made in the nineteenth century, by people who could read and write. I will not obey it, by God!" Frederick Douglass was quick to point out the effect of "this atrocious and shameless law" on free blacks. It subjected them to kidnapping. "The oaths of any two villains," Douglass observed, "were sufficient to consign a free man to slavery for life." Indeed, for several weeks following the passage of the Fugitive Slave Law, Douglass feared for his own safety. Friends posted guard around his house in Rochester. There was no trouble, but nearer to the South a virtual border war ensued.

This tense atmosphere formed the backdrop for the most spectacular of the fugitive slave cases occurring after the Compromise of 1850. On September 11, 1851, a Maryland planter named Edward Gorsuch came to the tiny hamlet of Christiana in southern Pennsylvania where, he heard, several of his fugitive slaves were harbored. The runaways were indeed there, but so were a group of blacks and some white sympathizers determined to prevent their recapture. The inevitable confrontation came at the house of William Parker, the black leader. As the slaves cowered upstairs, Parker met Gorsuch at the door. "My property is in this house. I've come for it," the slave-owner declared. Indignantly, Parker suggested that Gorsuch "go in the room . . . and see if there is anything there belonging to you. There are beds and a bureau, chairs and other things. Then go out to the barn; there you will find a cow and some hogs. See if any of them are yours." It was a case of right versus right; neither side would compromise principles each considered sacred.

At last a mob of blacks charged Gorsuch, knocking him down. When he struggled to his feet, he received a shot in the chest and slumped in the dust—dead. Never before had an owner been a victim in the fugitive slave business, and Parker and his colleagues were suddenly struck by the sure consequences of their action. Before nightfall on September 11 they were enroute to Canada via Frederick

Douglass's house in Rochester. Douglass received the men warmly. "I could not look upon them as murderers," he wrote, "to me, they were heroic defenders of the just rights of man against manstealers and murderers." Acting swiftly before news of the Christiana Riot reached Rochester, Douglass hurried the blacks on a steamboat bound for Toronto. Not until the gangplank lifted did he return home, carrying as a memento from Parker the pistol of Edward Gorsuch.

Although such resistance to the Fugitive Slave Law delighted Douglass, it caused despair among moderates in the North and South alike. They had hoped, desperately, that the Compromise of 1850 would be a final settlement of the sectional differences. But it seemed that the old belligerence had not died. Indeed sectional polarization continued with renewed vigor in the 1850s. Indicative was the reception accorded *Uncle Tom's Cabin,* which appeared in 1852. A searing indictment of the slave system by Harriet Beecher Stowe of Andover, Massachusetts, the novel sold over 1 million copies the first year. Southerners attacked *Uncle Tom's Cabin* as a gross distortion—the product of an oversentimental woman who had no first-hand knowledge of her subject. Many in the North, however, were deeply moved. Frederick Douglass, whose own life testified to the truth of much of what Mrs. Stowe wrote, called her account "a work of marvelous depth and power."

After *Uncle Tom's Cabin* opinion on both sides of the Mason-Dixon line hardened rapidly. Americans were increasingly less willing to discuss their differences, more inclined to fight to uphold their respective conceptions of "right." Once again the question of westward expansion brought the competing moralities into direct confrontation. This time the issue was over the status of slavery in the unorganized territory beyond Missouri. Stephen A. Douglas, a dynamic Senator from Illinois, triggered the controversy in January 1854 when he introduced a bill that made the fate of slavery in the territories of Kansas and Nebraska subject to local self-determination. Douglas's formula, known as popular sovereignty or squatter sovereignty, provided that the majority of residents of a territory, acting through their legislature, could vote slavery in or out before statehood. The Kansas-Nebraska Act, then, repealed the Missouri Compromise and its idea of a demarcation line between slavery and free soil. It made slavery at least a possibility in every part of the unorganized

West. Frederick Douglass called Stephen A. Douglas's plan "perfidious," and many in the North agreed. As Horace Greeley put it, Douglas and President Franklin Pierce "made more abolitionists in a month than Garrison and Phillips had made in a lifetime."

In Kansas itself, the result of popular sovereignty was civil war. Proslavery and antislavery partisans surged into previously uninhabited Kansas, each side set on becoming the determining majority. For two years they fought with ballots, but in 1856 they began to use bullets. Raiding parties from the slave state of Missouri attacked free soil communities in Kansas. The free soilers retaliated with "Beecher's Bibles," rifles collected by New England abolitionists at the suggestion of the Reverend Henry Ward Beecher, the brother of Harriet Beecher Stowe.

At this point the enigmatic figure of John Brown strode onto the Kansas prairie. Frederick Douglass had met him a decade earlier and been immensely impressed. "He was lean, strong, and sinewy," Douglass wrote, "of the best New England mould, built for times of trouble, fitted to grapple with the flintiest hardships." Brown hated slavery with the intensity of a fanatic. He told Douglass that the end of slavery justified any means. What Brown meant became apparent in Kansas. In May 1856, in the company of his sons (he had twenty children) and a few friends, Brown swooped down on the proslave settlements along Pottawatomie Creek. Arousing five settlers from their sleep, Brown proceeded to run them through with a sword in the name of the Lord. Afterward, he mutilated the corpses. Even Douglass called the act "a terrible remedy."

The shock waves emanating from "bleeding" Kansas were felt throughout the nation. Emotion took over, and both factions turned away from democracy in efforts to press their claims. Douglass noted "the display of pistols, bludgeons, and plantation manners in the Congress of the nation." In May 1856 Congressman Preston Brooks of South Carolina entered the Senate chamber and beat Massachusetts Senator Charles Sumner unconscious with a cane. Clearly, the cohesive forces holding the union together were weakening. The process was both reflected in and encouraged by the realignment of national politics. The Whig party succumbed to the slavery issue, and the Democrats split over it. In 1854 a new political coalition based on the principle of resistance to the expansion of slavery entered the lists under the name of the Republican party. By 1856, when Republican Presidential nominee John Frémont ran a strong second to Democrat James Buchanan, it was evident that Republicans and northerners were increasingly one and the same. Slavery expansion had come to symbolize sectional economic and political dominance. But in the final analysis it was the moral dimension of the issue that split the nation. As a rising Republican politician named Abraham Lincoln expressed it in a letter to a Georgian: "You think slavery is right and ought to be extended, while we think it is *wrong* and ought to be restricted. That I suppose is the rub."

The most disturbing event of the 1850s for Frederick Douglass was the Dred Scott decision of 1857. Scott was a slave whose master had taken him into the free soil state of Illinois. Anxious to construct a test case, Scott and his supporters sued for his freedom. When the case reached the Supreme Court, the justices decided to press the case to its ultimate implications for slavery in the United States. By a vote of 6 to 3 the Court sided with Chief Justice Roger Taney of Maryland in holding that as a slave Scott was property and must remain so no matter where his master decided to live. In effect this meant that Congress could not close a territory to slavery. The Missouri Compromise, already repealed by the Kansas-Nebraska Act, was now declared unconstitutional. The Taney Court went on to declare that slaves were not entitled to federal citizenship. Moreover, even free blacks—with the exception of those descended from people who were citizens before 1787—lacked the rights of citizenship.

Taney's majority opinion maintained that Americans had always regarded blacks as "being of an inferior order" with "no rights which any white man was bound to respect." Frederick Douglass, who was barred from citizenship under the Dred Scott decision, was astounded. Taney had cut the bottom out of his campaign to win blacks constitutional rights. On second thought, Douglass realized that the Supreme Court was "not the only power in the world. It is very great, but the Supreme Court of the Almighty is greater. Judge Taney . . . cannot change the essential nature of things—making evil good, and good, evil." Believing that the majority of Americans agreed with him rather than with Taney, Douglass took heart that the Dred Scott verdict might backfire by its very severity. He also knew that after the Taney decision, "the portentous shadow of a stupendous civil war became more and more visible."

In 1858 the trails of John Brown and Frederick Douglass crossed again. With his work in Kansas completed (Kansans rejected the pro-slavery Lecompton Constitution in 1858), Brown came east bent on new assaults against slavery. For several weeks he lived under Douglass's roof in Rochester, and the men discussed Brown's plan for attracting fugitive slaves to forts in the mountains of Virginia and Maryland. Overlooking Brown's record of dishonesty and crime, and a long history of insanity in his family, Douglass approved the idea. But when Brown abandoned guerrilla tactics in favor of capturing the federal arsenal at Harpers Ferry, Virginia, and starting a general slave insurrection, Douglass objected. The plan, he felt, was suicide. Undaunted, Brown persisted. On October 16, 1859, he struck at Harpers Ferry and succeeded in capturing the arsenal. But as Douglass predicted, he was quickly hemmed in by state and federal forces. John Brown's Raid ended October 17, when a force under United States Army Lieutenant-Colonel Robert E. Lee stormed the arsenal. Brown was captured, tried for treason, convicted, and sentenced to death by hanging. Northern pleas for leniency were rejected by a terrified and outraged South, which saw in the raid a threat to the whole fabric of Southern life. According to Virginia's governor, the slave insurrection Brown desired struck at "life, law, property, and civil liberty itself." Such things were sacred. Those who challenged them deserved to die.

In antislavery circles, on the contrary, John Brown became a hero and a martyr. Many Northerners thrilled to his last speech, in which he termed his raid "not wrong, but right" and welcomed the opportunity of mingling his blood with that shed by millions of slaves. Soon after the execution a song appeared to commemorate the event. The second verse of "John Brown's Body" suggested that many in the North associated their cause with God's: "He's gone to be a soldier in the army of the Lord! His soul is marching on." Ralph Waldo Emerson simply said that Brown's gallows had become a cross. Douglass called Brown a "noble old hero" and made no apologies for his violence against slaveholders who "voluntarily placed themselves beyond the laws of justice and honor." He had not joined the raiders, he explained, only because he disagreed with their means.

Just before John Brown's execution the governor of Virginia summed up the cause for the furor, and, incidentally, for the Civil War, in seven words. In speaking of the impossibility of pardoning Brown and of the radical divergence of opinion respecting him, the governor declared: "There is no middle ground of mitigation." The absence of such middle ground greatly increased the probability of war. The nation, in other words, had lost the consensus on fundamental definitions and values that holds a society together.

Soon after the capture of John Brown, Douglass learned that despite his disavowal of the raid, his name was implicated. Knowing he could expect no sympathy from the Buchanan Administration, Douglass hurriedly packed and, once more a fugitive, left for Canada and later for England. On returning in the summer of 1860 he found a tense Presidential campaign underway. The Democrats convened in April in Charleston, South Carolina, but their party was fatally torn. Stephen A. Douglas had the support of northern Democrats with his popular sovereignty formula for settling disputes over slavery. Southern Democrats believed that any restriction of the institution was illegal and the first step toward its abolition. The climax occurred when radical southerner William L. Yancey called on the convention to endorse a plank in the party platform stating that "slavery was right." The reply came from an Ohioan: "Gentlemen of the South, you mistake us—*we will not do it.*" Whereupon Yancey led the southern faction out of the convention hall. They later nominated John C. Breckinridge of Kentucky. Meanwhile, the northern Democrats chose Stephen A. Douglas. The schism virtually assured election of the Republican candidate, Abraham Lincoln.

Frederick Douglass was not happy with the Republican slogan for the 1860 campaign. He wished it read "Death to Slavery" rather than "No More Slave States." But as the election approached, Douglass gave up his efforts on behalf of Gerritt Smith, the candidate of the Radical Abolition party, and took the stump for Lincoln. His victory in November, with no electoral and very few popular votes from the South, Douglass termed a "glorious assertion of freedom and independence on the part of the North." The South was also prepared to assert its independence. South Carolina led the way on December 20, 1860, when a state convention unanimously approved an ordinance proclaiming the dissolution of the union between it and the other

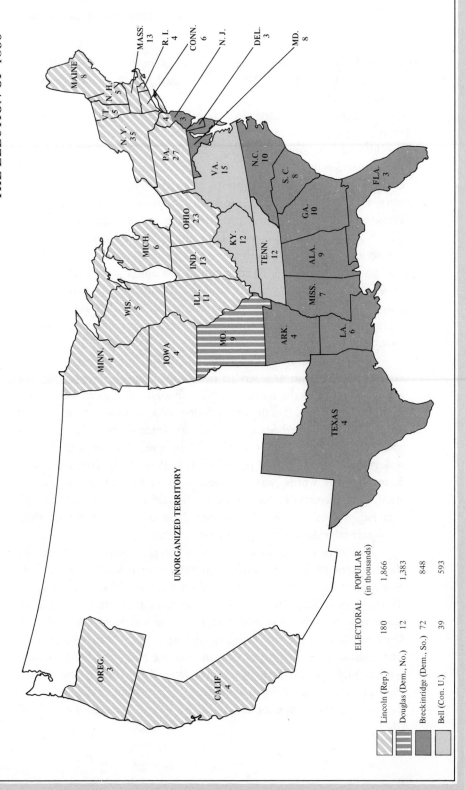

THE ELECTION OF 1860

		ELECTORAL	POPULAR (in thousands)
	Lincoln (Rep.)	180	1,866
	Douglas (Dem., No.)	12	1,383
	Breckinridge (Dem., So.)	72	848
	Bell (Con. U.)	39	593

UNORGANIZED TERRITORY

OREG. 3

CALIF. 4

MINN. 4

WIS. 5

IOWA 4

MO. 9

TEXAS 4

ARK. 4

LA. 6

MISS. 7

ALA. 9

TENN. 12

KY. 12

ILL. 11

IND. 13

MICH. 6

OHIO 23

N.Y. 35

PA. 27

VA. 15

N.C. 10

S.C. 8

GA. 10

FLA. 3

MAINE 8

VT. 5

N.H. 5

MASS. 13

R.I. 4

CONN. 6

N.J. 4

DEL. 3

MD. 8

states. Within six weeks, five other states in the Deep South also seceded, and in February 1861 they formed a new nation: the Confederate States of America.

The lame-duck Buchanan Administration struggled to repair the crumbling nation. Senator John J. Crittenden of Kentucky advanced the idea of a compromise along the lines of the old Missouri and popular sovereignty formulas. Douglass regarded these proposals as evasions, but many in both camps favored them. Eight slave states, after all, had not seceded. Moderate southerners pointed out that President-elect Lincoln had promised not to interfere with slavery where it already existed even if he did oppose its extension to the territories. And in the North there was a widespread feeling that although slavery was bad, the breakup of the union was worse. A wave of anger rose against the abolitionists. Douglass personally experienced mob action. "The talk," he observed, "was that the blood of some abolitionist must be shed to . . . restore peaceful relations between the two sections of the country."

Many Americans in the winter of 1860–1861 simply could not conceive of civil war as a serious possibility. Someone would engineer a solution short of the battlefield, they thought. But there were many in both North and South who nodded in agreement when Lincoln applied to the United States the biblical warning that " 'a house divided against itself cannot stand.' " "I believe," Lincoln added, "this government cannot endure permanently half slave and half free." The issue, in other words, was not the extension of slavery, but slavery itself. And slavery, or more precisely the ethical conflict that the system engendered, was social dynamite. Men do not compromise their fundamental values; they fight to preserve them.

Indicative of the presence of these deeper layers of conflict was the fact that the minor matter of provisioning federally owned Fort Sumter in Charleston harbor touched off the Civil War in early April 1861. "Thank God," Douglass sighed, grateful at last to have the issue come to a head. But the initial stages of the war were disappointing. On the field of battle the disorganized Union forces suffered a humiliating defeat in the first major encounter of the war—the Battle of Bull Run in July 1861. A little over a year later, the Second Battle of Bull Run produced a similar outcome. Confederate commander Robert E. Lee proved vastly superior to any of the several generals with whom

Lincoln experimented. The North fared better in its blockade of the Southern coast and in the Mississippi River theater of operations, but by 1863 the Union had not achieved military advantage in keeping with its marked superiority in numbers, wealth, and industrial capacity.

For people of Frederick Douglass's persuasion, the early stages of the Civil War were also frustrating on ideological grounds. President Lincoln steadfastly refused to define the conflict in terms of slavery. "My paramount object in this struggle," he wrote to *New York Tribune* editor Horace Greeley in 1862, *"is* to save the Union, and is *not* either to save or destroy Slavery." Douglass read these widely publicized words with a sense of profound discouragement. It was reinforced by Lincoln's initial refusal to accept black volunteers for the Union Army and his revival of the old African colonization scheme. The fact was, and Douglass knew it well, that much as Abraham Lincoln disliked slavery, he held no brief for blacks. The product of a self-made yeoman farming background, Lincoln resented the competition free blacks posed. And his prejudice ran deeper. In 1857 Lincoln spoke of the "natural disgust" which "indiscriminate amalgamation of the white and black races" produced in the minds of "nearly all white people." A year later he rejected the idea of political and social equality of the races on the grounds of a "physical difference." Lincoln candidly added that inasmuch as discrimination was necessary, "I am in favor of the race to which I belong having the superior position."

It was to Douglass's credit that he could overlook such expressions of prejudice in an attempt to understand and work with the President. Looking retrospectively at Lincoln's wartime record, Douglass remarked that in the first year of conflict the faith of black Americans in the federal government "was taxed and strained to the uttermost." On "genuine abolition grounds" Lincoln seemed to Douglass to be "tardy, cold, dull, and indifferent." Yet measuring his conduct in terms of the sentiment of the country as a whole, Lincoln appeared "swift, zealous, radical, and determined." The President, Douglass came to see, acted as a barometer, carefully gauging and expressing the public mind. Lincoln knew that to move too quickly against slavery would be to lose support vital to the prosecution of the war. The question of border states like Maryland and Tennessee was particularly delicate. Union, then, provided safer grounds than slavery on which to launch an attack on involuntary black servitude.

Lincoln was a master of practical politics, and his strategy became clearer on September 22, 1862, when he issued a preliminary draft of the Emancipation Proclamation. Carefully timed in the light of the progress of the war, Northern public opinion, and British relations to the Confederacy, the document stated Lincoln's intention on January 1, 1863, to free the slaves in all areas *not* under control of the Union. Douglass realized that this policy did not really free any slaves, but it nonetheless gave freedom higher priority as a war goal.

The Emancipation Proclamation restored Douglass's confidence in Lincoln's and the North's ultimate purposes. "The first of January 1863," he remarked, "was a memorable day in the progress of American liberty and civilization. It was the turning-point in the conflict between freedom and slavery." Shortly thereafter the War Department announced that it would accept black volunteers. Overjoyed, Douglass responded with a whirlwind of activity. Too old to fight personally, he traveled thousands of miles pleading with Northern blacks to enlist. The 54th and 55th Massachusetts regiments, which included two of Douglass's sons, were the result.

But it soon became clear that prejudice extended into the military. Not only were black regiments discriminated against in pay, equipment, and courts martial, they were regularly given preference over white troops for suicidal missions. Word came to Douglass in July 1863, for instance, that the Massachusetts 54th, exhausted from eight days of front-line service and forced marching, was ordered to storm a Confederate stronghold. Although the 54th fought bravely, 42 percent of its men were killed. Furious, Douglass stopped recruiting black soldiers and requested an interview with the President. Lincoln, who knew of Douglass's work, received him warmly, listened to his complaints, and responded, Douglass felt, honestly. Just the existence of black soldiers, Lincoln pointed out, was a gain. The remaining inequities would take time to eradicate. Disappointed as he was at such procrastination when blacks were paying the ultimate tribute to their nation on the field of battle, Douglass still campaigned in Lincoln's successful bid for reelection in 1864.

By this time the tide of war had swung toward the North. The turning point, many felt, came in early July 1863. On the third of that

CAMPAIGNS OF THE CIVIL WAR: 1861-1865

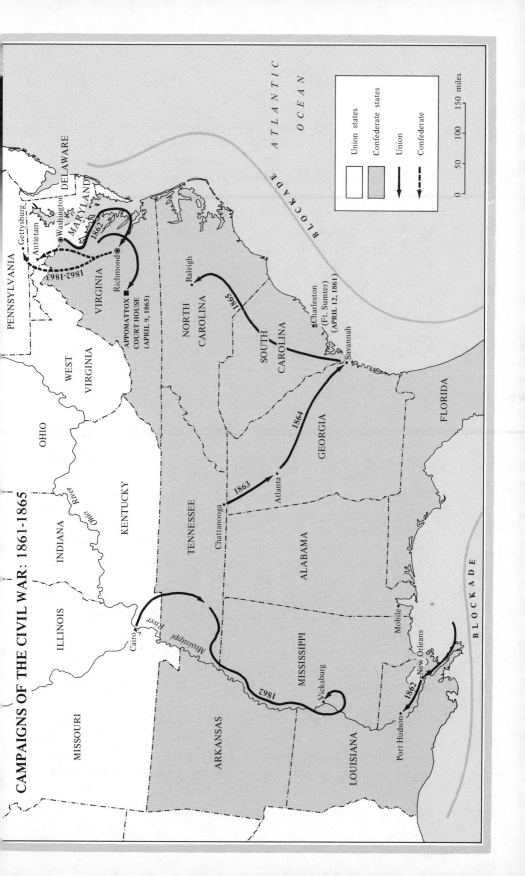

PENNSYLVANIA

DELAWARE

MARYLAND
• Gettysburg
• Antietam
• Washington
1862

WEST VIRGINIA

VIRGINIA
1862-1863
Richmond •
APPOMATTOX
COURT HOUSE
(APRIL 9, 1865)

OHIO

NORTH CAROLINA
Raleigh •

KENTUCKY
Ohio River

TENNESSEE
Chattanooga •
1863

SOUTH CAROLINA
1865
• Charleston
(Ft. Sumter)
(APRIL 12, 1861)
Savannah •

ILLINOIS

INDIANA

MISSOURI

Cairo •
Mississippi River

ARKANSAS

GEORGIA
Atlanta •
1864

ALABAMA

MISSISSIPPI
Vicksburg •
1862

ATLANTIC OCEAN

BLOCKADE

FLORIDA

LOUISIANA
Port Hudson •
New Orleans •
Mobile •
1862

BLOCKADE

Union states

Confederate states

Union

Confederate

0   50   100   150 miles

month at Gettysburg, Pennsylvania, an invading Confederate force under Robert E. Lee was repulsed, after furious fighting, by the army of George G. Meade. The next day, a thousand miles away, Ulysses S. Grant captured Vicksburg, Mississippi, and with it 30,000 Confederate soldiers and control of the Mississippi River. Lincoln then brought Grant east to confront Lee. After a series of bloody encounters, Grant settled in for a siege of the Confederate capital at Richmond. Meanwhile, in the western theater Major General William T. Sherman followed a Union victory at Chattanooga, Tennessee, in November 1863 with a march to the sea that isolated the Deep South. Late in 1864 Sherman turned north toward Grant's force. Caught in the pincers, Lee offered inspired resistance. Outnumbered and under-supplied, he still inflicted staggering losses on the dogged Grant. But in time the physical superiority of the North began to tell. Richmond fell on April 2, 1865. Seven days later Lee surrendered to Grant at Appomattox Court House in Virginia. Four years and over 600,000 American lives had been consumed in the Civil War.

Frederick Douglass received news of the collapse of the rebellion with mixed emotions. Speaking at a celebration in Boston's Faneuil Hall on April 4, 1865, he rejoiced in the fall of the slave power but questioned whether his countrymen, North as well as South, were prepared to accept blacks as citizens in the reconstructed United States. Douglass at first believed the best policy was to let the 4 million freedmen (ex-slaves) alone. "Do nothing with them," he advised white society, "mind your business and let them mind theirs." All black men needed was "simple justice, and an equal chance." Obtaining it, however, was not simple. While the war was still in progress, Lincoln had proposed a plan of reconstruction that restored citizenship to Southerners who pledged loyalty to the Constitution and who supported a Thirteenth Amendment abolishing slavery. When 10 percent of the voters in a state met this requirement, it would be readmitted to the Union. Douglass opposed the plan. Nothing in it guaranteed blacks the right to vote or any of the other privileges of citizenship.

Debate on the merits of Lincoln's plan ended abruptly on April 14, 1865, when John Wilkes Booth, a Southern fanatic, assassinated the President. Douglass hoped the resulting wave of Northern anger would encourage a harder line toward the South, but Vice-President

Andrew Johnson's reconstruction policy was, if anything, more lenient. The new President refused to support black suffrage on the grounds it would cause racial war, and in response to demands for black equality, he suggested African colonization. By the end of 1865 all the Confederate states except Texas were ready to be readmitted under Johnson's plan. Former slaveholders had regained political dominance. Black Codes had been adopted that made it a crime for a black to be unemployed. The ex-slaves, of course, had no work. Once arrested, they were hired to their former masters to pay off their fines. Douglass, who had had personal experience with such a hiring-out arrangement, loudly protested it as thinly disguised slavery. Freedom, it appeared, would make little difference to the Southern black. Abandoning plans to retire at the age of fifty, Douglass resumed his crusade for black dignity.

The attitude of Northern whites was crucial to the success of Douglass's effort. Some, like William Lloyd Garrison, ended their efforts on behalf of blacks when the Thirteenth Amendment was adopted in December 1865. As an abolitionist, Garrison maintained, his work was done. Douglass insisted it was just beginning. Fortunately for Douglass, his viewpoint was shared by the Radical Republicans. These Northern congressmen, led by Thaddeus Stevens of Pennsylvania and Charles Sumner of Massachusetts, favored harsher treatment of the defeated South. Their motives stemmed from political and economic ambitions for their party and section as well as from a humanitarian concern for blacks. They believed, moreover, that Congress, not the President, should control the reconstruction process.

By 1866 a civil war existed in the government. Presidential vetoes and congressional overrides were the weapons. Douglass, by now a national figure, took to the lecture circuit to denounce Johnson as "a traitor to the cause of freedom." The congressional elections of 1866 suggested that many Americans agreed. Emboldened, the Radical Republicans pushed their own plan of reconstruction over Johnson's veto. It rejected all existing state governments in the South and divided the section into five military districts. A guarantee of black citizenship and suffrage (subsequently embodied in the Fourteenth and Fifteenth Amendments) was set as a precondition for readmission to the Union. Douglass applauded this toughened federal policy toward the

South, but he also realized the importance of economic assistance at the grass-roots level. Without the much-discussed "forty acres and a mule," freedmen were destined to descend into the quasi-slavery of tenant farming and sharecropping. In the summer of 1867 Douglass had a chance to help when President Johnson offered him a position as head of the Freedman's Bureau. Although tempted by the power of this federal welfare agency, Douglass did not accept a post that he correctly interpreted as an insincere gesture to ward off political criticism. Praise for Douglass was widespread and lavish. "The greatest black man in the nation," wrote one editor, "did not become a tool of the meanest white." Douglass looked even better when a few months after his refusal a movement to impeach the President came within a single Senate vote of success. But the impeachment trial was only symbolic. Ulysses S. Grant had already won the election of 1868 with the crucial assistance of a half-million black voters. The Republicans' desire for black suffrage was not entirely altruistic.

Radical Reconstruction proved less advantageous for the freedmen than Douglass had hoped. Changing Southern laws was one thing; changing behavior quite another. The military protection was largely on paper. In practice the ex-slaves were victims of systematic repression and terror. Southern whites found ways to minimize the black vote by keeping the site of the polls secret or falsely arresting hundreds of blacks on election day. Plantation owners joined in a resolution not to sell land to any black. When a freedman managed to establish himself as an independent farmer, he was subjected to raids and vandalism. White terrorist groups such as the Pale Faces, the Knights of the White Camellia, and the Ku Klux Klan appeared throughout the South. Nominally these were rifle clubs, but Douglass well knew the nature of their favorite target. Other club activities consisted of burning the schools, churches, and homes of blacks who did not keep their white-defined place. But in truth there was surprisingly little desire among the ex-slaves to challenge the traditional social order. Many of them continued voluntarily in the old ruts of servility. Slavery, it appeared, had left scars on the black personality that were not quickly or easily erased.

By the 1870s Douglass sensed that the nation was tiring of the black problem. For half a century it had been wracked with controversy over race and section. Men of all parties yearned for peace and the chance to settle down to the business of business. Northern investors had a special desire for a final settlement of the sectional animosity. Despite its agricultural past, the South possessed the potential for an urban, industrial economy. If the tense, unsettled atmosphere of military Reconstruction could end, Northern money might combine with Southern managerial talent to build a "New South" of mines, mills, railroads, and cities.

This line of reasoning argued for returning control over Southern affairs to Southern whites. The gradual withdrawal of troops from the South in the early 1870s marked the beginning of this process. It ended in 1877 when the last troops departed after an informal agreement among sectional politicians: Rutherford B. Hayes, the Republican, would be awarded the Presidency in the disputed election of 1876; he in turn would terminate Reconstruction. The treatment of Southern blacks was tacitly understood to be a regional problem rather than a national one. In effect, this meant the end of all black rights except freedom from slavery.

For Frederick Douglass, now old in the service of his people, the postwar abandonment of the black was a bitter pill. The Fourteenth and Fifteenth Amendments still stood, but in practice black Americans were second-class citizens. When the Supreme Court declared the Civil Rights Act of 1875 unconstitutional, Douglass realized the full extent to which the federal government had turned its back on blacks. Now a black man could not even sit as an equal with whites on public conveyances or dine with them at public inns. The era of "Jim Crow" laws began. Douglass angrily attacked the decision as "a further illustration" of a "malignant, vulgar, and pitiless prejudice" in the United States.

Douglass devoted the closing years of his life to the problem of how such prejudice could be overcome. Resuming his old vocation as editor, he launched *The New Era*. Its motto was "Free men, free soil, free speech, a free press, everywhere in the land. The ballot for all, education for all, fair wages for all." Education was especially important in Douglass's eyes despite the fact that he had achieved his personal successes (climaxed by his appointment as minister to Haiti in 1891) without a single day of formal schooling. Reviving a plan he had discussed in the 1850s with Harriet Beecher Stowe, Douglass called for an "industrial college" for blacks. Remarkably well conceived, his plan rested on his conviction that black Americans were not sufficiently prepared to benefit from regular high schools and colleges. Anticipating the philosophy of Booker T. Washington and his Tuskegee Institute (founded in 1881), Douglass declared that his people "needed more to learn how to make a good living than to learn Latin and Greek." On the other hand, Douglass was not prepared to accept vocational education alone. A compromise was possible: blacks should be taught "to use their hands as well as their heads."

The most powerful weapon in Douglass's possession during the 1880s was persistent agitation of the American conscience. The man who had delivered thousands of lectures summoned the energy to give hundreds more. His last talk, at a women's rights meeting, took place just a few hours before his death on February 20, 1895. He also led by example, by simply refusing to accept discrimination when he encountered it in his personal life. On many occasions Douglass deliberately challenged Jim Crow laws and then patiently explained his viewpoint to irate whites. Sometimes he convinced them. On one occasion when he did not, he held on to his seat so tightly that when he was finally ejected, the chair went with him.

In 1884, eighteen months after the death of Anna, Douglass quietly married his secretary, Helen Pitts, a middle-aged, college-trained woman. The fact that she was white raised eyebrows and voices in both the white and black communities. Helen answered them by simply saying, "I was not afraid to marry the man I loved because of his color." Douglass, more philosophical, pointed out that the marriage was in keeping with his teachings of a lifetime. Color, he had always insisted, was an artificial issue raised to degrade and repress blacks. As for intermixing races, Douglass saw nothing unusual about what had been a fact of American life for two and a half centuries. Glancing with a smile at his own bronze skin, he liked to squelch his critics with the observation that his first wife "was the color of my mother, and the second, the color of my father."

SELECTED READINGS

The Person

*DOUGLASS, FREDERICK: *Life and Times of Frederick Douglass.*
Originally published in 1892 and subsequently rewritten several
times. The most convenient edition is that edited in 1962 by Ray-
ford W. Logan.

*ELKINS, STANLEY: *Slavery* (1959). An imaginative but controversial interpreation that Douglass's life does not support.

*FONER, PHILIP: *Frederick Douglass* (1963). A recent biographical
interpretation.

*FONER, PHILIP (ed.): *The Life and Writings of Frederick Douglass*
(4 vols., 1950–1955). The most extensive collection.

*GENOVESE, EUGENE D.: *The Political Economy of Slavery* (1965).
A recent Marxist interpretation.

*McPHERSON, JAMES M.: *The Struggle for Equality: Abolitionists
and the Negro in the Civil War and Reconstruction* (1964).
Social as well as political history.

*MEIER, AUGUST: *Negro Thought in America, 1880–1915* (1963).
An exploration of a forgotten corner of American intellectual
history.

*QUARLES, BENJAMIN: *Frederick Douglass* (1948). A frequently
laudatory early life.

*QUARLES, BENJAMIN (ed.): *Frederick Douglass* (1968). A sam-
pling of Douglass's writings, along with opinions of him by
representative figures of his time and today.

*STAMPP, KENNETH M.: *The Peculiar Institution* (1956). The most
balanced history of slavery in the United States.

The Period

*PHILLIPS, ULRICH B.: *American Negro Slavery* (1918). A controversial early portrayal of the institution in a relatively favorable light.

RANDALL, J. G., and DAVID DONALD: *The Civil War and Reconstruction* (2nd ed., 1961). The best one-volume account.

*WOODWARD, C. VANN: *Origins of the New South, 1877–1913*
(1951). The story of the South's recovery from the Civil War.

* Available in paperback.

CHAPTER SIX

Mark Twain

The young reporter with the slow Missouri drawl stamped the cold
of the high Nevada desert out of his feet as he entered the offices
of the Virginia City Territorial Enterprise. It was early in 1863. The
newspaper's editor, Joseph T. Goodman, looked puzzled at seeing
his Carson City correspondent in the home office, but Sam Clemens
came right to the point. "Joe, I want to sign my articles. I want
to be identified to a wider audience." The editor, already impressed
with his colleague of six months, readily agreed. Then came the

question of a pen name, since few aspiring writers of the time used their legal names. Clemens had something in mind: "I want to sign them 'Mark Twain,' " he declared. "It is an old river term, a leads-man's call, signifying two fathoms—twelve feet. It has a richness about it; it was always a pleasant sound for a pilot to hear on a dark night; it meant safe water."

For Mark Twain, the whole experience of growing up on the Mississippi River had "a richness about it." The flavor of that experience pervaded his best writing and happiest memories. But more and more Twain wrote about a myth. The river, the nation, and Twain himslf changed radically over his lifetime, and much of the old magic rubbed off. One factor was their passage through the searing fire of civil war into an often sordid and ugly Gilded Age of industrialization and urbanization. There was also an experiment with imperialism. By that time the frontier, which had been close to Twain's Missouri boyhood in the 1830s, had retreated to the far corners of the continent. In many ways Mark Twain and America grew up together—and neither aged gracefully. Gradually the sunny humor left Twain's writing; he died in 1910, bitter and pessimistic about his country and his countrymen.

Mark Twain was fond of tracing his ancestry to one Flavius Clemens, a literary character noted for his "want of energy." In reality, his roots ran back to a Gregory Clemens whose excessive energy on behalf of Oliver Cromwell in the English uprisings of the 1640s earned his severed head a place on a pole atop London's Westminster Hall. Gregory's family, however, escaped to the American colonies. Twain's grandfather owned property in Virginia, but his father, in characteristic American fashion, sought fresher fields over the mountains in Kentucky and Tennessee. Wealthy enough to own a few slaves and study law, John Clemens steadfastly pursued the material success that was the surest definition of status in the new society. In 1823 he married Jane Lampton. Twain's mother was descended from a long line of Kentucky pioneers, some of whom followed Daniel Boone through the Cumberland Gap in 1767 and remained to contest the ownership of the rich bluegrass country with bears and Indians.

For twelve years John and Jane Clemens followed a typical frontier pattern. There were children, frequent moves from one small town to another, and always the gnawing hunger for fame and fortune that Jacksonian America easily aroused but only grudgingly satisfied. For a time John Clemens pursued the law. But the mountain people frequently turned to more direct methods of settling their differences, so Clemens added storekeeping to his professions. And, like almost all frontiersmen, Clemens dabbled in land—75,000 acres of it, in fact, which he bought in eastern Tennessee about 1826 for an incredible $400. Even this price was high for the struggling Clemenses, but they fully expected the investment to yield millions. Mark Twain's first memories were of stories of the magical Tennessee land. By virtue of possessing so much land, John Clemens entered the social aristocracy of the Appalachian frontier. He bore the title "Squire" with a relish that seems surprising only to those who would make Jacksonians more democratic than in fact they were. Provided there was equality of opportunity, most Americans had no reservations about accepting the trappings of Old World social differentiation.

Despite their intensity, the hopes of Mark Twain's family for status and wealth were short-lived. In 1834 John and Jane Clemens became victims of the fierce and tangled financial wars of the early nineteenth century. The roots of the nation's financial difficulties ran back to the Panic of 1819, the first great financial dislocation in American history. As in most subsequent economic crises, a combination of optimism and greed that blinded people to the realities of the marketplace was the underlying problem. In this case three years of surging cotton-based prosperity following the conclusion of the War of 1812 pushed the price of prime land up to the unheard of level of $100 per acre. But even at this figure there was no shortage of buyers, because the Bank of the United States issued credit freely. In fact, the amount loaned exceeded by ten times the amount of hard cash in the Bank's possession.

The various state banks were even more irresponsible in their issuance of paper money, and the nation eagerly moved further and further out on the economic limb. It began to crack late in 1818 when a slackening demand for cotton coincided with a major banking failure in England. Inexorably the chain of credit, which extended across the Atlantic, began to tighten. First the Bank of the United States and then the smaller banks began to call in their loans. The paper money on which the boom had fed became virtually worthless scrap. Foreclosures multiplied, and panic gripped the public. There were even soup stations on the streets of major American cities. The depression, which lasted until 1822, was especially severe in the trans-Appalachian West where the Clemenses struggled for success.

Bewildered, afraid, and unwilling to blame their own excessive optimism, Americans turned savagely on banks in general, and particularly on the Bank of the United States. In popular parlance it became "the Monster," a mysterious and sinister presence that dwelled in the East and preyed on the common man of the South and West. Seeking to slay the dragon of paper money and offset the unfair advantage it allegedly gave the rich, political leaders like Thomas Hart "Old Bullion" Benton of Missouri fired the first shots in "the Bank War."

Andrew Jackson, from the Clemenses home state of Tennessee, was in the forefront of the assault. In his unsuccessful 1824 presidential campaign and in his successful 1828 and 1832 campaigns, Jackson made the Bank of the United States a primary issue. He had personally been burned by bankers, and as an old soldier he spared no quarter in his hatred. Jackson particularly distrusted Nicholas Biddle, the suave, wealthy Philadelphian who since 1823 had directed the Bank of the United States.

In point of fact, Biddle was a talented administrator who used the Bank to give some semblance of order to the growing nation's economy. But Jackson and his supporters saw in Biddle only a haughty aristocrat using "the Monster" to suppress men on the make. "The Bank," Jackson declared with typical frontier directness, "is trying to kill me, but I will kill it." An opportunity to do so arose in 1832, when Biddle applied to Congress for an extension of the Bank's charter. Congress approved but Jackson, confident of reelection in the fall, vetoed the bill with unconcealed relish on July 10, 1832. The President followed this act by withdrawing federal funds from the presumably moribund institution and distributing them to numerous state or "pet" banks.

Now it was Biddle's turn to fight. "The worthy President," he acidly remarked, "thinks that because he has scalped Indians, . . . he is to have his way with the Bank. He is mistaken." Choosing his weap-

ons carefully, Biddle called in loans, and just as in 1819 unemployment and business failure swept the nation. Among the hopeful entrepreneurs destroyed in the "Biddle panic" of 1833–1834 was John
Clemens. "In that storm," Mark Twain later wrote, "my Father's
fortunes were wrecked." Jackson, however, held firm. Centralized
banking was not restored, and, by the terms of the Specie Circular
(1836), paper money was rejected as a means of payment for public
lands.

A casualty of the Bank War, John Clemens looked for a new place
to pursue his dreams. His choice meant that Mark Twain would come
in contact with the Mississippi. The Clemenses' decision to go west—
men seeking to improve their position in this period hardly ever considered going east—was made in the spring of 1835. Their destination
was Florida, Missouri, a frontier town at the fork of the Salt River.
Some of Jane Clemens's relatives had settled the town a few years
previously, and in the best booster tradition urged everyone to come
and share a glorious future. Realism suggested that such confidence
was badly misplaced. Florida, Missouri, was in the middle of nowhere
and, in Mark Twain's words, "nearly invisible." It consisted, in fact,
of seventeen log and four frame houses, a long church that doubled as
a school, two stores, and about three hundred people. But 50 miles
down the Salt River lay the Mississippi, an established highway of
empire and potentially one of commerce as well. The first article of
faith in Florida was that the town's proximity to the great river was a
guarantee of prosperity. Dams and locks would make the stream navigable by steamboat. This meant direct water communication with
commercial centers like St. Louis, Cincinnati, and New Orleans. Beyond that entrepôt lay the world, and from the dirt streets of Florida
men's dreams spiraled upward and outward.

It was the same throughout the trans-Appalachian West. Every
village fully expected that the magic of internal improvements would
make it a major city. Navigational aids and canals figured in the first
wave of hope. Florida, Missouri, for example, anticipated transforming the shallow Salt River into an all-season, deep-water highway.
Twain's father headed a navigation company that obtained incorpora-
tion papers from the Missouri legislature. It built a dock and a small
boat—which never sailed. Missouri provided no help in building the
costly locks, and Andrew Jackson, in his 1830 veto of federal aid to

Kentucky's Maysville Road, closed the federal treasury to local improvement projects. But it was a revolutionary new form of transportation, railroads, that struck the final blow at Florida's dreams. Trains could run almost anywhere, at any season, and were less expensive than a canal-lock-dam system. Between 1830 and 1860 railroads came to dominate American transportation, and tiny Florida did not ·become part of the network of rails.

Jane Clemens was pregnant with Mark Twain when she arrived in Florida. He was born November 30, 1835. With five children now dependent on him, John Clemens struggled to make ends meet. He tried storekeeping and practiced law, but economic survival was a battle. One reason was the Specie Circular, which punctured the paper-money prosperity that followed the demise of the Bank of the United States. In 1837 tightening credit and a drop in land sales produced a panic that led to one of the worst depressions in American history. Not until the mid-1840s did the economy turn upward again.

The Clemenses responded to the renewal of hard times by moving once again. This time they went to Hannibal, Missouri, the town identified with Mark Twain's youth, his fondest memories, and his best writing. Hannibal had one distinct advantage over Florida and the Tennessee hamlets. It was directly on the Mississippi, 100 miles north of St. Louis. Mark Twain always remembered it as "a heavenly place for a boy," a "white town drowsing in the sunshine of a summer's morning; . . . the great Mississippi, the majestic, the magnificent Mississippi, rolling its mile-wide tide along, shining in the sun; the dense forest away on the other side." There were unlimited places to roam—woods and field and, if one dared, caves—and there was the river. After several narrow escapes from drowning, Twain mastered swimming. Thereafter there was no containing him. In company with a gang of contemporaries, many of whom made their way directly into *The Adventures of Tom Sawyer* and *The Adventures of Huckleberry Finn,* Twain turned the Mississippi into a giant playground. His days consisted of fishing, swimming, exploring islands, sneaking a ride on a raft or steamboat. School was only a temporary and distasteful interruption.

There was, to be sure, the seamier side of frontier life. The young Mark Twain saw an old man shot down on Hannibal's main street at high noon. He was present when a drunk stabbed an immigrant with a bowie knife and remarked on the way the blood spurted from the wound in powerful jets. Cowering in the bushes, he watched a widow mow down a local ruffian who had designs on her daughter. Fights and whippings were standard fare on the frontier, and Twain never seemed to be far from the center of action. On numerous occasions he stumbled over corpses in his rambles along the river. And there was the fact of slavery.

The Clemenses had owned a few slaves in Tennessee and, as a result of the Compromise of 1820, were able to take them to their new home in Missouri. Like the family's fancy two-horse carriage, slaves were both practical and an indication of status. A black house girl permitted Jane Clemens to at least approach the Southern ideal of ladyhood. A field hand allowed "Squire" Clemens to regard himself as something more than a storekeeper or farmer. Slaveholding, in sum, linked the Clemenses to the great planters whose several hundred slaves actually permitted the life of genteel ease that was the intellectual and emotional lifeblood of the antebellum South. To be sure, these big planters constituted only a small fragment of Southern society. Over half the slaveowners had less than five blacks, which was about the number John Clemens owned in good times. To own more than twenty slaves was exceptional and a mark of high standing. And the really large slaveholders, whose holdings in human property ran to one hundred or more, could have met together in a single hall. Yet it was this elite that dominated the South's economic and political life and set the social standards to which humbler men aspired. Significantly, of the South's total white population on the eve of the Civil War of 8,000,000, less than 400,000 owned slaves. But such was the hold of the planter ideal on the mind and institutions of the South that the tail wagged the dog. A civil war in defense of an institution that only a minority enjoyed was one result.

In time Mark Twain came to understand and despise slavery, but in his youth slaves were an accepted part of life. Jennie, the Clemens house girl, was a second mother to Twain, and the slave children were his playmates. On winter evenings the whole family, black and white, would gather in front of an open fire to hear Uncle Ned, a slave, tell weird and wonderful stories about ghosts, spells, charms, and other manifestations of the supernatural. On at least one occasion a slave saved Mark from drowning. Such human relationships with blacks were the source of Twain's tender account of Huckleberry Finn and the runaway slave Jim on their Mississippi raft. There is little doubt that Huck and, by implication, Mark Twain found more genuine affection and fatherly guidance in black men than he ever did in whites. The busy, cold John Clemens, in particular, was never close to his children. He died when Mark was twelve.

'Still, Twain came to appreciate at an early age the significance of the color line. The boy learned that blacks, unlike other people, could be bought and sold. They were property in a frighteningly absolute sense. For instance, during a trip in 1842 John Clemens wrote the family an account of the difficulties he was experiencing in selling one "Charlie." "The highest price I had offered for him in New Orleans was $50, in Vicksburg $40. After performing the journey to Tennessee, I expect to sell him for whatever he will bring." It was just a livestock transaction.

On another occasion the house girl snatched a whip from the upraised hand of Jane Clemens. This challenge to authority produced an immediate and violent response. John Clemens tied Jennie's wrists and lashed her shoulders with rawhide. Confused and afraid, Mark Twain watched in silence. He also saw a runaway slave cornered and beaten by six whites. He saw a slave killed with a rock for a trifling offense. He was present when a Hannibal mob attacked and almost lynched an abolitionist. The man was spared only through the efforts of a minister who convinced the mob that the intended victim was insane rather than serious. As for slave auctions, the raw nerve end of the institution, Twain's boyhood recollection is hazy. But he did "vividly remember," he later wrote, "seeing a dozen black men and women chained together lying in a group on the pavement, waiting shipment to a Southern slave-market. They had the saddest faces I ever saw."

After his father's death in 1847, Twain abandoned forever his career as a reluctant schoolboy and apprenticed himself to a Hannibal printer. The pay was in the usual form of board and clothes—"more board than clothes, and not much of either," Twain recollected. But the printing job opened Twain's eyes, as it had Benjamin Franklin's, to the larger world. In time Twain wanted to see it for himself. Again like Franklin, he left the printing shop to try his fortune in New York and Philadelphia. The two lives crossed briefly in 1853 when an unknown Twain stood before the grave of the famous Philadelphian. The young man recorded the event, without comment, in a letter home. He was more impressed with the size and pace of urban life. In awed tones the country boy described New York's Crystal Palace Fair, which had 6,000 visitors—double Hannibal's entire population—every day. New York itself contained an incredible 400,000 people and hummed with commercial activity.

It was during his year and a half in the East that Twain first became aware that the slaves who had been an accepted part of his Missouri boyhood were the subject of a national controversy of growing intensity. The newspaper offices in which he worked fairly buzzed with discussion of the Compromise of 1850, especially its Fugitive Slave Law. The efforts of the Free Soil party, organized in 1848, to exclude slaves from the western territories was highly controversial. For the first time Twain encountered widespread, vigorous abolitionism. Harriet Beecher Stowe's *Uncle Tom's Cabin* was the bestselling novel of the day, and the Missourian must have discussed it frequently. In Twain's small-farming upper South, the pictures Stowe painted of huge plantations and brutal overseers did not ring true. But her charges were undoubtedly the basis of a certain amount of harassment of Twain by his northern colleagues in the newspaper offices. On November 28, 1853, for example, Twain wrote to his brother Orion: "How do you like 'free soil'?—I would like amazingly to see a good old-fashioned negro." But the problem refused to disappear. Abolitionists like Stowe and blacks who refused to be "old-fashioned" like Frederick Douglass gave Twain's and the nation's conscience little rest.

Late in 1854, having proved his independence and obtained a not-altogether-pleasing taste of the outside world, Twain returned to his beloved Mississippi Valley. But the slavery controversy followed him West. By the fall of 1854 it was gnawing at the western edge of his home state. Missourians, in fact, played a major role in escalating the Kansas-Nebraska issue into a preview of the Civil War. Intensely proslave "border ruffians" from Twain's state swarmed into neighboring Kansas to vote and, after 1855, to fight the advocates of free soil.

On the great river to the east of "bleeding Kansas," however, the pace of life was still measured. Mark Twain pursued his calling as a printer in several locations and found time to dream of going to South

Western Steamboat, with full cargo.

Engineer on duty : two feet water on lower deck.

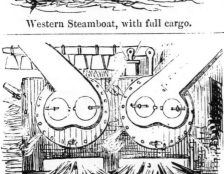

A Hot Boat.—Ten 56lbs. weights on safety-valve.

Pittsburgh on a clear morning.

Running on a Bank.

Going over Falls of Ohio.—[Not exaggerated.]

Harper's Monthly, *a leading American magazine, printed these impressions of travel on the Ohio and Mississippi rivers in its issue of December 1858. Mark Twain was piloting steamboats at this time and undoubtedly witnessed most of the scenes. The "hot boat" resulted from a captain's desire for maximum speed. The inoperative safety valve sometimes produced colossal explosions such as that which killed Twain's brother.*

America and making a fortune on the upper Amazon. But in the spring of 1857 he turned to an even older dream—steamboating. Twain's chance came when a veteran river pilot, Horace Bixby, agreed to take him on as an apprentice or "cub." The next step was to "learn the river" upstream and down, day and night, high water and low. After eighteen months Twain qualified as a pilot. The next two years were unquestionably the happiest of his life. He reveled in the glamour and excitement that came with being a star performer in the golden age of American steamboating. In peak periods there was a solid mile of the big black-stacked, triple-decked boats tied to the wharves of Cincinnati or St. Louis or New Orleans. Piles of produce lined the docks, and the waterfronts seethed with activity. There was power and growth in these scenes, and at least in the 1850s Twain was proud to be a part of them. He also loved the quiet moments when, high in his glass-walled pilothouse, the beauty of the river was overwhelming. He poured the magic of these moments into the best descriptive passages of *Huckleberry Finn*.

For the United States as well as for Mark Twain, the decades immediately preceding the Civil War were, on the whole, a time of confidence. To be sure, the rumblings of the sectional controversy were disturbing, but few before 1860 interpreted them as harbingers of real war. The nation's future appeared bright. The anxious, uncertain years after independence were well behind. The continuing growth of capitalism, combined with the natural abundance of the continent, promised unceasing prosperity. God, nature, and the course of history were on America's side. Reformers would take care of any problems that rapid growth might bring; progress, it appeared, was inevitable. Walt Whitman sensed this at his editor's desk in Brooklyn when he boasted in 1846 that "thirty years from this date, America will be confessed the first nation on earth." And Henry Adams, in his measured manner, recalled that as a young man in Massachusetts he too subscribed to the faith that held the world to be simple, moral, well-ordered, and secure. Mark Twain agreed. His pilot's view of the world bred confidence. Within a quarter of a century all three men would come to hold radically different opinions, but in the halcyon antebellum years there was little reason to question man's goodness or the nation's greatness.

Mark Twain had his first doubts about this idyllic world in June

1858. At the time Twain belonged to the crew of the sleek new *Pennsylvania*, a steamboat sufficiently fast to make the round trip between St. Louis and New Orleans in thirty-five days. Through his connections Mark obtained a clerkship on the *Pennsylvania* for his younger brother, Henry. Then disaster struck. While taking on wood from a flatboat 60 miles below Memphis, the *Pennsylvania*, for no apparent reason, exploded. The entire forward half of the boat blew out and scalding clouds of steam from the ship's boilers enveloped the trapped passengers and crew. By a quirk of fate Mark Twain was not among them. A quarrel with another pilot on the *Pennsylvania* had caused him to hire on a different boat and miss the ill-fated run. But Henry was present and horribly injured. Mark rushed to his bedside only to watch him die.

The personal loss was paramount for Mark Twain, but as he reflected on the explosion of the *Pennsylvania,* he perceived a level of tragedy at once broader and deeper. Technology, which the steamboat symbolized and which constituted so vital a part of the nineteenth-century American idea of progress, had betrayed its worshippers. For a horrible moment the machine had turned on its maker. The lesson was there for those who dared read it: the best condition for man might well be the unmechanized past and not the technological future. Of course, neither Twain nor America gave up on mechanization as a result of incidents like the *Pennsylvania* explosion. They could always be thought of as aberrations, temporary problems that a higher technology would surely solve. On the other hand, there were seeds of a later and deeper disillusionment in Twain's discovery of tragedy on the shining Mississippi.

The second shock to Twain's confidence in his nation was, of course, the Civil War. Few Americans who lived through that cataclysm were unaffected. In the first place, there was the spectacle of the vaunted democratic process shattering completely on the rocks of the slavery controversy. The Compromise of 1850, which many expected to be a final settlement of the sectional differences, proved only a temporary check. Westward expansion kept the old wounds open. Only three years after the compromise, Twain found "free soil" as burning an issue as ever. He also found American statesmen helpless. Franklin Pierce, a Democrat elected President in 1852, displayed an extraordinary lack of leadership during the Kansas-Nebraska controversy. His successor, James Buchanan, also proved adept at side-stepping the main issues. The best politician of the era, Senator Stephen A. Douglas of Illinois, could only devise a formula (popular sovereignty) that shifted the battlefield from the federal to the state and local level. By 1860, when the Republican Abraham Lincoln swept to victory without a single electoral vote from a slave state, it was clear that the national government was more a bone of contention than an agent of cohesion. Yet, in fairness to the politicians of the time, they faced a difficult—perhaps an impossible—problem of governing a house divided.

Mark Twain supported John Bell of Tennessee and his Constitutional Union party in the four-man election of 1860. It was the best of a poor slate for old-line Whigs like the Clemenses. But Bell, with his condemnation of sectional parties and loyalty to the Constitution and the Union, carried only three states, all in the upper South. Missouri, thoroughly divided, gave its nine electoral votes to the Northern Democrat Stephen A. Douglas. After the election Twain watched, only half-believing, as the secession process began. Along with most of his contemporaries, he fully expected that the nation would come to its senses long before it came to blows. Yet another compromiser would appear. But the firing on Fort Sumter, South Carolina, on April 12, 1861, and its surrender two days later ended all illusions. On the Mississippi River men began to take sides. Twain's instructor in piloting, Horace Bixby, went with the North and eventually rose to chief of the Union River Service. Mark Twain cast his lot with the Confederacy. But Twain and his associates were not radical; for a time, they saw validity in both positions. Moreover, the rivermen were in a sense men without a section. Their business was intersectional, and they thought in terms of long-distance trade and communication.

Gradually, however, attitudes hardened. On his last run up the Mississippi in April 1861, Twain heard plenty of war talk and saw men seriously preparing to fight. At Memphis he and a companion were in the pilothouse when a cannon roared on the shore. Ignorant of its meaning, they steamed on. A second blast, this time no warning, sent a ball screaming into the deck immediately in front of the pilots. "Good Lord Almighty!" Twain's friend gasped, "what do they mean by that?" Slowing and turning toward shore, Twain drawled, "I guess they want us to wait a minute." He was correct. After examination, the boat was allowed to pass. But it was the last steamboat to make the journey from New Orelans to St. Louis, for war severed the natural artery of the river. It also ended Twain's career as a riverman.

Undecided about his next step in a society crumbling before his eyes, Twain went home to Hannibal. In this border state the claims of the North and the South hung in the balance for most of the war. Governor Claiborne F. Jackson tried to lead Missouri out of the Union in March 1861, but failed to command the necessary legislative support. Neither was Missouri prepared to side with the Union. When Lincoln asked the state for troops for the Union Army, he was bluntly refused. As a result of this ambivalence, the state began to experience its own civil war as neighbors took up arms against one another. Still, in the beginning it was all very amusing and terribly romantic. Twain recalled how companies of soldiers formed in and around Hannibal without the slightest idea of the nature of their cause or the identity of their enemy. It was a gay military lark, with the bonus of kissing one's girlfriend goodbye before marching off to war. Twain himself went through this ritual after deciding, like Robert E. Lee, that he would defend his state from the Northern invaders. His older brother Orion, however, became a Union sympathizer, Lincoln Republican, and abolitionist.

As a Confederate soldier Mark Twain joined 30,000 other Missourians, but 109,000 men in that state eventually fought for the Union. Missouri as a whole never chose sides, remaining, along with Kentucky, Maryland, and Delaware, a slave state that did not join the Confederacy. Lincoln obviously wanted to preserve this indecision on the part of the border states and took every step, including some clearly illegal ones, to ensure the continuance of their neutrality. His success was a major factor in the outcome of the war.

For the first few weeks Mark Twain's military endeavors were only slightly more sophisticated than the games of war he had played as a child. The major armies had the same experience. Men dashed off to the First Battle of Bull Run, Virginia, in July 1861 in a holiday mood. No one expected the fighting to last more than a few months, but gradually the full meaning of civil war became apparent to Twain and to the nation. First of all there was the hard work of warfare. After the exciting farewells, Twain's band of fifteen self-styled Marion Rangers settled into an uncomfortable camp life from which all traces of grandeur quickly vanished. There were ludicrous blunders—a Ranger shot his horse as it approached him in the dark—and there was the genuine fear of actually encountering the enemy. But what finally soured Twain on the war was his recognition that its essence was organized killing.

He expressed his feelings in a short story centering on the panic murder by the Rangers of an unarmed stranger who innocently rode through their camp one night. The incident was fictitious, but unquestionably Twain felt it was possible, and the thought made him sick. Also distressing were the accounts of warfare in the East. At Bull Run troops only slightly better trained than the Marion Rangers engaged in a wild medley of mistakes that would have been funny if the costs were not calculated in lives. And the slaughter had just begun. Twain, however, had seen enough. He had no personal stake in slavery and did not sympathize with the political and social philosophies he allegedly defended. It was therefore with little regret that Second Lieutenant Twain allowed a sprained ankle to force him out of the war.

Quitting the war with a curse for both belligerents, Twain traveled to Iowa to join Orion Clemens. The disillusioned soldier found his brother in a frenzy of excitement. A friend in the Lincoln Administration had just secured for him an appointment as secretary of the territorial governor of Nevada. Orion, in turn, needed an assistant, and Mark did not hesitate to offer his services. Disgusted with the war that had transformed the happy valley of his youth into a nightmare, Twain was fully prepared to exercise the option he later extended to Huckleberry Finn and "light out for the Territory ahead of the rest." At the same time he intended to catch up to the rapidly retreating American frontier that had been such an important component of antebellum Hannibal's appeal.

On July 26, 1861, the Clemens brothers boarded a sixteen-horse stagecoach of the recently formed Butterfield Overland Mail Company at St. Joseph, Missouri. Nineteen days and 1700 miles later they arrived in Carson City, Nevada. It was a glorious trip, really an escape, for Mark Twain. There were just enough outlaws and Indians to lend excitement without creating serious danger. Twain described his feelings a decade later in *Roughing It*: "even at this day it thrills me through and through to think of the life, the gladness, and the wild sense of freedom that used to make the blood dance in my face on those fine Overland mornings." The stage followed the South Pass route Jim Bridger pioneered a quarter-century earlier and rumbled past Fort Bridger, which the old mountain man still operated. Twain enjoyed a few days of rest in Salt Lake City and later delighted in poking fun at the Mormon residents of that city. But Nevada was his goal, and soon the rejuvenated horses were racing across the Great Basin to the territorial capital on the eastern flanks of the Sierra.

When Mark Twain descended from the hot, dusty stagecoach in August 1861, he entered an extraordinary world. Only two years before Henry T. P. Comstock and several colleagues struck rich veins of gold and silver directly across the Sierra from the California strikes of 1849 that had launched the mining boom. By the time Twain arrived, the frantic heart of the bonanza had shifted from California and Colorado to Nevada. One of the richest single deposits ever found, the Comstock Lode yielded $350 million between 1859 and 1879. To harvest the wealth cities appeared in the wilderness almost overnight. They were raw and violent. Virginia City's first twenty-six graves were those of murdered men. Mark Twain was impressed with the entire spectacle. "The country is fabulously rich," he wrote back home, "in gold, silver, copper, lead . . . thieves, murderers, desperadoes, ladies . . . lawyers, Christians, Indians, Chinamen, Spaniards, gamblers, sharpers, coyotes . . . poets, preachers, and jackass rabbits." The desert environment, of course, was new and shocking for the man from well-watered Missouri. "The birds that fly over the land carry their provisions with them," he remarked with a flash of the wit that was to make him famous.

Twain originally intended to stay in the West a few months; he remained five and a half years. The principal reason was his enchantment with the region. It is apparent in his account of his first visit to Lake Tahoe. With another uprooted middle westerner, Twain hiked from Carson City to the lake soon after his arrival in Nevada. Deep blue and fully 20 miles long, Tahoe sits on the Sierra slope at 6300 feet. The surrounding snow-capped peaks rise several thousand feet higher. Twain was stunned by his first view: "as it lay there with the shadows of the mountains brilliantly photographed upon its surface I thought it must surely be the fairest picture the whole world affords." Twain and his friend had utilitarian reasons for coming to Tahoe. They intended to stake claims to several hundred acres of yellow pine forest on the lake shore. But the beauty and peacefulness of the location sapped their acquisitiveness. Drifting in a borrowed rowboat, much as Twain had drifted on the Mississippi, they joked, and smoked, and counted the massive trout plainly visible in a hundred feet of crystal water. Twain had indeed recaptured the magic of his Missouri boyhood. His happiness was nearly perfect. "Three months of camp life on Lake Tahoe," he wrote in *Roughing It*, "would restore an Egyptian mummy to his pristine vigor, and give him an appetite like an alligator." The only discordant note was a forest fire Twain's campfire ignited, but "conservation" was not yet in the American vocabulary, and the sight of bright flames licking up the hillsides struck Twain as a spectacle worthy of Tahoe's beauty.

While one part of Mark Twain's mind responded to the solitude and natural beauty of Tahoe, another part was infected by the get-rich-quick frenzy that seized western Nevada. In this ambivalence he was representative of American society in the middle decades of the nineteenth century. Here, too, was the frequently contradictory attraction to an older, simpler pastoralism and a future that was complex and increasingly urban. For Twain the call of the civilized sounded with a vengeance just after his return from Tahoe. By early 1862 he was fully engrossed in the silver fever. Racing from strike to strike, frantically laying out claims and abandoning them just as impulsively, he became part of a money-crazed society. Taking it for granted that he would become a millionaire before the year was out, Twain's fertile imagination dwelled on the life style such affluence would permit: "San Francisco . . . , Brown stone front—French plate glass—billiard-room off the dining-room—statuary and paintings—shrubbery and two-acre grass plot—greenhouse—iron dog on the front stoop—gray horses—landau, and a coachman with a bug on his hat!" It was a far cry from Hannibal or Tahoe, and Twain was also capable of bitterly attacking such materialism. But in this indecisiveness he expressed quite accurately the American dilemma about progress.

For Mark Twain as for so many other actors in the drama of bonanza mining, success always remained just out of reach. But after several rounds of near-misses, Twain gave up on precious metals and turned to the pursuit of his real bonanza—writing. This quest took him first, in August 1862, to the *Territorial Enterprise* of Virginia City, Nevada, in the heart of the Comstock Lode. The printer-riverman-secretary-miner with the most successful pen name in literary history fitted perfectly into the staff of the newspaper. All the reporters relied on a brand of irreverent humor that Mark Twain soon made his forte. In Virginia City, where he wrote until 1864, and then in San Francisco, the California mining camps, and, briefly, the Hawaiian Islands, Twain perfected his art. He learned much in these years from contact with Artemus Ward, the dean of American humorists, and Bret Harte, an aspiring local color writer. In 1865 Twain took a giant step toward literary recognition with the publication of "The Celebrated Jumping Frog of Calaveras County." Short, funny, and somewhat sadistic (the story concerned a live frog filled so completely with lead pellets that it could not jump), the tale was carefully constructed and used dialect adroitly. Widely circulated in the East, it put Twain's name before a national audience as a fresh, new talent.

By December 1866 Twain felt his literary apprenticeship was over. He was anxious to return to the "states" and claim the rewards of growing fame. An important factor in his decision to head East was the fact that the Civil War was over at last. Twain's side had lost, an outcome that had seemed improbable at the beginning. The South had had the advantage of being on the defensive. In order to win the Confederacy did not have to invade and defeat the North, but only protect its newly proclaimed sovereignty. On the Union fell the burden of aggression and the necessity of invasion. Like England in 1776, the North faced the task of forcing the rebels back into the fold. This involved fighting on the enemy's home ground and a dangerous extension of lines of communication and supply. (The English effort ultimately foundered on such rocks.) Moreover, the Southerners had the advantage of brilliant military leadership. Most of the officers in the United States Army on the eve of the Civil War were from the South, where traditions of militarism and gentlemanly bearing were closely entwined. Ironically, the federal military academy at West Point, New York, was the training ground for most Confederate officers, among them the talented Robert E. Lee. Also advantageous to the South was its dominance of world cotton production. Most observers initially felt this fact would bring textile producers like England and France hurrying to the aid of their principal supplier.

Beneath this optimistic surface, however, there were problems. "Cotton diplomacy" did not succeed in securing European assistance.

Not only did alternate sources of raw cotton appear, but England in particular was loath to support a society that condoned slavery. Without foreign aid, the South's advantage was gradually eliminated by the North's superiority in money, population, industry, and transportation. An agricultural society simply could not muster the munitions necessary to wage a prolonged war. But an important factor in the Union victory was the internal weakness of the Confederacy itself, which centered on the South's deification of the states rights philosophy, its abhorrence of centralized control. The problem existed on all levels. Confederate President Jefferson Davis, Vice-President Alexander Stephens, the Cabinet, and the Congress attacked each other with a vindictiveness unheard of in most nations, particularly in time of national emergency. This put a premium on the states, which was entirely consistent with Confederate political theory. But the various governors invariably put their own interests ahead of those of the Confederacy. Governor Joseph Brown of Georgia, for example, refused to allow Georgia troops to fight outside the state. Brown also dealt diplomatically with European nations as if Georgia were a sovereign entity. This was a case, it must be understood, of being too loyal, rather than disloyal, to Confederate ideals. The point is that they were poor ideals with which to prosecute a war.

In his brief tenure as second lieutenant of the Marion Rangers, Mark Twain had had ample confirmation that even at the lowest level no Southerner took orders easily. Everyone regarded himself as an officer. Twain's "The Private History of a Campaign That Failed" records the inevitable consequences. The ill-starred regiment's officers begged rather than ordered their soldiers to fight. A majority decision frequently obliged them to change their plans. Such methods of operation did not win many battles. Then, too, there was the question of slavery. For nonslaveholders like most of the Marion Rangers and most Confederate soldiers, the Civil War gradually came to make little sense. Why sacrifice to perpetuate an institution that benefited the planter elite? The war brought the social tension latent in the white South for decades boiling to the surface.

For Mark Twain full recognition of his "de-Southernizing," as a friend described it, came in Virginia City. His early writings for the *Territorial Enterprise* were intensely pro-South. Still associating himself with the old cavalier ideals, he was, in his own words, "the most conceited ass in the Territory." On one occasion he disparaged a dance staged in Carson City as a benefit for the Sanitary Commission (a kind of Red Cross organized by the Union), calling it a scheme to promote miscegenation. Several outraged readers of Twain's column immediately challenged him to duels. Ordinarily a Southern gentleman would have debated only the choice of weapons, but the challenges caused Twain to debate in his own mind the whole rationale of the southern way of life. Always frank, he concluded there wasn't much in it worth dueling about. The easiest way out of his predicament was to run away, and this he did, leaving Nevada for California in 1864. It was not that he was afraid; he simply was no longer committed to the Southern cause. This same lack of commitment among Twain's contemporaries back in the theater of war sapped the vigor of the Southern military effort. Without denying the valor of many Confederate troops in the heat of battle, it is plausible to think that the North did not win the war so much as the South lost it. Mark Twain would certainly have agreed with that analysis.

Whether in Nevada or California, the Civil War had an element of unreality for Twain. A fortnight away from even news dispatches, it was almost as if the battles took place in another country. The First Battle of Bull Run in Virginia, the encounter that shocked Americans into awareness that the war was real, took place in July 1861 when Twain was riding a stagecoach west. In April the following year 23,000 Americans lost their lives in the two-day Battle of Shiloh in Tennessee. It was the most deadly military engagement to that time in North America, but Twain's feverish pursuit of silver left him little time even to notice the event. In September 1862 over 20,000 men died in a single day of fighting along Antietam Creek in western Maryland. Technically Antietam was a draw, but in effect the encounter broke the back of Lee's northern advance and marked a decisive turning point in the general conflict. Twain, meanwhile, was beginning his career with the *Territorial Enterprise*. At Gettysburg, Pennsylvania, in July 1863 a do-or-die Confederate effort resulted in an incredible total loss of 50,000 men, more than a quarter of those participating. For Twain, however, it was a time to write witty newspaper essays such as "All About the Fashions" and "How to Cure a Cold." The war, obviously, was lightly regarded and easily dismissed by the one-time second lieutenant.

When Mark Twain returned to the East early in 1867, he sensed at once that the western sojourn which had spared him a confrontation with the full meaning of the Civil War made him an exception. The bulk of his countrymen knew that the war set them apart from earlier generations. A new mood prevailed. People had been forced to understand that for all America's pretensions to being a model society, a new Eden, the nation was not to be exempt from tragedy and suffering. The optimistic, innocent expectations of progress, even of perfection, that characterized the prewar decades seemed a mockery after four bloody years. Also mocked in the war-caused deaths of 600,000 Americans was the vaunted democratic process. Where was substance for the belief that majority rule was the key to the millennium? The war and the shocking assassination of Abraham Lincoln in its aftermath (April 15, 1865) left men with little choice but to accept the fact that force superseded reason and morality as a prime mover in human affairs. Perhaps, as the English biologist Charles Darwin argued in his 1859 *Origin of Species,* life on earth was best understood in terms of a struggle for existence in which only the fittest survived. Perhaps man was merely a pawn in the hands of forces beyond his control and even beyond his comprehension. Some said the nation grew up in the Civil War years; others felt it began to die. But no one disputed that it became sadder, wiser, and less certain about the future.

Twain could read the new mood in the faces he encountered after his return from California. He also found it in the awkward silence that followed his inquiry about old friends along the Mississippi. "The eight years in America from 1860 to 1868," Twain concluded, "uprooted institutions that were centuries old, changed the politics of a people, transformed the social life of half the country, and wrought so profoundly upon the entire national character that the influence cannot be measured short of two or three generations."

Twain's shock at discovering the Civil War after his lark on the frontier was certainly a factor in his acceptance of an opportunity to leave America once again—this time on one of the first organized pleasure cruises in maritime history. The *Quaker City* left New York June 8, 1867, for the Mediterranean. Twain sailed as a correspondent for the San Francisco *Alta California,* and his reaction to the Old World was thoroughly western. Confident in himself and in his country, Twain scoffed irreverently at the cultural treasures of Europe. Gone from his attitude was the embarrassed provincialism that caused earlier generations of Americans to disparage their native culture and slavishly imitate European social and esthetic taste. Poking fun at the cult of Michelangelo he encountered in Italy, Twain remarked that "the Creator made Italy from designs by Michelangelo." And his impressions on seeing the Czar of Russia were straight from the American frontier; this great personage was merely a man, and "if I chose I could knock him down."

Twain's patriotism is on display constantly in *Innocents Abroad*, the book that appeared in 1869 and described his tour. On one occasion in the Straits of Gibraltar, the *Quaker City* crossed the path of a strange sailing vessel. "She was one towering mass of bellying sail," Twain exulted, but when the ship displayed the American flag, his excitement knew no bounds. "She was beautiful before—she was radiant now." Then Twain philosophized on the meaning of the flag in a foreign locale: "to see it is to see a vision of home itself and its idols, and feel a thrill that would stir a very river of sluggish blood."

As Mark Twain gradually discovered after his return to New York in November 1867, it was easier to love America at a distance than up close. An era Twain later named "the Gilded Age" was already in full swing. As the Missourian began to fathom its ends and means, his disenchantment increased sharply. The vantage point for his initial investigations could not have been better. Before the *Quaker City* landed, Twain accepted a position as private secretary to Senator William M. Stewart of Nevada in Washington. The job was a complete sinecure and allowed Twain plenty of time to explore the quality of national politics and politicians. His notebooks recorded his findings. "Whiskey is taken into the committee rooms in demijohns," Twain reported, "and carried out in demagogues." Government, he discovered, was a business. Everyone was out to enrich himself, and corruption was the standard means. The openness with which bribery, graft, and influence peddling occurred shocked Twain. There seemed no checks on immorality. As Senator Roscoe Conkling of New York put it, "nothing counts except to win." And winning was defined in strictly material terms. Watching the near-impeachment of President Andrew Johnson play its ludicrous course, Twain lost respect for the whole political process. When he wrote "there are some pitiful intellects in this Congress," he likely understated his feelings.

Twain left Washington in disgust in 1868 to pursue a literary life, but the spoilsmen were just warming up. Under Ulysses S. Grant, who was elected President in 1868 and again in 1872, corrupt government flourished. The Civil War hero was not personally involved, but he was one of the most unqualified men ever to hold the office. Totally lacking in judgment in civilian situations, he let his administration become the tool of smarter but less principled men. For Twain, who met Grant early in 1868 and greatly admired him as a soldier, it was particularly painful to see the way the President allowed unscrupulous financial manipulators like Jim Fisk and Jay Gould to enjoy the protection of his friendship. Following close on the heels of Fisk's and Gould's attempts to corner the gold and the stock market in 1869 were scandals involving railroad contractors, whiskey distillers, and Indian traders. The threads of guilt in these cases ran through the House and Senate to the Cabinet and even as far as the Vice-Presidency. Still, in Twain's mind, Grant was untouchable, a rock of integrity in a sea of spoils. Henry Adams, who also observed Washington in the late 1860s, was not as charitable. The succession of Presidents from his great-grandfather to Grant, he thought, was evidence enough to destroy Darwin's argument for evolution. Grant, in Adam's opinion, was a Stone-Age President.

Although the Washington scandals were disturbing, the greatest moral explosion of the postwar decade for Mark Twain and many contemporaries involved a religious rather than a political figure. Henry Ward Beecher was the foremost clergyman of his time. Before the Civil War he had led a host of reform crusades, most prominently that of antislavery. In fact, the guns shipped to Kansas in the 1850s to defend free soil principles were popularly known as "Beecher's Bibles." The minister's sister was none other than the author of *Uncle Tom's Cabin*, Harriet Beecher Stowe. Striking in appearance and a master of eloquent expression, Beecher seemed to be the embodiment of morality and idealism. His writings, sermons, and lectures inspired millions of Americans with confidence that man could transcend base urges and, in the words of Ralph Waldo Emerson, hitch his wagon to a star.

Mark Twain had known and admired Henry Ward Beecher since

Travel in Mark Twain's day could be just as dangerous *as*
on today's freeways. The cause of this 1856 accident *was*
probably a front wheel catching on the logs of the brid*ge*
and snapping off. Twain went to Nevada in 1861 in *a*
larger coach pulled by sixteen hors*es.*

In 1859 Henry Comstock (left) staked the first claim on one of the world's most
concentrated deposits of gold and silver ore. It soon acquired the name Comstock
Lode. At this time wild game (foreground) was still plentiful, but by 1861, when
Twain arrived, miners were obliged to pay grossly inflated prices for provisions.

Virginia City, perched on the sides of a mountain in western Nevada, was Mark Twain's home from 1862 to 1864. The town literally rested on some of the world's richest gold and silver deposits.

On the afternoon of February 15, 1898, one of the United States mightiest battleships, the Maine, floated in the harbor of Havana, Cuba. The following morning it looked like this. An explosion that was never fully explained had sunk the ship and claimed 260 lives. Public furor, goaded by hysterial press coverage, led directly to war with Spain.

1867, when the celebrated clergyman had played a leading role in organizing the *Quaker City* tour. At the last minute Beecher found it impossible to join the cruise, but many members of his congregation did, and at its conclusion he entertained Twain at a dinner party. A brother of Henry Ward Beecher married Twain to Olivia Langdon early in 1870. When the couple settled in the fashionable Nook Farm area near Hartford, Connecticut, they became neighbors and friends of still more Beechers. Then the bomb dropped. In 1871 stories began to circulate in New York linking the Reverend Beecher to Mrs. Elizabeth Tilton in an adulterous relationship. Twain was outraged at what he considered a cruel slander of the magnificent Beecher. But the stories continued and, through the efforts of the militant feminist Victoria Woodhull, even appeared in pirnt.

Twain denounced them. Beecher was vitally important to him and to his time as a bastion of order and decency, an assurance that the nation had not lost its moral compass in a wilderness of material- ism. Gradually, however, Twain's eyes were forced open. Beecher's own sister declared that he was guilty of adultery. And Mrs. Tilton, who with her husband was a member of Beecher's congregation, quietly admitted being a party to the illicit relationship. Beecher even wrote a letter of apology to Mr. Tilton. Unsatisfied, Tilton in 1874 brought an alienation of affections suit against Beecher. The subsequent trial made headlines throughout the nation. Twain was, in the words of a friend, "tremendoulsy worked up" by the Beecher-Tilton affair and even attended a few of the court sessions. The ultimate inability or unwillingness of the jury to pin blame on Beecher was not really a relief. The whole business left a bad taste in Twain's mouth. Had considerations of right and wrong become so obscured or irrelevant that even the nation's foremost religious leader could ignore them? Was force—in this case, lust—more powerful than reason and morality? For Twain, the Beecher-Tilton affair, like the explosion of the *Pennsylvania* and the Civil War, was a shock that cast shadows of doubt over America's future. Antebellum expectations, at any rate, were made to appear innocent, naive, and unfounded.

Early in 1873 Mark Twain struck back at what he called the "moral ulcers" of his age with the best weapon he could muster—a book. The idea for *The Gilded Age* began at a dinner party at which Twain and his guest Charles Dudley Warner accepted a challenge from their wives to write a better novel than the current crop of best-sellers. The coauthors also intended to write a truer novel. The resulting manuscript, completed in three months of intense work, was a searing indictment of the social, economic, and political fabric of American life following the Civil War. Many of its characters and incidents came directly from the lives of Warner and Twain. There were the vote-buying congressman, the pretentious but hollow society ladies, the attractive younger ladies who parlayed their sexual favors into wealth and prominence, and a succession of various confidence men, frauds, and crooks. The protagonist of *The Gilded Age*, Harry Brierly, is a young idealist with plans for internal improvements in a middle western town strongly reminiscent of Twain's native Florida, Missouri. In the course of the novel Brierly learns the price of obtaining an appropriation from Congress. A series of bribes distributed to secure the grant finally leaves no funds to be used for the intended purposes. When he discovers this in the plush office of the bogus Columbia River Slackwater Navigation Company, Brierly's disillusionment and disgust are intense.

While satire like *The Gilded Age* was one outlet for Twain's feelings about the 1870s, the resurrection of earlier and allegedly better times was another. In the years after the Civil War, Twain found his thoughts straying back more and more to antebellum Hannibal and his boyhood on the river. In part this was a form of escape, just as the trip to Nevada had been. Old times on the Mississippi was a pleasant subject to contemplate compared with the "moral ulcers" of postbellum America. Moreover, in Twain's hands, nostalgia produced good literature. *The Adventures of Tom Sawyer*, which appeared in 1876, was the result of happy summer hours recollecting happy summer hours thirty years before. The book was, in large part, pure evocative writing, a thinly disguised autobiography. But just beneath the surface Twain snaps and snarls at the business-minded society in which he lived. *Tom Sawyer* is a paean to irresponsibility. The Franklinesque virtues of discipline, hard work, and material success are deliberately juxtaposed with the happy idleness and nonsense of boyhood on the river. At the root of this juxtaposition are disturbing questions about traditional American definitions of prosperity and progress.

Twain continued his oblique attack on the established national creed in a series of clever essays. In "Advice to Youth" he appeared to agree with Franklin in advising aspiring boys to get up with the birds, provided the birds slept until half-past nine. In "Autobiography of a Damned Fool" Twain parodies Franklin's famous autobiography by showing how the recommended cold swim every morning resulted in stolen clothing and death by exposure. Twain made his point explicit in two essays written about 1875. "The Story of the Bad Little Boy" and "The Story of the Good Little Boy" show that in terms of success, at least, wrong is right. The essays raised questions about ethical criteria as well as about success, and they presaged Huckleberry Finn's "wrong" decision with regard to his black rafting companion, Jim.[1] But at the same time Twain was challenging the validity of American values, most of his countrymen were cheering them. Horatio Alger's 119 books, beginning in 1868 with *Ragged Dick*, almost all dwelt on the theme of rising from rags to riches by dint of hard work, ability, and good luck. Expressing the heart of the American dream, Alger's books sold by the millions. Indeed, by the end of the century he was the only American writer with the same level of public recognition as Mark Twain.

While Twain might question Alger's easy acceptance of Franklinesque virtues, he could not deny that it was the Benjamin Franklins, not the Tom Sawyers, who dominated the nation in the Gilded Age. Awakened in the 1830s by the Jacksonian policy of liberating capitalism, the national economy survived the depressions that dashed John Clemens's hopes and, after 1843, entered a period of extraordinary expansion. The Civil War certainly slowed the economic growth rate, but the war also created opportunities. Moreover, Union victory placed the federal government in the hands of those who believed that the business of America was business. Industrial expansion became a major objective of wartime and postwar politics. With the South eliminated as a factor in national decision-making, there were few obstacles on the way to wealth.

The results of an accelerating economy boggled the mind of a small-town boy like Mark Twain. Between 1860 and 1900 the United States grew from a second-rate industrial power to the world's leader. In fact, the value of American manufactured goods almost equaled the total production of the three former leaders combined. New England

[1] See pages 260–262.

alone produced more goods per capita than any country in the world. The most intense economic surge occurred between 1877 and 1893, when a depression temporarily checked growth. In these sixteen years the national output of copper increased 7 times, crude oil 4 times, and manufacturing as a whole $2\frac{1}{2}$ times. The electric power industry, which did not even exist in 1877, was a 23-million-dollar business by 1893. By that date the United States had no equal in the timber, steel, oil, meatpacking, coal, iron, and telephone industries. American locomotives and American pianos were the best in the world.

The men who made this industrial bonanza possible were systems builders. They possessed the ability and accumulated the resources to order and integrate huge sectors of the American economy. Pragmatic, efficient, and extremely ambitious, they became the winners in the intense, wide-open competition that characterized the heyday of American capitalism. Consider Andrew Carnegie, a man Mark Twain knew and always regarded as the epitome of the self-made captain of industry. "Saint Andrew," Twain called the steel king and, naturally, received the appellation "Saint Mark" in return. Carnegie, like Twain, was born in 1835 in a small village, but the country was Scotland. When he was thirteen Carnegie came to America, settled with his impoverished parents in Pennsylvania, and began work as a bobbin boy in a cotton factory at a salary of $1.20 a *week*. Instead of being discouraged, Carnegie was thrilled at the prospect of being on the capitalistic ladder. In the next ten years he climbed it with astonishing speed. First railroads, then bridges, and finally steel occupied his attention. The huge Homestead steel plant on the Monongahela River near Pittsburgh, Pennsylvania, was started in 1872. By the end of the century the Carnegie Steel Company had emerged the victor in a struggle for existence that initially involved hundreds of competitors. In the course of the battle Carnegie became one of the richest men in America. In 1900 the one-time bobbin boy enjoyed an *income* of $25 million. The following year Carnegie sold his interests to the financier J. P. Morgan, the architect of an even larger conglomerate called United States Steel. The purchase price of the Carnegie Steel Company was nearly half a billion dollars.

Controversial figures in their own time, the verdict is still not in on Andrew Carnegie and his colleagues in industrial empire-building. Mark Twain, for example, could not suppress a sense of awe in the presence of Carnegie and his accomplishments. In an acquisitive age, Carnegie was a god. But Twain could also turn bitterly against acquisition. Once, according to Twain, Americans "desired money"; now they "fall down and worship it." The new gospel, he added, was: "get money. Get it quickly. Get it in abundance. Get it in prodigious abundance. Get it dishonestly if you can, honestly if you must." One of the problems Twain and his contemporaries encountered in evaluating industrialization as personified by a man like Carnegie was that the process involved new techniques of organization that seemed wrong only because they were strange. Early in his rise to prominence, for example, Carnegie discarded the old idea of small-unit competition— the free-for-all that characterized the Jacksonian economic ideal. The need for ordering giant, nationwide industries, Carnegie realized, simply could not be met by small companies. Their size did not permit the economies of scale that were the key to large-scale production. Nor could the small units possibly command sufficient capital to undertake such tasks as building a transcontinental railroad or moving a mountain of iron ore from northern Minnesota to Pittsburgh's refineries.

The new economic units Carnegie envisioned and developed were built around the principles of either vertical or horizontal ordering. In the former, the firm controlled all the steps in producing and marketing its product. Thus the Carnegie Steel Company did everything from mining the ore to producing finished steel. John D. Rockefeller's Standard Oil Company owned not only the wells, but the ships, refineries, distributorships, and even the barrel manufacturing companies necessary to market oil products. Horizontal ordering, on the other hand, meant controlling all the production at a particular stage in the industrial process—all barrel manufacturing in the nation, for instance. Two techniques existed. The *pool* preserved scattered ownership, but instituted corporate management; the *trust* (pioneered by Standard Oil in 1879) actually absorbed the participating units in a supercompany. Both these arrangements, as well as the holding companies that used stock control to accomplish their ends, worked to limit competition in the interest of efficiency and profits.

Many in Mark Twain's generation suspected the new economic combinations of foul play. After 1882, when a vocal critic of Standard Oil named Henry Demarest Lloyd coined it, the label "robber barons" was frequently attached to men like Carnegie, Rockefeller, and Cornelius Vanderbilt. These men undeniably mowed down competitors with ruthless precision, but they also made possible remarkable industrial progress from which the nation as a whole benefited. "Did Vanderbilt keep any of you down," Edward Atkinson asked a group of disgruntled citizens in 1886, "by saving you $2.75 on a barrel of flour, while he was making 14 cents?" Implicit in the statement was the idea that the large capitalists' achievement of greater efficiency should be a cause for national celebration. The defenders of the so-called industrial statesmen also pointed out that only the old, inefficient forms of competition had died. Newer and higher forms still held capitalism together. The market system still worked to punish errors in production and pricing. And competition still existed between *ways* of doing the same thing. The struggle between oil and electricity as a source of energy is a case in point. Mark Twain would learn to his sorrow that real competition also existed between alternative approaches to the mechanization of typesetting in the printing industry. The man who built a better mousetrap still had an advantage.

Although on occasion Twain could be highly critical of the modernization of America by machines and millionaires, a complete understanding of the man as well as his time demands recognition of a concurrent zeal for money and mechanization. In a period of rapid change such as the late nineteenth century it was natural to find aspirations split between the future and the past. Twain demonstrated such ambivalence when he alternated between awe at Lake Tahoe's wild beauty and delight at the prospect of striking it rich on the Comstock Lode. After his entrance into the national literary limelight in the late 1860s, Twain continued shifting back and forth. While idealizing Tom Sawyer's barefoot days on the Mississippi, he maintained and delighted in a grandiose standard of living. Twain's expenditures for the single year 1881 amounted to more than $100,000. The money came from his writing and from lecturing, as well as from his wife's substantial estate. But Twain remained unsatisfied, and his pursuit of success led him into a series of unfortunate investments. Indeed, Twain was so fascinated with the new technology that he became known as an easy mark for inventors interested in raising capital. In the early 1880s he poured thousands of dollars into a steam generator, a steam pulley, a new kind of watch, a device for marine telegraphy, and a new engraving process. There were lesser projects too, such as a hinged pants button, a self-pasting scrapbook, and a mechanical organ.

But Twain's most revealing and most disastrous speculation began innocuously enough when a Hartford jeweler cornered him in his billiard room and peddled $2000 worth of stock in a typesetting machine invented by James W. Paige. Twain paid the money sight unseen. A former printer, he knew the value of a device that could perform the most laborious task in the business. On seeing the typesetter in action, he immediately subscribed an additional $3000. The machine seemed almost human to Twain, a triumph of applied technology. Of Paige he wrote: "he is the Shakespeare of mechanical invention. In all the ages he has no peer." Paige came to Twain for more money, and the writer obliged first with $30,000, then $80,000, and ultimately a total of almost $200,000. Of course Twain expected to realize millions. He envisaged himself a Carnegie of typesetting, a new star in the national industrial constellation. But as with the Nevada mines, success always remained just beyond his grasp. Paige was a perfectionist who tended to overrefine his inventions beyond the point of practicality. While he tinkered and spent Twain's money, simpler devices like the linotype, which Twain spurned when offered an interest, captured the market. Finally, in 1894 the Paige machine was pronounced a failure and abandoned. Twain never realized a penny on his investments; in fact, the machine dragged him into an ignominious bankruptcy that filled his later years with bitterness. Ruefully, he recalled a conversation with Carnegie in 1893. Twain tried to interest the multimillionaire in the Paige typesetter, citing the old maxim about not putting all one's eggs in the same basket. Carnegie regarded him for a moment with his eyes half-closed; then he offered his own maxim: "put all your eggs in one basket—and watch that basket."

In the 1880s, while the Pagie debacle was in the making, Mark Twain wrote two of his most important books. Each contained an unfavorable commentary on progress and a critical assessment of modern America. Twain began *The Adventures of Huckleberry Finn* as a sequel to *The Adventures of Tom Sawyer*. When he started it in 1876, the pages flowed easily from his pen as they usually did when he wrote about his happy boyhood. Brilliantly employing the vernacular style of an untutored boy, Twain described Huck's relationship to St. Petersburg (Hannibal) and introduced him to the runaway slave Jim.

In the next block of chapters Huck and Jim begin drifting down the Mississippi. "You feel mighty free and easy and comfortable on a raft," Huck declares, and the picture Twain describes is indeed idyllic. But then, in Chapter 16, the raft drifts by the mouth of the Ohio River in a fog. The Ohio was to have been Jim's escape route to the North and freedom, but now the Mississippi was carrying him further and further into the heart of the South. At this point in the narrative Huck and Mark Twain faced a dilemma. Jim was a fugitive from justice; Huck, in effect, was stealing him. To continue to protect him on the raft demanded that Huck reject society and its institutions. As a white boy Huck felt the tug of duty, but as an individual he also felt strong affection for Jim, a surrogate father. What should he do? Twain's dilemma was somewhat larger. To have Huck support society and betray Jim involved a judgment on the merits of that society which Twain was not prepared to make. He therefore stopped writing. Before he could make Huck's decision, he had to make his own.

For six years Twain avoided the *Huckleberry Finn* manuscript except for the addition of a few chapters that did not bear on he dominant question of what to do about Jim. He even considered burning the entire manuscript. He continued, however, to gather impressions about his society pertinent to his impending judgment. Then, in 1882, he returned to the river, and took a steamboat over the route he used to pilot. The changes astonished and depressed him. Civilization had caught up to the Mississippi. Fields had replaced the forest Twain knew in his youth; factories dotted the river banks; towns that barely existed in Twain's day now boasted 50,000 people. And money dominated. Even steamboating had deteriorated from a romantic adventure to a crass business. "The world I knew in its blossoming youth," Twain wrote in his account of the 1882 trip, "is old and bowed and melancholy . . . the fire is gone out of its eyes. . . . In Hannibal the steamboatman is no longer a god." Part of the reason for Twain's disappointing reunion with the river was the fact that by 1882 he was no longer young. But neither was his country. Both had passed through a brothers' war and into an age of industrialization. The society he found, at any rate, seemed a far cry from that which he remembered and wrote about in the first half of *Huckleberry Finn*. Instead of the peacefulness and innate decency he associated with the earlier time, he found petty materialism, depravity, and callous inhumanity.

Returning to his studio in Hartford, Twain was ready to make his judgment and complete his novel. The last half of *Huckleberry Finn* is a series of exposures of a squalid civilization. Huck and Jim witness families engaged in bloody, pointless feuds; they see townsmen cheering as a drunk dies in the street; they watch as confidence men brazenly dupe a public which itself is gullible, cowardly, and hypocritical. Huck's verdict is also Twain's: "it was enough to make a body ashamed of the human race . . . I never seen anything so disgusting." Now it was easy to decide what to do about Jim. Huck would not betray him; America wasn't worthy of that decision. In a further gesture of rebellion, Huck heads west to the territories just as Twain had done in 1861. But for Twain in 1884, the year of *Huckleberry Finn's* publication, there was little territory left as an escape avenue. Considerations of debt and family further restricted him. Obliged, as a consequence, to remain and further contemplate the maladies of American civilization, Twain became increasingly bitter in his social criticism.

In *A Connecticut Yankee in King Arthur's Court*, published in 1889, Twain continued his scrutiny of modern America. When he wrote this novel he considered it his literary farewell. Twain opens the tale by transporting a nineteenth-century Yankee from Connecticut, Hank Morgan, back to the sixth-century England of King Arthur. With Yankee ingenuity, Hank proceeds to transform Arthurian England (a place strikingly similar to antebellum Hannibal) into a replica of America in the 1880s, complete with democracy, universal education, and a sophisticated technology. For a while the book conceals its purpose; Twain seems proud of the shining machines and towering edifices that Hank's leadership makes possible. Perhaps progress is beneficent, mankind innately good. But there are hints of a darker perspective. "There are times," Hank admits, "when one would like to hang the whole human race and finish the farce." Yet Hank himself is a large part of the problem. His technological knowhow not only makes schools, mines, factories, and labor-saving devices, but also revolvers, rifles, cannons, and huge bombs. Moreover, Hank's presence splits King Arthur's court into warring factions: the Yankees versus the knights. In the ensuing civil war the new order wins, slavery is abolished, and, Hank feels, society is firmly directed toward progress and prosperity.

Ended at this juncture, *A Connecticut Yankee in King Arthur's Court* might have taken its place among optimistic utopian novels of the time such as Edward Bellamy's *Looking Backward: 2000–1887.* Bellamy confidently predicted an America lifted to unprecedented heights by applied technology. His message captured the enthusiasm of millions of worried Americans. But Mark Twain was writing primarily for himself, and at the very time he wrote his book he was beginning to appreciate how misplaced was his confidence in James Paige (a technological genius comparable to Hank Morgan). So Twain prepared to give his own interpretation of the pursuit of progress. A new war breaks out in Arthurian England. Swarms of human "sheep" attack Hank and his elite corps of fifty-two boys armed with the latest weapons, including dynamite, Gatling guns, and electric fences. Their success in repelling the attack proves ironic. The stench from 25,000 rotting corpses pollutes Hank's stronghold and kills all the victors. Technology has turned against its creators; science is out of control; man's essential baseness has prevailed. In Mark Twain's opinion this was the way the world would end, and nineteenth-century America was on the right track, going full speed ahead.

Twain's involvement in national politics after the Civil War offers another way of tracing his growing disillusion and pessimism. In 1868 and again in 1872 Twain supported Ulysses S. Grant in his successful bids for the Presidency under the Republican banner. He knew Grant personally (later his publishing company produced Grant's memoirs), and he felt the Union hero would be good insurance against the possibility of the South rising again. On the other hand, Twain found much to like in the candidate of the Liberal Republicans and Democrats, *New York Tribune* editor Horace Greeley. Greeley's emphasis on reform, particularly his preference for civil service over patronage as a means of political appointment, appealed to Twain. But although Grant's scandal-marred administrations were hard to swallow, the cult of the General was strong. In 1876, however, Twain was released from his commitment to Grant and free to follow his inclinations to liberalism. This meant an aversion to political bosses, probusiness politics, and mob-supported demagogues.

The election of 1876 pitted Democrat Samuel J. Tilden against

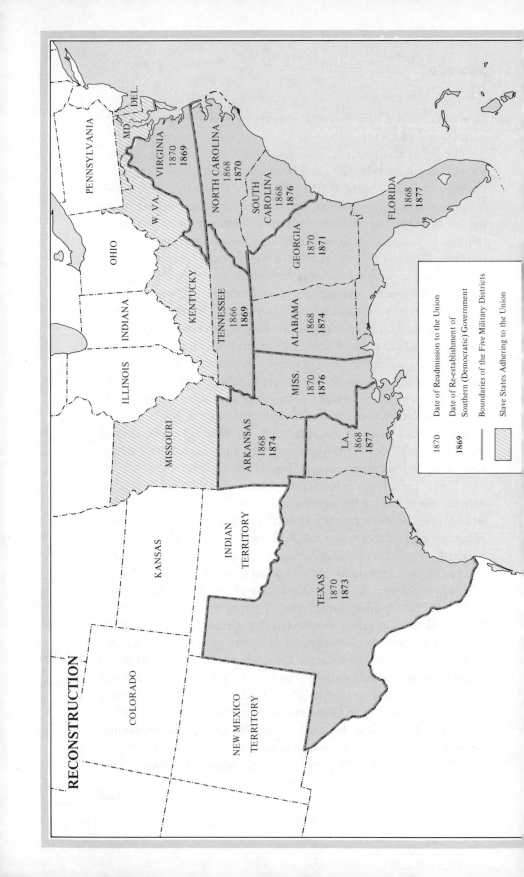

RECONSTRUCTION

PENNSYLVANIA

OHIO

INDIANA

ILLINOIS

MISSOURI

KANSAS

COLORADO

NEW MEXICO
TERRITORY

INDIAN
TERRITORY

MD.

DEL.

W. VA.

VIRGINIA
1870
1869

KENTUCKY

TENNESSEE
1866
1869

NORTH CAROLINA
1868
1870

SOUTH
CAROLINA
1868
1876

GEORGIA
1870
1871

ALABAMA
1868
1874

MISS.
1870
1876

ARKANSAS
1868
1874

LA.
1868
1877

TEXAS
1870
1873

FLORIDA
1868
1877

1870   Date of Readmission to the Union

1869   Date of Re-establishment of
      Southern (Democratic) Government

      Boundaries of the Five Military Districts

      Slave States Adhering to the Union

Republican Rutherford B. Hayes. As governor of New York Tilden had won Twain's admiration by smashing the infamous Tweed Ring of corrupt party hacks. On the financial front, Tilden was a "hard money" man, opposed to the expansion of currency (and consequent inflation) that the issuance of "soft" or paper money encouraged. Hayes, the Republican, was a comparatively unknown Ohio governor, but he enjoyed a reputation for clean politics, and the famous novelist threw his considerable weight behind the Republican ticket.

In the election itself, one of the most extraordinary in American political history, Tilden, in the opinion of most observers then and now, was elected—but Hayes went to the White House. This curious phenomenon came about as the result of Republican tampering with 20 disputed votes in the electoral college. Nineteen of these were from Southern states, where military Reconstruction still ensured Republican control. Accusing the Democrats of intimidating black voters at the polls, Republican negotiators awarded all the votes and the election to Hayes. But the Democratic South exacted its price for allowing "His Fraudulency" to win. By the unwritten Compromise of 1877 Reconstruction ended, and control of the South returned to white Southern Democrats.

Mark Twain's enthusiasm for Hayes did not last long. The Republican party, he discovered, stubbornly resisted permanent reform. Moreover, the Hayes Administration did little about the strikes and unemployment that were byproducts of industrialization. The human misery occasioned by this process troubled Twain deeply. To the consternation of his wealthy, conservative friends, he began openly sympathizing with the more militant labor organizations such as the Knights of Labor and the Greenback Labor party. Twain also worried about the continuing influence in Republican circles of James G. Blaine, "the filthy Blaine" Twain called him, and Roscoe Conkling. Yet in the election of 1880 Twain supported Republican James G. Garfield over Winfield S. Hancock, the Democrat. His decision reflected less admiration for Garfield and more fear that a now solidly Democratic South might revive the old sectional partisanship. Twain joined Republican orators whose evocation of Civil War atrocities to unify the North behind their party was known as "waving the bloody shirt." By stooping so low and even trotting out General Grant for a speaking tour in which Mark Twain also participated, Republican

THE ELECTION OF 1876

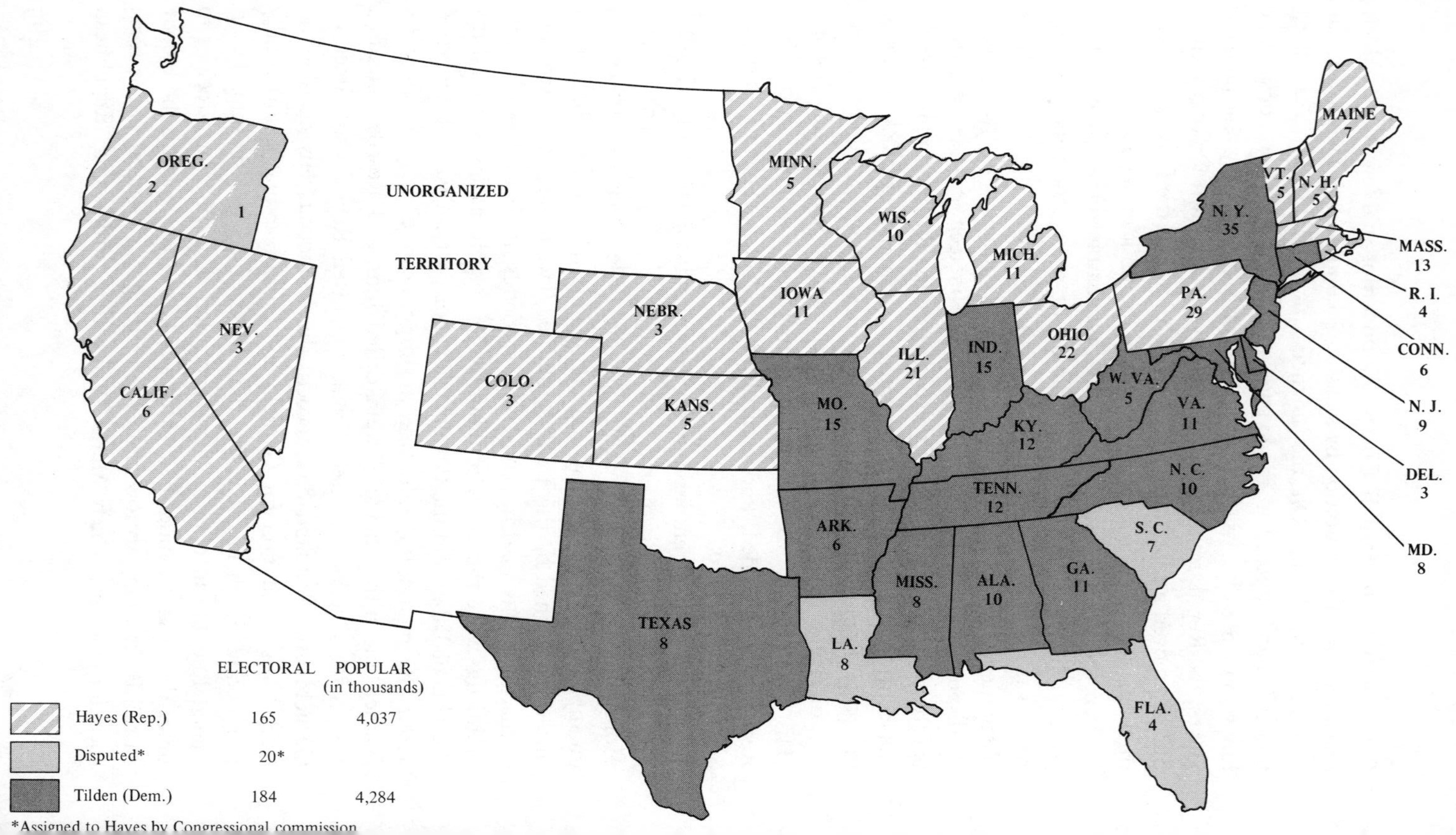

MASS. 13
R.I. 4
CONN. 6
N.J. 9
DEL. 3
MD. 8

MAINE 7
VT. 5
N.H. 5
N.Y. 35
PA. 29
VA. 11
N.C. 10
S.C. 7
FLA. 4
W.VA. 5
OHIO 22
MICH. 11
KY. 12
TENN. 12
GA. 11
ALA. 10
IND. 15
ILL. 21
WIS. 10
MISS. 8
LA. 8
MINN. 5
IOWA 11
MO. 15
ARK. 6
NEBR. 3
KANS. 5
TEXAS 8
COLO. 3

UNORGANIZED
TERRITORY

OREG. 2
NEV. 3
CALIF. 6
1

	ELECTORAL	POPULAR (in thousands)
Hayes (Rep.)	165	4,037
Disputed*	20*	
Tilden (Dem.)	184	4,284

*Assigned to Hayes by Congressional commission

leaders revealed their anxiety. In truth their long hold on the Presidency was nearing its end. Garfield, however, squeezed by Hancock, and the Republicans had four more years in which to prove themselves.

The beginning of the Garfield Administration was not auspicious from Twain's point of view. To his dismay, James G. Blaine became secretary of state. Then Garfield was assassinated on July 2, 1881, and succeeded by Vice-President Chester A. Arthur, a former colleague of Conkling in the domination of New York politics. But there were some encouraging signs. In 1881 the federal government succeeded in breaking Conkling's hold in New York and forcing his resignation from the Senate. Two years later the Pendleton Act created a bipartisan Civil Service Commission and instituted competitive exams for many government jobs. The act initially affected only one-tenth of the total federal work force, but it marked a watershed in the philosophy of government service.

The election of 1884 threw Mark Twain into a quandary, for the Republican nominee was his old nemesis Blaine. Deeply troubled, Twain and his fellow Connecticut intellectuals debated the question of party loyalty. Many bowed to the judgment of the smoke-filled rooms, but Twain remained true to his conscience. Throughout the fall of 1884 he tried to persuade Republicans to rise above orthodoxy and support the Democrat, Grover Cleveland. In this cause, which acquired the label "Mugwump," Twain joined such well-known reformers as George William Curtis, E. L. Godkin, Carl Schurz, and Charles Francis Adams.

The Blaine-Cleveland campaign was one of the bitterest ever seen in the United States, with the political smear reaching a new level of sophistication. Blaine's transgressions over the past decade received a full airing, and the Republicans countered with charges that the Democrats were the party of "Rum, Romanism, and Rebellion," a ploy that backfired in many quarters of American society. But the major issue in the campaign involved the Republican charge that Cleveland had fathered an illegitimate child. When the Democratic nominee humbly acknowledged that as a young bachelor he and a consenting widow had indeed had an offspring but added that he had cared for the mother and child ever since, public sympathy swung to his side.

Mark Twain was disgusted at the self-righteousness of Cleveland's detractors. They knew full well, Twain pointed out, "what the bachelor's other alternative was and . . . seem to prefer that to the widow." Then, in a statement suggestive of his growing misanthropy, Twain philosophized: "*isn't* human nature the most consummate sham and lie that was ever invented? Isn't man a creature to be ashamed of in pretty much all his aspects? Is he really fit for anything but to be stood up on a street corner as a convenience for dogs?"

Having campaigned hard for Cleveland, Twain watched his ensuing administration with great interest. Increasingly bitter at the hold of big business on American life, he applauded the passage in 1887 of the Interstate Commerce Act, which prohibited unreasonable, secret, and discriminatory railroad rates and practices. The act also created the Interstate Commerce Commission, the first federal agency authorized to regulate American private enterprise. But intention was one matter, practice quite another. As Twain watched in disgust, America's railroad magnates, aided by a sympathetic Supreme Court and a lukewarm President, systematically evaded the spirit and the letter of the Interstate Commerce Act.

A similar fate befell the Sherman Antitrust Act, passed in 1890 under President Benjamin Harrison, a Republican who spoiled Cleveland's bid for reelection. The Sherman Act grew out of the fear that trusts and other business conglomerates were conspiring to restrict competition and fleece the public. But once again a conservative judiciary was unwilling to apply what few teeth the act possessed. In fact, in a classic distortion of purpose, the antitrust legislation was turned against the emerging labor unions as a consequence of the Supreme Court decision in *United States* v. *Debs* (1894). Like the Interstate Commerce Act, the Sherman Act proved effective mainly as a deterrent to really meaningful reform.

From Mark Twain's perspective, the United States in the 1890s was a nation run by and for a wealthy, conservative elite. Benjamin Harrison's administration regularly favored the rich and powerful at the expense of farmers, laborers, small businessmen, and intellectuals like Twain. Monetary policy was a case in point. The Sherman Silver Purchase Act of 1890 did little to improve on the Bland-Allison Act passed twelve years previously. Neither really increased the amount of circulating currency or promoted inflation as critics of business had hoped. But when it came to the tariff, Congress and the President were quick to pass the highly protectionist (probusiness) McKinley Tariff of 1890.

Grover Cleveland was a personal friend of Mark Twain and entertained him frequently in the White House during his first administration. When Cleveland was elected to another term in 1892, Twain was pleased. He could not help noticing, however, that Cleveland's political and economic philosophy was strongly conservative and really differed little from that of the Republicans. Both camps were friendly to propertied interests and largely deaf to the demands of working people in the nation's farms and factories. Supporting Cleveland in this stance was a complex body of ideas about the nature of success in American history. In the first place, it was defined almost exclusively in material terms. The rich were generally conceded to be the top rung in American society. Second, success was believed possible for anyone possessing the requisite talent and determination. As Horatio Alger and Andrew Carnegie demonstrated in their separate ways, humble origin was not a handicap. This meant, in theory, that anyone could climb the magic ladder. But Mark Twain knew the facts. Even the most talented and energetic were often suppressed by the system. Yet insofar as Twain's contemporaries *believed* in the success myth, they proved willing to accept the prevailing social and economic framework. Rather than reform or abolish the free enterprise system, they hoped to become its beneficiary by trying a little harder. The elegant mansion of a Vanderbilt or a Morgan was an object of envy and aspiration rather than a hated symbol of injustice and oppression. The bona fide rags-to-riches success of a few, like Franklin or Carnegie, proved a narcotic for millions.

The rich in Mark Twain's America resisted reform by parading the philosophy of Social Darwinism and its conception of progress as something that stemmed from competition in which the unfit were weeded from the fit. A corollary of this was the idea that the government and the courts should let free enterprise alone. Only in this way could the scythe of competition do its beneficial work. To aid the unfit, according to this perspective, was to impede evolution—to sustain dinosaurs and other losers in the natural selection sweepstakes. But the major bulwark of the propertied elite was the old Protestant idea that worldly success was both a sign of God's favor and a way of glorifying God. It followed that the rich man could claim to be the beneficiary of divine selection too. As John D. Rockefeller said, "the good Lord gave me my money." Twain's old acquaintance Henry Ward Beecher added, "God has intended the great to be great and the little to be little." But the Reverend William Lawrence put it best when he wrote in 1901: "godliness is in league with riches." Implied was the idea that men with superior character were rewarded with success; poverty was the product of sinfulness, a kind of punishment meted out by an angry God. Russell Conwell, one of the few rivals to Mark Twain as a lecturer in the late nineteenth century, argued in his stock speech, "Acres of Diamonds," that "ninety-eight out of one hundred of the rich men of America are honest. That is why they are rich."

Twain was not fully convinced. The entire gospel of wealth, including the argument that through his philanthropy a rich man performed his obligation to society, seemed to him much like the confidence games he wrote about in the second half of *Huckleberry Finn*. In company with Henry George, whose *Progress and Poverty* appeared in 1879, Twain understood that a self-made man was as improbable as a self-laid egg. The success of individuals was the product of the growth of the whole American economy. Moreover, Twain recognized that while big business was applauding itself, the nation's morality and institutions were becoming so threadbare that they were unable "to protect the body from winter, disease, and death." A partial reckoning would come in the Progressive years, but like Huck Finn, Mark Twain had seen enough. The failure of the Paige typesetter and Twain's consequent backruptcy in 1894 were the last straws in his disenchantment with the cult of success.

Another shadow over Twain's last years was his country's entrance into the contest for international power and prestige called imperialism. Before the 1890s the nation had not been active in this endeavor. Mexico, to be sure, had been pushed out of the path of westward expansion in the 1840s, and in 1867 the United States made one of the best real estate deals in history by purchasing Alaska from Russia. But for the most part the development of the West and the economic colonization of the defeated South kept the imperialist urge in check. By the 1890s, however, a growing nation was pushing at its geographic boundaries. The frontier had vanished, and American appetites, whetted by 250 years of expansion, sought new morsels across the seas. For those requiring philosophic justification there was Josiah Strong's *Our Country* (1885), with its vindication of a "divinely-commissioned" America assuming the role of its "brother's keeper." Strong also employed Social Darwinism, arguing that in the worldwide competition of races it was either eat or be eaten. Naval power advocate Alfred T. Mahan agreed completely.

One of the first opportunities for American expansion was the Hawaiian Islands. Since Twain had visited the area in 1865, a surge of sugar production had made Hawaii a primary target of American business and American empire-building. In 1893, under heavy pressure from President Harrison and Secretary of State Blaine, Queen Liliuokalani capitulated. Republicans hoped for quick annexation of the islands, but Cleveland's return to the White House delayed it for five years. The Democrats, however, displayed their own brand of imperialism in 1895, when Secretary of State Richard Olney revived the Monroe Doctrine of 1823 to assert America's virtual sovereignty in Latin America. The immediate target of Olney's warning was Great Britain, and many restless Americans hoped for a chance to back the secretary's words with bullets. Theodore Roosevelt, then president of the New York police commissioners, confessed: "I rather hope that the fight will come soon. . . . This country needs a war."

Roosevelt got his wish in 1898. Mark Twain was on a round-the-world debt-paying lecture tour when the fever of the new Manifest Destiny infected the nation and produced a war with Spain. The immediate cause was American disapproval of Spain's conduct in a war with its colony, Cuba. Dispassionate analysis indicates that atrocities occurred on both sides, but sensation-hungry American newspapers cast Spain in the villain's role. When the United States battleship *Maine* blew up in the harbor of Havana, Cuba, on February 15, 1898, with the loss of 260 lives, a declaration of war was only a matter of time. It came on April 25, and in four months the most popular war in American history was over. First Commodore George Dewey captured the Philippine Islands and broke Spain's naval power in the Pacific. Then a badly disorganized American force, which included Theodore Roosevelt and his Rough Rider colleagues, managed to defeat an even more mismanaged Spanish army defending Cuba. But the imperialists saw only stars and stripes. As Secretary of State John Hay said, it was "a splendid little war." Roosevelt simply called it "bully." Only 379

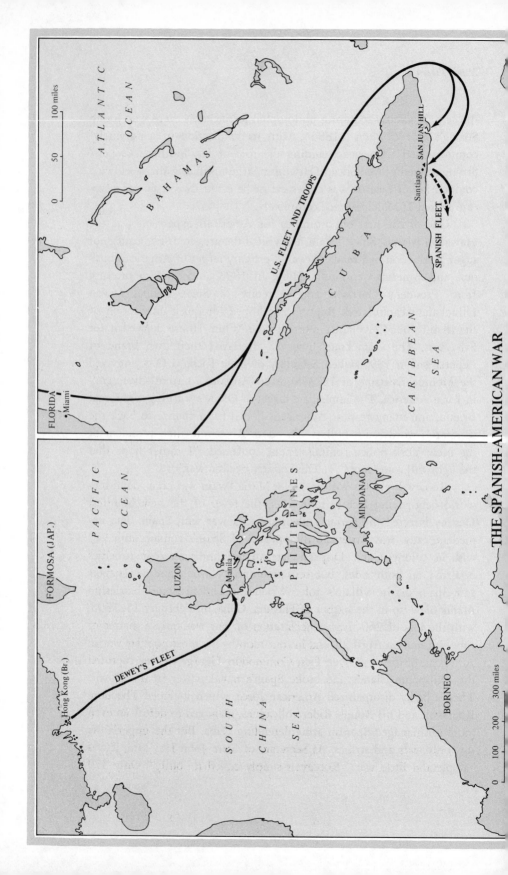

THE SPANISH-AMERICAN WAR

Americans died in combat, although disease, chiefly malaria, claimed more than 5000. Still is seemed a small price for assuaging the anxieties that accompanied America's entrance into national middle age.

By the terms of the Teller Amendment to the declaration of war with Spain, the United States forswore annexation of Cuba. But Guam, Puerto Rico, and the Philippines, all formerly Spanish, were a different matter. American hunger for empire led President William McKinley to support outright acquisition of these islands. The Philippines became the center of attention. Business interests, desirous of Pacific trade, and religious leaders trumpeting an "imperialism of righteousness" backed the administration. With money and God both on his side, McKinley rationalized that "duty determines destiny" and moved to annex the archipelago. The task proved considerably more difficult than defeating the Spanish. Philippine native leaders like Emilio Aguinaldo, whom the United States had supported in a mutual effort against Spain, resisted strenuously. They expected the United States to grant freedom and independence to the islands at the conclusion of the war. When it appeared that McKinley intended to substitute one foreign regime for another, the natives grew restless. For most of 1899 fighting raged on the islands. Thereafter Aguinaldo took his remaining forces to the hills in guerrilla resistance. Mop-up operations by American forces continued until 1902, when the Philippines were declared pacified.

Back in the United States, meanwhile, a groundswell of opposition rose against imperialism and particularly against McKinley's policy in the Philippines. A substantial portion of the American people wanted no part of a colonial empire on both idealistic and practical grounds. Even before the peace treaty with Spain was signed in December 1898, an Anti-Imperialism League was organized and attracted such diverse figures of national importance as Grover Cleveland, Andrew Carnegie, labor leader Samuel Gompers, Charles Eliot, the president of Harvard, and Mark Twain. Twain disliked imperialism from the beginning because he saw through the hypocrisy of its pious pretensions to the underlying considerations of power, profit, and the national ego. His views were contained in a letter written late in 1899. According to Twain, the departing nineteenth century might be seen as bequeathing to the approaching twentieth a Christian civilization "bedraggled, besmirched, and dishonored from pirate raids" throughout the world. "Her soul," Twain bitterly continued, is "full of meanness, her pockets full of boodle, and her mouth full of pious hypocrisies. Give her soap and towel, but hide the looking-glass."

It was soon apparent that Mark Twain was just sharpening his satirical guns against imperialism. His essay "To the Person Sitting in Darkness" in the *North American Review* for February 1901 was a devastating critique of the American foreign missions that carried civilization and the Gospel to allegedly backward peoples. The missions did their job, Twain explained, at the point of a bayonet. Those who really needed enlightenment, he continued, were the missionaries themselves. In another essay Twain reviewed the whole history of American involvement in the Philippines. Of the $20 million given Spain for the islands by the treaty ending the war, he observed, "we bought some islands from a party which did not own them." Of Aguinaldo he wrote, "we went back on an honored guest of the Stars and Stripes when we had no further use for him and chased him to the mountains." Then the nation which began the era of colonial revolutions systematically crushed the natives by destroying their villages, burning their fields, and exiling their leaders. The remaining 10 million were subjugated, according to Twain, by "Benevolent Assimilation, which is the pious new name of the musket."

Twain's essays on imperialism elicited a storm of public opinion. While some of his countrymen praised him for his frankness, others called him a traitor and worse. For these people, questioning imperialism was, in effect, doubting the whole value of America and its progress over the past century. Yet this was precisely Mark Twain's purpose.

By 1900 few could deny that America was greatly changed from what it was at the time of Mark Twain's birth sixty-five years before. Of course, human history is not static; change is the only constant. But the latter part of the nineteenth century brought a rate and scope of change unprecedented in the American experience. Any one of a number of indexes is revealing. Population, for instance, zoomed from about 15 million in 1835 to 75 million at the end of the century. Steel, which was not even produced in the United States until Twain was twenty, was being manufactured at the rate of 26 million tons annually by 1900. Coal surged from a production of 14 million tons when Twain was twenty-five to 257 million when he was sixty-five. Railroad mileage jumped from 30,000 miles on the eve of the Civil War to 193,000 at the century's end.

It is possible to find a spectrum of responses to the changes these figures suggest. At one extreme is the school of thought that applauded the differences. Growth, according to this perspective, was good, and America's progress unquestioned. Those problems that were acknowledged at all were attributed to un-American influences like the immigrants. As for America itself, the cheerleading philosophy could find nothing wrong with God's chosen people. The second broad category of response to a changing America was a free admission that progress had brought some serious problems. Unlike the cheerleaders, holders of this viewpoint did not hesitate to place responsibility on Americans themselves instead of on a scapegoat like the immigrant. But they did not despair in their criticism. Optimistically, they sought means whereby the nation could enjoy the blessings of growth without the blight. With the proper controls and reforms, the high promises of American life could be realized. This school of opinion was constructively critical and forward-looking in its reform endeavors.

On the pessimistic side of the turn-of-the-century spectrum of opinion were destructive critics or backward-looking reformers. Their point of view was that life had been better in the good old days before urbanization and industrialization. Growth brought only problems. Indeed, true progress consisted of restoring the values and institutions of the past. America could still reform, but only if it renounced the technological future toward which it appeared to be heading. Finally, directly opposite the affirming cheerleaders were those who rejected America completely. Reform, either of the forward- or backward-looking variety, was hopeless. The nation was moribund. Total collapse was only a matter of time and would be a blessing.

In his lifetime Mark Twain ranged the full gamut of these attitudes. As a young writer in Europe he cheered the American flag with the zeal of the most ardent imperialist. He devoted a large share of time and energy to the pursuit of material success. He was captivated by machines and their potential for progress. But Twain could also idealize the simple, pastoral America of his own boyhood and viciously attack the Gilded Age. By 1894, when he published *Pudd'n-head Wilson*, Twain was prepared to take the final step into despair.

"Whoever has lived long enough to find out what life is," Twain wrote in a *Pudd'nhead Wilson* chapter heading, "knows what a deep debt of gratitude we owe to Adam, the first great benefactor of our race. He brought death into the world." Most of the book is in a similar vein. In commenting on the anniversary of Columbus's discovery of America, Twain declared: "it was wonderful to find America but it would have been more wonderful to miss it." Only twenty-seven years before, Twain had stood with the crowd at the rail of the *Quaker City* and cheered wildly as a passing ship displayed the American flag. The mood of the two passages could not be more disparate nor the destruction of the American dream more complete. But Twain's misanthropy transcended the United States. In his later years he toyed with the prospect of shutting off the earth's oxygen supply for two minutes and enjoyed contemplating the course of history if Noah had missed the Ark.

It remained for *The Mysterious Stranger* (written about 1905 and published posthumously in 1916) to summarize the matured and final version of Twain's desperation. The setting is once again a town beside a river, but now the locale is Austria, the time the sixteenth century. In the course of the novel a mysterious stranger conducts a young boy (the Austrian equivalent of Tom Sawyer or Huck Finn) on a tour of the chamber of horrors that was and is human civilization. The revelations of cruelty, sadism, and suffering leave the boy with nothing but shame and contempt for his race. He realizes that the ideals of his childhood are naive dreams and that the only hope for men is early death or insanity. Civilization, Christianity, and material progress have left depravity and desolation in their wake. Progress is a myth. The future is revealed to be only a continuation of the errors of the past, but now multiplied by technology. The torture rack and wheel are replaced by bombs that kill thousands. Man's life is as meaningless, Twain decided, as that of the miniature race the mysterious stranger eliminated with the comment that "man is a museum of diseases, a home of impurities; he comes to-day and is gone to-morrow; he begins as dirt and departs as stench." Finally, at the end of *The Mysterious Stranger* the boy is told: "There is no God, no universe, no human race, no earthly life, no heaven, no hell. It is all a dream—a grotesque dream. Nothing exists but you. And you are but a *thought*—a vagrant thought, a useless thought, a homeless thought, wandering forlorn among the empty eternities!"

The dead, Twain concluded, were lucky. In 1910 he joined their ranks. He would no doubt have been astonished at the eulogies written in his honor, essays in which he was portrayed as America's happy humorist and an important source of national pride. The popular image of him is still that of a Tom Sawyer or a cracker-barrel story-teller. Yet perhaps Twain would not have been surprised at all at this distortion of the truth; for him it would have been just one more instance of the gullibility of what he called "the damned human race."

SELECTED READINGS

The Person

BENSON, IVAN: *Mark Twain's Western Years* (1966). The best history of Twain between 1861 and 1866.

*BROOKS, VAN WYCK: *The Ordeal of Mark Twain* (1920). The dark, pessimistic side of Twain's later life.

*DE VOTO, BERNARD: *Mark Twain's America* (1932). A rebuttal of the Brooks interpretation (see above).

LYNN, KENNETH S.: *Mark Twain and Southwestern Humor* (1959). Valuable for its insights into the relationship between Twain's life and his writings.

PAINE, ALBERT BIGELOW: *Mark Twain: A Biography* (4 vols., 1912). A detailed but laudatory account.

*SMITH, HENRY NASH: *Mark Twain: The Development of a Writer* (1962). A study of Twain's literary craftsmanship.

TWAIN, MARK: *Mark Twain's Autobiography* (2 vols., 1924). Part of *The Complete Works of Mark Twain*, the autobiography is neither complete nor entirely accurate.

The Period

*CALLOW, ALEXANDER B., JR.: *The Tweed Ring* (1966). An examination of the classic political machine of the Gilded Age in its New York City setting.

*CASH, W. J.: *The Mind of the South* (1941). Important for its insights into the Southern character and tradition.

*LAFEBER, WALTER: *The New Empire: An Interpretation of American Expansion, 1860–1898* (1963). The background to the controversy over American imperialism.

MCKELVEY, BLAKE: *The Urbanization of America, 1860–1915* (1963). A discussion of one of the main forces of change in Twain's America.

* Available in paperback.

*PAUL, RODMAN W.: *Mining Frontiers of the Far West, 1848–1880* (1963). The authoritative account of bonanza mining.
*PRATT, JULIUS: *Expansionists of 1898* (1964). An interpretation of the Spanish-American War.

* Available in paperback.

CHAPTER SEVEN

Jane Addams

Without knowing why, Jane Addams opened her eyes. It was pitch-black in her bedroom, and at first she heard nothing more than the muted night noises of the Chicago streets surrounding Hull House. Then she saw what had disturbed her sleep. A burglar had pried open the second-story window and was rifling her bureau drawers. Jane spoke quietly: "don't make a noise." The man whirled around, then prepared to leap out the window. "You'll be hurt if you go that way," Jane calmly observed. A conversation ensued in

the darkness. Addams learned that the intruder was not a
professional thief, but simply a desperate man who could find no
employment that winter of 1890 and had turned to crime to survive.
Hull House had been founded the previous fall as a social
"settlement" to serve just such people. It testified to Jane Addams's
belief that only unfavorable circumstances stood between the innate
dignity and worth of every individual and their realization.
Moreover, Jane believed that as a well-to-do, cultivated lady she
had a special responsibility for alleviating the social ills accompanying
the nation's growth. So she was in earnest when she promised her
unexpected visitor that if he would come back the next morning,
she would try to help. The burglar agreed, walked down the main
stairs, and left by the front door. At 9 A.M. he returned to learn that
Jane Addams had found him a job.

In contrast to most of those she helped in Chicago's slums, Jane Addams was a fifth-generation American. Her mother's roots ran back to a German immigrant who arrived in Philadelphia in 1727. John Huy Addams, her father, traced his ancestry to an Englishman who in 1681 received a grant of 500 choice Pennsylvania acres from William Penn himself. John Addams also had an eye for good land, and in 1844, at the age of twenty-two, he moved with his bride to northern Illinois. The region was barely settled, and the Addamses found an excellent location on Cedar Creek in the rural hamlet of Cedarville. A mill, a bank, a shrewdness about the value of land, and an unbending morality soon lifted John Addams to a position of prominence in the financial, political, and cultural life of his community. In 1847 he helped start the first subscription library, a sure sign that the area was no longer pioneer territory. Seven years later Addams went to the Illinois state senate. At the time, he was a Whig in politics, but by the mid-1850s he had grown unhappy with this affiliation. The Whig party was torn with dissension. Northern or "conscience" Whigs like Addams wanted nothing to do with Southern Whigs and their pro-slavery dogma. More and more they found themselves aligned with abolitionists, Free Soilers (the party had been organized in 1848), and some Northern Democrats on a platform emphasizing opposition to the expansion of slavery. In 1854 in Ripon, Wisconsin, men of this persuasion founded the Republican party.

The following year John Addams helped extend Republicanism to Illinois. Leadership of the new party had fallen to a Springfield lawyer-politician named Abraham Lincoln. Addams knew Lincoln well, and treasured the letters beginning "My dear Doubled-D'ed Addams." But others in the state rallied around Democrat Stephen A. Douglas. The 1858 debates between Lincoln and Douglas, rival candidates for the United States Senate, were a high point in antebellum Illinois politics. At Freeport, the nearest large town to the Addams home, Douglas asserted his belief in popular sovereignty with respect to slavery. This so-called Freeport doctrine held that each community could effectively, if not legally after the Supreme Court's Dred Scott decision, prevent slavery by refusing to pass the local codes supporting the institution. Conversely, a locality could enact the rules that made slavery feasible. Lincoln and Addams, on the other hand, believed slavery was a wrong that transcended local jurisdiction, that its extension, at least, should not be tolerated, and that Americans had a moral responsibility to face and solve the slave problem. It was precisely this kind of driving conscience that led Jane Addams to attack the social evils of a later era.

Jane Addams's birth in Cedarville September 6, 1860, came at one of the tensest periods of American history. The dissolution of the national Whig organization followed by the divorce of Northern and Southern Democrats had cleared the way for the election to the Presidency of a clearly sectional candidate. In November Lincoln was elected with virtually no support from the South. Five months later the nation plunged into civil war. John Addams did his part by recruiting and financing a company of Union soldiers, the Addams Guard, and Jane's girlhood was filled with stories of men risking their lives in the service of what they believed to be right. In later years she remembered standing on a thick dictionary and the family Bible to reach the plaque, crowned by an eagle, on which the names of the Guard were inscribed. She also recalled carefully putting the dictionary over the Bible so as not to profane that book with her feet!

The death of Mrs. Addams when Jane was a baby increased the influence of her father in her life to the point of an obsession. Her affection for him was, by her own admission, "doglike," and she lived constantly in the shadow of the ideals of conscience, integrity, and charity he set before her. Feelings of inadequacy quite understandably plagued Jane's early years. Her autobiography contains a characterization of herself as an "ugly, pigeon-toed little girl, whose crooked back obliged her to walk with her head held very much upon one side" and who lived in constant fear of being recognized as the child of her handsome, respected father.

Next to her father, the greatest influence on Jane's youth was Abraham Lincoln. Although only four at the time of his assassination in 1865, she distinctly recalled the American flags draped in black, the strange hush, and the tears of her father. Later she asserted that the memory, even the name, of Lincoln is "like a fresh breeze from off the prairie." He was the man who "cleared the title to our democracy" and confirmed the fact that democratic government was "the most valuable contribution America has made to the moral life of the world." For Jane Addams, Lincoln always remained "the greatest American." Many in her generation agreed.

After an indifferent education in the village school at Cedarville, Jane Addams, aged seventeen, contemplated college. The fact that such an option even existed for her testified to the emerging recognition of women's rights in the United States. But the movement was neither old nor well supported in the 1870s. Jane Addams and her contemporaries were expected to be demure and genteel—the custodians of morals and esthetics who freed men to concentrate on politics, power, and making money. In the sweep of Western history this had not always been the case. After the Reformation in Europe, women could vote and hold property, and the law recognized their rights. Gradually, however, they lost this parity with men, and became legal shadows of their fathers or husbands. Even in the New World, where pioneering women often did a man's work, the pall of Victorian morality gradually settled over a woman's life. Her sphere of influence was limited to the bedroom, kitchen, and nursery. Social approval of a career began and ended with marriage. Only very poor women "demeaned" themselves by taking jobs. Of course, this viewpoint improved men's chances in job competition. The American woman had no vote in federal (and most state) elections. She could not manage property or serve as a witness at a trial. She was, in short, a legal minor, a second-class citizen. After 1870, when ratification of the

Fifteenth Amendment guaranteed the right of blacks (men only, of course) to vote, she fell to the bottom rung of the American social ladder.

The countermovement for women's rights had its roots in the Enlightenment concept of the dignity and capability of every human being and the Enlightenment ideal of human freedom. The Industrial Revolution helped too, with its creation of job opportunities for women. In the United States they also benefited from the growth of the influence of the frontier. The attitudes and institutions that emerged from the successive series of American Wests favored equality of opportunity. It was no accident that the new territories and states of the West granted women the vote long before the older eastern regions. Another factor in the rise of the American woman was the ferment of reform that gripped the nation in the age of Andrew Jackson and Ralph Waldo Emerson. Everyone, it appeared, was organizing in an optimistic pursuit of a better life. This revolution of rising expectations could not be segregated by sex. In 1848 the first women's rights convention, Lucretia Mott and Elizabeth Cady Stanton presiding, took place at Seneca Falls, New York. The presence of Frederick Douglass at the meeting linked the cause of the nation's foremost minorities: blacks and women.

Male response to Seneca Falls was disappointing, but by the time Jane Addams was born the continued efforts of feminists such as Susan B. Anthony had at least transformed women's rights from a joke to a serious issue. The Civil War provided additional impetus. Women were needed as teachers, clerks, and nurses. In the absence of men, many served as farmers and mechanics. Some, particularly the nurse Clara Barton, won national acclaim for heroism on the battlefield. Older leaders like Stanton and Anthony raised money for the war effort through the National Women's Loyal League. But in the aftermath of the war women anxious to collect a toll of respect from a grateful nation were put down with the admonition that it was "the Negro's hour." Indignantly, in 1869 Stanton and Anthony organized the National Woman's Suffrage Association in New York. It demanded immediate suffrage for women and called for radical modification of the institution of marriage. A rival and more conservative organization, the American Women's Suffrage Association, formed in Boston the same year under Lucy Stone and Julia Ward Howe. This group moved to leadership of the women's movement in the mid-1870's, when the NWSA became associated in the public mind with the free-love and birth-control ideas of Victoria Woodhull.

While the radical feminists were making headlines and raising eyebrows, other women worked quietly in the crucial field of education. The problem here was to overcome the belief that, beyond the primary-school rudiments, education was a male possession. Even more damning was the widespread assumption that women's minds were incapable of being educated at the higher levels—that what advanced training ladies received should be restricted to such pursuits as embroidery, painting, French, singing, and playing the piano. Wealthy girls sometimes added a "finishing" tour to Europe's cultural capitals.

One of the first Americans to challenge this pattern was Mary Lyon, the founder, in 1837, of Mount Holyoke Seminary in South Hadley, Massachusetts. In a way that anticipated the career of Jane Addams, Mary Lyon rebelled against what she called the "genteel nothingness" that condemned women to protected, ineffective lives. Mount Holyoke made bold to offer a curriculum equal in content and rigor to the best men's colleges of the period. Oberlin College in Ohio went a step further in 1841 by graduating the nation's first coeds. In 1865 women's higher education achieved real distinction when the philanthropy of a brewer named Matthew Vassar enabled a women's college to open in Poughkeepsie, New York, with a physical plant and a faculty that most men's colleges could only envy. Vassar's most distinguished professor was a woman, the internationally acclaimed astronomer Maria Mitchell. Large-scale philanthropy also enabled Smith and Wellesley Colleges to open in 1875. Four years later Harvard blessed the beginnings of a women's annex that evolved into Radcliffe College.

Jane Addams wanted to attend Smith and even made the long journey to Northampton to take and pass the entrance examinations in the summer of 1877. But her father was adamant: Jane would attend the Rockford Female Seminary in Rockford, Illinois. Questioning her revered father never even occurred to the girl, and in the fall she dutifully, if unenthusiastically, packed her bags for "The Mount Holyoke of the West." The intellectual atmosphere at Rockford was intensely religious. Jane and many of her classmates chafed under the rigid discipline and the evangelical emphasis. Once Jane went for three months without praying and confessed she felt none the worse for the experience. She responded more positively to the doctrine of Christian usefulness, with its stress on taking religion out of the church and into society. Her sense of social responsibility was heightened by reading the works of English social thinkers such as Thomas Carlyle and John Ruskin. Ruskin particularly interested Jane because of his exposure of the injustices inherent in industrialism. At Rockford, Jane also studied Latin, Greek, French, natural science, ancient history, and moral philosophy. She was active in debate, edited the seminary magazine, and graduated in 1881 with the highest standing in her class.

For four years college filled Jane Addams's life, but after graduation she stepped into a world that had little interest in or use for a college-educated woman. Adding immeasurably to her bewilderment was the death of John Addams in August 1881. Deprived of his moral guidance and inspiration, Jane felt completely adrift. If this were not enough, a spinal operation cut short her study of medicine at the Woman's Medical College in Philadelphia and left her temporarily bedridden and permanently sterile. There seemed no alternative but to follow the Victorian feminine stereotype and immerse herself in culture. To that end Jane, her stepmother, and four other ladies toured England and the Continent for more than two years beginning in 1883. The group took language lessons, heard concerts and operas, and attended art galleries. But as for defining a purpose for her life, she was, by her own admission, "absolutely at sea." The pursuit of culture for its own sake seemed pointless, especially in view of the social problems that remained unsolved. Equally unappealing to Jane was the sheltered life of a gentlewoman-housewife, and motherhood was an impossibility. So she traveled idly, yearning for usefulness, hoping to break free of the trap of endless "preparation" and "construct the world anew."

At this low point in her life Jane Addams happened to glimpse the grinding poverty and depravity that existed beneath the polished surface of Europe's cities. The experience sowed seeds in her mind that later bore fruit in Hull House. The most significant moment of awakening came in April 1888 in Madrid, Spain, on her second trip abroad. Jane and her traveling companions attended a bullfight. As the bloody spectacle built to a climax, the friends, nauseated, excused themselves. Jane lingered on, delighting in the pageantry and its overtones of ancient gladiatorial combat. Later that evening, stung by the reprimands of her friends, she experienced "deep chagrin." She realized that by allowing cruelty to serve her personal pleasure, she had indirectly countenanced the whole system of exploitation that stripped many lives of dignity so that a few might flourish in luxury. After a restless night in Madrid, Jane arose determined to crystallize her vague ideals of social service into meaningful action. She began by describing to Ellen Gates Starr, a college friend and fellow traveler, a plan to rent a house in the most squalid section of an American city. There educated girls could both learn about and serve the real needs of the oppressed. London's Toynbee Hall offered a model of such a "settlement," and Jane used the remainder of her trip abroad to study it. The art galleries and operas were forgotten. After eight years of drifting, Jane Addams had found a career.

In June 1888 she returned to the United States eager to implement her ideas. The time was ripe for them. As urbanization and industrialization accelerated through the nineteenth century, they left in their wake social problems of unprecedented breadth and intensity. The abundance and opportunity that had always seemed a part of the New World simply did not materialize for millions of Americans. Mired in poverty and obliged to live in the slums of the larger cities, their lives were a nightmare of hard labor, poor health, and early death.

Although immigrants did not *cause* the slums, as some self-righteous "native" Americans maintained, they constituted an inordinate proportion of slum dwellers. And in the decades immediately preceding the beginning of Jane Addams's "settlement" in 1889, the stream of immigration increased to a flood. From 1850 to 1880 about 2.5 million foreign-born arrived in the United States each decade; in the 1880s, the figure leapt to 5.5 million. The year after Jane Addams graduated from college, 1882, almost 800,000 immigrants reached the New World. By 1890 approximately one-third of the population of Chicago was foreign-born. In the eastern seaboard cities the percentage was even higher. Because many newcomers spent their last money to reach America, they usually remained trapped in their port of entry. There were more Italians in Brooklyn (a borough of New York City) by 1900 than in Naples, Italy; three times as many Irish lived in New York as in Dublin. By 1900, of the 75 million Ameri-

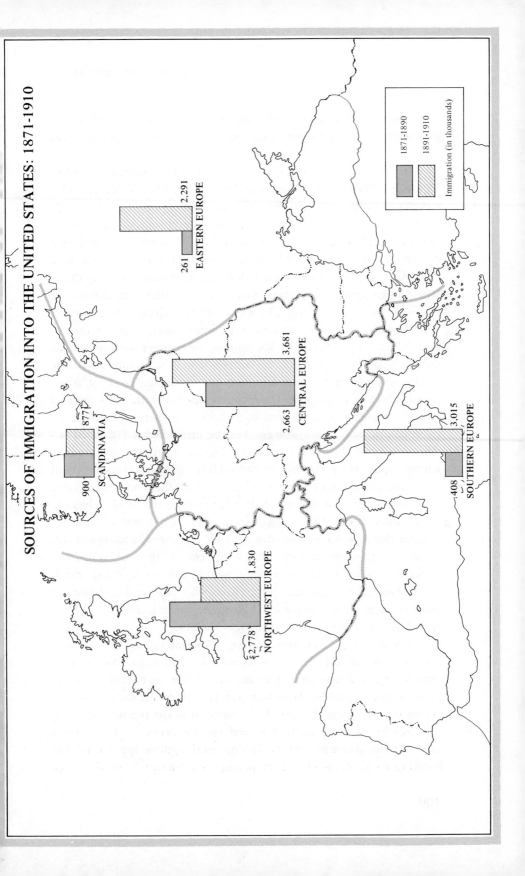

SOURCES OF IMMIGRATION INTO THE UNITED STATES: 1871-1910

EASTERN EUROPE
261
2,291

SCANDINAVIA
900
877

CENTRAL EUROPE
2,663
3,681

SOUTHERN EUROPE
408
3,015

NORTHWEST EUROPE
2,778
1,830

1871-1890
1891-1910
Immigration (in thousands)

cans, 10 million were foreign-born and 26 million of foreign-born parentage. By the third generation one was a native in America's fluid society.

Between Jane Addams's birth in 1860 and the founding of Hull House in 1889, the total population of the United States doubled. This was not as great a *rate* of increase as occurred in the early nineteenth century, but in effect the nation became more crowded. The explanation lies in urbanization. In 1830 only 1 of 15 Americans lived in a city (a community of over 800 persons). In 1860, the ratio was 1 in 6; in 1900, 1 in 3. By 1910 nearly half of all Americans were city dwellers. Viewed another way, there were 141 cities (the same definition) in 1860, and 778 in 1910. The impact of this change on American thought and institutions was profound. Before Jane Addams's generation the nation had been and had enjoyed thinking of itself as a rural society of pioneers and yeoman farmers with a scattering of village blacksmiths plying their trade under the spreading trees of small towns. Cities were suspect. The popular mind saw them as dens of aristocracy and inequity where rosy-cheeked farmers' daughters became painted and fallen women. Yet the bright lights fascinated another corner of the American mind. The cities were a new frontier where a "pioneering" lad like Horatio Alger's dime-novel heroes could climb the ladder from rags to riches. Feeding this dream of success were the palatial townhouses of the elite and the life of idle elegance lived within them. Very few Americans had the courage to confront the gulf that yawned between this life style and that of the urban poor. Fewer still protested the fact that 1 percent of the population controlled seven-eighths of the nation's wealth. But a few dared to ask the embarrassing questions. Jacob Riis, who published a blistering study of New York's slums in 1890 under the title *How the Other Half Lives*, was one. Jane Addams was another.

The meaning of industrialization, urbanization, and their attendant social frictions forced its way into the American consciousness with several headline-making events in the last quarter of the nineteenth century. Jane Addams was traveling to Smith College for an entrance exam when the first shock occurred in the summer of 1877. The weather was especially hot, and on the network of America's railroads the discontent of sweltering workingmen approached the breaking point. Railroad owners, playing free enterprise for all it was worth, had pared wages to the bone. The absence of safety features and employment compensation for injury were further sources of complaint. In July the railroads exploded in violence. A nationwide strike, the first in American history, paralyzed transportation. Mobs of workers derailed and burned trains. Beatings, stonings, and shootings were commonplace. In the case of the Baltimore and Ohio Railroad, federal troops crushed the protesters. But the Pennsylvania Railroad management found itself opposed by virtually the entire community of Pittsburgh. Company property amounting to $5 million was destroyed and a heavy loss of life sustained by both parties in the dispute. Similar violence flared in Chicago, St. Louis, and San Francisco. The United States Army finally came in to run the trains and halt the strike, but disturbing questions about capitalism and American society arose in its aftermath. And Jane Addams, wondering if the disrupted railroads would permit her to return to Rockford after her exam, had her first encounter with the social lesions that would be the object of her later reform endeavors.

The second major shock of the late nineteenth century occurred in 1886, when Jane Addams was between European trips and struggling unhappily with the question of a useful career. The locale was Chicago, and that fact may well have directed Jane's attention to this city as the subsequent site of her settlement. The background to the Haymarket Riot was widespread unemployment and unrest in America's industrial empire; the immediate cause was a clash between striking workers and police at the McCormick farm machinery factory. On the evening of May 4 some 1400 men gathered in Haymarket Square to hear labor leaders defend the eight-hour day. Just as the meeting began, a squad of 180 policemen entered the square and ordered the crowd to disperse. At that moment a blinding flash and deafening roar came from the midst of the policemen. Someone (the subsequent trial never ascertained who) had tossed a powerful bomb into the ranks of the police. The explosion killed seven and injured scores. The surviving police began firing into the mob, killing four more. As news of the Haymarket Riot spread over the nation, Jane Addams and her contemporaries were horrified. Such social violence might be the norm in Europe, but in the New World of democracy and opportunity it seemed incongruous indeed. The bright future of an industrializing America seemed suddenly clouded.

The third blow to American expectations took place in the countryside and, initially at least, involved natural rather than human violence. Beginning in 1880 the trans-Mississippi West had a series of abnormally wet years. Coupled with the rapid disappearance of unclaimed farmland further east, the weather reports tempted farmers into regions only marginally suited to agriculture. The propaganda of railroads and land developers spurred the westward push with promises of bumper crops and easy profits. Rain, it was illogically argued, followed the plow. In response hopeful men mortgaged everything to get a start in farming and ranching. The "garden" of the American West, men believed, would provide a safety valve for the nation's social troubles; the unemployed and discontented could go west to a cornucopia of plenty. The inevitable confrontation with reality came in the late 1880s. The climate reverted to its normal pattern, and fields turned to dust. Insects and lending institutions took care of whatever the fierce western sun spared. On top of this, howling blizzards in the winter of 1886–1887, the worst in the history of trans-Mississippi agriculture, decimated livestock. These bitter Americans who had paid the price searched for an explanation. Unwilling to blame themselves or nature, they turned on the political and economic establishment. Many of the alienated drifted back to the urban slums to provide additional subjects for reformers like Jane Addams.

In general, Americans responded to social problems in two ways. The first response simply denied that problems existed or blamed them on scapegoats. The high priest of this point of view, which was common in the ranks of the successful and powerful, was a Yale professor named William Graham Sumner. Its most visible exponent was the self-made Scottish immigrant named Andrew Carnegie. Sumner and Carnegie were Social Darwinists. Drawing on the evolutionary thinking of Charles Darwin and Herbert Spencer, they argued that the concept of "survival of the fittest" could be applied to contemporary society. And as Sumner and Carnegie saw it, wealth demarcated ability—the richest were the fittest. Successful men had emerged the winners in the social and economic sweepstakes; the poor deserved their fate. If poor people had possessed the requisite ability and determination, the Social Darwinists contended, they would not be poor. Carnegie habitually quoted Shakespeare in reply to dunning letters from impoverished acquaintances pleading hard times: "The fault, dear Brutus, is not in our stars, but in ourselves, that we are under-lings." It followed from this view that the competitive, free-enterprise system must be allowed to spin freely, rewarding talent with success and punishing incompetence with failure. Sumner, Carnegie, and their colleagues believed that the progress of the race depended upon the inexorable workings of this "natural law." Neither the government nor private philanthropists should meddle in the struggle for existence that was nineteenth-century American capitalism. To help the poor, the Social Darwinists maintained, was like trying to save the dinosaurs. Both were unfit to survive.

The second response to social problems, the one to which Jane Addams subscribed, broke sharply with the diagnosis and remedy offered by the Social Darwinists. It regarded much about American life in the late nineteenth century as neither desirable nor inevitable. While freely admitting that urbanization and industrialization made great achievements possible, people of this persuasion recognized that the changes created gross wrongs which should be remedied. Under-lying this position was a basic respect for the dignity of the individual regardless of his social and economic status, and the assumption that progress resulted from a planned, cooperative attack on problems rather than from the inevitable working of the grindstone of com-petition.

Foremost among the spokesmen of this reform philosophy in Jane Addams's youth were Lester Frank Ward, Henry George, and Edward Bellamy. Ward's *Dynamic Sociology* of 1883 excited Addams and other critics of the status quo with its argument that government must interpose itself between the strong and the weak, the privileged and the underprivileged, to ensure quality of opportunity, economic security, and a minimum standard of human dignity. Arguing that human beings could exert a creative, shaping force on evolution, Ward refused to accept the conservative Darwinists' conception of man as a helpless chip floating on the stream of time. Henry George and Ed-ward Bellamy attracted widespread attention with specific proposals for alleviating the nation's social and economic ills. A world traveler, George had long been troubled by the coexistence of progress and poverty in the industrializing nations. He was especially critical of the system of private land ownership that allowed a fortunate few to profit from the growth of society as a whole. In 1879 George published his ideas on the problem in *Progress and Poverty*. The book called for the abolition of all taxes except a massive single tax on real estate. Although not avowedly socialistic, the "single taxers" were clearly in revolt against many of capitalism's fundamental principles. The same was true of the followers of Edward Bellamy's "nationalism." The point of his *Looking Backward, 2000–1887* (1888) was to demonstrate that the unregulated, competitive profit system was an obstacle to human happiness and the true progress of the race. In Bellamy's America in the year 2000, an all-powerful but beneficent state had "nationalized" every aspect of the economy and thereby secured social justice. Every citizen in Bellamy's utopia lived an efficient, dignified, and enlightened life. The benefits of technological progress had been realized and the social liabilities left behind. It was a dream that inspired many of the reformers of Jane Addams's generation.

Social feminism was another expression of the concern that motivated Ward, George, and Bellamy. Beginning in the late 1870s a number of American women turned from agitating for the vote to various forms of social service and philanthropy. At first their activities centered around the church and the Sunday school, and consisted of aiding indigent mothers and children. Later the effectiveness and scope of the women's organizations broadened to the point of launching campaigns to eliminate or regulate prostitution, abolish alcohol (the Women's Christian Temperance Union was formed in 1874), and advance the general level of national morality (through the Social Purity League). In addition, many middle- and upper-class ladies joined local associations aimed at improving both themselves and their society. National leadership came from the General Federation of Women's Clubs (1890) and the Junior League (1901). But the high point of social feminism was the "settlement," and its showcase was Jane Addams's Hull House.

When Jane returned from Europe in 1888 she had a cause, a plan of attack, an income that permitted its implementation, and the energy born of almost thirty years of what she considered a useless life. January 1889 found her and Ellen Starr in Chicago, a city that Lincoln Steffens described as "first in violence, deepest in dirt; loud, lawless, unlovely, ill-smelling, new; an overgrown gawk of a village, the teeming tough among cities." Of course it was this condition that

294

attracted Jane Addams, and once in Chicago she deliberately searched out the rawest and most impoverished sections for a base of operations. Hull House at 800 South Halsted Street was ideal. Built in 1856 as a country home for a wealthy businessman, it stood thirty years later in the center of a squalid wilderness of tenements and factories populated largely by desperately poor immigrants. There were 7 churches and 255 saloons in the neighborhood. Mr. Hull, needless to say, had long since moved to greener fields beyond the sprawl of metropolitan Chicago, and Jane Addams was able to rent his mansion. On September 18, 1889, she moved in, and in company with a few other educated ladies of conscience and leisure began a comprehensive assault on human degradation.

After a short period of hesitance and mistrust, Jane Addams's new neighbors accepted her experiment with enthusiasm. Some 2000 people a week poured through the doors on Halsted Street. They received everything from hot lunches and child care services to instruction in English and lectures on art and philosophy. There was something for every age and interest. Jane Addams was convinced that the only way to reduce the influence of saloons, dance halls, and delinquency was to provide wholesome alternatives in the way of entertainment. Hull House therefore also organized parties and games at every opportunity to offer the hopeless something for which to live. Officially, according to its charter, Hull House existed "to provide a center for a higher civic and social life; to institute and maintain educational and philanthropic enterprises, and to investigate and improve the conditions in the industrial districts of Chicago." But for thousands of slum dwellers, the settlement simply meant that someone cared.

Alleviating human misery on a day-to-day, personal basis was only the start of Hull House's mission. Jane Addams was dedicated to making permanent improvements in the urban environment. To this end she campaigned for more effective garbage collection, won appointment as garbage inspector for her neighborhood, and in this capacity personally followed the wagons at 6 o'clock every morning. Encouraging her in these efforts was evidence that cleaner streets meant a greatly reduced death rate. On other occasions Jane organized a community improvement association that persuaded the city government to pave the streets, construct public baths, and build parks and playgrounds. People, she constantly insisted, were not machines, not objects of exploitation. They needed such things as playgrounds and baths and settlement houses to sustain a spark of joy and of hope. On another front Jane Addams took the lead in forming consumer co-operatives that secured better prices and higher quality in commodities such as coal and milk. Schools, in her estimation, were vital elements in long-range reform. Elected to the Chicago Board of Education, she pressed for reforms that made the schools better able to prevent delinquency and to prepare students for useful lives. As in the case of Hull House, her philosophy centered on stimulating rather than disciplining people.

Much of the activity at Hull House in the first decade of its existence had a close parallel in the Social Gospel movement. This attempt to make Christianity, particularly Protestantism, more useful in solving the problems of an industrial age took religion out of the churches and into society on a seven-day-a-week basis. Like Jane Addams, the Social Gospelers were not afraid to plunge into the heart of the ugliest parts of their social and physical environment. In Columbus, Ohio, Washington Gladden used his pulpit as a platform from which to negotiate a Christian solution to industrial strikes. Gladden's book, *Applied Christianity* (1886), was a defense of the new emphases. And by this time the Salvation Army, founded in London in 1878, had reached the United States. Its original intent was to save the souls of the urban poor, and its uniformed soldiers of both sexes leaned heavily on brass bands and similar revivalist techniques. But by the 1890s the Salvation Army had joined forces with settlements like Hull House in offering slum people ways to improve their condition short of the pearly gates. Social-service brigades went into the ghettos with relief and self-betterment programs.

Jane Addams's experiment on Halsted Street attracted many of the leading exponents of the Social Gospel. George Herron lectured there to overflow audiences on the incompatibility of modern capitalism and traditional Christianity. American society, he maintained, was on the verge of degenerating into atomized chaos. Herron called for a social ethic and a sense of community responsibility that would replace the dog-eat-dog relationships of free enterprise. William T. Stead also frequented Hull House. His biting indictment, *If Christ Came to Chicago*, published in 1894, appealed to the conscience of the city.

Stead was especially anxious to stop Chicago's flourishing white slave trade. Working closely with Jane Addams and other reformers, Stead managed to find homes and legitimate employment for some of the prostitutes. The greatest Social Gospeler of them all, however, was Charles M. Sheldon, whose book *In His Steps* (1897) eventually sold 23 million copies. Sheldon told the story of a town that decided to approach all questions of policy by asking, "what would Jesus have done?"

In real life, on the other hand, social problems proved less susceptible to reform; indeed, they seemed to grow in scope and intensity as the nineteenth century drew to a close. Hull House was only three years old when a depression of unprecedented severity paralyzed the economy. The poor, of course, suffered most. In the disastrous year of 1893 railroads, mills, factories, and mines went bankrupt and closed their doors. Dazed legions of unemployed walked the streets of the major cities. There was a shocking and ironic contrast between Chicago's Columbian Exposition, a world's fair in praise of technological progress, and the thousands of homeless men sleeping on its outskirts. Four hundred years after its discovery, the New World seemed to have fallen far short of the promise of its beginnings.

Jane Addams did her best. Hull House strained its resources in an effort to alleviate the social consequences of the Depression of 1893, but hardly made a dent in the misery of a single city. Thinking bigger, Jacob S. Coxey proposed a massive federal work-relief program centered on the idea of building good roads. When a conservative, business-oriented Congress rejected the idea, Coxey vowed to "send a petition to Washington with boots on." On Easter Sunday 1894 Coxey and his followers left Massillon, Ohio, and walked to the capital. On the way they recruited jobless workers in Pittsburgh, chiefly among the bitter losers of an 1892 strike in Andrew Carnegie's Homestead steel plant. When "Coxey's Army" reached Washington, their spirits were high; surely a democratic government would respond to the genuine needs of so many of its citizens. But the Grover Cleveland Administration regarded the march as a form of rebellion and met it with fixed bayonets, arrests, beatings, and even killing. Thoughtful Americans joined Jane Addams in taking a hard look at what they had assumed were established American rights and principles. Popular confidence in the government was further shaken when an 1895 ruling by the Supreme Court declared a modest 2 percent tax on incomes over $4000 unconstitutional. The wealthy, it appeared, were beyond challenge, and the election of 1896, in which the conservative Republican William McKinley trounced William Jennings Bryan despite the support Bryan received from most lower-income Americans, confirmed this impression.

For Jane Addams, the single most disturbing event of the 1890s was the Pullman Strike. Not only did it raise disconcerting questions about the beneficence of capitalism and the federal government; it took place just a few miles from Hull House in the Chicago suburb of Pullman, which George M. Pullman had created as a setting for his railroad car factory. Jane knew Pullman personally. She sat on the Citizens Arbitration Committee that endeavored futilely to settle the strike.

For Addams and most of her contemporaries the most shocking thing about the Pullman Strike was the fact that Pullman, Illinois, had been widely heralded as a model of enlightened labor-management relations. Although a company town, it was carefully planned with neat, comfortable housing; ample recreational facilities; beautiful parks; and excellent schools. Pullman seemed to prove that capitalism could benefit all parties—to dispel the gloom cast by Homestead, Haymarket, and the great railroad strike of 1877. George Pullman had apparently shown that the nation could advance peacefully into a future that was at once industrialized and just.

The Depression of 1893 gave the lie to such expectations. As Pullman's profits declined, management lowered wages again and again—a total of five times by the summer of 1894. Rents and food prices in the company town, however, remained at the predepression level. And George Pullman, standing firmly on the doctrine of benevolent paternalism, refused to hear his laborers' complaints or to submit them to arbitration. In June 1894 rising tensions exploded in a massive strike. The newly organized American Railway Union, under the leadership of Eugene V. Debs, voted to refuse service to all Pullman cars on America's railroads. Management responded by asking President Grover Cleveland to use the armed forces to invade the town of Pullman and end the strike. The President and his Attorney-General, Richard Olney, were more than agreeable. Ignoring the protests of Illinois Governor John P. Altgeld, the Cleveland Administration secured an injunction from a federal court and ordered 2000 troops to Pullman on July 4, 1894. Their arrival triggered a full-scale riot. Neither the union nor the army could preserve order. Mobs ranged the streets of Pullman. Before the troops prevailed, twelve men lay dead and millions of dollars of property were reduced to smoldering rubble.

The emotional currents generated by the Pullman Strike swirled around Hull House, and Jane Addams became deeply troubled by what she called "the growth of class bitterness." On the one hand were unemployed workers, wearing the white ribbons of the strikers, who told her about the perfidy of Pullman. Beneath the guise of benevolent paternalism, they charged, George Pullman was a tyrant, and his philosophy of labor-management relations little better than slavery. On the other hand, Jane Addams was a lady of wealth and breeding whose circle of friendships included capitalists. One acquaintance, who had lost thousands of dollars as a result of the strike, told Jane " 'the strikers ought all to be shot.' "

Sifting these competing claims in her own mind, Jane Addams wrote "A Modern Lear." The point of the essay was that George Pullman, like Shakespeare's King Lear, reaped ingratitude as the result of his peculiar form of dictatorial benevolence. In Jane's opinion, true friendship had to stem from genuine, unsolicited, and mutual respect. The Pullman Palace Car Company was, in the last analysis, a commercial operation. When pressed, it put commercial considerations before those of social welfare. Like Lear, Pullman affected kindliness only when it served his interests; his employees actually had no social identity save that of well-tended machines. The Pullman affair taught Jane Addams that if a capitalist was really interested in effective reform, he had to consult and if necessary compromise with the desires of the workers, even if this meant departing on occasion from strictly commercial criteria. Social progress, she concluded, "is not the result of [the capitalist's] . . . individual striving, as a solitary mountain climber beyond sight of the valley multitude." Instead, progress should be "lateral." The rise of the entire society, Jane Addams believed, constituted the only legitimate definition of progress.

The aftermath of the Pullman Strike found Jane Addams and her contemporaries doubtful about the susceptibility of American capitalism to reform. Perhaps there was an inherent incompatibility between

Leo, shown at his job in a textile
mill in Fayetteville, Tennessee, was
eight years old in this 1910
photograph. He earned fifteen cents
a day. Jane Addams campaigned
for laws prohibiting such
exploitation of children.

Jane Addams deliberately located her social settlement, Hull House, in a slum
neighborhood such as this one. Although the street shown has lighting, sidewalks, and
cobblestone paving, it was far above the average for American cities. And even
this street appears to lack an effective garbage collection system (note the dead
horse) and sewage system (the open gutters, left, carry the waste).

...e early feminists were assembled for the first International Convention of ...nen, held in Washington, D.C. in 1888. Only a few can be identified for sure. ...t row: *third from left, Susan B. Anthony; fourth from right, Elizabeth Cady ...on; third from right, Matilda J. Gage, a Civil War researcher and writer.* Second ... *third from left, Frances Willard, WCTU; fourth from left, Lillie Devereux ...e (nicknamed Tiger Lillie), author of "Fettered for Life."*

...Addams *(right), here ...onstrating with a friend, ...McDowell, was a leading ...cate of world peace all her ...life.*

The European immigrants who thronged to the United States in the late nineteenth and early twentieth centuries were a major recipient of Jane Addams's social service. The group here is on a 1906 ocean liner. Their hopeful faces suggest a lack of knowledge about conditions many of them would soon encounter.

the profit motive and social justice. Perhaps Hull House was only painkilling ointment for a chronic, deep-rooted disease. In this frame of mind Jane began to listen to the arguments of the Socialists, who proposed an alternative socioeconomic system based on mutual assistance rather than individual accumulation. The roots of this idea ran back half a century in the American context. The many utopian communities born of the great reform wave of the 1820s, 1830s, and 1840s operated on social and communal principles even before Karl Marx published his *Communist Manifesto* in 1848. In 1825 at a place significantly named "New Harmony," Robert Owen organized a commune based on the principles of cooperative labor and collective property ownership. The harmony at New Harmony was short-lived, but men continued to dream. Albert Brisbane revived communalism in the 1840s with the aid of the ideas of the French social thinker Charles Fourier. Brisbane's idea of economically efficient living units (he called them "phalanxes") inspired other undertakings, notably the Transcendentalists' Brook Farm. Perhaps the most visible of all the utopian communities was the one John Humphrey Noyes founded at Oneida, New York, in 1848. The Oneida perfectionists even extended their criticism of private property to a condemnation of the institution of marriage. In addition, there were various religious groups—the Shakers and the Mormons in particular—who successfully practiced forms of cooperative living.

After the Civil War the social abuses that came with the rapid growth and transformation of the American economy spurred renewed interest in socialism. Jane Addams was among those Americans who gave it serious consideration, and Hull House became a mecca for radical social thought. In 1890 its members formed the Working People's Social Science Club to discuss the various ways of organizing society. Marxist doctrine received considerable attention, but so did the American varieties of socialism propounded by Henry George and Edward Bellamy. A few years after his spectacular but unsuccessful campaign for the mayoralty of New York City, George personally addressed a Hull House audience. According to Jane Addams, this "great leader" received an ovation that rocked the building. On the whole, she welcomed such displays. "A Settlement," she wrote, "is above all a place for enthusiasms, a spot to which those who have a passion for the equalization of human joys and opportunities are early attracted."

Pursuing her personal exploration of alternatives to capitalism, Jane Addams journeyed to Russia in 1896 to study the life and thought of Count Leo Tolstoy. A disciple of Marx, Tolstoy had renounced his comfortable way of life to live communally with poor peasants in a remote village. Jane seemed to sense the similarities between Tolstoy's upbringing and her own. Perhaps, she reasoned, the Russian's refusal to live off the work of others' hands was the key to social justice. She therefore awaited her interview with great eagerness. But the meeting between the two reformers was short and to the point. Tolstoy had been working in the fields in his simple peasant garb. Upon seeing Jane Addams's elaborate dress, he remarked that it contained enough material in a single sleeve to make several peasant frocks. Didn't she find such clothes a barrier between herself and those she desired to help, Tolstoy demanded. His next questions concerned where Jane Addams's food and income came from. Mortified that she did not till the soil, the American returned to Chicago resolved to purify herself with humble work. Yet after a brief stint at bread baking in Hull House's kitchen, Jane abandoned Tolstoy's plan as "more logical than life warrants." The service of the poor, she concluded, could not be "pushed aside . . . while I saved my soul by . . . baking bread." The decision showed her commitment to reform within the capitalistic framework; she would elevate the underprivileged rather than join them.

Another indication of Addams's position was her relationship with the movement for organized socialism that gathered strength in the United States in the 1890s. On the one hand she admired the sincerity and the intensity of the Socialist attack on human degradation. Few Americans, she realized, were doing more to fulfill the ideals to which she subscribed than Eugene V. Debs, Victor Berger, and their colleagues. Yet the Socialists demanded a degree of intellectual conformity that repelled Jane Addams. "I should have been glad," she remarked, "to have had the comradeship of that gallant company had they not firmly insisted that fellowship depends upon identity of creed." On another occasion, at a street-corner rally, she angrily told an unruly crowd of laborers that she intended to resist the bullying of both millionaires and Socialists. If democratic institutions were to endure, she believed, the tyranny of both ends of the political spectrum had to be resisted.

Having thus rejected the alternative of dismantling the capitalistic system, Jane Addams directed her energies toward its improvement. One of the first fronts she attacked was the labor problem. Her neighbors around Hull House provided ample evidence of the depths of misery possible under the unregulated profit system. Wage slavery had a vivid meaning for Jane Addams. Most of her neighbors worked in Chicago's sweatshops making clothing, glass, and other products. Their hours were long—fourteen a day was the norm—and their wages so low as to necessitate the labor of the entire family. Children were not exempt. Jane Addams reported one case of a "little girl of four who pulled out basting threads hour after hour, sitting on a stool at the feet of her Bohemian mother, a little bunch of human misery." For Americans with social consciences, such a situation was intolerable.

Given the unwillingness of employers to alter a profitable system, two remedies seemed possible to Jane Addams. The older involved the organization of laboring people in their own behalf. The first such attempts in the United States came before the Civil War and involved skilled craftsmen such as machinists and carpenters. These craft unions managed to wring some concessions from employers dependent on their skills, but they did nothing for the great mass of unskilled workers. In 1869 Uriah Stephens attempted to organize this group in the Noble Order of the Knights of Labor. All workers except gamblers and bartenders were welcome, and under the leadership of Stephens and later of Terence V. Powderly the Knights of Labor grew prodigiously. But their calls for wages and hours reform and for an income tax went largely unheeded. After the Haymarket Riot of 1886, which many attributed to labor agitation, the Knights lost most of its membership. As the Knights fell, a new national union, the American Federation of Labor, rose. Organized in 1881, the AFL returned to the principle of skilled craft unionism. Samuel Gompers, a cigarmaker, provided the leadership that brought a million workers into the union fold by 1895.

Jane Addams made Hull House a center of union activities in the Chicago area. She believed that unions offered a means of constructive social change. Until the public and its government recognized and protected the rights of working people, unions had to fill the breach as best they could. Under AFL auspices bookbinders, shirtmakers, and glass processers organized at Hull House. So did various local unions and workingmen's clubs. For many of the participants, union activity marked the first faint stirrings of hope—the first light in dark and bewildered lives. Jane Addams stirred these sparks. She took special pleasure in the Jane Club, a cooperative living arrangement for working girls. Here was a demonstration of an alternative to the dog-eat-dog competition she saw at the root of so many of her nation's social and economic ills.

Although labor unions were an important forward step, Jane Addams recognized their limitations. Employers could, and customarily did, ignore their demands. It was a simple matter in the 1890s to fire "troublemaking" union workers and hire replacements from the masses of desperately poor immigrants. As for strikes like that at Pullman in 1894, Jane Addams saw them as little better than extensions of the old, unregulated competition on the part of both labor and management. What was needed, she felt, was the substitution of the rule of law for that of force in industrial relations. The government, in her opinion, had to be more than an observer at a prize fight. It had to make and enforce the rules which would ensure that the fight would be fought fairly and with dignity for all concerned.

This position gave rise to Jane Addams's interest in labor legislation. As early as 1891, the Hull House ladies helped push through the Illinois legislature a law limiting factory labor to persons older than thirteen. But the law proved a farce. Employees simply ignored it, and—to Jane Addams's surprise—so did the impoverished parents of working children. Regarding the latter as victims of the system, Jane persisted in her belief that child labor was a social evil. In 1893 she had the satisfaction of seeing a Hull House campaign result in tighter labor laws, including an unprecedented 8-hour maximum day for working women. At the same time a Hull House resident, Florence Kelley, received an appointment from prolabor governor John P. Altgeld as state factory inspector with the responsibility of reporting infractions. The honeymoon ended abruptly, however, in 1895 at the expiration of Altgeld's term. The new governor replaced Kelley with a factory owner. Moreover, the Illinois Supreme Court declared the 8-hour legislation unconstitutional on the grounds that women who wanted to should be allowed to work more than a third of a day. Bitter at what they considered a travesty of the concept of individual freedom, Hull House workers launched a vigorous campaign for new legislation. The Chicago business community chastised Jane Addams and her friends, labeled them flaming radicals, and finally offered them $30,000 to "keep quiet." Goaded by these insults, the ladies battled even harder. In 1903 they had the satisfaction of witnessing the passage of a second children's wages and hours act.

After 1903 the fight for labor legislation shifted from the state to the federal level. At first the United States Supreme Court ruled (*Lochner* v. *New York*, 1905) that acts limiting working hours were invalid, but a breakthrough came in 1908 in the case of *Muller* v. *Oregon*. The Supreme Court had been asked to rule on an Oregon statute limiting the hours of laundresses. Realizing that the verdict would affect Illinois legislation as well, Jane Addams followed the proceedings closely. Florence Kelley even helped secure the services of the brilliant lawyer (and later Supreme Court Justice), Louis Brandeis. In a famous legal brief, Brandeis dismissed precedent and the free enterprise system in two pages. He devoted the next hundred to a detailed examination of the harmful effects of unlimited working hours on society. This sociological approach convinced a majority of justices, and the Oregon law was upheld. Jane Addams breathed a sigh of relief. Perhaps, if pushed hard enough and long enough, capitalism was capable of self-reformation.

Political corruption also drew Jane Addams's fire in the late nineteenth and early twentieth centuries. Chicago provided a large target for her crusading zeal. In the 1890s she estimated that of the sixty-eight aldermen on the city council, fifty-seven were corrupt. Bribes and graft were their way of life. One of the worst aldermen represented Hull House's district. Three times the settlement campaigned to unseat him, and three times he triumphed with surprising ease. The reason, Jane Addams discovered, was that many voters were directly obligated to this political boss and his machine for jobs, favors, and protection. Continuing her analysis of the urban political situation, Jane came to understand that corrupt as he was, the boss was also a beneficial force in the community. With the exception of settlement workers like herself, he was the slum dwellers' only friend.

The boss, for example, might put a needy person on his payroll, or release someone from jail, or send medicine to a sick family, or pay the costs of a funeral. The Hull House alderman distributed 10 tons of turkey during the Christmas season in 1897. Needy recipients did not forget such kindnesses, and the politicos made certain their memories were fresh on election day.

For the immigrants, there was little need for reminders. The political boss was understood as the American equivalent of the European nobleman or feudal lord. He was a benevolent authority figure to be feared and revered. Of course his concern for the poor was insincere; votes and continued power were his real object. But the corrupt political system indisputably worked to alleviate some of the miseries of life in the ghetto. In this sense, Jane Addams realized, the boss was her colleague. Urban politics was an informal welfare agency. The boss raised funds from the wealthy and distributed them among the urban poor whose votes were vital to his political existence.

Although Jane Addams came to appreciate the social function of the city boss, she understood it as a poor substitute for sincere concern for the welfare of the urban masses. The real need was for honest, efficient, and democratic government that addressed the causes, rather than the symptoms, of human suffering. In this concern she had substantial help. "Good government" reformers had been at work since the 1870s. On the federal level the Pendleton Act of 1883, creating a Civil Service System, marked a major triumph over the spoilsmen. But the state and especially the local "rings" of corrupt politicians were harder to dislodge. In New York City, for instance, Boss William M. Tweed and his successors in Tammany Hall simply laughed at civil service and continued to surround themselves with partners in plundering the public. Beginning with a series of articles in *McClure's* in 1902, Lincoln Steffens gave Americans a frank look at their local governments. But his bitter exposé, collected under the title *The Shame of the Cities*, made it clear that the ultimate blame rested with the American people. Their apathy made the system of boss rule possible. Jane Addams agreed heartily. She took every opportunity to arouse the public in support of reform candidates throughout the nation. Samuel M. "Golden Rule" Jones, the mayor who cleaned up politics in the city of Toledo, Ohio, was a favorite speaker at Hull

House. So was Hazen S. Pingree, who did the same for Detroit and later, as governor, for Michigan.

Perhaps the most visible reformer on the state level was Robert M. "Fighting Bob" La Follette, the Wisconsin governor (1900) and United States Senator (1906). Jane Addams applauded his success in instituting civil service, direct primaries, lobbying regulations, popular referendums, and the first state income tax. She also thought well of Governors Hiram Johnson of California and Woodrow Wilson of New Jersey. As for her home state, she became one of the leaders of the Civic Federation and the Municipal Voters' League, which helped Mayor Carter Harrison make a dent in the multilayered corruption of Chicago. Other cities rejected mayors altogether in favor of government by a commission of experts or by an impartial city manager whose position was not dependent on elections. Those communities that retained elected officials made them more responsive to their electorates through adoption of new political devices such as the initiative, referendum, and recall.

In her role as reformer after the turn of the century, Jane Addams found herself in the company of a loosely knit band of fellow crusaders who assumed the label "Progressives." More a mood than an organized movement, progressivism was characterized by confidence in man's efforts to improve the quality of American life. Progressives like Jane Addams followed Lester Frank Ward and the reform Darwinists in rejecting the belief that man was a pawn in the hands of deterministic forces beyond his control. The future, as Herbert Croly put it, would *not* take care of itself. Mastery and control, Walter Lippmann added, should replace passivity and drift. The Progressives also agreed with John Dewey and the pragmatists that traditional ideas and institutions should be tested for their effectiveness in meeting current needs and, when ineffective, discarded. Most Progressives could agree on the matter of goals: justice in social relations, democracy in politics, and equal opportunity in business. The umbrella for all these was the goal of orderly, efficient progress toward the millennium that most Progressives believed lay at the end of the rainbow of reform.

Jane Addams was in complete accord with Progressive ideology, and she exemplified the social consciousness aspect of the crusade. She also personified the average Progressive. Differing sharply from the

Populists of the 1890s,[1] the Progressives were on the whole middle and upper class, urban, and comfortably wealthy. In fact, most of the Progressives had voted for William McKinley and against the Populist champion William Jennings Bryan in 1896. The typical Progressive felt threatened on several fronts. He feared, and to some extent envied, the growing might of big business and its affluent owners. Statistical compilations such as that of 1902, which revealed no less than 3561 millionaires in the United States, disturbed the Progressive mind. But so did the rising power of labor and immigrant groups. Blue collar radicalism, Progressives believed, was as dangerous as concentrated wealth. As a descendant, more often than not, of an old American family once accustomed to social dominance, the Progressive took for granted his right—indeed his duty—to lead his country out of the morass. Moreover, he saw in this leadership an opportunity to halt the slippage in his own status, to give himself an active role along with the new rich and the organized poor. Reform appealed, then, not only as a remedy for external evils, but as a means of personal reassertion.

In Jane Addams's case, this self-interest was clearly evident and, to her credit, frankly admitted. Social work had been her salvation. Her early life had consisted of a frustrating pursuit of genteel culture; founding Hull House had given her a purpose and, in time, an international reputation. It had given her the contact with reality she craved. In 1892, in the course of a lecture on "The Subjective Necessity for Social Settlements," Jane confessed that Hull House existed as much for frustrated upper-class, college-educated women as it did for the immigrants and urban poor. The "undirected" lives of the ladies, she declared, seemed "as pitiful as the other great mass of destitute lives." Later in the same address she referred to the "joys of self-sacrifice," not the least of which was "a love of approbation so vast that it is not content with the treble clapping of delicate hands, but wishes also to hear the brass notes from toughened palms." The Jane Club and Jane's willingness to be called "Saint Jane" by the Hull House community support this analysis. But Jane Addams was not saying anything new about human nature; she only called a spade a spade. And if egoism could be channeled into constructive social purposes, who was to deny

[1] See pages 344–345 for a discussion of populism.

its value? Reform, in sum, had clearly helped Jane Addams; but Jane Addams had unquestionably advanced reform.

By 1910 Jane Addams was famous. Her work at Hull House and her numerous writings, particularly *Twenty Years at Hull House* (1910), in a field one would now call sociology were known all over the world. In some quarters, to be sure, she was considered a radical and a crank, but in others she was seen as the first lady of American reform and one of progressivism's brightest lights. As such, she occupied a position of influence in national politics. Her first venture into this arena was in 1912, when she threw her weight behind the new Progressive party. This organization took shape in the last year of William Howard Taft's administration as a protest against his seeming indifference to the reform policies of his predecessor, Theodore Roosevelt. At first the dissatisfied Republicans rallied around Senator Robert La Follette, but early in 1912 Roosevelt, refreshed after an African safari, expressed an interest in opposing Taft. The organizers of the Roosevelt-for-President boom that immediately developed set their sights on the Republican National Convention scheduled for June 18 in Chicago. Jane Addams traveled uptown to attend. Her reputation got her a hearing before the Republican Platform Committee, and she used the opportunity to advocate the adoption of a plank favoring women's suffrage. But when the platform appeared, there was no reference to women and the vote. Jane had companions in frustration, for the Roosevelt supporters too had been thwarted by the Taft-controlled Republican Central Committee. After Taft received the party's nomination on June 22, they reconvened in another part of town to form a new party. A personal friend of Roosevelt, Jane decided to attend. When the Progressive, or Bull Moose, party endorsed women's suffrage as well as advanced reform measures on labor, health, and justice, she decided to join.

Theodore Roosevelt became the Progressive party's standard bearer; Jane Addams seconded his nomination. In doing so, she forced herself to swallow two unpalatable policies. One was Theodore Roosevelt's militarism and the other the Progressive party's deliberate silence on the problems of black Americans. Jane Addams rationalized the first with the fact that more people were killed or injured in industrial accidents than in war. The Progressives' proposals for reform in this area made their endorsement of war bearable. As for

THE ELECTION OF 1912

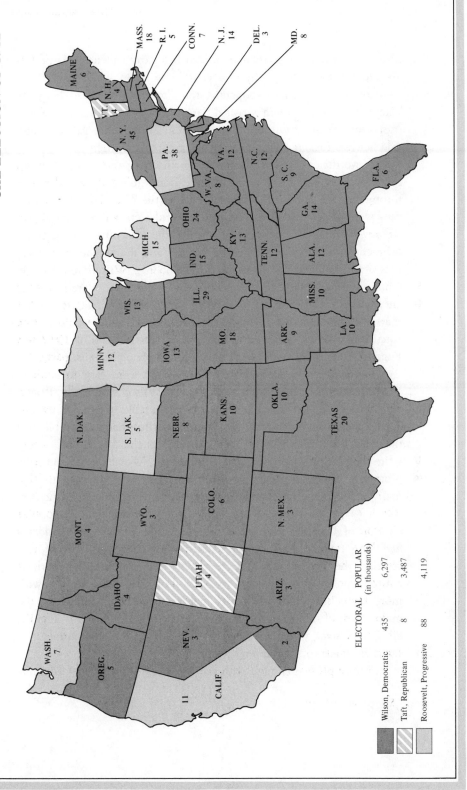

	ELECTORAL	POPULAR (in thousands)
Wilson, Democratic	435	6,297
Taft, Republican	8	3,487
Roosevelt, Progressive	88	4,119

MAINE 6
N.H. 4
VT. 4
N.Y. 45
PA. 38
MASS. 18
R.I. 5
CONN. 7
N.J. 14
DEL. 3
MD. 8
VA. 12
W.VA. 8
N.C. 12
S.C. 9
FLA. 6
OHIO 24
KY. 13
GA. 14
MICH. 15
IND. 15
TENN. 12
ALA. 12
WIS. 13
ILL. 29
MISS. 10
LA. 10
MINN. 12
IOWA 13
MO. 18
ARK. 9
N. DAK.
S. DAK. 5
NEBR. 8
KANS. 10
OKLA. 10
TEXAS 20
MONT. 4
WYO. 3
COLO. 6
N. MEX. 3
IDAHO 4
UTAH 4
ARIZ. 3
WASH. 7
OREG. 5
NEV. 3
CALIF. 11

blacks, she offered the explanation that her party's silence was preferable to the Republicans' hypocrisy. In time when white southerners were better prepared to cooperate, the Progressives would help the blacks. If such reasoning satisfied Jane Addams, it left many of her supporters deeply disturbed. A group from Hull House gathered outside her hotel room door and wept throughout the night.

Nevertheless Jane Addams took to the campaign trail, lecturing for Roosevelt and his running mate, Hiram Johnson of California, throughout the nation. It was an uphill battle. The nation's Republicans were sharply divided. The more liberal were willing to bolt for Roosevelt; the rich and powerful felt that the twin pillars of the establishment—the sanctity of private property and the autonomy of business—were safer in the hands of Taft. Woodrow Wilson, reform governor of New Jersey and, the Democrats' nominee offered another alternative. At the core of Wilson's "New Freedom" was the belief that an economy based on freely competing small units would restore equal opportunity. Completing the slate for the election of 1912 was Eugene V. Debs, the nominee of the rapidly growing Socialist party.

Given these options, the election results were easy to explain. With the Republicans disunited, Woodrow Wilson won easily. Roosevelt ran second, Taft third, and Debs a respectable fourth. Undiscouraged, Jane Addams felt that the Progressive effort had at least blocked the reelection of Taft. And "new parties," as she put it, "ultimately write the platforms for all parties." Moreover, Woodrow Wilson gave promise of continuing the age of reform. The next few years fulfilled many of her expectations. Two Constitutional amendments, the Sixteenth (a personal income tax) and the Seventeenth (direct popular election of United States Senators), instituted reforms Jane Addams had long favored. She also applauded the passage in 1914 of acts creating the Federal Trade Commission and establishing a stricter antitrust policy (the Clayton Act). Wilson also helped labor with more favorable wages and hours legislation, although, in truth, the main thrust of reform in this area was carried by Henry Ford.[1] Finally, all Progressives were heartened by Wilson's 1916 appointment of Louis Brandeis to the Supreme Court.

While pleased enough with the record of Wilson's first adminis-

[1] See pages 391–392.

tration to support him in the election of 1916, Jane Addams believed that progressivism could best be furthered by extending the vote to American women. Her argument was straightforward. Women were the traditional custodians of morality; they knew the value of the life they brought into the world better than did men. They would therefore be more responsive to problems such as child labor, prostitution, political corruption, and health. As women had disciplined families for generations, so they would discipline the nation. Their participation in elections could not fail but to advance reform.

The roots of Jane Addams's interest in woman suffrage lay in her father's support of the policy. By the time she graduated from college in 1881, she was an enthusiastic suffragist, but her interest in the movement faded as she became engrossed in the settlement idea. Jane Addams decided she was more concerned with alleviating misery in the ghettos than with women's rights. But after Hull House was well established, she turned once more to the suffrage crusade. In 1907 she led more than a hundred Chicago area women's clubs in a campaign for political status in that city. By 1916 twelve states had granted women the vote, and Carrie Chapman Catt had revived the National Woman's Suffrage Association as the spearhead in the campaign for a Constitutional amendment. The first success came in the House of Representatives in 1918, but it was not until August 26, 1920, that the thirty-sixth state approved the Nineteenth Amendment. Exactly fifty years after white American males granted the vote to blacks, they extended equal political rights to women. For Jane Addams, it was one of the triumphs of progressivism.

Peace rivaled social justice as an ideal in the mind of Jane Addams. True, her father had sponsored a company of soldiers during the Civil War, and the family always admired the brave men who fought so that the slaves could be free. By the time Jane Addams founded Hull House, however, she was beginning to have doubts about war. For one thing, it was inefficient and wasteful, and like most Progressives, Jane Addams reserved special hatred for these qualities. Why fight, she asked, when the alternative of reasoning together existed? War, in her opinion, was a rejection of human intelligence as a shaping influence on progress, a throwback to the tooth-and-claw existence of the jungle. In practice, armed conflict was a failure; it created far more problems than it solved. Moreover, in Jane Addams's view, war diverted the nation's attention from much needed social, political, and economic reforms. It was in this area, not in militarism, that she felt the nation's vigor could be both maintained and displayed. This was her answer to Theodore Roosevelt and the turn-of-the-century imperialists.

Another factor in Jane's pacifism and internationalism was her experience in the ghettos. Very different types of people, she became convinced, could coexist peacefully. If Chicago's immigrants, who constituted a microcosm of the Western world, could live together in a neighborhood, nations should be able to do the same. The end result would be a better life for all. Cooperation, not competition, held the answers to society's problems. On behalf of this belief, Jane Addams was willing to make pacifism aggressive. In 1907 she wrote that pacifists must renounce the "older dovelike ideal" and adopt a dynamic, forceful approach.

In that same year Jane Addams joined Samuel Gompers and William Jennings Bryan on the speakers' platform at the first National Peace Conference. The tone of this meeting and that of the following year was optimistic. "Physical force," as Jane Addams put it, "had ceased to be functional and would therefore disappear." It was the law of evolution. War was obsolete. Imagine, therefore, the shock of Jane Addams and other pacifists when on June 28, 1914, the assassination of Archduke Francis Ferdinand, heir to the Austro-Hungarian throne, ignited a major war in Europe. Initially the United States had no part in the conflict, and many Americans retreated smugly behind three centuries of believing themselves God's chosen people and three thousand miles of ocean. But for others, including Jane Addams, this position was extremely naive. She knew that the New World's immunity to European problems was not as complete as many of her contemporaries hoped. International trade and shipping linked the continents as did considerations of national security. There was also the sense of responsibility of many Americans for the kind of world in which they lived now and in the future.

In 1914 and 1915 Jane Addams played a leading role in putting into practice President Wilson's request for neutrality in thought as well as in deed. But for Jane the real goal was permanent world peace, and it was to this that she directed the bulk of her energies. In January 1915 she helped Carrie Chapman Catt found the Women's Peace party. At its first convention the party adopted eleven planks. Foremost among them was a proposal for a permanent neutral commission of international mediators to stop wars before they started. This harbinger of the League of Nations and the United Nations testified to the belief of Jane Addams and her colleagues that peace was a cause susceptible to scientific solution.

Three months after setting forth this plan, Jane Addams was at The Hague in Holland presiding over the first congress of the Women's International League for Peace and Freedom. Twelve nations sent delegations, and the united body expressed its conviction that women's natural concern with the preservation of human life should be capitalized upon in the interest of peace. The peace movement was allied with the suffrage movement. If women had the vote, it was implied, war would be less likely. At the conclusion of the Hague meeting, Jane toured the belligerent countries in the company of Dr. Aletta Jacobs, Holland's first female physician. They found the leaders of the warring nations receptive to their ideas, but reluctant to take a stand on peace for fear it would weaken their bargaining position with their enemies. Nonetheless, the press and the public in the various nations treated Jane's visit as a hopeful sign.

On returning to the United States in July 1915, Jane Addams found a climate of opinion markedly different from that she had encountered in Europe. The majority of Americans and their newspapers ridiculed the pacifists. Typical was the remark of Theodore Roosevelt, who otherwise had the highest opinion of Jane Addams. "Pacifists," said the hero of the Spanish-American War, "are cowards." Several factors figured in this hostility. First, German submarines, or U-boats, were making an all-out attack on the blockading British Navy. Neutral vessels were advised to remain clear of the North Atlantic in order to avoid unfortunate mistakes. Americans, however, insisted on their right to trade with whomever they pleased. Then the inevitable happened: an American ship, the *Gulflight*, was torpedoed. The country had scarcely absorbed this affront when news arrived that a German U-boat had sunk the British passenger liner *Lusitania* on May 7, 1915, with the loss of 1198 lives, including 128 Americans. Woodrow Wilson still kept the United States out of war, but he had less and less support for his neutralism.

Added to the submarine issue was an economic one. American

bankers were making heavy financial commitments to England and France. It followed that Allied defeat would mean the loss of billions of dollars. Moreover, American manufacturers enjoyed a lucrative business supplying munitions and other war products to the Allies. To a considerable extent, the prosperity of the United States was entwined with Allied military fortunes. Finally, there was the matter of historical and cultural ties. Most Americans felt closer to England than they did to Germany. American ideals, it was widely believed, were on the side of the Allies, and British propaganda skillfully nourished such thinking. In the public mind the Germans emerged as Stone-Age barbarians bent on the rape and pillage of innocent peoples.

The growing mood of sympathy for England explained in large part the ridicule and outright abuse heaped on Jane Addams and other pacifists. Criticism centered on the peace ship Henry Ford dispatched to Europe on December 4, 1915.[1] Jane Addams helped plan the venture despite her reservations about its seriousness. A few days before the sailing she fell ill with a serious kidney disease and was hospitalized. The Ford debacle was played out to its ineffective end without her.

Woodrow Wilson was reelected in 1916 on the campaign slogan "He Kept Us Out of War." The President personally hated war for many of the same reasons as Jane Addams, and he made a commendable struggle for peace and American noninvolvement. Twice he sent his top advisor, Colonel Edward M. House, to Europe in unsuccessful attempts to arrange peace negotiations. In December 1916 he tried once more to end the war by asking England and Germany to state their objectives as a prelude to compromise. But neither belligerent would give up the hope of a full-fledged victory. Even as Wilson urged "peace without victory," Germany planned a total military effort. Wilson had no choice but to prepare for the possibility of American involvement in the war. In 1916 Congress voted to increase the size of the army and to construct new warships, and Wilson created a Council of National Defense to facilitate industrial production.

Preparedness seemed to make sense when Germany announced on January 31, 1917, that she was beginning unrestricted submarine warfare. All ships, those of neutral nations included, were henceforth subject to attack. Wilson responded by breaking diplomatic relations

---

[1] Ford's peace ship is further discussed on pages 394–395.

with Germany, but he hesitated to take the final step to war. Three developments in the spring of 1917 changed his mind. First, an intercepted communication from German Foreign Minister Alfred Zimmermann revealed his country's interest in allying with Mexico and conquering part of the United States. Second, revolution against the Russian czar had put a democratic government in control of that country. Thus it now appeared that the Allies (England, France, Italy, Russia) were united in carrying the banner of popular sovereignty against autocracy. Finally, between February 3 and April 1, 1917, German submarines sank eight American ships in the North Atlantic.

In spite of these provocations, the actual decision to intervene as a belligerent in the European conflict was agonizing, particularly for a Progressive President who believed in reason and Christian brotherhood. Given this belief, Wilson had to state America's war objectives in highly idealistic terms. "The world must be made safe for democracy," he told the Congress on April 2, 1917, "we have no selfish ends to serve." As the President conceived it, the war was to be the greatest crusade of all; the goal was no less than freedom and justice for all mankind. On April 6, by a vast majority, Congress passed the war resolution.

Wilson deliberately phrased his rationale for war in terms that would appeal to the Progressive mind, and many Progressives followed him in supporting American intervention in World War I. They argued that this would be a war to end all war and that the federal government would begin assuming in wartime greater responsibility for the national welfare. John Dewey, Jane Addams's intellectual hero, defended the war as a practical step toward the advancement of permanent peace and liberal reform. But Jane was unconvinced. In her opinion war, for any reason, was a disaster, an admission that reason had given way to violence. As for domestic social advances that might be made during a war, she pointed out that many more might have been made if peace had prevailed.

In her opposition to World War I Jane Addams stood with some German-Americans and a handful of liberal intellectuals. But after April 6, 1917, most Americans regarded pacifists as traitors. Patriotism was easily warped into intolerance. George Creel's Committee on Public Information, created by the federal government to "sell the war to America," censored news, marshaled patriotic orators, and sat-

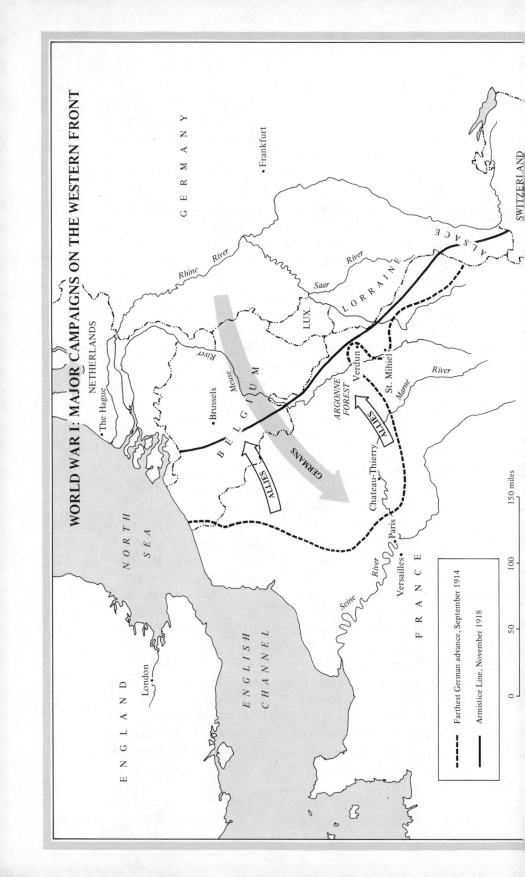

WORLD WAR I: MAJOR CAMPAIGNS ON THE WESTERN FRONT

ENGLAND

London

NORTH SEA

ENGLISH CHANNEL

NETHERLANDS

The Hague

Brussels

BELGIUM

LUX.

GERMANY

Frankfurt

Rhine River

Saar River

LORRAINE

ALSACE

SWITZERLAND

Meuse River

ALLIES

GERMANS

ARGONNE FOREST

Verdun

St. Mihiel

ALLIES

Chateau-Thierry

Marne River

Versailles

Paris

Seine River

FRANCE

- - - Farthest German advance, September 1914

——— Armistice Line, November 1918

0   50   100   150 miles

urated the country with anti-German propaganda. A wave of bigotry resulted. Many schools stopped teaching German; a mob pulled a German orchestra conductor off his podium. Sauerkraut was renamed "liberty cabbage"; frankfurters, "liberty pups." Those who openly opposed the war were subjected to vigilante justice. Hull House itself was "watched" by superpatriots from Chicago's American Protective League. The Espionage Act (1917) and the Sedition Acts (1918) provided mechanisms for punishing dissent. Jane Addams escaped personal abuse largely because she discontinued her public pacifist activities. Instead, she tried to humanize the war as much as possible. She argued for the right of conscientious objection and opposed the draft. Under Herbert Hoover, she served the United States Food Administration in an effort to promote food conservation and distribution to the needy. Occasionally, to be sure, she raised eyebrows by holding that hungry Germans should be fed as well as the citizens of the Allied nations. For Jane Addams, partisanship was inappropriate in the face of human suffering.

The armistice Jane Addams so anxiously awaited came on November 11, 1918. Americans had played a major role in bringing it about. Their initial contribution was in the form of morale, for when the United States joined the war in April 1917, the Allied will to resist was at low ebb. The U-boat blockade of food and supplies had proved so successful that the English doubted they could hold out for more than a few months. Russia had lost a million men in 1916 alone and was preoccupied with a revolution at home. On the western front, France seemed about to collapse before the German onslaught. In this context, America's decision to intervene began to have an effect even before troops could be mobilized. The United States Navy immediately challenged the submarine menace with convoys and mines. Within six months losses to the U-boats had decreased sharply. On the home front, American industry and agriculture launched a massive effort to feed and equip the Allies, and in Europe American troops confronted the German armies. Some 2 million "doughboys," many recruited under the Selective Service Act of 1917, manned the trenches across the path of the German advance into France. At Chateau-Thierry, only 50 miles from Paris, and at the Argonne, the American Expeditionary Force under General John J. Pershing provided vital assistance in turning back the invasion. Then the Americans joined the counter-offensive that ended the war.

After the armistice Jane Addams resumed her fight for world peace. Her first duty was to call another meeting of the Women's International League for Peace and Freedom, the first since 1915. The site selected was Zurich, Switzerland—a neutral vantage point from which delegates of all concerned nations could follow the course of the official peace negotiations in Paris. At both meetings discussion re-volved around the Fourteen Points Woodrow Wilson had set forth early in 1918 as a basis for a just and lasting peace. Eight of the points called for adjustments of European boundaries according to the principle of national self-determination. Five concerned guidelines for the conduct of nations, including the abolition of secret treaties and the freedom of the seas. The final point urged "a general association of nations . . . for the purpose of affording mutual guarantees of political independence and territorial integrity to great and small states alike." The Allied governments thought Wilson's formula too idealistic and too lenient in respect to Germany. In the course of the negotiations they gradually eroded the Wilsonian principles. When the final draft of the Treaty of Versailles was signed on June 28, 1919, Jane Addams joined Wilson in condemning it as punitive and calculated to increase, rather than lessen, the possibility of future war. Only the acceptance of the League of Nations idea, Wilson's fourteenth point, brightened the gloom.

Back in America, however, a quite different opinion of Wilson and the league was developing. Reacting against his crusading zeal, large segments of the American people turned away from their Presi-dent. His handling of the Paris negotiations created the impression that he was forcing his personal conception of world organization on the country. While such self-righteous leadership had its merits in beginning a war, it offended those seeking a return to normal condi-tions. In the congressional elections of 1918 voters returned Republi-can majorities to both houses of Congress.

After a sorrowful tour of the war-torn nations of Europe, Jane Addams returned to the United States to campaign for acceptance of the League of Nations. The Senate, which had to approve the Treaty of Versailles and the league, was sharply divided. Wilsonian Demo-crats favored ratification, but their number fell far short of the two-thirds needed for approval. Twelve to fifteen Senators, the Irreconcilables, opposed the treaty absolutely. They especially objected to the league on the ground that its provisions for collective security would involve the United States in an endless series of overseas wars. According to this viewpoint, America had erred in entering World War I and should henceforth isolate itself from Europe's problems. The remainder of the Senate was willing to accept a revised treaty—in particular, one that accorded more respect to national sovereignty.

Had Wilson been less of a moral idealist, he might have accepted some revisions and thereby gained enough votes for ratification. But despite the plea of his friends, Wilson chose not to compromise his principles. He was especially determined to resist the influence of Henry Cabot Lodge of Massachusetts, the prominent Republican chairman of the Senate Foreign Relations Committee and a bitter personal enemy. In September 1919 Wilson began an 8000-mile speaking tour to take his cause to the people. In the midst of it he collapsed, the victim of a paralyzing stroke. But still he refused compromise. When the election of 1920 resulted in the overwhelming defeat of the Democrats by Republican nominee and "normalcy" advocate Warren G. Harding, Wilson's last hopes died. The United States never joined the League of Nations and eventually made peace with Germany in a separate treaty.

Disillusioned as she was by these events, Jane Addams continued to make peace her overriding concern in the 1920s. Her most important contributions were writings analyzing why her countrymen were unable to enter into the cooperative internationalism on which world peace depended. The villain, she decided, was a virulent self-righteousness that deluded Americans into thinking they could best serve the world by looking after their own interests. The rejection of the league was clear evidence of this attitude. So, according to Addams, was American indifference to the spirit of the Washington Treaties of 1921–1922, which were an attempt to limit naval armaments and stabilize the situation in the Pacific. A similar insincerity marked American participation in the Kellogg-Briand Pact of 1928 outlawing war. Yet another instance of self-righteousness that troubled Jane Addams was the Red Scare of 1919, during which the government hounded thousands of alleged Communists. Jane Addams herself suffered verbal abuse from the American Legion, the Daughters of the American

Revolution, and other strongly patriotic organizations on account of her compassion for the peoples of Germany and Russia.

The same ugly nationalism appeared in even grosser form, in her estimation, in the trial of Nicola Sacco and Bartolomeo Vanzetti. These two Italian-Americans and admitted radicals were convicted on inconclusive evidence for a 1920 robbery and murder near Boston. Jane Addams was among the many liberal intellectuals who believed the men guilty only of being different. When Sacco and Vanzetti were electrocuted in 1927, she felt a part of American liberalism died with them.

The war debts and reparations question was another area in which American attitudes made no contribution to international peace. During World War I the United States had loaned the Allies considerable amounts of money. In the 1920s it demanded repayment, even though the debtor countries were experiencnig severe economic hardships. America also insisted on collecting the enormous reparations assessed against Germany as the cause of the war. Jane Addams did not expect forgiveness of these debts, but she felt her country could have been more understanding of the nations that had suffered so much.

Another development that disturbed Jane Addams in the 1920s was the growing opposition to immigration. She had long felt that immigrants constituted a vital and valuable component of American society. Indeed, with the exception of the Indians, every American had immigrant ancestry. The immigrant "problem," in her estimation, stemmed less from the immigrants themselves than from the injustices of American social and economic life. Given a chance, the foreign-born could become excellent Americans. Hull House existed to further this process. But many of her contemporaries disagreed. In their eyes immigrants, particularly the non-Aryans from Southern and Eastern Europe, were the cause of the nation's urban problems rather than their unfortunate victims.

The proponents of 100 percent Americanism gradually developed a case against immigration. One milestone was the forty-two-volume report of the United States Immigration Commission issued in 1910. It provided an elaborate, if heavily biased, correlation of immigration and vice, crime, poverty, and slums. Popular writing echoed these "conclusions." Madison Grant's *The Passing of the Great Race*

(1916) argued that the "melting pot" concept was a huge mistake. America could not continue to absorb undesirable racial elements and still maintain the "native" American type, characteristics, and institutions. "Maudlin sentimentalism" about the world's oppressed, Grant insisted, must be replaced with realism, the open door must be slammed shut. The *Saturday Evening Post* put it somewhat more bluntly: unless action were taken, one of its authors warned, Americans would become "a hybrid race of people as worthless and futile as the good-for-nothing mongrels of Central America and Southeastern Europe." Labor unions took up the cry for exclusion on the grounds that an abundance of immigrants depressed wages. Employers, of course, welcomed immigrants for the same reason, but by the 1920s mechanization had decreased the demand for unskilled labor.

The urgency of the immigration question increased suddenly after World War I as millions sought a sanctuary in the New World. More than 800,000 foreigners arrived in 1921 alone. Frightened, Congress passed an emergency measure establishing frankly discriminatory quotas. English-speaking immigrants and Aryans from Northern and Central Europe were given preference, and the total number of newcomers permitted to enter the country each year was sharply reduced. The National Origin (Immigration) Act of 1924 lowered quotas even further. In Jane Addams's eyes it was the sad and callous end of a three-century dream. America was no longer synonymous with opportunity and hope.

A heart attack in 1926 slowed Jane Addams down considerably. But she still maintained a keen interest in the American social scene and continued to write what ultimately amounted to over five hundred books and papers. Her stand on Prohibition was that drinking was not entirely evil. In the Hull House neighborhood the saloon provided an important element of social cohesion. And among immigrants, the drinking of beer, wine, and liquor was part of a cultural pattern. Of course she recognized and spoke out against abusive drinking, but in her view the disrespect for the law that Prohibition fostered was a comparable evil. And the bootlegging business that the policy spawned, especially in Al Capone's Chicago, was deplorable to her. It was with considerable relief that Jane Addams saw the Eighteenth Amendment to the Constitution repealed by the Twenty-First on December 5, 1933.

Reform also retained its interest for Jane Addams in the 1920s and early 1930s. Critical of the unimaginative conservatism of Republican Presidents Warren G. Harding and Calvin Coolidge, she voted in a losing cause for Eugene V. Debs, the Socialist, in the election of 1920, and for Robert La Follette, nominee of the revived Progressive party, in 1924. Of the latter and his accomplishments as governor and senator she wrote, "the political air of Wisconsin filled my lungs like a breath from the mountain tops of the finest American tradition." Also encouraging was the organization in 1920 of the American Civil Liberties Union, which took its stand on the people's capacity for self-government. But on the whole she felt that the American people in the 1920s were afraid of reform. They had seen the Russian Revolution wipe out private property rights, and any curbing of individual freedom by the government was suspect. From Jane Addams's perspective the period 1919–1929 was "inhibited" compared with the ten years preceding World War I.

Although Jane Addams voted for Herbert Hoover, a long-time personal friend, in the election of 1928 and again in that of 1932, she took considerable interest in the rising political star of Franklin D. Roosevelt. His sense of concern for the masses, as opposed to the rich, powerful, and established, was in line with her own. And his willingness to use the power of the federal government to achieve social justice delighted her after the timidity of the 1920s. Although she died some months before it was enacted, the Social Security Act of August 8, 1935, was the kind of law she had long advocated. But in the last analysis she approved of Roosevelt because even in the trying times created by the Great Depression, he avoided the extremes of communism on the one hand and totalitarianism on the other. Roosevelt reformed the American system in order to preserve its essence, and this, in Jane Addams's estimation,, was the central purpose of the previous half-century of American reform.

SELECTED READINGS

The Person

*ADDAMS, JANE: *Twenty Years at Hull-House* (1910). Along with her *The Second Twenty Years at Hull-House* (1930), these are

* Available in paperback.

the best sources of Jane Addams's thought and of information about her life.

FARRELL, JOHN C.: *Beloved Lady: A History of Jane Addams' Ideas on Reform and Peace* (1967). A summary of her involvement in two of her major interests.

*LASCH, CHRISTOPHER (ed): *The Social Thought of Jane Addams* (1965). A useful selection of key articles by Jane Addams.

LEVINE, DANIEL: *Jane Addams and the Liberal Tradition* (1971). The interrelation of a life and a political philosophy.

LINN, JAMES WEBER: *Jane Addams: A Biography* (1935). The only full-scale study.

The Period

*BREMER, ROBERT: *From the Depths: The Discovery of Poverty in the United States* (1964). The beginnings of the social welfare crusade.

*FLEXNER, ELEANOR: *Century of Struggle: The Women's Rights Movement in the United States* (1970). A reliable general survey.

*GRAHAM, OTIS L., JR.: *The Great Campaigns: Reform and War in America, 1900–1928* (1971). National politics.

*HOFSTADTER, RICHARD: *The Age of Reform: From Bryan to F.D.R.* (1960). A pioneering interpretation of the liberal impulse from Populism to the New Deal.

*LASCH, CHRISTOPHER: *The New Radicalism in America, 1889–1963* (1965). An analysis of the intellectuals, including Jane Addams, who questioned values and institutions in the twentieth century.

*LINK, ARTHUR: *Woodrow Wilson and the Progressive Era: 1910–1917* (1954). The best general survey by the author of a multivolume Wilson biography.

*MOWRY, GEORGE: *The Era of Theodore Roosevent and the Birth of Modern America* (1958). A broad look at the Progressive years.

*WHITE, MORTON: *Social Thought in America: The Revolt against Formalism* (1957). Intellectual cross-currents of the late nineteenth and early twentieth centuries.

* Available in paperback.

CHAPTER EIGHT

Gifford Pinchot

In the fading light of a February afternoon in 1907 a solitary horseman moved slowly along a trail in Rock Creek Park in Washington, D.C. Gifford Pinchot was mulling over an idea. As head of the young United States Forest Service, Pinchot had charge of administering the national forests. It was a big job, but he saw still larger horizons. Trees, after all, were only one natural resource. On that same day Pinchot had dealt with questions of stream flow, navigation, irrigation, flood control, water power, soil erosion,

*minerals, grassland, and wildlife. Yet these matters were
pigeonholed in separate government bureaus, and that, Pinchot
mused, was part of the problem. "Suddenly," in his words, "the idea
flashed through my head that there was a unity in this complication."
The "island" approach to environmental management was not
compatible with the indivisibility of the environment.*

*For Pinchot, the revelation in Rock Creek Park "was a good deal
like coming out of a dark tunnel." Now he saw the landscape as a
whole and the need for an equally comprehensive, long-range
administrative policy. A few days after the ride, in consultation
with his associates in the Forest Service and with his close friend
President Theodore Roosevelt, he coined the term* conservation.
*During the next four decades he saw it become a household word as
increasing numbers of Americans came to share his concern over
environmental deterioration.*

The young Gifford Pinchot did not seem destined to be a reformer.
His family had a firm position in the uppermost social and economic
echelon of nineteenth-century America, a group for whom conservatism was a way of life. Grandfather Cyril Pinchot had fought with
Napoleon. In 1816, after the restoration of the French monarchy,
Cyril fled to the United States. Settling in Milford, Pennsylvania, near
the Delaware River, he quickly established a prosperous dry goods
and transportation business. His son and Gifford's father, James
Pinchot, inherited the knack for success. After a decade of business in
New York City, money was no longer a problem. The rich got richer in
1864, when James married Mary Jane Eno, the daughter of real estate
mogul Amos Eno.

Gifford Pinchot was born August 11, 1865 at the elegant Connecticut estate of his maternal grandfather. His early life was typical
of a small number of very rich Americans. There were tutors and
governesses who shined and polished their little charges for parental
audiences. Private preparatory schools and colleges, Phillips Exeter
Academy and Yale in Pinchot's case, intensified the polishing. Summers passed pleasantly at the shore or in the mountains. The former
meant Newport, Rhode Island, a village on Narragansett Bay that

328

the Pinchots, along with Ward McAllister and New York's socially prominent "Four Hundred," discovered after the Civil War. The inland alternative took the Pinchots to upstate New York's Adirondack Mountains. There, in a comfortable sportsmen's lodge setting, Gifford acquired a love of hunting and especially of fishing that he never lost. For shorter vacations the Pinchots repaired to their manor house at Milford. Grey Towers, as it was called, was designed by Richard Morris Hunt, architect to the affluent in the late nineteenth century. It was taken for granted that such houses would be in the European mold; America's gentry of this era almost frantically sought to reproduce the aura surrounding Europe's nobility. A half-century elapsed before Frank Lloyd Wright and other architects of a native American style received recognition. With Wright's buildings, so sharply in contrast to the palaces of the Pinchots, the nation finally dared to be itself.

Of course, the Pinchot family was well connected. In later years Gifford could state as a simple fact that he knew every President from Ulysses S. Grant to Harry S. Truman. When such connections smoothed his way into Yale in 1885, it appeared he was well launched on a life of genteel ease. But the young man had a different orientation. Like Jane Addams, he chafed at the uselessness of his situation. In a note written to a friend in 1914 during his campaign for the United States Senate, Pinchot said: "my own money came from the unearned increment on land in New York held by my grandfather.... Having got my wages in advance in that way, I am now trying to work them out." Comfort, in short, was no challenge. In company with other overprivileged children (one thinks especially of Theodore Roosevelt), Pinchot felt compelled to strive, to excel, to lead. Public service of a reforming nature offered an outlet for these drives. Find a cause and become its champion—here was the formula for the genuine achievement people like Addams, Roosevelt, and Pinchot craved.

In Jane Addams's case the human refuse of growth provided the opportunity to serve. Gifford Pinchot chose another victim of capitalistic exploitation: the American forest. James Pinchot started his son's career when he suggested in 1885, on the eve of Gifford's departure for his freshman year at Yale, that forestry might be an exciting vocation. Certainly it would be new; the profession simply did not exist in the United States at that time. Gifford Pinchot recalled that when his father made the suggestion, he had "no more conception of what it meant to be a forester than the man in the moon." The only image the word conjured up was that of a man who "wore green cap and leather jerkin and shot cloth-yard arrows at the King's deer." But Gifford "loved the woods" and, with breadwinning beside the point, he was willing to experiment with his life.

In the 1880s neither Yale nor any other American college or university offered instruction in forestry. Pinchot therefore chose courses in biology, geology, meteorology, and astronomy. He also found time for participation in the clubs, teams, literary societies, and class "rushes" that were so much a part of collegiate life in that era. Tall, lean, and ruggedly handsome, Pinchot made friends easily and took keen pleasure in his college years. As commencement approached, a classmate asked him the inevitable question: "what are you going to do after graduation?" Be a forester, Pinchot replied. "What's that?" responded the friend. "That's why I am going to be a forester," Pinchot rejoined. Being one, however, demanded special training available only in Europe. In the Old World, where supplies of wood were limited, forests had long been regarded as crops and carefully managed so as to ensure a sustained yield of lumber. This, in fact, was the definition of forestry that Pinchot should have provided his inquiring classmate.

Gifford's first stops on his postgraduate tour were England and Germany, where he talked with the men responsible for introducing forestry to British India. From these interviews the trail led to France and the French Forest School at Nancy. Bilingual as a result of years of tutoring, Pinchot learned easily and eagerly. He was especially impressed with the seriousness of European forest management. The foresters in charge were powerful government officers, and the penalties for burning or illegally cutting trees were severe. Every scrap of wood, down to pencil-sized sticks, was carefully collected and utilized. The annual revenue of the forests of France and Germany astonished the young American, and he was amazed to learn that their level of productivity had remained constant since the time of Columbus. Here was sustained yield for sure!

Returning to the United States late in 1890, Pinchot faced a discouraging situation. "So far as . . . natural resources were concerned," he observed, "we were still a nation of pioneers." With very few exceptions, Americans subscribed to the myth of inexhaustibility. The environment, they assumed, was a cornucopia from which could be wrung a never-ending bounty of raw materials. Attitudes had not changed appreciably since the seventeenth century. Progress was synonymous with exploitation; profit was god; and the environment's sole function was to line American pockets. Armed with such ideas and unrestrained by government regulation, Americans raped their land. In lumbering, a strip-and-run philosophy prevailed. Rather than harvesting timber on sustained yield principles, as a crop, loggers clear-cut the forests, moving westward like a swarm of locusts. A scarcity of trees? Absurd! Over the next ridge there were more and more. Indeed, the problem was too many, not too few, trees. The long-term interests of society made little difference to a people who measured their history in decades rather than millennia. What, the typical American demanded, did posterity ever do for me?

Bolstering the economic rationale for exploiting the environment was the assumption that undeveloped land was not only useless, but evil. The first settlers carried from Europe, and particularly from the Christian tradition, the idea that a wilderness was a cursed place, the abode of Satan and lesser devils like the heathen Indians. The wilderness was feared and, whenever possible, avoided until its redemption by the twin forces of civilization and Christianity. It followed that the conquest of the land was the pioneer's special pride. Symbolic of that victory was the destruction of trees, the clearing of the land. The result, both literally and figuratively, was the substitution of light for darkness.

The pioneer situation was simply not conducive to conservation. Here, trees were enemies. When the land was covered with trees and settlements were specks in a vast wilderness, forest management would not even be a consideration. The difficulty was that pioneer priorities remained long after true pioneer circumstances had vanished. This frontier hangover worked against every conservation effort.

Pinchot's postgraduate year in Europe made him keenly aware of the price Americans paid for the lack of government regulation of the use of the environment. Government, indeed, seemed in league with the exploiters. For over a century the state and federal land agencies had diligently pursued a policy of selling the land to private owners at prices that could best be labeled handouts. North Carolina sold some of the finest hardwood forest in the world at 10 cents an acre. The federal government bettered even this price by giving millions of acres free to mining and railroad interests. The Northern Pacific Railroad alone received more land than the total area of Pennsylvania, New Jersey, and Rhode Island combined. Under the Timber and Stone Act of 1878 a citizen could obtain up to 160 acres of forest land supposedly "unfit for cultivation" at a price of $2.50 per acre. In theory the act was intended to help individual settlers, but in practice it invited corruption. Lumber companies quickly lined up stooges whose "claims" soon became part of their sprawling empires. But such circumvention was not really necessary. Many companies operated on cut-out-and-get-out principles wherever they pleased, "stealing timber," as Pinchot put it, from the nation. Enforcement of existing forest laws was out of the question in the vastness of the American West. Moreover, the whole issue of federal land administration was, in Pinchot's words, "dripping with politics."

According to Pinchot, the most unfortunate part of the disposal of the public domain was that once the land left government ownership, so did all power to regulate its use. The sacred cows of individualism, free enterprise, and Anglo-American law combined to ensure that a man could do as he pleased with land he possessed. Ownership, for all intents and purposes, was absolute.

The forest fire question typified the American attitude toward resources in the late nineteenth century. Nobody cared. In 1891 alone Pinchot estimated that at least 12 million acres of forest burned in the United States. The fact elicited only yawns. In Europe, by way of contrast, Pinchot found that a single fire of less than 6000 acres was still lamented *ninety years* after it occurred. He concluded that the nation to which he returned to practice forestry was "obsessed . . . by a fury of development. The American Colossus was fiercely intent on appropriating and exploiting the riches of the richest of all continents—grasping with both hands, reaping where he had not sown, wasting what he thought would last forever."

Gifford Pinchot obviously bucked the mainstream of American environmental thinking in the 1890s, but he could find some reasons for optimism in the nation's past. As early as 1626 cracks appeared in the illusion of inexhaustibility. After only six years of occupying the region, the colonists around the Plymouth settlement in Massachusetts found that convenient supplies of timber were disappearing. They therefore passed a law regulating the cutting and sale of timber, the first conservation measure in American history. Thirteen years later Rhode Islanders looked at their shrinking meat supply and instituted a protective policy for deer for six months of the year. The first large-scale instance of enlightened environmental planning occurred in Pennsylvania in 1681. William Penn, the proprietor, decreed that "in clearing the ground, care be taken to leave an acre of trees for every five acres cleared." Penn even appointed a "woodsman" to supervise the cutting, and took steps to eliminate forest fires. Over the next century and a half there were a number of similar responses to regional shortages of natural resources.

A new note sounded in the 1840s, however, with the emergence of the American sportsman. He was a gentleman hunter or fisherman who believed that game and fish had value other than as food. With his finely tooled shotgun and light bamboo flyrod, he elevated hunting and fishing to the level of sport. The sportsmen also launched a protest against the market hunters' wholesale slaughter, which threatened the end of the game supply. In 1850 the New York Game Protective Association became the nation's first private conservation organization. In the West the pioneer perspective held sway; it was the older states, where the first pinches of scarcity occurred, that were the first to respond. A social factor also figured in the emergence of a conservation mentality. Upper-class easterners, particularly those who lived in cities, did not have to wrest a living from the land. From the perspective of paved streets and townshouse libraries, nature took on a quite different meaning. Less a threat, the natural world could be appreciated and even protected. Pinchot illustrates the point. Had he been the son of a Minnesota lumberman instead of a Manhattan millionaire, it is doubtful that he would have become a champion of conservation.

As Pinchot reviewed the progress of environmental protection in his own lifetime, the work of several foresighted men gave him reason for encouragement. One was George Perkins Marsh, scientist, diplomat, and world traveler, whose book, *Man and Nature*, appeared in 1864. Pinchot read the book as a student at Yale and found it exciting and inspiring. Marsh contended that the condition of the environment was as much a product of man as of nature. Man's power to transform the natural world should entail a commensurate sense of responsibility. That it did not, he warned, was one of the gravest threats to the welfare, and indeed to the survival, of civilization. Focusing most of his book on the disastrous consequences of deforestation for the water supply, Marsh pointed to ancient empires around the Mediterranean Sea whose declines paralleled that of their woodlands. Would the United States follow the same suicidal course? In Marsh's opinion there were already strong indications that this would be the case. His book was written to stem the tide of environmental destruction, and he called for immediate reforms in forest and watershed management. One sentence stuck in young Pinchot's mind: "man has too long forgotten," Marsh wrote, "that the earth was given to him for usufruct alone, not for consumption, still less for profligate waste."

The second giant in early American conservation history was John Wesley Powell, a scientist-explorer whose loss of one arm in a Civil War battle did not prevent him from leading the first descent of the Colorado River in 1869. Powell subsequently conducted detailed investigations into the geography and hydrology of the Great Basin between the Rocky Mountains and California's Sierra. In 1878 he presented to Congress a *Report on the Lands of the Arid Region of the United States*, and three years later he assumed direction of the United States Geological Survey. Powell challenged traditional American ideas in three important ways. First, he showed the Great Basin to be neither an agrarian paradise nor a "Great American Desert," but rather a region suited to limited, carefully controlled agriculture. The second element of Powell's challenge was his insistence that the dams and irrigation projects necessary for agriculture in the Far West could not be built by private enterprise. Money and manpower on a scale only the federal government could provide would be required for reclamation of arid lands. Finally, Powell dared to question the beneficence of the widely heralded Homestead Act of 1862 and its 160-acre allotments of virtually free land. Beyond the 100th meridian of longitude where the annual rainfall seldom exceeded 20 inches, Powell felt that 160 acres was an unworkable unit. It was much too small for grazing stock and much too large for intensive irrigation. The overall import of Powell's report was clear. Instead of allowing preconceived hopes and fears to determine environmental policy, Americans should base it on a long, realistic look at their landed heritage and their future needs.

Another American who commanded Pinchot's respect was Carl Schurz. As Secretary of the Interior from 1877 to 1881 under President Rutherford B. Hayes, Schurz brought the European perspective of his native Germany to the question of resource management in the New World. During his tenure as secretary he called repeatedly for federal forest management. It was time, he believed, to stop selling the public domain to private exploiters; the land should be leased to responsible developers. In this way tight federal control could be maintained. In view of this stand, Pinchot correctly identified Schurz as the father of the national forests.

Marsh, Powell, and Schurz led a small group of Americans bold enough to challenge the prevailing conception of the land's purpose and to expose inexhaustibility as a myth. They were also prepared to question the free enterprise dogma that rejected the prospect of government regulation even in society's interest. In their lifetimes Marsh, Powell, and Schurz were dismissed as hysterical alarmists and dangerous radicals. It would fall to Pinchot and other second-generation conservationists to implement their ideas in federal institutions such as the Reclamation Service (1902) and the Forest Service (1905).

Utilitarianism was the primary defense for early American conservation and the one that always made the most sense to Gifford Pinchot. Natural resources were useful, so they should be conserved. Economics explained everything. Forests, Pinchot learned in Europe, must *pay*. But esthetic considerations also had a place in the growing conservation movement. Those concerned with the preservation of beauty agreed with Ralph Waldo Emerson that nature could serve many purposes. A tree might be lumber; it might also be the inspiration for poetry and religion. The roots of esthetic appreciation of the American environment ran back a century before Pinchot's birth to Romantics like the Virginia country gentleman William Byrd, the botanist William Bartram, and the ornithologist John James Audubon. In the first half of the nineteenth century painters like Thomas Cole, writers like James Fenimore Cooper, and poets like William Cullen Bryant led the way. But the preeminent champion of the beauty and spirituality of unspoiled nature was Henry David Thoreau. Beginning in the late 1830s, Thoreau used the ideas of his fellow Transcendentalist Emerson to build a philosophy of the value of the wild. At its heart was the idea that nature reflected moral laws and spiritual truths. "In Wildness," he declared, "is the preservation of the World." Both physical and intellectual vigor depended on occasional contact with nature. Thoreau deplored the commercialism of the Age of Jackson. In 1845 he deliberately turned his back on it and sought in an isolated cabin at Walden Pond ways to simplify his existence and commune with nature.

For esthetic conservationists like Thoreau, the preservation of unspoiled nature against the encroachments of American enterprise was imperative. The institutional embodiments of such thinking were national and state parks and forest preserves. The calls for wilderness protection that began with George Catlin in 1832 were climaxed exactly forty years later with the establishment of Yellowstone National Park. This designation of over 2 million acres in northwestern Wyoming as a "public park or pleasuring ground for the benefit and enjoyment of the people" marked the first instance in history of large-scale wilderness preservation in the public interest. The second milestone was the establishment in 1885 of a state Forest Preserve in New York's Adirondack Mountains, and in 1890 naturalist John Muir successfully persuaded Congress to designate 1500 square miles of California's Sierra Nevada as Yosemite National Park.

Gifford Pinchot was skeptical about esthetic conservation and national parks. He welcomed men like Muir as allies in the crusade against enviornmental exploitation, but as a professional forester accustomed to thinking of trees as a crop, he could not accept simple preservation. The science of forestry demanded periodic cutting of selected mature trees. This was illegal in the national parks. As a consequence, Pinchot and Muir were uneasy colleagues in the 1890s, uncertain about one another's ultimate intentions.

The Forest Reserve Act of 1891 increased the confusion. This law, which slipped through Congress almost unnoticed, gave the President power to withdraw from private sale and proclaim as a public reservation any forest land owned by the federal government. Within a month after its passage, President Benjamin Harrison designated 13 million acres in various parts of the West as forest reserves. At the time, no one in the federal government had a clear idea of what to do with the land in question. John Muir, who founded the Sierra Club in

THE DECLINE OF U. S. VIRGIN FORESTS

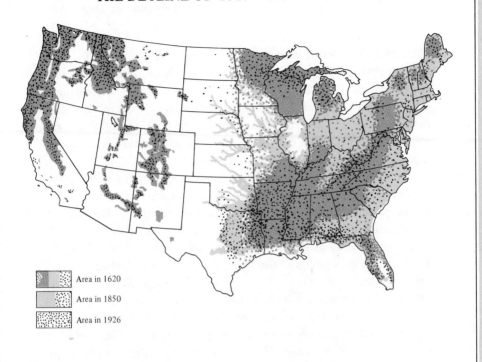

Area in 1620
Area in 1850
Area in 1926

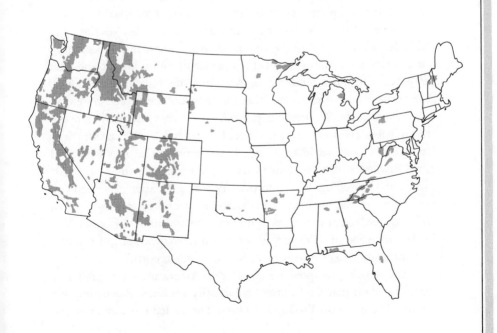

NATIONAL FORESTS 1930

1892 as a defender of wilderness, hoped the reserves would be managed as national parks. Pinchot, on the other hand, assumed the new reserves marked the beginning of federal involvement in sustained-yield forestry. The conflict inherent in these different philosophies came to a head in the summers of 1896 and 1897, when Muir and Pinchot served together on a federal commission charged with recommending a management policy for the reserves.

At first Muir's views prevailed, and on February 22, 1897, President Grover Cleveland created over 21 million acres of forest reserves in the West with no mention of utilitarian objectives. But western congressmen and businessmen, by now fully aware of the Forest Reserve Act, howled in protest. There was even talk of impeaching the President. In the opinion of the West, the reserves "locked up" natural resources and with them growth, jobs, and prosperity. On June 4, 1897, western votes helped pass the Forest Management Act, which left no doubt that the reserves would be developed. According to the act, the primary purpose of the government forests was "to furnish a continuous supply of timber for the use and necessities of citizens of the United States." It also opened the reserves to mining and grazing. Pinchot's philosophy of environmental management had been vindicated; Muir could no longer expect the reserves to remain wild.

Gifford Pinchot's crusade benefited considerably during the 1890s from the impact of the ending of the frontier. In the beginning all America was a frontier, and the presence of virgin land to the west exerted an enormous influence on American life and thought. Indeed, Americans mistakenly assumed that the frontier, like natural resources, was inexhaustible. Westward expansion, however, went on at an accelerating pace. The frontier shifted decade by decade as a growing population carved out settlements in the wilderness. The inevitable end came, marked with terse, bureaucratic finality in the census of 1890: "up to and including 1880 the country had a frontier of settlement, but at present the unsettled area has been so broken into by isolated bodies of settlement that there can hardly be said to be a frontier line. In the discussion of its extent, its westward movement, etc., it can not, therefore, any longer have a place in the census reports."

The shock prompted disbelief. But Americans were gradually forced to admit that the frontier had actually vanished. Pioneering was history. The historian Frederick Jackson Turner led the way in assessing its meaning. In 1893, three years after the census report, he published an essay entitled "The Significance of the Frontier in American History." Turner's ideas cut the channels in which a great deal of American thought on this subject subsequently flowed. The crux of his argument was the belief that the frontier had played the dominant role in shaping American character and institutions. Democracy, he contended, was a forest product. Individualism, self-reliance, respect for common men, and an urge to perfect society emerged from the opportunities inherent in wilderness conditions. The New World, according to Turner, had been a clean slate on which idealists had drawn their dreams for a better life. By virtue of being exposed to the transforming influence of the frontier, the American was a better man than the European. Although Turner occasionally recognized that frontier democracy had some liabilities, his attempts at scholarly impartiality only thinly masked a conviction of the superiority of democracy.

Even if we grant the oversimplifications in Turner's thesis, there was enough truth in his environmental explanation of American development to cause his contemporaries to think of the frontier as a valuable part of the national heritage. Concern over the disappearance of frontier conditions followed. Turner himself wondered whether American ideals "have acquired sufficient momentum to sustain themselves under conditions so radically unlike those in the days of their origin." The implication was that with the passing of the frontier, America might have seen the passing of its greatest age. The course of the nation might now be a downhill slide.

By the turn of the century many Americans had joined Turner in his uneasiness about the ending of the frontier. One did not have to read his essay to perceive that for two and a half centuries the frontier largely explained America's remarkable material growth as well as many characteristics of its citizenry. One result of this frame of mind, and the one that helped Gifford Pinchot, was a tendency to be receptive to the conservation idea. It seemed logical that conservation would preserve the remainder of America's abundance, deny the chilling implications of the census pronouncement, and assuage anxiety over the nation's advancing age. Conservation, to be sure, was not the only beneficiary of turn-of-the-century anxieties. Imperialism, which in some eyes represented a search for new frontiers, also reflected the prevailing mood. But conservation had special appeal because it at-

339

Along with Gifford Pinchot, Theodore Roosevelt (left) and John Muir (right) dominated the early American conservation movement. Here they stand on the rim of Yosemite Valley, part of the national park Muir played a major role in establishing. The year of the photograph is 1903.

The opening of the last Indian territories in the West occasioned wild scrambles for land claims and signified the ending of the frontier. Here homestead claimants rush into Oklahoma's "Cherokee Strip" on September 16, 1893.

The Tennessee Valley Authority and its work after 1933 in the upper South climaxed the dream of men like Gifford Pinchot for a completely and efficiently managed environment. This is Norris Dam on the Clinch River, completed in 1936 and named after the most important advocate of the TVA idea, Senator George Norris. The spillway (background) is almost 40 feet higher than Niagara Falls.

vironmental irresponsibility came home to roost with a vengeance in the Middle est in the 1930s. With the grass ploughed under, the soil literally blew away. ousands of people were broken both financially and spiritually. This eloquent otograph was taken as part of a federal project by Arthur Rothstein in the heart the "Dust Bowl."

tacked the problem, which was basically environmental, directly. Conservation would be, in a sense, the new frontier, keeping the nation young, vigorous, prosperous, democratic, and wholesome. For a civilization that had begun to notice its first gray hairs, conservation was welcome psychological as well as environmental tonic.

Pinchot's plea for environmental realism and responsibility also received support in the 1890s from national recognition of the plight of American agriculture. The trouble on the farms began shortly after the Civil War, when agricultural prices started a thirty-year decline. Increased productivity, the result of mechanized cultivation of ever-larger fields, overburdened the market, and at this time there were no federal price supports for commodity prices. The more farmers produced, the less they earned. Moreover, American farmers were for the first time competing in a world market. Nonperishable products such as wheat could be grown in Australia or South America, shipped to the United States, and still hold at competitive prices. On a smaller scale, the bulk produce of huge "bonanza" farms in the trans-Mississippi West affected agricultural prices in other parts of the nation.

As farm income declined throughout the 1870s and 1880s, more and more farmers found it necessary to mortgage their land either to banks or, under the lien system prevalent in the South, to the local general store. As debtors in an age of deflationary fiscal policy and falling crop prices, farmers found it increasingly difficult to pay what they owed. For example, a debt equivalent to 100 bushels of potatoes might, five years later, require 125 bushels to pay off. Indebtedness hung on year after year, embittering farmers and raising visions of a sinister eastern money-lending conspiracy. The government also received a share of criticism for both its deflationary monetary policy and a tariff policy that discriminated against agriculture and in favor of industry. The prices farmers paid for manufactured goods, in other words, were supported artificially, whereas agricultural goods had to compete in an unprotected market.

A psychological factor also figured in the frustration of late nineteenth-century American farmers. Since New World settlement began, those who labored in the earth had been regarded by a grateful nation as God's chosen people. Agriculture, as Thomas Jefferson so often said, was the backbone of the Republic. America could take pride in being a nation of sturdy yeoman farmers. But the Jacksonian and Civil

War eras accelerated a process that gradually substituted the industrialist and businessman for the farmer in the hierarchy of American esteem. The action, people discovered, was in the cities. More and more, the business of America was business. The farmer, meanwhile, acquired the image of an uncouth drudge—the hayseed or hick. In contrast to the glitter of the urban scene, farm life seemed an impossibly dull round of backbreaking chores. From an American nobleman the farmer declined into an American joke. And at the same time the American West, that "Garden of the World," became a prison. This dual transformation unquestionably played a part in the growth of agrarian bitterness.

Of course the farmer was a cause as well as a victim of hard times. Gifford Pinchot understood the problem very well. The soil, like the forest, was not a cornucopia. Even the incredibly rich land of the tidewater South and the Mississippi Valley in time showed the effects of intensive one-crop farming. Cotton and tobacco were particularly hard on the soil, but men desperate for money felt they could not afford to let their fields lie fallow to recover fertility. They demanded bumper crops year after year. For a while the land obliged, but then the reckoning came. Productivity dropped, and men left the worn-out land for fresh fields in the West. The system worked as long as fertile, well-watered land was abundant. But as Pinchot knew, the farmers, devouring their capital, were living on borrowed time.

The trans-Mississippi West was the farmers' last frontier. After the Civil War they followed the railroads onto the Great Plains, breaking the rough prairie sod with James Oliver's improved plow and fencing the tilled land with Joseph F. Glidden's invention—barbed wire. But as John Wesley Powell pointed out, men could not invent water. This lesson was seared into the minds of western farmers by a series of droughts in the late 1880s. Crops and credit withered. Desperate men, accustomed to "go West" in the face of such adversity, found themselves at the limits of agriculture with no place to turn. As they reviewed "the farm problem" of the 1890s, all Americans gained a keener appreciation of the meaning of scarcity and the necessity of environmental management.

The farmers themselves were more inclined to shift blame for their predicament from themselves and from the environment to political and economic injustices. The organization of agricultural in-

343

terests on a national level was the most visible response to this interpretation of their plight. Oliver H. Kelley launched the first farmers'
organization in 1867 under the grandiose title Patrons of Husbandry.
Better known as the Grange from the name of its local units, Kelley's
group included over a million farmers by the mid-1870s. The Gran-
gers began cooperative buying and selling arrangements, pressed for
state regulation of railroads and grain elevators, and supported the
efforts of the Greenback party to increase the supply and value of
paper currency. When in 1877 the United States Supreme Court upheld a Grange-sponsored law respecting railroad rates in the case of
Munn v. *Illinois*, organized farming won an encouraging victory. In
the *Wabash* case nine years later, however, the Court invalidated all
state laws on interstate commerce and left the farmers once again
without legal recourse in the face of rate discrimination.

The Farmers Alliance continued the work of the Grange in the
1880s. By now the farmers' demands had expanded to include the free
coinage of silver (an attempt to increase the amount of money in
circulation, alleviate the plight of debtors, and raise farm prices), a
reduction in tariff rates, a federal income tax, a system of government
loans to farmers, and tight government control—if not outright ownership—of railroads. By 1890 the Alliance was a major factor in state
and local elections, particularly in rural regions of the South and West.
Two years later organized farmers and some laborers were ready to
enter the national political arena under the banner of the Populist or
People's party. A convention in Omaha, Nebraska, wrote a platform
based on the familiar agrarian grievances. In the ensuing election the
Populist nominee, James B. Weaver of Iowa, received over a million
popular and twenty-two electoral votes. A speech by Ignatius Don-
nelly of Minnesota typified the emotionalism surrounding the 1892
effort: he thundered from the soapbox that "the fruits of the toil of
millions are boldly stolen to build up colossal fortunes for a few."

As one of the fortunate few, Gifford Pinchot looked askance at
the often ill-informed and violent accusations of the rural radicals.
Populist leaders such as "Sockless" Jerry Simpson of Kansas and
Mary Ellen Lease, the "raise-less-corn-and-more-hell" girl, were about
as far from the social and political style of the Pinchots as it was
possible to get. So, for that matter, was William Jennings Bryan, the
Nebraska orator who skyrocketed into leadership of both the Demo-

cratic and Populist parties in an unsuccessful bid for the Presidency in 1896. William McKinley, the conservative, portly Republican, was the natural choice of established people like the Pinchots. But Gifford recognized that the Populists were his allies in protesting a situation that resulted, at least in part, from unwise exploitation of the environment. And he was learning to appreciate the efforts of those who championed the rights of the people against entrenched power and privilege. As for the farmers, they lost the battle in 1896 but won the war. Within a few years, most of their seemingly radical demands were American institutions, and the American farmer found himself a relatively pampered and prosperous individual.

By the end of the 1890s Gifford Pinchot was widely recognized as the foremost American forester. He had demonstrated his ability on the private forest lands of the Vanderbilt family's estate, Biltmore, near Asheville, North Carolina. The sustained yield and sustained profits Pinchot extracted from Biltmore's hardwood stands persuaded the Vanderbilts to purchase 100,000 adjoining acres. Pinchot took charge and made western North Carolina the birthplace of American forestry. Meanwhile, he opened an office in New York City as a consulting forester and enjoyed a succession of private and state clients. The customer he desired most, however, was the United States. In 1898 opportunity knocked. Bernhard E. Fernow resigned as head of the federal Division of Forestry, and President William McKinley's secretary of agriculture offered Pinchot the job. At the time the division was little more than in information agency, a forestry organization without forests. But Pinchot was delighted to join the federal team. His vision was fixed not on what federal forestry was, but on what it might become. In particular, his hopes centered on the forest reserves and the possibility of consolidating their management under the direction of his office.

At this point in his career Gifford Pinchot and conservation became the beneficiaries of two significant national developments: the advent of progressivism and the succession to the Presidency of Theodore Roosevelt. Roosevelt succeeded to the nation's highest office September 14, 1901. President William McKinley had died from an assassin's bullet fired a week earlier. Quite in character, the Vice President was on a mountain-climbing expedition when news of the shooting reached him. At forty-two he was the youngest chief executive in American history to that date. In background and character he closely resembled Pinchot. Roosevelt's family was equally wealthy and of the patrician class. His youth had been spent in private schools, on European tours, and in an Ivy League college—Harvard in his case. After graduating in 1880, Roosevelt faced the choice of a career with mixed emotions. His strong sense of personal morality and social consciousness, along with his distaste for the crass materialism of the newly rich, ruled out business. For a time he considered teaching and writing, and actually published several creditable volumes of history, but a literary life left his passion for physical challenge and leadership unsatisfied. Being a gentleman-sportsman appealed to his obsession with virility and his love of outdoor adventure, but did little for his sense of duty. So Roosevelt decided to become a politician and lead the nation to greatness.

With this decision behind him, he rose rapidly. He served as New York state assemblyman, police commissioner of New York City, assistant secretary of the navy, and governor of New York. In 1898 Roosevelt's participation in the Spanish-American War gave him the national reputation he needed for federal office. Two years later the hero of San Juan Hill was elected vice-president under McKinley. New York's political boss, Senator Thomas C. Platt, was delighted to see the unmanageable governor removed to the relatively innocuous pastures of the vice-presidency. But many Republican leaders had their doubts about the impetuous Roosevelt. Republican strategist Mark Hanna dourly warned, "There's only one life between this madman and the White House." But while Roosevelt's rhetoric and general aggressiveness gave promise of radicalism, he had a self-confessed "horror of extremes." He preferred a compromising middle way that would champion reform and still preserve the best of the old order. He would act—but as he told Mark Hanna, he would "go slow."

The trails of Pinchot and Roosevelt first crossed in 1894 when Pinchot was a consulting forester in New York. From their correspondence it appears that Pinchot had no difficulty convincing Roosevelt of the need for scientific forest management. In 1897 Roosevelt sponsored Pinchot's election to the Boone and Crocket Club, an elite group of trophy hunters. Two years later, when Roosevelt was governor, the relationship of the two men seems to have taken a more personal turn. Pinchot's autobiography notes that on one visit to the

346

executive mansion, "T.R. and I did a little wrestling, at which he beat me; and some boxing, during which I had the honor of knocking the future President of the United States off his very solid pins." In later years in Washington, D.C., the President and his chief forester expanded their activities to include hiking, riding, and a great deal of tennis. Indeed, Pinchot was in the circle of close Roosevelt friends, enjoying the kind of access to the President about which most bureaucrats only dream. Such personal contact goes a long way toward explaining the rise of the conservation movement in the early twentieth century.

When Roosevelt entered the White House to complete McKinley's term, the alleged abuses of big business were a leading national issue. Beginning in the 1890s a number of journalists threw off illusion and restraint in their anger over economic and political injustice. Their purpose was protest and, ultimately, reform; their target was the concentrated power of the nation's largest companies and corporations. Popular magazines provided the primary outlet for these exposés. Ida M. Tarbell continued Henry Demarest Lloyd's criticism of the oil industry in a series of bitter articles in *McClure's*. Ray Stannard Baker used the same journal to lash out at the railroads. In the widely read pages of *Everybody's* and *Cosmopolitan*, Thomas W. Lawson and David Graham Phillips added fuel to the fire under high finance and high politics. Such articles obviously contained exaggeration as well as fact, but they influenced millions of readers. Novels also made a significant contribution. Theodore Dreiser, Frank Norris, and Jack London portrayed economic and social conditions in a way calculated to arouse the wrath of idealistic Americans. Another novelist, Upton Sinclair, described the lack of standards in the meat-packing industry in such graphic detail as to cause many readers of *The Jungle* (1906) to become physically ill.

Roosevelt was not sympathetic to such one-sided criticism. In fact, it was he who coined the deprecatory term *muckraking* to describe those writers who could see only the sordid. But while the muckrakers were clearly on the angry fringe of progressivism, they provided the vital spark that stimulated many of their more moderate countrymen to concern and action.

Criticism of the free enterprise system, with its unrestrained competition and resulting concentration of wealth and power, represented a considerable change for beneficiaries of that system such as Theodore Roosevelt and Gifford Pinchot. As an undergraduate at Yale in the 1880s Pinchot swallowed William Graham Sumner's brand of Social Darwinism whole. When asked in an assignment to discuss government regulation of railroad rates, Pinchot responded as a conservative: "the railroads own the tracks and the cars, don't they? Then why shouldn't they charge what they please?" It was dog-eat-dog, and the victor deserved the spoils. But as he matured Pinchot began to see flaws in this philosophy. He noticed that unrestrained lumber companies left environmental chaos in their wake. And he saw how concentrated wealth could warp the purposes of laws. In time Pinchot became convinced that despite its blessings, private enterprise sometimes thwarted the long-term public interest. He also came to see that the only organization strong enough to make business socially responsible was the federal government. With this perspective, Pinchot was well on his way to becoming a Progressive.

Theodore Roosevelt felt much the same way about big business. He admitted that "this is an age of combination," and he readily acknowledged the contributions that efficient, large-scale businesses made to American life. But he also understood that large corporations often acted without regard to the common good. The solution, as Roosevelt and Pinchot saw it, was for the federal government, in the name of the people, to control and regulate the giant trusts and corporations. They had no intention of destroying the basis of the American free enterprise system, but they would use the state as a positive force to preserve fair play. This stewardship concept most nearly defined Roosevelt's and Pinchot's variety of progressivism.

Seeking tools to implement his reform philosophy, Roosevelt dusted off the Sherman Antitrust Act, which had been notoriously ineffective since its passage in 1890. His Attorney General, Philander C. Knox, announced soon after Roosevelt became President that the federal government was planning a suit under the Sherman Act with the purpose of breaking up the Northern Securities Company, the huge financial empire that resulted from the merger of the railroads of James J. Hill and Edward H. Harriman. Since the names of Rockefeller and Morgan were also involved, the Northern Securities Company was the preeminent symbol in the public mind of consolidated, unprincipled wealth. Roosevelt's challenge to its legitimacy met with widespread approval. When in 1903 a federal court order directed the company to dissolve and a year later the Supreme Court upheld the decision, the President became a shining knight. The cheers continued as the Roosevelt Administration undertook prosecution of forty-four more corporations in such industries as meat, tobacco, and oil.

It was an indication of the political genius of Pinchot and the rest of the Roosevelt team that they could satisfy both sides of the trust question. Even while developing a national reputation as a "trust buster," the Roosevelt Administration managed to assure capitalists that it was not their enemy. Big businessmen quickly perceived that progressivism was their best protection against more radical reform proposals such as those of the Populists, the labor organizations, and the Socialists. Roosevelt satisfied the public demand for reform, yet left the American economy essentially unchanged. He reformed in order to preserve, and in many cases he allowed the representatives of business to write and implement their own reform proposals. Only to those who accept the trust-busting myth is it surprising that the Morgans, Rockefellers, and other captains of industry donated generously to Roosevelt's war chest in the 1904 Presidential campaign.

After trouncing the Democrats, Populists, and Socialists in the election of 1904, Roosevelt and his colleagues pressed forward with what came to be known as the Square Deal. At the top of the program was the regulation of business in the public interest, and the business the Progressives most desired to regulate was the railroads. Despite previous attempts at reform such as the Interstate Commerce Act (1887) and the Elkins Act (1903), railroad companies continued to set rates and grant privileges many citizens regarded as grossly unfair. Roosevelt's efforts to obtain an effective law were initially thwarted by strong opposition from congressional conservatives. Finally, after months of political haggling, the administration obtained passage of the Hepburn Act (1906).

The new legislation empowered the Interstate Commerce Commission to set and enforce railroad rates in response to shippers' demands. The railroads might protest through the courts, but meanwhile the altered rate schedule would be in effect. The Hepburn Act disappointed the more radical Progressives, particularly those who noticed the railroads' ability to infiltrate the regulating agency, but it greatly expanded the idea of federal control of business. When Congress passed the Pure Food and Drug Act and the Meat Inspection Act, 1906 became a banner year for the Roosevelt Progressives. Widely demanded by muckrakers, these laws made it clear that not only interstate commerce, but any industry directly affecting public health and safety was subject to federal control. And the President seemed to be moving even further to the political Left. "Every man," he believed, "holds his property subject to the general rights of the community to regulate its use to whatever degree the public welfare may require it."

In such a concept Gifford Pinchot saw fertile soil for conservation. Indeed, Pinchot had been pressing his cause since Roosevelt's succession to the Presidency. The forester's first goal was securing the transfer of the forest reserves from the jurisdiction of the Department of the Interior to that of the Department of Agriculture, where they would be under the supervision of his division. Roosevelt arranged the transfer in 1905, and shortly thereafter the reserves were renamed National Forests. An eager Pinchot swung into action, planning sustained yield management policies for the vast domain in his charge and in the process molding the United States Forest Service into one of the most effective bureaus in the government. An unusual esprit de corps animated the members of Pinchot's team. Sensing from their chief and from the President that they had a mission, not merely a job, they plunged into the task with astonishing zeal. A familiar sight in the closing years of Roosevelt's administration was Pinchot, his associates in the Forest Service, and sometimes even the President himself sprawled on the floor of a map-covered room creating millions of acres of new National Forests.

The Forest Service's enthusiasm did not meet with universal approval. In the West, where the reality of a frontier died hard, "Pinchotism" was especially resented. From the western point of view the chief forester was an obstacle to progress and prosperity. As a rich and aristocratic easterner, it was said, he had no conception of the need for continued exploitation of undeveloped land. Try as he might to convince his critics that he too favored prosperity, but on a long-term basis, Pinchot nevertheless became a political target both in the West and among certain members of Congress. "This enormous territory of the forest reserves," one detractor declared, "is an empire within a republic, ruled by a despot with as much power as the Czar of Russia."

Partly in answer to such criticism, Pinchot decided to give conservation maximum publicity after he hit upon the idea during that 1907 ride in Rock Creek Park. Writing and speaking constantly in the next few years, the chief forester sought to explain the significance of his brainchild. First of all, he explained, conservation involved the management of the total environment, not just the forests or grasslands or rivers. Second, "conservation is development, the use of the natural resources now existing on this continent for the benefit of the people who live here now." Obviously Pinchot intended this as an answer to those who took conservation to mean permanent preservation, the "lockup" idea so hateful to westerners. The third principle of conservation was the prevention of waste. Along with many Progressives, Pinchot deified efficiency. Through scientific planning and applied technology, he believed, mankind had the ability to control every aspect of his existence. "Experts" held the keys to the millennium. Finally, Pinchot linked conservation to the mainstream of progressivism with his insistence that "natural resources must be developed and preserved for the benefit of the many, and not merely for the profit of a few." In this light, conservation was an extension of democracy, and Pinchot capitalized fully on the early twentieth-century enthusiasm for this cause. At every opportunity he stressed the public's interest in and right to the environment and its resources. It was clever politics, for by implication it allied the opponents of conservation with self-seeking trusts, monopolies, and what Pinchot called "concentrated wealth."

The zenith of the Progressive conservation drive was 1908. On February 26 the Inland Waterways Commission, which Roosevelt had appointed the previous year, submitted plans for multipurpose river development. Under the guidance of Pinchot and a talented protégé of Powell named William John McGee, the commission pioneered in treating rivers as a single unit from source to mouth. This kind of comprehensive environmental planning became the special province of the United States Bureau of Reclamation. Implementing progressivism's faith in science, efficiency, and federal control, the Bureau of Reclamation's planners and engineers had twenty-five major water projects under way by 1908. Located for the most part in the arid

West, the projects had as their goal the reclamation by irrigation of over 2 million acres.

In May 1908 a thousand national leaders, including the state governors, met at the White House at the President's invitation for a conference on conservation. Gifford Pinchot was the moving force behind the unprecedented gathering. He wrote many of the speeches the conferees heard and underwrote a large share of the conference expenses. President Roosevelt himself opened the meetings with a ringing plea for concern for "the weightiest problem now before the Nation." The rest of his speech reflected Pinchot's utilitarianism. Roosevelt called for the elimination of waste by more efficient methods of harvesting natural resources. The specter that haunted him and the other delegates was "running out" of vital raw materials. National prosperity and greatness were the ends to be served. Near the close of his address, Roosevelt lashed out at "unrestricted individualism." Previously, he thundered, "we have admitted the right of the individual to injure the future of the Republic for his own present profit. . . . The time has come for a change." Pinchot thought it had already occurred. In his opinion, the 1908 conference marked "a turning point in human history."

The White House Conservation Conference, and the Pinchot-chaired commission Roosevelt subsequently appointed to inventory the nation's natural resources, helped make conservation part of the American vocabulary. Pinchot had high hopes that the movement would spread throughout North America and then to the world. Along with Roosevelt he planned a series of international conferences. But Congress, the expected source of funds, was not impressed. Congressional leaders in fact actively resented the aggressive executive leadership Roosevelt and Pinchot personified. The legislators were particularly unwilling to be swept off their feet by conservation in view of Roosevelt's announcement that he would not run for reelection in the fall of 1908. Added to these political problems were certain intellectual shortcomings of the conservation idea itself. Pinchot's neat formulas, such as his definition of conservation as "the greatest good to the greatest number for the longest time" and the multiple-use dogma, proved on close examination to be unsatisfactory guidelines for policy-making. Consensus could not often be reached on what in fact was the "greatest good," and the "greatest number" principle left no room for minority interests in the environment like those of wilderness preservationists. The multiple-use idea offered no means for adjudicating the claims of competing uses.

Some of these shortcomings became apparent after 1908 in the bitter battle over the Hetch Hetchy Valley in California's Yosemite National Park. The City of San Francisco wanted Hetch Hetchy as the site for a municipal reservoir and hydropower station, and applied to the federal government for permission to build a dam there. Friends of wilderness and parks leaped forward to oppose the dam and defend the national park concept. As "Mr. Conservation," Gifford Pinchot found his opinion on Hetch Hetchy eagerly sought. He had little difficulty making up his mind. Parks, in Pinchot's view, were nice, but they had to give way to the material needs of a large city. Explaining his reasoning to a congressional committee, Pinchot declared that "the fundamental principle of the whole conservation policy is that of use, to take every part of the land and its resources and put it to that use in which it will serve the most people." For him, "use" had a distinctly economic connotation; looking at a free-flowing river or backpacking in a wilderness were not legitimate definitions of the term.

John Muir did not agree. Long hostile to Pinchot's utilitarianism, which he regarded as little better than that of the pioneers, Muir made the defense of Hetch Hetchy a personal challenge. A national park, he insisted, should be safe for all time from "ravaging commercialism." Otherwise the amenities were lost and life degenerated into a race for the feed trough. As for damming Hetch Hetchy, Muir was incredulous that anyone would even consider flooding a valley that in many ways was the scenic equal of the famous Yosemite just to the south. "Dam Hetch Hetchy!" Muir roared, "as well dam for water-tanks the people's cathedrals and churches, for no holier temple has ever been consecrated by the heart of man." Muir's point was that the use of the environment had to encompass esthetic and spiritual as well as economic dimensions.

Since the multiple-use management philosophy was no help in solving the Hetch Hetchy problem (obviously the valley could not be *both* a wilderness and a hydropower development), the antagonists took their differences to higher authority. Opinion there was also divided. Only after six years of nationwide controversy and three separate congressional hearings did a bill granting Hetch Hetchy to San

Francisco become law in 1913. John Muir and most of his Sierra Club colleagues were deeply disappointed. Evil, in Muir's estimation, had triumphed over good; Americans had shown "a perfect contempt for Nature, and instead of lifting their eyes to the God of the Mountains, lift them to the Almighty Dollar."

Although those who held the esthetic conservationist or preservationist position lost the Hetch Hetchy fight to defenders of Pinchot's "wise use" school of thought, there was an element of victory in their defeat. Indeed, the most significant thing about the Hetch Hetchy controversy was that it occurred at all. One hundred or even fifty years earlier a similar proposal to dam a wild river would not have occasioned the slightest ripple of public protest. Traditional American assumptions about the use of undeveloped country did not include reserving it in national parks for its recreational and inspirational values. The emphasis was all the other way—on civilizing it in the name of progress and prosperity. Older generations conceived of the thrust of civilization into the wilderness as the working out of divine intentions. But Muir and his colleagues had been successful in generating widespread resistance to this very process. What had formerly been the subject of national celebration was made to appear in many eyes as a national tragedy. Moreover, scattered sentiment for wilderness preservation had jelled in the course of the Hetch Hetchy controversy into the beginnings of a national movement. And in Hetch Hetchy preservationists had a symbol which, like the *Maine*, would not easily be forgotten. In fact, in 1916 the passage of the National Park Service Act made economic development of the parks much less likely.

Another impetus to the preservation idea was the growth and refinement of an American cult of the primitive. With the ending of the frontier and the corresponding burst of urbanization, more and more Americans had become enthusiastic about getting back to nature. They moved to the suburbs, planted gardens, joined country clubs, and vacationed in the nation's parks and wildernesses. The interest in preserving outdoor virtues and skills also accounts for the emergence of the Boy Scouts as the nation's most popular youth organization after 1910.

Literature also reflected the new taste for nature. After Owen Wister invented the "western" in 1902 with *The Virginian*, it became a staple in the literary diet of millions of Americans. Cowboys became national heroes. No one contributed more to this process in Gifford Pinchot's lifetime than Zane Grey. Endlessly riding the purple sage, Grey's characters reminded Americans of an older, and many were prepared to say a better, way of life. Other best-selling books, such as Jack London's *The Call of the Wild* (1903) and Edgar Rice Burrough's *Tarzan of the Apes* (1912), were even more explicit in their message that wildness—in man as well as nature—could be an asset. Spurred by such writings and by a general sense of malaise that accompanied the beginning of the frontierless twentieth century, Americans began to consider the possibility that they might be overcivilized. The doubts about growth and prosperity implicit in such thinking were important reasons for the rise of esthetic conservation and the wilderness preservation movement. The majority still clung to the traditional exploitative ethic, but as the Hetch Hetchy protest demonstrated, their views were no longer unchallenged.

While the battle over Hetch Hetchy was still in progress, Gifford Pinchot's name also came to national prominence in another conservation cause célèbre. The explanation of the Ballinger-Pinchot controversy of 1909 and 1910 lay in the struggle over the issue of reform within the Republican party. When Theodore Roosevelt left office in the spring of 1909 and departed for an African safari, he had the satisfaction of knowing that his Secretary of War and hand-picked successor, William Howard Taft, would enter the White House. In the election of the previous fall Taft had easily defeated the perennial Democratic loser William Jennings Bryan. But thereafter Republican fortunes declined. Granted that Roosevelt was a tough act for anyone to follow, still Taft's Presidency was not a success. Within a year after he took office, the unity that had elected four successive Republican Presidents shattered into bitter factionalism. Taft, it quickly appeared, was not about to follow in Roosevelt's footsteps with respect to reform. As his administration began, he endorsed the conservative Speaker of the House, Joseph Cannon, in preference to reform-minded insurgents such as Representative George Norris. The President's support of the highly protective Payne-Aldrich Tariff of 1909 further angered Progressives, who expected lower rates. But the darkest cloud over Taft's term in office involved Gifford Pinchot.

It was inevitable that Pinchot and Taft would clash. The chief forester had been too close to Roosevelt, both personally and ideologi-

DISGUISED AS THE FAITHFUL SHEPHERD DOG A WOLF IS FOUND WITHIN THE CORRAL

Two newspaper cartoons of 1910 present the contrasting public images of Gifford Pinchot. Above, Pinchot is represented as the faithful watchdog guarding the nation's natural resources from Secretary of the Interior Richard A. Ballinger and other "wolfish" special interests. The sleeping shepherd, President William Howard Taft, has not maintained the corral constructed from "big sticks" by his predecessor Theodore Roosevelt.

The second cartoon (below) depicts Pinchot unfavorably as the enemy of traditional pioneer ideals. Note the dress of Pinchot, a reference to his eastern, aristocratic background, which was widely condemned in the West.

THE WILD AND WOOLLY EAST.

cally, to accept the new President's redefinitions. Within a month after Roosevelt left Washington, Pinchot found the federal government "dead." The passage of time only deepened his disappointment. Roosevelt, in his view, had "made" Taft, and Taft had pledged his support of Roosevelt's policies. But Pinchot found little evidence of continuity between the administrations. Overlooking the Taft Administration's passage of the Mann-Elkins Act (1910) tightening federal regulation of railroads and its institution of almost twice the number of antitrust suits as under Roosevelt, Pinchot saw only the growth in power of conservative Republicanism. The Old Guard and the special interests were back in the federal saddle at the expense of the public interest. Summarizing his impressions, Pinchot remarked that replacing Roosevelt with Taft was "as though a sharp sword was succeeded by a roll of paper, legal size."

Symbolic of this change in Pinchot's eyes was the way Taft's Secretary of the Interior, Richard A. Ballinger, administered federal lands. Alaska was the focal point. In summer of 1909, just when Pinchot's rage at Taft was at the boiling point over the latter's refusal to support Roosevelt's plans for a world conservation conference that fall, charges of fraudulent federal sale of Alaskan coal fields reached his receptive ear. According to the informant, a young Department of the Interior land inspector named Louis R. Glavis, Ballinger had cleared the way for some of the nation's most powerful financial syndicates, including that of J. P. Morgan, to acquire valuable lands on what amounted to the nation's last frontier. Pinchot felt the public interest had been violated, Roosevelt repudiated, and the whole conservation movement ridiculed. Furiously he attacked Ballinger and, by implication, the Taft Administration's leniency toward big business. Ballinger, as expected, professed his innocence in the face of the chief forester's headline-making criticism, and the President stood behind his cabinet officer.

The Ballinger-Pinchot controversy was stalemated as 1910 began. But as Pinchot left his house for a dinner engagement on the evening of January 7, a messenger from the White House arrived with an envelope for him. Without bothering to open it, he reentered his house, waved the letter at his mother and announced, "I'm fired." Then he left for dinner, glorifying in what he regarded as martyrdom to the ideals of Roosevelt and conservation. In retrospect it appears that Ballinger, while not a conservationist, was not a crook. And it would seem that Taft had little alternative but to fire Pinchot for blatant insubordination. Political realities, not conservation, determined the outcome of the Ballinger-Pinchot controversy. Yet in the public mind its resolution was either a deserved rebuke of progressivism's interference in free enterprise or confirmation that reformers must struggle still harder to protect the environment from exploitation.

After January 7, 1910, Gifford Pinchot found himself without a job, and even worse for a man who harbored political ambitions, without a party. Naturally his thoughts turned to Roosevelt, still on safari, and in April Pinchot traveled to the Italian Riviera to meet with the former President. They talked again, between sets of tennis, when Roosevelt returned to the United States in June. The immediate outcome of the discussions was discouraging for Pinchot. Despite the wave of national sympathy that followed his dismissal (thirty newspaper editors even suggested he should run for the Presidency against Taft), Roosevelt was noncommittal about the Ballinger issue. He urged his friend to keep cool and keep the Republican party united. Taft had faults, Roosevelt conceded, but still retained his confidence.

In the next two years Roosevelt's faith in Taft withered into bitter enmity, to the delight of Gifford Pinchot. Throughout the summer of 1910 Ballinger and the Department of the Interior were the subjects of a congressional investigation provoked by Pinchot's charges. The sessions were highlighted by the brilliance of Louis D. Brandeis, the lawyer who carried the case against Ballinger, and the mismanagement of the administration's case. Public suspicions were reflected in the congressional elections of 1910, in which the Republicans lost control of the House of Representatives for the first time since 1892. And Ballinger, still under heated criticism, resigned his seat in Taft's cabinet early in 1911.

Thanks in part to Pinchot's influence, the significance of these developments was not lost on Theodore Roosevelt. As early as August 31, 1910, he made an impassioned reaffirmation of his reform philosophy in the course of a speech at Pottawatomie (sometimes Osawatomie), Kansas. Pinchot, who was with Roosevelt on this occasion, had actually ghostwritten the President's speech. Drawing on the memory of John Brown, whose antislavery fanaticism put the town on the map in the 1850s, Roosevelt and Pinchot called for the central government to become sufficiently powerful to ensure equal opportunity and social justice. Following the argument in Herbert Croly's 1909 book *The Promise of American Life*, they asserted that America could not retreat to an economy of small, competitive units. Concentration was a fact of twentieth-century life. The task of the reformer was to build a federal government strong enough to counter the strength of big business, big labor, and other concentrations of power in the private sector. On behalf of the people the federal government would become a mighty welfare state, regulating, controlling, and stabilizing American life. Only in this way, Pinchot and Roosevelt believed, could popular sovereignty be preserved and the blessings of an urban-industrial age separated from its liabilities. The New Nationalism, as they called their plan, harked back to Alexander Hamilton and anticipated many aspects of Franklin D. Roosevelt's New Deal.

The Pottawatomie blast provided a reference point for the political maneuverings of the next two years. Taft and the conservative Republican Old Guard regarded Roosevelt and Pinchot as wild-eyed radicals out to destroy the capitalistic system. Democrats distrusted the New Nationalism for quite different reasons. Following the lead of Woodrow Wilson, the scholarly governor of New Jersey who would head the party's ticket in the election of 1912, they protested Roosevelt's advocacy of big government. "Free men," Wilson explained, "need no guardians." What they did need, in his estimation, was a return to free competition, equal opportunity, and respect for the individual in the tradition of Thomas Jefferson. Concentrations of power, according to Wilson, should be destroyed, not accepted and countered with even more power. The government should be a referee, not a participant, in the economic game. "I don't care how benevolent the master is going to be," Wilson declared, "I will not live under a master." And whereas Roosevelt accepted the label New Nationalism, Wilson referred to his approach to reform as the New Freedom. The difference, according to Wilson, was between "regulated monopoly" and "regulated competition."

On January 21, 1911, Gifford Pinchot and a small group of Republican Progressives or "insurgents" met in Washington at the home of Senator Robert M. La Follette of Wisconsin to organize the National Progressive Republican League. For his part, Pinchot was determined to use the group as a lever to force the Republican party toward the political Left. If this failed, it would make a fine nucleus for a new third party. At first most of Pinchot's colleagues were unwilling to go along with the idea of a schism, and gradually La Follette emerged as a challenger to Taft. Pinchot supported his candidacy with time and substantial gifts of money. By early 1912, however, he sensed with mounting excitement that Roosevelt himself might oppose Taft for the Republican nomination. Embarrassed, Pinchot hurriedly changed bandwagons and took to the stump on behalf of his former chief. The campaign trail led to the Republican National Convention in Chicago. Roosevelt arrived in high spirits. Asked by reporters how he felt, he replied, "like a Bull Moose." The term stuck as the emblem of his cause. But in the smoke-filled rooms of the convention, the moose proved no match for the establishment. Taft's control of the national party machinery was so complete that he effectively excluded Roosevelt's delegates and captured the Republican nomination in spite of what was probably a grass-roots preference for Roosevelt.

Pinchot, who had been helping mastermind Roosevelt's candidacy, immediately walked out of the convention and on June 22, in company with Jane Addams and several thousand other Progressives, gave birth to a new party. In the weeks that followed Pinchot helped write a party platform that expressed advanced reform thinking on a variety of topics from conservation to child labor. Roosevelt promised his followers that they would stand at Armageddon and "battle for the Lord."

As the campaign of 1912 began in earnest, Pinchot was confident Roosevelt could beat Taft, but he was less confident about the Democratic nominee, Woodrow Wilson. Subsequent events proved his fears well founded. The Progressive party had a wealth of enthusiasm, a platform aimed at controlling the powerful and privileged, and the biggest name in American politics. But it lacked a network of organization. Moreover, Wilson's variety of reform proved highly attractive, particularly on the farm, in the small town, and among the urban middle classes. Pinchot campaigned furiously for Roosevelt and his running mate, Governor Hiram Johnson of California. In October he expressed the inevitable election-eve optimism, declaring "the Republican party is done for." But it was the Bull Mooose that died. Roosevelt ran well ahead of Taft in both the popular and electoral vote, but

Wilson, taking advantage of the schism in Republican ranks, swept to victory with 41 percent of the popular vote. Now the Democrats would have their innings in the game of reform.

In the aftermath of the election of 1912 Pinchot conferred with several leading members of the Progressive party, including Jane Addams, in an effort to keep the organization alive. His own preference was to push the party to the political Left—to advocate outright government ownership of key businesses and utilities. Extreme individual wealth, he believed, could not be tolerated in a republic. The only exception he admitted was "a man who earned it as Henry Ford has done." In going this far Pinchot pleased the Socialists and the radical fringe of Progressives, but he parted ways with the great majority of reformers. Undaunted, he set out to finish in Pennsylvania what the Roosevelt Administration had started on the national level. His immediate goal was the seat in the United States Senate then occupied by the powerful Republican boss of Pennsylvania, Boies Penrose. Armed with the nomination of the state's Progressive or Washington party and, for the first time, with a wife (the former Cornelia Bryce), Pinchot waged a spirited campaign in 1914. He had the backing of some of the foremost names in the liberal constellation—Jane Addams, Booker T. Washington, Hiram Johnson, and Roosevelt himself. Indeed, the former President mailed over a million post cards to Pennsylvania voters saying that Pinchot was "fighting . . . for the same things for which we fought in 1912." The verdict, however, was the same. Penrose walloped Pinchot, gaining almost twice as many popular votes. Promising not to abandon the fight "for political and economic freedom," the loser and his bride left for Europe.

On the national level the Progressive party foundered on the shoals of disinterest. When Roosevelt announced he would not accept the nomination tendered him by the Progressive delegates at their 1916 convention, Pinchot and most other Bull Moosers threw what support they had behind the Republican nominee, Charles Evans Hughes. The real reason for the third party's demise, however, was Woodrow Wilson's striking success as a reformer. Not only did the Democrats pass the series of social and economic reforms that delighted Jane Addams, they also designed a new tariff policy (the Underwood Tariff of 1913) that lowered rates and eliminated favoritism. The same act instituted a small tax on personal incomes and shifted other federal taxes to bear more heavily on the rich. Another signal accomplishment of 1913 was the Federal Reserve Act, which made the nation's banking system more susceptible to public control. By 1916 Wilson could boast with a considerable degree of justification that he had "come very near carrying out the platform of the Progressive party" as well as that of the Democrats.

Gifford Pinchot, however, was not impressed. Wilson struck him as a weak and vacillating leader who was not to be trusted. "I have come," he wrote on the eve of Wilson's reelection in 1916, "to have not only a complete disbelief in his sincerity but a more bitter contempt for him than I have ever had for any other man in public life." On the basis of the record, this was a biased, sour-grapes estimation. As Pinchot's brother Amos recognized, Wilson had in many ways brought progressivism to its zenith and deserved the support of sincere reformers. But Gifford wore Roosevelt blinders and could see only Wilson's flaws. Moreover, Pinchot possessed such a strong sense of personal righteousness that he habitually regarded those who disagreed with him as villains. Before Wilson, it had been Ballinger and Taft who elicited his contempt.

Woodrow Wilson's foreign policy came in for special criticism from Gifford Pinchot. In particular, he attacked the President's conduct toward Latin America and Germany which, he stated, "seems to me to have reached the final limit of cowardice and dishonor." With reference to Latin America, Pinchot meant the Democrats had abandoned the "big stick" and big-money methods of Roosevelt and his imperialistic associates in favor of a diplomacy of morality and restraint. In fact, Wilson took pains to make amends to Colombia for Roosevelt's virtual seizure of the Panama Canal route in 1903. Wilson also succeeded in preventing the strained relations between the United States and Mexico in the years 1913 to 1916 from leading to the full-scale war Roosevelt would almost certainly have demanded.

If Wilsonian policy toward Latin America distressed Pinchot, the President's conduct in terms of the European war that began in 1914 outraged him. Pinchot could not believe any sane man could plead for total neutrality. In his eyes there was no question that the Allies, especially England, were fighting for the ideals of "liberty, democracy, and civilization" against the barbarous "military autocracy" espoused by Germany. It was equally clear on what side of the fight the United

States should enlist. When the *Lusitania* was sunk by a German submarine in 1915, Pinchot went into a frenzy of pro-Allied crusading. The "Lusitania murderers" and the rapers of Belgian nuns, he told his audiences and correspondents, must be crushed by the world's enlightened peoples. It seemed to Pinchot that the Allied cause was simply an international extension of the Progressive crusade for justice and fair play.

Along with Theodore Roosevelt, he hungered for the opportunity of leading a volunteer expeditionary force to Europe. When Wilson denied them a commission, the one-time Rough Rider fumed in frustration, and Pinchot made plans, which never materialized, to lead a private "regiment of foresters" to the battle line in France. In 1917 Pinchot did obtain an appointment in Herbert Hoover's Food Administration, a wartime emergency operation, but resigned in disgust three months later with a fine contempt for its head. The experience pointed up one of Pinchot's chronic personal shortcomings, a tendency to see men and policies in black and white terms, all good or all bad. Compromise was not a Pinchot specialty, and the widespread recognition of this fact may well have cost him the term in the White House he coveted for so many years.

At the conclusion of World War I, Pinchot's attention turned back to politics. He hungered for office. With Roosevelt now a memory (he died January 6, 1919), his chief lieutenant felt responsible for carrying on his reform ideals. As the election of 1920 approached, Pinchot first supported General Leonard Wood, a Roosevelt man, for the Republican nomination. Senator Warren G. Harding of Ohio, he told one audience, "would make a fine President to look at, but that is about all you can say of him." Yet when the smoke cleared from the convention rooms, Harding was the Republican choice. Mending fences as best he could, Pinchot unenthusaistically supported a man who promised to steer the nation back toward the "normalcy" that Pinchot, the reformer, chronically opposed. After Harding's election Pinchot watched with increasing disappointment as the administration descended to depths of inefficiency and corruption not seen in the United States since the Gilded Age. Determined at least to sustain progressivism in Pennsylvania, Pinchot first accepted an appointment as the state's commissioner of forestry and then threw his hat into the ring for the governorship.

The death of Boies Penrose in 1921, the year before the election, removed the biggest obstacle to Pinchot's ambitions, and with the state's political machine in disarray, he swept to victory in the fall of 1922. Overjoyed to be back in the mainstream after a dozen years, Pinchot poured an extraordinary amount of his seemingly boundless energy into his new job. For guidelines he understandably drew on his recollection of the philosophy, methods, and style of Theodore Roosevelt, whose picture reposed above the governor's desk throughout his four-year term. But some new gimmicks appeared. For six hours every week, Pinchot hung a sign saying "Walk Right In" on his office door and, without the buffer of a secretary, faced the people of Pennsylvania.

Progressivism came to Pennsylvania in other ways as well. Governor Pinchot instituted numerous reforms in the financial and administrative structure of the state government in the interest of efficiency. For instance, he managed to consolidate 139 separate offices into 15 cabinet posts and 3 commissions. In 1924 he launched a battle against the utility companies of the state and, in particular, against those who would monopolize the production and sale of electric power. Pinchot's interest in this cause began in the earliest phases of Progressive conservation and climaxed in 1920 with the passage of the Federal Water Power Act. This legislation created a Federal Power Commission with authority to license and, if necessary, to take over and operate all private developments on navigable waterways. Pinchot saw it as a direct blow at the exploitation of natural resources and, like the Forest Service, a demonstration of the regulative potential of big government. He hoped to apply the same principle to Pennsylvania by instituting tight government control over a consolidated energy industry in the interest of the common welfare. But in the mid 1920s he was partially thwarted by the "power crowd's" ability to influence the regulatory commission and even the state court system. Pinchot's greatest achievement in regard to power in these years was a book-length report on the problem that became a conservation classic. As for forests, Governor Pinchot's acknowledged expertise enabled him to push through a series of important reforms.

It was comforting for Pinchot to know that conservation was alive and well in Pennsylvania, because on the federal level there were strong indications of relapse. Under Harding the federal government returned to a policy of environmental giveaway. The most notorious instance, and the worst of a series of scandals in the Harding years, concerned oil. The problem began with the appointment of Albert B. Fall as Harding's secretary of the interior. On learning of it in 1921, Pinchot remarked that it might have been possible to pick a worse man for the job, "but not altogether easy." Events soon substantiated Pinchot's fears. Fall was no sooner in office than he arranged for the President to transfer federal oil reserves from the jurisdiction of the Department of the Navy to that of his own Interior operation. It was like putting sheep in the care of a wolf. Fall promptly leased the oil fields at Teapot Dome and Elk Hills, Wyoming, to private developers in return for bribes amounting to almost $500,000. Two years later, in 1924, a Senate investigating committee exposed the crooked dealings. Fall was eventually found guilty, fined, and jailed for a year—the first cabinet member in American history to achieve this distinction. More important from Gifford Pinchot's viewpoint, the Wyoming leases were canceled and the principle of responsible federal management of the environment upheld.

In 1924 and again in 1928 Pinchot's Presidential ambitions flickered intermittently. Among the kingmakers his name occasionally came up as a dark horse, but for too long he had made too strong a wake through American politics to be considered very seriously. Still, as one of the chief bearers of the legacy of Theodore Roosevelt, Pinchot's opinions were significant. As a Republican governor in 1924, Pinchot turned his back on Robert La Follette's revival of the Progressive party and supported Calvin Coolidge. He was not, however, enthusiastic about the dour Vermonter, whose murmured epithets seemed to put him squarely in the camp of big business. Much more to Pinchot's taste was the Progressive platform, with its emphasis on conservation, government ownership of utilities, and prolabor laws. But Pinchot and La Follette had crossed swords in 1912, and Gifford Pinchot was not the kind of man to forget easily.

Reviewing the field in 1928, Pinchot could not muster much enthusiasm for either of the major candidates. The Republican nominee, Herbert Hoover, was also on Pinchot's blacklist since their disagreements over the Food Administration during World War I. Moreover, Hoover did not take a hard line on the question of regulating electric power monopolies, the problem Pinchot regarded as the most serious of the decade. If the government did not move quickly, he feared, "the hand that turns the electric switch . . . will rule the land." The fact that by 1930 ten utility companies controlled three-quarters of America's light and power business lent some substance to Pinchot's position.

Senator George Norris of Nebraska, whom Pinchot termed the "most useful man" sitting in Congress during a forty-year period, had long waged an almost single-handed fight against the power trust. To Norris's credit were the blocking of Henry Ford's bid for control of the Tennessee River and the passage, in 1928, of a bill authorizing federal control of the giant Boulder Dam on the lower Colorado River. But Hoover, in company with most conservative Republicans in the 1920s, clung tightly to the ideal of free and unregulated enterprise that men like Norris and Pinchot spent their lives trying to modify.

It appeared, as a consequence, that Pinchot might switch from his accustomed Republican affiliation in the election of 1928. The Democratic candidate, New York's talented governor Alfred E. Smith, agreed completely with Pinchot on the utilities issue; he advocated government ownership and operation of generating facilities. Public welfare, Smith believed, must come before private profit. Smith was willing to use big government to achieve this end. He favored, for example, the McNary-Haugen plan whereby the federal government bought and sold agricultural produce and thus maintained a floor or "parity" under farm prices. Indeed, Smith was in the direct Progressive tradition, clearly the best hope for continuing reform in 1928. But in Pinchot's mind and that of many of his contemporaries, there was one damning black mark against Smith's name. He was a "wet" on the question of prohibiting alcoholic beverages. The fact that Smith was also Catholic and thoroughly urban in his orientation did not disturb Pinchot as much as it did some of his less sophisticated rural and small-town countrymen. With considerable reluctance, Pinchot endorsed Hoover in 1928 and watched him roll to a crushing victory. But Smith's ability to draw votes from the nation's metropolitan areas was a straw in the wind for an urbanizing nation.

In 1929, the year the economy crashed, Gifford Pinchot and his wife were fulfilling a lifelong dream, sailing a 148-foot yacht in the South Pacific. He enjoyed the rest, but politics was in his blood. On his return from the cruise in 1930 he sought and won a second four-year term as governor of Pennsylvania. The comeback, rare in American politics, called attention to Pinchot as a liberal Republican or third-party candidate for the Presidency in 1932. He could not hide his excitement about the idea. The advent of the Great Depression seemed to him proof positive that the relatively probusiness policies of Harding, Coolidge, and Hoover were in need of an overhaul by reformers of the Theodore Roosevelt mold. Pinchot was especially upset at the Hoover Administration's reluctance to take positive action to control the economy and alleviate the suffering of poverty-stricken Americans. But the real villain in Pinchot's eyes was Secretary of the Treasury Andrew Mellon, who calmly advised letting the economy spiral down to equilibrium regardless of the attendant social costs. If necessary, Mellon recommended, "liquidate labor . . . liquidate farmers."

In Pennsylvania, by way of contrast, Pinchot launched what came to be known as the "little New Deal." Even before his inauguration as governor in 1931, he appointed a committee on unemployment. Relief of the poor was another Pinchot objective. After pleading unsuccessfully with Mellon and Hoover for federal relief, Pinchot proposed that the richest men in Pennsylvania voluntarily support a relief program for the duration of the depression. Leading the way, he pledged a contribution of one-quarter of his income for 1930. The legislature, however, preferred to appropriate $10 million for direct relief. Additional millions appeared as hard times continued. Pinchot also pioneered in work relief. Long before Franklin Delano Roosevelt and his various work relief projects (the Works Progress Administration, the Public Works Administration, and the Civilian Conservation Corps are the best known), Pinchot launched a campaign to improve rural transportation in his state. Its purpose was twofold: to get the farmers out of the mud and to get dollars into their pockets. The thousands of miles of paved "Pinchot roads" that resulted became a symbol of the governor's concern for the common man.

Similarly expressive of this concern were a series of social security measures, some defeated by a suspicious legislature, and a generally friendly attitude toward organized labor. Applying Progressive ideals to the 1930s, Pinchot contended that human rights had to be given precedence over property rights. Indeed the whole depression, in Pinchot's eyes, was explained by the "selfish and short-sighted" refusal of business "to share with labor and with the consuming public the tremendous profits of mass production." The conduct of Henry Ford, for one, did not fully support this generalization, but it was about as accurate a brief analysis of the economic dislocation as it was possible to make.

Although only Pinchot knew for sure, there is little doubt that he voted Democratic in the election of 1932, crossing party lines for the first time in his life, with the exception of the Bull Moose bolt in 1912. The Democrats' standard bearer that year, Governor Franklin D. Roosevelt of New York, was a friend, a social peer, and a subscriber to Pinchot's political ideals. Moreover, he was related to Theodore, and it was impossible, at any rate, to support Hoover. Roosevelt's triumph in the election delighted Pinchot, and his enthusiasm did not diminish as the new President completed his "Hundred Days" of federal assault on the problems of the depression. Yet the New Deal Roosevelt promised and delivered to the American people could not help but arouse a certain wistfulness in Gifford Pinchot. For decades he had been advocating many of the policies with which Roosevelt won political fame. Indeed, the New Deal was in many ways reminiscent of the Square Deal and the New Nationalism. The Pottawatomie address Pinchot wrote for Theodore Roosevelt in 1910 could well have served his cousin in 1933. Concentration, control, and planning by a strong central government were the watchwords of the early phases of the New Deal. The first Roosevelt would have fully approved of the second's "brain trust" of management experts. The most significant difference between the two Roosevelts was that Theodore operated in relatively prosperous times, whereas Franklin took office in one of the nation's darkest hours.

Pinchot was in a mood in 1933 to cooperate with Franklin Roosevelt, and even to join his team. Several "Dear Franklin" letters had the covert purpose of fishing for an appointment. Two liberal Republicans and long-time friends of Pinchot had already received posts, Henry A. Wallace as secretary of agriculture and Harold L. Ickes as secretary of the interior. But there was nothing for Pinchot. Politics is a partial explanation. Roosevelt wanted to strengthen the Democrats in a key state such as Pennsylvania. More important, Pinchot's uncompromising temperament did not fit the style of the pragmatic Roosevelt. A "broker" President, he mediated among various points of view, habitually avoiding the black-and-white approach so characteristic of Pinchot. In fact, compromise was the signal achievement of the New Deal. Roosevelt succeeded in avoiding the extremes of both unregulated capitalism and completely regulated collectivism. He demonstrated that even in a time of national emergency a middle way was possible. By moving, as he put it, "slightly to the left of center," Roosevelt was able to combine valuable features of both socioeconomic alternatives.

The President's refusal to respond to Pinchot's overtures turned the governor against the New Deal in the closing years of Roosevelt's first term. In this posture Pinchot joined a growing number of Roosevelt critics. On the political Right was the Liberty League, organized in 1934 by conservative businessmen to protest the New Deal's modification of the American free enterprise system. Those who did not feel Roosevelt modified it enough constituted the other source of criticism. Their leading spokesman was the Louisiana "Kingfish," Huey Long, who rose to national prominence in the year before his assassination (September 1935) with his "Share Our Wealth" plan. Dr. Francis E. Townsend of California and Father Charles E. Coughlin of Michigan had similar plans for becoming American Robin Hoods, taking from the rich and giving to the poor. This was also the essence, of course, of the Socialist and Communist proposals that commanded considerable interest among American intellectuals, if not among workingmen, in the 1930s.

Some of the criticism of the early New Deal resulted from its own internal problems. Roosevelt's vigor, charm, and confidence in the country had largely dispelled the paralyzing fear and despair that gripped the nation at the end of Hoover's term, but his assault on the broader problems of economic recovery and permanent reform were less successful. In 1935, despite the Agricultural Adjustment Administration's ability to raise farm prices through a program of planned scarcity, the gross national product was still way down and unemployment way up, compared with predepression standards. Moreover, the invalidation of the National Recovery Administration and parts of the Agricultural Adjustment Administration in 1935 and 1936 by the Supreme Court cut the heart from Roosevelt's attempt at national economic planning. Undaunted and always the experimenter, the President prepared for a new approach. Abandoning the idea of cooperating with consolidated businesses, Roosevelt took a turn at breaking up concentration and restoring competition. This "second New Deal" also emphasized compensatory fiscal policy as outlined by Marriner Eccles of the Federal Reserve Board and the British economist John Maynard Keynes. According to this theory, economic recovery could be promoted and prosperity maintained by a program of heavy government spending at times when private spending declined.

Before the second New Deal could be fully tested, Roosevelt faced the election of 1936. Pinchot was outspoken in his support of the Republican nominee, Governor Alfred M. Landon of Kansas, a former Bull Moose Progressive. But Roosevelt had the support of the people and succeeded in making his opponents appear to be tools of the same plutocracy that had brought on the depression. The tactic worked beautifully. Roosevelt carried every state except Maine and Vermont. Uneasily Pinchot watched his second term unfold. He was especially concerned about the President's abortive attempt in 1937 to alter the composition of the Supreme Court so as to make it more amenable to New Deal legislation. He also observed with growing worry the economic recession of 1937 and 1938, which left the American economy in nearly the same condition as when Roosevelt first took office. More and more, it appeared that the nation's economic salvation would come from a foreign rather than a domestic source.

The prospects for a second world war grew steadily throughout the 1930s. The hopes that Jane Addams and other pacifists pinned on the Kellogg-Briand Pact (1928) outlawing war evaporated under the heat of aggressively expansionist governments in Japan and Germany. The Japanese moved first: in 1931, Japan occupied the Chinese province of Manchuria. Hoover's Secretary of State, Henry L. Stimson, condemned the invasion, as did the League of Nations. But Japan, knowing full well that the economic plight of the Western nations permitted nothing stronger than words, simply withdrew from the league and continued an imperialistic course. A parallel situation soon developed in Europe. The aggressor was a new Germany, recovered from World War I and determined, under the leadership of Adolf Hitler's Nazi party, to right the alleged wrongs of the Treaty of Versailles. In 1933 Germany also left the league. Meanwhile the United States, preoccupied with the depression, pulled the security blanket of isolationism even further over its head. Throughout the mid-1930s the general opinion in this country was that intervention in World War I had been a dreadful mistake engineered by a group of profit-hungry munitions makers and rabid imperialists. Far from messianic idealism, Woodrow Wilson's foreign policy of 1917 seemed either blind stupidity or outright treachery. Having been burned once, Americans of this persuasion were unwilling to touch the hot stove again. Roosevelt knew the fallacy of this argument, but he also knew the political consequences of bucking too strong a current.

In October 1935 Italy joined the imperialist game, invading and conquering Ethiopia. The following year Spain exploded into a civil war that sent other European nations scurrying to take sides. All the while Roosevelt, often against his better judgment, worked to satisfy isolationism with a blanket policy of neutrality and noninvolvement. Gifford Pinchot, for one, objected. Just as in the years before World War I, he condemned militarism, particularly that of Germany, and urged the United States to aid the forces of democracy. The neutrality laws, in his opinion, should be modified to permit the sale of munitions to England and France. Yet even as Hitler rampaged through Europe in total disregard of the national sovereignties established at Versailles, the isolationists prevailed. To one of them, who argued that the United States was safe from attack and should allow the Europeans to fight out their differences among themselves, Pinchot wrote: "every now and then in this world of imperfections a man comes across a statement so perfect and rounded in its wrong-headedness as to make it worth preserving." He was consequently delighted when on November 4, 1939, Roosevelt finally signed a new neutrality law permitting arms trade on a cash-and-carry basis. The arrangement clearly favored the Allies, who had the sea power necessary for buying the materials of war from the United States.

The next two years brought a succession of disasters abroad. France fell in June 1940, and it seemed England would soon be next. By this time Roosevelt was mobilizing American industry for the possibility of war. The resultant spurt of economic activity had the effect of ending the depression, while the sense of national emergency contributed to Roosevelt's reelection, this time with Pinchot's support, in 1940. The defeated Republican was Wendell L. Willkie, a utility company executive whom Pinchot could not stomach.

After the election Roosevelt moved more boldly on the war question. In March 1941 he pushed through Congress the Lend-Lease Act, which committed the United States to being, in the President's words, an "arsenal of democracy." But the persistence of isolationism was an impossible obstacle to intervention. Japan ended the stalemate. The aggressions of that country in the Far East had, by the fall of 1941, reached a point of no return. It seemed that nothing less than domination of the Pacific would content the militarist Japanese regime. Roosevelt retaliated with a series of economic boycotts, and everyone knew that relations between the two countries were at the breaking point. Nonetheless, Japan's beautifully executed carrier-based air attack of December 7, 1941, on the American naval base at Pearl Harbor in the Hawaiian Islands caught the nation by surprise.

Pinchot called the Pearl Harbor strike the highest kind of treachery, but—characteristically—he castigated his own country for "the very ultimate in brass-hat dumbness" to be caught utterly napping. But dumb or not, the United States was at war with Japan and, four days later, with Germany and Italy. In Roosevelt's words, a "terrible lesson"—the illusion of American isolation—had been learned. But for Gifford Pinchot, now nearing eighty and the victim of a series of heart attacks (he died October 4, 1946), the international events of the next few years were of secondary importance. His thoughts turned back to the past and to conservation.

"I have . . . been a Governor every now and then," Pinchot wrote in his memoirs in the early 1940s, "but I am a forester all the time." As such, he had reason for encouragement in reviewing the history of American conservation in the 1930s. To be sure, environmental problems continued. The great Middle West dust storms early in the decade darkened skies across half the republic and sent thousands of desperate families migrating to California. Yet the very magnitude of the Dust Bowl disaster proved an ironic blessing, for it elicited concern and action. The Civilian Conservation Corps, which Roosevelt established during the Hundred Days, put 2 million unemployed young Americans to work repairing the environment. The prevention of soil erosion was one of their principal concerns. Pinchot had nothing but praise for the CCC, although he was disappointed in not being asked to play a role in it. However, the former chief forester could take satisfaction in the role he played in resisting the transfer of the United States Forest Service from the Department of Agriculture to the Department of the Interior, which Secretary Ickes hoped to convert into a catch-all "Department of Conservation." In Pinchot's mind, forests were a crop and should remain under the administration of Agriculture.

In 1935 the creation of the United States Soil Conservation Service under Hugh H. Bennett did for the land what Pinchot and the Forest Service had done for the trees. It was the direct response of the Roosevelt Administration to the Dust Bowl. But the showpiece of New Deal environmental policy was the Tennessee Valley Authority. Also a product of the busy Hundred Days, but long the object of environmental planners such as William J. McGee, George Norris, and Pinchot himself, TVA proposed the management of the environment of an entire region as one unit, in the public interest, by a team of federal experts. To some extent, the lives of the people of the Tennessee Valley were "planned" in ways they openly resented or did not understand, but the project remained a favorite New Deal example of how to find the coveted middle way between individualism and collectivism. And as a dozen dams tamed the Tennessee River and its tributaries and the resultant hydroelectric power modernized the surrounding country, TVA became a byword for regional planning throughout the world.

The most significant long-term development in environmental history in the 1930s was the emergence and refinement of an ecological perspective and an attendant ethic for man-land relations. The seminal figure was Aldo Leopold, a graduate of the Yale Forest School, which the Pinchot family underwrote to the extent of several hundred thousand dollars. At first Leopold carried Pinchot's utilitarian gospel into his work on the National Forests of the Southwest, but he came to see that the environment's ability to serve man was not the ultimate criterion of conservation. Rather, Leopold believed, it was the health of the environment itself and of all its myriad, interrelated life forms. Man was just a part of the whole; a member, not the master, of a community of living things. It followed that ethics, not economics, should govern man's relationship to the environment. Preserving the delicate balance of nature, not sustained yield, should be the goal of conservation.

Gifford Pinchot had little sympathy for or understanding of ecology and the land ethic. But, in fairness to him, these are still novel concepts to most Americans. What Pinchot and his utilitarian conservation did was to provide the necessary bridge from a pioneer to an ecological perspective.

SELECTED READINGS

The Person

FAUSOLD, MARTIN L.: *Gifford Pinchot, Bull Moose Progressive* (1961). Pinchot's early political interests as they centered around the election of 1912.

MCGEARY, M. NELSON: *Gifford Pinchot: Forester-Politician* (1960). The most balanced biography.

PENICK, JAMES L.: *Progressive Politics and Conservation: the Ballinger-Pinchot Affair* (1968). The most recent study of the controversy that in 1910 cost Pinchot his job as chief forester.

PINKETT, HAROLD T.: *Gifford Pinchot: Private and Public Forester* (1970). Limited to Pinchot's involvement in forestry.

The Period

*BLUM, JOHN: *The Republican Roosevelt* (1954). An excellent short interpretation of Theodore Roosevelt.

*GINGER, RAY: *The Age of Excess: The United States from 1877 to 1914* (1967). A lively interpretation of the years in which modern America took shape.

*HAYS, SAMUEL: *Conservation and the Gospel of Efficiency* (1959). Places the Progressive conservation movement in a context of science and engineering.

*HOFSTADTER, RICHARD: *Social Darwinism in American Thought* (1944). Interpretation of how the rich justified themselves by application of the evolutionary theses of Charles Darwin.

*JOSEPHSON, MATTHEW: *The Robber Barons* (1934). Criticism of the new breed of industrial leaders who dominated the nation's economic life in the late nineteenth century.

*LEUCHTENBERG, WILLIAM E.: *The Perils of Prosperity, 1914–1932* (1958). Succinct economic and political history.

* Available in paperback.

*NASH, RODERICK: *Wilderness and the American Mind* (1967). Analysis of the growth of American concern for the environment.

*SCHLESINGER, ARTHUR M., JR.: *The Age of Roosevelt* (1957). A study of the background to and achievements of the administrations of Franklin D. Roosevelt.

* Available in paperback.

CHAPTER NINE

Henry Ford

The rope tightened, strained, and an automobile chassis began to inch along a 250-foot track on the floor of the Ford Motor Company factory. Henry Ford's eyes narrowed in concentration as he watched workmen add part after part. Five hours and fifty minutes later, a finished Model T coughed into life and rolled off the assembly line under its own power. Ford permitted himself a fleeting smile. The previous production record was cut in half. But for Ford the breakthrough of August 1913 was just a start. Even as he left the

*experiment he was thinking about refinements that soon reduced
production time to ninety-three minutes. The unbelievable day of
a-car-a-minute was not far ahead. By 1920 every other motor
vehicle in the world was a Ford, and Ford himself was a living
legend.*

The advance guard of the Ford family came to Michigan from
Ireland in 1832. Henry's father, William, joined them in 1847, the
second year of the great potato famine that persuaded so many Irish
to try their luck in the New World. After crossing the Atlantic, the
Fords used wagons, canal boats, and finally larger vessels on Lake
Erie to reach Detroit.

One day's wagon ride west of Detroit on the road to Chicago lay
Dearbornville, or Dearborn, and the River Rouge. At the time William
Ford arrived, the region was only a few decades past the frontier stage.
Bears and wolves were still part of the everyday scene. for the settlers,
and dense forests dominated the landscape. But once they were
cleared and the swamps drained, southeastern Michigan provided
deep, loamy soil, ideal for agriculture. William began as a carpenter
for the Michigan Central Railroad, acquired a little cash, 40 acres of
land, a wife, and a family. Henry, born July 30, 1863, was the first
child to live beyond infancy.

The Ford farm in Dearborn typified the variegated pattern of
northern agriculture. In sharp contrast to the staple crop system of
southern plantations where cotton was king, William kept a variety of
livestock, grew several crops, maintained an orchard, tanned hides, cut
wood, tapped maple trees for sugar, and supplemented the family
income by hunting, fishing, and trapping. Mary Ford churned butter,
made candles and soap, fashioned clothes from homespun cloth, kept
a vegetable garden, and preserved its harvests. In the absence of slaves
or cash for hired hands, Henry got his fill of "chores" at an early age.
School was therefore something of a vacation. Henry's formal education began and ended in the one-room Scotch Settlement School a mile
and half walk from the homestead. The curriculum consisted of *Mc-
Guffey's Readers* and rulers strong enough for serious spanking. The
readers, written by William Holmes McGuffey, were one of the major

influences on the American mind in the nineteenth century. McGuffey's six books, published between 1836 and 1857, sold an estimated
122 million copies—more than three times the population of the
United States when Ford was a schoolboy. Several generations of
Americans grew up on McGuffey's moral-coated language lessons. As
in the Puritan sermon, virtue was always rewarded and delinquency
brought instant catastrophe. Benjamin Franklin's prose also graced
McGuffey's pages, and young Henry Ford gained from them a clear, if
unbending, ethic of hard work and clean living. He never abandoned
this system of values. Years after his school days, the billionaire Ford
bought and transported to his hometown museum the log cabin birthplace of William Holmes McGuffey.

Another harbinger of the mature Ford was his early fascination
with machinery. He was a born mechanic, a natural tinkerer. Clocks
and watches were his first love. Before he entered his teens, the neighborhood relied on him as a repairman of timepieces. He could also
build them, as he proved when some friends jokingly gave him a
completely empty watch to "repair." In less than an hour Ford returned the watch, running perfectly.

From watches Ford graduated to larger machines. He studied the
village sawmill to learn the way a sliding steam valve operated. His
father's occasional jobs with the Michigan Central provided a chance
to learn about locomotives. In Dearborn Henry built water wheels,
wagons, and even a steam turbine that blew up a section of fence and
drove a piece of metal through his lip. Sometimes his abilities proved
more immediately useful, as when he constructed a device for opening
the farm gate without dismounting from the wagon. As a result, the
family accepted his obsession good-naturedly, with only an occasional
warning to keep new toys out of Henry's hands for fear he would take
them apart.

The history of invention is filled with sudden insights. Ford's first
one came on a clear, hot July day in 1876 as he and his father drove
the team toward Detroit. The noise came first, a hissing and clanking
that shattered the country stillness. Then around a bend lumbered a
huge machine—a boiler and engine mounted on wheels with a trailer
full of coal in the rear. Of course Ford had seen trains move on tracks,
and he knew about stationary engines that used steam to power mills
and threshers, but this one moved overland under its own power. The

potential rather than the actual appearance of the awkward monster captivated Ford. In an instant the twelve-year-old was off the wagon, questioning the operator of the vehicle. The answers were disappointing, but Ford could hardly contain his excitement. A whole new challenge—self-propelled overland transportation, a horseless carriage— opened before him. A half-century later the automobile king declared, "I remember that engine as though I had seen it only yesterday." He even recalled that it made 200 revolutions per minute.

The year 1876 was the centennial of the United States, and to mark it Philadelphia, the "birthplace of liberty," staged a spectacular Centennial Exposition. Machinery was the star of the show. Ford's father made his first long trip since immigrating three decades before in order to attend. He returned to the farm with glowing reports of giant engines. Henry absorbed every detail and in 1879 sought seasonal employment in Detroit's factories, foundries, and jewelry stores. Oblivious to considerations of diet and sleep when absorbed in mechanical problems, he worked a grueling schedule. Everything took second place to engineering. Despite a boyhood of Sunday school, Ford, exactly like Benjamin Franklin, came to a practical conclusion about religion. "I think I saved a lot of valuable time," he noted, "by staying away from church." More to the point, his god was in the machine shop.

Returning to Dearborn to help at harvest time, Ford gained experience operating the kind of self-propelled steam engine he first saw running on the road when he was twelve. Chancing to meet the agent for the company that manufactured the engines, Ford became a mechanic and demonstrator for it throughout southern Michigan. He even built a primitive steam-propelled tractor. But steam vehicles were slow, unwieldy, inefficient, and voracious consumers of bulky fuel. So in his little farm workshop Ford began experimenting with alternative sources of power: electricity, illuminating gas, and a little-known liquid called gasoline.

He was in good company. The nineteenth century was the golden age of American invention. The Industrial Revolution, spreading from England, met the challenges of an undeveloped continent and a burgeoning America. The result was an explosion of revolutionary inventions. Ford's obsession with "building a better mousetrap" sprang from the same ambition that produced the steamboat (1807), the reaper (1834), the typewriter (1843), the telegraph (1844), and the sewing machine (1846). Cable streetcars appeared on San Francisco's hills in 1873, and the next year electrically powered cars operated in New York. But the giants of American invention in Ford's youth were Alexander Graham Bell and Thomas A. Edison. The Bell telephone revolutionized communication in 1876, while Edison's phonograph (1877) and incandescent bulb (1879) were only the best known of over a thousand Edison patents.

By 1890 a number of young engineers with prophetic names like Dodge, Buick, Studebaker, and Olds had joined in the pursuit of Ford's dream of a self-propelled carriage. Two breakthroughs inspired their efforts. One was the bicycle. Lightweight, spoke-wheeled, highly maneuverable, and relatively fast, it directed attention to the possibility of independent, long-distance travel over ordinary roads. A novelty in the 1880s, bicycles became a national craze in the next decade, and many of the first attempts to build cars took bikes, rather than wagons or carriages, as models. The second significant development was the emergence of an efficient gasoline engine from the shop of Nikolaus Otto in Germany. Otto did not immediately think of his invention as a source of power for vehicles, but several dozen Americans, among them Henry Ford, did. In 1891 Henry excitedly told Clara Bryant Ford, his wife of three years, that he could adapt the Otto engine to move vehicles. A practical girl for whom transportation meant horses, Clara wondered how. Seizing a convenient piece of sheet music, Henry drew a quick and convincing sketch. He also convinced Clara of the need to settle permanently in Detroit, where he could obtain experience in the field of electrical ignition. The Fords made the move that year, facilitating Henry's work at the Edison Illuminating Company.

Detroit at the start of the 1890s was in the process of rapid growth. The streets were still lined with trees and Belle Isle in the Detroit River afforded pleasant outdoor recreation, but expansion brought problems. Horse-drawn vehicles and bicycles jammed unpaved streets that in wet weather turned to quagmires. City politics were equally dirty, a condition Mayor Hazen S. Pingree's reform campaign only partially alleviated. Factories, tenements, and saloons tended to replace the fine downtown residences. Their former owners, in turn, took the lead in replacing the surrounding countryside with suburbs. Sprawl was becoming a fact of American city life.

At the Edison plant Ford's abilities as a machinist earned him a modest but respectable $50 per month, but his heart was in his home-work—building a gasoline engine. Although Ford attended the Co-lumbian Exposition in 1893 in Chicago, he probably was not aware of the progress German and French inventors had already made. So it was with the trepidation and the thrill of the pioneer that he began his labors. The finished product was only about 18 inches long. On Christmas Eve 1893, Ford clamped it to his kitchen sink and called to Clara for help. Busy with seven-week-old Edsel and Christmas prepa-rations, she was not pleased with her assignment of dribbling gas down the intake opening while Henry spun the flywheel. At first nothing happened, and Clara's frown deepened. Then, with a spurt of flame, the tiny motor roared into life. After 30 seconds Henry shut it off.

Now hot on the trail of his car, Ford worked like one obsessed. Every dollar and every hour he could find went into materials and construction. It was a trial-and-error process conducted in a wood-shed. In the absence of auto parts shops, everything had to be built from scratch; the finished product represented not one invention, but dozens. By June of 1896 Ford was ready. A warm rain was falling as he applied the finishing touches to the car at 2 A.M. in the presence of a fellow Edison employee and the faithful Clara. The tension mounted as Ford pushed the vehicle to the doorway of the woodshed. Suddenly he stopped, puzzled and embarrassed. The woodshed door was too small to permit the exit of the car. Impulsively Ford grabbed an ax and widened the doorway. He turned on the current from the battery, engaged the choke, and fired the engine. Then he sprang into the driver's seat (taken from a bicycle), pulled the lever transmitting power to the wheels, bumped down the alley onto Bagley Avenue, and disappeared into the rainy night.

Ford's car was not the first gas-powered vehicle to be built in the United States (an honor earned by J. Frank Duryea in the early 1890s), but it was an outstanding achievement. Trim, rugged, reliable, and capable of speeds up to 25 miles per hour, the first Ford car still stands in the Ford Museum, ready to run. But in 1896 its future was highly uncertain. Henry Ford was an unknown, unfinanced mechanic who had built a car in a woodshed. He had lots of ambitious competition. Ford, however, caught the wind that drove him to world leadership in less than two decades. His motive? Probably not money (he could, after all, have stopped working and lived far more sumptuously than he actually ever did with his first half-million dollars) so much as achievement and self-expression. Putting the nation on cheap yet efficient wheels was for Ford the same kind of challenge as repairing a schoolmate's watch or building his first engine in Clara's kitchen.

The summer of 1896 found Ford in New York at the annual convention of the Edison Illuminating Company snapping photographs like any gawking tourist from the hinterland. His film records his interest in the Brooklyn Bridge, opened in 1883 and still one of the engineering wonders of the world, and in another engineering wonder: Thomas A. Edison. Like Ford, Edison was a midwesterner and largely self-educated. The men were also similar in their love of machinery and their capacity for sustained application to mechanical problems. Edison, Americans believed, never went to bed, and he encouraged the notion by predicting that in time man would evolve beyond the need for sleep—like a machine!

At first Ford circled warily around the great man, taking an occasional photograph, but his moment came at the end of a banquet when his Detroit superior offhandedly remarked to Edison that this "young fellow here has made a gas car." The statement was made as a joke in the expectation that the assembly would laugh Ford out of his foolish ideas. Instead the humor backfired. The diners, including Edison himself, expressed great interest. Soon Ford was the center of attention. With the aid of sketches on a menu he explained the details of his ignition system. Edison brought his fist down on the table so hard the dishes jumped. "Young man," he roared, "that's the thing! You have it—the self-contained unit carrying its own fuel. Keep at it." Here was the encouragement Ford needed. He later remarked: "I had hoped I was right, sometimes I knew I was, sometimes I only wondered if I was, but here . . . out of a clear sky the greatest inventive genius in the world had given me a complete approval."

Returning to Detroit, Ford began to assemble a team of associates and to search for financial backing. By 1899 he had both, and as chief engineer of the Detroit Automobile Company, a golden opportunity to produce cars commercially. The result was total failure. The high point of the company's life was a headline in the Detroit *News-*

Tribune for February 4, 1900, which read: "Swifter Than A Race-Horse It Flew Over the Icy Streets." The following article described a journalist's wild ride at speeds up to 25 miles per hour in one of Ford's new vehicles. But this was exceptional. Usually the heavy, truck-like machines stood stalled at the curb while horses flew by on the streets.

Discouraged and now considerably behind rival car makers like Ransom Olds, Ford tried another approach. He would build a fast car and go to the races. Not only was there publicity and cash support for the winner, but, Ford believed, the best opportunity to test and improve the automobile. In 1901 he had his racer and his first trophy, a cut-glass punch bowl. A year later he developed a car of 100 horsepower. With daredevil Barney Oldfield at the wheel, Ford's car beat the best field of racers in the country by half a mile with a speed of close to a mile a minute. Later Ford himself drove the car 90 miles per hour over the ice of Lake St. Clair for a new world record.

With the racing program going nicely, Alex Y. Malcomson and Ford organized a group of Detroiters as the Ford Motor Company. Money was hard to raise, but the dozen investors Malcomson talked into contributing were fortunate. They eventually realized the greatest return on their investment in the history of American business. The $100 that a sister of one of the founders contributed ultimately earned her $355,000.

The key to the success of the Ford Motor Company was the vision of Henry Ford. He left something to be desired as a businessman and personnel director, and in truth there were better automobile engineers in the country, but as an associate remarked of Ford, "he had the dream." Its essence was a light, rugged, reliable, and above all, inexpensive car that the average American could afford. Cars had been rich men's toys. Constructed individually and by hand, they cost between $3000 and $5000. Around Newport, Rhode Island, and other playgrounds of the wealthy cars were common, but for most turn-of-the-century Americans they were inconceivable luxuries.

Ford had a different idea. "I will build a motor car for the multitude," he declared. "It will be built of honest materials, by the best workmen that money can hire, after the simplest design that modern engineering can devise. But it shall be so low in price that the man of moderate means may own one." But how? In 1903 it did not seem possible to make something as complicated as a car cheaply. Ford, however, had a plan. "The way to make automobiles," he explained, "is to make one automobile just like another automobile, to make them all alike, to make them come from the factory just alike— just like one pin is like another pin when it comes from a pin factory."

The roots of the mass production system with which Ford revolutionized the manufacture of automobiles were as old as the first American factories. Before 1790 a Delaware farmer's son named Oliver Evans applied the principle of automation to the milling of flour. Previously, millers carried bags of wheat to a loft from which the grain fell between the grindstones. Then the flour was again toted upstairs for drying and sifting. Evans devised a network of vertical and horizontal conveyors that utilized the power of the water wheel instead of manual labor. Only two men were needed in Evans's mill. One poured wheat into the system; the other rolled away barrels of flour. A few years later in Pawtucket, Rhode Island, Samuel Slater constructed a cotton-spinning mill with seventy-two spindles. Falling water provided the power for this pioneering mechanization of textile production in the United States. Subsequent refinements made it possible to transform raw cotton into finished cloth in a continuous process under a single roof. The first factory was the Boston Manufacturing Company's plant at Waltham, Massachusetts, established in 1813. The American merchant capitalists involved in this undertaking also experimented with a new form of business organization—the corporation. In this arrangement a group of investors pooled their assets, but profited, or lost, only in proportion to their individual involvement. This concept of limited liability made possible the capital accumulation that launched large-scale industry in the middle decades of the nineteenth century.

Along with mass production, corporate financing ended the era of home and small-shop manufacturing. The artisan or craftsman producing an item from start to finish on a single workbench was replaced by machine operators responsible for only a small portion of the production process. Eli Whitney was the pioneer who turned from his cotton gin to gunmaking in the late 1790s. Before this time guns had always been fashioned individually by skilled gunsmiths. Whitney thought that unskilled laborers could do the job at less expense and in a shorter time if production was standardized. The key was to make identical parts (Whitney used metal molds) that could be assembled in a series of simple operations. Standardization also facilitated gun repair. From firearms Whitney turned his attention to timepieces, transforming the industry and, incidentally, making it possible for a young Henry Ford to interchange parts among the watches and clocks in his collection.

In Ford's time the mantle of Oliver Evans and Eli Whitney fell on the shoulders of Frederick W. Taylor. In company with Ford and his contemporaries, Taylor deified efficiency. The concept demanded an obsession with speed, a faith in science and technology, and a pragmatic orientation that put production results above all other considerations. Establishing the nation's first consulting service in a field that came to be known as scientific management, Taylor dissected the manufacturing process. With a stop watch and a tape measure as his constant companions, he conducted a series of time and motion studies. Taylor demonstrated, for example, that if a worker on an assembly line spent an extra second reaching into a drawer for a screwdriver, time could be saved and production increased by having the tool on a cord as close to the screw in question as possible. In the course of a day, Taylor maintained, the economies were significant.

Going a step further, Taylor made it a basic principle to replace a man with a machine whenever possible. Machines, he reasoned, were more precise—and they did not gossip with their neighbors or require sick leaves or strike for higher wages. When a man was essential, Taylor advised that he be compensated according to the piecework system, in which production, rather than elapsed time, determined pay. Another Taylor axiom was specialization. Whenever feasible, he broke the manufacturing process into small parts. A man whose sole function consisted of endlessly tightening the same six screws as they moved past him on the assembly line would develop remarkable efficiency. His sanity, however, was another matter. Finally, Taylor stressed the importance of synchronization. All the operations in a plant had to mesh smoothly if maximum speed was to be achieved.

In 1911, when Taylor distilled his ideas into a book entitled *The Principles of Scientific Management*, the automotive industry offered the most fertile ground in the American economy for the application of his ideas. Indeed, Henry Ford had already drawn upon them and made some refinements of his own. Efficient production explained why the Ford Motor Company was able to sell a car for $850. This comparatively low price, in turn, was the chief reason for the company's remarkable early record of sales and profits. Ford at first sacrificed efficiency by tinkering with his car and changing the design almost annually, but in 1908 he built the Model T and recognized it as a superior vehicle. Then he made a crucial decision: He would build the Model T and no other for the next twenty years. This policy opened the way to unprecedented efficiency and enormous economies of scale. Consumer choice, to be sure, was a casualty and the subject of endless humorous stories, such as Ford dealers telling purchasers they could have the Model T in any shade of black they desired.

The home of the Model T after 1910 was the Ford Motor Company's new Highland Park plant northwest of Detroit. It was also the showcase of American industry. The factory began by producing about three hundred cars a day, but one by one the various manufacturing processes were improved according to the principles of Frederick Taylor and the genius of Henry Ford and his associates. A giant leap forward occurred in the early spring of 1913, when construction of the electrical generator or magneto was placed on a continuously moving assembly line. Before, an individual worker sat down before a pile of materials and put a magneto together in about 20 minutes. The assembly-line technique divided the operation into twenty-nine parts and involved twenty-nine men. It also lowered construction time to 5 minutes. Now one man, working "on the line" as part of a team, could do the work of four.

After this success it was only a matter of months before Ford put the whole car on a moving assembly line. Branch lines, such as that which produced magnetos, fed into the main track. Again the results were spectacular. From 12 hours and 30 minutes, production time per car dropped to 5 hours and 50 minutes. Further refinement lowered the record in April 1914 to 1 hour and 33 minutes. In 1920, with several plants around Detroit in operation, Ford achieved his dream of producing one car for every minute of the working day. Still he was not satisfied. On October 31, 1925, the Ford Motor Company made 9109 Model Ts, one every 10 seconds! Sales kept pace, largely because Ford made it a policy to pass on the economies of mass production to the consumer. In 1910, for instance, the basic Model T cost $725, and 34,528 Americans became proud owners. Six years later the price was down to $345 for the 730,041 purchasers. Eventually it reached an all-time low of $290. Meanwhile, Ford made millions of dollars. By 1920 every other car in the world was a Model T, and the Germans, searching for a word to describe revolutionary industrial reorganization, coined *Fordismus*.

As the Ford Motor Company grew, Henry Ford gradually assumed the role of spokesman for the American business establishment. With the assistance of a stable of ghost writers, he expounded his philosophy of industry and life to an admiring nation. Predictably, Ford defended the economic and political system under which he had succeeded. His idea of reform was to improve upon existing patterns. He had little patience with Progressive reformers, especially those critical of the free enterprise system. Such a person, Ford declared, "wants to smash things. He is the sort of man who would tear up a whole shirt because the collar button did not fit the buttonhole. It would never occur to him to enlarge the buttonhole."

Ford singled out for special criticism the reformers who tried to "start a new world in Russia" with the Revolution of 1917. Their basic error, he opined, was to violate "Nature" by instituting a communistic economy that denied the individual the fruits of his ability and his effort. To Ford, private property was a sacred pillar of civilization and competition the crux of social relations. On the other hand, he did not defend the status quo. A static "life of ease" or the accumulation of money for its own sake were invitations to decay in a society as in an individual. With frequent references to his own life, Ford explained how there was always room for improvement. And Ford looked forward to the day when machinery, "the new messiah," would usher in a golden age of truth, beauty, and peace.

As the employer of over 32,000 workers in 1916, Ford was acutely conscious of the labor problem in the United States. Since the violence of the 1890s at Homestead, Pullman, and other urban-industrial areas, the workingman had made little progress toward obtaining his fair share of the profits of American business. He still worked long hours at poor pay and under trying, often dangerous, conditions. Labor unions like the American Federation of Labor tried to do their best for the skilled laborer, but the unskilled masses had few friends. And even organized workers encountered massive resistance on the part of management.

This is a difficult route to follow and care should be taken, for there is danger in getting off the route.

The roads are good to Carr; small hills and good if dry the balance of the way.

---

357   CHEYENNE TO RAWLINS, WYO.—188.3 m.

Inter-mediate Mileage.	TOWNS.		Inter-mediate Mileage.		TOWNS.
0	0	Cheyenne, Wyo.	18.3	103.4	Rock River
			24.9	128.3	Medicine Bow
20.	20.	Granite Canon	15.3	143.6	Hanna
21.1	41.2	Kask's Ranch	20.7	164.3	Walcott
16.8	58.	Laramie	8.	172.3	Ft. Steele
27.1	85.1	Lookout	16.	188.3	Rawlins, Wyo.

This is the direct route to Rawlins and probably best in dry weather. In wet weather go directly north to Rock Creek 103 m. (June 17th) thence to Medicine Bow. The road gradually rises over the Sherman Divide, through an open grazing country. Good dirt roads with some short steep hills; altitude of 8,000 and 9,000 feet is attained; snow capped peaks in various directions. Route some of the way parallels wire fences; law permits cutting of fences to avoid bad mud holes. From Rock Creek follow old Union Pacific R.R. bed; road good. Just before reaching Medicine Bow cross bridge at a ranch house. Road to Hanna is also over U. P. R.R. and fairly good. Leaving Hanna pass by cemetery on hill and go south of R.R. thru a sage brush country with no water. Road is bad with high centers (and some hills) being nothing but a trail.

At Ft. Steele cross North Platte River on ties of R.R. bridge. Telegraph R.R. office in Omaha for permit if not obtained en-route. Rawlins has the last blacksmith shop before reaching Green River.

423

Motoring in the early twentieth century often resembled an expedition, as this 1912 description from a guide of the Automobile Association of America suggests. For some years blacksmith shops did double duty for horses and cars.

In May 1902 anthracite coal miners in the United Mine Workers struck for higher wages and shorter hours. The mine owners, who did not even recognize the union's existence much less its right to influence management policy, were incensed. George F. Baer spoke for the owners when he declared that "the rights and interests of the laboring man will be protected and cared for—not by labor agitators, but by the Christian men to whom God in His infinite wisdom has given the control of the property interests of the country."[1] But the miners, abstaining from violence and asking only for the opportunity to arbitrate, won widespread sympathy. As the strike dragged on into the summer and fall of 1902 with no sign of settlement, President Theodore Roosevelt decided to act. The owners were told that unless they took steps to settle their differences with their employees, the United States Army would work the mines in the national interest. At the same time the President secured the assistance of J. P. Morgan in putting financial pressure on the mine owners. Frightened at this unprecedented show of executive power, the owners capitulated and granted a 10 percent wage increase.

Labor's celebration of the anthracite settlement was tempered by the knowledge that with Roosevelt's blessing the owners "paid" for their concession by raising the price of coal 10 percent. And there was no union recognition in the settlement. Indeed, the completely unionized or "closed" shop had few defenders outside the unions. In the Progressive mind, big labor was as much a threat to the public welfare as big business. Several events reflected this point of view. One was the 1905 decision of the United States Supreme Court in the case of *Lochner* v. *New York* which invalidated a maximum-hour law for bakers on the grounds that it interfered with the free enterprise system. Three years later the Supreme Court unanimously upheld the application of the Sherman Antitrust Act to labor organizations that acted in restraint of trade. This decision in *Loewe* v. *Lawler* (the Danbury Hatters case) created the possibility of declaring strikes illegal.

Disgusted, many workingmen began to turn to radical alternatives. Founded in 1905, the Industrial Workers of the World grew under the leadership of William "Big Bill" Haywood to have a sizable

[1] For a discussion of the premises on which Baer's statement was based, including Social Darwinism, see pages 292–293.

following in agriculture, mining, and lumbering, particularly in the Pacific Northwest. The IWW advocated abolition of the wage system, the creation of "one big union" for all laborers, and the creation of a proletarian class consciousness in the Marxist tradition. Also on the political Left was the Socialist party of America, which had been organized in 1900 by the veteran labor leader Eugene V. Debs. Starting in that year, Debs offered himself as a candidate for the Presidency of the United States. At first it was a joke, but capitalists like Henry Ford gradually became aware that the Socialists struck responsive chords in a significant number of American minds. In the election of 1908 Debs received 420,000 votes; four years later, the figure was 900,000, or almost 6 percent of the national vote. In industrial centers and depressed agricultural regions the percentage was considerably higher. Milwaukee even elected a Socialist to the House of Representatives. Still more frightening to the Establishment was the violence that labor agitation could generate. In 1905 a former governor of Idaho was assassinated, and in 1910 the Los Angeles Times Building was bombed in an act of terrorism attributed to the IWW.

In Detroit Henry Ford faced his own set of problems. The city had a strong open-shop, anti-union tradition. Employers were accustomed to exploiting the concentrations of East European immigrants in the community at virtual slave wages. The Ford Motor Company, for example, adhered to a standard wage of $2.34 a day or 26 cents an hour. By 1913 the situation in the automotive industry was tense. The Studebaker plant suffered a paralyzing strike that summer, and by fall IWW agents were active at Ford's Highland Park complex. To his credit, Ford recognized the problem. His labor force had long been too large for the kind of personal, inspirational management that was his forte. Lacking it, the existing wage scale and the monotonous, assembly-line assignments provided little incentive. The result was a massive turnover among Ford employees. The company had to hire 53,000 men a year in order to keep 14,000 on the job. Constant retraining of this labor force cost Ford millions of dollars annually. Pondering the problem in the winter of 1913–1914, Ford hit upon a brilliant solution. On January 5, 1914, he announced a new policy. Henceforth every Ford employee over twenty-two years of age would receive "a share in the profits of the house" sufficient to make the minimum wage

$5 daily. Moreover, the standard "day" was reduced from nine hours to eight.

Ford grandiosely termed the new plan "the greatest revolution in the matter of rewards for its workers ever known to the industrial world." Previously, by his own admission, Ford had paid "whatever it was necessary to pay." After January 5, 1914, he adopted profit-sharing. Labor and capital would pull together; everyone was a partner down to the lowliest sweeper of floors. The workers would rise with the organization they served.

The nation and the world learned about the $5 minimum day with amazement. Financiers declared the Ford Motor Company would be bankrupt within two years. But Henry did not have to worry. Thousands thronged Detroit seeking jobs at Ford. Those who secured or already possessed them were caught up in a wave of enthusiasm for making automobiles. Production records soared. The IWW organizers quietly left Highland Park, and talk of a union to match the power of management stopped abruptly. So did the costly turnover in the labor force; and despite the higher wages, Ford made more money than ever. At the same time he restored faith in the capitalistic system. The $5 day was a dramatic, concrete rebuttal to the criticisms of Socialists and Communists. Instead of resenting the rich man, the average American resumed his traditional attempt to become one.

With mass production and the $5 day well launched and sales setting new records each year, Henry Ford was free to turn his remarkable energies elsewhere. For the first time in his life he lifted his eyes from the workbench and turned to the larger sphere of world affairs. The result was not always happy. Henry might leave the machine shop, but a machine-shop mentality would not leave Henry. As a master mechanic, he tended to think that all problems were susceptible of mechanical solutions. It was simply a matter of finding the right tools and using them properly according to clearly defined laws. Good planning and careful design, in Ford's opinion, guaranteed a world that would function with the same efficient smoothness as the engine of a Model T. To achieve perfection, human nature and human conduct awaited only the coming of men who, in Ford's words, "can create the working design for all that is right and good and desirable." Such engineers "can mould the political, social, industrial, and moral mass into a sound and shapely whole." Here was a revival of the old idea of American mission complete with its innocence, its confidence, and its faith in man as reformer.

Beginning in 1915, Ford began to offer himself to mankind in this messianic capacity. The first dragon against which he threw his energies and his bank accounts was World War I. When war began in Europe in 1914, President Woodrow Wilson urged impartiality in word and deed. Ford supported the President wholeheartedly. Breaking with his economic peers, the automobile king branded the conflict a capitalists' war. He resurrected the old Populist suspicion of New York and Wall Street in attacking the bankers (chiefly J. P. Morgan) and manufacturers who supplied England and her allies with loans and munitions. This, Ford agreed with Secretary of State William Jennings Bryan, was a clear violation of the spirit, if not the letter, of neutrality. By heavily underwriting the Allied war effort with loans and trade, the United States was, in effect, marrying itself to the Allied cause. Even though most of the loans were secured with collateral, the economic repercussions of Allied defeat would shake America. The stakes, moreover, were high. American loans, mainly to England, amounted to $2.3 billion by 1917. The corresponding figure for Germany and the Central Powers was only $27 million.

For his own part, Ford vowed that he would sooner burn his factory to the ground than build a single vehicle for war purposes. Furthermore, he completely rejected preparedness—the idea that the United States should get ready for the possibility of war. But his position was not universally popular in the Ford Motor Company. James Couzens, an original partner and the company treasurer, led the dissent. A Canadian of English parentage, Couzens was vigorously pro-Allies. When a German submarine sank the British liner *Lusitania* on May 7, 1915, Couzens joined many Americans in crying for a declaration of war against Germany. Ford, however, stood firm. Of the *Lusitania*'s passengers he drily remarked, "well, they were fools to go on that boat, because they were warned." Furious, Couzens quit the Ford Motor Company in October.

The following month Henry Ford's pacificism took a more active turn. The occasion was a meeting with Rosika Schwimmer, a dashing Hungarian, and Louis Lochner, the young American secretary of the International Federation of Students. Both were militant pacifists and expert persuaders. Ford soon found himself committed to the idea of establishing a commission of neutral nations to devise an acceptable peace for the belligerents. On November 21 in New York Ford jumped at Lochner's half-humorous idea of chartering a ship to take the peace delegates to Europe. Jane Addams, who attended the meeting, protested the flamboyance of the idea, but for Ford that was precisely the point. Before nightfall *Oscar II* had been chartered from an amazed steamship company, and Ford was preparing to meet Woodrow Wilson in Washington. There he received his first reversal. The President was polite, even to the point of sharing his favorite joke about Ford cars with his guests, but would not endorse the idea of a peace commission. Disgusted, Ford branded Wilson "a small man" who had missed a great opportunity.

With the project hanging in the balance, Ford decided to persevere. Years of engineering experiments had given him a where-there's-a-will-there's-a-way doggedness. On November 24, 1915, he called a news conference in New York. Always an embarrassed public speaker, he managed to tell the assembled reporters that "we're going to get the boys out of the trenches before Christmas. I've chartered a ship, and some of us are going to Europe." The seasoned newspapermen, who also tended to be pro-British, were first astonished and then convulsed with laughter. Their stories poked fun at the rich rustic who thought he could build a peace like he built a car. *Oscar II* was termed a "loon ship" and the original "ship of fools." On the floor of the United States Senate Ford's delegation was styled "an aggregation of neurotics." Even Ford's wife and closest friends begged him to drop the project. But on December 4 *Oscar II* left New York harbor after a rousing sendoff. On board were the most distinguished group of Americans Ford's representatives had been able to accumulate with just nine days' notice. But most of the big names, including the now ill Jane Addams, were missing.

During the voyage to Norway, Ford wandered aimlessly among his guests, striking one reporter as "the vaguest of the vague, a comic, charming child." The only exception was when he slipped below deck to study the ship's engines. In Europe the inevitable debacle played itself out quickly. Ford became ill in the bitter Norwegian winter and returned to the United States within a week. Before following him the delegates toured the nonbelligerent nations and established a Neutral Conference for Continuous Mediation. But the animosities of the

394

belligerents proved too strong to settle at the conference table. When Ford withdrew support early in 1917, the conference collapsed. His flirtation with pacifism had cost him over $450,000. But in retrospect Ford's attempt to end the war does not seem as quixotic as it did to some of his countrymen in 1915. The underlying principles of peace the conference advanced were remarkably similar to Woodrow Wilson's Fourteen Points. And the idea of a permanent organization devoted to world peace subsequently bore fruit in the League of Nations and the United Nations.

Although Ford was a pacifist, he was also a fervent nationalist—a believer in and an exponent of the American way. When the United States declared war on Germany in April 1917, Ford was therefore quick to agree that "we must stand behind the President." Indeed he had changed his mind about Wilson since the abortive peace ship interview. The President, Ford felt, had sincerely tried to mediate the European war. His "peace without victory" speech of January 22, 1917, seemed to Ford to express some of the ideals behind the *Oscar II*. But Wilson had also failed and come to the reluctant conclusion that militarism could best be fought with militarism, a war to end war. Ford agreed, and after American entrance into World War I placed his factory at the disposal of the United States government and its allies. In the next eighteen months the Ford Motor Company built aircraft engines, ambulances, tanks, submarine chasers, and even helmets and gas masks. When the armistice came on November 11, 1918, Ford had the satisfaction of knowing he had made a major economic contribution to the victory.

In the 1920s Henry Ford reached the zenith of his career. Few names were better known in the United States. Whether one read his publications (mostly ghostwritten), followed his headline-making public life, or merely drove the Model T, Ford was an inescapable part of the postwar culture. The flivver—as Americans dubbed the Model T—the flask, and the flapper seemed to symbolize the age. Cars, especially, characterized what many thought was a new era. They upset familiar patterns of living, loving, working, recreating, even thinking. Much of the roar of the twenties came from the internal combustion engine. While providing portable bedrooms in which to enjoy sexual freedom, cars also helped gangsters and bootleggers get away. The image of two cars in every garage helped elect a President in 1928. The "lost"

395

generation was a generation on wheels, supposedly spinning to endless parties through the pages of F. Scott Fitzgerald novels. And Henry Ford, preaching the gospel of the machine, seemed to herald the coming of modernity.

Beneath the surface, however, such generalizations ring hollow. Neither Ford nor the 1920s merit the clichés with which each has so frequently been saddled. In the case of the man, both the old and the new mingled in his mind. On the one hand, Ford was a builder and bulwark of the modern, mechanized, urbanized nation; on the other, he devoted a remarkable amount of effort and expense to sustaining traditional America. The nostalgic, backward-looking Ford repeatedly deplored the very conditions that Ford the revolutionary industrialist did so much to bring about.

This ambivalence did not signify a lack of values so much as a superfluity of them. Hardly "lost," Ford's faith was strong, if bigoted and contradictory. His prescriptions for America were clear, if sometimes simpleminded. To the mass of citizens, Ford seemed to demonstrate that there could be change without disruption, and in doing so he eased the anxieties engendered by a time of rapid and often bewildering change. "The average citizen," editorialized the *New Republic* in 1923, "sees Ford as a sort of enlarged crayon portrait of himself; the man able to fulfill his own suppressed desires, who has achieved enormous riches, fame and power without departing from the pioneer-and-homespun tradition." In this nervous clinging to old values, even while undermining them, Ford was indeed a "crayon portrait" of the 1920s.

But was Ford typical of Americans in these years? Can he really be said to symbolize the postwar age? He was, after all, in his middle fifties when the decade began. But a great many Americans were also middle-aged in the 1920s, far more, in fact, than the twenty-year-old collegians who have hitherto characterzied these years. And at one point even a group of college students ranked Ford as the third greatest figure of all time, behind Napoleon and Jesus. It is also relevant that Ford possessed considerable political appeal after World War I. He narrowly lost the race for United States Senator from Michigan in 1918, and five years later his candidacy for President of the United States was widely discussed and supported. For many Americans, Ford was the most respected public figure of the time.

Fortunately for the historian, if not always for himself, Ford tended to state his opinions forthrightly on a wide variety of subjects outside his field of competence. He also had the money to publish and otherwise implement his ideas. The resulting portrait is that of a mind steeped in traditional Americanism. For Ford in the 1920s agrarian simplicity and McGuffey morality were still sacred. So was America with its heritage of freedom, fairness, and hard, honest labor. Ford's confidence in the old-fashioned virtues verged on the fanatical. The "Spirit of '76," equal-opportunity democracy, rugged individualism, the home, and motherhood were his touchstones. "More men are beaten than fail," he declared in 1928. "It is not wisdom they need, or money, or brilliance, or pull, but just plain gristle and bone." In the Dearborn *Independent*, "Mr. Ford's Page" stated that "one of the great things about the American people is that they are pioneers." This thought led easily to a restatement of the concept of American mission. "No one can contemplate the nation to which we belong," Ford continued, "without realizing the distinctive prophetic character of its obvious mission to the world. We are pioneers. We are the pathfinders. We are the road-builders. We are the guides, the vanguards of Humanity." Theodore Roosevelt and Woodrow Wilson had said as much, but Ford was writing *after* the war that allegedly ended the nation's innocence and mocked its mission.

Ford's intense commitment to the traditional American faith led him to suspect and ultimately to detest whatever was un-American. The same loyalties compelled him to search for explanations for the unpleasant aspects of American civilization in the 1920s that exonerated the old-time, "native" citizen. The immigrants were the primary targets of Ford's fire. In editorial after editorial and in several books, Ford argued that aliens who had no conception of "the principles which have made our civilization" were responsible for its "marked deterioration" in the twenties. He enthusiastically supported the Immigration Acts of 1921 and 1924, which used the quota system to reduce sharply the number of immigrants entering the country.

Ford also became a subscriber to the tired myth of an international Jewish conspiracy. When he could not find sufficient evidence for such a plot to take over the country, if not the world, Ford dispatched special agents to probe the affairs of prominent Jews and collect documentation. The search resulted in the "discovery" of the so-called Protocols of the Learned Elders of Zion. Although they were exposed as a forgery in 1921, Ford continued to use the Protocols to prove the existence of a Jewish scheme to overthrow the gentile elite, He also managed to blame everything wrong with modern America from jazz to the "fixing" of the 1919 World Series on the Jewish presence.

Ford's attack on the Jews was only a part of a general wave of insecurity and intolerance that swept through American society after World War I. First came the Red Scare of 1919, in which suspected Communists were hounded and in some cases deported by self-styled patriots. The distorted nativism of nervous minds continued in the 1920s under the white gowns and masks of the second edition of the Ku Klux Klan. Launched in 1915 by a never-say-die southerner, the KKK rose to nationwide power and a membership of 5 million by 1924. Ford was not a Klansman, but his anti-Semitism found a receptive audience in the Klan. In addition, the KKK hated Roman Catholics, blacks, urbanites, "wets" (anti-prohibitionists) and liberals of all shades. In the minds of its members, who were concentrated in rural areas and small towns in the South and Middle West, the KKK was a bastion of the national morality—America's front line of defense against evil, degeneracy, and, as it frequently happened, modernism. Nervous about the present and fearful of the future, the Klansmen yearned for a seemingly simpler and purer past.

So did Ford. The tension in his thought between old and new, nostalgia and progress, is dramatically illustrated in his attitude toward farming and farmers. On the one hand he believed farm life to be a ceaseless round of inefficient drudgery. Indeed, he had abundant personal evidence from his Dearborn boyhood. "I have traveled ten thousand miles behind a plow," he remarked at one point. "I hated the grueling grind of farm work." With the incentive of sparing others this painful experience, Ford addressed himself to the problem of industrializing agriculture. The farmer, in Ford's opinion, should become a technician and businessman. Tractors (Fords, of course) should replace horses. Mechanization would make it possible to produce in twenty-five working days what formerly required an entire year. Fences would come down and vast economies of scale take place. Agriculture, in a word, would be revolutionized by the same techniques of mass production that transformed American industry. And

Ford's modern farmer would not even live on his farm, but instead commute from a city home. To prove his point, Ford bought and operated a 9000-acre farm near Dearborn.

Yet Ford the so-called father of modern agriculture was only part of the man. He also retained a strong streak of old-fashioned, horse-and-buggy agrarianism. Farming, from this perspective, was more than a challenge in production; it was a moral act. So even while his cars made it possible, Ford lashed out at the modern city as a "pestiferous growth." In the manner of Thomas Jefferson he continually contrasted the "unnatural," "twisted," and "cooped up" lives of city dwellers with the "wholesome" life of "independence" and "sterling honesty" that the rural environment offered. "What children and adults need," he told one reporter, "is a chance to breathe God's fresh air and to stretch their legs and have a little garden in the soil." This ideal led Ford to choose small towns instead of cities as the sites of his branch factories. "Turning back to village industry," Ford declared in 1926, would enable Americans to reestablish a sense of community—with nature and with each other—that urbanization had destroyed.

Ford's enthusiasm for nature did not stop with ruralism. From 1914 to 1924 he sought a more complete escape from civilization on a series of camping trips with Thomas Edison, the naturalist and writer John Burroughs, and the tire king Harvey Firestone. Although the gear these self-styled "vagabonds" took to the woods was far from primitive, they apparently shared a genuine love of the outdoors. In Burroughs's words, Ford and his friends "cheerfully endure wet, cold, smoke, mosquitoes, black flies, and sleepless nights, just to touch naked reality once more." Ford had a special fondness for birds. Characteristically, he had five hundred birdhouses built on his Michigan farm, including one with seventy-six apartments—the "bird hotel." There were also electric heaters and brooders for Ford's fortunate birds. The whole production mixed technology and nature in a way that symbolized his ambivalence.

As for roads and automobiles, Ford saw them not as a threat to natural conditions, but rather as a way for the average American to come into contact with nature. The machine and the garden were not incompatible. Ford declared he could not agree with those who saw mechanization leading to a "cold, metallic sort of world in which great factories will drive away the trees, the flowers, the birds and the green fields." According to Ford, "unless we know more about machines and their use . . . we cannot have the time to enjoy" nature. But such statements only partly covered Ford's nervousness about the mechanized, urbanized future. The contradictions persisted. The same man who envisaged fenceless bonanza farms could say, "I love to walk across country and jump fences." The lover of trees could state, in utmost seriousness, "better wood can be made than is grown."

Ford's attitude toward history has been the subject of considerable misunderstanding. The principal source of confusion is a statement that received wide publicity in 1919 in connection with his libel suit against the *Chicago Tribune*. "History," Ford is supposed to have said, "is more or less the bunk. It is tradition. We don't want tradition. We want to live in the present, and the only history that is worth a tinker's dam is the history we make today." On another occasion Ford admitted that he "wouldn't give a nickel for all the history in the world." Complementing this sentiment is Ford's reputation as a forward-looking inventor and revolutionary industrialist dissatisfied with the old processes. Here, it seems, is a man fully home in the alleged new era of the 1920s. But in fact Ford idolized the past. His "history . . . is bunk" remark referred to ancient history as it was taught in the schools. For what actually happened in America's past, and its tangible evidence, Ford had only praise.

The most obvious evidence of Ford's enthusiasm for history was his collector's instinct. He began with that bastion of his own youth, the *McGuffey Readers*. By sending agents to scour the countryside with no limits on cost, Ford by 1925 had accumulated one of the few complete collections of the many McGuffey editions. To share their wisdom with his contemporaries, he had thousands of copies of *Old Favorites from the McGuffey Readers* printed in 1926. The book contained such classics as "Try, Try Again" and "The Hare and the Tortoise." It dispensed an ideal of individualism and self-reliance at the same time that Ford's assembly lines were transforming men into cogs in an impersonal machine.

From books Ford turned to the collection of things, and during the 1920s he amassed the most extensive collection of Americana in existence. He bought so widely and so aggressively that he became a major factor in antique market prices. Everything was fair game. Lamps and dolls, bells and grandfather clocks made their way to his museum, along with machines of all descriptions. Ford delighted in showing visitors around. Playing a few chords on an antique organ, he would remark: "that takes me back to my boyhood days. They were beautiful days." This sentiment undoubtedly figured in Ford's decision to restore his boyhood home. Everything had to be exactly as he remembered it. Furniture, china, and rugs were rehabilitated or reconstructed. He even hired archeologists to dig the ground around the family homestead to a depth of 6 feet in the hope of recovering Ford artifacts.

After restoring the homestead, Ford turned to reconstructing an entire pioneer town. Greenfield Village, Michigan, became a monument to Ford's reverence for the past. "I am trying," he explained, "to help America take a step . . . toward the saner and sweeter idea of life that prevailed in pre-war days." Greenfield had gravel roads, gas street lamps, a grassy common, and an old-fashioned country store. The automobile king permitted only horse-drawn vehicles on the premises. The genius of the assembly line engaged individual artisans to practice their crafts in the traditional—and obsolete— manner. In time, the boyhood cottages of Walt Whitman, Patrick Henry, and William Holmes McGuffey were purchased and transported to Greenfield.

Ford's money also saved historic sites in other parts of the country. In 1922 he bought the celebrated Wayside Inn at Sudbury, Massachusetts, and opened it as a museum for the edification of the public. But a new highway ran too near; the roar of the automobile disturbed the horse-and-buggy atmosphere. So, Ford had the state highway rerouted around the shrine at a cost of $250,000. He also restored the schoolhouse in Sudbury, which was supposed to be the site where Mary gamboled with her little lamb, and the village blacksmith's shop. History then, was not "bunk" to Henry Ford. The speed of change seemed to increase proportionately with his desire to retain contact with a past he believed had been wholesome, happy, and secure. "The Old Ways," as the *Dearborn Independent* declared, "Were Good."

Ford's opinion of the new morality of the jazz age was predictably low. He deplored the use of tobacco and even went so far as to publish tracts against smoking. When he had the power, he went beyond exhortation. "No one smokes in the Ford industries," their

leader proclaimed in 1929. As for alcohol, Ford was a fanatical Pro-
hibitionist. The Eighteenth Amendment and the Volstead Act, which
in theory made the United States "dry" after January 16, 1920, was
for Ford a great triumph. Any Ford workman detected drinking publicly or even keeping liquor at home was immediately dismissed.
"There are a million boys growing up in the United States," Ford
exulted, "who have never seen a saloon and who will never know the
handicap of liquor." When confronted with evidence of bootlegging
and the existence of speakeasies, Ford offered his standard explanation of evil—a Jewish conspiracy. The mass of Americans, he believed, "were, like himself, dry by moral conviction as well as by law."
And, in truth, the glamorous violations of Prohibition have been exaggerated out of all proportion. The 1920s roared largely in the pages of
its novelists and historians. Henry Ford, in other words, was far more
typical of Americans as a whole than F. Scott Fitzgerald.

Sex was too delicate a matter to be addressed directly, but Ford
conveyed his opinions through a discussion of music and dancing. Few
things about the twenties worried him more than jazz. The new music
clashed squarely with his ruralism and Bible-belt morality. In 1921
Ford struck out savagely at the "sly suggestion and abandoned sen-
suousness" of jazz, which sounded like "monkey talk, jungle squeals,
grunts and squeaks and gasps suggestive of cave love." To counter the
unhealthy influence, Ford promoted traditional folk dances. Not only
the scores but the backwoods fiddlers themselves were invited to Dearborn to play "Old Zip Coon" and "Arkansas Traveler." Ford also
undertook the revival of traditional social dancing. In 1926 a guidebook appeared entitled *"Good Morning": After a Sleep of Twenty-five
Years Old-fashioned Dancing Is Being Revived by Mr. and Mrs.
Henry Ford*. The essential purpose of the book, however, was to revive old-fashioned morality. It began by condemning as promiscuous
the newer dances such as the Charleston and the whole flapper syndrome. "A gentleman," the book explained, "should be able to guide
his partner through a dance without embracing her as if he were her
lover." Proper deportment, according to Ford, minimized physical
contact. There were elaborate rules regarding gloves, handkerchiefs,
and ways to request a dance. The guidebook, in short, was a monument to nineteenth-century conceptions of morality, decorum, and
order. So were the dances Ford and his wife hosted at Dearborn.

Precisely at nine, Ford's guests convened in evening dress in a lavish tribute to Victorianism.

Ambivalence is the key to the mind of Henry Ford. He looked both forward and backward. Confidently progressive as he was in some respects, he remained uneasy about the new ways. And the more conditions changed, the more Ford groped nostalgically for the security of traditional values and institutions. He was neither lost nor dissipated and roaring. And in the Jazz Age, he hated jazz. Yet Ford was popular to the point of being a deity in the 1920s. As a plain, honest, old-fashioned billionaire, a technological genius who loved to camp out, he seemed to his contemporaries to resolve the moral dilemmas of the age. Like Charles A. Lindbergh, another god of the era who combined the characteristics of pioneer and technologist, Ford testified to the nation's ability to move into the future without losing sight of the past.

While Ford labored to shape the nation's morality, the continued expansion of his company and his reputation involved him in the mainstream of its politics and economy. Over two decades of effort had left Americans weary of heroics; the ideal of reform now gave way to the pursuit of personal success. The insipid Warren G. Harding was well qualified to preside over the return to what he called "normalcy" in the years immediately following World War I. Ford did not support Harding in the election of 1920. Still a pacifist and a believer in international cooperation such as the League of Nations represented, he voted for and contributed to the unsuccessful Democratic team of James M. Cox and Franklin D. Roosevelt. Two years later Ford found himself seriously considered as a successor to Harding. The "Ford for President" movement gained momentum rapidly in 1922, and by 1923 Henry seemed ahead of the pack. His stern ethical code and anti-Semitism attracted followers in the South and Middle West, while his success as a manufacturer had nationwide appeal. At first Ford was not interested. His narrow loss to Truman H. Newberry in the 1918 Michigan senatorial election had left him disenchanted with politics. But the Presidential fever was hard to resist. Running the government, Ford began to think, was no different from running a factory.

The people closest to Henry Ford were amazed at his Presidential ambitions. Edison reminded his friend of his chronic shyness in public situations, adding: "you can't speak. You wouldn't say a damned

With this assembly line, instituted in 1913, Henry Ford reduced t
time needed for constructing electrical generators for his Model T fro
twenty minutes to fi

Americans exercised considerable
imagination in finding ways
to use the mobile powerplant
that Henry Ford perfected. This
Model T has been converted
into a snowmobile.

A large amount of
national pride surrounded
these four men whose
association included
camping trips. From the
left they are Thomas
Edison, John Burroughs,
Ford, and Harvey Firestone.
As the attire of the men
suggests, some of their
camping ventures were not
too primitive.

Ten thousand impoverished New Yorkers were given a free meal on Christmas Day, 1931 at the Municipal Lodging House. Such "bread lines" became a symbol of the Depression.

The human pathos of the Great Depression is reflected in this March 1933 photograph of Seattle, Washington. Shanty towns like the one in the foreground were known as "Hoovervilles" in remembrance of the President whose term coincided with the beginning of hard times. Looking from this misery to the skyscrapers in the background, many wondered what had gone wrong with the American dream.

word. You'd be mum." Less friendly critics such as Oswald Garrison Villard of the *Nation* declared they had never encountered a candidate "so absolutely unfit" for the Presidency. Even Clara Ford wrote indignantly to her husband's staff: "since you got him into it, you can just get him out of it. I hate this idea of the name of Ford being dragged down into the gutters of political filth. My name is Ford, and I'm proud of it! If Mr. Ford wants to go to Washington, he can go, but I'll go to England." With this kind of support at home, Ford must have had second thoughts, but the decisive blow came when Harding died on August 2, 1923. Calvin Coolidge, the taciturn Vermonter who had gained a nationwide reputation by using the power of the governorship of Massachusetts to break a Boston police strike in 1919, proved politically attractive. The professional politicians who had previously shown an interest in Ford now switched to Coolidge. Late in 1923, Ford himself came out for Coolidge.

Behind Ford's decision lay the story of Muscle Shoals, which was a major rapid on the Tennessee River in northern Alabama. During World War I the federal government made plans to harness its power and develop nitrate plants. Over $100 million went into the Muscle Shoals complex, but funds ran out before it was operative. In 1921 the installations were rusting away, to the disgust of a disciple of efficiency like Henry Ford. So he offered the government $5 million for Muscle Shoals, provided that the United States completed the Wilson Dam at a cost of $50 million. From Ford's point of view, this was surely one of the best buys in the history of business. Furthermore, it opened the possibility of acquiring extensive land holdings in the Tennessee Valley and reaping the monetary rewards of the region's rebirth.

Ford's critics, chiefly Senator George W. Norris of Nebraska, denounced the entire proposition as "the most wonderful real estate speculation since Adam and Eve lost title to the Garden of Eden." Hostile journalists branded Muscle Shoals "The Biggest GRAB Ever Attempted in America." Still, many fully expected that Ford could do for the Tennessee Valley what he had done for the automobile. Thousands of "pioneers" swarmed into the upper South in 1922. The Ford organization stood ready to swing into action, and the political climate of Harding's Washington was generally favorable. But George Norris, doggedly insisting that the government should develop the area in the public interest, held Ford at bay almost singlehandedly.

This was the context in which Henry Ford and Calvin Coolidge met for private interviews in September and again in December 1923. We will never know precisely what was said, but the topics of discussion were almost certainly the election of 1924 and Muscle Shoals. A few days after the December meeting Coolidge recommended to Congress the sale of Muscle Shoals to an unnamed private interest. Almost simultaneously Ford publicly announced the abandonment of his Presidential plans, thereby clearing the way for Coolidge in the election of 1924. Ford got the worst of the deal. Coolidge won in 1924, but Ford never got Muscle Shoals. Senator Norris, whose dream eventually materialized into the Tennessee Valley Authority, blocked approval of the sale.

The collapse of Ford's Muscle Shoals bid was one of the few reversals big business suffered in the United States during the 1920s. Determined to undo the "damage" inflicted on capitalism by the Progressive reformers, Harding and his cabinet were unabashedly pro-business. Herbert Hoover, the Secretary of Commerce, was a self-made millionaire who construed his function as protecting fortunes such as his own. Secretary of the Treasury Andrew Mellon, a multimillionaire from Pittsburgh, declared that "the Government is just a business and can and should be run on business principles." To Mellon, this meant that the taxation of the rich should be sharply reduced. He believed it was better strategy to tax the lower-income groups heavily and thus free the rich to promote economic growth by investment. In time, Mellon argued, the benefits would trickle down to the less fortunate. Ford was a case in point. His enormous, largely tax-free profits allowed him to institute the $5 and later the $6 and $7 days for his employees.

Andrew Mellon did not see his soak-the-poor tax structure fully implemented, but the Harding Administration was able to help big business with the tariff. The Fordney-McCumber Act of 1922 made possible duties so high as to exclude foreign competition completely. Businesses confined to the United States applauded the protection as a step toward monopoly, but for the Ford Motor Company and other internationally-oriented concerns, high tariffs hurt trade. Ford's protest, however, was a minority voice in the business community.

The Harding Administration left office on a wave of scandal, but Coolidge continued the postwar Republican tradition of favoritism of the rich. After prevailing in 1924 over Democrat John Davis and Progressive Robert LaFollette, Coolidge declared forthrightly that "the business of America is business." On another occasion, perhaps with Henry Ford in mind, he stated that "the man who builds a factory builds a temple." The federal government, Coolidge believed, should withdraw as much as possible from involvement in the economy. Within the broad framework of the law, business should have an unobstructed opportunity to pursue the main chance. The 1920s witnessed a revival of the socioeconomic philosophy of Andrew Carnegie's Gilded Age.

Herbert Hoover, who defeated Democrat Alfred E. Smith for the Presidency in 1928, typified in his career and his thought the ideals of the age. In fact, Hoover was probably the only real competition Henry Ford encountered in the gallery of public heroes of the twenties. Left an orphan in 1884 at the age of ten, Hoover grew up to an international mining career that made him rich. During World War I he became famous as head of the American Relief Commission abroad and the Food Administration at home. A genius in matters of large-scale efficiency, like Ford, Hoover neatly executed apparent miracles. In 1922, while secretary of commerce under Harding, he set forth his creed in a slender volume entitled *American Individualism*. Its message was one of rugged individualism and free enterprise. Hoover staunchly defended the unregulated profit system. Society and government owed the people only three things: "liberty, justice, and equality of opportunity." Competition took care of the rest, carrying the deserving to their just rewards and the failures to deserved defeat. Any interference, such as philanthropy or favoritism, only dulled "the emery wheel of competition" and retarded progress. Hoover paid lip service to restricting the strong in the interest of society as a whole, but the main thrust of his thought was directed toward awarding the victors their spoils.

When Hoover began his term in the White House early in 1929, there were few surface indications of the economic collapse just around the corner. "I have no fear for the future of our country," the President announced in company with most members of the establishment; "It is bright with hope." On the surface, there was much to support this prognosis. Riding the momentum of a five-year boom, the stock market pushed to ever higher levels. Business seemed good. In

Detroit the Ford Motor Company had just completed a changeover from the Model T to the Model A and, after two lean years, was solidly in the black. Its mighty River Rouge plant was now in full operation in a location accessible to ocean-going vessels using the St. Lawrence—Great Lakes waterway. Like Carnegie before him, Ford gradually consolidated all phases of production under his ownership. Ford iron ore, Ford logs, and Ford coal came to the Rouge and were converted by Ford smelters and mills into Ford cars by an army of more than 100,000 workers. Prosperity seemed a permanent American possession. When breaks in speculators' confidence in 1928 and early 1929 caused sudden, sharp drops in stock prices, most Americans were not overly concerned. The buyers would return. Ford and Hoover agreed with Andrew Mellon, who offered the calm if unfounded assurance that "there is no cause for worry. The high tide of prosperity will continue."

By the late summer of 1929, however, Mellon's "tide" was sustained largely by statements like his own. The nation's prosperity was one of belief rather than fact, of paper rather than property. Granted that hindsight is always twenty-twenty, still it is surprising that the nation's business and political leaders did not recognize the symptoms. Perhaps they did not want to see, because the signs were there for those who dared to look. One was the limited nature of the prosperity of the 1920s. Substantial segments of the American people simply did not share in the allegedly good years of the decade. It was not that they lost money, but rather that the gap between their incomes and the cost of living widened steadily. A dollar bought less and less. The result was a tendency for consumption to lag behind production. America's economy was top-heavy and, consequently, unstable.

Farmers were a case in point. After weathering a postwar price slump in agricultural commodities, the farmer's lot began to improve slowly. But the prices he had to pay for things like Ford tractors rose too and often more quickly. To combat this situation, farmers lobbied for government support of agricultural prices. Many ideals coalesced in bills sponsored by Senator Charles McNary of Oregon and Representative Gilbert Haugen of Iowa. They proposed that the federal government purchase agricultural surplus and thereby support prices at "parity" (the pre-World War I level). Advocates of the McNary-Haugen plan argued they were asking no more than the equivalent of the protective tariff that supported prices on manufactured goods. But in the 1920s the business of America was business, and Coolidge vetoed McNary-Haugen bills in 1927 and again in 1928. Hoover followed suit. Farm incomes, and American purchasing power, continued to decline.

The American laboring man also experienced harder and harder times after World War I. In Detroit inflation and the rising cost of living ate into Ford's renowned $5 minimum wage. By the end of 1918 the $5 was worth $2.80 in prewar currency. To his credit, Ford realized that high wages meant high production, high consumption, and general prosperity. In 1919 he set the minimum in his factories at $6 per day. But this gave the worker only $3.36 in 1914 dollars. Labor unions and collective bargaining, which might have alleviated the situation, faced widespread hostility after the war. In 1919 attempts of steel and coal workers to improve their lot by strikes were put down by the combined might of the federal government and business management. Courts issued injunctions that forced striking workers back to their jobs. They also upheld anti-union "yellow-dog" contracts and allowed the Clayton Act, originally construed as pro-labor, to be turned against unions. A decision of the Supreme Court in *Hamer* v. *Dagenhart* (1918) invalidated all laws aimed at restricting child labor. In 1922 Harding used the threat of federal troops to reopen coal mines with wages slashed 50 percent.

Labor leaders added to their own problems. The craft unions like the American Federation of Labor were still afraid to attempt to organize masses of unskilled workers on an industrywide basis. Without organization, laborers in industries such as steel, food packing, chemicals, and automobiles were helpless. Ford, for example, steadfastly refused to permit unions to gain a foothold in his plants; he claimed he knew best how to take care of his men. Granted that working conditions and wages at Ford in the 1920s were better than the national average, still the refusal of the foremost industrialist of the age to sanction unions had an adverse national effect. Ford had pioneered in wage reforms; he might have set the pace in making negotiation rather than dictation the norm in labor-management relations. As it was, union membership declined steadily in the twenties.

Farmers and laborers were not alone in unsuccessful efforts to gain a larger share of the nation's wealth in the years before the Great

Crash. Small businessmen and professional people such as doctors, lawyers, and teachers felt the economic pinch. Until late 1929, the luxury and investment of the rich gave the appearance of national prosperity, but a situation in which one-third of all personal income went to one-twentieth of the population was highly vulnerable. When the crash and subsequent depression curtailed high-income spending, there was insufficient lower- and middle-income consumption to support the economy. Exports might have alleviated the falling demand, but the high tariff policies of Republican administrations since Harding discouraged foreign trade just when it was most needed.

Another weakness was the unstable nature of America's corporate and banking structure. Like a row of dominoes, poorly financed organizations were poised to fall en masse. The problem was rampant speculation that in the late 1920s reached the proportions of a national mania. Borrowing far beyond their means, men and companies gambled on paper profits. Lending institutions facilitated the overextension. In time, the tangled threads of financial dependency were stretched thinner and thinner. When a break occurred, the whole structure came down with a crash.

With his new Model A outstripping General Motors' Chevrolet and Plymouth lines, Henry Ford was in the midst of a very good year when the bottom fell out of the American economy. It happened with sickening suddenness. In early September 1929 *The New York Times* average of selected industrial stocks stood at 452, up an unbelieveable 200 points since early the previous year. By mid-November the *Times* average was 224. Panic selling, particularly on "Black Thursday" (October 24) and "Black Tuesday" (October 29), caused a paper loss of $26 billion in securities. By the middle of 1932 the *Times* average had dropped to 58. In Detroit Henry Ford kept close watch on the collapsing market, but derived considerable satisfaction from the thought that "Ford" was not among the big losers on the stock exchange. Indeed, it was not even listed. Many years before Ford had consolidated ownership of the Ford Motor Company in his immediate family. No stock was sold to the investing public. As a result, the crash left Ford completely untouched in the short run.

Herbert Hoover, however, was worried. On November 29, 1929, he summoned Ford and other leaders of American business to a conference in Washington, where he pleaded with them not to cut wages or raise prices. Ford was glad to cooperate; in fact, he went the President one better. To the astonishment and dismay of some of the conferees, he walked out of the meeting and announced that he was *lowering* prices on the Model A coupe by $35 and that his minimum daily wage would be *increased* from $6 to $7.

Ford's spectacular announcements can be understood as a symptom of his instinctive ability to grab the limelight, but they also reflected a basic confidence in the American economy. The crash was certainly disturbing, but along with Herbert Hoover and most fiscal experts of the day, Ford believed almost religiously in the self-regulating nature of the economy. In his opinion, the law of supply and demand would correct temporary economic imbalances provided it was allowed to operate without interference. America's only problem was too many people forsaking business for speculation. "A market," he blithely declared in *Moving Forward* (1930), "is never saturated with a good product." If Americans had concentrated on making good products (like the Model A, one presumes), rather than on making dollars, the depression would have never occurred. For the same reason, its cure lay in "quantities of goods pushed out into the world" at low prices and in "building buying power" with high wages. In Ford's mind, "the wages of the workmen are more important to the country than the dividends to stockholders."

As the depression deepened, Ford was unable to live up to these ideals. The $7 day lasted only a year and three-quarters. And even those who received this rate found their weekly pay envelopes contained less money because of cutbacks in the number of hours worked. Also, there were fewer laborers. From a high of 174,000 men in 1929, Ford employment declined to less than 50,000 in 1933. River Rouge workers earned a total of $181 million in 1929; four years later the figure had declined to $32.5 million.

The human meaning of these statistics and of comparable ones throughout the country is difficult for a generation that has known only affluence to comprehend. There was suffering, fear, anger, and discontent approaching the point of revolution in large segments of the population. In Ford's Detroit and other urban-industrial areas throughout the nation, sullen-faced jobless men formed bread lines to receive what doles there were. Others trapped gophers for stew or combed garbage dumps in search of edible food. Panhandlers, with their inevitable "brother, can you spare a dime," were legion, but few brothers could. Some women were obliged to turn to prostitution to feed their husbands and children. Home for thousands of Americans was a shack in a "Hooverville." For bedding they used "Hoover blankets"—old newspapers. In the New World, that promised land of abundance and opportunity, a dark age had come.

Aside from a few token contributions to local relief efforts in Dearborn, Ford dismissed the depression as bad judgment on the part of some men and bad luck on the part of others. His belief, like that of Herbert Hoover, was that welfare sapped the strength of American traditions of individualism and self-help. He also agreed with the President that the national budget should not be unbalanced in efforts to revive the economy or even to relieve suffering. This philosophy made Henry Ford appear the essence of heartless capitalism. In September 1930, as he boarded a luxurious ocean liner for a European vacation, he casually told the press: "it's a good thing the recovery is prolonged. Otherwise the people won't profit by the illness." In *Moving Forward,* published the same year, Ford echoed William Graham Sumner and Andrew Carnegie in declaring that "the very poor are recruited almost solely from the people who refuse to . . . work diligently." The jobless were urged by farm-boy Ford to "cultivate a plot of land" in the "good old pioneer way."

Despite such platitudes, it was clear that by 1932 Detroit was near the breaking point. In March almost half the city's wage earners were unemployed, with no relief in sight. In this climate of desperation Communist organizers succeeded in promoting a "hunger march" to dramatize the plight of the people. The target of the march was Ford's River Rouge plant, and many of the marchers were sometime Ford employees. A mile from the Rouge, Dearborn police intercepted the column and a running battle involving tear gas, bricks, and bullets ensued. At the end, four marchers lay dead and the Ford empire, guarded by Harry Bennett's corps of private police, was untouched.

Simultaneously in Washington, D.C., thousands of unemployed veterans of World War I marched to reinforce demands for bonuses. Their effort was likewise in vain. Two men were killed in the forcible eviction of this Bonus Army from its shantytown near the capitol. Thoughtful Americans were beginning to wonder if the political and economic system of their country could withstand the strain of hard times and, even more disturbingly, if it *should*.

Held in an atmosphere of tension verging on desperation, the election of 1932 loomed as the most significant since that of 1860. President Hoover had worked hard with a variety of political and economic tools to halt the depression, but his commitment to free enterprise and the balanced budget hobbled his efforts. Ironically, the hero of American relief efforts in postwar Europe proved ineffective in alleviating the suffering of his own countrymen. Nonetheless, the Republicans renominated him. The Democrats chose the governor of New York, Franklin Delano Roosevelt. A distant cousin of Theodore, Franklin Roosevelt had attracted attention by his courageous conquest of a crippling attack of poliomyelitis and his humanitarian attitude toward welfare problems in New York. He exuded a confidence that, in the depths of the depression, proved almost magnetic.

Henry Ford, however, was not swept off his feet. He had voted Democratic for Wilson and peace in 1916. Four years later he again supported the Democrats in a losing cause. But in 1924, after the collapse of his own Presidential boom, he switched parties and voted for Calvin Coolidge. He was a Hoover man in 1928, and in 1932 he continued to support the man so like him in origin and philosophy. Signs in Ford plants read: "to prevent times from getting worse and to help them get better, President Hoover must be reelected." In view of the scanty evidence for such an assumption, one must seek the real reasons for Ford's decision in 1932 in his incompatibility with Roosevelt.

Although the men knew each other during World War I when Roosevelt, as assistant secretary of the navy, handled Ford war contracts, they had little in common. Roosevelt was a patrician, born to wealth and educated at Harvard. Moreover, Ford clung to a belief in the open, opportunity-filled world of Horatio Alger, William Holmes McGuffey, and the pioneers, a world in which effort and ability were always rewarded. Let things alone, he insisted, and in time the free enterprise system would find solutions to America's problems. Roosevelt, on the contrary, believed that with the ending of the frontier the era of relatively equal opportunity had also ended. The government, he reasoned, must do for the country what the frontier had once done—ensure opportunity, security, and prosperity for the individual and for the nation as a whole. In the manner of his cousin Theodore's New Nationalism, Franklin Roosevelt proposed to meet concentrated economic power with the concentrated power of the federal government. The depression would be legislated away even if it meant stepping on some traditionally sacrosanct toes.

Roosevelt campaigned on the theme of federal action, of "bold, persistent experimentation." He was, to be sure, vague about what this meant, and his economic thinking in 1932 was almost as conservative as Hoover's, but he seemed unafraid to lead in new directions. "Let it be . . . symbolic," he declared after making an unprecedented flight to Chicago to accept the Democratic nomination in person, "that . . . I broke traditions." And he concluded his acceptance speech: "I pledge you, I pledge myself to a new deal for the American people."

Despite Ford's opposition, Roosevelt gained a convincing victory (57 percent of the popular vote) in the election of 1932. It is significant that only 1 million out of 40 million voting Americans opted against repairing the old system by supporting Socialist or Communist candidates. The nation sweated out the last months of the Hoover Administration which, by its own admission, was "at the end of our rope" as far as economic recovery was concerned. With Roosevelt's inauguration on March 4, 1933, the psychological depression, at least, was over. "The only thing we have to fear," the new President shouted into the cold, gray air of his inauguration day, "is fear itself." A whirlwind of action followed. Attacking simultaneously the problems of relief, recovery, and permanent reform, the New Deal at first commanded Henry Ford's respect. On May 8, 1933, he included a personal message in a company advertisement acknowledging Roosevelt as the man who "turned the Ship of State around" and set America's face toward the future. In particular, Ford approved of the new administration's concern for farmers (the Agricultural Adjustment Act) and its decision to use the neglected resources of Muscle Shoals and other hydropower sites in the Tennessee Valley.

But Ford's attitude changed after June 16, 1933, when Roosevelt signed the National Industrial Recovery Act (NIRA). This climax of the New Deal's first "Hundred Days" created the National Recovery Administration (NRA) under Hugh S. Johnson, a hard-boiled veteran of both military and business campaigns. The NRA's purpose was to persuade American employers to stop cutting wages and firing employees, thus reducing demand and deepening the depression. The tools for this task were "codes" of fair competition that established minimum wage and hour standards. Promulgated by the President, the codes had the force of law. They also benefited from favorable public opinion. Johnson exploited this advantage by branding the NRA the nation's best hope to check "the murderous doctrine of savage and wolfish individualism" and calling on everyone to ostracize code violators. Another important part of the National Industrial Recovery Act was contained in its Section 7a, a guarantee to labor unions of the right to organize and bargain collectively.

Initially, the NRA was a decided success. Two million employers placed the administration's symbol, a blue eagle, in their places of business and tried to terminate wage and price cutting. Part of the automobile industry cooperated. Chrysler flew blue eagles from every flagstaff, and Chevrolet advertised that it was "proud and glad to do our part." Ford, however, held back. "We know that President Roosevelt wants to do the right and helpful thing," he told reporters on the day the NIRA was signed, but "I was always under the impression that to manage a business properly you ought to know something about it." Even the fact that codes were to be drawn up by the industrialists themselves did not lessen Ford's opposition. He believed, with considerable justification, that his company had already taken steps to maintain high wages, and in his private notes he grumbled at the New Deal's efforts to "kill competition." Another note read: "I do not think that this country is ready to be treated like Russia for a while. There is a lot of the pioneer spirit here yet." Of course this was unrealistic. It was the New Deal's great achievement that it managed to preserve the essence of capitalism while making it more responsive to national needs. In the desperate atmosphere of 1933 Roosevelt could well have moved toward the extremes of government control that Josef Stalin and Adolf Hitler were imposing elsewhere at precisely the same time. Instead, the New Deal followed a middle way, reforming the free enterprise system in order to preserve it. In this endeavor Roosevelt had the support of the great majority.

Ford remained firmly in the minority. Despite Hugh Johnson's friendly pleadings and subsequent threats to administer a "sock in the nose" to "chiselers" who did not join the code agreements, the Ford

Motor Company, with 24 percent of the nation's automobile production, refused to cooperate. Its leader advised his fellow industrialists to "forget these alphabet schemes [such as NRA] and take hold of their industries and run them with good, sound, American business sense." As a result of his resistance, Ford became a hero to right-wing opponents of the Roosevelt Administration who in 1934 organized the Liberty League. Ford's reputation increased as Johnson unwisely overextended his bureau's efforts and invited the 1936 ruling of the Supreme Court (*Schechter Poultry* v. *U.S.*) that declared the NIRA unconstitutional. There was even talk of the seventy-three-year-old Ford as an opponent to Roosevelt in the election of 1936.

Henry Ford also stood athwart the mainstream of American thinking in his opposition to the organization of labor. As with the NRA codes, he felt the Ford Motor Company knew the interests of the working man and how best to serve them through company welfare programs. The bulk of his workers disagreed. Moreover, they believed they had the support of the majority of their countrymen. The New Deal had revived unionism after a sleep of a quarter-century. Even after the invalidation of Section 7a of the NIRA, the National Labor Relations (Wagner) Act of 1935 maintained the principle of labor's right to organize and management's obligation to bargain in good faith. The American Federation of Labor responded with a successful campaign to organize skilled workers according to the philosophy of craft unionism. But in 1935 a powerful new force, operating on a new philosophy, entered the labor scene. The Committee (later Congress) of Industrial Organizations, under the leadership of John L. Lewis, operated on the belief that all the workers in a given industry should be organized in one big union. The automobile industry was a prime target of CIO attack. Working through the United Automobile Workers under Walter Reuther, the CIO carried the fight to General Motors in the winter of 1936–1937. Using a new weapon, the "sitdown strike," which prevented operation of a plant with nonunion men, the UAW forced General Motors to the negotiating table in February 1937.

Ford was unmoved and determined to resist the unions, with force if necessary. What his policy meant became clear on May 26, 1937, when Reuther and other union leaders arrived at the gates of the Rouge to distribute circulars. A gang of Ford toughs, including professional wrestlers and boxers, constituted the reception committee. The union men were ordered to leave. As they started to obey, they were slugged from behind, kicked in the groin, head, and abdomen, and finally thrown down a flight of iron steps. The press was on hand to describe and photograph the entire proceedings of the "Battle of the Overpass." These documents later became part of the evidence the National Labor Relations Board and were used to accuse the Ford Motor Company of violating federal labor laws and discriminating against unions. Henry Ford personally denounced the charges as gross falsehoods even as similar cases of brutality occurred at Ford plants in Dallas and Kansas City. In lieu of the UAW, he offered workers his own Blue Card Union and seemed to have evaded both unionization and federal authority.

In the winter of 1940–1941 the UAW renewed its attempts to organize the Ford Motor Company. On its side were recent Supreme Court decisions favorable to labor, including the upholding of the Wagner Act. Also influential was the revival of the economy as a consequence of the United States' assumption of a major share of war production for a new set of European belligerents. With workers in increasing demand, Ford could not pick and choose between union and nonunion men as easily as before. On April 1, 1941, the UAW struck at the Rouge and closed the plant. Growling that he would "never submit to any union," Ford wanted to unleash Harry Bennett's squads of plant police with tear gas and machine guns. But he consented to an election under the auspices of the National Labor Relations Board. The results of the May 21 balloting were definitive: 70 percent of Ford's workers supported the UAW, 27 percent the AFL, and only 2.7 percent Ford's no-union principle.

Deeply hurt, Ford vowed he would quit business rather than accept the verdict of his employees. "Close the plant!" he thundered to his aides. The government, they quickly pointed out, would take it over to service war contracts. Let it be so, Ford snapped back. But he was losing his grip. The judgment that had built an industrial empire was lost. Already the victim of a stroke, Ford had only two more years of autocratic company management and seven more years of life remaining. His son Edsel pleaded with him to alter a business philosophy of rugged individualism that had lost its usefulness decades earlier. Clara Ford threatened divorce if he did not accept unionization. At length Ford was persuaded to enter, or more exactly, was dragged kicking and screaming into the modern world he had done so much to create.

SELECTED READINGS

The Person

BENNETT, HARRY H.: *We Never Called Him Henry* (1951). A reminiscence by one of Ford's close business associates.

*HERNDON, BOOTON: *Ford: An Unconventional Biography of the Men and Their Times* (1969). The most recent account of Henry Ford, his son, and their company.

JARDIM, ANNE: *The First Henry Ford: A Study in Personality and Business Leadership* (1970). Incisive, dispassionate analysis.

NEVIS, ALLAN, and FRANK ERNEST HILL: *Ford* (3 vols., 1954–1963). The best source for the man and the company. A fair, thorough treatment.

*RAE, JOHN B. (ed.): *Henry Ford* (1969). Ford's own writing and the evaluations of others.

*SWARD, KEITH: *The Legend of Henry Ford* (1948). A comprehensive account, frequently critical of Ford.

WIK, REYNOLD M.: *Henry Ford and Grass-roots America* (1972). Ford's relationship to the ideas and feelings of common people in the United States.

The Period

*BERNSTEIN, IRVING: *The Lean Years: A History of the American Worker, 1920–1933* (1960).

*BURNS, JAMES M.: *Roosevelt: The Lion and the Fox* (1956). The best analysis of Franklin D. Roosevelt as a politician.

*CONKIN, PAUL: *The New Deal* (1967). A good brief analysis.

*DEGLER, CARL: *The Age of the Economic Revolution, 1876–1901* (1967). The background to the emergence of the Ford Motor Company and similar enterprises.

*HAYS, SAMUEL: *The Response to Industrialism, 1885–1914* (1957). A sweeping, often provocative interpretation of one of the forces transforming American life.

*HIGHAM, JOHN: *Strangers in the Land* (1955). The immigrant and the response of "native" Americans to him in the late nineteenth and early twentieth centuries.

* Available in paperback.

*MAY, ERNEST: *The World War and American Isolation, 1914–1917* (1959). The changing relationship of the United States to the first general European war of the twentieth century.

*MAY, HENRY: *The End of American Innocence* (1959). Intellectual and social history focusing on the impact of World War I.

*NASH, RODERICK: *The Nervous Generation: American Thought, 1917–1930* (1970). A revisionist treatment of the social and intellectual history of a much-mythologized era.

*WIEBE, ROBERT: *The Search for Order: 1877–1920* (1967). An imaginative generalization concerning the major forces for change in the life of a maturing nation.

* Available in paperback.

CHAPTER TEN

Martin Luther King, Jr.

Perspiring in the sweltering heat of a Washington August afternoon, Martin Luther King looked down from the steps of the Lincoln Memorial at the largest assembly ever congregated in the United States. Well over 200,000 people, 70 percent of them blacks, jammed the mile-long mall that swept away to the Washington Monument. Angry yet hopeful, they had come to the nation's capital in 1963, the centennial of the Emancipation Proclamation, to personify black demands for equality in American society. But the

*speakers and singers who preceded King had not been particularly
effective, the heat was oppressive, and the great crowd was starting to
thin around the edges. As he mounted the podium King sensed this
restlessness and the need for a focus. At first his deep voice was husky,
but it soon became resonant with a purpose that quieted and
transfixed the multitude and millions of television viewers. King's
eloquence dramatized the anguish of black history. One hundred
years after slavery, he pointed out, the black man was still "an exile
in his own land." It was the future, however, that mattered. "I have a
dream," he cried repeatedly, as he sketched his vision of freedom,
justice, and brotherhood. At the end of his speech King prophesized
that one day all people would be able to join together in singing
the words of an old Negro spiritual: "Free at last! Free at last!
Thank God Almighty, we are free at last!" There was an awed
silence; then an ear-shattering roar; the crowd was on its feet
applauding wildly. King had galvanized the massive assembly. At
that moment he stood at the crest of a mounting wave of black
protest. Yet, as King must have known, his dream would have an
agonizing birth. Just five years after his Washington address, he lay
dead on the balcony of a Memphis motel, the victim of the violence
he had devoted his life to overcoming.*

On September 2, 1864, the great-grandparents of Martin Luther
King looked on with astonishment as 100,000 Union soldiers under
the command of General William T. Sherman marched triumphantly
into their home town, Atlanta, Georgia. Sherman, on his way from
Tennessee to the Atlantic Ocean, was slicing the Confederacy apart.
For slaves like the Kings, his presence in Atlanta was reason for both
joy and fear. On the one hand it promised freedom; on the other, it
meant changes with which the ex-slaves were ill prepared to cope.
Some of the bitter fruits of liberation were already apparent. Sherman's scorched-earth policy had left Atlanta a smoldering ruin. Equally
searing were the hatreds and rivalries that swept over the South
during Reconstruction. The Kings were caught in the middle of a
power struggle in a conquered province. The participants were North-

ern whites ("carpetbaggers"), Southern whites willing to play the North's game ("scalawags"), and old-line Confederates anxious to regain control of their region. In addition, Republican and Democratic politicians fought for control of the votes of a reunified South.

This competition briefly elevated Southern blacks to a position of prominence. Between 1868 and 1871 military occupation of the South made "Black Reconstruction" possible. Black votes sent a few blacks to the United States Senate and House of Representatives. In South Carolina's lower house, blacks even constituted the majority. But if freedmen such as the Kings interpreted this as genuine power, they were sadly mistaken. At best, many of the black voters were puppets in the hands of self-seeking white politicians. And when northern zeal for forcing Reconstruction flagged in the late 1870s, the freedmen found themselves virtually friendless. Restoration of white supremacy in the South followed immediately. For blacks like Frederick Douglass, the promise of the Civil War had turned to ashes. True freedom, it appeared, would not come all at once. The old social relationships would be slow to erode.

Martin Luther King's grandfather, James Albert King, was a case in point. He was born in 1863, the Emancipation Proclamation year, and the Union victory two years later seemed to guarantee him equality of opportunity. As James grew up, he too had a dream for the future. It consisted of ownership of a small farm, economic independence, and a measure of self-respect. But even these modest hopes were doomed to frustration. Despite the efforts of the Freedmen's Bureau created by Congress in 1865 to assist ex-slaves and the intentions of radical Republicans such as Thaddeus Stevens to divide the great plantations so as to give every black 40 acres and a mule, James King's fortunes declined. Within a few years he had sunk to a condition of economic dependence that was tantamount to slavery.

For James King the process began when he moved from Atlanta to Stockbridge, Georgia, in the late 1870s and took work as a sharecropper for a white landlord. Under this arrangement he farmed a white man's land, and took a share of the harvest as his wages. He hoped eventually to accumulate the means to purchase his own land, but his economic situation never improved. And even if he had managed to surmount the legal, social, and economic obstacles southern whites put in the way of would-be black landowners, the crop-lien system waited to strip him of any gains. The local merchant would lend the black farmer equipment and provisions against his future crop. At the harvest the merchant stepped in to claim all the crop and more. Keeping black farmers in a state of continual debt worked as a subtle but effective system of social repression. Looking back on his father's life, Martin Luther King, Sr., bitterly commented that James worked "from sun up to sun down for a whole year and still owed 'the man' $400 for the privilege of working."

In the last two decades of the nineteenth century the southern states took steps to make sure that the James Kings remained on the bottom of their political, economic, and social structure. Segregation laws and customs took firm root after the withdrawal of the last northern troops in 1877. Most southern states eventually revised their constitutions to include discriminatory regulations against blacks. James King found himself in a divided world. Racial ostracism extended to churches, schools, housing, jobs, restaurants, and transportation. Even cemeteries were segregated. Indeed, the separation of the races in the post-bellum South was sharper than it had ever been in the slave era. The reason is not hard to find. When the South had slavery, it felt more confident of its ability to control the region's 4 million blacks. Most of them were property and could be treated as such. After emancipation, however, new means of social control had to be improvised. And now blacks were, at least on paper, human beings who possessed the basic rights of citizenship and suffrage. Feeling more threatened, and lacking the power to control blacks by owning them, the white South developed the rigid patterns of segregation that James King's grandson assaulted.

In 1883 the United States Supreme Court found the Civil Rights Act of 1875 guaranteeing blacks "free and equal enjoyment" of public accommodations unconstitutional. The court's finding symbolized the growing feeling in the North that, once freed, black people had to fend for themselves in a Darwinistic struggle for existence. Even former abolitionists and other liberal reformers were reluctant to take up the lance in the blacks' behalf. Slavery, it seemed, was one thing; equal opportunity for the former slaves another. It was quite true that many whites who detested slavery also detested the prospect of having black people as social, economic, and political equals. A backlash of sympathy for the southern whites' "problem" spread rapidly in the North after the Civil War. Few Americans protested when in 1890 Mississippi led a parade of southern states in instituting a poll tax. These measures in effect snuffed out black suffrage and with it the Fifteenth Amendment, which only twenty years earlier had been the pride of Radical Reconstruction.

Although James King and millions like him received no schooling, education offered one way out of the morass that was black life in the postbellum South. Not only did it promise economic rewards and a genuine role in self-government, but it also offered a road to social respect. John C. Calhoun of South Carolina had inadvertently suggested this before the Civil War, when he remarked: "if a Negro could be found who could parse Greek or explain Euclid, I should be constrained to think he had human possibilities." Calhoun clearly dismissed the possibility, but his remark was obviously a challenge to those of a different persuasion. After the Civil War many white educators and philanthropists were determined to call Calhoun's bluff. With the help of the Freedmen's Bureau and the tiny corps of educated southern blacks, they launched a system of elementary education for blacks of all ages. A few black colleges appeared, notably Hampton, Fisk, Howard, and—near where James King labored for "the man"—Atlanta University. Wealthy northerners such as George Peabody and John D. Rockefeller gave millions for black education. Northern churches contributed additional money as well as numbers of young people who attacked the challenge of educating the freedmen with energy and idealism.

Southern blacks were glad to have these friends, but frequently the idealism of the educational missionaries did not match the ex-slaves' immediate capacities and needs. Impressive as parsing Greek and explaining Euclid might be in demonstrating innate ability, the usual nineteenth-century college curriculum had little relevance to the black situation. The man who discerned this problem most clearly and, in solving it, became the most significant black American in the generation before Martin Luther King's birth was Booker T. Washington.

Born a slave on a plantation in Franklin County, Virginia, in 1856, Washington determined at an early age to make something of his life. And his autobiography, *Up from Slavery* (1901), reads very much like Benjamin Franklin's. After the Civil War, Washington worked in West Virginia's coal mines and attended school at night. In

1872 he entered the Hampton Institute, Virginia, and worked his way through school as a janitor. At Hampton, Washington came under the influence of Samuel Chapman Armstrong, a teacher who emphasized the importance of personal industry and honesty as prerequisites to success. Washington learned, in his words, "thrift, economy and push [in] an atmosphere of business, Christian influences, and the spirit of self help." These values became the hallmark of his approach to the black problem.

After graduating from Hampton in 1875 and teaching for several years, Washington was selected in 1881 to organize a school for blacks at Tuskegee, Alabama. The resulting Normal and Industrial Institute became Washington's life work and his key to fame and influence. Martin Luther King always referred to Washington's method for uplifting his race as "patient persuasion." It was an apt characterization. Washington believed in a conciliatory approach to the white establishment. He urged blacks to subordinate considerations of political and social equality to those of economic advancement. Respect for the law and cooperation with authority followed. So did turning the other cheek, but Washington's approach succeeded in winning a broad base of support.

Washington's formula for black advancement was the one he had learned at Hampton. Using Franklin's virtues of dedication, thrift, and industry, blacks would establish the firm economic base necessary, Washington believed, for first-class citizenship. "Let down your buckets where you are," was his advice. "Be content," Martin Luther King interpreted this as meaning, "with doing well what the times permit you to do." The fact that the result was most often humble, manual labor for an elite did not disturb Washington in the least. "The opportunity to earn a dollar in a factory just now," he once remarked, "is worth infinitely more than the opportunity to spend a dollar in an opera house." And he illustrated this philosophy by personal example. On one occasion Washington, by then famous as the president of Tuskegee Institute, was on his way to his office when a wealthy white lady demanded that he stop and chop a pile of wood. Without a word, Washington removed his coat, cut the wood, and carried it to the kitchen. After he left a maid told the lady that her woodcutter was Professor Booker T. Washington. Mortified, she appeared at his office the next day to make an awkward apology. "It's entirely all right, madam," Washington replied. "I like to work, and I'm delighted to do favors for my friends." From that day on the lady became one of Tuskegee's most generous benefactors; her gifts and those of her friends amounted to hundreds of thousands of dollars.

Whites everywhere, particularly those in the South, were delighted at Washington's lack of emphasis on civil rights and social equality. Especially after his 1895 address at the Cotton States Exposition in the Kings' hometown of Atlanta, Washington became the national symbol of the "good" black. The Atlanta Compromise, as his doctrine came to be known, and his emphasis on vocational instead of college education seemed to whites to mark an acceptance by blacks of a servile status. Under Washington's leadership, conservative whites felt confident blacks would "keep their place."

To Martin Luther King, Washington's approach to black equality at the turn of the century "had too little freedom in its present and too little promise in its future." King did not call Washington an "Uncle Tom" who compromised rights for the sake of peace; Tuskegee's leader was sincere in desiring full equality for blacks. The problem, King felt, was Washington's optimistic belief that white men would in time reward the hardworking, well-behaved black with respect. Looking back on Washington's time and analyzing his own, King believed this confidence was misplaced. Washington, according to King, underestimated the depth of evil that permeated racial discrimination. "As a consequence," King continued, "his philosophy of pressureless persuasion only served as a springboard for racist Southerners to dive into deeper and more ruthless oppression of the Negro." For this reason King favored adding "persistent . . . nonviolent pressure" to Washington's patient persuasion. It was this viewpoint that inspired King's 1964 book, *Why We Can't Wait*.

Washington's philosophy also met criticism in his own time among his own people. William Monroe Trotter and William E. B. Du Bois led the attack on Washington's compromise. The result of it, they feared, would be an American caste system with the black permanently at the bottom. Du Bois was the leader of the attack on gradualism. A decade younger than Washington, a northerner from Great Barrington, Massachusetts, and the son of a reasonably well-to-do family, Du Bois's perspective was worlds apart from that of the exslave. A companion of whites since childhood, he regarded himself as their equal. In intelligence he felt himself superior, and he hoped to enter Harvard. Lack of funds thwarted these plans temporarily, and Du Bois accepted a church scholarship at Fisk. Travel and study in Europe followed, and in 1895, the same year that Washington proclaimed the Atlanta Compromise, Du Bois received the Ph.D. from Harvard University.

In view of their backgrounds, it was to be expected that Du Bois and Washington would differ sharply in their analysis of and prescription for the black problem. Du Bois believed strongly in the value of higher as opposed to vocational education. Proficient himself in science, social science, and literature, Du Bois saw no reason why blacks could not compete as equals with whites and forge. to the top. In contrast to Washington's stress on practical, manual training for the masses, Du Bois believed in giving the "exceptional men" of his race intensive higher education. This "talented tenth," to use his phrase, would enter professions like law, medicine, and teaching and win respect for the rest of their race.

Du Bois taught at Wilberforce University in Ohio and at the University of Pennsylvania before moving to Atlanta in 1900 to pursue his pioneering sociological studies of black Americans. Until this time Du Bois had not appreciated the full strength of racism in the Deep South. But his experience in Atlanta, which included witnessing a lynching, removed his illusions. Increasingly militant, he became impatient with Washington and conciliation. Such accommodation, he believed, might work for some blacks, but others should be encouraged to reach for excellence. Refusing an invitation to teach at Tuskegee, Du Bois publicly attacked the "Tuskegee machine" and accused Washington of advocating quasi-slavery. In 1905 Du Bois joined with William Trotter, editor of the Boston *Guardian*, and other black intellectuals in the first organized opposition to postbellum racism. The Niagara Movement proposed to assail America's conscience with loud and unceasing protest, but it lacked funds, and white support. As Washington was fond of pointing out, it accomplished little—but a seed had been planted, a seed that men like King would later nourish.

In his impatience with patience Martin Luther King was in tune with William Du Bois. But in regard to the "talented tenth" idea, the men were at odds. According to King, the Du Bois program excluded

430

the masses. "It was," in King's words, "a tactic for an aristocratic elite who would themselves be benefited while leaving behind the 'untalented' 90 percent." King's dream did not leave anyone behind.

For black Americans, the Progressive movement offered promise without fulfillment. While writers and politicians filled the air with cries for social justice, the black man's lot continued to be one of broken dreams. The hopes that flared in 1901 when Theodore Roosevelt invited Booker T. Washington to luncheon in the White House quickly died. Neither of the three Progressive administrations passed significant legislation on behalf of blacks. If anything, discrimination increased in these years. Almost everywhere blacks found themselves stripped of the right to vote, barred from labor unions, denied decent housing, and as a result of the Supreme Court decision in *Plessy* v. *Ferguson* (1896), confined to separate and usually unequal public schools. President Woodrow Wilson even segregated federal employees.

Moreover, the Progressive years witnessed a bitter white backlash. Racial violence increased in the North as well as the South. Over 1000 blacks were lynched between 1900 and 1914. In Brownsville, Texas (1906), and Springfield, Illinois (1908), angry mobs ran roughshod over black communities. One of the worst riots of this period occurred in Atlanta and must have touched the lives of people like the James Kings. At the height of the disturbance in September 1906, whites, enraged by alleged rape charges, attacked every black in sight. Upon encountering resistance, tempers flared even higher. White and black eyes could not meet without suspicion, and fear haunted the soft southern nights much as it had in the times of slave insurrections. Like immigrants, blacks were regarded as aliens and resented by a society uneasy over the pangs of rapid growth and change.

The increase in discrimination in the early twentieth century tested the incipient civil rights movement. Booker T. Washington, maintaining his optimism, remarked that no matter how bad his situation in the United States, he was still far better off than the depressed classes of Europe. But even Washington finally wearied of the continual abuse and called racism a cancer in the nation's heart. William Du Bois continued his militance. In 1909 he joined a number of white liberals, including Jane Addams, to found the National Association for the Advancement of Colored People. Although dominated by whites (Du Bois was the only black officer), the NAACP became the most substantial and long-lived organization of its kind. Its Legal Redress Committee attacked all forms of discrimination in an effort to obtain constitutional rights for black people. The NAACP's magazine, *The Crisis*, which Du Bois edited for many years, had 100,000 readers by the end of World War I. After 1911 the NAACP was joined in its crusade by the National Urban League, whose particular concern was the plight of blacks in cities.

These developments did not have much meaning, however, in Stockbridge, Georgia, where James King struggled on under the crushing weight of the crop-lien system. By this time in the Deep South "the man" was fully in charge, and among poor, illiterate blacks the spark of resistance had long been extinguished. Fortunately, it was periodically rekindled in the young. James King's son, Martin Luther, Sr., was bright and ambitious. As a teenager he became disgusted with his father's poverty and passivity. Determined not to inherit this condition, Martin left the worn-out fields and crumbling shacks of Stockbridge in 1916. He was seventeen years old, and he was going to try his luck in Atlanta. In the larger city, he reasoned, there would be more job opportunities and, he hoped, more freedom. In time there might be economic security, perhaps a house he could call his own. Moreover, the bloody race riots of 1906 had left in their aftermath the Atlanta Civic League and a group of white and black citizens determined to ease the city's social tensions. Atlanta was as good a place as any to start the climb toward dignity.

In leaving the rural South, Martin Luther King, Sr., joined a stream of younger, dissatisfied blacks. By the end of World War I emigration from the South reached flood proportions. Martin chose a southern city, but many of his contemporaries moved to the metropolitan areas of the North and Middle West, where defense industries were hungry for labor. Hundreds of thousands traveled up the Mississippi River to St. Louis and on to Chicago, Detroit, and Cleveland. Another path of migration terminated in New York City's Harlem. Those who followed these escape routes from the rural South brought little but hope and frequently found frustration. In fact, the urban ghettos were epitomes of segregation, and the barriers between blacks and success were just as high as in the southern countryside. Occasionally, however, an individual emerged from the squalor and frustration that was the usual lot of urban blacks. Such was the case with Martin Luther King, Sr. A decade of diligent work in Atlanta left him with a modest bank account and, thanks to evening classes, a high school diploma. He also found time to preside over two small Baptist churches and to marry the daughter of one of Atlanta's foremost black clergymen. The Kings were living with him in Atlanta's best black neighborhood when Martin, Jr., was born, January 15, 1929.

At the time of Martin Luther King's birth the prospects for black Americans were far from promising. Of course the democratic rhetoric and the emphasis on national unity during World War I raised hopes in much the same way as had the Civil War. Blacks proved eager customers for war bonds and thronged to enlist in the armed forces. Fighting for their nation, they believed, would be a sure way of winning gratitude and respect. But most whites thought otherwise. Military leaders refused to integrate the armed forces or appoint black officers. The most menial and dangerous tasks fell to black soldiers. Discrimination persisted even in the trenches in Europe. Blacks received far fairer treatment at the hands of the French than they did from their own countrymen. There were even reports that the Germans treated captured black soldiers with more consideration than they received from their colleagues in arms.

Nonetheless World War I inspired blacks, particularly those who fought in Europe, to press forward the crusade for civil rights. William Du Bois expressed the prevalent attitude in *Crisis* for May 1919 when he wrote: "*We return. We return from fighting. We return fighting.* Make way for Democracy! We saved it in France, and by the Great Jehovah, we will save it in the U.S.A., or know the reason why." But the war to make the world safe for democracy had not secured it in the United States. Equality, it appeared, was still a white possession. The troops had scarcely returned from "over there" when a series of bloody race riots turned the summer of 1919 into a nightmare for blacks. In Chicago alone, thirty-eight persons died in four days of what amounted to civil war. A revived Ku Klux Klan spurred the racial strife. Long lines of white-robbed whites marched slowly yet menacingly through the black neighborhood. They were still marching in the 1930s when Martin Luther King recalled seeing them from his window. If these tactics did not intimidate minorities, the KKK administered floggings and worse. Hardly a lunatic fringe, the organization's 5 million members were scattered by the mid-1920s from Mississippi to Maine. Still, much of the bloodshed of the post-World War I years was the consequence of a new spirit among black people. For the first time since the era of slave insurrections, urban blacks fought back from their ghettos in a more or less organized manner. The poet Claude McKay caught the mood of defiance when he wrote that blacks would no longer die "like hogs, hunted and penned in an inglorious spot," but rather "pressed to the wall, dying but fighting back."

The pride implicit in McKay's statement became a factor of increasing importance in American black history during the decade of Martin Luther King's birth. It also provided the bedrock of confidence on which King subsequently helped construct the freedom movement. Several components figured in the growth of white and black appreciation of black cultural values and traditions. One, of course, was simply the passage of time. The experience of slavery left a scar on the black mind that healed slowly. Slaves, or the children of slaves, could not easily regard themselves with esteem. But those like Martin Luther King, Jr., who were three generations removed from slavery, could begin to look upon themselves and their heritage with new eyes.

The first important herald of race pride was Marcus Moziah Garvey. A Jamaica-born black with piercing eyes and a talent for charismatic leadership, Garvey organized the Universal Negro Improvement Association in New York City in 1916. Its motto was "Back to Africa." Garvey called upon blacks to leave the United States, return to their African homeland, and build a mighty nation. The idea, to be sure, was neither new nor universally accepted among American blacks. King, for example, later termed Garvey's program an admission of defeat, a confession that black people were incapable of winning a just release from discrimination. Moreover, King pointed out, most blacks in the United States could not easily go back to Africa on both practical and psychological grounds. For better or worse, they were Americans. Garvey's grandiose plans, which included orders of nobility such as the Knights of the Nile and a costly Black Star Steamship Line, aroused only jeers on the part of the more sophisticated protest leadership.

Yet, as King recognized, Garvey's message transcended a sim-

434

plistic back-to-Africanism. "He called," as King put it in 1964, long after Garvey had been arrested for mail violations and deported to Jamaica, "for a resurgence of race pride." In a manner that anticipated the Black Power advocates of King's own time, Garvey drew attention to a truth long dormant in the black mind—there was no disgrace to being black. Indeed, Garvey went further to suggest that black was beautiful, that black people had a heritage as old and as distinguished as that of the allegedly master race. The idea brought a ray of hope to the ghetto. Millions of blacks thrilled to Garvey in the 1920s with a degree of emotionalism that testified to the depth of their former sense of inferiority.

Music was one of the first tangible expressions of the black pride Garvey did so much to advance. Since the 1890s, black Americans had played an increasingly important role in influencing popular music in the United States. Ragtime, blues, and jazz were successive outgrowths of black talent and the black experience. Moving north from New Orleans as cultural baggage in the great migration, jazz, especially, took the country by storm. The music of Joe "King" Oliver, Kid Ory, and Louis Armstrong crossed the color line in its appeal. The Harlem area of New York eventually became the nation's jazz capital, and the compelling, improvised sounds became closely associated with the black identity. Behind the appeal of jazz was the assumption that black culture was freer, wilder, more sensuous, more joyous than that of whites. Perhaps, more Americans than ever before concluded, these people had a distinctive and distinguished contribution to make to American cultural life. In fact, jazz gained enough prominence to name the age in which Martin Luther King was born.

The sense of black identity that Marcus Garvey promoted and jazz portrayed also flowered in the Harlem Renaissance. The term refers to the artistic and intellectual explosion that took place among the residents of New York's black ghetto during the 1920s. The renaissance was the work of the "new Negroes"—militant, proud of their blackness, wanting to contribute to American culture, yet determined to preserve their racial identity. Writers like Langston Hughes, Claude McKay, Countee Cullen, and Jean Toomer managed to do just that. Also making major contributions to the rise of black art and letters were the Harlem-published journals of the NAACP and the National Urban League, *Crisis* and *Opportunity*. One of the most significant aspects of the Harlem Renaissance was the way it attracted white admirers. Blacks were suddenly more than laborers and servants. The allegedly exotic, primitive, unrepressed quality of black life fascinated white Americans. Many thronged uptown to Harlem's clubs and cafés to partake of a commodity a later generation would deify as "soul." Although the stereotype they constructed was no more accurate than that of the melon-eating darkie, whites too were beginning to find value in blackness.

Although he was born on the brink of America's terrifying skid into the Great Depression, Martin Luther King's childhood was more secure and comfortable than that of most southern blacks. Martin Sr.'s determination to break the chains of poverty and illiteracy paid dividends for his son. Sixty-five percent of Atlanta's black population was on relief at one time or another during the depression, but around the King's spacious home on Auburn Avenue, sandlot ball games and Christian fellowship continued without interruption. Of course all was not base hits and love for young Martin; inevitably his life crossed the "color line," and he learned the meaning of prejudice. For Martin, the dream was shattered at the age of six. He had been accustomed to playing ball with two white boys in the neighborhood. One day their mother told him in no uncertain terms to leave and not come back because her sons were white and he was black. After tearfully relating the story to his mother, he received an explanation of the extent of race hatred. But he was cautioned never to hate in return. Quite probably Alberta King, the daughter of an NAACP leader, had read in that organization's journal a letter the Indian pacifist Mahatma Gandhi wrote to American blacks. Gandhi counseled them to put their trust in love and nonviolence. He also reminded Americans of color not to be ashamed of their heritage of slavery; there was dishonor only in having been slaveholders. The prejudiced person, in other words, was more to be pitied than the objects of his prejudice. Turning the other cheek was a sign of superiority. It was a message that stayed with Martin Luther King as he became one of the greatest proponents of nonviolent protest in American history.

Like many black mothers, Alberta King concluded most of her discussions of race with her son by pointing out, "you are just as good as anyone else, and don't you forget it." But the reality of southern life taught a different lesson. Martin never forgot his father's indignation

Martin Luther King, Jr.

when an Atlanta shoestore refused him equal service. Taking the bewildered Martin's hand, he stalked from the store utilizing the boycott idea Martin would later employ with great effectiveness on a larger scale. The boy also learned how to organize and influence people from observing his father in action. Martin Sr. was the local leader of the NAACP, an active member of the Atlanta Voters League, and a director of Morehouse College. Understandably, talk at the King dining table frequently turned to the subject of black rights and the struggle for their realization. Martin Jr. was never far from the freedom movement he led as an adult.

While Martin Luther King moved through elementary and secondary school at a grade-skipping pace that prepared him for college at the age of fifteen, the nation staggered through the most traumatic decade in its economic history. The Great Depression worked special hardship on American blacks. In times of unemployment they invariably found themselves "the first fired and the last hired." In 1935 the percentage of unemployed blacks was nearly double that of whites. Job discrimination was never more rampant than during hard times.

Because of their traditional allegiance to the "liberating" Republican party, the bulk of the black vote in the election of 1932 went to Herbert Hoover. In November 1932 the shape of Franklin D. Roosevelt's New Deal was still unformed, its effectiveness uncertain. But after the 1934 congressional elections, it was apparent that the Democrats were making massive gains among blacks. By 1936 the majority supported Roosevelt. Their vote was in direct response to the effectiveness of New Deal relief and recovery measures in easing their particular plight.

One of the most important New Deal agencies in this regard was the Public Works Administration. Its head, Secretary of the Interior Harold Ickes, was a former local officer of the NAACP and a champion of the principle of equal opportunity employment. This was especially the case when federal construction projects were concerned. Moreover, Ickes made sure that a substantial part of the PWA's efforts went toward renewal of the urban slums where many blacks lived. The Civilian Conservation Corps also responded to Roosevelt's wish to avoid discrimination in dispensing work relief, and hired 200,000 black youths. Occasionally, to be sure, federal money was administered, in the words of black labor leader A. Philip Randolph, "by the whim of southern prejudice, in the mood of arrogant superiority." At the massive construction camps that build Boulder (later Hoover) Dam and the Tennessee Valley Authority projects, for instance, government agents allowed segregated housing.

The New Deal tried to give new hope to farmers whose lot had worsened steadily since World War I. The Agricultural Adjustment Act of 1933 provided a system for paying farmers to take land out of production. Roosevelt's advisers believed such restrictions would raise farm prices, but for blacks the AAA was deadly. Thousands of tenant farmers and sharecroppers lost what little security they had and were forced from the country to cities already crowded with jobless men. Their plight became the worst in America at the height of the depression. Martin Luther King, Sr., had many occasions to be thankful he had cut the cord with sharecropping two decades earlier. One result was that Martin Jr. could attend school while many of his contemporaries struggled simply to exist.

The National Recovery Administration also had disadvantages for the black. Designed to allow responsible self-government for industry, the NRA gave little protection to black labor. The blacks who were consequently laid off nicknamed the agency "Negroes Ruined Again." Through the Works Progress Administration of 1935, howver, the New Deal recouped many of its losses as far as blacks were concerned. The WPA's director, Harry Hopkins, distributed billions of dollars in the form of work relief. At the close of the 1930s more than a million black Americans owed their living to the WPA. Characteristically, they celebrated it in a song. The lyrics of a popular blues tune of the period ran:

> Please Mr. President, Listen to what I've got to say,
>> You can take away all the alphabet, but please
>>> leave the WPA
> I went to the polls and voted, I know I voted the
>> right way,
>>> So I'm asking you, Mr. President, don't take away
>>> that WPA.

Overall, the New Deal laid the foundations for better days for black Americans. For the first time since Reconstruction, the federal government recognized and endeavored to ease their conditions of life and work. As President, Franklin D. Roosevelt did more than any of his predecessors. Blacks were included in nearly every phase of his administration, and some achieved high federal posts. The economist Robert C. Weaver, for example, headed the President's informal "Black Cabinet." Roosevelt's highly publicized refusal to sign an antilynching bill in 1938 for fear of losing the support of southern Democrats should be seen in the broader perspective of his entire record. Summing it up, *Crisis* reported that "for the first time in their lives government [had] taken on meaning and substance for the Negro masses." The 1930s also witnessed the continued growth in effectiveness of the NAACP. Concentrating on legal rights and aided by brilliant black lawyers such as Thurgood Marshall, later a Supreme Court justice, and Hamilton Houston, the NAACP struggled to make the Fourteenth Amendment a reality. In 1930 the association put enough pressure on the United States Senate to block confirmation of President Hoover's Supreme Court nominee, John H. Parker, an opponent of black suffrage. Two years later Nathan R. Margold, head of the NAACP legal defense committee, decided to attack the principle of "separate but equal" education. He did not succeed, but he laid the legal foundation that ultimately led to the desegregation decision of 1954.

While attempting to achieve civil rights reform, the NAACP experienced a sharp internal struggle over ideology. William E. B. Du Bois headed the faction that by the 1930s had become thoroughly disillusioned at the prospects of reform within the American economic and political system. He proposed that blacks voluntarily segregate themselves from that system and turn instead to Marxism. Immensely impressed with his visit to Russia in 1927, Du Bois believed that if blacks sided with Communists, their combined force could topple a capitalistic order already reeling from the Great Depression. The National Negro Congress, founded in 1935 by Ralph Bunche and E. Franklin Frazier among others, was a step toward organization of a black proletariat. More conservative leaders of the NAACP such as Roy Wilkins, Walter White, and Martin Luther King, Sr., disagreed strongly with this approach. Pointing to the success of the Congress of Industrial Organizations (CIO) in advancing the interests of black laborers, they were not prepared to abandon capitalism or white America. Eventually they forced Du Bois out of the NAACP and into the Communist Party.

After skipping the ninth grade, Martin Luther King entered Atlanta's Booker T. Washington High School as a sophomore in 1942. Already he possessed a flair for oratory and a growing understanding of how to use it on behalf of his people. Part of this insight came from observing the course of the national civil rights movement. The ongoing controversy between his father's position and that of Du Bois and the black radicals, for instance, sharpened the young King's faith in the power of love and reason to transcend racial separatism of both the white and the black varieties. He also received a lesson in the power of nonviolent protest from black labor leader A. Philip Randolph. The background to Randolph's campaign was discrimination in the armed services and defense industries during World War II. Despite the explicit provisions of the Selective Service Act (1940), prejudice permeated the drafting and training of blacks. Defense workers were treated similarly. In early 1941 Randolph, who was president of the Brotherhood of Pullman Porters, threatened President Franklin D. Roosevelt with a massive march on the capital to protest this discrimination.

Roosevelt faced the prospect of international embarrassment. He had publicly referred to the United States as the "great arsenal of democracy" and now feared that Germany would use racial problems in anti-American propaganda. But keen politician that he was, Roosevelt was reluctant to alienate southern Democrats by enforcing civil rights legislation. The President begged Randolph to cancel the march. Randolph held firm, and an estimated 100,000 blacks prepared for the protest. Finally, on June 25, 1941, one week before the scheduled demonstration, Roosevelt issued an executive order banning "discrimination in the employment of workers in defense industries and government because of race, creed, color or national origin." He also established the Fair Employment Practices Committee. Old enough to appreciate what had happened, King filed the knowledge for future reference. He had occasion to recall it six years later, when Randolph again threatened massive civil disobedience and again secured his goal —desegregation of the armed forces.

World War II was in full swing in 1944 when Martin Luther King entered Morehouse College in Atlanta. He responded at once to the "freer atmosphere" and to professors who "were not caught up in the clutches of state funds and could teach what they wanted with academic freedom." Much of Morehouse's concern was with racial problems, and King wanted to help his people, but when his thoughts turned to a career he found himself undecided. His father hoped he would enter the ministry, but King was suspicious. Too often, he felt, religion had been an anesthetic for blacks, the substitution of a vague heavenly afterlife for happiness and justice in the here and now. Business was another possibility, and King had the ability and the contacts to go to the top. Yet here, too, there were problems. The successful "black bourgeoisie," King observed, frequently cared more for personal success than for the condition of the masses. Law seemed more promising. As a Southern black man King continued to experience a series of degrading confrontations with prejudice that suggested the importance of legal redress. A particularly bitter experience occurred when King returned from an oratorical contest in Valdosta, Georgia, on a public bus. Ordered by the driver to move from seats reserved for whites, King and his friends at first refused. After the driver became enraged, the students reluctantly moved, but King admitted he would never forget the depth of his anger. There was a need for lawyers to break down, as King put it, "the legal barriers to Negro rights."

Gradually, however, King came back to religion as his life work. Contact with Morehouse's minister-teachers like Benjamin E. Mays and George D. Kelsey showed him how religion could be made socially relevant and practically useful. Ordained in 1947, a year before graduation, King became assistant pastor in his father's church. He also worked with Atlanta's integrated Intercollegiate Council, an experience that softened his previous resentment of whites. Some of them, he realized, were genuinely sympathetic with the condition of black Americans and worthy colleagues in the fight to improve it.

Following Morehouse, King embarked on three years of graduate study at Crozer Theological Seminary in Pennsylvania. These were years of intellectual quest, as King sought a philosophy for coping with the race problem. His reading of the German philosopher Hegel helped. King responded positively to Hegel's idea that progress can come only through the painful struggle of one condition against its opposite. He also liked the notion that an individual was capable of advancing, if not causing, great historical changes. Marxism, with its emphasis on breaking the hold of the Establishment on the underprivileged, seemed relevant to the black situation. "Power," he wrote in agreement with Marx, "concedes nothing without a demand. It never did and never will." But unlike the black Marxists of the 1930s, King could not accept Marx's rejection of God as a moving force in human affairs. More to his taste, as a consequence, was the teaching of Walter Rauschenbusch and other proponents of the Social Gospel. Their advice to take religion out of the churches and into the streets struck responsive chords in King. Any faith that was content with men's souls and oblivious to their social and economic condition, he decided, was "spiritually moribund . . . only waiting for the day to be buried."

The most exciting ideas King encountered at Crozer, however, were those of the Indian pacifist Mahatma Gandhi. Deeply influenced in turn by Henry David Thoreau's *On the Duty of Civil Disobedience* (1849), for two decades Gandhi used nonviolent resistance in the struggle to liberate 350 million Indians from British rule. His success in 1948 made a great impression on the youthful King. Gandhi seemed to prove that love and passive resistance might be a powerful agent of social change. This was not, King realized, to deny the reality of hatred and of evil. Like the American theologian Reinhold Niebuhr, King was learning to set aside superficial optimism in constructing a meaningful philosophy of reform. He would face evil, and overcome it, with compassion and love. This was close, of course, to the method of Jesus of Nazareth, whose teachings remained King's principal guide.

At Boston University, where King enrolled in 1951 to seek a doctorate in philosophy, the preparation for leadership continued. An important part of it consisted of meeting and marrying Coretta Scott. She was the daughter of an Alabama family whose color had not prevented them from retaining considerable land holdings ever since Reconstruction. Coretta attended public schools in Alabama and, in 1945, Antioch College in Ohio. Although conscious of her role as a "token of integration," Coretta pursued a program of study in elementary education with high enthusiasm. When it came time to practice teach, however, she was barred from the local school system. Thoroughly disillusioned, Coretta told herself that as a black she had to face "the problem" no matter how educated or wealthy she became. "This is the first time it has hit you in the face," she thought, "you might as well accept the fact."

After graduating from Antioch in 1951 without the teaching certificate she had hoped to receive, Coretta Scott turned to music and planned her future around the concert stage. She was studying at the New England Conservatory of Music in Boston when she met Martin Luther King. His driving sense of mission "to do something for humanity" in general and blacks in particular was contagious. And in Coretta, Martin found someone to share his dream.

Married in 1953 during Martin's final year of graduate school, the Kings faced a nation whose climate of opinion was slowly but steadily shifting toward greater understanding of black conditions and black demands. After his favorable 1947 response to A. Philip Randolph's call for an end to discrimination in the military, President Harry S Truman set the tone of the new mood. At his inuaguration in 1949, for the first time in American history blacks were invited to the major social events. Truman also ordered (July 1948) complete integration of all units of the military, a process that American involvement in the Korean War hastened considerably. Truman's Fair Deal, in the words of NAACP head Walter White, reflected a nationwide recognition "of the new place of all ordinary Americans." The blacks among them were further heartened by the beginnings of African independence. Beginning in the early 1950s over two dozen black nations emerged from the wreckage of Europe's colonial system. Another object of pride in these years was Ralph Bunche. A political scientist from the University of California at Los Angeles, Bunche rose to importance in the Department of State and, after World War II, emerged as a world figure as a result of his role in founding the United Nations. Bunche also negotiated a settlement of the Arab-Israeli dispute of 1948 and for his efforts received the Nobel Peace Prize.

Unquestionably, however, the most encouraging development in the 1950s, and in many ways since the Emancipation Proclamation, was the Supreme Court's reversal of its stand on school segregation. Since the 1930s the NAACP picked away steadily at the principle of "separate but equal" as laid down by the Court in *Plessy* v. *Ferguson* (1896). In 1945 Thurgood Marshall assumed leadership of the legal assault, and for the next decade a steady stream of cases filed by the NAACP sought to test the law. There were signs of a thaw in 1950. Then on May 17, 1954, the Supreme Court handed down an opinion in the school segregation case of *Brown* v. *Board of Education of Topeka.* When Chief Justice Earl Warren declared that "separate educational facilities are inherently unequal," the long struggle was over. But as Martin Luther King soon realized, in many ways it had just begun.

The gap between principle and practice was apparent immediately after the Brown decision. Having cleared its conscience with a declaration, the Supreme Court proved a reluctant reformer. Refraining from setting a timetable for desegregation, the Court in May 1955 merely urged school boards to proceed "with all deliberate speed." In many parts of the country it was deliberate indeed! Emboldened by hesitant national leadership, reactionary forces, particularly in the South, "declared war" on the Brown decision. In a manner reminiscent of Reconstruction and of the 1920s, White Citizens' Councils sprang up across the South, and the Ku Klux Klan was reactivated to obstruct integration. Tom Brady, a judge in Mississippi, epitomized the revived contempt for blacks when he urged white southerners to "blow again and stronger on the dying embers of racial hate." But even responsible southern white leadership was agitated. One hundred United States congressmen issued a manifesto pledging their support of those organized "to resist forced integration by lawful means."

In this atmosphere of tense race relations, Martin Luther King arrived in Montgomery, Alabama, in September 1954 to take charge of the Dexter Avenue Baptist Church. For a little more than a year the Kings tried to avoid controversy while quietly building a following for their church. But on December 1, 1955, the main current of the freedom movement swung in their direction. On that day a seamstress named Rosa Parks boarded a Montgomery bus and refused to sit in the black section. Arrested for violating city segregation ordinances, Rosa Parks sparked a storm of discontent. E. D. Nixon, a long-time civil rights activist in Montgomery, paid her bail and then conferred with King and Ralph Abernathy about a one-day bus boycott. The idea, as King later suggested, was not simply to protest the arrest of Rosa Parks, but to protest the "series of injustices and indignities that have existed over the years." Recalling Thoreau's resistance to the Mexican War in the 1840s, King became convinced that the time had come for blacks to refuse to cooperate with "an evil system."

With Montgomery's entire black population supporting the bus boycott, it soon became evident that it would be possible to prolong and coordinate the protest. As president of the newly formed Mont-

444

gomery Improvement Association, King presided over this expansion. His first step was to set forth his philosophy of protest. Putting together what he had learned from Hegel, Rauschenbusch, and Gandhi with his Christian principles, he convinced his colleagues to operate through "persuasion, not coercion." Love was central to his method. Quoting Booker T. Washington, he warned Montgomery blacks: "let no man pull you so low as to make you hate him." The nonviolent resister, King explained, refuses to hate. He does not seek "to defeat or humiliate the opponent, but to win his friendship and understanding." All life, in King's view, was interrelated, all men were ultimately brothers. It followed that "along the way of life, someone must have the sense enough and the morality enough to cut off the chain of hate." It required courage to take this step. Again and again King explained that *"nonviolent resistance does resist."*

On this note King and his Montgomery Improvement Association launched a boycott that ultimately lasted for 382 days. Before it was over, the city's black population had organized their own, highly efficient transportation system utilizing private cars. Passive resistance prevailed throughout. There were no riots, no fights. Even when King's house was bombed, he admonished angry blacks to love their enemies and trust in God. Finally in November 1956 the Supreme Court upheld a lower court decision declaring unconstitutional Alabama's laws requiring segregation on public buses. On December 21, King, Abernathy, E. D. Nixon, and a host of newsmen joyfully boarded the first integrated bus in Montgomery.

The *idea* of nonviolent resistance was not unknown in the history of black protest. William Lloyd Garrison had advocated it before the Civil War as a response to slavery, and A. Philip Randolph urged its adoption during World War II. In fact, in 1942 James Farmer organized the Congress of Racial Equality (CORE) for purposes of instituting massive, relentless noncooperation. But it was not until Montgomery that the hopes of earlier leaders became reality. King demonstrated the ability and the willingness of blacks to challenge the system without "violence of spirit." Granted the boycott did not noticeably improve the overall social situation of blacks in Montgomery, it did signal, in King's words, "a new sense of dignity and destiny" among blacks that would henceforth underlie the freedom movement.

As evidence, bus boycotts soon spread to other southern cities,

When a federal court order failed to open Little Rock's Central High Sch[ool]
to black students, President Dwight D. Eisenhower had no alternative but to send
troops. With their assistance people like Elizabeth Echford, 15, we[re]
able to attend classes, but at the price of insults such as she is receiving he[re].

When Martin Luther King, Jr., decided to take the freedom movement [to]
Birmingham, Alabama in the Spring of 1963, he deliberately challenged one of th[e]
bastions of race prejudice in the United States. Widely publicized photographs [of]
the protest, like this one of May 3, 1963, aroused the conscience of th[e]
nation and the worl[d].

Martin Luther King, Jr., helped lead 200,000 people in an August 1963 March on Washington. Shortly after this photograph was taken King delivered his "I have a dream" speech from the steps of the Lincoln Memorial.

In the riots in the Watts area of Los Angeles in 1965 looting and arson were commonplace. The usual targets were white-owned businesses, but A. Z. Smith, who owned this barbershop, was an exception. Martin Luther King, Jr., found that the Watts rioters had little patience with his philosophy of non-violence.

and thirty-five eventually voluntarily abolished bus segregation. Moreover, Montgomery marked the entrance of the masses into the freedom movement. Organizers like Martin Luther King made it possible for thousands of black voices to be added to those of the NAACP's corps of lawyers. The result could only strengthen black demands.

After Montgomery the recognized leader of nonviolent resistance, King gathered black religious leaders together in Atlanta in January 1957 for the purpose of forming the Southern Christian Leadership Conference. King, as expected, became president, and immediately put pressure on President Dwight D. Eisenhower to come South and personally support civil rights laws. When he sidestepped the invitation, King and Roy Wilkins of the NAACP went to Washington in May as part of a Prayer Pilgrimage 35,000 strong. The conviction and the eloquence of the young minister (King was only twenty-seven) dominated the assembly even in competition with figures of the stature of entertainer Sammy Davis, Jr., and baseball star Jackie Robinson. In the major speech of the Prayer Pilgrimage King demanded that southern blacks be given an opportunity to vote without restriction so that they might "quietly, lawfully implement the Supreme Court desegregation decisions." He followed up his speech with a conference with Vice-President Richard M. Nixon and in June had the satisfaction of seeing Congress pass a Civil Rights Act, the first since Reconstruction. A Texas Senator, Lyndon B. Johnson, led the fight for the measure, which empowered judges to jail anyone who prevented qualified persons from voting. The act also established a Commission on Civil Rights to investigate alleged violations.

As one who put his faith in nonviolence, King's reactions to the Little Rock crisis of September 1957 were mixed. It began when Arkansas Governor Orville Faubus defied a court ruling giving black children the right to attend Little Rock's Central High School. The next move was President Eisenhower's. He was reluctant to enforce integration, but as a military man he knew the necessity of enforcing the principle of federal supremacy. For two months federal troops with fixed bayonets escorted nine black children to and from Central High. A unit of the National Guard remained stationed at the school for the entire 1957–1958 academic year. Feelings ran high throughout the country. Little Rock was unquestionably the most serious challenge to federal authority since the Civil War. In some parts of the

South the show of federal force hardened resistance to assertions of black rights. There was a rash of attacks on the persons and property of blacks. But even the diehards could not mistake the significance of active federal involvement. American blacks had a powerful friend. The confidence this inspired explains in large part the growth in militancy in the freedom movement after the Brown decision.

Late in 1958 King's nonviolent philosophy received a severe challenge. On Saturday afternoon, September 20, he was seated in a Harlem shoestore autographing copies of his new book, *Stride Toward Freedom*, which described the Montgomery boycott. Looking up, he saw a black woman pushing through the crowd toward him. She asked his name, and on hearing it drew a long letter-opener from her dress and plunged it into King's chest. She had not used the loaded pistol police later found in her handbag, but, as doctors discovered after a three-hour operation, the point of the letter-opener rested against King's heart. A sudden movement, or even a cough, would have killed him instantly. After he recovered, King told a crowded press conference that he felt "no ill will" toward his assailant; he hoped she would receive the help she obviously needed. Then he added that the real tragedy of the incident was not the injury to himself, but the demonstration "that a climate of hatred and bitterness so permeates areas of our nation that inevitably deeds of extreme violence must erupt." It was King's mission to abolish such violence and still secure freedom for his race.

In February 1959 Martin and Coretta King made a pilgrimage of their own to India. Their host was none other than Prime Minister Nehru, a close observer of America's racial problems and an admirer of King. After visiting the places where Gandhi had worked and taught, the Kings were even more deeply convinced that his technique of massive, nonviolent resistance was applicable to black social protest. But on his return to the United States King found a challenge to his philosophy in the growing impatience of black youth and in the ideas of Elijah Muhammad and the Black Muslims. Indeed, in Malcolm X the Muslims had an emerging leader as compelling as King himself. And Malcolm gave no quarter in his criticism of King's methods. Passive resistance, the Muslim contended, made the black defenseless in the face of white hatred. He called for race pride, black nationalism, and the end of integration. The Black Muslims wanted no

449

part of what they considered an inferior white civilization. A campaign for civil rights within that civilization was meaningless. America's 20 million blacks, Malcolm declared, should think in terms of their own superior culture.

Martin Luther King did not agree. There was no salvation for blacks or anyone else, he believed, through separatism and isolation. The only real solution to the problem was the establishment of the true brotherhood of all men. In the eyes of many frustrated black Americans, however, the Muslim solution glittered. King realized that his leadership of the freedom movement hung in the balance, so did non-violence. He resigned as pastor of the Dexter Avenue Church in Montgomery and on January 24, 1960, moved to Atlanta and prepared to devote his life to "a bold, broad advance of the Southern campaign for equality." In particular, he sought "new methods of struggle involving the masses of people"—methods, moreover, that were not violent or unlawful.

The sit-in was one answer. It started as an idea in the minds of several students at North Carolina Agricultural and Technical College in Greensboro. Like most southern blacks, they knew and revered Martin Luther King as the man who took on the power structure in Montgomery and won. The students also owned *Martin Luther King and the Montgomery Story*, a booklet written and illustrated in a comic-book format, which had sold over 200,000 copies since the bus boycott. King's example and an insult suffered by one of the boys the day before inspired a group of four to sit down at a Woolworth's lunch counter in Greensboro and order coffee. The date was February 1, 1960. The students expected to be refused service by the white waitress, and they were not disappointed. What was unusual was they remained sitting, in silent protest, until the counter closed. And they returned for many days thereafter, suffering verbal and even physical abuse, but supported by the conviction that this was the kind of non-violent protest King would endorse. On February 4 the blacks were joined at Woolworth's by sympathetic white students from a local women's college. A news story about the sit-in followed, and a new chapter in the freedom movement began.

From Greensboro sit-ins spread across the South to more than fifty cities, and there were marches and other expressions of support throughout the nation. King and the Southern Christian Leadership

Conference presided over the growing movement. It pleased him to hear reports such as one in May 1960 from Nashville, Tennessee, which described the behavior of participants in a sit-in. "When called names, they keep quiet. When hit, they do not strike back. Even when hostile white youth pull hair and snuff out burning cigarettes on the backs of Negro girls, the girls do not retaliate. They pray and take what comes, in dignity." This was the essence of nonviolence, and as its chief exponent, King's stature increased daily. The demonstrators in many parts of the South carried with them a printed card: "Remember the teachings of Jesus Christ, Mahatma Gandhi and Martin Luther King. Remember love and nonviolence." When harassed, they asked one another what King's response would have been. When arrested and jailed, as many were, they sang and prayed as King had taught. But sometimes there was victory. Not only did nonviolence put the onus of brutality on the white segregationists, it also exerted considerable economic leverage. After several weeks of sit-ins, store owners in twenty-seven southern cities agreed to desegregate their operations.

To expand and coordinate the sit-in form of protest, King and his associates in the Southern Christian Leadership Conference helped students organize the Student Nonviolent Coordinating Committee (SNCC) in April and May 1960. Along with a revived Congress of Racial Equality (CORE), it sponsored a series of Freedom Rides across the South. Using interstate buses for transportation and determined to test civil rights laws everywhere they went, riders of both colors "put the sit-ins on the road." In May 1961 in Anniston, Birmingham, and Montgomery, Alabama, local police stood aside as white mobs beat the Freedom Riders savagely. Unfortunately for the cause of segregation, they also beat several representatives of the national news services. The resulting pictures were front-page news everywhere. Southern white resistance had also backfired the previous autumn when the story of Martin Luther King being placed in leg irons and sentenced to four months at hard labor for failing to renew his Georgia driving license made the headlines. The commotion not only brought the intervention of Senator John F. Kennedy, then running for the Presidency, on King's behalf, but discredited and ridiculed the white supremacists. Nonviolent resistance seemed to be working.

Still, there were moments during the acceleration of the freedom movement in the early 1960s when King had doubts about its future. He knew the line between passive and violent resistance was very thin. The black protest he had done so much to arouse would be increasingly hard to control and discipline. Young blacks, especially, were chafing at the bit on nonviolence. They demanded action, now, and they were not oblivious to the example of Africa, where dynamic native leaders were violently asserting the independence of their countries. The members of SNCC and CORE, in particular, had serious reservations about King's Southern Christian Leadership Conference and the still more conservative NAACP and Urban League.

Seeking ways to reassert his philosophy and his leadership, King lashed out with criticism of the Kennedy Administration. There was too little civil rights legislation and too little enforcement of what laws existed. Responding to Kennedy's promise to put a man on the moon within a decade, King pointed out the absence of a plan "to put a Negro in the state legislature of Alabama" in the same amount of time. The latter, he implied, would be more difficult. It was not just a matter of justice long overdue. King warned Kennedy that he would have to act quickly and decisively if he wished to prevent black discontent from reaching "an explosion point." He also warned him about tokenism. In the fall of 1962 federal authorities literally forced a black named James Meredith into the University of Mississippi. The Kennedy Administration and the nation as a whole made much of the "breakthrough," but King pointed out that Meredith's admission was merely a crumb thrown black Americans in lieu of real equality for all. King contended further that tokenism was worse than useless: "it is a palliative which relieves emotional distress, but leaves the disease and its ravages unaffected. It tends to demobilize and relax the militant spirit which alone drives us forward to real change." On another occasion, he put it more bluntly: "it does no good to apply Vaseline to a cancer."

What did do good, in King's opinion, was a massive, nonviolent protest campaign like the one he conducted in Montgomery, which left in its wake a real and permanent change in institutions and attitudes. With this in mind, in 1962 he led a prolonged effort to "liberate" Albany, Georgia. The local power structure retaliated calmly and efficiently, arresting marchers and closing facilities threatened with integration. As a result, the blacks accomplished little. Even King's supporters had to recognize the ineffectiveness of nonviolent protest against the well-organized, hard-core prejudice it encountered in Albany.

The disappointment of Albany and the rising criticism of impatient black militants left King keenly aware of the need to make passive resistance work. Early in 1963 he set his strategy. He would take the freedom movement to Birmingham, Alabama. He would lead a nonviolent attack on the power structure of what he called "the most segregated city in America." And he would avoid the spontaneity of Albany in favor of meticulous planning and coordination. The results justified his hopes. Birmingham became another great stride toward freedom. The explanation lay partly in King's talent for leadership, but even more in the conduct of his opponents. Albany's white officials successfully resisted the temptation to crush the black demonstrators and thereby avoided adverse publicity. But the Birmingham group, led by the racist commissioner of public safety, Eugene "Bull" Conner, responded in a manner calculated to advance King's cause. Connor and his policemen met every move of peaceful protest King staged with brutal repression. Men, women, and children were swept down streets and sidewalks by powerful streams of water from fire hoses. Snarling police dogs were unleased on crowds. Clubbings and beatings of demonstrators were commonplace. And thanks to comprehensive newspaper and television coverage, all of it occurred in full view of the country and the world. The shock was general. Many Americans agreed with one senator, who declared Birmingham a "national debacle." White supremacists had not appeared in so unfavorable a light since before the Civil War.

The demonstrators, on the other hand, won widespread respect for their ability to withstand provocation. King and the other black leaders succeeded in controlling the protest. The urge to riot and attack Bull Connor's men was sublimated, for the most part, into prayer and into singing the battle hymn of Birmingham—folk singer Pete Seeger's adaptation of the old hymn "We Shall Overcome." Still, thousands were arrested in April of 1963, including King himself, who was placed in solitary confinement and denied communication. Many feared for his life, but a telephone call from Coretta, who had just given birth to their fourth child, to President John F. Kennedy brought an immediate improvement in the conditions of King's detention.

While he waited for release, he received news that Birmingham's white religious leaders had publicly denounced both the demonstrations and King's right to be called a man of God. In response, King wrote his widely publicized "Letter from Birmingham Jail," dated April 16, 1963. A ringing defense of nonviolent protest and civil disobedience, it linked his cause to that of Lincoln, Jefferson, and Jesus. Accepting the label of "extremist," King defended the role of "creative extremists" as agents for righting wrongs. Finally, he expressed his deep disappointment that clergymen of any color could align themselves against the black struggle for equality.

After serving eight days in prison, King accepted bond money raised by entertainer Harry Belafonte and left Birmingham jail. He plunged at once into the task of keeping the pressure on the city's leadership. Demonstrations and an effective boycott of segregated businesses continued. At the same time, he struggled desperately to keep the movement nonviolent in the face of bombings and beatings. By May 1963 there were signs of success. A large number of Birmingham businessmen were prepared to come to terms with the blacks. A program of desegregation was arranged for stores and restaurants. Bull Connor was ousted. Plans were made to integrate schools the following autumn. Hearts, to be sure, did not change as fast as rules, but for the blacks of Birmingham, Alabama, there was a new sense of dignity. And on the national level the events in Birmingham spurred the campaign for more effective federal civil rights legislation. On June 11, over national television, John F. Kennedy became the first President to declare racial discrimination a moral as well as a legal issue. It was time, he said, for government at every level to act on behalf of equality for every American. "Those who do nothing," Kennedy added, "are inviting shame as well as violence." A week later he submitted to Congress a program calling for complete desegregation of all public accommodations.

Looking back on Birmingham, Martin Luther King believed the freedom movement turned an important corner in Alabama in 1963. Nonviolence had produced meaningful change, and there was hope for black Americans. "I have this hope," King wrote in *Why We Can't Wait*, "because, once on a summer day, a dream came true. The city of Birmingham discovered a conscience."

Despite the satisfactions of Birmingham and the great March on

Washington, 1963 was a bitter year for Martin Luther King. On June 12 Medgar Evers, NAACP field secretary and King's counterpart in the Jackson, Mississippi, demonstrations, was shot and killed by a white terrorist. For King and his family, it must have been clear that sooner or later he would become prey to this kind of violence. But pausing only to grieve for Evers, he launched a nationwide speaking tour that was interrupted by tragedy on September 14. A bomb had been thrown through a window of the Sixteenth Street Baptist Church in Birmingham. When the smoke cleared, four little girls who had been attending a Sunday school class lay dead. The event threatened to undo the settlements of May and precipitate a full-scale racial war. King rushed back to Birmingham and, with the help of local clergy, barely managed to avert violence. On November 22 of this tense, emotion-charged year, the nation lost its President to an assassin's bullet. For King, who thought John F. Kennedy had undergone a "transformation from hesitant leader to a strong figure with deeply appealing objectives," the sense of loss was great.

The new President, Lyndon B. Johnson, immediately dedicated his considerable talents at political infighting to securing passage of Kennedy's still-pending Civil Rights Bill. Finally passed in June 1964, it prohibited racial discrimination in accommodations and employment. The bill's teeth came from a section withdrawing federal funds from states found practicing discrimination. Many Americans celebrated the measure as an important milestone toward equality. King regarded it as the outcome of Montgomery, Birmingham, and the Washington March. But a few dissented. Diehard segregationist Strom Thurmond, for example, the senator from South Carolina, greeted the Civil Rights Act with the opinion, "this is a sad day for America."

At the other end of the spectrum, black radicals were also sad. The accelerating freedom movement (there were 758 separate civil rights demonstrations in 186 cities in the ten weeks following King's Birmingham campaign) also produced an acceleration in militancy. King had long anticipated and dreaded such a development. Speaking shortly after Birmingham, he warned that the urban ghettos in particular contained "certain elements [which] . . . will respond with violence if the people of the nation do not recognize the desperate plight of the Negro. . . . The brutality they are experiencing as a result of their quest for equality may call for retaliation." King, of course, did not advocate such a development; he never wavered from a nonviolent stand. But he realized that nonviolent protest was no substitute for freedom. Unless the Civil Rights Bill and other legislation brought tangible gains for black Americans, he foresaw "a season of terror and violence."

In October 1964 Martin Luther King learned from a radio bulletin that he had been awarded the Nobel Peace Prize for his efforts in furthering "brotherhood among men." The award stirred controversy. In many eyes King's role had been anything but that of peacemaker. On the other hand, if the roots of true brotherhood lay in social equality, as others believed, then King's honor was richly deserved. But for King personally, the award was an added burden. After it he felt even more responsible for the course of American race relations. And by 1964 he was increasingly uneasy. What disturbed him most was the prospect of losing control of the black protest movement he had done so much to bring about. More radical aspirants to black leadership, preaching a doctrine of black nationalism and retaliatory violence, were waiting for King to falter. They were evident at the Washington rally in the person of John Lewis, who asserted that a revolutionary change in American institutions was a necessary prelude to freedom. His speech broke the otherwise solid front of the civil rights movement and portended a deeper split in the future. The rioting that engulfed Harlem in the summer of 1964 despite King's plea for peace was evidence that the schism in the freedom movement would not be restricted to philosophical grounds.

The new year began with several indications that the movement was nearing the boiling point. In February Malcolm X became the victim of black terrorism encouraged, apparently, by the estranged Black Muslim leader Elijah Muhammed. Fearing a black civil war, King volunteered to mediate the dispute, but was rejected by both sides. The militants wanted no part of a man they regarded as patient and docile to a fault—an "Uncle Tom." A month later in Selma, Alabama, King again encountered the stinging charge of "chickening out." The occasion was a series of marches protesting the denial of suffrage, and the critics were the young blacks King himself had rallied to the movement just a few years before. Even when President Lyndon B. Johnson, in a direct response to Selma, submitted a strong Voting Rights Bill to Congress, these men questioned his credibility. Finally, in August 1965 the most shocking of a series of riots by urban blacks erupted in the Watts district of Los Angeles. King left a religious convention in Puerto Rico to rush to the West Coast. In King's opinion, rioting was "absolutely wrong" as a form of protest, "socially detestable and self-defeating." But the blacks of Watts proved indifferent or openly hostile to King's efforts at mediation. Their anger transcended passive resistance; their feeling of powerlessness was not alleviated by King's philosophy of nonviolent dignity.

Moved by both the dejection of urban blacks and the pressure of the radicals, King went to Chicago in January 1966 to launch a massive campaign against social and economic deprivation. For nine months he directed the Chicago Movement from a slum tenement. It was not a success. Despite the fact that one-third of Chicago's population was black, the scarcity of local black leadership and a boss-dominated city government combined to limit King's effectiveness. Moreover, the movement got away from King on several occasions. A vicious three-day riot, for instance, was touched off when police denied the use of a fire hydrant to children trying to get some relief from the sweltering heat. And to his dismay King found that many Chicago blacks, like those in Watts the year before, were proud of the riot, proud to have "shaken Whitey up." The compromise settlement that ended the Chicago Movement in September was vague and unsatisfying. Black militants seized on it as an example of the ineffectiveness of nonviolence and jeered King publicly.

King understood the radical position put forth in 1966 by Stokely Carmichael, the new leader of SNCC; Floyd McKissick of CORE; and black power advocate H. Rap Brown. He knew the reason for the organization that year in Oakland, California, of the Black Panther Party for Self-defense under the leadership of Huey Newton and Bobby Seale. Nor was he surprised to see the Black Muslims recover from the defection of Malcolm X and go on to gain the support of many young people, including heavyweight boxing champion Cassius Clay (Muhammad Ali). "I had urged them," King wrote, "to have faith in America and in white society. Their hopes had soared. . . . They were now hostile because they were watching the dream that they had so readily accepted turn into a frustrating nightmare." Still King clung to his original postulates—nonviolent protest, reform through the existing system, acceptance by and integration into white

America. With an ecologist's insight, King constantly maintained that "all life is interrelated—tied into a single garment of destiny."

When James Meredith, who had integrated the University of Mississippi, was shot on June 6, 1966, while marching alone near Memphis, King rushed to the scene pleading for peace. He preserved it too, although at one point he had to physically restrain Stokely Carmichael from lunging at a state trooper. It was more difficult, in a way, to restrain the growth of black hatred, black separatism, and reverse racism. In King's view these would only call forth a backlash of white racism that inevitably would crush the black minority (only 15 percent of the American people). Black violence, moreover, would undo King's painstaking efforts to encourage respect for a people brave enough to turn the other cheek. He cringed, therefore, when young militants altered his theme song to "We Shall Overrun." He was similarly disturbed at their growing reluctance to accept the aid of white liberals. Carmichael and his colleagues, King came to realize on the Meredith March, were of a different generation. Lacking the Christian element that figured so strongly in King's life and thought, they were children of violence. Carmichael had been arrested twenty-seven times between the ages of nineteen and twenty-four. He had seen nonviolent blacks abused too often. Like H. Rap Brown, he was prepared to admit that "violence was as American as apple pie." And he was prepared to use that violence on behalf of black Americans.

On the Meredith March from Memphis to Jackson, Mississippi, in the summer of 1966, King and Carmichael engaged in a running debate. Carmichael was anxious to have the freedom movement accept his "Black Power" slogan. King preferred "Black Equality" or "Power for Poor People" or "Freedom Now." For hours on end he attempted to bring the militants around to his view, but to no avail. "Black Power" prevailed in Jackson and, a year later, in Cambridge, Maryland, when H. Rap Brown told a rally to "burn this town to the ground if [it] don't grant the demands of Negroes." King could only shudder and watch the white backlash gather force. It took various forms, from the defeat of a civil rights bill in 1966 to segregationist George Wallace's relatively strong showing (13 percent of the national vote) as a third-party candidate in the election of 1968.

But, in the vicious circle King dreaded, blacks responded to the growing white backlash with behavior calculated to accelerate it still more. The summer of 1967 brought the most serious race riots yet to American cities—forty-one incidents in thirty-nine communities. With every new headline white resistance to civil rights stiffened. King remained convinced that only a reemphasis on nonviolence and civil disobedience could regain white support and bring real improvement. The riots were killing the freedom movement, King explained in a 1967 book, *Where Do We Go from Here: Chaos or Community?*

With this problem in mind, King, Ralph Abernathy, and the Southern Christian Leadership Conference began preparations in the winter of 1967–1968 for a Poor People's March on Washington. In keeping with King's beliefs, it would be a fully integrated, nonviolent appeal to the nation's conscience. The marchers planned to request federal support in the amount of $12 billion to fund the proposals in an "economic bill of rights." There was reason to think President Johnson would respond to such a request, even though King had broken sharply with him over the issue of the Vietnam War. As a proponent of peace and nonviolence, King could not accept the rationales advanced in support of that conflict. He maintained his position even in the face of pointed criticism by the NAACP and the Urban League, whose leaders preferred to keep the issues of war and civil rights separate in the hopes of gaining support from the administration.

The Poor People's March was set for June 1968, but the whirlwind pace King had kept since the beginning of the decade allowed him only occasional participation in the planning. One of the detours took him to Memphis, where a garbage strike theatened to evolve into racial encounter of crisis proportions. Local black leaders wanted King to organize a peaceful demonstration, but once again he had difficulty working with black power militants. Uncontrollable black looters, arsonists, and street fighters were another source of difficulty. On March 28 they transformed a nonviolent march into an orgy of destruction that provoked an even greater measure of police brutality. As a self-styled "riot preventer," King was sick at heart. If Memphis exploded, he feared the approaching summer of 1968 would be chaos. Already black leaders, like the Harlem Congressman Adam Clayton Powell, were arousing the urban masses and, as part of their campaign, making references to "Martin Loser King" and his Uncle Tom tactics. Nonviolence, King felt, was on trial in Memphis.

On April 3, 1968, on the eve of the crucial Memphis march, King addressed a capacity crowd at the Masonic Temple of that city. His mood was strangely somber, introspective. "Like anybody," he mused, "I would like to live a long life." But longevity, he added, was not his chief concern; he would rather do God's will. Some of his aides were reminded of the great Washington rally of 1963, where King had expressed his belief "that if a man hasn't discovered something that he will die for, he isn't fit to live!" The following evening, on the way to yet another mass meeting, King walked onto the balcony of his motel room and leaned over the railing to talk with a colleague. A moment later he crumpled to the ground. An assassin's bullet, fired from a hotel room across the street, had pierced his skull. The killer, arrested two months later and identified as James Earl Ray, was a white drifter with a long criminal record.

The murder of Martin Luther King moved the American people as had few events in recent years. The immediate response in all but the most prejudiced white minds was shame. Millions of whites felt compelled to apologize to black people as a whole and went to their churches for services honoring King. But even among the mourners, white and black eyes did not meet easily. Everyone seemed to recognize that with King had gone a powerful influence for interracial compassion and understanding—the basis of ordered change and reform. The evidence came almost at once in the rioting that broke out in over 130 cities. Black people were furious. Stokely Carmichael summed up the prevalent feeling when he declared that white America "declared war on us" in killing King. Floyd McKissick added that "nonviolence is a dead philosophy, and it was not the black people that killed it." Black Panther spokesman Eldridge Cleaver made it clear that he saw in King's death the "final repudiation by white America of any hope of reconciliation, of any hope of change by peaceful and nonviolent means." Added to this bitterness was the discouraging March 1968 report of President Johnson's National Advisory Commission on Civil Disorders, which found white racism at the root of a process of polarization that threatened democratic values and the nation itself. Although unrelated to the race issue, the assassination of Presidential aspirant Robert F. Kennedy on June 5 deepened the pessimism of 1968.

Slowly, however, those who hoped for better days shook off their discouragement. Ralph Abernathy, King's colleague since Montgomery and the first to bend over his fallen body in Memphis, tried to overcome. The Poor People's March that came to Washington in June 1968 was a living testimony to Abernathy's determination to carry on the traditions of King and the SCLC. In his memory Abernathy named the marchers' encampment around the Lincoln Memorial Resurrection City. For many participants in the freedom movement, King was indeed a black Jesus, "a man," as Coretta King wrote a month after her husband's death, "who refused to lose faith in the ultimate redemption of mankind."

The same faith, this same belief that America was capable of giving her black citizens equal justice and opportunity, has characterized the mainstream of the freedom movement since King fell. The riots that so many feared would turn the nation into clusters of armed camps did not recur with the vehemence or the frequency of the 1964–1967 period. Nor did black militance advance very far beyond a fringe of young radicals from the urban ghettos (there were only about 1000 Black Panthers by 1970). One reason, to be sure, was the death, arrest, and self-exile of many of the radical leaders. By 1971 Huey Newton, Bobby Seale, and Angela Davis were in various stages of complex court trials. Eldridge Cleaver escaped the same treatment only by fleeing to Algeria. Stokely Carmichael also went to Africa. George Jackson, the Californian who wrote *Soledad Brother* in his jail cell, and Fred Hampton, a Chicago Panther, were shot to death. Still, Newton could declare early in 1972 that the Black Panthers had decided to put away their guns and work within the American system. The new challenge, Newton explained, was "to organize the black communities politically."

Another reason for the decline of militancy was dissension among the radicals themselves. Soon after King's death, some black power advocates softened their black-only policy to the extent of collaborating with white radicals in the Peace and Freedom party's effort in the 1968 elections and in the Students for a Democratic Society organization. But others insisted on not mixing races, and the result was a splintering and weakening of the radical movement. A compromise position commanded the greatest respect. It applauded the black-is-beautiful part of black nationalism, but saw it as part of the pluralism that lent vitality to American culture.

King never lost this conviction, and it was given substance after his death by the ability of blacks to make significant gains in the American political and economic structure. Carl Stokes and Richard Hatcher, for instance, were elected to the mayoralties of Cleveland, Ohio, and Gary, Indiana, in 1967 and reelected two years later. Although in a much smaller arena, the achievement of Charles Evers in July 1969 was equally great and just as important as a symbol for black Americans. The brother of the slain freedom worker Medgar Evers, Charles was inaugurated mayor of Fayette, Mississippi. His administration won biracial respect for its fairness to all people, and by 1971 Evers was talking about running for the governorship. That a black in Mississippi could be serious about this was tangible evidence of changing times and tangible food for black hopes.

Abandoning the marches and prayers that were King's means, blacks of the 1970s used the civil rights legislation, particularly the Voting Rights Act of 1965, to attain King's goals. Blacks were gaining power, but it was not black power. Julian Bond, the handsome young black elected to Georgia's House of Representatives in 1965 and mentioned for the vice-presidency at the 1968 Democratic National Convention, made it clear that he meant to use the system rather than destroy it. Bond called for blacks to come home, come South, and use the ballot box and the new federal guarantees of suffrage to usher in a new day. He would play the American game and win an honest victory. For Bond and many of his contemporaries, elective politics was by 1972 the cutting edge of the black revolution.

In the economic sphere, to be sure, black people still lagged far behind the national average. But Jesse Jackson, another protégé of King who saw his hero fall in Memphis, typified the determination of younger blacks to see a better day. Jackson was radical and sharply critical of Ralph Abernathy, but he gave his radicalism constructive expression in the highly successful Operation Breadbasket in Chicago and similar organizations in other cities. Aimed at consolidating and applying black economic power, the Breadbasket campaigns stressed boycotts, cooperative buying, the development of black-operated business alternatives, and the end of job discrimination. Early in 1972

Jackson reorganized Operation Breadbasket as People United to Save Humanity (PUSH). Its membership, he stated, would be a "rainbow coalition" of poor people of all colors. On higher business levels, it was possible in 1972 to say that a black alternative existed in the worlds of construction, banking, insurance, and finance.

Progress towards King's dream was also evident in the broad trend of southern political life. Prior to the passage of the Voting Rights Act in 1965, there were only 72 elected black officials in the eleven states that had comprised the Confederacy. Early in 1971, there were 711. They ranged from city councilmen to school board officials, judges, and sheriffs. Every southern state had at least one black in its legislature. True, there were in 1971 only 40 blacks among 1805 state lawmakers in the South, but a start had been made. And considering the distance traveled since Rosa Parks refused to leave her seat in a Montgomery bus, it was an impressive achievement. Socially, to be sure, there was little progress. Laws and officials might change, but the general love and brotherhood that Martin Luther King extolled seemed generations away. Yet blacks had risen, in the persons of Thurgood Marshall and Edward Brooke, as high as the United States Supreme Court and Senate. And by 1972 it was no longer outrageous or amusing in many quarters to consider the possibility of a black President. In fact, New York Congresswoman Shirley Chisholm broke two barriers by campaigning for this office.

It was in the grass roots of local politics, however, that the freedom movement achieved its greatest vitality and, for most blacks, its greatest meaning. In Greene County in the heart of Alabama's black belt, the SCLC helped black citizens place representatives on the county commission and school board. Getting out the vote on election day was not easy among a people accustomed to intimidation, but one campaign poster was especially effective. Beneath the date of the election, it stated simply: "Martin Luther King died for this day."

SELECTED READINGS

The Person

*BENNETT, LERONE: *What Manner of Man: A Biography of Martin Luther King, Jr.* (3rd ed., 1968). The best biography by a black author.

BISHOP, JIM: *The Days of Martin Luther King, Jr.* (1971). The full story behind King's assassination, with details of his earlier life.

*KING, CORETTA SCOTT: *My Life with Martin Luther King, Jr.* (1969). King's widow's reminiscences.

*KING, MARTIN LUTHER, JR.: *Stride Toward Freedom: The Montgomery Story* (1958). King's own account of his struggle to end segregation in public transportation in Montgomery, Alabama.

*KING, MARTIN LUTHER, JR.: *Where Do We Go from Here: Chaos or Community?* (1967). A review of black history and the civil rights movement since 1964 plus speculation about the future.

*LEWIS, DAVID L.: *King: A Critical Biography* (1970). Another perspective on a controversial figure.

*LINCOLN, ERIC (ed.): *Martin Luther King, Jr.* (1970). A collection of profiles of King by his contemporaries.

*MILLER, WILLIAM ROBERT: *Martin Luther King, Jr.: His Life, Martrydom, and Meaning for the World* (1968). A full, factual account.

The Period

*FRANKLIN, JOHN HOPE: *From Slavery to Freedom: A History of American Negroes* (3rd. ed., 1967). General treatment of black history by a distinguished black scholar.

GOLDEN, HARRY: *Mr. Kennedy and the Negroes* (1964). John F. Kennedy's involvement in civil rights.

*HARRINGTON, MICHAEL: *The Other America* (1962). The history of poor people of all colors.

*LINCOLN, ERIC: *The Black Muslims in America* (1961). An examination of the more radical wing of the black revolution.

LOMAX, LOUIS: *The Negro Revolt* (1963). An analysis of the freedom movement since 1955.

* Available in paperback.

*MEIER, AUGUST, and ELLIOTT M. RUDWICK: *From Plantation to Ghetto* (rev. ed., 1970). An interpretive history of blacks in America valuable especially for its use of recent scholarly findings.

*MUSE, BENJAMIN: *The American Negro Revolution: From Nonviolence to Black Power, 1963–1967* (1968). The best general account of the developing freedom movement.

*PEEKS, EDWARD: *The Long Struggle for Black Power* (1971). Interpretation of recent black history in the United States.

* Available in paperback.

CHAPTER ELEVEN

Neil Armstrong

As television beamed the greatest technological feat in history to an incredulous world, Neil Armstrong prepared to enter a totally new environment. Moving awkwardly in his cumbersome spacesuit, he entered the range of a television camera mounted on the Eagle. *The next moment he became the first man to stand on land that was not earth. There were few surprises. The surface of the moon at 10:56 P.M. Eastern Daylight Time on July 21, 1969, looked just as Armstrong had been trained to expect it would. Everything*

467

connected with the flight of Apollo 11 had been carefully rehearsed hundreds of times. Characteristically, Armstrong had his lines prepared. "That's one small step for [a] man," his voice crackled across 200,000 miles, "one giant leap for mankind." His tone was calm, almost matter-of-fact.

In all of American history it would be difficult to choose a less auspicious summer for the birth of a child than that of 1930. The stock-market crash the previous autumn punctured the bubble of the 1920s prosperity, and only the most naive or hypocritical could deny that the nation was spiraling rapidly toward economic disaster. Realists saw the start of America's worst depression as an event that cast shadows of doubt on the vision of national greatness nourished so carefully first by Progressive reformers and then by post-World War I spokesmen for the status quo. At the time of Neil Armstrong's birth, August 5, the trends were already clear. Unemployment was rising rapidly; national income was falling with comparable speed, as were industrial production, profits, and investment. It was a time for failure, foreclosure, and bankruptcy.

In 1930 banks failed at the rate of several hundred every month. Frightened people reacted by transferring their funds from the surviving banks to cookie jars and mattresses. This only increased economic stagnation, for then there was no money to prime the pumps of recovery. Even as prices were slashed in an effort to find markets, buyers disappeared. The nation ran scared. Fears multiplied when the federal government under Herbert Hoover gave little indication of being either willing or able to arrest the downward slide. Some of the states and the cities were willing, but the worse the depression became, the less they could do in the way of relief. By Neil Armstrong's first winter, soup lines of desperate men were forming in the major metropolitan areas. His own prospects for success seemed equally bleak. With hard work and luck, he might have enough to eat and wear. Perhaps he could complete high school and hope for a job. Beyond that was uncertainty. By any standard it seemed highly improbable in 1930 that Armstrong, or anybody, would stand on the moon.

A farm owned by his grandparents outside Wapakoneta, Ohio,

was Neil Armstrong's birthplace. "Wapak," the local name, contained about 7000 people and was the epitome of small-town middle America. Neil's father was among the more fortunate members of the white collar labor force. As auditor of county records in the state of Ohio, he kept his job during the depression. Moving his wife, Neil, and two younger children from one small Ohio town to another, he managed to weather the economic storm. But the Great Depression left an intellectual scar on Neil Armstrong, as it did on many other Americans who passed through this trauma. They grew up in an atmosphere of no-nonsense efficiency. Children like Neil were expected to do home chores, earn what they could at odd jobs in the neighborhood, never yearn for things they could not afford, keep a stiff upper lip, and pray. When youthful dedication to this ethic flagged, "the depression" was unveiled to enforce compliance. There were frequent family discussions about the need for personal sacrifice, careful planning, and hard work. Neil never forgot this gospel of hard work. "The single thing which makes any man happiest," he remarked just before the Apollo 11 mission, "is the realization that he has worked up to the limits of his ability, his capacity." According to this formula, Armstrong's own nearly total absorption in aviation and later in space flight must have made him a happy man.

When Neil Armstrong was two years old, his mother took him to the Chicago airport to watch the planes. Years later she recalled that she had a difficult time persuading him to leave, and she thought that might have been significant. At six Armstrong had his first flight, over Warren, Ohio, in a rattling old Ford trimotor. His father was pale with fright, but the experience made Neil a flying fanatic. He began with magazines and books on aviation, then entered a long model-building stage. There was even a recurring dream, later dramatized by the press, that by holding his breath he could hover over the ground. Of course the depression still gripped the nation, and the Armstrongs made sure that Neil's hobby did not interfere with education and family chores. But school was a breeze for Armstrong, who skipped several grades and impressed his teachers as a dreamer with the ability and diligence to carry his dreams to realization. His schoolmates felt the same way. The epigram below Armstrong's picture in the yearbook of Blume Senior High School stated: "he thinks, he acts, 'tis done."

As a result of his ability to get things done, Armstrong found time for music (he played baritone horn for a high school group called the Mississippi Moonshiners), the Boy Scouts (he attained the rank of Eagle), and church activities. He also financed his passion for flying with a variety of odd jobs ranging from the usual lawn mowing to cleaning the mixing vats in a bakery, a position he got because he was small enough to climb right into the vat. But his biggest bonanza was the 40 cents an hour he earned sweeping the Rhine-Bradings Drugstore. Starting in 1945, when he was fifteen, Armstrong used his earnings to pay for flying lessons at Wapakoneta's grassy field. One hour in the air cost $9, but the next year, even before he could legally drive a car, he had his pilot's license.

While Neil Armstrong was playing for the Mississippi Moonshiners and flying whenever he could afford it, his country was playing a leading role in the second global war of the twentieth century. Except for the fact that it ended the depression, World War II did not have much impact on everyday life in Wapakoneta, Ohio. But the war was the most important factor in a restructuring of international relations that would in time profoundly affect Neil's life.

The Japanese attack on Pearl Harbor ended a long period of agonizing American uncertainty about the war that had enveloped the rest of the world's major powers. In a little more than eight hours, the Hawaiian base suffered the loss of 19 ships, 150 planes, and 2335 lives. It was by far the most devastating attack on American soil by a foreign power. Indeed, the only precedents were the several battles of the War of 1812, the skirmishes of 1846 that launched the Mexican War, and the firing on Provincetown, Massachusetts, by a German submarine during World War I. Congress reacted immediately, on December 8, 1941, with a declaration of war against Japan. Germany and Italy responded on December 11 by declaring war against the United States. Although millions of Americans had vowed not to repeat the "mistake" of intervening in World War I, the nation now found itself faced with the need to prepare for its second major war in a quarter-century.

In view of the widespread misgivings among the American people, President Franklin D. Roosevelt felt compelled to justify warfare in idealistic terms clothed in the concept of mission: "when we resort to force, as now we must," he declared, "we are determined that this force shall be directed toward ultimate good as well as against immediate evil. We Americans are not destroyers—we are builders." Earlier, in January 1941, Roosevelt had enunciated "four essential human freedoms" which the United States was determined to defend around the world: freedom of speech, freedom of worship, freedom from want, and freedom from fear. A similarly altruistic statement, the Atlantic Charter of August 14, 1941, was a joint effort with Prime Minister Winston Churchill of Great Britain. This document rejected gain of any kind as a war aim and asserted the principle of popular self-determination for people everywhere. America would be the champion of liberty. It was a gospel that boys like Neil Armstrong accepted unquestioningly. The "Japs" and "Nazis" were hated villains.

Similar zeal on the part of adults explains why World War II was highly popular with Americans in general. There were no significant antiwar protests during the war, and national morale remained high. One result was the remarkable achievement of mobilization. Between 1939 and 1945, the United States Army grew from 174,000 to 8,300,000. An additional 7 million men and women enrolled in other branches of the armed forces. Thirty-one million Americans registered for the draft under the Selective Service Act of 1940 and its extensions. Most young Americans could not wait to fight. For Neil Armstrong, flying his model planes off model aircraft carriers in Wapakoneta, inaction must have seemed especially cruel. His chance, however, was coming.

Mobilization also entailed industrial redirection. Once again the United States became the arsenal of democracy. In 1939 the nation could muster only 2000 airplanes. Its capacity to produce more was also negligible. But by the end of the war, thanks to the adoption of the mass-production techniques Henry Ford pioneered in the automobile industry, 100,000 planes were in service. All told, American factories built 300,000 aircraft in the five years after France fell to Germany in June 1940. In addition, the United States produced 3 million machine guns and over 60 million tons of shipping capacity. Naturally this demanded money, and federal expenditures, which never exceeded $8 million annually in the 1930s, soared to $100 million in 1945. One pleasant byproduct of this outlay was the ending of the Great Depression.

At the beginning of 1942 the United States and its chief allies,

Great Britain and Russia, faced the task of reversing the momentum that had carried the Axis powers (Germany, Italy, Japan) to dominance of a substantial portion of the earth. Strategy was a moot question. Roosevelt and Premier Josef Stalin of the Soviet Union preferred to create a front in western Europe and move through France at the German homeland. Winston Churchill demurred. It seemed to him that a better strategy was to flank Europe by moving through North Africa, then strike at its "soft underbelly" via Italy and the Near East. Churchill ultimately prevailed, and on November 8, 1942, a combined English and Amercian force under General Dwight D. Eisenhower invaded North Africa. Allied leaders met at Casablanca in Morocco in January 1943 to make the unconditional surrender of the enemy their goal. Next they moved slowly against the Germans in Africa and their often-brilliant "Desert Fox," General Erwin Rommel. Surrender in Africa came on May 12, 1943, and the Allies moved their forces across the Mediterranean and into Italy. The Fascist government of Benito Mussolini fell on July 25, 1943, but the Germans dug in behind the Volturno Line in central Italy and resisted the Allied advance yard by bloody yard.

On June 6, 1944, Great Britain and the United States opened a second front in Europe. This time the landing craft, carrying 3 million men, hit the beaches on France's Normandy coast. The success of D-Day in establishing a beachhead 70 miles wide and 5 miles deep marked the beginning of the end for Germany. The Allies moved inexorably across France, and by the spring of 1945 were in the heart of Germany. So were the Russians, who closed in from the east with the aid of American munitions. When the two forces met in late April, the war was over for Germany. Adolf Hitler committed suicide. On May 7, 1945, the remnants of his nation surrendered to Eisenhower. V-E (Victory in Europe) Day was a cause for massive celebration throughout America.

Wapakoneta, Ohio, was no exception, and V-E Day brought a thrill of patriotism to Neil Armstrong. By this time he was flying regularly over Ohio, and he was entranced by the B-17 bombers used in the invasion of Germany. Since the start of the war the big England-based aircraft had pounded the centers of Axis industry. But Armstrong's imagination was really captured by the role of planes in the vast, watery expanses of the Pacific military theater. After Pearl Har-

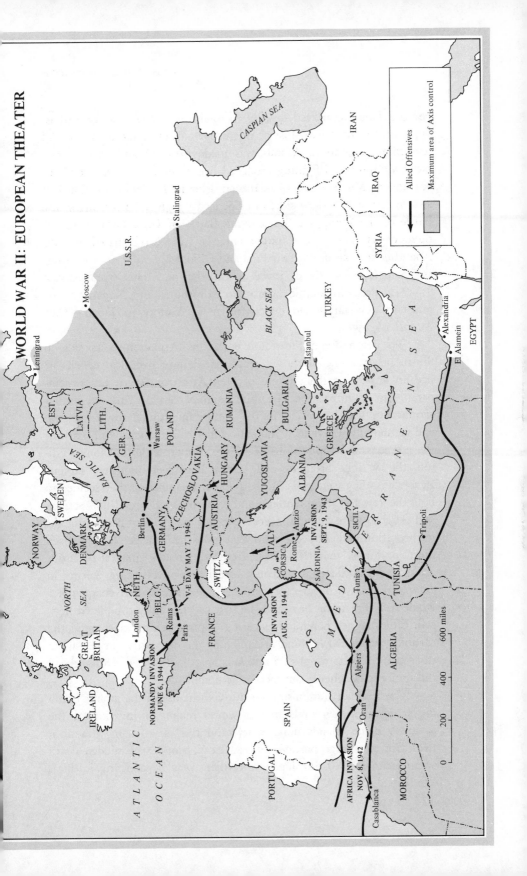

WORLD WAR II: EUROPEAN THEATER

Allied Offensives

Maximum area of Axis control

ATLANTIC OCEAN

NORTH SEA

IRELAND

GREAT BRITAIN
London

NORWAY

SWEDEN

DENMARK

BALTIC SEA

GER.

EST.

LATVIA

LITH.

Leningrad

Moscow

U.S.S.R.

Stalingrad

CASPIAN SEA

NETH.

BELG.

Reims

Paris

NORMANDY INVASION
JUNE 6, 1944

FRANCE

SWITZ.

V-E DAY MAY 7, 1945

GERMANY

Berlin

Warsaw

POLAND

CZECHOSLOVAKIA

AUSTRIA

HUNGARY

RUMANIA

YUGOSLAVIA

ALBANIA

BULGARIA

GREECE

BLACK SEA

Istanbul

TURKEY

IRAN

IRAQ

SYRIA

INVASION
AUG. 15, 1944

PORTUGAL

SPAIN

CORSICA

SARDINIA

ITALY
Rome Anzio

INVASION
SEPT. 9, 1943

SICILY

Tripoli

M E D I T E R R A N E A N   S E A

Tunis

TUNISIA

Alexandria

El Alamein

EGYPT

Algiers

Oran

AFRICA INVASION
NOV. 8, 1942

Casablanca

MOROCCO

ALGERIA

0   200   400   600 miles

bor the Japanese moved quickly to establish a shield of fortified islands across the ocean. Just as in Europe, America faced the task of reversing momentum. A start was made in 1942 and 1943, when bitter air and naval fighting produced American victories in the Coral Sea and at Midway and Guadalcanal Islands. By 1944 the tide had swung to the American side, as evidenced by pivotal triumphs in the Battle of the Philippine Sea and the Battle of Leyte Gulf. Many of these engagements were fought entirely with carrier-based aircraft. And after the capture of Iwo Jima and Okinawa, only 750 miles from the main Japanese islands, it was aircraft that on August 6 and August 9, 1945, dropped atomic bombs on Hiroshima and Nagasaki. The resultant devastation led directly to V-J (Victory in Japan) Day, August 14, 1945.

The detonation of the atomic bomb, like Armstrong's first step on the moon, was one of those events that delimit historical epochs. It had an impact on the thought of Neil Armstrong's generation comparable to its impact on Hiroshima and Nagasaki. This intellectual significance was bound up in the American attitude toward science and technology. Previously, the nation had had unquestioning faith in the methods and applications of science. Robert Fulton, Thomas Edison, the Wright brothers, and Henry Ford were not just famous Americans, they were gods. In the popular imagination they seemed to hold the keys to the millennium and certainly to the good life. Science and progress were thought inseparable. But the chain of breakthroughs in theoretical and applied physics that unleashed nuclear energy raised more problems than it solved. Ironically, man's greatest scientific achievement produced the greatest threat to his well-being. Science in control was science out of control. Although man had conquered a whole new dimension of nature, he still had not fully conquered himself. Ethics lagged behind engineering; morals behind machinery; the capability to destroy behind discipline of the destructive urge. Like a three-year-old who weighs 250 pounds, man had power before he had the ability to channel it into socially acceptable uses.

The Truman Administration justified the use of the atomic bomb in Japan on the grounds that it would make an invasion of the Japanese home islands unnecessary, and thus save many American lives. But to a large portion the American people, the sudden death of an estimated 80,000 Japanese civilians was beyond any justifica-

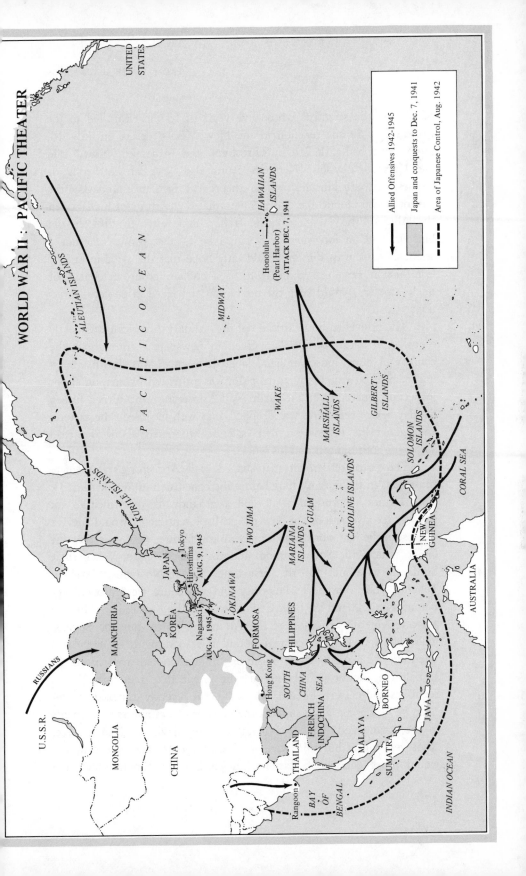

WORLD WAR II : PACIFIC THEATER

UNITED STATES

PACIFIC OCEAN

ALEUTIAN ISLANDS

MIDWAY

Honolulu
(Pearl Harbor)
HAWAIIAN ISLANDS
ATTACK DEC. 7, 1941

WAKE

MARSHALL ISLANDS

GILBERT ISLANDS

KURILE ISLANDS

SOLOMON ISLANDS

CAROLINE ISLANDS

CORAL SEA

IWO JIMA

GUAM

MARIANA ISLANDS

NEW GUINEA

Tokyo
Hiroshima
AUG. 9, 1945
JAPAN
OKINAWA

KOREA
Nagasaki
AUG. 6, 1945

FORMOSA

PHILIPPINES

MANCHURIA

RUSSIANS

U.S.S.R.

MONGOLIA

CHINA

Hong Kong

SOUTH CHINA SEA

FRENCH INDOCHINA

THAILAND

Rangoon

BAY OF BENGAL

MALAYA

BORNEO

SUMATRA

JAVA

AUSTRALIA

INDIAN OCEAN

Allied Offensives 1942-1945

Japan and conquests to Dec. 7, 1941

Area of Japanese Control, Aug. 1942

tion. Even the scientists whose five years of frantic effort led to the world's first atomic reaction in the New Mexico desert on July 16, 1945, were badly shaken by Hiroshima and Nagasaki. "Now," said the Harvard physicist Kenneth Bainbridge, "we are all sons of bitches." Albert Einstein, whose theoretical brilliance underlay the advent of the atomic age, sadly contemplated the fruits of his labor in the ashes of the Japanese cities. If he could relive his life, an old Einstein told an interviewer, it would be as a carpenter and not a scientist. As it was, Einstein could only hope that the Atomic Energy Commission (established in 1946 as a civilian group in charge of nuclear policy) could keep the new monster headed in peaceful directions.

The post-Hiroshima attitude of the ordinary American was neatly captured in a cartoon that appeared in newspapers throughout the country. A huge, muscular hand labeled "Science" was shown emerging from turbulent clouds. In its palm was a tiny ball which, on closer inspection, proved to be the earth. Neil Armstrong, who turned fifteen the day before the bomb was dropped, may well have seen the cartoon and, given his fascination with science, wondered about the road ahead for both himself and his world.

The peace settlement that shaped Neil Armstrong's immediate future was in the making long before the conclusion of World War II. The Atlantic Charter of 1941 laid a groundwork of principles for postwar reconstruction, but how its idealistic sentiments would survive the test of the real world was largely up to the three new superpowers: Great Britain, the Soviet Union, and the United States. When their heads of state met for the first time late in November 1943 at Teheran, Iran, differences in policy and procedure were already apparent. England and the United States were willing to abide by the "no aggrandizement" provision of the Atlantic Charter. But the Soviets, who also signed this document, found it at odds with their avowed intention of advancing communism on an international front. Stalin, in fact, left no doubt at Teheran that he intended to retain the Baltic republics and eastern Poland, which he had recently annexed. Moreover, he was prepared to support the newborn Communist movements in the unannexed part of Poland, in Yugoslavia, and in Greece. Roosevelt and Churchill were well aware that Russia's "support" would prove decisive in Eastern Europe, but at Teheran they were prepared to play down their misgivings in the interest of winning the war.

The next meeting of the Big Three took place at Yalta in the Crimea in February 1945. An aging and weary but courageous Roosevelt had been elected to an unprecedented fourth term the previous November over the young Republican Governor of New York, Thomas E. Dewey. With the victory Roosevelt received a mandate from the majority of Americans to construct the peace. The aftermath of World War I relatively fresh in their minds, the people hoped this one would be a just and lasting settlement. Yalta was a crucial milestone, and it provided few reasons for encouragement. Great Britain and the United States, still anxious about winning the war and feeling the need of Soviet support, gave in to Russia's demands for territory in Eastern Europe and in the Far East. Churchill and Stalin also accepted without close scrutiny the concept of "free popular elections" in the European countries liberated from Axis control.

Roosevelt was too experienced a politician to accept the assurances Stalin extended at Yalta. Almost as soon as the conference ended, he had misgivings, and by April 1945 he was exchanging angry charges and countercharges with the Soviet leader. It now appeared that Russia was intent on installing a chain of satellite states along its western frontier. On April 12 Roosevelt wrote to Churchill that in regard to the extension of Soviet power, "we must be firm." Later that same day Roosevelt died suddenly, and Vice-President Harry S Truman, a former senator from Missouri, assumed the burden of concluding World War II. Although victory over the Axis powers was sweet, it was tempered with the realization that the end result might be only the replacement of the Nazi juggernaut with a new version under the red flag of communism. By the summer of 1945 Churchill was already speaking of an "iron curtain" between Russia and the West. What went on behind it, he implied, was unknown and, presumably, unfree. Stalin confirmed this impression before a shocked and angry Churchill and Truman at the last Big Three conference at Potsdam, Germany, late in July. The pledges of Yalta, it appeared, were only so much paper in the face of Russia's postwar ambitions for communism. Once again, the United States had won the war but lost the peace.

By the time Neil Armstrong graduated from high school in

June 1947, it was clear that conflict with the Soviet Union was the dominant theme of American foreign relations. The expectations of the 1930s and the early war years that democracy and communism shared a common denominator of respect for popular self-determination gave way to the realization that these systems, as defined by the current leadership, were implacably opposed. Indeed, the term *cold war* became associated with the growing Soviet-American tension that kept Armstrong's world on edge.

The United States had several strategies available for meeting the postwar Communist challenge. One was liberation. It called for positive American action aimed at freeing peoples trapped behind the Iron Curtain—the Poles, Czechs, Hungarians, Yugoslavs, and, some argued, the Russians themselves. The rationale here was to force Russia to keep its Yalta pledges concerning free elections. Apathy was immoral. "What we need to do," declared the belligerent Secretary of State John Foster Dulles, "is recapture the kind of crusading spirit of the early days of the Republic." America had a mission to liberate the world. The second strategy also took a hard line. "Massive retaliation," as it was called, entailed immediate and all-out (that is, nuclear) response to Russian expansion whenever and wherever it appeared. The hope was that the threat of such a severe reprisal would stop Soviet aggression before it began. The result was an arms race between the world's two major powers and a dark cloud of fear over all mankind. Alternative three, "disengagement," involved reducing Soviet-American tension by withdrawing the American presence from hotspots such as Central Europe and Southeast Asia. Its proponents were willing to allow the peoples of these regions to choose the political system they desired. If the choice went against democracy, it had to be accepted. In its extreme form, disengagement compared to the isolationism that had been the major theme in American foreign policy after World War I.

A fourth alternative was the United Nations. A successor to the League of Nations, the UN began as a wartime coalition of Allied countries. Its function in times of peace was defined at the Dumbarton Oaks Conference held near Washington, D.C., in 1944 and at the Yalta meeting early the following year. The final charter was adopted April 29, 1945, in San Francisco; it provided for a General Assembly and a Security Council. The latter body consisted of five permanent members (the United States, Great Britain, Russia, France, and China) and six elected members. It had the power to invoke military sanctions against actions threatening world peace, but any one of the permanent members could veto such a decision. Still, the United Nations was a possible deterrent to Soviet aggression. In marked contrast to its policy toward the League of Nations, the United States gave the new world organizations its full support. Within a decade this commitment would send Neil Armstrong to the Far East as a fighter pilot.

The fifth response of Neil Armstrong's America to the Soviet presence in the postwar world was "containment." The term was that of a foreign service officer, George Kennan, and the concept entailed "the adroit and vigilant application of counterforce" at every point where Russia attempted to expand its circle of influence. Full-scale war was not contemplated. Indeed, the proponents of containment hoped never to engage the Russians face to face and never to involve nuclear weapons. Rather, a series of limited wars and wars of nerves were envisaged, many of them to be fought "second-hand" for the superpowers by other peoples or by the United Nations. Containment, in essence, meant a patient snuffing out of sparks before they ignited a third world war. The strategy rested on the belief that if communism did not grow, it would eventually mellow or even wither and die.

A vital aspect of containment was the creation and maintainence of sufficient strength, both material and ideological, in the non-Communist world to resist Soviet pressures. President Harry S Truman took the first step in this direction on March 12, 1947, when he announced that the United States would not stand by and watch Greece and Turkey fall to the Communists. "I believe," Truman told the Congress, "that it must be the policy of the United States to support free peoples who are resisting attempted subjugation by armed minorities or outside pressures." The President further suggested that totalitarianism was "nurtured by misery and want." It followed that the United States could support freedom by economic and financial aid to hard-pressed peoples. The Truman Doctrine resulted in the immediate appropriation of $400 million in foreign aid for Greece and Turkey, and eventually it ended the Communist revolutions in those countries. America's security, it seemed certain, could not be divorced from that of the free world as a whole.

On June 5, 1947, three months after Truman set forth his doctrine, Secretary of State George C. Marshall proposed a broader plan for helping Europe recover from the ravages of war. Directed at the causes rather than the symptoms, the Marshall Plan called for the commitment of billions of dollars to fight poverty, increase production and trade, and promote economic cooperation in Europe. The long-range objective was to create a social and economic setting conducive to free institutions. Surprisingly, the Soviet Union was initially included in America's program for European recovery. "Our policy," Marshall declared, "is directed not against any country or doctrine but against hunger, poverty, desperation, and chaos." Yet after just one preliminary meeting of the nations involved, the Russians abandoned the attempt to cooperate with the West. A few months later, in the fall of 1947, they announced their own plan for helping the world: The Cominform, a new agency dedicated to the extension of communism, would assist any nation in launching a Communist revolution. A demonstration of what the Russians had in mind occurred February 25, 1948, when a coup d'etat and several key assassinations and convenient suicides gave Communists control of Czechoslovakia. The next month the United States Congress answered with the first of what in time amounted to $12 billion in appropriations under the Marshall Plan.

The next move in the cold war chess game was Russia's, and on June 24, 1948, she blockaded the divided city of Berlin, which lay deep in the Soviet-occupied part of Germany. This meant that the American, French, and British zones of Berlin, and the 2 million people who lived there, were isolated behind the Iron Curtain. The Western nations faced a crisis. They could not afford to yield to this show of Russian strength if communism was to be contained; neither could they risk a major war by invading Russian-held Germany. The way out of the dilemma was an airlift that supplied West Berlin for 321 days, until Russia lifted the blockade. It was a dramatic demonstration of the value of patience and determination and of the vitality of the non-Communist world. The Berlin airlift helped inspire the founding of the North Atlantic Treaty Organization (NATO), which established mutual defense arrangements among twelve nations on April 4, 1949. But Americans still preferred to fight with dollars rather than bullets, and President Truman's Point 4 Program early the same year extended the Marshall Plan concept to the entire underdeveloped world. Russia's detonation of an atomic bomb in September 1949, however, struck fear into the hearts of men everywhere, posing as it did the threat of a nuclear holocaust that would leave few survivors on any side.

By this time Neil Armstrong was preparing to take an active role in the cold war. The chain of events began innocently enough in the spring of 1947 when Armstrong rushed home from high school with news that he had won a scholarship in the United States Navy Air Cadet program. His mother became so excited at the news that she dropped a jar of raspberries on her foot and broke a toe. But the Armstrong family could not have been happier. For years a college education for Neil and the other children had seemed like one of the many casualties of the depression. Now Neil had a chance. Although he would have preferred the Massachusetts Institute of Technology (to which he applied unsuccessfully), he gladly enrolled at Purdue University in West Lafayette, Indiana, in the fall. Armstrong's major in aeronautical engineering was demanding, but he managed to find time to join a fraternity, play the baritone horn in the Purdue marching band, write a musical score for a variety show, and preside over the campus flying club. He also took time during his freshman year to complete the requirements for the Eagle rank in the Boy Scouts. Armstrong was not the kind of person to stop short of a goal.

By the terms of his scholarship, Armstrong interrupted his college career after two years for a tour of active duty with the Navy. While in the service, he turned his principal hobby into a vocation. The Navy first sent him to Pensacola, Florida, for flight training. By the time he won his wings in 1950, a chain of events in the Far East had produced an eruption in the cold war that would soon demand his talents. The area of contention was the Korean peninsula. Japan held Korea during World War II, and at the conclusion of that conflict Russia, which entered the war in the Pacific only a week before Japan surrendered, and the United States began joint occupation. The 38th parallel of latitude was the dividing line between the zones. Eventually, the American leadership expected, all troops could be withdrawn and the Koreans allowed to establish a free and unified nation.

For a few years immediately after the war the joint occupation of Korea worked satisfactorily. But to the north, in China, a civil war between Mao Tse-tung's Communists and Chiang Kai-shek's Nationalists cast lengthening shadows over Korea. In 1949 the Chinese Communists prevailed; the Nationalist government was driven to the island of Formosa. At about the same time, the bulk of the American force left South Korea. The way was now clear for Communist expansion, and on June 25, 1950, North Korean troops crossed the 38th parallel in an effort to conquer South Korea. They almost succeeded. The forces of the United Nations, whose Security Council had voted to resist the North Korean aggression on a day when the Russian delegate was not present, dug in at the very tip of the Korean peninsula and stopped the invasion. In September the tide turned in the UN's favor as the American General Douglas MacArthur landed an amphibious force behind the enemy lines. Oblivious to the tactics of containment and intent only on pressing for total victory with nuclear weapons, MacArthur was dismissed in April 1951 by President Truman. Thereafter the Korean War, carefully limited in size and weaponry, ground on for two more years while peace negotiations took place. The settlement of June 26, 1953, left North and South Korea in approximately the same geographical positions they had occupied three years earlier. But communism had been contained in the severest test to that date.

Neil Armstrong had no sooner qualified to fly in combat than he was ordered to Korea. He was nineteen years old. There were the usual soul searchings. But as a pilot of Phantom jets based on the carrier *Essex*, Armstrong must have killed people. Time and again, seventy-eight times in all, he blazed over enemy territory, strafing concentrations of men and machines. In the course of his duty, Armstrong collected three Air Medals and, almost inevitably, some close brushes with death. "Every day," he recalled, "was an unusual experience. You see that big orange puff from the antiaircraft gun, then see the shell whiz by the cockpit—believe me, it's an experience." On one occasion his jet limped back to the *Essex* riddled with bullet holes and missing a wing tip. On another, antiaircraft fire knocked out the landing system and much of the controlling mechanism of Armstrong's plane. Characteristically calm under pressure, he veered the streaking aircraft back toward South Korea, waited until he thought he was over friendly territory, and parachuted safely into a rice paddy. A few days later he was airborne again in a new Phantom. Armstrong left Korea with a reputation as one of the nation's hottest pilots.

When Neil Armstrong returned from Korea in 1953 to resume his career as a Purdue undergraduate, he found the nation relatively content under the leadership of the principal hero of World War II, Dwight D. Eisenhower. After twenty years of Democratic Presidents and grandiose reform programs like Roosevelt's New and Truman's Fair Deal, Eisenhower was content to steer the country as he liked to steer a golf ball—straight down the middle. His goal was normality. If it resembled that of Warren G. Harding and the other Republican Presidents who followed the Progressives and World War I, it was because there was in fact much in common between the 1920s and the 1950s. Signs of a conservative reaction were visible even before Truman's second term. In June 1947 a Republican-dominated Congress reversed the prolabor trend of the 1930s by passing the Taft-Hartley Act over Truman's veto. The legislation outlawed the closed shop, in which only members of labor unions were permitted to work, and revived the injunction as a means of breaking strikes. Conservatism was also apparent in 1947 in the passage of a proposal for a constitutional amendment forbidding a President from serving more than two terms. When it was finally ratified four years later, the Roosevelt haters received a measure of satisfaction.

Going into the election year of 1948, the Republicans appeared to have the upper hand, but a tireless, fiery campaign by Truman again frustrated Thomas E. Dewey by a narrow margin. Still, the majority of the American people were noticeably retreating from the liberal tolerance of the Roosevelt-Truman years. And just as in the aftermath of World War I, Communists became the subject of national hysteria. The major factor in this development was the growing public awareness of the cold war. Russia's achievement of nuclear capability in the fall of 1949 heightened public anxieties, particularly when it became known that Soviet espionage played a crucial role in this process. In the most shocking exposure, Whittaker Chambers, an admitted Russian spy turned state's witness, implicated Alger Hiss, a one-time State Department official. Liberals rushed to defend Hiss, much as they had defended Sacco and Vanzetti in the 1920s. But further investigation, spearheaded by a young California congressman named Richard M. Nixon, led to Hiss's conviction on a charge of perjury, and to the discrediting of liberalism. Another headline case in 1950 revealed how scientist Klaus Fuchs had systematically handed atomic secrets to the Russians throughout the 1940s.

In view of this espionage it seemed foolish to many Americans to adopt anything but an attitude of unswerving suspicion and hatred toward Communists. Particularly during the early 1950s, when young Americans like Neil Armstrong were putting their lives on the line in Korea, the fires of emotional hate burned brightly. The American who benefited most from this paranoia was the junior senator from Wisconsin, Joseph R. McCarthy. In a speech at Wheeling, West Virginia, February 9, 1950, McCarthy claimed to be in possession of a list of fifty-seven avowed Communists who worked for the Department of State. A series of similar charges followed, and McCarthy quickly assumed the role of the dragon slayer. Reasonable men, led by President Truman, might dismiss him as an unprincipled demagogue, but there was no denying his power. Public opinion polls revealed that more than half the American people approved of McCarthy and his virulent anticommunism. Those who did not were frequently smeared with charges of being Communist sympathizers and found their credibility and their careers permanently damaged.

In the spring of 1954, Joe McCarthy met his match when he attempted to implicate the United States Army in a Communist plot. The hearings were televised nationally. At the Phi Delta Theta fraternity at Purdue, Armstrong joined the throngs who peered intently at the flickering image of a man running out of lies. Indeed, the Army-McCarthy hearings marked the first time that television exerted a shaping influence on history. Yet many Americans were sorry to see McCarthy broken. For a time he had offered an alternative to the frustrations of the cold war. Substantive or not, his crusade created a cause that gave millions of uncertain people something in which to believe.

The election of Eisenhower in 1952 capped the trend toward conservatism. Running on a famous smile and the slogan "I Like Ike," the old soldier crushed the Democrats' urbane and eloquent candidate, Adlai E. Stevenson, the Governor of Illinois. Just as in 1828, when frontiersman Andrew Jackson defeated the Harvard-trained aristocrat John Quincy Adams, and in 1872, when newspaper editor Horace Greeley lost to the Union hero Ulysses S. Grant, the man of ideas proved no match for the man of action. Eisenhower well summarized the nation's traditional anti-intellectualism when he defined an intellectual as someone "who takes more words than are necessary to tell more than he knows." For others, it was sufficient to dismiss Stevenson and his liberal-intellectual followers as "eggheads." But as Neil Armstrong, the budding aeronautical engineer, was beginning to appreciate, the increasing complexity of American civilization was also increasing the need for intelligence and expertise.

While Armstrong struggled toward the degree he received from Purdue in June 1955, Eisenhower lived up to his conservative billing. He appointed a General Motors executive, Charles Wilson, to the position of secretary of defense. Wilson's biases were so ingrained he could not even understand the uproar which greeted a casual statement that he had always believed that "what was good for our country was good for General Motors, and vice versa." Another millionaire headed the Department of the Treasury, and Eisenhower's secretary of the interior, ex-Chevrolet dealer Douglas McKay, frankly stated that the Republicans were "in the saddle as an Administration representing business and industry." The President himself subscribed to the Whig theory of politics. In his view, Roosevelt and Truman had dangerously increased the power of the executive branch of the federal government at the expense of the Congress, the courts, and the states. Eisenhower deplored the Presidential steamrolling of the early New Deal and Roosevelt's later efforts to pack the Supreme Court. Deliberately refusing to cast the shadow of his office over Capitol Hill, the President hid his preferences behind the orderly veneer of an efficient, military-style staff.

The other hallmark of Eisenhower's domestic policy was a preference for economic stability with as little federal management as possible. For him, as for Herbert Hoover and Calvin Coolidge, free enterprise was the taproot of America's strength. Eisenhower distrusted the government's entrance into the nation's socioeconomic life with projects like the Tennessee Valley Authority. Such developments represented "creeping socialism," and in 1954 and 1955 the Eisenhower Administration unsuccessfully attempted to provide a private alternative to TVA hydropower with the Dixon-Yates contract for a steam generating facility. The Republicans did manage, however, to reduce the federal budget by 10 percent, and they allowed economic controls imposed during the Korean War and some New Deal agencies to expire. But overall, Eisenhower accepted far more of the New Deal than he rejected. Especially after his second electoral victory, another landslide over Stevenson in 1956, he quietly abandoned the ideal of a balanced budget when economic recession threatened. Just like Roosevelt, Eisenhower loosened credit, increased subsidies, reduced taxes, and raised federal spending in an effort to pump vigor into the economy. Even the arch-conservative Secretary of Agriculture, Ezra Taft Benson, was obliged to relent and pay out billions of dollars in an abortive effort to support farm prices. This compensatory fiscal policy ended the recessions of 1953, 1957, and 1960, but it is certain that the Eisenhower Republicans regretted every departure from the balanced budget and the ideal of federal nonintervention. Their years in office clearly marked a retrenchment after the bold experimentation of the Roosevelt-Truman decades.

Neil Armstrong found little to criticize about the Eisenhower administrations. In the first place, he was not intensely interested in politics. When he did think about it, he tended to go along with the Republicanism of his parents and to appreciate Eisenhower's efforts to preserve an even-keeled social and economic environment conducive to the building of modest savings and a family. Such considerations became important to Armstrong after he added a new interest to music and flying. Janet Shearon was a beauty queen at Purdue and a member of the Chi Omega sorority. A home economics major, she had a number of early-morning laboratory courses and met Neil in the chilly Indiana dawns as he delivered campus newspapers. Each admired the other's industry. A further bond was Janet's considerable knowledge of airplanes. After almost two years of admiration, Armstrong finally asked her for a date. "He is not," Janet later remarked, "one to rush into anything." They were married in January 1956.

Armstrong left Purdue with a degree in aeronautics and a good reputation. One of his professors recalled that "he was a good student, not outstanding, but quite good, very thorough. I . . . made a notation in my grade book: 'completes work when others do not.'" Such recommendations and Armstrong's skill as a pilot secured him a job after graduation in June 1955 with the National Advisory Council on Aeronautics at the Lewis Propulsion Laboratory in Cleveland, Ohio. But the densely populated Middle West was not the best place to test the experimental aircraft NACA assigned him. Armstrong soon found himself bound for Edwards Air Force Base, California, and the wide-open spaces of the Mojave Desert. At the High Speed Flight Center located at Edwards, Armstrong worked as a civilian test pilot as well as an engineer and researcher. His specialties became supersonic fighter planes, paragliders, and rocket aircraft piggybacked aloft by larger, slower airplanes. In one of them, the X-15, Armstrong frequently flew to the edge of space, going as high as 40 miles at speeds of up to 4000 miles per hour.

There were risks in the business, of course. On several occasions Armstrong's experimental plane failed to function upon release in mid-air, but Neil managed to start the engines even as he plummeted toward earth. At least there were no antiaircraft guns, and Armstrong relished total involvement in a world of flight. His ability was unquestioned. "He flies an airplane," one admirer remarked, "like he's wearing it." Flashing over the mountain cabin that he and Janet called home while he flew out of Edwards, Neil like to roll his plane and waggle its wings at her and their infant son. Watching with binoculars, she waved back. Recreation for Armstrong also came in the air, in nonmotorized gliders that rode the great uplifts created by the Tehachapi Mountains and the Sierra Nevada. The delicate, silent world of powerless flight appealed to his sense of privacy. Never a team-sport player or a fitness enthusiast, Armstrong saved his energies for flying, his family, and sometimes music. "I believe," he told an interviewer, "that every human being has a finite number of heartbeats available to him, and I don't intend to waste any of mine running around doing exercises."

In 1958 NACA became NASA, the National Aeronautics and Space Agency (later Administration), and Armstrong, along with America, was beginning to think about space. The roots of the space race lay buried in the same Soviet-American competition that produced the cold war and sent Neil Armstrong into the air over Korea. It was more than a question of military advantage or even technological competence. Prestige was involved. Leadership in space was thought to be a symbol of general cultural vitality. At a time when communism and democracy were competing for the allegiance of people throughout the world, this was no slight consideration.

In the early 1950s, however, the United States showed little interest in beating the Russians into space. The budget-conscious Eisen-

Pictured here at the final dinner of the Crimea (Yalta) Conference of February
are (left to right, center) Joseph Stalin, Franklin D. Roosevelt, and Winston Chur
Others in the party are U.S. Secretary of State Edward R. Stettinius, Jr. (
British Foreign Minister Anthony Eden (partly hidden by Stettinius, rear)
Russian Foreign Minister Vyacheslav Molotov (far right). President Roos
clearly shows the strains of his office. He died two months later, saddened b
realization that the Yalta meetings had not laid the foundations for world

The moon's orbit around the earth during the Apollo 11 mission is shown here
by its different positions during the flight. The bottom shows the moon's position at
launch; the middle shows positions during the flight; and the top shows
positions at splashdown. The numbered positions show fifteen key steps: (1) liftoff,
(2) earth orbit checkout, (3) injection on path to the moon, (4) turnaround and
docking, (5) course correction, (6) retro-firing for lunar orbit, (7) elliptical lunar orbit,
(8) lunar module separates, (9) landing on the moon, (10) ascent stage docking,
(11) ascent stage is left in orbit, (12) injection on homeward trip, (13) course
correction, (14) service module is jettisoned, and (15) chutes lower
men to earth splashdown.

Sea-based aircraft were an important component of the United Nations offensive power during the Korean War, 1950–1953. Neil Armstrong flew seventy-eight missions off a similar carrier in the course of the conflict.

One of the most valuable dividends of space exploration was the attainment of a new perspective for viewing the earth. The billions of people who saw this photograph by the moon-orbiting Apollo 8 astronauts had dramatic evidence of the smallness and the fragility of man's only home. The need for environmental protection was self-evident, as was the need for brotherhood among men. Especially for Americans, accustomed to "limitless" frontiers, the view from the moon was shocking and sobering.

hower Administration, in particular, regarded a space program as nothing more than an expensive and useless stunt. Only a few military leaders and scientists kept the dream of space alive in these years. Even after Russia astonished the world on October 4, 1957, by placing Sputnik I in orbit around the earth, many Americans remained blasé. "One small ball in the air," Eisenhower casually remarked, "does not raise my apprehensions, not one iota." A White House staffer added that Sputnik was merely "a silly bauble . . . a bubble in the sky." And Sherman Adams, the President's closest aide, disclaimed any interest in "an outer space basketball game." Still, for other Americans who watched the new "star" move across the night sky, Sputnik was cause for both awe and alarm. Neil Armstrong was unquestionably among those who watched and for whom the manmade satellite was a source of both wonder and challenge.

The most insistent opposition to Republican indifference toward space came, appropriately, from the Democrats. Leading the cry of "Shame!" after Sputnik was the powerful Democratic floor leader in the Senate, Lyndon Baines Johnson of Texas. For Johnson, success in space was not only imperative in the context of the cold war; it was also a way to embarrass the Republicans and perhaps ease his own way into the White House. As chairman of a Senate subcommittee on preparedness that opened hearings in November 1957 shortly after Sputnik II successfully carried live dogs into space, Johnson paraded a succession of scientists and strategists before the nation. The mounting concern reached frenzied proportions after December 6, 1957, when the United States' highly publicized Vanguard rocket, designed to orbit our first satellite, collapsed in a burning heap after rising only inches from the launching pad. From around the world came guffaws of ridicule and labels like "Flopnik," "Kaputnik," and "Stayputnik." At home it was a source of general embarrassment as well as a goad to action. When General James Doolittle, chairman of the Scientific Advisory Board, suggested that Sputnik was the result of Russian children working harder in school, Americans responded with a frantic campaign for educational excellence. One result was the National Defense Education Act of 1958. Russia, meanwhile, continued its disturbing string of space successes. A satellite was placed in orbit around the moon on the second anniversary of Sputnik I.

Early in 1958 Lyndon B. Johnson, already running hard for the

1960 Democratic nomination, delivered his own version of the State of the Union address. Space figured prominently in his remarks, and he turned to history to reinforce them. "The Roman Empire controlled the world because it could build roads," Johnson argued. "Later, when men moved to the sea, the British Empire was dominant because it had ships. Now the Communists have established a foothold in outer space." He hardly needed to draw the conclusion that "total control over earth lies somewhere out in space." It was a question, in Johnson's mind, of who would achieve this control—the enslaving Russians or the American children of light and liberty. If this juxtaposition was simplistic and self-serving, it was also the staple ingredient in the American concept of mission since John Winthrop extolled his "city upon a hill." As for American scientists, Edward Teller, the father of the hydrogen bomb, solemnly stated that the nation's post-Sputnik situation was as great an emergency as that which obtained after Albert Einstein alleged Hitler's Germany was close to completing an atomic weapon. But Eisenhower still had doubts. Rising to a statesmanship rare in the history of the American Presidency, the former general concluded his two terms with a farewell warning for the nation "to guard against the acquisition of unwarranted influence . . . by the military-industrial complex." He was afraid that a combination of generals backed by their clients in industry and their patrons in Congress would pressure the nation into a premature ordering of priorities in which space came first.

On the other side, the urgency of the space boosters' message was heightened by continuing friction with the Soviet Union. The efforts of Neil Armstrong and his colleagues that ended the Korean War in 1953, it is true, lowered the temperature of the cold war, but it continued to simmer. One reason was the emergence of a comprehensive new Soviet strategy aimed at winning over the uncommitted and, for the most part, underdeveloped world to communism. Joseph Stalin, before his death in March 1953, and his eventual successor Nikita S. Khrushchev made it clear that Russia welcomed revolutionary movements anywhere. Soviet economic and technical assistance stood ready to support those who challenged the control of the older colonial powers. If that challenge took a Communist form, so much the better. An important aspect of this plan was providing evidence that Russia, rather than America, was the power of the future. To that end Moscow delighted in pointing out that the growth rate of the Soviet economy in the 1950s averaged three times that of the United States. Breakthroughs in weaponry, led by the intercontinental ballistic missile and the hydrogen bomb (1953), and in space also supported these claims.

In response, American foreign policy changed from containment to the harder lines of liberation and massive retaliation. Richard Nixon, running hard for the vice-presidency with Eisenhower in 1952, forecast the new emphasis when he attacked Stevenson as "Adlai the appeaser . . . who got a Ph.D. from Dean Acheson's [Truman's Secretary of State] College of Cowardly Communist Containment." In place of this allegedly soft strategy, Nixon and Eisenhower's Secretary of State, John Foster Dulles, argued for an offensive against communism. They even went so far as to suggest the desirability of using nuclear weapons and of striking directly at the Soviet Union rather than at the fringes of Communist influence. Russians, these Republicans believed, could be intimidated by a show of force. The "necessary art," Dulles maintained, was "the ability to get to the verge without getting into the war." "If you are scared to go to the brink," he added, "you are lost."

Such "brinks," and the opportunity for what came to be called "brinksmanship," appeared with frightening frequency in the 1950s and lent substance to the argument that the United States must not be second best in space. One of the more explosive meeting places of the cold war was Indochina. No sooner had an uneasy peace settled over Korea than France found its colonial interests in this teeming corner of Southeast Asia threatened. Despite massive transfusions of American supplies and dollars, Communist revolutionaries led by Ho Chi Minh and backed by China and Russia threatened to overrun the French. In March 1954 France informed the United States that it could not hold its fortress at Dien Bien Phu without direct assistance. Dulles and Nixon, among others, were willing to intervene on a Korean scale if necessary, but for the time being cooler heads prevailed. Eisenhower allowed Dien Bien Phu to fall on May 7. In the settlement following French withdrawal, the independent nations of Laos, Cambodia, and Vietnam were organized but without the free elections Americans expected. Vietnam was divided at the 17th parallel: a Communist regime held North Vietnam, and an Amercian-supported regime held the south. Another Korea seemed in the making, particularly after September 8, 1954, when Dulles engineered a mutual-defense scheme known as the Southeast Asia Treaty Organization (SEATO)—an Asian counterpart of NATO. Thereafter the United States was committed to maintaining the balance of power on the very doorstep of the Communist world.

The situation in Indochina was bad enough, but Americans soon found that the cold war had to be fought on a worldwide front. To the north and east of Indochina lay the island of Taiwan (Formosa), from which Chiang Kai-Shek continued to voice his determination to return to the Chinese mainland. Any such move threatened to implicate his supporters, chiefly the United States, in a major Asian war. Half a world away, Germany remained divided and the source of continuing tension as thousands of refugees from Russian-controlled East Germany fled to the west. There was even an abortive attempt at revolution in East Germany. In Hungary an uprising in October 1956 proved successful in overthrowing the local Communist party. Although the Hungarians immediately appealed to the United Nations for support, Russia moved quickly with troops and tanks. For once John Foster Dulles was not willing to risk a confrontation, and the non-Communist world stood by as the Hungarians were brutally forced back into the Soviet camp. Then the focus of the cold war shifted to the Suez Canal, where Russia's support of Egypt and the military strong man Gamal Abdel Nasser threatened freedom of access to this vital waterway. In the ensuing war between Israel, France, and Great Britain, on the one hand, and a Soviet-backed Egypt on the other, the United States managed to alienate both sides. Finally, in the late 1950s, the cold war reached the New World in a series of Communist uprisings in Latin America. For the United States, the most serious of these occurred only 90 miles away on the island of Cuba in 1959 and placed the charismatic young Fidel Castro in power. Almost immediately he turned to Russia for guidance and support.

Dwight Eisenhower was seriously ill in the closing years of his second administration, but he retained the hope that as a final contribution to his country and the world, he could be the prime mover in the creation of a permanent peace. As part of this endeavor, a series of international meetings on disarmament, nuclear test bans, and the issue of Germany and Berlin received full American support. They were carefully pyramided to lead to "summit" meetings in which the leaders of the superpowers could sit down to talk together. The first of these, at Geneva in 1955, gave promise of breaking the vicious circle of American-Soviet relations since World War II. An informal meeting between Eisenhower and Khrushchev on American soil in 1959 raised hopes still further. But just before the next summit in May 1960, the United States was embarrassed by Russia's announcement that an American high-altitude reconnaissance plane, a U-2, had been shot down 1200 miles inside the Soviet Union. For a few days the Eisenhower Administration had no comment, but on May 7 Khrushchev announced that the pilot of the U-2 was alive and had confessed to espionage. To his credit, Eisenhower quickly accepted full responsibility for the mission and saw plans for the summit and for peace crash along with the U-2.

At the beginning of the 1960s Neil Armstrong was keenly aware of the possibility of space flight and its role in the cold war, but he honestly believed that the way to space was through the kind of high-speed aircraft he was testing over the California desert. For the rocket-launched capsule of Project Mercury, which Eisenhower reluctantly approved, and the original seven astronauts selected in 1959, Armstrong initially had little respect. The astronauts, he felt, were "babes in the woods." Coming from a man who had flown higher than any American, in the X-15, this sentiment was understandable. So was Armstrong's annoyed comment that he "tended to regard the Mercury people as inexperienced intruders in our business." He was therefore surprised and rather shocked in September 1962 when NASA notified him that he had been selected for the second group of astronauts. He accepted, with some reluctance. But he quickly discovered that by this time the federal government was fully committed to space via rockets and was shooting for the moon. A sheepish Armstrong reassessed his earlier opinion of the rocketry group: "I am frank to admit I gave them too little credit."

The developments that brought Neil Armstrong into the astronaut program and put his country on the path to the moon began in 1960 with the election of Senator John F. Kennedy of Massachusetts to the Presidency. His opponent, Vice-President Richard M. Nixon, lost in one of the closest elections in American history. Out of a total of 68.3 million popular votes cast, Kennedy's margin of victory was just over 100,000. Many observers felt the delicate balance of national favor tipped his way as the result of a series of television debates with his Republican opponent. Before an audience of 70 million, Kennedy proved a master of the medium. Dynamic, articulate, handsome, only forty-three years of age, he seemed to offer the nation, to use one of his own favorite words, renewed "vigor." As far as space was concerned, Kennedy had no strong feelings. But he was convinced that the relative conservatism of the Eisenhower administrations cost the United States precious ground in its race with the Soviet Union for world prestige and power. In Kennedy's view the first requirement of the 1960s was to "get the country moving again," to define and attack a "New Frontier." In this context, the moon loomed increasingly larger.

Kennedy had been in office less than three months when news reached the United States that on April 12, 1961 the Russians had succeeded in orbiting the first man in space, Yuri Gagarin. The cosmonaut's ride lasted only 108 minutes—one complete orbit of the earth —but it struck at the heart of the New Frontier mentality and the vigorous Kennedy image. On April 14 the President summoned his closest advisors to consider what had suddenly become a crisis in space research and development. He did not, it appeared, intend to be second best in this race or any other. "What can we do?" Kennedy pleaded. "Can we go around the moon before them? Can we put a man on the moon before them? . . . if somebody can just tell me how to catch up. There is nothing more important." The cost, he made it plain, was a minor consideration.

Three days later, April 17, 1961, Kennedy's anxiety about making a dramatic demonstration of American superiority increased sharply when an American-supported invasion of Cuba by Cuban refugees opposed to Fidel Castro's Communist government failed miserably at the Bay of Pigs. The President's willingness to assume full blame for the fiasco did not lessen its unfavorable impact on the image of his administration. Coupled with the Gagarin flight, the Bay of Pigs seemed to show that Kennedy's stirring ideals were just so many words. The tide had to be turned. On April 19 Kennedy met for forty-five minutes with his vice-president and a long-time advocate of space flight, Lyndon B. Johnson. Their conversation was secret, but according to a top Kennedy aide, when Johnson left, America "was already halfway to the moon." The formal commitment came a month later, after Alan Shepard broke the United States man-in-space barrier with a 15-minute flight. On May 25 Kennedy told an assembled Congress: "I believe this nation should commit itself to achieving the goal, before this decade is out, of landing a man on the moon and returning him safely to the earth." Part of the commitment, of course, was financial; even conservative estimates of the cost of preparing for and executing a manned lunar landing were in the neighborhood of 20 *billion* dollars.

Misgivings about Kennedy's moon decision of 1961 were mostly overridden in the next several years by considerations of the ongoing cold war. After Eisenhower's hopes for "peaceful coexistence" with the Communist world foundered on the U-2 debacle and the collapse of the 1960 summit meeting, American-Russian tensions rose sharply. Indochina continued to fester. When Kennedy entered the White House in January 1961, a bitter civil war was in progress in the swamps and jungles of Laos. And despite American aid that amounted to $150 for every Laotian, pro-Western government in that country remained in jeopardy. The same was true in neighboring South Vietnam, where a Communist guerrilla group, the Viet Cong, was challenging the republican regime. The government of Ho Chi Minh in North Vietnam supported the Viet Cong. The United States, in turn, rushed to the support of the incumbent Diem administration with supplies and, after 1961, with military advisers and special "green beret" troops. But in November 1963 Diem was overthrown and murdered by his own people. By this time it was becoming evident that Vietnam had the potential for entangling the United States to a far greater extent than any previous cold war commitment.

In Europe, the inability of the superpowers to deal with the problems of a conquered Germany continued to undermine peace. For fifteen years an ideological wall had separated East and West Germany as well as the Soviet and Western-controlled sectors of Berlin. In August 1961, after a summit-level showdown between Kennedy and Khrushchev in Vienna, the Russians transformed the wall into concrete and barbed wire. They also vowed to drive the West out of Berlin by the end of the year. They were concerned that since World War II over 3 million East Germans fled from Communist control and sought refuge in the Western sector. In the battle for world prestige, this unequivocal demonstration of communism's lack of appeal had the same effect on the Soviet ego as Sputnik and the Gagarin flight had on America's. The Berlin Wall stopped the flow of defectors, but Kennedy's firmness caused Khrushchev to lift his end-of-the-year deadline.

As the 1961 Berlin crisis showed, neither Russia nor the United States was willing, in the last analysis, to press to the point of direct war. Both sides realized that given their possession of nuclear bombs thousands of times more powerful than those which devastated Hiroshima and Nagasaki, there would be no victors and few survivors of an unlimited war. This bipartisan realization also figured in the settlement of the Cuban Missile Crisis of 1962. This frightening confrontation arose as a result of Soviet delivery to Cuba of long-range missiles capable of reaching most of the United States. When U-2 reconnaissance flights in October confirmed the presence of the missile stations, Kennedy faced the most serious possibility of a world war since 1945. His response was to establish a naval blockade of Cuba, demand the removal of existing missiles, and inform Khrushchev in no uncertain terms that a Cuban missile attack on the United States would result in instant, direct retaliation on the Soviet Union. For several days a war of nerves prevailed. Then the Russians and Cubans backed down and removed the missiles. It was a great day for Kennedy's foreign policy, but the real credit belonged to universal fear at the prospect of a nuclear holocaust. Fear also inspired the 1963 treaty banning atmospheric nuclear tests that ended the radioactive fallout panic.

By the summer of 1963 John Kennedy's style in international politics had matured considerably. He came to see the arrogance and the danger inherent in the assumption of American infallibility. "We must face the fact," he declared, "that the United States is neither omnipotent nor omniscient—that we are only six percent of the world's population—that we cannot impose our will upon the other ninety-four percent of mankind—that we cannot right every wrong or reverse each adversity—and that therefore there cannot be an American solution to every world problem." The corollary of this belief was the acceptance of the ideas and institutions of others. "If we cannot end now all our differences," the President asserted, "at least we can help make the world safe for diversity." Here was a direct repudiation of Woodrow Wilson's ideal of safeguarding worldwide

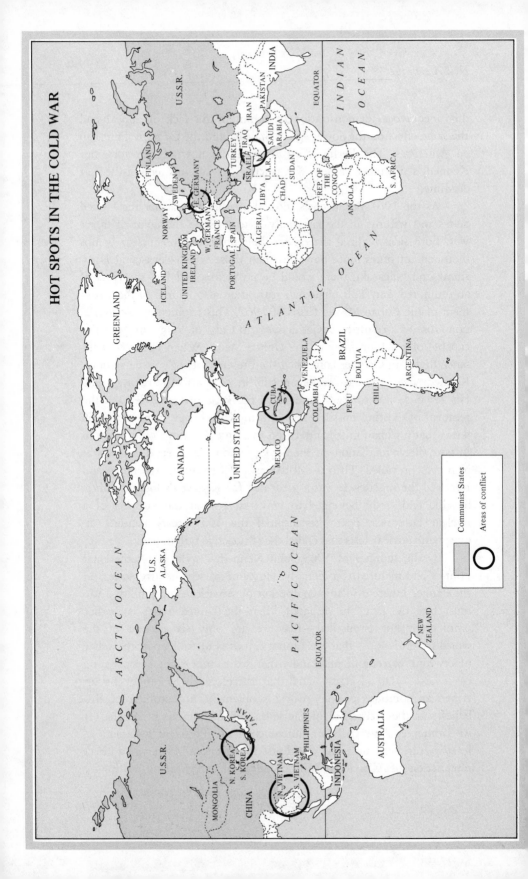

HOT SPOTS IN THE COLD WAR

democracy and of the cold war strategy of liberation. Kennedy's position was essentially an application of the philosophy that inspired his 1961 inaugural address, in which he acknowledged the impossibility of achieving perfection but still affirmed it as a goal. It was a new, sadder-but-wiser liberalism, one founded on the real rather than the ideal. The consequences for the cold war were apparent at once. Khrushchev termed the President's "diversity" speech the greatest by an American since Franklin D. Roosevelt. Shortly thereafter, in September 1963, he agreed to the test-ban treaty.

Kennedy's attitude toward space also matured measurably during his years in the White House. His decision to go to the moon in the spring of 1961 was the shoot-from-the-hip response of a frightened, angry man. By 1962, however, the President was able to separate the space venture from the cold war context. "We choose to go to the moon," he explained, "not because [it is] easy, but because [it is] hard; because that goal will serve to organize and measure the best of our energies and skills." Later in this speech Kennedy referred to the famous mountaineer who declared that he wanted to climb Mount Everest " 'because it is there.' " "Well," Kennedy concluded, "space is there, and . . . the moon and the planets are there, and new hopes for knowledge and peace are there." In September 1963 the President went to the United Nations to propose that the moon mission become a cooperative venture of the earth as a whole. A race with Russia, he implied, involved both needless duplication of effort and prolongation of the old selfish nationalism. And then Kennedy died. Like three American Presidents before him, he fell victim to an assassin's bullet. The news of the shooting on November 22, 1963 by a crazed fanatic, who himself was shot before a trial could elicit a full explanation, plunged the country into a paroxysm of shame and grief. For many it seemed that much of the promise of American life died with its young President. "He stood," one editorial commented, "for excellence in an era of indifference—for hope in an era of doubt. He had confidence in man and gave men confidence in the future."

Neil Armstrong was living in the space-boom community of El Lago, Texas (near Houston), the day John Kennedy died in Dallas. His selection as an astronaut required that he move near NASA's Manned Spacecraft Center, the training ground for spacemen and the home of Mission Control. The new job also brought a degree of public attention appalling to the quiet, introverted Armstrong. Ever since John Glenn had orbited the earth three times in February 1962, space had captured the American imagination. The astronauts became the new frontiersmen, pioneer heroes in a technological age. Every scrap of news about them found a ready audience.

Armstrong, however, provided lean pickings for reporters. "Silence," his wife remarked, "is a Neil Armstrong answer. The word 'no' is an argument." Others who knew the man testified that he seldom rose to any bait. "He'll smile at you," one acquaintance reported, "and you'll think he is agreeing. Later on you'll remember that he didn't say a word." But if he did not make good copy, in other respects Armstrong fitted NASA's bill to perfection. He was immensely dedicated; extraordinarily precise, efficient, and confident; cool under pressure; and quite possibly the best technical pilot in the world. Moreover, Armstrong had the white, Anglo-Saxon, Protestant, Establishment-oriented background and the clean-cut all-Americanness that NASA seemed to favor in the men who represented its multibillion dollar enterprise. Before acceptance as astronauts, a candidate and his family were thoroughly screened to ensure that they were proper symbols of middle America. In one sense exceptional, Armstrong and his colleagues were also exceptionally ordinary.

Armstrong's work at the Manned Spacecraft Center and at Cape Canaveral (Cape Kennedy after the assassination) in Florida began with assignments as a back-up command pilot. In this role, Armstrong, like an understudy in the theater, went through complete training for the actual performance in the event the principal proved unable to fulfill his assignment. But in March 1966 Armstrong moved up to the starting team as command pilot of Gemini 8. By this time Lyndon Johnson had entered the White House on his own merits by defeating conservative Republican Barry Goldwater in a landslide election victory in 1964.

The moon definitely figured in Johnson's plans for what he termed the "Great Society." So, of course, did a "War on Poverty," civil rights, Medicare, and a clean environment, but success in space was, for Johnson, an essential index of American greatness. As a result the space program forged ahead. After no less than thirteen successive failures between 1958 and 1964, unmanned American spacecraft succeeded in orbiting and landing on the moon. The data collected suggested the feasibility of a manned landing, and Congress, under Johnson's masterful prodding, responded munificently. In 1966, the year of Armstrong's debut in space, the NASA empire extended to 400,000 Americans in 120 universities and laboratories. Twenty thousand industrial firms made contributions, and the budget for 1966 alone was $5.9 billion.

The attention of this vast assembly of talent and money was focused on Armstrong and his co-pilot, David R. Scott, on March 16, 1966, as they sat on top of the rocket that was to lift Gemini 8 into earth orbit for the purpose of testing the rendezvous and docking procedure vital to a moon mission. The blastoff from Cape Kennedy was normal, and Armstrong succeeded in locating and attaching his craft to a previously orbited target satellite. But 30 minutes after docking a thruster rocket malfunction sent the coupled vehicles into a near-fatal spin. Keeping his head in a life-and-death situation, Armstrong eased the Gemini craft out of the docking alignment. The roll now increased to almost a revolution a second. Searching for a solution to the problem, Armstrong used sixteen different jets to stabilize the craft in an extraordinary application of piloting skill. Perhaps the mission could have continued its programmed three days, but a shaken Mission Control ordered reentry, and Armstrong brought his spacecraft down in the Pacific Ocean less than 11 hours after blast off.

Gemini 8 was a reminder that for all its technological sophistication, space flight was not exempt from malfunction and from fear. A more dramatic and tragic demonstration of the same point occurred on January 27, 1967, when three astronauts burned to death during a ground test of the new Apollo moonship. Shock, quickly succeeded by waves of doubt about the whole moon mission, spread through the nation. But the space program by this time had generated considerable momentum, not a small part of which was provided by the bureau-cratic-industrial complex that fed off the appropriated billions. After several rounds of investigations and angry recrimination, Apollo went ahead. The successful flight of the 180 million horsepower, $200 million Saturn V rocket on November 9, 1967, silenced most criticism of a technological nature.

From a philosophic and economic perspective, however, America's involvement in space was still subject to widespread questioning. In many minds the race riots that seared America's cities in the mid-

1960s, the emergence of a counterculture, and the escalating Vietnam War were of far greater concern than placing a man on the moon. Particularly after the assassinations of Martin Luther King on April 4, 1968, and of Presidential contender Robert F. Kennedy on June 5 of the same year, it seemed undeniable that the most challenging problems were right here on earth rather than on a satellite 238,000 miles away. In this connection, some recalled the belief of Albert Einstein that "politics is much harder than physics."

But Einstein's logic also suggested why many Americans delighted in the nation's growing space capability. For them it was a relief to look up instead of down, to confront a tangible, physical problem comparable to clearing the land of trees or building a transcontinental railroad. Such tasks, involving muscles and machines, had long been America's forte. There was comfort in doing them, in measuring progress rather than chronicling failure. And by the dark summer of 1968 when King and Kennedy died, the moon was definitely a realizable goal.

Neil Armstrong was testing a jet-powered lunar landing model that year when his next brush with death occurred. The simulator was hovering 200 feet above the ground when it suddenly and unpredictably went out of control in much the same manner as Gemini 8. Armstrong fought to recover stability as long as he dared. He finally ejected only seconds before the module crashed and burned. The next day, after treatment for minor injuries sustained when his parachute dragged him along the ground, Armstrong was back at his desk investigating what went wrong.

His impressive performance here and in the Gemini 8 emergency were not lost on NASA officials. They also were aware of the way Armstrong had responded when his house burned one night and when his two-year-old daughter died of a brain tumor. Important too was the knowledge that Armstrong was a civilian. It was therefore not especially surprising to the space community that on January 9, 1969, Armstrong was selected to command Apollo 11 and thereby to become the first man on the moon.

Apollo 11's blastoff was scheduled for July 16, and in the preceding months Neil Armstrong turned the full force of his disciplined energies to the enormous labor of preparation. The demands of the job mercifully left little time for thoughts of failure, particularly the possibility of being stranded on the moon. But it was not in Armstrong's nature to entertain doubts about himself or about his mission. "I have been in a relatively high-risk business," he told an interviewer, "all of my adult life." Yet few of the other undertakings had had such possibilities for expanding human knowledge, and this impressed the astronaut. "I have confidence," he added, "in the equipment, the planning, the training. I suspect that on a risk-gain ratio, this project would compare very, very favorably with those to which I've been accustomed in the past 20 years." Indeed, the part of the mission Armstrong dreaded most was the necessity of meeting the press. But along with his colleagues on Apollo 11, Colonel Edwin E. Aldrin and Lieutenant Colonel Michael Collins, he dutifully presented himself on July 5 for one hour of questioning. Novelist-reporter Norman Mailer was among the most perceptive of the observers. He noted immediately Armstrong's painful, hesitant manner of speaking and his preference for the unemotional, jargon-filled dialect Mailer named "computerese." But he saw other things as well. Armstrong, wrote Mailer, was "simply not like other men." Behind his thin-lipped, half-mocking smile was a quality Mailer could only label "presence." Perhaps, the novelist speculated, it came from feeling the winds of death so frequently during his thousands of hours aloft. Armstrong, at any rate, seemed "in communion with some string in the universe others did not think to play."

The question of being stranded on the moon inevitably arose in the interviews. What if the lunar module proved unable to rise from the moon's surface? "Well," Armstrong's disgust with such a question showed in his face, "that's an unpleasant thing to think about." Pressed further about what he would do with a dead engine or an overturned spaceship, Armstrong finally faced the inevitable: "at the present time we're left without recourse should that occur." As for another obvious question concerning Armstrong's relationship to Christopher Columbus, the astronaut exhibited predictable modesty. He was a team man. There were ten others who could do his job equally well. Thousands of people had contributed to and would control the mission. Armstrong refused to be a hero. The day of the interviews ended with reporters digging hard for Armstrong's philosophy of the moon flight. Why was this being done? The astronaut evaded the question, but the press, annoyed, according to Mailer, at his unimaginative submersion in aerospace jargon, gave him no peace. Finally, and awkwardly, an answer came. "I think we're going to the moon," Armstrong managed, "because it's in the nature of the human being to face challenges. It's in the nature of his deep inner soul to do those things, just as salmon swim upstream."

The July 5 interviews left Norman Mailer vaguely dissatisfied. Somehow Armstrong and his fellow astronauts did not measure up to the drama of their mission. In some ways they represented the worst, not the best, about America. "The astronauts," Mailer wrote, "were the core of some magnetic human force called Americanism, Protestantism, or Waspitude. . . . They were the knights of the Silent Majority, the Wasp emerging from human history to take us to the stars." But Wernher von Braun, the father of the Saturn rocket that would start Apollo 11 on its way to the moon, provided an alternative to Armstrong's businesslike perspective: "I think [putting a man on the moon] is equal in importance to that moment in evolution when aquatic life came crawling up on the land." The press, Mailer reported, actually applauded von Braun's remark. Here, at last, was a headline.

The man who would do that first crawling emerged from the ready room at Cape Kennedy at 6:25 A.M. on July 16, 1969. There was the accustomed calmness, the enigmatic smile, a quick wave. Then Neil Armstrong entered a van for the 3-minute ride to the launching pad. Among the million people watching the countdown in person was Martin Luther King's successor, Reverend Ralph Abernathy. He had led a Poor People's March to the Cape to protest the priorities that put the moon ahead of jobs and human dignity. But NASA persuaded Abernathy to select some of his poor people and take seats in the VIP stands with congressmen and with former President Lyndon Johnson. The hope was that while Apollo 11 was in space Americans could put aside their grievances and differences. And as the fiery Saturn lifted the spacecraft into the Florida dawn, even the severest critics were momentarily silenced. There was wonder in this beginning of a new age. "A ship of flames," observed Mailer, "is on its way to the moon."

Ralph Abernathy agreed that the launching pad was "holy ground." But, he added, "it will be more holy once we feed the hungry, care for the sick, and provide for those who do not have homes."

Other members of minority groups had less patience. Almost immediately after the launch a biracial group of protesters invaded the Manned Spacecraft Center in Texas, settled down by a dummy lunar module, and displayed placards calling for a commitment to social justice comparable in size and effectiveness to that which was speeding Armstrong to the moon.

For over 230,000 miles the flight of Apollo 11 progressed, in the NASA jargon, with "zero defects." Armstrong ran his ship, according to an official, "with an iron fist." Even the periodic telecasts from the command module were excellent, and the world was able to see how astronauts worked and relaxed. But the last 3000 feet of the mission were something else. By this time the lunar landing module *Eagle*, bearing Armstrong and Aldrin, had left Collins and the command module, *Columbia*, orbiting the moon. Descending rapidly, Armstrong trusted the computer-directed automatic guidance system until the 3000-foot level. Then he glanced out the window to get his bearings and experienced the closest thing Neil Armstrong ever felt to fear: instead of heading for the expected smooth landing ground, *Eagle* was entering a crater the size of a football field, filled with huge boulders.

A slight navigational error had left the astronauts 4 miles from their planned landing site on the southwestern shore of the dry Sea of Tranquillity. To continue on their present course was to risk landing on terrain so uneven that the *Eagle* might easily have tipped over. There was a moment of indecision. Armstrong's eyes flicked to the ABORT button in the center of his control panel. One push and *Eagle* would blast away from the descent stage and go back into lunar orbit where Collins waited in *Columbia*. But everything in Neil Armstrong's background and character resisted such a surrender. Seizing instead the horizontal and tilt control levers and abandoning the automatic landing system, the master pilot began to skim *Eagle* across the surface of the moon. As Aldrin read off data concerning the rate and progress of the descent, Armstrong searched for a safe landing site. Several possibilities proved on closer inspection to be unsuitable. Finally, only seconds from a mandatory abort situation, which would have been brought about by shortage of fuel for the descent engine, Armstrong saw a relatively flat plain and eased *Eagle* onto it. "Houston," his voice crackled back to earth, "Tranquillity Base here. The *Eagle* has landed."

Few watching the televised report of the flight of Apollo 11 realized to what extent the decade-long work of thousands of people and billions of dollars depended, in the ultimate moments, on the flying ability of Neil Armstrong. So, of course, did his life and that of Edwin Aldrin, but in this respect at least, Armstrong had been there before. In a sense Armstrong's success was a vindication of the importance of the human component. Many observers back on earth took heart from the fact that in a crisis a man, not a machine, saved the day. To this extent the traditional American conception of heroism survived the emasculating supervision of Mission Control.

The next twenty-two hours were certainly the most intensely chronicled of Neil Armstrong's life. In complete contrast to Christopher Columbus and Jim Bridger, Armstrong's moments of discovery were witnessed, via television, by an international audience estimated at 528 million. The awe-filled first step on the moon was accompanied by Armstrong's "that's one small step for [a] man; one giant leap for mankind"—words he claimed to have conceived while riding Apollo 11 on the way to the moon. Many had speculated and even bet on what the first man on the moon would say, and Armstrong surprised his critics by rising above "computerese" to make a dignified and moving statement. Next, in accordance with long-established plans, Armstrong walked on the moon, took photographs, collected samples of rock, deployed scientific instruments, received a telephone call from President Nixon, and erected an American flag, despite extensive criticism that the act perpetuated the old territorial syndrome that had frustrated peace on earth so frequently. The successful firing of the ascent engine ended man's first lunar visit, and on July 24, 1969, the Apollo 11 team, now reunited, splashed down in the Pacific Ocean.

After eighteen days of quarantine, a precaution against the possibility of moon germs, Armstrong stepped forth into the glare of a hero's welcome. Personally he found the dramatization of his performance distasteful. "If historians are fair," he said, "they won't see this flight like Lindbergh's.[1] They'll recognize that the landing is only

[1] In 1927 Charles A. Lindbergh flew nonstop and alone from New York to Paris amid the cheers of the world.

one small part of a large program." Armstrong also hoped, it would be possible for him and his family to live a "private life . . . within the context of such an achievement." He was not disappointed when poll takers found that the typical man on the street had difficulty recalling Armstrong's name a year after the landing.

But the nation that had picked up Apollo's huge tab for almost a decade demanded a hero, and Armstrong, along with Aldrin and Collins, was displayed at state dinners, ticker-tape parades, and in twenty-two foreign nations on a world tour. He was, after all, the answer to Sputnik, a trump in the cold war, and in a deeper sense, a symbol of the vitality of his civilization. As *Time* magazine editorialized, the moon landing "was a vindication of some traditional strengths and precepts in the American character and experience: perseverance, organizational skill, the willingness to respond to competition, even the belief that the United States enjoys a special destiny in the world." But, predictably, the honors that meant most to Neil Armstrong were those bestowed on him by his home town. Wapakoneta renamed its airport and a street in his honor and erected a sign on the main highway: "Wapakoneta: The Home of Neil Armstrong— First Man on the Moon." On Neil Armstrong Day he told the assembled 7000 citizens: "you are my people, and I'm proud to be one of you."

Armstrong hoped his flight into space would promote a sense of worldwide community. It was, after all, a very small planet Armstrong had looked back on from the moon, and this perspective underscored the need for gratitude, humility, and brotherhood. In his postflight speeches, Armstrong dwelled on a "spirit of Apollo," the essence of which was that man "can attack a very difficult goal and achieve it if you can all agree on what the goal is . . . and will work together to achieve that goal." Success in space, in other words, was evidence for Armstrong that no problems were beyond solution.

Despite his hopes, the "spirit of Apollo" showed signs of flagging even as the astronaut sped home from the moon. For many ordinary Americans the mission, exciting as it was, seemed totally unrelated to their everyday concerns. "My car just had $250 worth of repairs, and the price of steak is 40¢ higher than last April," a woman from Illinois wrote to *Life* magazine, and so, she added, "pardon me for not giving a darn about the moon." From a New Jersey man came the complaint, heard widely before and after, if not during, the lunar landing, that earthly problems like population control, poverty, and war should take precedence on the list of American and world priorities. "When we get down to about [problem number] 649 on the list," he concluded, "we can begin to indulge in space exploration." One answer to this kind of criticism came from a lady in Maryland: "let me remind those persons who are beating their breasts about the money spent on the moon landing instead of on poverty and city slums that, had Isabella waited to clean up the slums of Palos, Columbus would never have discovered the Western Hemisphere. And that voyage did more to alleviate the suffering of the world's poor than anything that had come before it."

Still, American opinion about Armstrong's achievement remained mixed. Norman Mailer wondered if the moon flight was "the noblest expression of a technological age, or the best evidence of its utter insanity." San Francisco columnist Herb Caen had no such doubts. He termed Apollo 11 "history's greatest ego trip." The black militant Eldridge Cleaver, speaking from exile in Africa, saw diabolical intentions in the moon shot, and denounced it as "a circus to distract people's minds from the real problems, which are here on the ground." One of these, unquestionably, was social justice, particularly for the residents of America's cities. After World War II urbanites were more and more members of lower income groups and frequently of ethnic minorities as well. Those who could afford it moved out of the center city to suburban sanctuaries. But the crime, violence, drug abuse, misgovernment, poor schools, and ill health in the inner cities remained national problems.

Those who tried to stem the tide of deterioration, like Mayor John Lindsay of New York City, realized that massive expenditures— on the order of several Apollos—would be required to resuscitate his city alone. Killing rats and rehabilitating addicts, however, had considerably less appeal to the bulk of American voters and taxpayers than exploring space. The cities continued to languish. When Neil Armstrong left the astronaut program in November 1970 and moved to Washington, D.C., to assume an administrative post in NASA's Office of Advanced Research and Technology, he placed himself in the heart of one of the nation's worst urban settings. Armstrong's salary of over $30,000 made possible an escape from the central city, but it constituted a constant background of concern, even of fear, for his kind of American.

The urban problem was just a part of a larger concern of Neil Armstrong's America: maintaining environmental quality. By the late 1960s, in fact, environment and the related concept of ecology became key indexes of American thought like faith for the Puritans and efficiency for the Progressives. Alerted by books such as Rachael Carson's *Silent Spring* (1962) and Paul Ehrlich's *The Population Bomb* (1968), and by ecocatastrophes such as the Santa Barbara oil spill of January 28, 1969, many concluded that pollution was the foremost menace to man. If the environmental problem was not solved, they reasoned, all others became inconsequential. A healthy habitat was the first prerequisite.

As an astronaut Armstrong had vivid evidence of the earth's fragility and the consequent need for responsibility. He was one of the first human beings to see the earth as a tiny blue ball hanging in an infinity of space. This experience, and the resulting color photographs, dramatized for people everywhere Adlai Stevenson's concept that the earth itself was a spaceship, needing for survival all the care and love that NASA lavished on its smaller versions. Indeed, the earth needed more because, unlike the astronauts, mankind had no second home. This was dramatized by the explosion on the 1971 Apollo 13 mission when it was 200,000 miles out on the way to the moon. With their main supplies of energy, oxygen, and water severely depleted, the astronauts barely limped back to earth. If a similar breakdown of the earth's natural life-support systems occurred, there would be no alternative for man.

On the question of avoiding ecocatastrophe, Armstrong was optimistic. He had an abiding faith in the power of technological man to preserve the ecosystem. "If we can find people skillful enough to reach the moon," he told a San Francisco convention in April 1972, "we . . . can find people to solve our environmental problems." In the same talk Armstrong stated his belief that by the end of the century man would have complete control of the weather, including the capacity to abolish natural calamities like hurricanes and droughts. Others might argue that the really fundamental solutions to environmental problems lay in man's mind, not his machines. Values were involved. Reverence might be a more crucial part of the man-nature relationship than control. But Armstrong at least spoke in a manner consistent with his education, career, and life style.

Neil Armstrong is now a professor of aerospace engineering at the University of Cincinnati. When he accepted this position in 1971, he knew it meant a final break with NASA and almost certainly the end of his chances to return to space. But the number of Americans who would do so in Armstrong's lifetime was uncertain. After Apollo 11 and several subsequent manned moon landings, the space program entered a period of relative quiescence. Earth-orbiting laboratories took precedence over the more dramatic flights to the moon. Moreover, the pressure to beat the Russians, who abandoned the competition in manned lunar landings, was gone and with it the incentive to pour billions of dollars into space. Indeed, the possibilities of collaboration with the Soviet Union in space before the end of the 1970s appeared excellent.

In early December 1971 Armstrong declared that "it is my considered judgment it is possible to land men on Mars within this century." In view of the success of the Mariner reconnaissance flights to the red planet, few challenged his opinion. But beyond the nearest planets there were immense difficulties, chiefly that of time. As Armstrong pointed out early in 1972, "By our present means, it would take sixteen centuries to reach the nearest star. . . . You'd have to provide the means whereby 100 generations could be born, live and die during the journey." And assuming Mission Control could solve even these problems, many Americans still threw the question of priorities in the face of any space proposal. From this perspective Neil Armstrong and his moon walk signify little or nothing. Yet in this connection the observation of Stanford physicist Robert Hofstadter demands attention. "In a thousand years," he remarked, "there will be few things remembered, but this will be one of them."

SELECTED READING

The Person

FARMER, GENE, and DORA JANE HAMBLIN (eds.): *First on the Moon* (1970). Documents, including transcripts of radio communications with the crew of Apollo 11.

HAMBLIN, DORA JANE: "Neil Armstrong Refuses to Waste Any Heartbeats," *Life* (July 4, 1969). A lively article based on personal interviews.

*MAILER, NORMAN: *Of a Fire on the Moon* (1970). A novelist turns journalist to interpret Apollo 11 and place it in its historical setting.

RECER, PAUL: "The Man They Chose to Be First on the Moon," *New York Post*, July 14, 1969. Useful biographical data.

The Period

*BUCHANAN, ALBERT RUSSELL: *The United States and World War II* (1964). Comprehensive coverage of diplomatic and military history.

COLE, WAYNE: *America First: The Battle Against Intervention* (1953). A study of those who opposed America's entering World War II.

*KAHIN, GEORGE M., and JOHN W. LEWIS: *The United States in Vietnam* (1967). The story of America's deepening involvement in Southeast Asia.

*LAFEBER, WALTER: *America, Russia, and the Cold War, 1945–1966* (1967). Highly interpretive.

*ROVERE, RICHARD: *Senator Joe McCarthy* (1959). The rise and fall of the most successful demagogue in recent American history.

*SCHLESINGER, ARTHUR M., JR.: *A Thousand Days* (1965). An insider's view of the John F. Kennedy Administration.

*SCHLESINGER, ARTHUR M., JR.: *The Bitter Heritage: Vietnam and American Democracy, 1941–1968* (rev. ed., 1968). A review of the antecedents and conduct of the Vietnam War.

*SPANIER, JOHN W.: *American Foreign Policy Since World War II* (3rd. ed., 1968). A solid, factual account.

YOUNG, HUGO, BRYAN SILCOCK, and PETER DUNN: *Journey to Tranquility* (1970). A study that places the entire American space effort since World War II in the context of national and international events.

* Available in paperback.

Bob Dylan

By traditional standards the figure behind the microphone at New York's prestigious Town Hall the evening of April 12, 1963, was not impressive. Thin and sallow, with long unkempt hair and wrinkled blue workshirt, he looked younger than his twenty-one years. Moreover, it was his first major concert. But soon after Bob Dylan began to riffle his guitar and sing, it was evident that in his case the traditional standards did not apply. Neither Dylan nor his youthful audience felt them to be important. In fact,

*most of Dylan's songs protested established attitudes and
long-accepted actions. In one song Dylan turned historian,
reviewing America's wars against "devils" from Indians to
Communists. These crusades had occurred, he implied, because of
the nation's smug self-righteousness. "You never ask questions," the
lyrics said, "when God's on your side." But by the time of that Town
Hall concert, Dylan and many of his contemporaries were in a
questioning mood. And through the remainder of the decade, they
became sufficiently disgusted and angry to revive American
bohemianism, support a New Left, and transform the restless
frustration of youth into a full-fledged counterculture. "For the times,"
Bob Dylan sang, "they are a-changin'!" As the Town Hall audience
rose in wildly enthusiastic ovations, it was apparent that Dylan
would be both a cause and a beneficiary—and in some ways a
casualty—of that change.*

The winters in northern Minnesota are long and brutal. The prevailing northwest wind howls across a thousand miles of pine and
prairie stretching to the Canadian Rockies and drives the temperature
many degrees below zero. At such times, civilization huddles, very
small, in the face of natural forces. Spring in the north country is a
hopeful season; the lake ice breaks up, and new leaves appear on the
birches. On May 24, 1941, Robert Allen Zimmerman was born in
Duluth.

Both sides of Dylan's family ("Zimmerman" was abandoned late
in 1959 as part of a rejection of his background) were small shopkeepers. Their hardware, furniture, and clothing stores provided
enough money to maintain a piano in the living room. When Bob was
six, the family moved from Duluth, at the western tip of Lake Superior, to Hibbing, an iron mining town of 17,000 up on the Mesabi
Range near the Canadian border. Most of Hibbing's residents were
immigrants, or the children of immigrants, with names that reflected
Scandinavian, Polish, Slavic, and Italian antecedents. Most were
Catholic. The Zimmermans, however, were Jewish, and Bob therefore
received an early taste of what it meant to be different, to be an
outsider. There were some advantages in this. As Dylan told a maga-

zine interviewer, "I see things that other people don't see. I feel things that other people don't feel." In Hibbing, such sensitivity was rare. "The thing you have to know about the Iron Range," a contemporary who knew Dylan volunteered, "is that it is very suppressed. It's astounding that Bob came out of a nonthinking area, and that's exactly what it is—narrow-minded, everyone conforming to the same point of view, the kids expected to think like their parents and be like their parents. Not much was expected of you, except to make enough to live on and raise a family and be like everyone else."

In general, this characterization could also serve to describe the United States in the decade and a half following World War II. It was a time of prudent, crewcut complacency. Even the young and energetic shunned commitment, ideas, involvement. Politics was in bad taste. Daniel Bell explored this mood in a book entitled *The End of Ideology: On the Exhaustion of Political Ideas in the Fifties.* Risks were to be minimized at all costs. The ideal was to keep one's cool, to refrain from rocking the boat or veering it off course. With the Great Depression of the 1930s and austerity of World War II still facts of enormous significance in American society, aspirations centered on security. The accepted credo emphasized a college degree, a steady job, a house in the suburbs, a family, and a station wagon. Girls were obsessed with making a "good" marriage, boys with advantageous retirement plans.

Success through competition remained a paramount virtue in the United States, but now the competitive unit was the organization rather than the individual. The person who succeeded in this setting was what *Fortune* editor William Whyte termed in 1956 "the organization man." His chief traits were loyalty to the company and a thoroughgoing conservatism. Dressed in gray flannel suit and white shirt with button-down collar, legions of junior executives practiced the art of getting ahead by getting along. Values and goals were absorbed from one's peers rather than evolved from personal preferences, a characteristic sociologist David Riesman labeled "other-direction." The perfection and omnipresence of advertising that Vance Packard described in *The Hidden Persuaders* (1957) also contributed to this standardization of attitudes and life styles. And the advent of television gave the process of social homogenization an enormous boost. Two years after the end of World War II, there were approximately 10,000 TV sets in American homes; in 1957, there were 40 *million*. By that time, the taste makers could use the new media to reach half the population simultaneously.

Bob Dylan was in the vanguard of those Americans who began to look critically at the priorities and life style of what pundits afterward dubbed the "silent generation." The hard times of the 1930s and the tension of war were not the same realities for him that they were for those even a few years older, like Neil Armstrong. To him, security and conformity seemed unimportant, even boring. Hibbing of the 1950s, Dylan told a *Playboy* columnist, "couldn't give me anything. It was very void-like . . . I didn't want to die there." But in Hibbing and places like it across the nation, where "if you were different they would pick you to pieces," as an old girlfriend of Bob's asserted, rebellion was not easy. For the adolescent Dylan, there were two alternatives. One was running away, and on this point Dylan long left a confusing trail of fact and fiction. For a number of years at the peak of his fame in the middle 1960s, he maintained that leaving home had been almost an annual occurrence for him since the age of ten. The story supported the aspiring Dylan's attempts to create the myth of himself as a modern troubadour who had seen and done practically everything before he was twenty. There were other tales about his having been an orphan from Oklahoma or having grown up following a traveling circus. Anything was preferable, it seemed, to being a Jewish storekeeper's son from Hibbing, Minnesota. But the evidence and, in soberer moments, Bob Dylan himself testify that his rebellion actually took a quite different form—withdrawal into himself and into the world of music.

Dylan began to play the family piano when he was eight. He had no formal instruction. In the next few years he applied the same trial-and-error techniques to the harmonica and a Sears Roebuck guitar. A wire neck rack enabled him to play both instruments simultaneously, and the ungainly arrangement became and remains a Dylan trademark. Without the technology that made recording and broadcasting possible, Dylan might well have ended his musical development at this point with a handful of campfire melodies. But records and radios brought the larger, constantly changing world of American popular music to his Hibbing doorstep. One of his first idols was Hank Williams, a white songwriter and guitarist whose forte was hillbilly or, as it was sometimes called, country music. Dylan bought every Williams record available and played them incessantly. Another important influence was black music, especially blues, rhythm and blues, and spirituals. The best source of these sounds in Hibbing was a Little Rock, Arkansas, midnight disk jockey show. Inspired, Dylan borrowed his father's car to travel to Minneapolis and talk to the handful of black musicians in that city.

In 1955 a film called *Blackboard Jungle* came to Hibbing. The town fathers feared the effect of its glamorous portrayal of juvenile delinquency, but for Dylan the theme song by Bill Haley and the Comets, "Rock Around the Clock," was its most memorable feature. Loud, raw, and sensual, the tune named and launched rock-and-roll music. "Hey, that's our music," the adolescent Dylan exclaimed to a friend, "that's written for us." Rock and roll seemed to be musical rebellion. It was an expression of the streets, the minorities, the young rather than the conservatories or the polished popular music industry.

Close behind Bill Haley in the mid-1950s came rock-and-roll superstars like Elvis Presley and Richard "Little Richard" Penniman. Many among the older generation despised their sound and style, but this only served to increase their appeal to Dylan and his contemporaries. And no one could deny their impact. Little Richard alone sold 32 million records in the first explosion of rock. Bob Dylan was among the most enthusiastic purchasers, and his first performances at Hibbing talent shows and high school dances had all the wild, screaming marks of Little Richard's style. But Dylan learned and grew by imitating. By the time he graduated from high school in June 1959, he had encountered and assimilated several more musical styles. One was the "talking blues" and folk balladry of Woody Guthrie. Born in 1912 in Oklahoma, Guthrie actually lived the kind of impoverished, vagabond existence Dylan tried to build into the public image of his own early life. The depression and the Dust Bowl were Guthrie's milieu, and he sang of and for the starving, the homeless, and the unemployed. Along with a Harvard dropout named Pete Seeger and a black ex-convict called Huddie Ledbetter but better known as Leadbelly, Guthrie created a people's music, songs for the underprivileged in modern America. The popularity of such folk music marked an early stage in the politicization of Bob Dylan's generation.

Guthrie and Seeger, whom Dylan discovered as his high school

graduation approached, had also dabbled in radical politics. During
the depression of the 1930s, when capitalism seemed powerless to
alleviate the misery of large segments of American society, alternate
economic and political systems attracted sympathizers. The folk singers experimented with communal living, discussed communism, and
lent their talents to the People's Artists and various other labor and
youth groups with leftist leanings. Seeger and Guthrie also popularized
the institution and the nonsense word *hootenanny* to describe a gathering of folk singers. In 1948 Seeger organized a quartet called the
Weavers and made the top of the Hit Parade with a recording of
Leadbelly's "Goodnight, Irene." But the group also did protest songs
with references to Fascist oppression and the people's struggle for
liberation. By the early 1950s these songs aroused right-wingers whose
suspicions had been whetted to near-hysteria by the anti-Communist
demagoguery of Senator Joseph R. McCarthy.[1] The word was passed
to the masters of the media that Seeger and his colleagues were unacceptable. By 1952, the Weavers found their access to a national
audience blocked.

In 1955 Pete Seeger's role in the Depression years came to the
attention of Bob Dylan's generation. The House of Representatives
Committee on Un-American Activities subpoenaed Seeger for questioning concerning his attitude toward communism. The committee
also hoped Seeger would reveal the names of other allegedly dangerous
colleagues. The incident made headlines when Seeger, disdaining the
protection afforded by the Fifth Amendment, simply told the committee he would not cooperate. An indictment for contempt of Congress followed in March 1957. Seeger was ultimately cleared, but not
before his reputation had been nearly ruined. His name, along with
those of many other entertainers, appeared on an unofficial blacklist
that effectively barred him from radio, television, films, and the major
record companies. Seeger might have left the country along with
other political malcontents like Charlie Chaplin, but he remained to
sing his protest songs, which he regarded as the mainstay of his self-
styled "theory of cultural guerrilla tactics." For Bob Dylan, the spectacle was impressive. A man had dared to buck the American cultural

[1] See page 484.

mainstream. The fact that this man was a folk singer was, to the impressionable young Minnesotan, even more significant.

The Seeger affair was just one crack in the cultural consensus of the 1950s. Another example of rebellion, and a powerful influence on Bob Dylan during his high school years, was the career of James Dean. The son of a Quaker dentist from Indiana, Dean dropped out of college to pursue an acting career. His movies of the early 1950s showed resentful adolescents looking for ways to express their frustration at a world that failed to fulfill their expectations. Although rebellious, these people had no creed except their discontent with middle-class America. Dean's best-known film, pointedly titled *Rebel Without a Cause*, showed three styles of rebellion: juvenile delinquency, violence, and driving fast cars. Dylan saw the film at every opportunity.

What made James Dean so charismatic for Dylan and his contemporaries was that he lived the life he portrayed on the screen. The dress was the same—black leather jacket, blue jeans, boots—and so was the hard, scornful expression, the suspicious eyes, the dangling cigarette. In the jargon of the time, Dean was a "hood." Then, in 1955 Dean paid the supreme price for his way of life when his white Porsche Spyder, moving at well over 100 miles per hour, slammed into another vehicle near Paso Robles, California. The steering column of the Porsche passed completely through Dean's body. He was dead at twenty-four.

The reaction to Dean's death was a product of the anxieties and ambitions of his youthful admirers. Dean provided an alternative to conventional ways of living and dying. Some of his fans hysterically insisted that he had not died, but was recuperating in secret and, like a messiah, would return. Thousands of teenagers wrote to him every month; a year after his death, the mail still poured in. Fan clubs flourished. Magazines, books, and even plastic casts of his head enjoyed a brisk sale. Dylan and his Hibbing friends were eager consumers of the Dean legend. "Bob," a contemporary recollected, "dug James Dean."

If Dean's violence was one expression of youthful frustration, the quiet desperation of Holden Caulfield was another. Caulfield appeared in 1951 as the protagonist of J. D. Salinger's novel *The Catcher in the Rye.* He was an adolescent with all the alleged advantages of wealth and education, but his life was a series of dissatisfactions that ended in expulsion from a private school. Nothing had meaning—school, society, the standard definitions of success. Caulfield's struggle was for what Dylan's generation came to call "identity," and Salinger's novel became a kind of bible for those similarly searching.

The "beatniks" or "beats" of the 1950s also gave direction to Bob Dylan's unfolding life. They were heirs of an American bohemian tradition dating back to the art colonies of the 1920s and the itinerant existence of Depression vagabonds. Only a handful actually lived the life Jack Kerouac described in *On the Road* (1955), but beatniks were important as symbols of nonconformity. Expressing contempt for the social norms that governed relations between the sexes for most Americans, they followed a sexual style their defenders called "liberated" and their critics, "irresponsible." The beatniks also began experimenting with drugs and Far Eastern philosophies and talking about forms of perception that transcended rational intelligence. Their emphasis was on personal freedom rather than public issues. Like James Dean, their rebellion had no clear cause. "We gotta go and never stop going till we get there," a Kerouac character declared. "Where we going, man?" his friend inquired. "I don't know, but we gotta go." It was almost a decade before this restless discontent found places to go in the civil rights and international peace movements.

While still in high school, Dylan's conception of social injustice in the United States sharpened considerably when he encountered the novels of John Steinbeck. Characteristically, Bob read every one. Especially important to him were *Tortilla Flat* (1935) and *The Grapes of Wrath* (1939), which detailed the agonies of poverty among migrants to California. Closer to home, Dylan heard tales of the strikes that swept the Iron Range in 1907 and again in 1916. There had been bloodshed, even killings, and the intense hatred of "the company" still revived whenever miners were laid off. Dylan encountered the emotions associated with joblessness most directly in connection with his father's furniture business. For several years, he had the unhappy assignment of reclaiming the furniture that unemployed miners had bought on credit during better times. "It just destroyed Bob to do that," a friend remembered.

In senior high school Bob Dylan's contemporaries regarded him as somewhat "hoody" in the manner of James Dean. Indeed, shortly after Dean's death Dylan bought a motorcycle and, inevitably, a black leather jacket, tight "pegged" pants, and big boots. But those close to Bob, like his first girlfriend Echo Helstrom, realized he was in fact no more a part of the motorcycle crowd than he was of the groups who ran student government or supported athletics. Dylan, according to Echo, might be seen with one crowd or another, but he "didn't fit in with anyone in town, really." One reason was that Bob wrote poetry, something he had done since he was twelve. Most of the poems were immediately forgotten, but now he sang some of the verses, and began to develop the instinctive feeling for words and music that underlay his later achievements.

Another surprise to those who thought they had categorized Dylan was the fact that in the fall of 1959 he entered the University of Minnesota on a state scholarship and took up residence in a Jewish fraternity house, Sigma Alpha Mu. His dress then was equally "straight" or "cleancut," and consisted of pressed chino pants, striped button-down shirts, tweed sports jackets, and white buck shoes. But the nervous, chubby-faced Dylan brought his guitar to Minneapolis, along with the ambition to make the big time in popular music. Both drew him to Dinkytown, a district of small shops and cheap apartment houses on the edge of the campus that harbored what little radicalism existed in American college communities at that time. It was in a Dinkytown coffeehouse late in 1959 that the aspiring musician first used the name "Bob Dylan."

After six months, Dylan stopped attending classes. He was an unsuccessful student. He later told an interviewer, "colleges are like old-age homes . . . except for the fact that more people die in colleges." Dylan, in other words, was beginning that winter of 1959–1960 to regard established institutions as dead. What was alive was his music and the handful of beatniks (they were just starting to be called "hippies") in Dinkytown. Dylan gradually adopted their life style. He abandoned the collegiate uniform for rumpled workclothes. He ate and slept irregularly and indiscriminately. He seldom washed. His hair crept down over his collar. An occasional check from Hibbing kept him in wine and cigarettes and paid the rent for his dingy furnished room. But since Dylan was trying desperately to hide his ordinary past, the contact with Hibbing was embarrassing. He fabricated dozens of stories about where he came from and what he had done.

*Demonstrations against college and
university policies, such as this "sit in" at
Sproul Hall on the campus of the
University of California at Berkeley in
1964, were harbingers of an American
counterculture. Folksinger Joan Baez
(center, hand on her head) provided
entertainment and publicity for the event.*

A large part of the American protest against the Vietnam war was i
the name of the Vietnamese civilians destroyed or disrupted in the course of battle
The women in this news photograph are refugees, homeless victims of wa

Typical of some parts of the counterculture are these participants in the rock music festival at Woodstock, New York, August 15, 1969. Drugs played a major role in this and similar gatherings.

The efforts of Bob Dylan and others to politicize the nation's youth bore its major fruit in the 1960s in the massive street demonstrations for peace during the Democratic National Convention in Chicago in August 1968. Here a demonstrator confronts the National Guard in front of the Hilton Hotel. The extensive newspaper and television coverage of the protest multiplied its effect many fold.

Few believed them, but most Dinkytown regulars were impressed by the intense, nervously energetic kid with his guitar and his growing collection of songs.

In the fall of 1960 Dylan rediscovered Woody Guthrie. He remembered his songs from Hibbing, but now a friend introduced him to Guthrie's autobiography, *Bound for Glory*. Dylan devoured the book, played Guthrie's records endlessly, and literally fused his identity with that of the hobo troubadour from Oklahoma. The results were striking. Almost overnight, Dylan's musical and personal eclecticism was channeled into a single direction. "It took him about a week," a folk music devotee at the university commented, "to become the finest interpreter I have yet heard of the songs of Woody Guthrie." Interpretation of this quality demanded sympathy with Guthrie's social consciousness, his concern for the helpless little people at the bottom of the pile, and his anger, in his words, at "those who steal with their pens." For Guthrie, music was a social weapon; for Dylan, this realization was the key to the well springs of his own creativity as a bard of the counterculture.

Just before Christmas 1960, twenty-year-old Bob Dylan left the Midwest. Like F. Scott Fitzgerald and Charles A. Lindbergh, young Minnesotans of an earlier era, Dylan was off to seek a place in the American pantheon of heroes. Inevitably, he headed for New York. Not only was this the popular music capital of the country, but Woody Guthrie lived in a hospital in nearby New Jersey. Upon arriving, Dylan went directly to Greenwich Village, the downtown district famous for free living and free thinking since the 1920s. Using his guitar as a calling card, he found a few meals and a bed. Within a few days he had located Guthrie and visited the old songmaker. The evidence suggests the visit was a success. The men talked and played songs for each other. Within a few weeks Guthrie was characterizing Pete Seeger as "a singer of folk songs," but Dylan as "a folk singer." It was an apt distinction. Dylan was developing a style totally lacking in the polished grace and calculated, commercial showmanship of big-name folk performers of the early 1960s such as the Kingston Trio and Harry Belafonte. But he was not ineffective in performance; he had, after all, been singing in public almost constantly for a decade. He had a knack with a song and an audience that was soon sensed by the coterie of professional folk singers in Greenwich Village. Seeger ventured the opinion that the high-strung Dylan might become the nation's greatest troubadour "if he doesn't explode." Robert Shelton, folk music critic for *The New York Times*, concurred when he heard Dylan for the first time on September 26, 1961, at Gerde's Folk City, a Village club. A contract with Columbia Records followed, and in February 1962, Dylan's first album appeared.

Although only two of Dylan's own songs were in the first album, he had never stopped writing. Early in 1962 he turned to social protest as a theme. "The Ballad of Emmett Till" told the story of a young black from Chicago who was beaten and killed in Mississippi for whistling at a white girl. Here was new folk song material, a departure from the rich man–poor man motif of the Guthrie school. It seems clear that the inspiration for "Emmett Till" and the other race songs that followed came from Suze Rotolo, a beautiful, intelligent girl who worked in the New York office of the Congress of Racial Equality and lived with Dylan. Another contemporary concern, the nuclear fallout scare, lay behind Dylan's "I Will Not Go Under the Ground."

In April 1962, following a long, pensive beer-drinking session with a friend in a Greenwich Village club, Dylan went home and quickly wrote "Blowin' in the Wind." The song dazzled those who first heard it and went on to become the spiritual anthem of the civil rights and antiwar movements. Like most of Dylan's best work, it was understated—simply a series of questions about when justice and peace would come. But there was poetry in the lyrics, and the music conveyed the growing tension of a gathering storm.

Incredible as it seemed to those around him in 1962 and 1963, Dylan could produce a dozen new songs a day. He frequently worked on several at once, like a chess master playing multiple games. But unlike many topical songwriters, Dylan did not pay much attention to the news. He said he *felt* the issues and reacted spontaneously. "The song was there," according to Dylan, "before I came along." The folk music world was astounded. An unknown who, in the words of one observer, was "practically a freak, scruffy-looking and a twerp" was writing songs "every bit as good as Guthrie's . . . or Seeger's." Seeger himself felt the whole process was "spooky" and concluded, "the kid has to be a genius . . . a reincarnation of *all* the folk geniuses there ever were." And Joan Baez, already gaining prominence as a singer of protest songs, heard the bitterly satiric "With God on Our Side" the night Dylan wrote it and admitted to a "state of disbelief that anybody was turning out something like that."

The autumn of 1962 brought James Meredith's dramatic effort to break the color line on the Oxford campus of the University of Mississippi and the tension of the Cuban missile crisis.[1] Dylan responded with two of his better "finger-pointin' songs," as he termed them, "Oxford Town" and "A Hard Rain's A Gonna Fall." The latter employed rich but veiled imagery to drive home Dylan's point that lies, hatred, and inhumanity were on the verge of undoing civilization. Fear and anger underlay the song, and Dylan found himself expressing the emotions of many of his contemporaries. Their world, their lives were on the thin line of survival. Continuing to explore this theme, Dylan composed "Only a Pawn in Their Game." Ostensibly about the shooting of black civil rights leader Medgar Evers, the song implied that evil was largely the result of the establishment's game of power politics. In April 1963, at the Town Hall concert, Dylan unveiled another ballad about a victim of greed, this time a boxer killed in the ring because no one had the courage to stop the fight.

By now a second album was ready for release, and under the aggressive management of Albert Grossman, Dylan was rapidly becoming a national figure. He was also making money, a fact some regarded as a tragedy. A *successful* folk singer seemed to be a contradiction. Dylan, too, was a pawn in the game of the barons of popular music. Protest songs were important, from this perspective, because they *sold*. But for the most part, the youthful audience who responded to Dylan in 1963 saw only the rumpled clothing, the pained, bony face, and the intense manner reminiscent of both Holden Caulfield and James Dean. Dylan acquired added stature in the counterculture in May 1963 when he refused to appear on the prestigious *Ed Sullivan Show* rather than accept the Columbia Broadcasting System's stipulation that he not play his "Talkin' John Birch Society Blues." The song satirized the radical right organization's paranoia about communism, and CBS feared repercussions. By preserving his integrity in the face of what was coming to be termed "the establishment," Dylan seemed to be following in Pete Seeger's footsteps as hero as well as bard.

[1] See pages 452 and 497.

The summer of 1963 found Dylan's "Blowin' in the Wind" a smash hit throughout the nation. Peter, Paul, and Mary, a leading singing group, began to use the song on their concert tours of colleges and universities. "Now we'd like to sing a song," Peter Yarrow would say by way of introduction, "written by the most important folk artist in America today, Bob Dylan." When Peter, Paul, and Mary released a single of the song in mid-1963, it sold 300,000 copies in two weeks. Then came Dylan's sensational appearance with Joan Baez at the Newport Folk Festival in July. When it was over, Dylan was a counterculture hero, a prime mover in the surge of restless, rebellious youth against an authority they no longer respected. Dylan captured this mood in "The Times They Are A-Changin'." It was a battle song with a revolutionary message. Losers were becoming winners, Dylan said, "and the first one now / will later be last." If intellectuals, parents, and politicians were unwilling to leave the "old road," they should at least "get out of the new one." Failure to do so, Dylan made clear, was to invite obliteration. Analyzing Dylan's popularity at this time, one college student stressed his uncanny ability to sing what people, young ones in particular, were feeling. Then he explained that "this was the most together period in recent American history. . . . The word began to spread and college kids . . . realized something incredible was happening, like the age was filled with tremendous spirits. . . . That whole [counterculture] scene was generating a lot of vibes, and Dylan had the heaviest vibes of them all. Dylan was sowing the seeds of the decade."

As Dylan sensed so well, a change was occurring in the American temper in the mid-1960s, and it largely explained his own rise to stardom. The new mood emanated from the young, and at this point half the total population of the United States was under twenty-five. Like Dylan, these Americans were not scarred by the Depression or World War II. The obsession of earlier generations with success and security seemed sterile and unsatisfying. Rather than accept the world as handed to them and strive for a place within it, Dylan's contemporaries turned critical and rebellious. In sharp contrast to the youth of the 1950s, they craved involvement and felt responsibility. Impatience with the American status quo became commonplace, and political activism became a way of life. So did folk and rock music, freer love, drugs, peace, nature, mysticism, the quest for human values, and the struggle to preserve the dignity and integrity of the individual. Fusing these strands into what came to be known as the "youth movement" and, toward the end of the decade, as the "counterculture" was a perception of social crisis and a sudden sense of community among those determined to meet it.

The politicization of Dylan's generation received a great boost from the election of John F. Kennedy in the fall of 1960. In the first place, Kennedy was young—the youngest President, in fact, ever to be elected. Moreover, Kennedy was handsome, dynamic, and articulate. His beautiful wife, Jacqueline, was by any calculation the most exciting First Lady in American history. For many, the Kennedys restored pride in the nation and faith in the political process. His election and the stirring words of his inaugural address brought new hope, a release of moral energy. Ideals once again became fashionable.

Civil rights was the immediate beneficiary of Kennedy and the New Frontier mentality. For many young Americans of the 1960s, the Freedom Movement that Martin Luther King ignited created their first opportunity to work against "the system". There was a delicious thrill in defying the establishment with sit-ins, marches, and boycotts; even the danger inherent in civil rights work in the South was an attraction. It was nice, for a change, to believe in something enough to take risks.

The atmosphere of protest and idealism that pervaded the early 1960s was an excellent background for the reinvigoration of American radicalism. Much of it took place under the label "New Left." The term referred more to a point of view than an organized political movement. It stressed the presence of oppression in the United States and the world and, as a remedial measure, proposed a largely ideological fight against the established power structure. One of the principal institutional expressions of the New Left was Students for a Democratic Society (SDS), which a University of Michigan group, inspired by Thomas Hayden, organized shortly after the decade began. A year older than Bob Dylan, Hayden had remained in college and was a graduate student in sociology at Michigan at the time he fathered SDS. In company with most New Left pioneers, Hayden believed that racial prejudice was only a part of a broader and deeper malaise in American society. Ultimately, he argued, the Establishment's fixation on power and profit explained America's involvement in wars of aggression abroad. This linkage of antidemocratic practices at home and imperialism abroad was one base of SDS ideology. The other was that the mainstay of the New Left would not be the laboring classes, but the campus communities. In the words of the 1962 Port Huron Statement, largely the work of Hayden, "social relevance, the accessibility of knowledge, and internal openness—these together make the university a potential base and agency in a movement of social change."

Tom Hayden seemed a prophet of extraordinary ability in the fall of 1964, when students at the Berkeley campus of the University of California escalated the civil rights movement into a full-blown assault against the establishment. The immediate issue was university opposition to campus-based political activism. For several months a virtual state of war existed between university and local law enforcement authorities on the one hand and social activists, informally organized as the Free Speech Movement, on the other. At the height of the confrontation in December, a student leader named Mario Savio applied protest techniques learned the previous summer in Mississippi. Students took over several university buildings, and when police arrived, went limp in the nonviolent manner advocated by Martin Luther King. When Joan Baez appeared on the disrupted campus and sang "We Shall Overcome," the connection between the causes of students and blacks was clearly drawn. Both social groups contended they were second-class citizens and the victims of a repressive, powerful elite. The remedy, Savio declared, was to "put our bodies against the gears, against the wheels . . . and make the machine stop until we're free." The success of the Berkeley militants in actually stopping academic processes and the subsequent resignation of University of California President Clark Kerr lent credibility to Savio's formula. But the establishment showed its own muscle when conservative Republican Ronald Reagan won the governorship of California in 1966 on a "get tough" platform aimed particularly at the university community. Older people, in general, supported Reagan, a fact that prompted the student slogan, "You can't trust anyone over thirty." In such a sentiment was the flowering of the generation gap implicit from the beginning of the counterculture protest.

For many young Americans of Bob Dylan's generation, however, rebellion continued to have inward, personal, nonpolitical connotations. From this perspective, "freedom" meant the opportunity to "do your own thing." The unconventional nature of the things that were usually done lent added appeal to the life-style revolution. In its vanguard were the "hippies" (those "hip" to what was happening), who first became noticeable as a social group in Berkeley and in San Francisco's Haight-Ashbury district in the aftermath of the Free Speech Movement. Invariably under thirty, poor, long-haired, bearded, sexually "liberated," and determined to create a viable alternative to "square" values and culture, hippies became a symbol of what was wrong—or right—about America in the 1960s.

Drugs were a symbol within this symbol and, in many eyes, the paramount source of contemporary social friction. Although the use of hallucinogens was not new in American culture, many felt the modern popularity of drug-induced "trips" began with Harvard research scientist Timothy Leary. In 1961 Leary's study of a compound called LSD convinced him that drugs opened the way to higher levels of beauty, sensitivity, and truth. A future of peace, love, and brotherhood was supposed to follow such transcendence. Although fired by Harvard for using undergraduates in his experiments, Leary toured the country urging everyone to "tune in" to his message, "turn on" with drugs, and "drop out" of antiquated ways of living and thinking. By 1965 the social smoking of marijuana was commonplace on the American college campus, and "pot" or "grass" had begun to penetrate the high schools. Opinions about the physiological consequences of using marijuana varied widely. For many it was important mainly as a symbol of independence, like drinking alcohol during Prohibition in the 1920s, and a badge of brotherhood. But others moved on from marijuana to increasingly lethal drugs like heroin.

Bob Dylan's relationship to the counterculture protest gaining momentum in the mid-1960s was complex. Characteristically, he walked well in advance of the masses of his contemporaries. While they were discovering politics and protest, Dylan was moving on, both musically and personally, toward more inward, mystical concerns. One of the major factors in this change was the assassination of John F. Kennedy. Dylan was going uptown to confer with his manager on Friday, November 22, 1963, when he learned that the President had been shot in Dallas, Texas. As stunned as if the victim were a close friend, Dylan, like most Americans, sat glued to his television set for several days, absorbing the bizarre murder of the assassin and the moving solemnity of Kennedy's funeral. It seemed to him that what promise there was in the traditional American way died with Kennedy, who had stood, as one obituary put it, "for excellence in an era of indifference—for hope in an era of doubt." Now there was nothing between Dylan's kind of American and the rising anger of the Establishment. Dylan even feared for his own life. He was a public figure, and he knew that what he was saying and singing might well bring forth a madman's bullet.

But fear was not the only factor drawing Dylan away from social activism after 1963. Kennedy's murder underscored his growing sense of futility. "Something," as he put it, "had gone haywire in the country . . . I couldn't understand anything." Specifically, it seemed that reform crusades were trivial and ineffective. In December 1963 Dylan viciously attacked the older liberals in the Emergency Civil Liberties Committee who were honoring him with a formal dinner and the Tom Paine Award. Such people, he now felt, were "hung up." Even in the name of reform, they "used" other people. Moreover, he believed, their pat formulas stopped short of the ultimate solutions, which had to do with individuals as individuals, not as members of groups. The real oppression was internal; the real goals were integrity and self-respect.

From this perspective Dylan saw his earlier protest or "message" songs as foolish. "Only college newspaper editors and single girls under fourteen," he told an interviewer, "could possibly have use for them." He said he was through writing songs "*for* people," through being a "spokesman," through carrying "the world on my shoulders." The prospect of nuclear holocaust, for example, once elicited Dylan's best creative efforts. But by 1964, in his words, "the bomb is getting boring, because what's wrong goes much deeper than the bomb. What's wrong is how few people are free." By this Dylan no longer meant release from oppressive political and social institutions; he had an inward kind of freedom in mind. "From now on," he made clear, "I want to write from inside me."

Eastern religion, existential poetry, and a wide assortment of drugs were all part of the new Dylan. So were ambiguous, irrational, mystical, and frequently bitter songs that grappled with concepts like general guilt and absolute freedom. He was still caustically anti-establishment, as "Subterranean Homesick Blues," "Maggie's Farm," and "Like a Rolling Stone" (all 1965) proved. But these songs did not speak to public issues so much as they voiced the private agony of individuals. Love gone sour figured prominently in the album Dylan released at this time, which was significantly entitled *Another Side of Bob Dylan*. His own relationship with Suze was deteriorating, and music allowed him to express his feelings.

The rediscovery of rock-and-roll was also part of the other side. In 1965, to the horror of his folk singing following, he abandoned the single guitar, put a group of electric-powered instruments behind him, and turned the amplifiers up. Many of his Greenwich Village associates thought Dylan had sold out to commercialism, that he was trying for a share of the big audience and the big money that the English rock group, the Beatles, found after their spectacular American television debut on February 9, 1964. Almost overnight, with such apolitical but musically exciting numbers as "I Want to Hold Your Hand," they had eight of the top ten hit songs in the United States. Unquestionably Dylan was impressed. He went to England, met the Beatles (and introduced them to marijuana), and returned to perfect a style of music soon dubbed "folk-rock." But if more fame was Dylan's objective, the results proved to be ironic. By 1966 he was one of the biggest phenomena in American popular music and an increasingly unhappy man. The spotlight of public attention left him no place to hide. The inner self, on which Dylan's art had always fed, was itself being devoured. Desperately he searched for an escape. A motorcycle accident on July 29, 1966, helped. Seriously injured and hospitalized for a long period, Dylan seized the opportunity to wipe clean his concert and recording calendar and retire from public view. The lyrics of "Mr. Tambourine Man" (1964) anticipated his feelings: "I'm ready for to fade / Into my own parade."

The parade, however, went on and on. Even as Bob Dylan was moving away from protest and a public life, his contemporaries were using his songs as inspiration for a wave of social criticism of a magnitude unprecedented in recent American history. Civil rights continued to receive a share of reforming energies, but white liberals found themselves suspect and unwanted in what was becoming a black concern. In its place, international peace became *the* crusade of the last half of the 1960s. One reason was that the temperature of the cold war, particularly in Indochina, was increasing. Large-scale American involvement in Vietnam began in 1964 after an alleged North Viet-

SOUTHEAST ASIA

CHINA

Red River

• Thanuyen   • Pingsiang

• Dien Bien Phu

Hanoi ◉   • Haiphong

BURMA   N O R T H

Thanhoa •   G U L F

V I E T N A M   O F

LAOS   • Vinh   T O N K I N

• Vang Vieng

◉ Vientiane   Mekong River   Donhoi •
                                              Vinhlinh •   DEMARCATION LINE 1954
• Udon   HO CHI MINH TRAIL   DEMILITARIZED ZONE (DMZ)

• Phitsanulok   • Hue

          Savannokhet •

T H A I L A N D   • Roiet   → Danang

          Saravane •

          • Pakse

• Ratchasima

                              • Pleiku   • Quinhon

◉ Bangkok   • Pleime

          C A M B O D I A   S O U T H

Battambang •

          • Konpong Thom

                              • Bo Duc   • Camranh Bay

Pnompenh ◉   V I E T N A M

Takeo •   ◉ Saigon   S O U T H

G U L F   Vinhlong •
                    Rachgia •   C H I N A
O F

S I A M   • Camau   S E A

0   100   200   300 miles

namese attack on U.S. ships in the Gulf of Tonkin. In retaliation, the United States began bombing North Vietnam. By early 1965, 23,000 American soldiers were actively fighting on the South Vietnamese side. The opposition, counting on America's inability to sustain enthusiasm for a distant war, dug in for a long haul. But the Lyndon Johnson Administration was just as determined to prove its vitality and the sincerity of its opposition to Communist expansion. The war, as a result, escalated rapidly.

In 1966, the cost of containing communism in Vietnam was $6.1 billion; in 1967, it was $20 billion. Moreover, the number of American troops involved soared to 500,000. The mounting death toll, which soon surpassed that of the entire Korean conflict a decade earlier, could only be justified, in President Johnson's words, as necessary to deter "a wider pattern of aggressive purpose" comparable to Hitler's in the 1930s and Stalin's in the early 1950s. According to this line of reasoning, the only hope of stopping the Communists was to present a firm, unyielding front. Escalating the war, the President tried to explain, would demonstrate the credibility of America's commitment and cause the Communists to back down. But as every American escalation of the war met with a counterescalation, it was Johnson's credibility that came into question.

America's growing involvement in the ever-thickening morass of the Vietnam war brought Bob Dylan's generation to the boiling point. Dylan anticipated their anger and their frustration in "Masters of War" (1963), which lashed out at the militarists who "play with my world/Like it's your little toy." In the hope of defusing the war, many young Americans, including the Students for a Democratic Society, had gone "part of the way with LBJ" in the election of 1964. The subsequent escalation left them feeling betrayed. The war, in a word, seemed immoral. By the spring of 1967 journalist Walter Lippmann could brand Vietnam "the most unpopular war in American history." Antiwar protestors pointed out that the United States lacked evidence that the North Vietnamese resistance was really part of a global Communist offensive. They argued that growing polycentrism in the Communist world and the long-standing Vietnamese distrust of China made such an international conspiracy unlikely. Perhaps, it was openly suggested, the Johnson Administration and the Pentagon did not recognize who the enemy was. Perhaps the United States had invited itself into what amounted to a civil war among the Vietnamese people. Such interference might well be thwarting a legitimate process of self-determination.

The peace movement did not, of course, limit its efforts to this kind of reasoned analysis and argument. Beginning in the fall of 1965, demonstration followed demonstration on college campuses throughout the country. Antiwar marches and rallies drew other segments of society into the movement. As expected, the Selective Service System and industries involved in the munitions business were favorite targets. But in the background was the vision of a sinister military-industrial complex, the core of the establishment, about which Dwight Eisenhower had spoken[1] and Bob Dylan sung. The more radical proponents of peace, like Yale professor Staughton Lynd and SDS organizer Tom Hayden, traveled to Hanoi to let the North Vietnamese know their feelings. Others burned draft cards, applied for the status of "conscientious objector," or fled to Canada. In the spring of 1968, 221 major demonstrations occurred at 101 American colleges and universities. The most spectacular took place at New York City's venerable Columbia University in defense of a mixed bag of minorities including blacks, hippies, students, Socialists, and the Vietnamese people. The idea was to support all "movements of liberation," foreign and domestic, by revolution if necessary. This philosophy received its most extreme statement in a radical wing of SDS known as the Weathermen. The group's name came from Bob Dylan's "Subterranean Homesick Blues," which contained the line: "You don't need a weather man / To know which way the wind blows."

While campus violence and confrontation politics dominated headlines at the end of the 1960s, many critics of the war in Vietnam and injustice at home attempted to work within the American political system. There were notable successes, particularly the victory of antiwar Senator Eugene McCarthy in the 1968 New Hampshire Presidential primary. With a zeal that was almost religious, thousands of young Americans descended on New Hampshire to sell their man and their philosophy. Their success and the continued nationwide unrest were important factors behind President Johnson's March 1968 decision not to seek reelection. The counterculture celebrated ecstatically.

[1] See page 491.

The system had responded to the pressure of the people. But almost as quickly as they had lifted, the clouds descended again. On June 5, 1968, Robert F. Kennedy, another opponent of the war whose chances of nomination seemed better than those of McCarthy, was assassinated by a deranged Palestinian refugee. The fact that Kennedy had just won the California Presidential primary made the loss all the more disheartening for his supporters.

In August of that tense summer of 1968, the Democratic party's national convention took place in Chicago. The most memorable events, however, occurred in the streets outside the hall. Young leftist activists, led by Abbie Hoffman's and Jerry Rubin's Youth International Party (the Yippies), planned and publicized protest demonstrations for peace and freedom. Chicago's old-style political boss, Mayor Richard J. Daley, and his police force were ready and eager to put them down. The result was bloody street fighting in which the police crushed the demonstrators. Much of the brutality was captured by television cameras. Some Americans, the ones soon to be called the "silent majority," cheered Daley's show of force. The contempt Dylan and his colleagues had long showered on bourgeois life was being avenged. Others saw in the Chicago streets the seeds of a tragic social schism, possibly even a civil war.

Once again, however, the American political system showed its resilience. In Chicago the Democrats' organization man, Vice-President Hubert H. Humphrey, received the nomination, and then narrowly lost the election to Republican Richard M. Nixon. The surprise of the 1968 election was the relatively strong showing (13.5 percent of the popular vote) of third-party candidate George Wallace, the governor of Alabama. An avowed segregationist who favored winning the war in Vietnam and restoring law and order at home, Wallace struck responsive chords in many quarters.

The ongoing war in Vietnam was the most difficult problem Richard Nixon inherited. Despite an abundance of promises and plans, how to get out of Southeast Asia without reneging on America's promise to defend freedom remained a problem. Protracted peace negotiations produced little more than rhetoric, and Nixon began a policy of unilateral troop withdrawals. Although nothing was done or said about the billions of dollars the United States continued to pour into the war and bombing missions continued, the number of American ground troops in Vietnam was reduced by a publicity-conscious Nixon Administration to less than 50,000 by the summer of 1972. Periodically, however, American muscles flexed in invasions of Cambodia and Laos or in the form of intensified bombing and the mining of North Vietnamese harbors. Each intensification of the war produced a flare-up in the peace movement at home. Campus demonstrations continued. In Isla Vista, adjacent to the campus of The University of California at Santa Barbara, a branch of the Bank of America was burned down. At Kent State in Ohio and Jackson State in Mississippi, inexperienced troops and police fired into groups of students and took several lives. The peace protests of late 1969 were the largest public demonstrations in American history. An estimated 500,000 people gathered for a "March Against Death" in Washington.

The Nixon Administration was not unmoved. While the official Paris peace talks dragged on, Hanoi Radio startled most of the world on October 26, 1972 by publicizing positions of "final negotiations" between Le Duc Tho, North Vietnam's chief delegate, and the President's special foreign policy adviser, Dr. Henry Kissinger. Peace, according to Kissinger's elaboration, seemed finally "at hand."

Richard Nixon's overwhelming reelection in November 1972 came at the expense of George McGovern, standard-bearer of a badly divided Democratic party. Groundwork for the landslide was laid the previous March, when Nixon's visit to the People's Republic of China foreshadowed resumption of communication and commerce for the first time in twenty-three years. His state trip of May 1972 to the Soviet Union presaged large-scale trade agreements. The intensity of the cold war, Nixon could claim, was declining. The governments of a still-divided Korea agreed at least to talk to one another about settling their problems. And diplomatic "signalling" between Washington and Havana indicated hope for resuming a relationship after twelve years.

At home, however, the tensions Bob Dylan helped define remained vigorous in 1973. A computerized America of technological expertise, the Puritan work ethic, and the frontier fixation on conquest —the pride of older Americans—appeared to be challenged by newly enfranchised youth and politically conscious blacks. But according to columnist Tom Wicker, "The irony is that the counterculture and black militancy are based at least partially on an effort to redeem the old values,' rather than just paying lip service to them." While the Apollo lunar-landing program, the most visible symbol of techno-logical progress, ended without fanfare in December 1972, a small but significant trickle of educated blacks began to migrate from northern cities to a more promising south. At the same time the Dow-Jones average (30 large industrial corporation stocks traded on the New York Stock Exchange) closed above the 1000 level for the first time, young people flocked to organic farms worked with their grand-parents' implements. One farm manager sought "an ecological and satisfying means of being in the world. . . . Here you can find . . . the wind in your face, your hands in the dirt."

In January 1968, Bob Dylan ended seventeen months of self-imposed silence by appearing in concert and releasing a new album, *John Wesley Harding*. It was apparent at once that the retirement had wrought still more changes in his music and in his manner. Retreating from the electronic and drug-induced absurdities of "acid rock," Dylan found a refuge in country music and blues. He returned to folk singing. His style mellowed and became more gentle and relaxed. Two more albums, *Nashville Skyline* (1969) and *New Morning* (1970), confirmed Dylan's new directions. By this time he was thirty, married (to Sarah Lowndes), and the father of several children. He was also very rich and lived in a large home in the country about 100 miles north of New York City. His songs and conversation in this period were acutely personal, focused on such things as love, redemption, renewal, and the search for a joyous life. Both drugs and social protest were put away. He discovered nature and the Bible as themes for his art. And there were other surprises. In August 1969 Dylan returned to a reunion of his high school class in Hibbing, Minnesota. The follow-ing June he astonished the counterculture by accepting in person an honorary degree from Princeton University. Shortly thereafter, "Dr." Bob Dylan discovered his Jewish heritage, donated to Jewish philan-thropies, and visited Israel.

As Dylan's new image took shape in the 1970s, it elicited cries of disbelief and disappointment. He was accused of abandoning his role as the conscience of an age, of joining the establishment, and even of "ripping off" the youth movement. Yet once again the evidence sug-gests that Bob Dylan was in the vanguard of his generation. The 1970s opened with a different mood. Although environmental pollu-

Richard Nixon was met by an enthusiastic crowd as he arrived at Miami on August 22, 1972, for the Republican National Convention. He was renominated that night, and he was reelected by a landslide that November.

tion and women's rights claimed considerable attention, as focuses of social protest many Americans, including the young, returned to an emphasis on private matters. It appeared that the traumas of the 1960s had left American liberalism limp. Crusading demanded expenditures of energy that could not be sustained over long periods. Politics, as a consequence, lost some of its appeal. Security, success, and conformity made corresponding gains. Indeed, the 1970s seemed reminiscent in some respects of the 1950s. There were those who contended that the establishment had repressed and crushed its critics; but for others, it did not matter any more.

This change in the temper of the times was evident at the gigantic Woodstock, New York "happening" of August 15, 1969. Dylan did not attend the rock festival, but the gathering of over 300,000 young Americans reflected his new orientation. The anger so evident earlier in the decade was gone. There was a gentleness about Woodstock; love, nature, sex, marijuana-fed reveries, and being nice to others were the primary concerns of the self-styled "flower people." In the supreme tribute of the new wave of youth, Woodstock was a "beautiful experience." The fact that it was not politically important was inconsequential.

Dylan in 1972 was in possession of himself once again. He might be a leader, but on his own terms and in his own good time. He could on occasion support a social cause, as he did at the concert for Bangladesh in New York in August 1971. But now Dylan was singing for a cause, not embodying the cause in his songs. He was detached, reserved, complacent. It was enough, he implied, to survive and enjoy what was rather than burn for what could be. But the prodigious musical talent was still there, along with the enormous reputation. The problems of the nation and the world are also there, and the answers, as Dylan knows, are still "blowin' in the wind."

SELECTED READINGS

The Person

*DYLAN, BOB: *Tarantula* (1971). A book long in the making in which Dylan expressed his feelings about life in a stream-of-consciousness fashion. Difficult for all but the devoted Dylan fan.

HENTOFF, NAT: "Profiles: Bob Dylan," *The New Yorker* (October 1964). The first extended discussion of Dylan and his impact.

KERMODE, FRANK, and STEPHEN SPENDER: "Bob Dylan: The Metaphor at the End of the Funnel," *Esquire* (May 1972). Kermode and Spender have written separate and contrasting analyses of Dylan's significance.

*McGREGOR, CRAIG: *Bob Dylan: A Retrospective* (1971). Collected essays interpreting Dylan and his music.

SCADUTO, ANTHONY: *Bob Dylan: An Intimate Biography* (1971). A complete and unbiased personal history, especially remarkable in view of the subject's passion for privacy.

THOMPSON, TOBY: *Positively Main Street* (1971). An interpretation of life and thought in Hibbing, Minnesota, during Bob Dylan's youth.

"Playboy Interview: Bob Dylan," *Playboy* (March 1966). An example of Dylan mythologizing his life and partially obscuring his ideas.

The Period

*BERMAN, RONALD: *America in the Sixties: An Intellectual History* (1968). Especially good on the emergence and various manifestations of the New Left.

*GOLDMAN, ERIC F.: *The Crucial Decade: America, 1945–1955.* (1965). Political and social history.

O'NEILL, WILLIAM L.: *Coming Apart: An Informal History of America in the 1960s* (1971). The best account of American thought and society in Dylan's time.

*ROSZAK, THEODORE: *The Making of a Counter Culture* (1969). Reviews the history of American social and cultural criticism in the 1960s.

* Available in paperback.

Index

NOTE: Entries set in large and small capitals refer to the main subject headings covered in this book. Page numbers in *italic* refer to illustrations.

75 76 9 8 7 6 5